ARCHIPELAGIC
AMERICAN STUDIES

ARCHIPELAGIC AMERICAN STUDIES

BRIAN RUSSELL ROBERTS
&
MICHELLE ANN STEPHENS,
EDITORS

DUKE UNIVERSITY PRESS
Durham and London | 2017

© 2017 Duke University Press
All rights reserved

Text designed by Jennifer Hill
Typeset in Minion Pro
by Westchester
Publishing Services

Library of Congress
Cataloging-in-Publication Data
Names: Roberts, Brian Russell, editor. |
Stephens, Michelle Ann, [date] editor.
Title: Archipelagic American studies /
Brian Russell Roberts and
Michelle Ann Stephens, editors.
Description: Durham : Duke University
Press, 2017. | Includes bibliographical
references and index.
Identifiers: LCCN 2016050803 (print) |
LCCN 2016056567 (ebook)
ISBN 9780822363354 (hardcover : alk. paper)
ISBN 9780822363460 (pbk. : alk. paper)
ISBN 9780822373209 (e-book)
Subjects: LCSH: United States—Insular
possessions—History. | United States—
Territories and possessions—History. |
United States—Colonial question. |
Caribbean Area—History. | Islands of the
Pacific—History. |Philippines—History.
Classification: LCC F970 .A734 2017 (print) |
LCC F970 (ebook) | DDC 973—dc23
LC record available at
https://lccn.loc.gov/2016050803

Cover art: Fidalis Buehler, *White Cloud
Caution Flasher*, oil painting on panel,
18" × 20". Courtesy of the artist.

For our parents—
Carole Audrey Stephens,
George Stephens,
Catherine Lee Roberts,
and Roland Keith Roberts—
whose lives have shaped the ways
we see this terraqueous world

CONTENTS

Editors' Acknowledgments   xi

INTRODUCTION
ARCHIPELAGIC AMERICAN STUDIES
Decontinentalizing the Study of American Culture
Brian Russell Roberts & Michelle Ann Stephens   1

PART I | **THEORIES AND METHODS FOR AN ARCHIPELAGIC AMERICAN STUDIES**

CHAPTER 1
HEURISTIC GEOGRAPHIES
Territories and Areas, Islands and Archipelagoes
Lanny Thompson   57

CHAPTER 2
IMAGINING THE ARCHIPELAGO
Elaine Stratford   74

PART II | **ARCHIPELAGIC MAPPINGS AND META-GEOGRAPHIES**

CHAPTER 3
GUAM AND ARCHIPELAGIC AMERICAN STUDIES
Craig Santos Perez   97

CHAPTER 4
THE ARCHIPELAGIC BLACK GLOBAL IMAGINARY
Walter White's Pacific Island Hopping
Etsuko Taketani   113

CHAPTER 5
IT TAKES AN ARCHIPELAGO TO COMPARE OTHERWISE
Susan Gillman   133

PART III | EMPIRES AND ARCHIPELAGOES

CHAPTER 6
COLONIAL AND MEXICAN ARCHIPELAGOES
Reimagining Colonial Caribbean Studies
Yolanda Martínez-San Miguel   155

CHAPTER 7
INVISIBLE ISLANDS
Remapping the Transpacific Archipelago of US Empire in Carlos Bulosan's *America Is in the Heart*
Joseph Keith   174

CHAPTER 8
"MYTH OF THE CONTINENTS"
American Vulnerabilities and "Rum and Coca-Cola"
Nicole A. Waligora-Davis   191

PART IV | ISLANDS OF RESISTANCE

CHAPTER 9
"SHADES OF PARADISE"
Craig Santos Perez's Transpacific Voyages
John Carlos Rowe   213

CHAPTER 10
INSUBORDINATE ISLANDS AND COASTAL CHAOS
Pauline Hopkins's Literary Land/Seascapes
Cherene Sherrard-Johnson   232

CHAPTER 11
"WE ARE NOT AMERICAN"
Competing Rhetorical Archipelagoes in Hawai'i
Brandy Nālani McDougall   259

PART V | ECOLOGIES OF RELATION

CHAPTER 12
PERFORMING ARCHIPELAGIC IDENTITIES IN BILL REID, ROBERT SULLIVAN, AND SYAMAN RAPONGAN
Hsinya Huang   281

CHAPTER 13
ARCHIPELAGIC TRASH
Despised Forms in the Cultural History of the Americas
Ramón E. Soto-Crespo   302

CHAPTER 14
THE GREAT PACIFIC GARBAGE PATCH AS METAPHOR
The (American) Pacific You Can't See
Alice Te Punga Somerville   320

PART VI | INSULAR IMAGINARIES

CHAPTER 15
THE TROPICS OF JOSEPHINE
Space, Time, and Hybrid Movements
Matthew Pratt Guterl   341

CHAPTER 16
THE STRANGER BY THE SHORE
The Archipelization of Caliban in Antillean Theatre
J. Michael Dash   356

PART VII | MIGRATING IDENTITIES, MOVING BORDERS

CHAPTER 17
THE GOVERNORS-GENERAL
Caribbean Canadian and Pacific New Zealand Success Stories
Birte Blascheck & Teresia Teaiwa   373

CHAPTER 18
LIVING THE WEST INDIAN DREAM
Archipelagic Cosmopolitanism and Triangulated Economies of Desire in Jamaican Popular Culture
Ifeoma Kiddoe Nwankwo   390

CHAPTER 19
OFFSHORE IDENTITIES
Ruptures in the 300-Second Average Handling Time
Allan Punzalan Isaac   411

AFTERWORD
THE ARCHIPELAGIC ACCRETION
Paul Giles   427

Selected Bibliography   437
Contributors   453
Index   459

EDITORS' ACKNOWLEDGMENTS

THIS BOOK'S FRAMEWORK AND COMMUNITY grew in significant ways out of a series of four special conference sessions that Brian and Michelle organized from 2010 to 2014: "Island Chains, Insularity, and the American Archipelago" for the 2010 ASA Convention; "Archipelagic American Discourses: Decontinentalizing American Studies" for the 2012 MLA Convention; "Archipelagic American Studies" for the 2012 ASA Convention; and a second session titled "Archipelagic American Studies" for the 2014 ASA Convention. Participation in other conferences further expanded our thinking and set of interlocutors: "Archipelagic Thinking: Redefining Caribbean Studies in Dialogue with Archipelago and Island Studies" at the 2013 Caribbean Philosophical Association Conference; "The Grave Wave Off the Shores: Pacific and Caribbean Island Ecologies and Imaginaries" at the 2014 ASA Convention; and "Rethinking Postwar Anglophone Caribbean Literature" at the 34th West Indian Literature Conference at the University of Puerto Rico, Rio Piedras, in 2015. During these sessions, we found a stellar set of interlocutors in our fellow participants, many of whom became contributors to this volume, and all of whom have provocatively directed our thinking along routes we might not have considered otherwise: Keith Camacho, Elizabeth DeLoughrey, Elizabeth Maddock Dillon, Beatriz Llenín Figueroa, Paul Giles, Matthew Pratt Guterl, Susan K. Harris, Hsinya Huang, Allan Isaac, Iping Joy Liang, Judith Madera, Yolanda Martínez-San Miguel, William J. Maxwell, Sean Aaron Metzger, Ifeoma Kiddoe Nwankwo, Lizabeth Paravisini-Gebert, Ramón E. Soto-Crespo, and Lanny Thompson.

At Brigham Young University the project has benefited from Brian's association with two research groups and numerous colleagues. Early on, the American Modernity Research Group workshopped a project overview/proposal, where we received valuable feedback from Frank Christianson, Jamin Rowan, Emron Esplin, Jill Rudy, Jesse Crisler, Ed Cutler, and Stacey Margolis (who joined us from the University of Utah). More recently, the Humanities Center's Archipelagoes/

Oceans/Americas research group has afforded a lively set of interlocutors: Mary Eyring, Fidalis Buehler, George Handley, Scott Miller, and Trent Hickman. Visiting speakers for these two research groups have also offered encouragement and new directions in thought: Gordon Hutner invited an *American Literary History* article review with an archipelagic frame; Wai Chee Dimock entertained questions on continents and Americanist transnationalism; Doug Mao read and commented on writing that later came to bear on the book's introduction; Priscilla Wald pointed toward others interested in the archipelagic; and Mari Yoshihara spoke on the significance of *American Quarterly*'s move to Hawai'i in the context of archipelagic and oceanic thought. During the past several years at BYU, Billy Hall, Matt Wickman, Kristin Matthews, Mike Taylor, Jamin Rowan, and Emron Esplin have also been important and recurrent sounding boards for the project. David Penry was generous in preparing the Koch island iterations used in the introduction, and Daryl Lee kindly helped with French-language permissions issues. Deep gratitude to Phil Snyder, who as department chair has been an enthusiastic supporter and provided funding for a 2014 research trip to Honolulu, where Brian benefited (when not in the archive) from illuminating discussions with Craig Santos Perez, Alice Te Punga Somerville, Paul Lyons, and Florence "Johnny" Frisbie.

At Rutgers the project has benefited from the support of the scholars and administrators involved in the Rutgers Advanced Institute for Critical Caribbean Studies, the members of the research cluster on Archipelagic Studies and Creolization, participants in faculty seminars on Caribbean Studies sponsored by RAICCS and the Center for Race and Ethnicity, and on Archipelagoes sponsored by the Center for Cultural Analysis. The project has also benefited from Rutgers colleagues interested in archipelagoes more broadly. Participants and scholars whose conversations and works have played a key role include Nelson Maldonado-Torres, Yolanda Martínez-San Miguel, Carter Mathes, Yarimar Bonilla, Tatiana Flores, Matt Matsuda, Allan Isaac, and Chris Iannini.

In writing the introduction and conceptualizing the shape of the collection more generally, we have benefited from our colleagues' feedback during invited talks and workshops for the American Studies Program at BYU, the Critical Caribbean Studies Group at Rutgers, the University of Sydney's English Department, National Sun Yat-sen's English Department, National Taiwan Normal University's English Department, the Centre for United States Studies at the University of Sydney, the American Studies Program at Universitas Sebelas Maret, the American Studies Faculty Workshop at Haverford College, the Asian and Asian American Institute Seminar Series at the University of Connecticut, the American Territorialities Symposium at the University of Potsdam, and both the Caribbean Conferences Series and the Workshop for Seminar on Caribbean and Diaspora, sponsored by the social sciences faculty of the Department of Sociology and Anthropology, the social sciences faculty of the Institute for Caribbean Studies, and the humanities faculty of the Red de Proyectos Interdisciplinarios at the University of Puerto Rico, Rio Piedras. We are also indebted to Belinda Edmondson and Donette Francis, editors of the *Journal of Transnational American Studies* special forum "American Studies: Caribbean Edition," who invited us to write an early article on archipelagic American studies. Gary Okihiro, Vince Rafael, Peter Hulme, Elizabeth DeLoughrey, and Shelley Fisher Fishkin have been encouraging as we have discussed the project with them from time to time.

At Duke University Press, Courtney Berger has been a wise and enthusiastic guide since we began talking with her about this collection in 2012, and the comments of Duke's three anonymous reviewers have offered crucial perspectives, suggestions, and enthusiasm, helping shape and refine the project as it moved from the proposal stage to the manuscript stage and to its final published form. Sandra Korn was an excellent help as we navigated permissions.

For this book, our greatest gratitude goes to the volume's contributors, who have worked with us through multiple essay drafts as the project's coherence came into focus, and whose work in theorizing and seeing the ramifications of an archipelagic frame within American studies has been an inspiration. Michelle would also like to thank, with love, Louis and Alexandria for their support over the years it took to bring this project to fruition, and Sandra for doing her part to contribute to the collection's visual works. Brian thanks William and Sierra, and, as always, Norma.

INTRODUCTION | **ARCHIPELAGIC AMERICAN STUDIES**

Brian Russell Roberts &
Michelle Ann Stephens

DECONTINENTALIZING
THE STUDY OF AMERICAN
CULTURE

TOWARD A VISION OF THE ARCHIPELAGIC AMERICAS

Every grade-schooler in the United States is taught to view President Thomas Jefferson's 1803 Louisiana Purchase as a landmark event in "American history." This purchase, as the famous narrative goes, doubled the size of the United States and ousted France (and the threat of its powerful army) from continental North America.[1] But consider the Louisiana Purchase's fame in comparison to that of the United States' nearly forgotten 1941 agreement to build military bases on six British colonial possessions in the Caribbean, which President Franklin D. Roosevelt trumpeted as "the most important action in the reinforcement of our national defense . . . since the Louisiana Purchase."[2] Or consider the Louisiana Purchase side by side with President Harry S. Truman's seldom-discussed Cold War instigation of a US trusteeship in Micronesia, which more than doubled the size of the United States in terms of total land and water area, thereby constituting a massive geographical grounding for its emergence as the dominant Pacific power (see figure I.1).[3] Juxtaposing the Louisiana Purchase's fame with these enormously significant yet comparatively unknown events in the Caribbean and Pacific, one must ask how the narrative of continental America (which has been a geographical story central to US historiography and self-conception) has so completely eclipsed the narrative of what we are terming "the archipelagic Americas," or the temporally shifting and spatially splayed set of islands, island chains, and island-ocean-continent relations which have exceeded US-Americanism and have been affiliated with and indeed constitutive of competing notions of the Americas since at least 1492.

This archipelagic version of America has spanned more than five centuries, and hence the archipelagic Americas are clearly not confined to the islands and waters that have been appropriated by the United States via (to borrow a phrase from Richard Drinnon) the United States' dedication to "seagoing Manifest Destiny."[4] Yet within the interdisciplinary field of American studies (which has

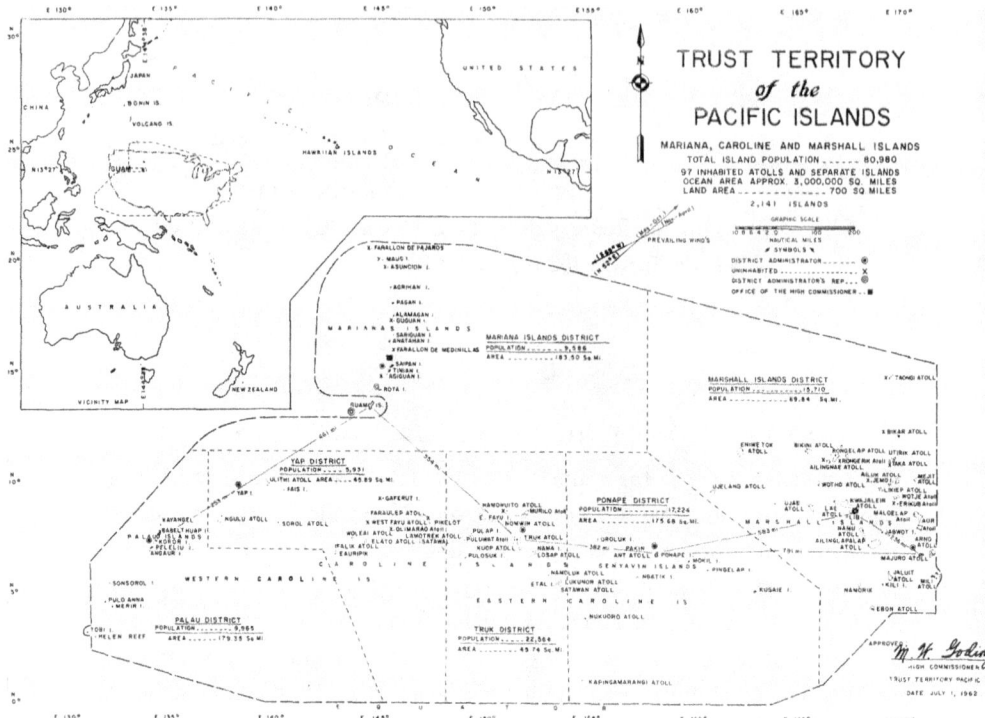

Figure I.1. US government map of the Trust Territory of the Pacific Islands, published in 1962, highlights the Trust Territory's size by overlaying it (in the upper left) with an outline of the lower continental United States and noting that the territory occupies a land area of seven hundred square miles and an ocean area of approximately three million square miles. Courtesy of Map Collection, University of Hawai'i at Mānoa Library.

traditionally taken the United States as a primary object of analysis),[5] the United States' imperial subset of the archipelagic Americas offers a familiar starting place for the mapping of an archipelagic version of the Americas. This is because over the course of the past quarter century, the new American studies—or what Donald Pease has called the "postexceptionalist American studies"—has sought to undercut the US-American exceptionalism of Cold War American studies and to turn our attention toward "US imperialism and US global interdependencies."[6] These critical interests have drawn intense attention to a number of island spaces. For instance, the US Supreme Court's Insular Cases, or the post–Spanish-American War cases that framed Puerto Rico as "foreign . . . in a domestic sense,"[7] in many ways have emerged as paradigmatic of US imperialism as they have received recurrent treatment within Americanist scholarship.[8] The specific treatment Puerto Rico has received within the context of US imperialism is of a piece with postexceptionalist American studies' more general treatments of island-based US territories in the Pacific and Caribbean,[9] and as an upshot of this anti-imperialist and postcolonial tack, transnational American studies has increasingly tended to highlight a view of the United States as imbricated with insular and archipelagic spaces.

Consider, as a litmus test, the presence or absence of the term "archipelago" within the American Studies Association's official journal, *American Quarterly*, from its founding in 1949 through the present. Whereas the half century ranging from 1949 through 1999 saw only six articles that used the term "archipelago," the first fifteen years of the twenty-first century saw thirty-eight articles using the term.[10] And indeed, the journal's 2014 and 2015 special issues, respectively titled *Las Américas Quarterly* and *Pacific Currents*, both offer content that not only addresses individual archipelagoes but also engages with questions of the archipelago as a geographical form and the archipelagic as an analytical framework. The 2014 special issue concludes with a part titled "Archipelagic Thought," composed of a cluster of four essays whose "authors . . . refuse the status of islands as merely insular or as bound by their natural topographies."[11] Meanwhile, the 2015 special issue has an introduction remarking on archipelagoes as models of "subterranean contiguities and undercurrents that extend to the conceptual," while one of the essays discusses the "archipelagic" frame as offering "a promising analytic to navigate the transnational, transatlantic, transpacific, transindigenous, and transhemispheric turns in the now discontiguous archipelago of American studies."[12] No doubt appearances of the term "archipelago"—and, more significantly, treatments of the archipelagic Americas—will proliferate in the pages of *American Quarterly* at a faster clip in the coming years. Taken together, these special issues of AQ mark a significant transition from continental to archipelagic geography and institutional context: the September 2014 issue was the final special issue produced at the University of Southern California, while the September 2015 issue was the first special issue published after *American Quarterly* made the institutional transition to its new home, as of January 2015, in the University of Hawai'i at Mānoa's American Studies Department.[13]

These thematic, geopolitical, and institutional transitions demand increasingly self-reflexive assessments of and engagements with the US imperial subset of the archipelagic Americas. As outlined by the US Department of Interior's Office of Insular Affairs (OIA), this subset includes the US commonwealths of Puerto Rico and the Northern Mariana Islands (CNMI); the US territories of American Sāmoa, Guåhan/Guam, and the US Virgin Islands; and the independent nation-states that are freely associated with the United States: the Federated States of Micronesia (FSM), the Republic of the Marshall Islands (RMI), and the Republic of Palau (ROP).[14] Leaving the OIA's website, but still thinking in terms of the robust US investment in pursuing a seagoing Manifest Destiny, one must also acknowledge at least a partial roster of the United States' former island territories. On the heels of an illegal overthrow of the Kingdom of Hawai'i's government in 1893, the United States took the Hawaiian Islands as a protectorate and then annexed them as a territory in 1898 before they became the fiftieth state in 1959.[15] The United States also administered the Trust Territory of the Pacific Islands (now CNMI and the freely associated FSM, RMI, and ROP) from 1947 through the 1980s and 90s, and at various times it controlled Cuba, Haiti, and the Dominican Republic as occupied or protectorate territories.[16] The United States governed the Philippines for nearly half a century, from 1898 through 1946, with a hiatus from 1942 through 1945 during the Philippines' World War II occupation by Japan. Additionally, the seldom-discussed Guano Islands Act of 1856 authorized the following: "That when any citizen . . . of the United States may have discovered, or shall hereafter discover, a deposit of guano on any island, rock, or key not within the lawful jurisdiction of any other government, and not occupied by the citizens of any other government, and shall take peaceable possession thereof, and occupy the same, said island, rock, or key may, at the discretion of the President of the United States, be considered as appertaining to the United States."[17] This act has resulted in a planet-spanning archipelago of over one hundred past and present-day US claims, ranging from Pukapuka (acquired in 1860 and ceded to the Cook Islands in 1980) to the Swan Islands (acquired in 1862 and transferred to Honduras in 1972) to the equatorial Pacific's Palmyra Atoll (acquired in 1860 and persisting as an unorganized US territory to this day) to several nonexistent islands in the Pacific and Caribbean.[18] The splayed set of islands claimed by the United States—across space and time—may be conceived of as (to draw on the work of Lanny Thompson) an "imperial archipelago" of "overseas territories under the control of the United States" (see figure I.2).[19]

But of course our term "archipelagic Americas" both includes and extends beyond the United States' imperial archipelago. The term designates islands that have been America-affiliated and America-constituting in ways that precede and exceed traditional narratives of US imperialism and US governmentality. In recent turns toward plantation and Creole networks in colonial American studies, scholars describe seventeenth- and eighteenth-century conceptions of the tropical and subtropical Americas as the "Greater Caribbean," an "archipelago of island and coastal colonies" "extending (roughly) from Guiana and Surinam in the south, through the islands of the Greater and Lesser Antilles, to Louisiana, Florida, and South Carolina."[20] Hence the archipelagic Americas overlap with and help constitute what José David Saldívar has recently described as a predominantly North-South oriented sphere of trans-Americanity.[21] But from here, the archipelagic Americas also extend outward

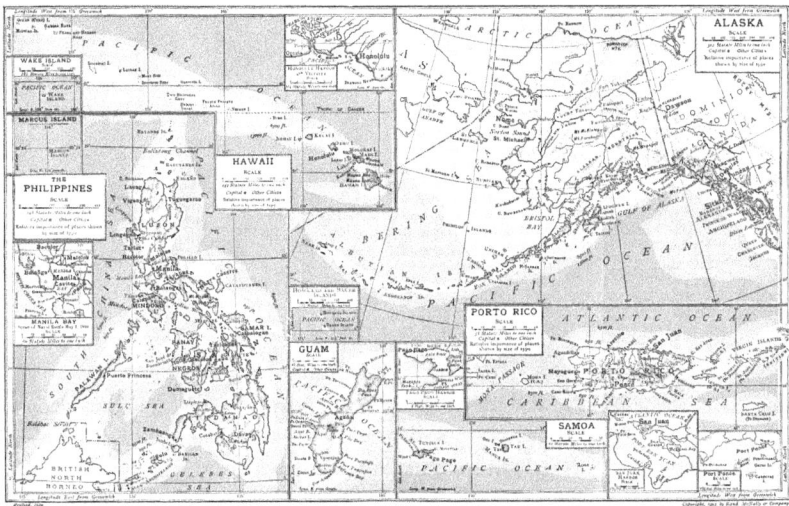

Figure I.2. Foldout map of the United States' early twentieth-century imperial archipelago. Colonies and dependencies represented: Wake Island, Marcus Island, the Philippines, Hawai'i, Howland and Baker Islands, Guam, Puerto Rico, Sāmoa, and Alaska. From William D. Boyce, *United States Colonies and Dependencies* (Chicago: Rand McNally, 1914).

laterally, beyond the American hemisphere, as great numbers of workers were imported to Surinam from the Southeast Asian island of Java, and as slavery and the plantation economy linked the Caribbean to archipelagic and continental regions of Africa, Asia, and Europe.[22] These connections included historical routes (as commemorated during the Philippines' Día del Galeón Festival in 2010) that involved the globe-spanning journeys of Spanish galleons of the colonial era, as they traveled across waterways that linked the Philippines with Mexico and Spain (see figure I.3).[23] Deploying models that range from US-American to generally American, and from centuries old to the present day, this broader cartography of the archipelagic Americas reaches from the Summer Isles of British subject John Smith's *General History of Virginia, New England, and the Summer Isles* (1624) to the Galápagos Archipelago of Charles Darwin's *The Voyage of the Beagle* (1839).[24] It extends from Roanoke Island of the lost sixteenth-century Roanoke Colony to the islands in the China Sea that in 2014 President Barack Obama noted the United States was treaty-bound to protect against Chinese incursions.[25] The network further ranges from the Arawak island of Guanahani in the Caribbean to the Inuit Sea and the Arctic Archipelago claimed by Canada, from the Aleutian Islands of Alaska to Turtle Island of the Six Nations, from the Netherlands' Manhattan Island to the

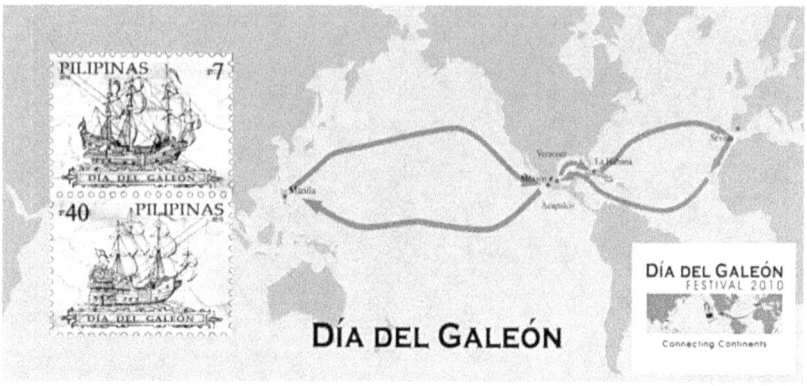

Figure I.3. Commemorative stamps issued by the Philippine government in conjunction with the Día del Galeón Festival. Various routes depicted in the accompanying map were used from the fifteenth through the nineteenth centuries.

Marshall Islands' Bikini Atoll, and from the channel-cut islands at the mouth of the Oronoco River to the island in Lake Texcoco upon which Tenochtitlan (later Mexico City) was built.[26]

Admittedly, at first glance this expansive view of the archipelagic Americas will not resemble the archipelagoes with which many readers are acquainted. An archipelago, one might intuitively assert, is a natural grouping of islands: a group of islands situated in close proximity (as seen in the Philippines), a set of islands on the same tectonic plate (as seen in the British Isles), a series of islands created by the same undersea hotspot (as seen in Hawai'i), or, inspired by a folk etymology of the term "archipelago," a string of islands forming an arc (as seen in the Lesser Antilles). And yet, as accurate as it is to say that an archipelago requires the apparently natural materiality of land and ocean, the geographical form of the archipelago is as culturally contingent as the geographical form of the continent, whose contingency was laid out persuasively in Martin W. Lewis and Kären E. Wigen's influential study *The Myth of Continents: A Critique of Metageography* (1997). In this study, Lewis and Wigen unsettle readers' easy acceptance of "the standard seven-part continental scheme employed in the United States," convincingly arguing that "a sophisticated understanding of global geography [can] be reached" only after abandoning traditional geographical models and recognizing, at the most basic level, that "the division between Europe and Asia is entirely arbitrary," that in common parlance the area referred to as "Africa begins south of the Sahara Desert," and that North and South America's separation has been only putative, with "little importance for either social history or the animal and plant kingdoms."[27] In his essay "Dividing the Ocean Sea," Lewis further demonstrates that how we see the oceans—organized as discrete units into separate ocean basins in relation to their adjacent continents—is also culturally constructed and historically contingent.[28] Lewis and Wigen's demystifications of continents and oceans—their strong arguments regarding these spatial forms' cultural contingency—are enhanced as they trace the radically shifting notion of a continent and an ocean across time, from the ancient Greek geographers through the final years of the twentieth century.

Though seldom attaining the prominence of continents or even oceans in dominant geographical accounts of the planet, archipelagoes are equally culturally contingent. One may take the planet's largest archipelagic state, the Republic of Indonesia, as a case in point. Although Indonesia's first president, Soekarno, confidently asserted that "even a child, if he looks at the map of the world, can show that the Indonesian Archipelago forms one entity,"[29] this archipelagic nation-state defies the intuitive modes that would identify an archipelago by recourse to nature. Whereas received wisdom says the islands of an archipelago ought to attain coherence through proximity, the Indonesian archipelago's province of Papua, occupying most of the western half of the island of New Guinea, is closer to the Philippines and the islands identified as Micronesia and Melanesia than it is to Indonesia's administrative center on the island of Java. Or, if the islands of an archipelago ought to be situated on one tectonic plate, Indonesian lands and waters overlap with four, the Eurasian, Australian, Philippine, and Pacific plates. Or, if an archipelago ought to be made up of islands affiliated with a single volcanic hotspot, Indonesia is composed of volcanic and nonvolcanic islands. The case of the Indonesian archipelago is significant because, even as it is regarded as the largest archipelagic state, it functions to undercut a view of the archipelago as a naturally coherent entity, pushing the archipelagic form toward what for some may feel like an uncomfortably tropological or metaphorical model.

Yet what we are describing is a push and pull between the metaphoric and the material, in which the concept of archipelago serves to mediate the phenomenology of humans' cultural relation to the solid and liquid materiality of geography. Viewed from this perspective, the archipelago emerges as neither strictly natural nor as wholly cultural but always as at the intersection of the Earth's materiality and humans' penchant for metaphoricity.[30] In addition, this acknowledges the metaphoric deployment of the original term from which the English "archipelago" derives. "Archipelago" derives from the Italian term *arcipélago* (with *arci-* signifying "principal" or "chief," and *-pélago* signifying "pool" or "abyss"), which arose during the thirteenth century. It emerged as a name for Hellas's chief sea, the Aegean, and by metonymy it came to describe not the sea but the set of islands that studded the Aegean.[31] During Europe's so-called Age of Discovery, explorers traveling to other regions experienced an uncanny

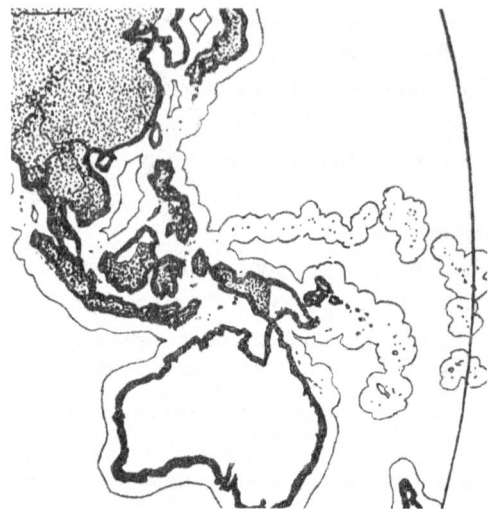

Figure I.4. In 1955, the government of Indonesia published a map representing sea-based lines extending out from continental and archipelagic shorelines. This excerpt from the map reveals Indonesia's converging water borders with the United States via the Philippines (1898–1946) and Micronesia (1947–90s). Excerpted from the end-paper map in *Asia-Africa Speaks from Bandung* ([Jakarta]: Ministry of Foreign Affairs, Republic of Indonesia, 1955).

and formal recognition of the Aegean in the island-studded zones they now beheld and wrote about.[32] Consequently, the term "archipelago" ceased to name a specific sea and began structuring and describing a formal and indeed tropological human relation to material geographies that span the planet. Though the term's self-conscious metaphoricity has fallen by the wayside for most of its everyday users, the concept of "archipelago" repays and indeed demands engagement through a critical awareness that takes into account its situation as a prime metaphor within the structuring grammar of colonial modernity.[33]

Beyond undercutting a notion of the archipelago as an unimpeachably natural form, the case of Indonesia is significant to the project of contemplating the archipelagic Americas because, as far removed as Indonesia has generally seemed to most denizens of the American hemisphere, the Indonesian archipelago has been a long-term—and indeed bordering—neighbor of the United States of America. From 1898 through the end of World War II, the US territory/commonwealth of the Philippines was as much a US claim as were the prestate territories or districts of, say, Oklahoma (1890–1907), New Mexico (1850–1912), or Hawai'i (1898–1959). During this time, the United States, via the Philippines, shared a watery border with the Dutch East Indies, which eventually emerged as the Republic of Indonesia after World War II. If the Philippines, like Indonesia, gained independence after World War II, the United States nonetheless remained Indonesia's neighbor through the 1990s, via US control of Micronesia as the UN Trust Territory of the Pacific Islands. Even today, in light of its continuing compact with the Republic of Palau, the United States continues to border Indonesia through freely associated partnership (see figure I.4).

American studies scholarship of recent years has not made visible this century of shared US-Indonesian borderwaters, in spite of transnational and postcolonial American studies' fixation on borderlands to such a degree that it has sometimes been referred to as "the borders school," with Shelley Fisher Fishkin's landmark presidential address to the American Studies Association taking Gloria Anzaldúa's famous work on US-Mexico borderlands as emblematic of American studies' "transnational turn."[34] In noting this blind spot concerning the US-Indonesian borderwaters, we are much less concerned with geography (simply recovering a watery border) than we are with metageography, or interrogating the geographical assumptions that have made the borderwaters illegible not only among Americans generally (US and hemispheric) but even among American studies scholars who have been of the borders school. The received metageographical assumption regarding the American hemisphere and the United States in particular has been that these sites are fundamentally continental spaces, and continental presumptions—which are the bedrock of what Michael Denning once described as "the heart of the method, content, and politics of American Studies"[35]—have persisted into the American studies of the twenty-first century. Indeed, we would argue, the epistemic gravity of both the United States' and the Americas' mythic continentalism has obscured the materiality of the Americas' archipelagic status.[36] Consider how the Americas' continental presumptions have tended to disrupt a hemispheric consciousness of Canada's Arctic Archipelago as constituted by 36,000 islands (twice as many as are counted in what is regarded as the largest archipelagic state, Indonesia).[37] Elsewhere, continental exceptionalism has disrupted perception of the United States' planet-spanning archipelagic territories as affording it control over an oceanic exclusive economic zone (EEZ) that is more extensive than US land area and larger than the EEZ of nearly any other nation.[38] Continentalism has also stymied general acknowledgment of the Caribbean as an archipelago of jolting geopolitical diversity, with multiple political affiliations (in addition to independent nation-states, we see affiliations with the Netherlands, the United States, Britain, France, the European Union, etc.) mediated by proliferating modes of governmentality (territory, department, protectorate, municipality, commonwealth, and others).[39]

Given the ways these major archipelagic American attributes have been eclipsed within both popular and scholarly narratives, we would suggest that the Americas' dominant continental narrative has precipitated a general relation to the archipelagic Americas that might be described as a collective negative hallucination, that is, a hallucination that does not involve perceiving something that is *not* present, but rather a hallucination that involves *the nonperception* of something (e.g., an immense archipelago, the archipelagic Americas) that is present.⁴⁰ Archipelagic American studies not only involves the project of unraveling this negative hallucination but also emerges as a mode of American studies dedicated to tracing the interrelations of America (as a contingent and elastic space constellated by oceanic waterways, two continents, and uncounted islands both within the hemisphere and beyond via the sinews of empire) and the broader planetary archipelago. This tracing of the interactive and constitutive relationships between (to borrow a phrase from W. E. B. Du Bois) "America and the islands of the sea" holds in productive tension the insights produced by such newly emerging fields as island studies and ocean studies, attentive to the materialities of archipelagic existence as well as to the ways in which the island's wide deployment as a metaphor has continually exerted influence on those materialities.⁴¹

Such questions of material geography have often hung rather precariously in the balance vis-à-vis the transnational American studies. This problematic was already clear in 1998, when Janice Radway, in her ASA presidential address, discussed the prospect of a globalized transnational American studies and warned of scenarios in which the project of tracing cultural continuums across national borders might attain such prominence that "space and geography . . . [may] be thrown out entirely as an organizing rubric for the investigation of human culture."⁴² During subsequent years, this tendency has not been the absolute rule, but it has nonetheless been pervasive enough that the Americanist and oceanic studies scholar Hester Blum has recently noted the sea's uneven centrality to the "transnational turn" while offering a succinct corrective to a scholarly tendency to overlook the ocean's materiality: "The sea is not a metaphor."⁴³ Blum's is a reminder of the material and formal geographies that, as Radway foresaw, may sometimes be jettisoned by Americanist scholarship focused on transnational geographies produced by cultural contestations and cultural continuities. Affording an archipelagic translation to Radway's and Blum's warnings on the danger of neglecting to hew closely to the materiality of space and geography, we would suggest that (just as scholarly writing about women does not necessarily constitute an engaged and informed gender studies) the simple act of writing about cultures and events on islands has not required archipelagic thought nor has it constituted archipelagic studies. That is to say, analyses of US imbrications with, say, Cuba, Hawai'i, and the Philippines may be found wanting to the degree that these analyses bear only casual concern for the geographically material and formal attributes of their archipelagic objects of study. Indeed, an American studies that is archipelagic must go far beyond simply acknowledging or seeing islands. Much more than a recovery project, thinking with and through the archipelago involves attentiveness to what George B. Handley describes as "the phenomenological encounter with natural forms,"⁴⁴ and this tack—which is both materially and formally aware—has much to teach us regarding archipelagic thought's potential to renovate American studies reading practices.

To this point, we have defined the terms "archipelagic Americas" and "archipelagic American studies" vis-à-vis the material and metaphorical imbrications of the concept of an "archipelago," as well as in terms of an expansive yet inevitably incomplete set of islands that might be taken to constitute an American archipelago. We have further suggested that the conceptual, cultural, and political marginalization of archipelagic space is fundamentally grounded in the dominance of the Americas' mythic continental models. In what follows, we discuss, first, the nature of US-American continentalism and what it means to decontinentalize our approaches to the Americas. We then trace key features of a postcontinental, insular imaginary and, further, describe archipelagic imaginaries and reading practices that foreground the Americas' embeddedness within a planetary archipelago that holds in tension the supraregional and the microregional. We close by describing the collection of essays included here as in and of itself constituting an archipelagic formation, a self-conscious assemblage that aims to crystallize what is already in solution discursively and epistemologically within emergent Americanist scholarship, namely, a turn toward approaching islands, island-sea assemblages, and littoral formations that goes beyond colonialist tropes and requires a new world of archipelagic understanding.

DECONTINENTALIZING AMERICAN STUDIES: NEW PLANETARY TOPOGRAPHIES AND TOPOLOGIES

In juxtaposing continental and archipelagic American models, the distinction between topography and topology becomes critical. While topography involves the study of the surface shape and features of the Earth's terrain, topology is concerned with more abstract relations between spatial entities. The level of abstraction available through topology means that spatial surfaces may take a variety of forms, or deformations. Taken to the extreme (e.g., in cases of extreme twisting or stretching), topology reveals the multiple shapes a single surface may take before undergoing, finally, a fundamental ontological shift. At these shift points (points of breaking or tearing), a shape or feature assumes a new topology.[45] Conceptualized in these terms, the United States' Louisiana Purchase may be said to have precipitated a shift (westward) in US continental topography without resulting in a change to the country's perceived continental topology. But as the energies of Manifest Destiny shifted from wayfaring across the continent to seafaring in the Caribbean and the Pacific, the United States constructed an imperial archipelago that deformed—stretched, twisted, and finally fractured—its entity status to the point of a topological shift. And yet this archipelagic and imperial view of the United States has been consistently disrupted by what we have discussed elsewhere as a long US tradition of continental exceptionalism, or its self-aggrandizement as exceptional specifically by recourse to its continental land claims. These claims range from Thomas Paine's protest against the purported absurdity of the small English island ruling the vast American continent in 1776, to the emergence of the Continental Army and the Continental Congress as the founding institutions of US-American democracy, to the strong scholarly reinforcement of US continental presumptions in American studies scholarship ranging from the mid-twentieth-century focus on the continent as virgin land and garden through the transnational turn of the present day.[46]

American studies' persistent if usually unintentional continental exceptionalism is visible in one of the transnational turn's most prominent and generative volumes, Wai Chee Dimock's *Through Other Continents: American Literature across Deep Time* (2006), which of course bears a title marking the centrality of the continental model to a general practice of transnational analysis. Defining "deep time," or history of a *longue durée,* in terms of the continent's epic vastness, Dimock directs our sights toward "a crisscrossing set of pathways, open-ended and ever multiplying," wherein "continents and millennia" are linked into "many loops of relations."[47] Here, although this crisscrossing set of pathways might have found an apt geographical metaphor in the interisland relations of an archipelago (and in fact *longue durée* as a historiographical frame developed in tandem with Fernand Braudel's landmark book on the Mediterranean world), the US-American tradition of affording primacy to the continent persists, implicitly inviting those who contemplate the multimillennial vastness of deep time to take up the corresponding vastness of continents (as opposed to islands) as their temporal frame's geographical grounding and metaphor for transnationalism.[48] This continental-transnational model is evident in the work of other prominent American studies scholars as well as in the discourse of the United States' most prominent political leaders.[49]

We would suggest that a residual Americanist bias toward the continent also inhabits the field's persistent anti-insularity or anti-islandness. Time and again, and in ways that are critically analogous to Thomas Paine's foundational dismissal of the small island as a politically inferior form, major transnationalist methodological discussions have argued against "the *insularity* of an American studies that imagines the nation as . . . fixed . . . and self-enclosed," against an old "American Studies that is . . . *insular* and parochial." Major voices have privileged "complex hemispheric history" in opposition to "*insular* and nationalist" accounts, trumpeting "international embeddedness" against an earlier tendency to "look at the United States . . . in an *insular* way."[50] To be sure, major postexceptionalist scholars have only deployed the term "insular" according to a widely accepted usage, namely to describe (as the *Oxford English Dictionary* has it) a state of being "cut off from intercourse with other nations, isolated; self-contained; narrow or prejudiced in feelings, ideas, or manners."[51] And yet, precisely because this definition stands uncontested, it is important to remark on the epistemic violence resulting from and perpetuated by a continentally oriented (neo)colonial modernity that has associated the island's defining geoformal feature with devalued categories such as the fixed, the self-enclosed, the parochial, the narrowly nationalist, and the internationally disembedded.[52]

Undertaking the process of decontinentalizing our methods and biases asks that Americanists carefully consider such perspectives as those expressed in Hawaiian writer Joseph P. Balaz's poem "Da Mainland to Me" (1989):

Eh, howzit brah,
I heard you goin mainland, eh?

    No, I goin to da continent.

Wat? I taught you goin San Jose
for visit your bradda?

    Dats right.

Den you goin mainland brah!

    No, I goin to da continent.

Wat you mean continent brah?!
Da mainland is da mainland,
dats where you goin, eh?!

    Eh, like I told you,
    dats da continent—
    Hawai'i
    is da mainland to me.[53]

While the poem's first speaker (represented in italics) portrays the propensity of even island residents to sometimes assume a continentalist perspective that views the continent as the *main* land, the poem's second speaker (represented in roman script) patiently yet resolutely and incisively denaturalizes any easy conflation of the categories of *continent* and *mainland,* advancing instead a decontinentalized stance in which the island—or, within the poem, the archipelago—becomes that which is main, while the continent continues to exist (indeed as a place that may be worth traveling to) but in the absence of its long-naturalized centrality to perceptions of the planet.[54]

As we are using the term, the project of "decontinentalizing" does not of necessity require an antagonistic relation to American continental spaces, though such a stance will be justified in many cases, analogous to the antagonism of José Martí's famous term *nuestra América* (our America) toward an imperial United States.[55] However, whether or not it assumes an antagonistic stance, decontinentalizing involves—as showcased in Balaz's poem—a patient, resolute, and incisive skepticism regarding continental presumptions to uniquely *main*land status, combined with a dedication to the project of reimagining insular, oceanic, and archipelagic spaces as *main*lands and *main*waters, crucial spaces, participants, nodes, and networks within planetary history. Decontinentalizing also involves recovering the insular and archipelagic status of spaces that have sometimes been casually perceived as easily continental (such as New York City, much of Canada, or the Florida Keys),[56] as well as tracing the cultural lives of insular and archipelagic spaces that have existed while surrounded by continental regions, such as the islands in Utah's Great Salt Lake, the natural and created islands in Lake Texcoco upon which Tenochtitlan (later Mexico City) was built, and the many islands of the US-Canada Great Lakes borderwaters. Beyond historicizing and denaturalizing continentalism while deconstructing anti-insularity as it appears in Americanist and transnational discourse, decontinentalizing requires that we interrogate the image of the desert isle that has become so constitutive of colonial appropriations of island territories. Indeed, against a continentalist model in which the figure of the island and its surrounding ocean are constructed as ineluctably isolated and empty, and in the spirit of what has recently been discussed as a "critical insularity" that refuses the romance of an idealized tropical isle,[57] Americanists may draw upon rich and self-consciously archipelagic theorizations and models that during the past half century have attained increasing prominence among island-based and island-oriented scholars, intellectuals, and governmental officials.

In the mid-1950s, in opposition to US affirmations of the tradition that waters extending over three miles past a shoreline "are high seas over which no state exercises sovereignty,"[58] the postcolonial nations of the Philippines and Indonesia declared the political ramifications of their countries' archipelagic topology. The Philippines announced in 1956 that "all waters around, between and connecting different islands belonging to the Philippines Archipelago, irrespective of their width or dimension, are necessary appurtenances of its land territory, forming an integral part of the national or inland waters, subject to the exclusive sovereignty of the Philippines."[59] The following year, Indonesia made an analogous declaration that "all waters surrounding, between and connecting the islands constituting the Indonesian State, regardless of their extension and breadth, are integral parts of the territory of the Indonesian State and therefore parts of the internal or national waters which are under the exclusive sovereignty of the Indonesian State."⁶⁰ Although the United States sent protests to both the Philippines and Indonesia,⁶¹ these postcolonial nation-states eventually joined with Mauritius and Fiji in the 1970s and finally triumphed when their "archipelago principle" was encoded as a principle of international law with the ratification of the United Nations Convention on the Law of the Sea in 1994.⁶²

The Caribbean has also been a major center of archipelagic theorization and practice. In the 1950s, just as the Philippines and Indonesia were asserting archipelagic principles within the waters spanning the Pacific and Indian Oceans, Trinidadian intellectual C. L. R. James was advocating for the federation of the British West Indies around the principle that they too functioned culturally as one interrelated unit.⁶³ Also theorizing the Caribbean not as being composed of isolated islands but as an interconnected archipelago, Jamaican intellectual Sylvia Wynter has described an "ex-slave-labor archipelago of the post-1492 Caribbean and the Americas," while Martinican writer Édouard Glissant wrote that "insularity" is not "a mode of isolation" but is constitutive of a world in which "each island is an opening. . . . The Antillean imaginary frees us from suffocation."⁶⁴ Glissant saw "the whole world . . . becoming archipelagized," a mode of thought allied with that of Cuban theorist and novelist Antonio Benítez-Rojo, who took the Caribbean template as key to viewing a vast and world-spanning archipelago, a "meta-archipelago (an exalted quality that Hellas possessed, and the great Malay archipelago as well) . . . having neither a boundary nor a center," flowing from a Balinese temple to a Bristol pub to a barrio in Manhattan.⁶⁵

Flowing outward, the Caribbean meta-archipelago has surfaced in the work of Pacific and Indian Ocean practitioners and theorists. Relying upon Glissant's *Caribbean Discourse* and his *Poetics of Relation* to discuss creolization in the Indian Ocean's archipelagic spaces, Françoise Lionnet offers a modern reinterpretation of a Dutch portolan map of the East Indies.⁶⁶ The Caribbean also surfaces in collaborative ways in the collection *A New Oceania: Rediscovering Our Sea of Islands* (1993), which borrowed its epigraph from Trinidadian poet Derek Walcott's poem "The Sea Is History." *A New Oceania* republished and celebrated Pacific Island intellectual Epeli Hau'ofa's influential essay "Our Sea of Islands." In his essay, Hau'ofa rejected the perspective of "those who hail from continents" and who believe "islands are tiny, isolated dots in a vast ocean"; Hau'ofa advocated instead for the recovery of an Indigenous model of Oceania as an interconnected "sea of islands" in which Pacific "peoples and cultures moved and mingled unhindered" in "a large world." As he argued, Pacific cultures and peoples have circulated throughout Oceania and among "regions of the Pacific Rim."⁶⁷

Situated on what is sometimes called the Rim, and also concerned about encroaching continental perspectives, a group of faculty at the University of the Philippines published a collection titled *Archipelagic Studies: Charting New Waters* (1998). The collection's lead essay cautions that Philippine intellectuals and larger populations have assessed their world via "the Procrustean framework of an externally-sourced paradigm."[68] This externally sourced paradigm, as outlined in the collection's concluding essay by Jay Batongbacal, is a continental paradigm that gained ascendancy in the Philippines and throughout the world through "decades of ... training in disciplines developed and dominated by Western continental countries."[69] The essay argues that the university's new Archipelagic Studies Program, in taking up this "commonly-known idea [of] the archipelago," poses "a common challenge to almost all the major academic fields," questioning "the very assumptions of academic disciplines and perspectives."[70]

The disciplinary disruptions precipitated by an archipelagic frame have been playing out in archipelagic arenas beyond the postcolonial world. Within one portion of archipelagic Europe, this has been the case for over four decades, since J. G. A. Pocock published his paper "British History: A Plea for a New Subject" in 1975. Pocock argued that "English history" ought to become the "old" subject, while "British history" ought to emerge as the "new subject."[71] Within this British history, "the Atlantic archipelago" (Pocock's replacement term for the vexed "British Isles") was a starting place for a pluralistic rather than England-centered narrative. Affording competition to continental narratives of Europe, Pocock's Atlantic archipelago was "a large—dare I say a sub-subcontinental?—island group."[72] Decades after this archipelagic intervention, Philip Schwyzer has observed that "the archipelagic perspective," with its essential "willingness to challenge traditional boundaries," has helped this "New British History" to "reshape ... our image of these islands in all historical periods."[73]

The archipelagic perspective has been foundational to shapings and reshapings that have taken place within—and emanated from—another swath of archipelagic Europe, namely the Mediterranean's island-studded Aegean Sea. As we have previously discussed, human perception of, and interaction with, the Aegean (inasmuch as the very term "archipelago" emerged from this crucible) was a starting point for the archipelagic metaphor itself. Complementing the Mediterranean's role in providing the planet with a structuring geographical grammar of ancient origin, contemporary scholars of the Mediterranean—such as Irad Malkin and Christy Constantakopoulou—have recovered forgotten insular themes and networks that point toward the centrality of archipelagic geography to Hellenic identity and cultural formations.[74]

In tandem with the archipelagic theorization that has emanated from these regionally defined archipelagoes, a field of island studies has also begun to flourish, with the founding of two English-language journals, *Island Studies Journal* (2006) and *Shima* (2007), the instigation of the book series *Rethinking the Island* (2013), and the recent publication of special issues on islands in international journals, including *New Literatures Review* (2011), *International Journal of Okinawan Studies* (2012), *Southerly* and *Diaspora* (2013), and *Third Text* (2014).[75] As defined in the first issue of *Island Studies Journal* in 2006, the "core of 'island studies'" was the study of "the constitution of 'islandness' and its possible . . . influence and impact" on ecology, human and animal behavior, academic disciplines, and policy issues.[76] Yet by 2011, major voices in the field had recognized the urgency of an "archipelagic turn" to compensate for island studies' trend toward leaving "island-to-island relations . . . under-theorized," and shortly thereafter, in the journal's special issue titled *Reframing Islandness: Thinking with the Archipelago* (2013), Jonathan Pugh suggested that using the archipelago as a thought template permits space to become "more than [a] mere backcloth," providing access to islands' "transfigurative originality."[77] In ways that are intellectually and institutionally imbricated with island studies' "archipelagic turn," UCLA-based scholars such as Elizabeth DeLoughrey have been dedicated to deep and transregional thinking routed through the geographical form of the archipelago.[78]

Taking inspiration from these islanders and other island-oriented thinkers, we are calling for a decontinentalization of perceptions of US and generally American space, and a shift toward recognizing the Americas as a set of spaces that has been persistently intertwined with, constituted by, and grounded in the archipelagic. To do so is to strive for different ways of seeing, recovering marginalized metageographies and concomitantly imagining new metageographies in ways analogous, say, to Jacques Dominique Cassini's polar projection map of 1696, which countered a basin-based model for the world's oceans and instead linked them as one continuous sea or arc that surrounds a world island (see figure I.5). Or consider Jesse Levine's map, published nearly three centuries later in 1982, which strives for "a new world of understanding" by flipping the conventional map of the Americas upside down, challenging prevalent assumptions that the countries at the top of a map are more important than those at the bottom (see figure I.6). Contemplating analogously radical revisions of spatial perception, how might we imagine maps—visual and conceptual—that challenge widely held American assumptions that larger countries situated on continental landmasses are more important than smaller countries situated on islands and among archipelagoes? Answering this question will not be so simple as rotating the map by 180 degrees. Even as decontinentalized frameworks will find common cause with other transnational frames of analysis that seek what Lisa Lowe and David Lloyd describe as "a comprehension of the lateral relationships between sites in which alternative practices emerge,"[79] archipelagic approaches will

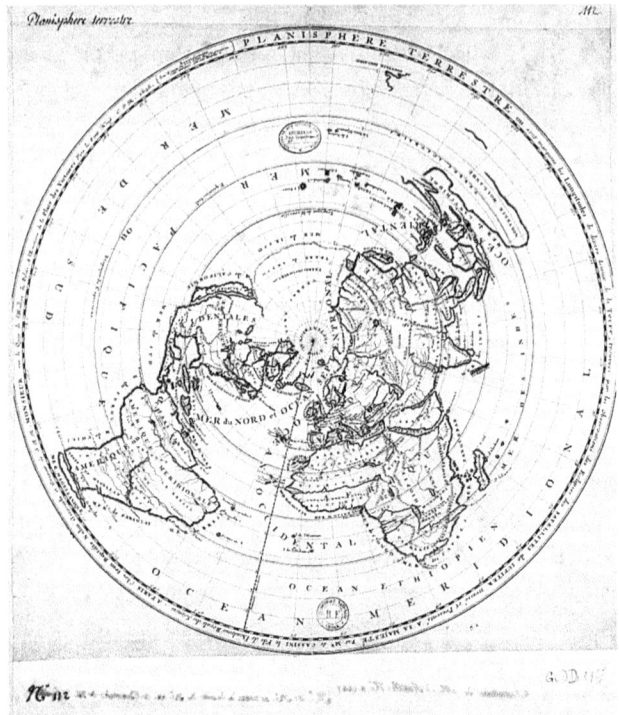

Figure I.5. Jacques Dominique Cassini's polar projection map (1696). Courtesy of World Digital Library, Library of Congress.

exist in productive and generative tension with postcolonial and world-systems frameworks that center on core-periphery topologies, with hemispheric models that hinge implicitly on border-like Euclidian latitudinal or longitudinal lines, with ocean-specific models in which ocean basins circumscribe the sphere of inquiry, with global South models that focus on states and regions that lack capital advantage in the global economy, and with planetary approaches that have taken the continent as their central metaphor.

In attempting to imagine maps whose provocation is the work of imagining continent-island relations in ways that feel decentered or upside down, we need schemas that take into account region and power but that also reorient, reimagine, and sometimes exceed these categories, dedicating themselves to an analytical preoccupation with the geographical form of the island (wherever found) as well as with the cultural mechanisms by which islands have cohered as watery archipelagoes throughout the planet. Engaging in what Grant McCall in 1994 termed "nissology," or "the study of islands on their own terms," we seek schemas that move beyond Western discourse's tendency to deploy the desert island for clichéd purposes of metaphorical abstraction, and toward metageographical

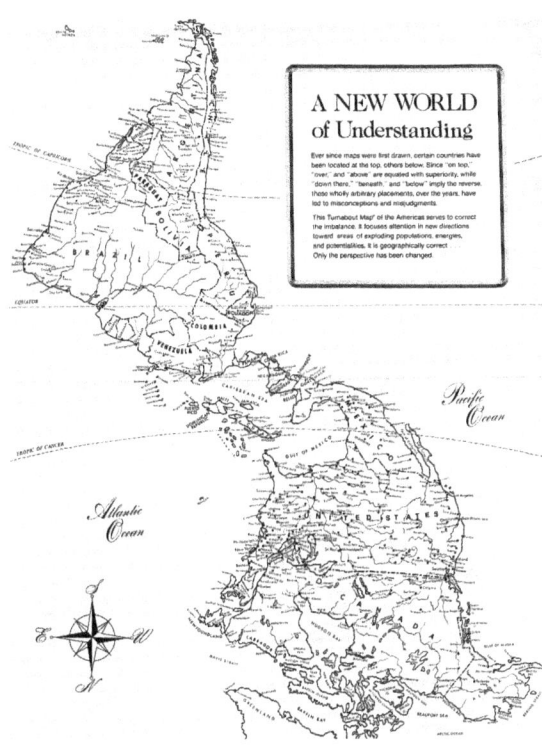

Figure I.6. "A New World of Understanding" carries a caption explaining: "Ever since maps were first drawn, certain countries have been located at the top, others below. . . . These wholly arbitrary placements over the years . . . have led to misconceptions and misjudgments. . . . This Turnabout Map of the Americas serves to correct the imbalance." Used with permission of Susan Levine Kaplan.

remappings that offer new methodologies and methods of reading for the emergence of an American studies that is truly archipelagic.[80] In contributing to this project of critical insularity (in which "insularity" implies not narrowness but interconnectedness), we dedicate the space below to outlining a set of methodologies and reading practices that we refer to collectively as "an archipelagic nissology of the anti-explorer." This mode of nissology approaches islands by means of such notions as the anti-explorer, the infinite island, the insular-real, the mise en abyme, and the catachrestic. Such reading practices and methodologies promise to permit Americanists to reenvision the geographical form of the island, to reconceive of the planetary map as archipelagically fractal, and, consequently, to imagine radically new phenomenological relations to the Americas.

THINKING WITH THE ISLAND: A NISSOLOGY OF THE ANTI-EXPLORER AND THE COASTLINE

Many who study and live on islands have been drawn to the coastline, that place where water meets land, as a material and protean site where islands attain meaning within human cultures and consciousnesses.[81] For Simone Pinet, human tracings of the shoreline stand as "the primary cartographic gesture" of imperial "appropriation."[82] Greg Dening sees the beach not only as a place of conquest but also as one of cross-cultural encounter and exchange.[83] Peter Hay describes an island's circumscribing coast as evoking an "edgy" quality. While acknowledging that an island's edginess may for some represent containment, Hay's preference is to think of "the island edge [as] . . . the portal to roads and sea-trails."[84] Marc Shell goes even further in his contemplation of the meeting of land and water, reminding us that "islandness . . . resides in a shifting tension between the definition of *island* as 'land as opposed to water' and the countervailing definition as 'land as identical with water.'"[85] He describes the etymology of the word "island" further by stating, "The English term *island* includes two meanings" in conflict: "the French-influenced meaning as something like 'insulet.' . . . [which] involves the separation, or 'cutting' off, of land from water at the coast. . . . The other meaning of *island* . . . is historically prior. It is of Norse origin: 'water-land.' . . . and indicates the mixture of water and land at the limiting, or defining, coast."[86] Other evocative terms for Shell include "*marshland, muck, mud . . . bog*," "the sort of malleable, ever-changing humid material, or clay . . . familiar to coastal cultures."[87] Shell adds that "the older meaning of *island* . . . as 'water-land' morphed [during] the Renaissance into the newer meaning . . . as 'water defined against land.'"[88] In the wake of these historical and critical assessments of the meeting between water and land, how might further interrogations of the notion of the coastline help to shape, methodologically and conceptually, what we in this collection are advancing as a postcontinental insular imaginary?

For an answer to this question, we need to follow a path laid down by the Caribbean poets Derek Walcott and Édouard Glissant, and by the mathematician Benoit Mandelbrot. This is a path that leads us away from uninterrogated images of the desert isle and toward a mathematically and poetically theorized infinite island. "What is the nature of the island?" Derek Walcott asks in his essay "Isla Incognita" (1973). He answers less with an answer than with a hint toward a method for imagining a possible answer: "[This question] has stuck . . . [with me] for over thirty-five years. I do not know if I am ready to answer it. . . . Except by. . . . the opposite method to the explorer's."[89] In following this hint toward a method, we ask what an anti-explorer's method might look like. The explorer, we would suggest, is a figure who, traditionally speaking, sallies forth with confidence that if the world is as yet unknown, then it at least may be surveyed and hence known via the Euclidean geometry of a latitudinal and longitudinal grid superimposed upon an idealized sphere.[90] In the explorer's world, space is mapped, before it is known, by a globe-enveloping set of bisecting lines that drive toward human efforts at discovering or knowing the portions of the grid that contain *terra incognita* and *mare incognitum* (see figure I.7). In contrast to

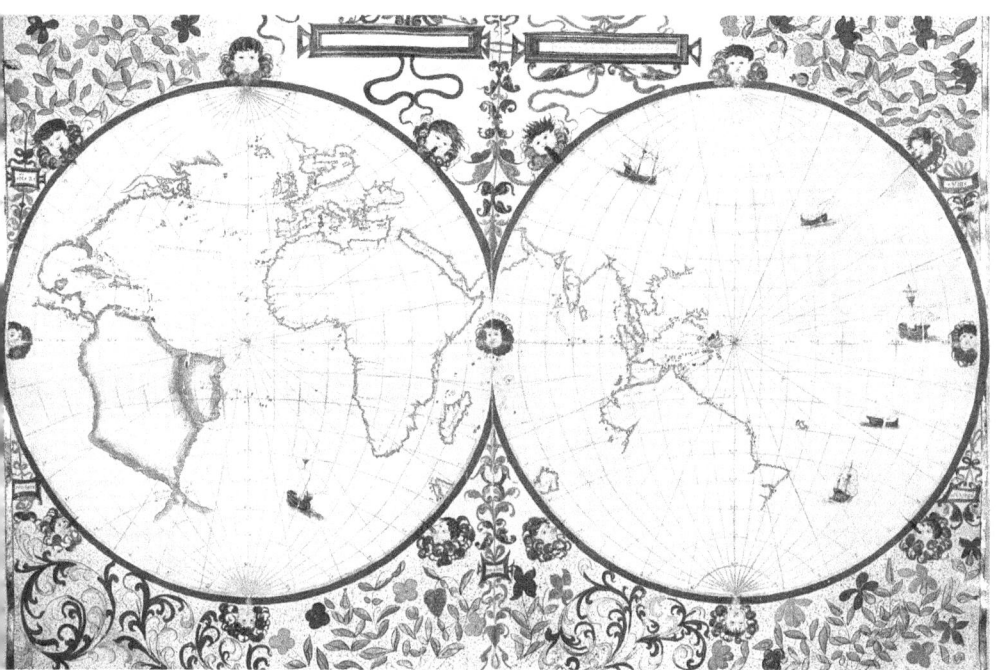

Figure I.7. Jean Rotz's eastern and western hemisphere map illustrates the latitudinal and longitudinal grid and perceptions of space associated with the explorer's method. From Jean Rotz's *Boke of Idrography* (ca. 1535–42). © The British Library Board, Royal 20 E IX f29v–30r.

the explorer's method, an anti-explorer's method appears in the work of several Caribbean thinkers who have conceptualized the world not by means of the Euclidean set of lines that constitute the latitudinal and longitudinal grid, but rather by means of the post-Euclidean schemas of chaos and fractal geometry. Antonio Benítez-Rojo's notion of meta-archipelago relies on "the new scientific perspective" in which "*Chaos*" refers to "regularities that repeat themselves globally" within what we "know of as Nature." For Benítez-Rojo, the regular repetitions of the stars in the Milky Way find an oceanic mirror in the meta-archipelagic islands of the sea.[91] Like Benítez-Rojo's meta-archipelago, Édouard Glissant's famous theorizations of Relation are also fundamentally imbricated in chaos's repeating regularities, with the "poetics of Relation" emerging as a subset of "*chaos-monde*," or the aesthetics of the universe.[92]

These Caribbean gestures toward chaos and self-similarity constitute direct recourse to the pioneering mathematics of Benoit Mandelbrot, as innovated in his article "How Long Is the Coast of Britain?" (1967), his book *Fractals: Form,*

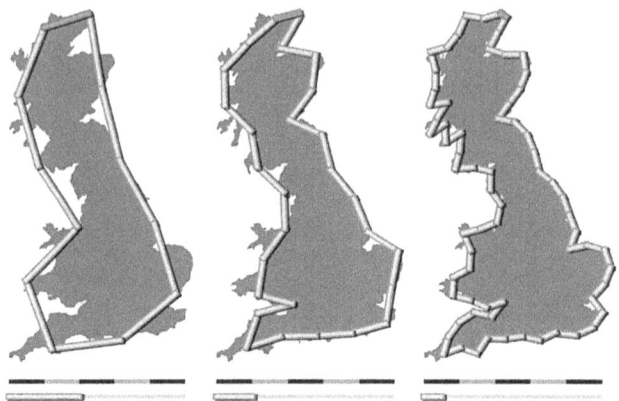

Figure I.8. As the unit of measurement decreases in length from two hundred to one hundred to fifty kilometers, the length of Britain's coast increases from about 2,350 to 2,775 to 3425 kilometers; the shorter the unit of measurement, the greater the measured length of the coast. Alexandre Van de Sande, "Britain Fractal Coastline Combined," 2005. Available at https://commons.wikimedia.org/wiki/File:Britain-fractal-coastline-combined.jpg. GNU Free Documentation License.

Figure I.9. Mathematician Alexis Monnerot-Dumaine renders one of Mandelbrot's signature fractal figures as an island. Available at https://commons.wikimedia.org/wiki/User:Prokofiev#/media/File:Mandelbrot_island2.jpg. GNU Free Documentation License.

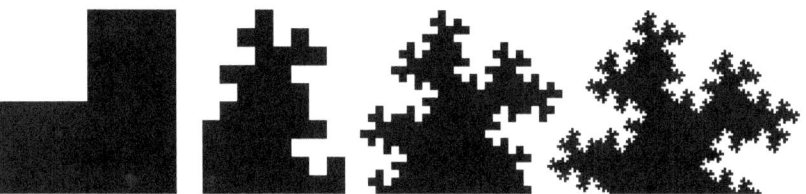

Figure I.10. Inspired by Mandelbrot's iterative "Koch Island" sequence in *The Fractal Geometry of Nature* (plate 51), this is a series of four iterations (*left to right*) of a mathematically generated Koch island peninsula, suggestive of an island's lengthening coastline when its shores are resolved according to increasingly smaller units of measurement. Koch island iterations generated by David Penry in 2016; peninsula arrangement by Christine Riggio.

Chance, and Dimension (1977), and his book *The Fractal Geometry of Nature* (1983).[93] In his article Mandelbrot asks, "How Long Is the Coast of Britain?"[94] He later answers that the coast of the island of Britain is infinite, explaining, "It is evident that [the coast's] length is at least equal to the distance measured along a straight line. . . . However, the typical coastline is irregular and winding, and there is no question it is much longer than the straight line" (see figure I.8).[95] Remarking on this irregularity's effect on length measurements, Mandelbrot elaborates, "When a bay or peninsula noticed on a map scaled to 1/100,000 is reexamined on a map at 1/10,000, subbays and subpeninsulas become visible. On a 1/1,000 scale map, sub-subbays and sub-subpeninsulas appear, and so forth. Each adds to the measured length."[96] This is also what Mandelbrot calls "corrugation," the edginess of the land masses of the Earth when magnified at finer and finer scales, which the mathematician modeled using fractal formulas that produced images uncannily like an island's corrugated edges (see figure I.9). As the scale or unit of measurement becomes increasingly "smaller and smaller," the measured length of the coastline "tends to increase steadily without bound"[97] (see figure I.10). Later, Mandelbrot draws upon these observations on infinite perimeter to arrive at an island's infinite area: "Since earth's relief is finely 'corrugated,' there is no doubt that, just like a coastline's length, an island's total area is geographically infinite."[98]

To embrace Mandelbrot's apprehension of the island as infinite is not to enter into a contest of comparative magnitude with the continent. It is not to say, *If you have the massive continent, then we have the infinite island*. Rather, an apprehension of the island's fractal infinitude is the foundation for moving away from the explorer's method (which looks at the as yet unknown world and attests to its fundamental knowability) and toward the anti-explorer's method, which involves looking at the putatively known world and attesting to its final unknowability. To borrow terminology from Glissant, the anti-explorer's method would be to look toward the seemingly easily graspable or "minute" to see the unknowable and "infinite."[99] One might even suggest, as do Pinet and Shell, that the island appears as a trope precisely when one encounters the unknowable and the unfamiliar, that is, phenomena in the Real, that uncanny Lacanian space of a reality that cannot be measured and has not been integrated into the symbolic orders of language and knowledge.[100] When Sean Metzger, Francisco-J. Hernández Adrián, and Michaeline Crichlow call on us to focus on an "insular-real," they mean to describe those experiences of islands that have not or have yet to be integrated into our discourses, our measurements, our archives, and our tropes.[101] These may be local, island knowledges, some of which are lost, contingently receding, or resurgent within the dominance of other epistemological frames, ranging from the most local use of an herb to the cosmic navigational worldview of Pacific Island canoers who have perceived the islands as moving in relation to the stars.[102]

The anti-explorer's method, then, is premised on the figure of the infinite island as a hyperobjective space that is like one of the foundational images of fractal geometry, the Mandelbrot set, which Mandelbrot used to exemplify fractal geometric shapes that are "'rough' at all scales. No matter how close you look, they never get simpler, much as the section of a rocky coastline you can see at your feet looks just as jagged as the stretch you can see from space"[103] (see figure I.11). Describing this as "a new geometry of nature," Mandelbrot devised these shapes to "study those forms that Euclid leaves aside as being 'formless' . . . [and] 'amorphous.'"[104] We access the infinite island through what Mandelbrot calls a mathematics of the "irregular and fragmented," a "Natural Geometry of certain 'wiggles,'" in which the chaotic wiggles (or fractal shapes) are a "'gallery of monsters'" in the eyes of Euclid or Newton.[105] In terms of an insular epistemology, the infinite island takes us far away from fantasy desert isle that is knowable, even predictable, in its clichéd tropological dimensions, to an uncanny and unknowable island that calls into question what we know and how we know.

The anti-explorer walks the infinite island's coastline. Mandelbrot's fractal geometry has its genesis in this figure, a man walking along a rocky shore of non-Euclidean wiggles. Mandelbrot invites the reader, "Imagine a man walking along the coastline . . . taking the shortest path." When "the tide is low and the waves are negligible," this man might follow the rocky coastline's fractal roughness "down to finer details by harnessing a mouse, then an ant, and so forth. Again, as our walker stays increasingly closer to the coastline, the distance to be covered continues to increase with no limit."[106] So too does Édouard Glissant use the beach walker metaphor to describe the "poetics of Relation" in his book of that title: "The movement of the beach, this rhythmic rhetoric of a shore, do not seem to me gratuitous. . . . This is where I first saw a ghostly young man go by;

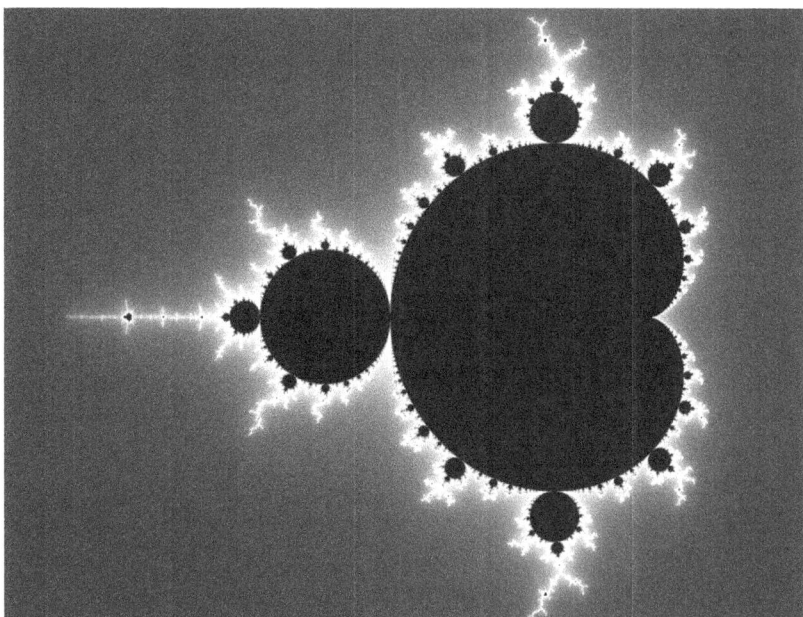

Figure I.11. In a "Mandelbrot set," the shape's boundaries incorporate endlessly smaller versions of the shape itself, creating fractal self-similarity at any scale. This image resembles plate 188 in Mandelbrot's *The Fractal Geometry of Nature*. Created by Wolfgang Beyer with the program *Ultra Fractal 3*. Available at https://en.wikipedia.org/wiki/Mandelbrot_set#/media/File:Mandel_zoom_00_mandelbrot_set.jpg. GNU Free Documentation License.

his tireless wandering traced a frontier between the land and water."[107] When this man appears at the end of *Poetics,* he merges with Mandelbrot's beach walker, the figure who traces the fractals—the broken, scabrous, wiggling shapes—that constitute the chaos of Nature: "The man who walks . . . is making sense of the beach. . . . This enclosed errantry, this circular nomadism—but one with no goal or end or recommencing. . . . His traveling . . . traces repeated figures here on the earth, whose pattern we would catch if we had the means to discover it. This man who walks . . . represents chaos without realizing it."[108] In tracing "repeated figures" and subtle "patterns," this anti-explorer leads us to read in reference to the category of form, or self-similar patterns that repeat across space and as an object is subjected to increasing magnification.[109]

No doubt the infinite island's logic moves against much of transnationalism's dedication to vastness as conventionally conceived. Rather, it is aligned with what Americanist Terrell Scott Herring has recently valorized as a study of "microregion" that might counterbalance Americanists' "'planetary turn'" with "an interpretive scale" that "does not preclude the infinitely subnational."[110] In defense—and advocacy—of a move toward the infinitely small analytical frames proffered by Mandelbrot and Glissant's infinite island, one might consider several arenas in which the very small becomes highly significant. Think of the Large Hadron Collider's role in testing for theorized and inconceivably small particles that are then linked to questions of extra dimensions and warped geometries with universal implications.[111] Or think of what Cook Island writer Florence "Johnny" Frisbie has referred to as the existential/ecological import of eating just one coconut crab on the Pacific atoll of Pukapuka; speaking of the lagoon and one of the small islands on its edge, Frisbie recalls, "Nine months of the year, ten months of the year, nobody goes to the little island. . . . If we go . . . and kill the turtle and eat the coconut crab, we're not going to have anything. The lagoon is like a womb."[112] Or consider the growth (i.e., the endless elaborations conducing toward infinitely small details) of the Koch island or Mandelbrot set (see figures I.10 and I.11), and think of the pantun verse of peninsular and archipelagic Southeast Asia, "a verse that grows and develops upon itself as coral flowers upon a reef."[113]

Here on the infinite island, frames of analysis become simultaneously infinite in their smallness and in their unending capacity for reaching ever greater levels of resolution: the bay, when examined within a closer frame, is shown to contain many subbays, and each subbay, when examined within a still closer frame, contains many sub-subbays, and the sub-subbays further resolve into sub-sub-subbays in an infinite regress of recursively smaller analytic frames, as animated in "Koch Snowflake, Koch Curve," which is accessible online.[114] This is an estranging view of the island as mise en abyme, a trope that literally means "placed into abyss" (recall that -*pelago*, from *archipelago*, refers to an abyss) but is widely used to describe an artistic work that contains an inset image of itself, where the inset image then contains a further image of itself, and so on, with the pattern continuing into infinity (see figure I.12). Fractal geometry's mise en abyme, which Mandelbrot derived from the geographical form of the island, is taken back up again in relation to the island by Jamaican–New Yorker artist Sandra Stephens. Stephens is keenly aware of the aesthetic qualities evoked by repeating regularities, and her digital artwork self-consciously draws upon Mandelbrot's geometry to visualize and figure the island via fractal self-similarity.[115] Stephens's *Fractal 3* advances a set of repeating and mirroring wiggles, rather than easy Euclidean straight lines, and as the coastline is represented by an even more roughened outline of Mandelbrot's fractal shape, it blurs the relations between land/sand, shoreline, and water (see figure I.13). On Stephens's island, fractal repetition and regression inhabit not only the shore but also the interior of the island, as seashells and small images of the island itself plummet into the abyss of what Mandelbrot describes as the fine corrugations that produce the island's infinite area.

Figure I.12. Sandra Stephens, digital manipulation of Tyler Kane, *Successors of the Unknown*, 2015. Charcoal drawing, 22×30 in. Used with permission of the artists.

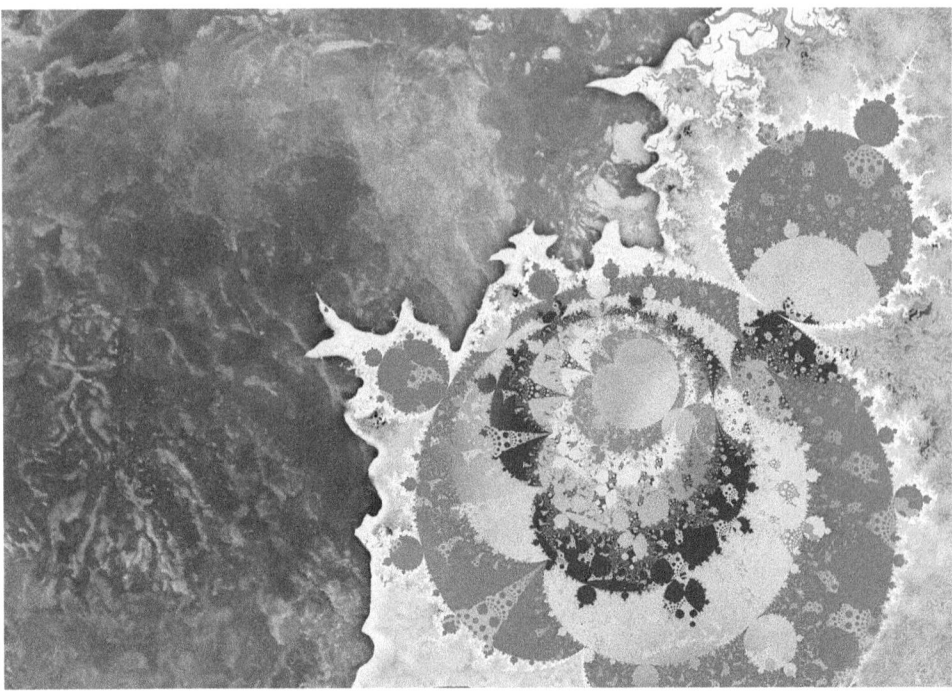

Figure I.13. Sandra Stephens, *Fractal 3*, 2012. Digital image with background texture from painting by Jenna North. Used with permission of the artists.

If the island has often functioned throughout colonial and postcolonial history as a fixed space that is easily accessed and assessed, the infinite island reflects a deeper experience and understanding of insularity that intersects with Glissant's notion of errancy, or the open and curious relationship to the Real that he advocates. This is again that insular-real of island experiences that have not been fully symbolized and codified. This anti-explorer's island, with its myriad seashells and other forms that recursively plunge into a corrugated abyss, dashes the aspirations of would-be close readers who fantasize of a "shipwreck" and a "deserted island" where they might "enjoy some close reading," peacefully and simply, far from the maddening and "inconceivable quantity of texts" long available in libraries and archives and, now, "from electronic databases."[116] Rather than offering an idyllic return to close reading, the anti-explorer's island is a maelstrom, a place constituted by infinitely large numbers of analytical frames moving toward the infinitely minute, matching and even exceeding the sheer capaciousness of what Franco Moretti, beginning in the year 2000, has described as "distant reading."[117] Approaching this island brings us closer to what is both unknowable and unscalable in the Real. But it also requires us to think about how such phenomena as repetition and self-similarity, the infinitude of minute effects imaged in the mathematical Mandelbrot set and troped in the notion of mise en abyme, can magnify up into linked archipelagic networks that are also attributes of an "insularity" for which we barely have a name.

THINKING WITH THE ARCHIPELAGO: THE DISTANT READER AND THE NETWORK-ASSEMBLAGE

Drawing directly on evolutionary theory's reliance on archipelagoes' tendency to give rise to various interrelated species, Moretti in *Distant Reading* (2013) has written of European literature as arising from a "discontinuous, fractured... European space [that] functions as a sort of archipelago of (national) sub-spaces, each of them specializing in one formal variation."[118] In his repeated use of the archipelago as both metaphor and model, Moretti's move is an acknowledgment of the archipelago's power to hold in tension and undercut both the myopia of nationalism and transnationalism's tendency to paper over difference.[119] Yet before Moretti arrived at the archipelago as a geographical grounding for the practice of distant reading, Glissant was addressing distant readers who inhabit an archipelagic world.[120] In the very moment at which Glissant in his *Poetics of Relation* (1990) enjoined us to consider the infinite patterns and textures traced by the beach-walking anti-explorer, he addressed his reader directly: "Distant reader, as you recreate these imperceptible details on the horizon, ... look at him," look at "the man who walks."[121] Glissant's *distant reader,* we would suggest, is an anti-explorer who not only merges with the beach walker in tracing the island's infinite mise en abyme but also who apprehends, as Glissant observes elsewhere, that "each island is an opening," an opening onto other islands, figuring the individual island (any individual island) as a participant within a world genre of islands, which, in their insular interlinkings, emerge as a planet-spanning archipelagic assemblage.[122] This mode of thought, expressed powerfully in Hau'ofa's image of an expansive sea of islands, is less about *island interchangeability* than it is about *island interchange.*

The fraught discourse of insular interchangeability has been of longue durée. As a quick case in point we might look toward Bali Ha'i, a fictional island that was popularized in the mid-twentieth-century United States. Portrayed in Rodgers and Hammerstein's *South Pacific* (musical 1949 and film 1958), Bali Ha'i emerged as a wide ranging fusion of apparently Indonesian, French Polynesian, Tongan, and Puerto Rican elements, such that Puerto Rican actresses seemed to pose as ethnically Tongan while interacting with French planters and singing of an island whose name evoked one of the most widely known sites in Indonesia.[123] Like the trope of the desert isle, the idea of island interchangeability takes the idea of a "repeating island" and reduces it to a place out of time, with a mishmash of cultural elements whose contours—whose ties and links to other historical and cultural elements very near or very far away—are flattened out and become meaningless, organized instead around more reified notions of the tropical island idyll, and exoticized understandings of cultural hybridity and creolization.

Against this flattening, it is from an understanding of both the regularities and irregularities, the patterns and ruptures, that accumulate when dealing with individual items within a large and ever-multiplying, ever-evolving set, that distant readers of the world genre of islands will see repeating regularities (a reef structure, a wave's curl, a shore's contour, an introduced tree or feral animal species, a mise en abyme, an opening). Anti-explorers will also note, with Mandelbrot, that chaos's fractal repetitions may be *statistical* but they are not exact.[124] Against the discourse of insular interchangeability, anti-explorers understand, with Florence Frisbie, that no two islands are the same.[125] A more networked idea of *island interchange* suggests that islanders have always, in contradistinction to our colloquial notions of insularity as bounded and closed-in, been aware of, curious about, and able to distinguish themselves from their connections to formations beyond their island shores.

Looking beyond the individual and infinite island, we would suggest that the wide-ranging human project of describing—and conjuring into existence—the coherence of groups of islands has been a prime example of *catachresis,* one that has taken place across historical epochs and across cultures and regions. In the classical sense referred to by the first-century Roman rhetorician Quintilian, catachresis is "the practice of adapting the nearest available term to describe something for which no actual term exists," as in the *tooth* of a comb or the *leg* of a table.[126] We want to frame archipelago formation in terms of this trope of catachresis, whereby "archipelago" itself becomes a term deployed in the attempt to name connections—the "submarine" unities between land and sea, island and island, island and continent—that are harder to see from the shores of landlocked, above-ground, territorial epistemologies and ways of thinking.[127] Analogous to the Mediterranean term "archipelago" in its catachrestic work to conjure an interisland grouping, the Javanese notion of *nusantara* ("the *other* islands") emerged in the fourteenth century as a catachrestic and island-centric mode of envisioning the world beyond Java.[128] The island interchange (rather than insular interchangeability) that we advocate for rests on islanders' interest in apprehending, and naming for themselves, their relations—both converging and diverging—with others beyond (and within) their shores. To the degree that this is always an open, uncertain, anxious, exhilarating, repeating process of discovery, familiarity, and threat, what is exchanged, the mobile processes that drive and facilitate those exchanges, slip just outside the boundaries of what can be precisely named and discursively coded.

One might say that as "mise en abyme" is to islands (an estranging yet unexpectedly apropos trope), "catachresis" is to islands that humans have envisioned as interconnected. This archipelagic catachresis inheres in the very dissensus that has surrounded the description of putatively related islands: Are interconnected islands *scattered? Splayed? Groups? Arcs? Far-flung? Links in a chain?* This dissensus in terminology reveals the ways in which island groups are discursively constructed, with the groups' topographical coherence existing as power-constituted and only in relation to national, imperial, linguistic, racial, ethnic, tectonic, or other heuristics.[129] Island naming practices, especially across island clusters, reveal multiple modes of catachresis—creating names and links and overarching networks of meaning for relations across water that seem to have no accepted inherent terminology. Polynesians have historically thought in terms of insular analogy (seen in place names like Savai'i, Hawai'i, Havai'i, and the legendary homeland Hawaiki); English and other European languages strain toward evoking insular interconnection by using the definite article "the" in front of a pluralized proper noun (as in "the Philippines," "the Azores," or "the Antilles"), as if each distinct island were a singular—yet self-cloning—Philippine, Azore, or Antille. Where Benítez-Rojo has seen "meta-archipelago," Hau'ofa has seen a "sea of islands," and Samoan writer Albert Wendt has viewed the "scatter of islands" as a coherent "dazzling . . . creature."[130]

Within the context of catachrestic naming practices that forge archipelagoes, the influential injunction to rethink the United States and America *through other continents* might be reconceptualized so that the networked continents become a cluster of islands in search of their forgotten archipelagic geography, hanging together and yet separated. This image can be contingently emblematized by the Dymaxion map presented by US inventor Richard Buckminster Fuller in 1943, which deforms traditional views of the planet into an icosahedron net with nearly contiguous landmasses (see figure I.14). Here, the spherical shape of the planet unfolds such that the world itself becomes an island. The continental landmasses maintain separation while the map's radical topological shift reconfigures them in a way consistent with the look of an archipelago. We have returned again to that older cartographic specter of a world island surrounded by an ocean sea, as projected by Cassini's map from 1696 (see figure I.5). We use Fuller's map here to image the implied topological shift toward which the study of the archipelagic Americas gestures. It is one in which spaces traditionally conceived of as continental become legible as islands in an archipelago, consistent with Barbadian intellectual George Lamming's commentary on continental

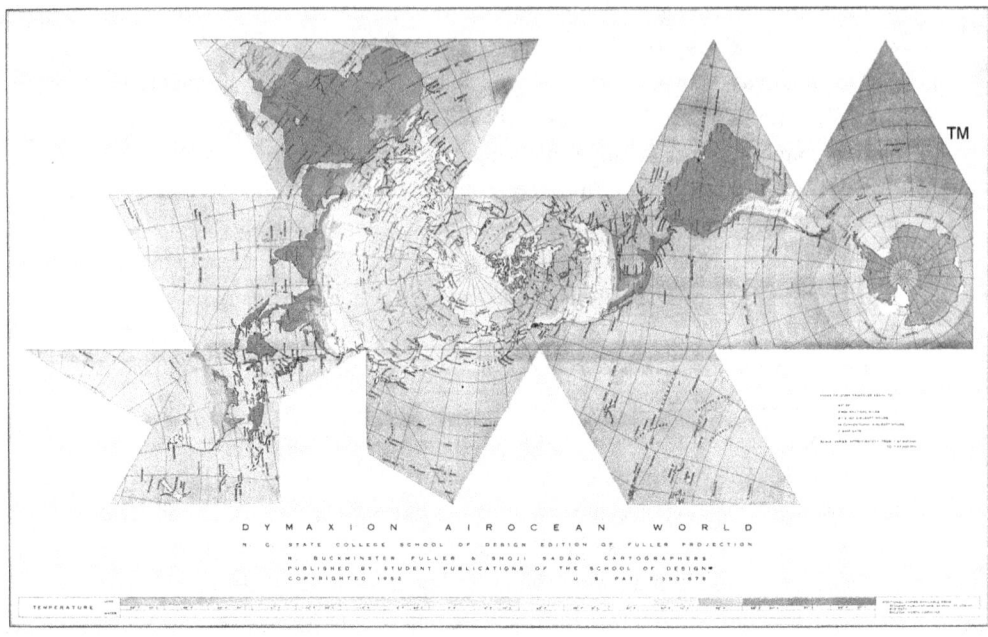

Figure I.14. The Fuller Projection Map design is a trademark of the Buckminster Fuller Institute. ©1938, 1967, and 1992. All rights reserved. www.bfi.org.

America as "one island only" among "the island of China, and the island of Africa and the island of India."[131]

And yet, as useful as Fuller's map may be in terms of reenvisioning continents vis-à-vis islands and archipelagoes, the map's deficiencies are stark with regard to its representation of the planet's major archipelagic networks. It privileges the coherence of large landmasses over the coherence of oceanic spaces, rendering Madagascar as continental Africa's satellite rather than a node within the Indian Ocean world, and dissevering the Caribbean from the Atlantic.[132] Even Wendt's "dazzling . . . creature," that "vast . . . [and] varied . . . scatter of islands" in the Pacific,[133] is drawn and quartered, with blank space repeatedly fracturing the Pacific's oceanic networks of migration and exchange. Papua New Guinea and Aotearoa/New Zealand orbit Australia on the map's far left; a broken ocean divides these Oceanian nodes from the Micronesian islands that float on the map's lower central panel. And the Micronesian islands are further isolated, by yet another broken ocean, from such island groups as Hawai'i, Fiji, and Sāmoa, which reside on the map's lower right panel. Rapa Nui/Easter Island, which sits to the far right, off the southwestern coast of South America, seems more affiliated with Antarctica than with the islands of the Pacific, a view that unfortunately

Figure I.15. Fidalis Buehler, *Bali Hai Series-II*, 2012. Digital print, 54 × 54 in. Used with permission of Fidalis Buehler.

imagines out of existence the waka/canoe routes of a topologically and topographically connected Pacific.

As a map of island-continent interchange (rather than interchangeability), and a catachrestic trope of interconnectedness, the Dymaxion map is expansive in some directions, limited in others. To compensate, we want to return to one of those emblematic islands of interchangeability, Bali Ha'i, and complement Fuller's map with the map proffered by Gilbertese-American visual artist Fidalis Buehler in *Bali Hai Series-II,* a work exhibited in 2012 at the Katherine E. Nash Gallery at the University of Minnesota (figure I.15). Here, rather than seeing islands of the Pacific as broken up and nearly erased, viewers see in the foreground a cross-section of two islands that are geomorphologically connected by submarine topography. These islands' connection is also achieved via a set of filamentous networks, simultaneously evocative of airline routes, communications cables, kinship ties, Internet connections, social networks, and waka/canoe voyages undertaken with the aid of maps perhaps similar to Marshall Island stick charts (figure I.16).[134] These connections proliferate among nodes and across a sea of islands, moving toward a horizon that is represented in the mid-ground. This horizon is not a straight line but is, rather, granular, as if permitting viewers access to—even from a fantastic distance—the bubbles within a wave or the grains of sand on a beach. Here, in resonance with Mandelbrot's fractal geometry, a vast horizon of archipelagic islands shares its scale with the ephemeral air

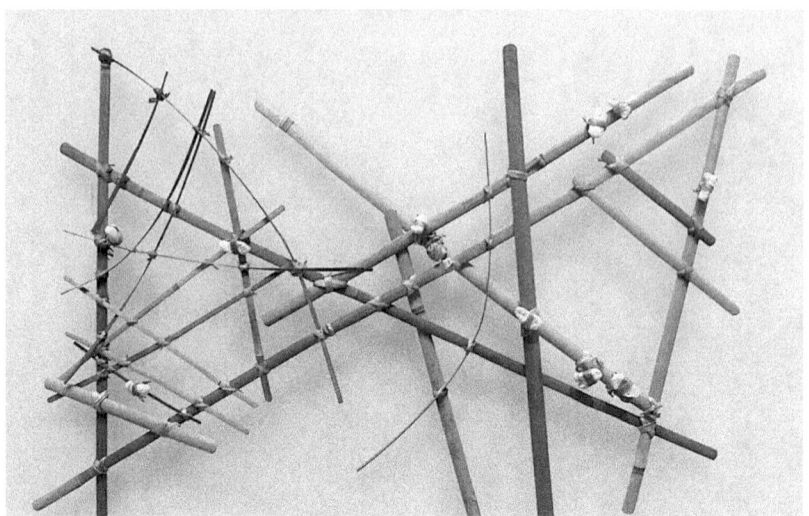

Figure I.16. Navigational stick chart from the Marshall Islands (creation date unknown), displayed at the Berkeley Art Museum and Pacific Film Archive. From the collection of the Phoebe A. Hearst Museum of Anthropology at the University of California, Berkeley. Photo by Jim Heaphy, 2016. Available at https://commons.wikimedia.org/wiki/File%3AMicronesian_navigational_chart.jpg. Creative Commons License (CC BY-SA 3.0), https://creativecommons.org/licenses/by-sa/3.0/.

bubble or the infinite untrackable sand grains tumbling in a wave. The supraregional horizon melds with the islands' microregional corrugations. Meanwhile, over and beyond the horizon, the infinite islands' multidirectional networks proliferate still, even if the islands themselves are no longer visible due to the Earth's curvature. Rather than a palimpsest of undifferentiated "island" characteristics and tropes thrown inward and dumped on a fictional Bali Ha'i's shores, filaments reach outward connecting the real referents for Bali Ha'i, say, to the island of America, the islands of the Azores, the island of China, the islands of Trinidad and Tobago, the island of Africa, the Chagos Archipelago, the island of India, or the islands of the Galapagos.

During the opening ceremony of the 2014 UN Climate Change Summit, Marshallese poet Kathy Jetnil-Kijiner catalogued an archipelago of sites that, although long-since mapped according to the explorer's method, have not existed according to the explorer's imaginary: "there are those / hidden behind platinum tiles / who like to pretend / that we don't exist / that the marshall islands / tuvalu / kiribati / maldives / and typhoon haiyan in the philippines / and floods of pakistan, algeria, columbia / and all the hurricanes, earthquakes, and tidalwaves / didn't exist."[135] Jetnil-Kijiner's poem works in tandem with Buehler's *Bali Hai Series-II*.

Against imagined nonexistence, and in the spirit of what has recently been described as the "vital need within 'isolated' archipelagoes to break through the strictures of an area studies imaginary and its conceptual limits,"[136] Buehler's *Bali Hai Series-II* and Jetnil-Kijiner's poem take the anti-explorer's tack, turning toward sites already mapped and dismissed for their smallness, refiguring them as infinite both in terms of site-specific corrugations and in terms of their catachrestic coherence as an assemblage, their networked proliferations beyond the horizon.

AN ARCHIPELAGIC COLLECTION FOR AN AMERICAN ARCHIPELAGO

In this introduction, we have referred repeatedly to the archipelagic Americas, or the temporally shifting and spatially splayed set of islands, island chains, and island-ocean-continent relations that have exceeded US-America and have been affiliated with and indeed constitutive of competing notions of the Americas since at least 1492. Taken together, the essays in this collection do not treat some sort of idealized space (i.e., *the* American archipelago) but rather offer a contingent view of what a protean, material, and messy space (i.e., *an* American archipelago, among many possible visions) might look like, as a subset of the much larger archipelagic Americas. Because of this collection's disciplinary grounding in the field of American studies, it continues to take the United States, with its cultures of imperial and global interdependencies, as a notable object of study.[137] Hence, within the current volume, the United States has a persistent if ever-shifting presence, in some chapters emerging as the main object of much needed archipelagic analysis and reevaluation, while elsewhere becoming a coprotagonist with the cultures of other nation-states or regions in new narratives of broader American archipelagic relations. Still elsewhere, the United States becomes an antagonist against which Indigenous archipelagoes struggle for recognition of sovereignty, and in other cases the United States fades into the deep background while non-US archipelagic American relations come into sharp focus across the planet. The geographical diversity, frequently within single essays, spans from Canada to New Zealand, from the early eighteenth century's Archipiélago de México to the present-day Caribbean, from José Martí's Cuba to José Rizal's Philippines, from the Bahamas to an island set in the US-Canada borderwaters, from Haida Gwaii (off the coast of British Columbia) to Pongso no Tau (of the Taiwanese archipelago) to Aotearoa (New Zealand), from Kamehameha I's Pae ʻĀina (Hawaiʻi) to Italy, from Jamaica to England, from the Philippines to its planetary diaspora, from the French Antilles to the contested site of Guam, to theoretical and imagined geographies, to subaltern archipelagoes within the continental United States. Because of this geographical diversity, and because of the varieties of ways in which a site or person may embrace or contest imperatives that they *be American* (to borrow a phrase from Carlos Bulosan),[138] the essays here cannot permit the term "American" to function as a stand-in or abbreviation for the "United States of America." Rather, in referring to the United States of America we use the terms "US-America" and "United States," although we retain certain standard US-American-oriented terms, such as "Native American," "African American," "Asian American," and "American Pacific."[139] Otherwise, terms such as "American," "Americas," and "America" (as in the "American Culture" of our introduction's title) are reserved for references to notions of America that may include not only the United States but also hemispheric frames as well as frames that exceed or precede the United States as an entity.

Of course, this is an approach to American studies that bears the deep impress of the field's transnational turn. And in bearing that impress, it also shares with transnational American studies a common set of purviews and problematics that point toward the question of critical genre. Whereas the 1950s and 1960s myth-and-symbol school of American studies found its central critical genre in the monograph (with new monographs vying to either embellish upon or overthrow and replace the United States' fundamental myth), the transnational American studies found one of its central critical genres in the essay collection, as scholars with differentiated specialties have collaborated to bring into focus something beyond what their individual arenas of expertise might render legible.[140] The situation is similar in the context of an American studies that is becoming archipelagic. No individual scholar will be acquainted with the expanse of uncounted and oftentimes unacknowledged islands that have constituted the archipelagic Americas' place within the larger planetary archipelago. Yet to the degree that the very project of distant reading is an archipelagic project, the collection itself becomes not simply a *reader* (or anthology) on archipelagic American studies but also a *distant reader* of the Americas' constitution by and intersections with the world genre of islands. Hence, we would see *Archipelagic American Studies*' collaborative dedication to reading discontinuous yet interlinked geographies in analogy to Alice Te Punga Somerville's 2010 commentary on anthologies of Pacific literature: "These . . . anthologies become waka: taking on things and travellers, dropping them off in new places, accruing value and meaning from the diversity of their cargoes."[141] As a collection, then, our canoe-anthology undertakes its voyage with the intention to promote a transition from an archipelagic American studies in-solution (or suspended in water, practiced as a structure of feeling by various scholars) to an archipelagic American studies precipitated, or an archipelagic American studies crystallizing into what is already in the water, an emergent conceptual formation and epistemological framework.[142] *Archipelagic American Studies* becomes an interisland shuttle—a networking canoe or waka—helping to trace the United States and the Americas' imbrications with "transnational insularity" as it cuts across a "world of archipelagic regions."[143]

In parts I and II, *Theories and Methods for an Archipelagic American Studies* and *Archipelagic Mappings and Meta-Geographies,* the authors theorize the ways in which archipelagic heuristics can function as new epistemological frameworks, the archipelagic island itself becoming a figure for methodological and conceptual approaches to US and generally American cultural and historical material. These opening parts reflect the idea that islands have often stood in, as tropes, for the boundaries of new knowledge, as thresholds for new cartographic understandings of the Real. In "Heuristic Geographies: Territories and Areas, Islands and Archipelagoes," Lanny Thompson powerfully sets forth the archipelagic model as a heuristic that facilitates an interlinked vision of states, areas, islands, and the world more generally. The essay brings a social-scientific approach to these interrelations, and further examines the archipelago's analytical utility vis-à-vis the key categories of spatiality and temporality. Elaine Stratford's "Imagining the Archipelago" permits readers to perceive an archipelagic United States, situating the continental United States within a continuum between the local and the global. Stratford bases her notion of "the United States as an archipelago" on "five modes of archipelagicity," which she elaborates on using Elizabeth DeLoughrey's notion of "archipelagraphy" to describe how thinking about the continent in terms of island-continent-ocean assemblages can unfix the continent from the older paradigms of a discourse of Manifest Destiny.

In "Guam and Archipelagic American Studies," Craig Santos Perez places Guam at the center of, rather than as a footnote to, US-American history. His idea of the "auto-archipelago" plots Guam's, and any island's, archipelagic relation to its multiversioned self, while his notion of the "terripelago" captures both the determining structures and fissures in the notions of territoriality that have shaped the US empire. Etsuko Taketani's focus in "The Archipelagic Black Global Imaginary: Walter White's Pacific Island Hopping" is on a spatial paradigm shift occurring in the 1940s that had an impact specifically on an African American global imaginary. The shift transforms the maritime, equatorially based perspective provided since Mercator's seventeenth-century mapping of the world, into a polar-based cartography of an "aerial (transcontinental) Atlantic," useful for military endeavors during World War II. If "air-age globalism" began White's questioning of the boundaries of and relations between hemispheres and continents, it was his island hopping through the archipelagic Pacific, Taketani argues, that allowed him to chart a new political geography of race. The final essay of the second part, Susan Gillman's "It Takes an Archipelago to Compare Otherwise," offers a bold reimagining of comparativism as a methodology. Gillman suggests that the "archipelagic challenge" provides an opportunity for us to justify a model of comparison that is truly multinodal, self-conscious in the way it theorizes simultaneous disjunctions and conjunctions. Using a "Mediterraneanizing" approach to examine the complex set of interrelations among C. L. R. James and W. Adolphe Roberts (two West Indian nationalists of the mid-twentieth century) and José Martí and José Rizal (founding figures of Cuban and Philippine nationalism in the late nineteenth century), she identifies the analogical relations paired with disjunctions that have typically stymied their comparison. Her essay showcases the payoffs of taking up the "archipelagic challenge" of routing comparativist methodologies through self-consciously archipelagic templates. All together the essays in these two opening parts offer new terminology and frameworks for thinking with the archipelago as an epistemological heuristic, for demonstrating new methodological interventions facilitated by archipelagic investigations, and for mapping new islandic, oceanic, and continental topologies.

In parts III and IV, *Empires and Archipelagoes* and *Islands of Resistance,* the authors use historical, literary, and cultural criticism to deconstruct colonial discourses and tropes of the island and anti-insular ideologies. The essays in these two parts grapple with the various legacies—historical, political, cultural, economic, linguistic, ideological, and subjective—of imperialism and the colonial world system in America-affiliated and America-constituting island spaces, and the negotiation and rearticulation of these legacies in various literary and cultural forms in contexts ranging from the Pacific to the Caribbean and from Mexico to the United States and Canada. Yolanda Martínez-San Miguel's "Colonial and Mexican Archipelagoes: Reimagining Colonial Caribbean Studies" describes the historical formation and present existence of what she terms "colonial archipelagoes," which are archipelagic spaces that have been territorialized by multiple imperial powers. In delineating the concept of the colonial archipelago, Martínez-San Miguel illustrates Greater Mexico's importance to pursuing an American studies that is archipelagic, as she reminds us that what we now think of as the Caribbean was during the seventeenth and eighteenth centuries constructed as the Archipelago of Mexico, an archipelago networked with the Philippines. In addition to official imperial cartographies, she describes a colonial archipelagic cartography in which islands function as navigational nodes central to the networks created between ports by the Spanish flota system. The logic of the historical Mexican Archipelago then shadows a contemporary US Virgin Islands writer's short story about an archipelago in the process of collapse, as older colonial frameworks fragment into new decolonial realities. In "Invisible Islands: Remapping the Transpacific Archipelago of US Empire in Carlos Bulosan's *America Is in the Heart,*" Joseph Keith begins with the desert island trope as deployed in *Robinson Crusoe,* "one of the canonical narratives of the colonial imagination." Bulosan updates the Robinsonade trope in his semiautobiographical novel of a young Filipino migrant laborer's transition from the Philippines to an itinerant life in the continental United States. Keith argues that, over the course of the novel, Bulosan also maps an alternative, subaltern geography of the United States, an "insular topography of racialized and 'unincorporated' subjects and spaces" that stretches between and beyond the nation's conventionally identified borders to the Philippines. Recasting the "island castaway" narrative as a bildungsroman, the protagonist's story emerges within a setting in which the archipelagic comes to represent both a repressive sociopolitical geography, much like Mike Davies's "urban archipelago" or Amy Kaplan's "penal archipelago,"[144] but also a new kind of community, "a multiracial archipelago of global migrants laboring at the limits of citizenship" within the nation. Nicole Waligora-Davis's "'Myth of the Continents': American Vulnerabilities and 'Rum and Coca-Cola,'" examines some of the tensions and relations between US continentalism and US imperial interests in the islands of the Caribbean just before the mid-twentieth century, as they coalesced around the Andrews sisters' famous 1945 hit song "Rum and Coca-Cola." Waligora-Davis argues that "the circulation of this song, the copyright infringement cases pursued (1945–1948), and the social histories marshaled in its lyrics, provide an entry-point for understanding US militarization in the West Indies and its reciprocal social, political, economic, and cultural effects."

In "'Shades of Paradise': Craig Santos Perez's Transpacific Voyages," John Carlos Rowe uses the poet's work to demonstrate how an anticolonial poet-activist (and contributor to the present collection) reclaims Indigenous traditions while still drawing on the colonial archive as an inescapable, determining force. For Rowe, transpacific studies and archipelagic American studies are linked in their common attention to the ways colonial world systems have deeply structured and affected archipelagic regions. Rowe argues that an archipelagic methodology "is more than merely a scholarly approach; it is also an alternative ontology for peoples who have experienced the multiple occupations of colonial powers." Cherene Sherrard-Johnson's focus, in "Insubordinate Islands and Coastal Chaos: Pauline Hopkins's Literary Land/Seascapes," is on the ways in which the late nineteenth-century African American author uses "island openings" or "island prologues" in her otherwise fully continental narratives. Sherrard-Johnson argues that Hopkins pits these islands as "exemplars of hybrid ethnic and ecological harmony" against imperial understandings of nationhood, but also, that she does this by mixing imperial tropes of the islands as paradise with her more historical understanding of islands as insurgent spaces. Utilizing Paul Giles's notion of the parallax zone to triangulate Hopkins's islands, both internal and external to the North American continent, with continental coastlines and circum-Caribbean maritime tides, Sherrard-Johnson offers another frame within which to understand the archipelagic as offering a comparativist reading practice and methodology. Finally, in "'We Are Not American': Competing Rhetorical Archipelagoes in Hawai'i," Brandy Nālani McDougall discusses a sovereign Hawai'i's challenges, both historically and in the present, to a US-American "rhetorical archipelago" that naturalizes the Hawaiian Islands as part of the United States' imperial archipelago. She argues that rhetorics of unification have been a part of the Hawaiian archipelago's history prior to its current status as a US state. Through discussion of a number of cultural and material objects, McDougall narrates both how the Hawaiian Kingdom unified itself, and also how many of these symbols of unification mark both the co-optation and the resistance of the archipelago in relation to US claims.

Parts V and VI, *Ecologies of Relation* and *Insular Imaginaries,* include essays discussing various literary forms and cultural discourses of the "insular-real," that is, material from the archive of actual insular products, cultures, discourses, and cultural forms representing and encompassing island experiences. Situating the canoe as a voyaging technology and trope that unexpectedly connects Indigenous cultures associated with three seemingly disparate island sites throughout the Pacific, Hsinya Huang's "Performing Archipelagic Identities in Bill Reid, Robert Sullivan, and Syaman Rapongan" turns toward the interlinked work of First Nations artist Bill Reid, Aotearoan poet Robert Sullivan, and Indigenous Taiwanese writer Syaman Rapongan to trace the ways that canoes facilitate not only transpacific human connections but also interspecies ecologies as well as correspondences among the living and nonliving. As Huang elucidates, attentiveness to these archipelagic interconnections can counteract continental biases in both American and Native studies. Ramón E. Soto-Crespo's "Archipelagic Trash: Despised Forms in the Cultural History of the Americas" makes a valuable intervention in a number of arenas: as it unearths a new and fascinating archive for both Caribbean studies and the literature of the Americas more broadly, it engages with archipelagic theory to rethink how we conceptualize archives and canons, and other literary forms' relationships to canons. Soto-Crespo identifies archives of trashy fiction that gather together the flotsam and jetsam of a decapitalized whiteness, drifting in the unbounded space of a Sargasso-like Sea that floats in the midst of the circum-Atlantic, within circuits flowing between the postcolonial Caribbean and the United States. Innovatively using and expanding on Moretti's reliance on the archipelago to theorize vast transnational literary systems, he showcases a type of archipelagic antifoundationalism that counters the national foundationalism identified by Doris Sommer and others, undoing national jurisdiction through the logic of less organized and bounded forms of political belonging. In an illuminating essay that complements and interlinks with Soto-Crespo's treatment of the Sargasso and the literary gyres of the Atlantic, Alice Te Punga Somerville contemplates the Pacific and the intersecting cultural and natural gyres that have given rise to the great Pacific garbage patch, a vast soup of plastic particles that circulates in the world's largest ocean, in "The Great Pacific Garbage Patch as Metaphor: The (American) Pacific You Can't See." For Te Punga Somerville, these microscopic and otherwise small plastic particles tell stories not only about the cultures that produced them and set them adrift but also about the Indigenous cultures whose ocean they pollute, and whose presence and migrations within US-American culture and life have remained difficult to detect because of the way general US culture has conceived of the categories of smallness and bigness, island and continent. Te Punga Somerville's rich essay, we hope, works powerfully against her prediction that "most American studies scholars will complete their whole careers without engaging with (perhaps even reading) a Pacific scholar."

Examining two of Josephine Baker's films from the late 1920s and early 1930s, Matthew Pratt Guterl's chapter "The Tropics of Josephine: Space, Time, and Hybrid Movements" interrogates Baker's fascination with and investment in insular and archipelagic spaces and tropes, explaining that although she is well loved for her comedic timing, "it is her melodramatic turn toward loneliness that spotlights her political point, and that draws our eye to islands." Translating Baker's investments in islands into an archipelagic imperative for American studies, Guterl argues for a shift away from the frequently conflated categories of the cosmopolitan and the continental, toward attaining a "better sense of the strange, of the distant, of the seemingly obscure, and of those things that fall outside." J. Michael Dash's "The Stranger by the Shore: The Archipelization of Caliban in Antillean Theatre" introduces Anglophone readers to less-well-known features of Édouard Glissant's work that have to do with his particular poetic notions of space. Specifically, Dash argues that the notion of *naitre au monde,* or "being born or precipitated into the world," represents Glissant's "unceasing concern with how we might inhabit the world poetically or how we might renounce territorial claims in earthly dwelling." The archipelago becomes Glissant's central metaphor and site for a form of "poetic thought" that dwells in a world experienced as a "new liberatory, dream space" rather than in "mapped or geometric" Euclidean terms. Dash uses Glissant's notion of open and archipelagic sites to read more critically "nativist ways of dwelling." Dash's delineation of these ways of dwelling is organized around claims of sovereignty as they are represented, more or less, in three plays from the Francophone world, by Glissant, Aimé Césaire, and José Pliya. In so doing, Dash offers a review of Caribbean theatre as a form in which writers struggle both to define the meaning of Antillean space and to work through the traumatic psychodramas produced in archipelagic subjects by colonial histories.

The essays in part VII, *Migrating Identities, Moving Borders,* focus primarily on how archipelagic formations, movements, and identities transfigure and reconfigure the transnational/global. Birte Blascheck and Teresia Teaiwa's "The Governors-General: Caribbean Canadian and Pacific New Zealand Success Stories" compellingly integrates interviews with younger-generation New Zealanders and Canadians, community newspapers reflecting the views of more established immigrant groups, and the words of minority world leaders. In so doing, their essay examines the interrelation of diaspora and nation, and these categories' relation to the increasingly globalized narrative of "celebritized success" regarding minority political candidates. In the notion of "archipelagic diasporas" the authors also seek to model a comparative method for studying transnational migration phenomena across noncontiguous but articulated spaces, linking relations between islanders and the states they migrate to. Ifeoma Kiddoe Nwankwo's essay "Living the West Indian Dream: Archipelagic Cosmopolitanism and Triangulated Economies of Desire in Jamaican Popular Culture" innovatively maps the economies of desire for the exotic that undergird, in counterintuitive ways, the representational relations between the Caribbean archipelago and the continental United States. Nwankwo's alternative mapping goes beyond center-periphery dynamics in describing the triangulated relations among the Caribbean, the United States, and the United Kingdom, facilitating an increased awareness of Anglophone Caribbean agency in shaping the relationships between and among the three. This permits her to focus on the class and gendered aspects of the Jamaican dream (of travel sophistication and know-how) as it relates to a perhaps more often discussed (US) American Dream. Allan Punzalan Isaac's "Offshore Identities: Ruptures in the 300-Second Average Handling Time," focuses on call center agents in the Philippines who link the "outsourced voices of the global South" to the "lightning speed of capital consumption of goods, technologies, and services." Relying on interviews with these agents, as workers who "work abroad and live at home," Isaac examines how their nighttime work lives are structured by an archipelagic logic that pits corporate global time against everyday nation time. At the same time, their "after the call" identities as national consumers and domestic tourists create a national reimagining of "offshore" archipelagic space as a tourist destination. Citizens of the Philippines in the call center industry become new "offshore subjects," with simultaneously national and transnational identities.

The afterword, "The Archipelagic Accretion," by Paul Giles, frames archipelagic American studies' relation to the larger field not as based on the type of "theoretical parricide" associated with anxiety-of-influence approaches to advancing "some new critical method." Rather, for Giles, an archipelagic Americanist approach is "constructed in a more organic way around spatial and temporal accretion." Giles's term "accretion," by which he refers to a gradual buildup, reminds us of the organic accretions that have helped produce shorelines in many parts of the world, as the limestone skeletons of coral and other organisms have become sand, and then have been gradually built up to form beaches and entire islands in many cases. This image of accretion (in which small stones that at first may appear to be nonbiological are recalled, counterintuitively, as foundational building blocks of sea life and its environment) is consistent with Giles's assertion that the archipelagic will have the "capacity to turn [the notion of America] inside out," "the capacity to enable an imaginative inversion of the domestic premises that have traditionally underpinned the field of American studies."

NOTES

1. Sanford Levinson and Bartholomew H. Sparrow, introduction to *The Louisiana Purchase and American Expansionism, 1803–1898* (Lanham: Rowman & Littlefield Publishers, 2005), 2; "Louisiana Purchase Lesson Plan," Stanford History Education Group, accessed January 6, 2016, http://sheg.stanford.edu/upload/Lessons/Unit%204 _Expansion%20and%20Slavery/Louisiana%20Purchase%20Lesson%20Plan.pdf.

2. Richard W. Van Alstyn, *American Diplomacy in Action: A Series of Case Studies*, 2nd ed. (Palo Alto, CA: Sanford University Press, 1947), 135.

3. On the US trusteeship in (or annexation of) Micronesia, see Elizabeth M. DeLoughrey, *Routes and Roots: Navigating Caribbean and Pacific Island Literatures* (Honolulu: University of Hawai'i Press, 2007), 17–18 and 31; and Oleg Kurochkin, *The Annexation of Micronesia: US Colonialism in the Twentieth Century* (Moscow: Novosti, 1986).

4. Richard Drinnon, *Facing West: The Metaphysics of Indian-Hating and Empire-Building* (1980; repr., Norman: University of Oklahoma Press, 1997), 129.

5. In spite of its transnationalization, American studies as a field continues to have its center of gravity in the study of US culture's presence and contestations inside and outside of the United States.

6. Donald Pease, "Re-thinking 'American Studies after US Exceptionalism,'" *American Literary History* 21, no. 1 (2009): 19, 20.

7. Quoted in Christina Duffy Burnett and Burke Marshall, "Between the Foreign and the Domestic: The Doctrine of Territorial Incorporation, Invented and Reinvented," in *Foreign in a Domestic Sense: Puerto Rico, American Expansion, and the Constitution*, ed. Christina Duffy Burnett and Burke Marshall (Durham, NC: Duke University Press, 2001), 1.

8. Although Guam and the Philippines were also declared to be "foreign in a domestic sense" (Burnett and Marshall, "Between the Foreign," 1), Puerto Rico has attracted more attention among Americanists for being assigned this anomalous status. See, for instance, Amy Kaplan, *The Anarchy of Empire in the Making of U.S. Culture* (Cambridge, MA: Harvard University Press, 2002), 2–4; Priscilla Wald, *Constituting Americans:*

Cultural Anxiety and Narrative Form (Durham, NC: Duke University Press, 1995), 224; Ramón Soto-Crespo, *Mainland Passages: The Cultural Anomaly of Puerto Rico* (Minneapolis: University of Minnesota Press, 2009), 59–60 and 101–2; Nicole Waligora-Davis, *Sanctuary: African Americans and Empire* (New York: Oxford University Press, 2011), xiv, 94–104.

9. See Rob Wilson, *Reimagining the American Pacific: From "South Pacific" to Bamboo Ridge and Beyond* (Durham, NC: Duke University Press, 2000); Allan Punzalan Isaac, *American Tropics: Articulating Filipino America* (Minneapolis: University of Minnesota Press, 2006); Mary A. Renda, *Taking Haiti: Military Occupation and the Culture of U.S. Imperialism, 1915–1940* (Chapel Hill: University of North Carolina Press, 2001); and Matthew Pratt Guterl, *American Mediterranean: Southern Slaveholders in the Age of Emancipation* (Cambridge, MA: Harvard University Press, 2008).

10. Figures for 1949 through 1999 are based on JSTOR Advanced Search, using "archipelago," "archipelagoes," "archipelagos," "archip," and "pelago," and then searching through individual articles to confirm that "archipelago" (or any derivative form of the word) indeed appears. Figures for 2000 through 2015 are based on Project Muse Advanced Search, using "archipelago," "archipelagoes," "archipelagos," "archip," and "pelago," and then searching through individual articles to determine that "archipelago" (or any derivative form of the word) indeed appears. In calculating the number of articles appearing during the two timeframes, we used a loose definition of "article" that includes not only standard articles but also issue introductions, forum contributions, and book reviews.

11. Macarena Gómez-Barris and Licia Fiol-Matta, "Introduction: Las Américas Quarterly," *American Quarterly* 66, no. 3 (2014): 501–2. Just one of the four essays in this section uses any derivative of the term "archipelago": Alexandra T. Vazquez's essay frames itself as contributing to "work . . . in the surround of Archipelagic American studies"; Alexandra T. Vazquez, "Learning to Live in Miami," *American Quarterly* 66, no. 3 (2014): 872n10.

12. Paul Lyons and Ty P. Kāwika Tengan, "Introduction: Pacific Currents," *American Quarterly* 67, no. 3 (2015): 553; Craig Santos Perez, "Transterritorial Currents and the Imperial Terripelago," *American Quarterly* 67, no. 3 (September 2015): 619.

13. Sarah Banet-Weiser, "Editor's Note," *American Quarterly* 66, no. 3 (September 2014): v.

14. "All OIA Jurisdictions," U.S. Department of the Interior, Office of Insular Affairs, accessed June 30, 2014, http://www.doi.gov/oia/islands/index.cfm.

15. On this history, see Haunani-Kay Trask, *From a Native Daughter: Colonialism and Sovereignty in Hawai'i* (1993; repr., Honolulu: University of Hawai'i Press, 1999), 4–16.

16. On these three later countries, see Isaac, *American Tropics*, 2.

17. Quoted in Jimmy M. Skaggs, *The Great Guano Rush: Entrepreneurs and American Overseas Expansion* (New York: St. Martin's, 1994), 227.

18. Skaggs, *Great Guano Rush*, 230–36, 77, and 123.

19. Lanny Thompson, *Imperial Archipelago: Representation and Rule in the Insular Territories under U.S. Dominion after 1898* (Honolulu: University of Hawai'i Press, 2010), 1.

20. Chris Iannini, *Fatal Revolutions: Natural History, West Indian Slavery, and the Routes of American Literature* (Chapel Hill: University of North Carolina Press, 2012), 4, 91, 10. See also Keith Sandiford, *Theorizing a Colonial Caribbean Atlantic Imaginary: Sugar and Obeah* (New York: Routledge, 2011); and Monique Allewaert, *Ariel's Ecology: Plantations, Personhood, and Colonialism in the American Tropics* (Minneapolis: University of Minnesota Press, 2013).

21. José David Saldívar, *Trans-Americanity: Subaltern Modernities, Global Coloniality, and the Cultures of Greater Mexico* (Durham, NC: Duke University Press, 2011). On the "American tropics" paradigm, see Maria Cristina Fumagalli, Peter Hulme, Owen Robinson, and Lesley Wylie, eds., *Surveying the American Tropics: A Literary Geography from New York to Rio* (Liverpool, UK: Liverpool University Press, 2013).

22. See Annemarie de Waal Malefijit, *The Javanese of Surinam: Segment of Plurality* (Assen, Netherlands: Van Gorcum, 1963), 25–31; and Paul Gilroy, *The Black Atlantic: Modernity and Double Consciousness* (Cambridge, MA: Harvard University Press, 1993).

23. Matt K. Matsuda, *Pacific Worlds: A History of Seas, Peoples, and Cultures* (New York: Cambridge University Press, 2012), 114–26.

24. For Smith's account of Bermuda, see John Smith, *Generall Historie of Virginia, New-England, and the Summer Isles* (London: Blackmore, 1632), 169–201; for Darwin's account of "oceanic islands" and natural selection, see Charles Darwin, *On the Origin of Species by Means of Natural Selection* (1859; repr., London: Murray, 1861), 414–42.

25. Anna Brickhouse, *The Unsettlement of America: Translation, Interpretation, and the Story of Don Luis Velasco, 1560–1945* (New York: Oxford University Press, 2014), 245–52; "Obama Says US Will Defend Japan in Island Dispute with China," *Guardian*, April 24, 2014, http://www.theguardian.com/world/2014/apr/24/obama-in-japan-backs-status-quo-in-island-dispute-with-china.

26. On Guanahani, see Washington Irving, *History of the Life and Voyages of Christopher Columbus,* vols. 1–2 (Philadelphia, PA: Lea & Blanchard, 1841), 287–88; on the Inuit Sea, see Rosemarie Kuptana, "The Inuit Sea," in *Nilliajut: Inuit Perspectives on Security, Patriotism and Sovereignty* (Ottowa: Inuit Tapiriit Kanatami, 2013), 10–12; on the Arctic Archipelago, see Phillip Vannini et al., "Reterritorializing Canada: Arctic Ice's Liquid Modernity and the Imagining of a Canadian Archipelago," *Island Studies Journal* 4, no. 2 (2009): 121–38; on the Aleutians, see Debra G. Corbett, Christine Lefevre, and Douglas Siegel-Causey, "The Western Aleutians: Cultural Isolation and Environmental Change," *Human Ecology* 25, no. 3 (1997): 459–79; on "turtle island," see David Cusick, *Sketches of the Ancient History of the Six Nations* (1827; repr., Lockport, NY: Turner & McCollum, 1848), 13; on England and the Netherlands' 1664 exchange of the Southeast Asian nutmeg island of Run for the island of Manhattan, see Jill Forshee, *Culture and Customs of Indonesia* (Westport, CT: Greenwood, 2006), 15; on the Bikini Atoll, see Jack Niedenthal, *For the Good of Mankind: A History of the People of Bikini and Their Islands* (Majuro, Marshall Islands: Bravo Publishers, 2001); on the Oronoco, see Sir Walter Raleigh, *The Discovery of the Large, Rich, and Beautiful Empire of Guiana* (1596; repr., Cambridge University Press, 2010), 48–49; on Mexico City, see Jonathan Kandell, *La Capital: The Biography of Mexico City* (New York: Random House, 1988), 29–32.

27. Martin W. Lewis and Kären E. Wigen, *The Myth of Continents: A Critique of Metageography* (Berkeley: University of California Press, 1997), 3.

28. Martin W. Lewis, "Dividing the Ocean Sea," *Geographical Review* 89, no. 2 (1999): 188–214.

29. Soekarno, *"Lahirnja Pantjasila" (The Birth of Pantjasila): An Outline of the Five Principles of the Indonesian State* ([Jakarta]: Ministry of Information, Republic of Indonesia, 1952), 20.

30. Our point on archipelagoes is analogous to John R. Gillis's discussion of "islands [as] the master metaphors" that have permitted oceanic navigation; John R. Gillis, *Islands of the Mind: How the Human Imagination Created the Atlantic World* (New York: Palgrave Macmillan, 2004), 5. For Marc Shell, since "human imagination of islandness has variably informed cultures" and "islandness" marks "identity confronting difference" more broadly, "islandology" represents the "study of how we speak about islands" as both empirical and symbolic entities; *Islandology: Geography, Rhetoric, Politics* (Stanford, CA: Stanford University Press, 2014), 1, 3, 5.

31. "Archipelago," *Oxford English Dictionary,* 2nd ed. (Oxford: Clarendon Press, 1989).

32. "Archipelago," *Oxford English Dictionary*.

33. On the place of the island within colonial modernity, see Antonis Balasopoulos, "Nesologies: Island Form and Postcolonial Geopoetics," *Postcolonial Studies* 11, no. 1 (2008): 12–17.

34. Amritjit Singh and Peter Schmidt, "On the Borders Between U.S. Studies and Postcolonial Theory," introduction to *Postcolonial Literature and the United States: Race, Ethnicity, and Literature* (Jackson: University Press of Mississippi, 2000): 3–72; Shelley Fisher Fishkin, "Crossroads of Cultures: The Transnational Turn in American Studies—Presidential Address to the American Studies Association, November 12, 2004," *American Quarterly* 57, no. 1 (2005): 17–57.

35. Michael Denning, "'The Special American Conditions': Marxism and American Studies," *American Quarterly* 38, no. 3 (1986): 364.

36. Against use of the term "America" as a shortened form of "United States of America," Latin American commentators have often relied on a mythic continentalism, reclaiming the term "America" by stating, "América es un continente" (America is a continent) rather than a single country. This phrase was used by Rosa-Linda Fregoso during her presentation for the special session on *AQ*'s special issue *Las Américas Quarterly* at the 2014 American Studies Convention. This mode of Latin American continentalism is consistent with Mexican poet Octavio Paz's 1941 essay "América, ¿Es un Continente?," which advocates for a retrenchment of (Latin) American "continental consciousness" in the face of the United States' imperial work to turn (Latin) America into "a group of islands lacking cohesion and consciousness"; Octavio Paz, "América, ¿Es un Continente?" *Primeras Letras (1931–1943),* ed. Enrico Mario Santí (Mexico City, Mex.: Vuelta, 1988), 191, 192. Translations from the Spanish by Brian Russell Roberts.

37. Robert Cribb and Michele Ford, "Indonesia as an Archipelago: Managing Islands, Managing the Seas," in *Indonesia beyond the Water's Edge: Managing an Archipelagic State* (Singapore: Institute of Southeast Asian Studies, 2009), 1.

38. "Exclusive Economic Zone," *Wikipedia,* accessed Sept. 24, 2016: http://en.wikipedia.org/wiki/Exclusive_economic_zone; and "The United States is an Ocean Nation," NOAA *Office of General Counsel,* accessed Sept. 24, 2016: http://www.gc.noaa.gov/documents/2011/012711_gcil_maritime_eez_map.pdf.

39. For more on issues of sovereignty and nonsovereignty, see Godfrey Baldacchino and David Milne, eds., *The Case for Non-Sovereignty: Lessons from Sub-National Island Jurisdictions* (New York: Routledge, 2008); and Yarimar Bonilla, *Non-Sovereign Futures: French Caribbean Politics in the Wake of Disenchantment* (Chicago: University of Chicago Press), 2015.

40. See André Green, *Key Ideas for a Contemporary Psychoanalysis: Misrecognition and Recognition of the Unconscious* (New York: Brunner-Routledge, 2005), 218.

41. For this definition of archipelagic American studies, we have drawn on previous work in Brian Russell Roberts and Michelle Stephens, "Archipelagic American Studies and the Caribbean," *Journal of Transnational American Studies* 5, no. 1 (2013): 4, 6, 7. For the quotation from Du Bois, see W. E. B. Du Bois, *The Souls of Black Folk,* ed. Brent Hayes Edwards (1903; repr., Oxford: Oxford University Press, 2008), 15.

42. Janice Radway, "What's in a Name? Presidential Address to the American Studies Association, 20 November, 1998," *American Quarterly* 51, no. 1 (1999): 22.

43. Hester Blum, "The Prospect of Oceanic Studies," PMLA 125, no. 3 (2010): 670.

44. George B. Handley, "Toward an Environmental Phenomenology of Diaspora," *Modern Fiction Studies* 55, no. 3 (2009): 656.

45. For a basic overview of topology, see Donald M. Davis, "Topology," in *Encyclopedia of Mathematics Education,* ed. Louise S. Grinstein and Sally I. Lipsey (New York: Routledge-Falmer, 2001), 764–66. Thanks to Matthew Wickman for conversations on topology.

46. For more extensive discussions of continental exceptionalism, see Roberts and Stephens, "Archipelagic American Studies and the Caribbean," 8; and Brian Russell Roberts, "Archipelagic American Literary History and the Philippines," *American Literary History* 27, no. 1 (2015): 129–30.

47. Wai Chee Dimock, *Through Other Continents: American Literature across Deep Time* (Princeton, NJ: Princeton University Press, 2006), 3.

48. For Dimock's reliance on Braudel, see Dimock, *Through Other Continents,* 4–5. On *longue durée* and seas, coasts, and islands as the "heart" of the Mediterranean, see also Fernand Braudel, *The Mediterranean and the Mediterranean World in the Age of Philip II,* vol. 1, trans. Siân Reynolds (1949; repr., Berkeley: University of California Press, 1995), 23–24, 103–67. For her commentary on the continent as a metaphor for transnationalism, see Wai Chee Dimock and Matthew Wickman, "The Wai Chee Dimock Approach," ThinkingAloud, Classical 89, accessed Oct. 10, 2016, http://www.classical89.org/thinkingaloud/archive/episode/?id=4/14/2014.

49. See, for instance, Lisa Lowe's *The Intimacies of Four Continents* (Durham, NC: Duke University Press), 2015. See also Barack Obama's 2009 commentary, "I have known Islam on three continents," on having interacted with Muslims on the island of Java, hailing from his father's Kenyan family, and in the city of Chicago; Barack Obama, "Remarks by the President at Cairo University, 6-04-09," accessed Oct. 11, 2016, https://www.whitehouse.gov/the-press-office/remarks-president-cairo-university-6-04-09.

50. Amy Kaplan, "Manifest Domesticity," *American Literature* 70, no. 3 (1998): 583; John Carlos Rowe et al., introduction to *Post-Nationalist American Studies,* ed. John Carlos Rowe (Berkeley: University of California Press, 2000), 2; Anna Brickhouse, "Hemispheric Jamestown," in *Hemispheric American Studies,* ed. Caroline F. Levander and Robert S. Levine (New Brunswick, NJ: Rutgers University Press, 2008), 21; and Winfried Fluck, "A New Beginning? Transnationalisms," *New Literary History* 42, no. 3 (2011): 381. Emphasis added.

51. "Insular," def. 4.a., *Oxford English Dictionary,* 2nd ed. (Oxford: Clarendon Press, 1989).

52. On islands and cosmopolitanism, see Françoise Lionnet, "Cosmopolitan or Creole Lives? Globalized Oceans and Insular Identities," *Profession* (2011): 27–29.

53. Joseph P. Balaz, "Da Mainland to Me," *Chaminade Literary Review* 2.2 (1989): 109.

54. For an illuminating discussion of Balaz's poem, see Wilson, *Reimagining the American Pacific,* 129–31.

55. José Martí, "Nuestra América," in *Obras Completas / José Martí,* vol. 6 (Havana: Editorial Nacional, 1963), 15–23. Martí's antagonism has frequently animated transnational American studies projects, as in, for instance, Sandhya Shukla and Heidi Tinsman, ed., *Imagining Our Americas: Toward a Transnational Frame* (Durham, NC: Duke University Press, 2007).

56. Key West of the Florida Keys is frequently described as "the southernmost point in the continental United States." See, for instance, Lynn M. Homan and Thomas Reilly, *Images of America: Key West* (Charleston, SC: Arcadia, 2000), 21.

57. Sean Metzger, Francisco-J. Hernández Adrián, and Michaeline Crichlow, "Introduction: Islands, Images, Imaginaries," *Third Text* 28, nos. 4–5 (2014): 338.

58. Quoted in Muhammad Munavvar, *Ocean States: Archipelagic Regimes in the Law of the Sea* (Dordrecht, Neth.: Nijhoff, 1995), 62.

59. John C. Butcher, "Becoming an Archipelagic State: The Juanda Declaration of 1957 and the 'Struggle' to Gain International Recognition of the Archipelagic Principle," in *Indonesia Beyond the Water's Edge: Managing an Archipelagic State* (Singapore: Institute of Southeast Asian Studies, 2009), 35–36.

60. Munavvar, *Ocean States,* 64. One of the Indonesian declaration's architects later recalled that Indonesia was worried about US involvement in the regional unrest of the era: "We had all these big boys interfering, trying to keep us apart because they had their own designs. So this archipelago principle seemed to be a good thing for the important political unity of Indonesia" (Butcher, "Becoming an Archipelagic State," 39).

61. Munavvar, *Ocean States,* 64 and 65.

62. Munavvar, *Ocean States,* 87, 93, 94. Butcher, "Becoming an Archipelagic State," 45.

63. See C. L. R. James's discussions of the West Indian Federation in *Modern Politics* (Detroit, MI: Bewick/Ed, 1973), 81–86; and in C. L. R. James, *At the Rendezvous of Victory: Selected Writings* (London: Allison and Busby, 1984), 85–128. For more of a comparative discussion of James's archipelagic writings at midcentury and the international struggle over the "archipelago principle," see Michelle Stephens, "Federated Ocean States: Archipelagic Visions of the Third World at Midcentury," in *Beyond Windrush: Rethinking Postwar Anglophone Caribbean Literature,* ed. J. Dillon Brown and Leah Rosenberg (Jackson: University of Mississippi Press, 2015), 222–38.

64. Sylvia Wynter and Katherine McKittrick, "Unparalleled Catastrophe for Our Species? Or, to Give Humanness a Different Future: Conversations," in *Sylvia Wynter: On Being Human as Praxis* (Durham, NC: Duke University Press, 2015), 41. Glissant is quoted in Kaiama L. Glover, *Haiti Unbound: A Spiralist Challenge to the Postcolonial Canon* (Liverpool, UK: Liverpool University Press, 2010), 1.

65. Quoted in Celia M. Britton, *Édouard Glissant and Postcolonial Theory: Strategies of Language and Resistance* (Charlottesville: University of Virginia Press, 1999), 179; Antonio Benítez-Rojo, *The Repeating Island: The Caribbean and the Postmodern Perspective*, 2nd ed., trans. James E. Maraniss (Durham, NC: Duke University Press, 1996), 4.

66. Lionnet, "Cosmopolitanism or Creole Lives?," 24.

67. Epeli Hau'ofa, "Our Sea of Islands," in *A New Oceania: Rediscovering Our Sea of Islands*, ed. Eric Waddell, Vijay Naidu, and Epeli Hau'ofa (Suva, Fiji: University of the South Pacific, Beake House, 1993), 6, 7, 8, 13. Our volume's capitalization of the term "Indigenous" takes into consideration the following guidelines suggested by the academic journal *Decolonization: Indigeneity, Education & Society*, which asks contributors to capitalize the word by stating: "These terms are deeply political. When we capitalize them we evoke shared historical memory, cultural meanings, and particular political interests. By spelling indigenous with a lower case I we un/knowingly reproduce dominant writing traditions that seek to minimize and subjugate Indigenous knowledges and people." Oct. 15, 2016: http://decolonization.org/index.php/des/about/submissions. Our sense of appropriate exceptions here and throughout the collection include: references to indigenous plants or animal or things, uses of derivative terms (such as "indigeneity"), appearances of the term in quoted material, and appearances of the term in which capitalization could inadvertently imply that certain members of Indigenous groups are not Indigenous. Taking up the latter example: to say "Indigenous Chamorro populations" or "Indigenous Pacific Islanders" may imply that some Chamorro populations or some Pacific Islanders are not Indigenous, as if Chamorros or Pacific Islanders were groups made up of an Indigenous subset and a settler-colonial subset. In these cases, where the term is redundant but cannot be deleted because it importantly functions to mark a group's indigeneity for readers who may be unaware of it, we have used phrases such as "indigenous Chamorro populations" or "indigenous Pacific Islanders." (We have taken analogous approaches to the terms "Native" and "Aboriginal.") Thanks to Alice Te Punga Somerville for much appreciated help thinking through these editorial practices.

68. For landmark commentary on the fraught use of the term "Pacific Rim," see Arif Dirlik, "Introducing the Pacific," in *What Is in a Rim? Critical Perspectives on the Pacific Region Idea*, ed. Arif Dirlik (Boulder, CO: Westview Press, 1993): 3–11; and Bruce Cumings, "Rimspeak; or, The Discourse of the 'Pacific Rim,'" in Dirlik, *What Is in a Rim*, 29–47. Merlin M. Magallona, "Reflections on Strategic Research: Towards an Archipelagic Studies and Ocean Policy Program," in *Archipelagic Studies: Charting New Waters*, ed. Jay L. Batongbacal (Quezon City: University of Philippines Printery, 1998), 8.

69. Jay L. Batongbacal, "Defining Archipelagic Studies," in Batongbacal, *Archipelagic Studies*, 1998), 183.

70. Batongbacal, "Defining Archipelagic Studies," 194.

71. J. G. A. Pocock, "British History: A Plea for a New Subject," *Journal of Modern History* 47, no. 4 (1975): 613.

72. Pocock, "British History," 606.

73. Philip Schwyzer, introduction to *Archipelagic Identities: Literature and Identity in the Atlantic Archipelago, 1550–1800*, eds. Philip Schwyzer and Simon Mealor (Hampshire, UK: Ashgate, 2004), 4, 3.

74. Irad Malkin, *A Small Greek World: Networks in the Ancient Mediterranean* (New York: Oxford University Press, 2011); and Christy Constantakopoulou, *The Dance of the Islands: Insularity, Networks, the Athenian Empire and the Aegean World* (New York: Oxford University Press, 2007).

75. For an extensive list of pre-2007 island-oriented journal issues, see Godfrey Baldacchino, "Islands, Island Studies, Island Studies Journal," *Island Studies Journal* 1, no. 1 (May 2006): 8.

76. Baldacchino, "Islands," 9.

77. Elaine Stratford et al., "Envisioning the Archipelago," *Island Studies Journal* 6, no. 2 (2011): 123, 115; Jonathan Pugh, "Island Movements: Thinking with the Archipelago," *Island Studies Journal* 8, no. 1 (2013): 10.

78. See DeLoughrey, *Routes and Roots*; and Françoise Lionnet, "Continents and Archipelagoes: From *E Pluribus Unum* to Creolized Solidarities," PMLA 123, no. 5 (2008): 1503–15. DeLoughrey has served on *Island Studies Journal*'s editorial board since its founding. Lionnet moved from UCLA to Harvard in 2015.

79. Lisa Lowe and David Lloyd, introduction to *The Politics of Culture in the Shadow of Capital*, ed. Lisa Lowe and David Lloyd (Durham, NC: Duke University Press, 1997), 5.

80. Grant McCall, "Nissology: A Proposal for Consideration," *Journal of the Pacific Society* 17, nos. 2–3 (1994): 1. For an insightful follow-up discussion of nissology, see Godfrey Baldacchino, "Studying Islands: On Whose Terms? Some Epistemological and Methodological Challenges to the Pursuit of Island Studies," *Island Studies Journal* 3, no. 1 (2008): 37–56. On islands and metaphorical abstraction, see Gillis, *Islands*; and Peter Hay, "A Phenomenology of Islands," *Island Studies Journal* 1, no. 1 (2006): 19–42.

81. Offering a phrase that inspires the heading above, Gillis describes the ancient Greeks as "thinking *with* islands" even before settling them (Gillis, *Islands*, 5).

82. Simone Pinet, *Archipelagoes: Insular Fictions from Chivalric Romance to the Novel* (Minneapolis: University of Minnesota Press, 2011), 30, 31.

83. Greg Dening, *Beach Crossings: Voyaging across Times, Cultures, and Self* (Philadelphia: University of Pennsylvania Press, 2004), 13, 17, 19.

84. Hay, "Phenomenology of Islands," 23.

85. Shell, *Islandology*, 1.

86. Shell, *Islandology*, 18.

87. Shell, *Islandology*, 18.

88. Shell, *Islandology*, 19.

89. Derek Walcott, "Isla Incognita," in *Caribbean Literature and the Environment: Between Nature and Culture*, ed. Elizabeth M. DeLoughrey, Renée K. Gosson, and George B. Handley (Charlottesville: University of Virginia Press, 2005), 52. Although the essay was not published until 2005, Walcott wrote it in 1973 (Walcott, "Isla Incognita," 57). We thank Beatriz Llenín-Figueroa for drawing our attention to the project of thinking about what might be the opposite of the explorer's method.

90. Elsewhere, the explorer's approach has been discussed as "a European project" of "planetary consciousness" involving the double project of circumnavigating the globe and "the mapping of the world's coastlines"; Mary Louise Pratt, *Imperial Eyes: Travel Writing and Transculturation*, 2nd ed. (1992; repr., New York: Routledge, 2008), 29. Hence, the type of explorer we are describing is closely linked to and freighted with European colonial and imperial presumptions. Meanwhile, we are intrigued by the alternative explorational epistemologies offered by David Chang's recent book, which begins: "What if we were to understand indigenous people as the active agents of global exploration, rather than the passive objects of that exploration?"; David A. Chang, *The World and All the Things Upon It: Native Hawaiian Geographies of Exploration* (Minneapolis: University of Minnesota Press, 2016), vii. Chang seeks to wrest the category of exploration from European epistemologies and practices while we (with the figure of the anti-explorer) are seeking to negate the category in favor of alternative epistemologies and practices. Even so, we find common cause with Chang in his description of explorers (or we would say anti-explorers) who are "reshaping their place in the globe in ways and spaces we do not yet even suspect"; Chang, *The World*, 257.

91. Benítez-Rojo, *Repeating Island*, 2.

92. Édouard Glissant, *Poetics of Relation*, trans. Betsy Wing (Ann Arbor: University of Michigan Press, 2009), 94.

93. Benoit Mandelbrot, "How Long Is the Coast of Britain? Statistical Self-Similarity and Fractional Dimension," *Science* NS 156, no. 3775 (May 5, 1967): 636–38; Benoit Mandelbrot, *Fractals: Form, Chance, and Dimension* (San Francisco: Freeman, 1977); Benoit Mandelbrot, *The Fractal Geometry of Nature* (New York: Freeman, 1983). Glissant nods directly toward Mandelbrot; Glissant, *Poetics*, 93.

94. Mandelbrot, "How Long Is the Coast of Britain?," 636.

95. Mandelbrot, *Fractal Geometry*, 25.

96. Mandelbrot, *Fractal Geometry*, 26.

97. Mandelbrot, *Fractal Geometry*, 26–27.

98. Mandelbrot, *Fractal Geometry*, 116.

99. Édouard Glissant, *Traite du Tout-Monde* (Paris: Gallimard, 1997), 120.

100. Pinet, *Archipelagoes*, xxxii, 66–71; Shell, *Islandology*, 3–4, 15, 17. For more on Jacques Lacan's discussions of the Real, see *The Four Fundamental Concepts of Psychoanalysis* (New York: W. W. Norton & Company, 1998), 22, 41, 54, and 69.

101. Metzger, Adrián, and Crichlow, "Introduction," 339.

102. On islands moving in relation to the stars, see Vicente M. Diaz, "No Island Is an Island," in *Native Studies Keywords*, ed. Stephanie Nohelani Teves, Andrea Smith, and Michelle H. Raheja (Tucson: University of Arizona Press, 2015), 97.

103. Stephen Wolfram, "The Father of Fractals," *Wall Street Journal*, November 22, 2012. With the term "hyperobjective" we allude to Timothy Morton's notion of the "hyperobject," something that is "massively distributed in time and space relative to humans"; Timothy Morton, *Hyperobjects: Philosophy and Ecology after the End of the World* (Minneapolis: University of Minnesota Press, 2013), 1.

104. Mandelbrot, *Fractal Geometry*, 1.

105. Mandelbrot, *Fractal Geometry*, 1, plate C2, 3.

106. Mandelbrot, *Fractal Geometry,* 26.

107. Glissant, *Poetics,* 122.

108. Glissant, *Poetics,* 208.

109. On self-similarity, see Mandelbrot, "How Long Is the Coast?," 637.

110. Terrell Scott Herring, "Micro: Region, History, Literature," *American Literary History* 22, no. 3 (2010): 627.

111. Lisa Randall, "Extra Dimensions and Warped Geometries," *Science* 296 (May 24, 2002): 1422–27.

112. Florence "Johnny" Frisbie and Brian Russell Roberts, conversation, February 11, 2014, Mānoa neighborhood, Honolulu, Hawai'i.

113. Katherine Sim, *More Than a Pantun: Understanding Malay Verse* (Singapore: Times Books International, 1987), 12.

114. "Koch Snowflake, Koch Curve," Wikipedia Commons, accessed Oct. 12, 2016, http://commons.wikimedia.org/wiki/File:KochSnowGif16_800x500_2.gif.

115. Michelle Stephens, "What Is an Island? Caribbean Studies and the Contemporary Visual Artist," *Small Axe* 17, no. 2 41 (2013): 12.

116. Maurice S. Lee, "Deserted Islands and Overwhelmed Readers," *American Literary History* 26, no. 2 (2014): 207.

117. Moretti's first reference to "distant reading" appears in his essay "Conjectures on World Literature," originally published in 2000 and now appearing as the second chapter of his book *Distant Reading* (London: Verso, 2013), 47–49.

118. Moretti, *Distant Reading,* 12. In terms of this section's header, Jonathan Pugh offers a provocative essay on "thinking with the archipelago" in "Island Movements: Thinking with the Archipelago," *Island Studies Journal* 8, no. 1 (2013): 9–24.

119. For other moments when Moretti theorizes through the archipelago, see *Distant Reading,* 1, 18, 63, 128.

120. Originally published in 1994, Moretti's essay "Modern European Literature: A Geographical Sketch" offers his initial references to Europe as an archipelago. This essay now appears as the first chapter of *Distant Reading.*

121. Glissant, *Poetics,* 208.

122. Glissant quoted in Glover, *Haiti Unbound,* 1. For a discussion of islands and continents in terms of geographical genres, see Brian Russell Roberts, "Abolitionist Archipelago: Pre- and Post-Emancipation Islands of Slavery and Emancipation," *Atlantic Studies* 8, no. 2 (2011): 234.

123. The name "Bali Ha'i" inevitably recalls the Indonesian island of Bali. And although James A. Michener's *Tales of the South Pacific* (upon which the Rodgers and Hammerstein adaptations are based) explains that Tonkinese people have come to the islands "from Tonkin China" as indentured laborers (Michener, *Tales of the South Pacific* [1947; rprt., New York: Dial, 2014], 153), the musical and film adaptations do not provide this context and hence have left many viewers to assume that perhaps the term "Tonkinese" is an idiosyncratic term for inhabitants of Tonga. *South Pacific*'s portrayal of French planters draws on social conditions in French Polynesia. Meanwhile, the Tonkinese character Bloody Mary was originally played by Puerto Rican actress Juanita Hall and subsequently by another Puerto Rican actress, Diosa Costello; see Jesús Colón, *A Puerto Rican in New York and Other Sketches* (New York: Arno Press, 1975), 156.

124. See Mandelbrot, "How Long Is the Coast?," 636.

125. Florence (Johnny) Frisbie, *Miss Ulysses from Puka-puka: The Autobiography of a South Sea Trader's Daughter* (New York: Macmillan Company, 1948), 158; and Frisbie and Roberts conversation.

126. Quintilian, *Institutio Oratoria, Books VII–IX*, trans. H. E. Butler (Cambridge, MA: Harvard University Press, 1921), 321 (8.6.34).

127. Edward Brathwaite, *Contradictory Omens: Cultural Diversity and Integration in the Caribbean* (Mona, Jamaica: Savacou, 1974), 64.

128. Jennifer L. Gaynor, "Maritime Ideologies and Ethnic Anomalies: Sea Space and the Structure of Subalternity in the Southeast Asian Littoral," in *Seascapes: Maritime Histories, Littoral Cultures, and Transoceanic Exchanges,* ed. Jerry H. Bentley, Renate Bridenthal, and Kären Wigen (Honolulu: University of Hawai'i Press, 2007), 60.

129. Brian Russell Roberts, "Archipelagic Diaspora, Geographical Form, and Hurston's *Their Eyes Were Watching God*," *American Literature* 85, no. 1 (2013): 122.

130. For more on island name resemblances see, S. Brink, "The Onomasticon and the Role of Analogy in Name Formation," *Namn och Bygd* 84 (1996): 73; also see Benítez-Rojo, *Repeating Island,* where the idea of a "meta-archipelago" is first mentioned on page 4; and Hau'ofa, "Our Sea of Islands," 4–8; Albert Wendt, "Towards a New Oceania," in *Writers in East-West Encounter: New Cultural Beginnings,* ed. Guy Amirthanayagam (London: Palgrave-Macmillan, 1981), 202.

131. George Lamming, *The Pleasures of Exile* (1960; repr., New York: Alison and Busby, 1984), 154.

132. This view of the Caribbean and Madagascar would roll back such paradigms as Paul Gilroy's "black Atlantic" and Vicente M. Diaz's oceanic thesis that "no island is an island." See Gilroy, *Black Atlantic;* and Diaz, "No Island Is an Island."

133. Wendt, "Towards a New Oceania," 202.

134. Marshall Island stick charts were constructed using fibers from plants, with sticks representing wave patterns, while cowrie shells or coral pieces generally represented islands; Richard Feinberg et al., "'Drawing the Coral Heads': Mental Mapping and Its Physical Representation in a Polynesian Community," *Cartographic Journal* 40, no. 3 (2003): 245.

135. Kathy Jetnil-Kijiner, "United Nations Climate Summit Opening Ceremony—A Poem to My Daughter," on *Iep Jeltok: A Basket of Poetry and Writing from Kathy Jetnil-Kijiner,* accessed Oct. 11, 2016, https://jkijiner.wordpress.com/2014/09/24/united-nations-climate-summit-opening-ceremony-my-poem-to-my-daughter/.

136. Metzger, Adrián, and Crichlow, "Introduction," 340.

137. This tack is consistent with the *American Quarterly*'s stance, expressed on the final page of each issue (including the recent special issues *Las Américas Quarterly* and *Pacific Currents*), on a dedication to examining "American societies and cultures, past and present, in global and local contexts," including "work that contributes to our understanding of the United States in its diversity, its relations with hemispheric neighbors, and its impact on world politics and culture."

138. Carlos Bulosan, "Be American," in *On Becoming Filipino: Selected Writings of Carlos Bulosan,* ed. E. San Juan, Jr. (Philadelphia, PA: Temple University Press, 1995): 66–72.

139. In our use of variations on the term "American," we are inspired by Janice Radway and others' conscientious deliberations on the hemispheric implications of using this term; Janice Radway, "What's in a Name? Presidential Address to the American Studies Association, 20 November, 1998," *American Quarterly* 51, no. 1 (1999): 1–32. See also Renda's "Note on Usage" in *Taking Haiti*, xvii. In retaining certain US-oriented usages of the term (e.g., "American studies" as a field name and "Americanists" as scholars of American studies), we are inspired by Donald Pease's pragmatic *description rather than prescription* vis-à-vis the question of usage, as he acknowledges that "'America' remains the commonly accepted self-representation in American studies associations"; Donald E. Pease, introduction to *Reframing the Transnational Turn in American Studies*, ed. Winfried Fluck, Donald E. Pease, and John Carlos Rowe (Hanover, NH: Dartmouth College Press, 2011), 1.

140. This myth-and-symbol school trend, in which scholars wrote monographs seeking to overthrow previous scholars' favored US myths, is emblematized in Alan Trachtenberg's dismissal of Henry Nash Smith's 1950 thesis on "virgin land" and Leo Marx's 1964 thesis on the "machine in the garden": "Not the land, not the garden, but the road . . . has expressed the essential way of American life"; Alan Trachtenberg, *Brooklyn Bridge: Fact and Symbol* (Chicago: University of Chicago Press, 1965), 21. In contrast, transnational Americanists' engagement with the world has necessitated a turn toward the anthology genre since, as Moretti has suggested, studying world literature (and, we would add, world culture more generally) eventually requires a "sort of cosmic and inevitable division of labour"; Moretti, *Distant Reading*, 59.

141. Alice Te Punga Somerville, "Our Sea of Anthologies: Collection, Display, and the Deep Blue Sea," in *Cultural Crossings / A la croisée des cultures: Negotiating Identities in Francophone and Anglophone Pacific Literature / De la négociation des identités dans les litteratures francophones et anglophones du Pacifique,* ed. Raylene Ramsay (Brussels, Bel.: Peter Lang, 2010), 219.

142. See Raymond Williams, *Marxism and Literature* (Oxford: Oxford University Press, 1977), 133–34.

143. Metzger, Adrián, and Crichlow, "Introduction," 341.

144. In *Contemporary Housing Issues in a Globalized World* (Farnham, UK: Ashgate, 2014, 13), Padraic Kenna uses the phrase "urban archipelago" in reference to Mike Davis's work *Planet of Slums* (London: Verso, 2006), where Davis also uses the term "archipelago" (46, 105, 172). Amy Kaplan describes the Guantánamo Bay detainee camp as "one island in a global penal archipelago" in "Where Is Guantánamo?" *American Quarterly* 57, no. 3 (2005): 831. Also on the archipelago metaphor and coercive state power, see Paul Amar, *The Security Archipelago: Human-Security States, Sexuality Politics, and the End of Neoliberalism* (Durham, NC: Duke University Press, 2013).

PART I | THEORIES AND METHODS FOR AN ARCHIPELAGIC AMERICAN STUDIES

1 HEURISTIC GEOGRAPHIES

TERRITORIES AND AREAS, ISLANDS AND ARCHIPELAGOES

Lanny Thompson

THIS CHAPTER WILL EXAMINE the heuristics of various geographical metaphors that shape theoretical and empirical analyses, especially in the social sciences and humanities. I understand a heuristic to be a practical method that attempts the solution of theoretical, empirical, or interpretative problems, while geographical metaphors are ways of seeing and of framing these problems. Some of the most important geographical metaphors have been territories (as delimited by states), regions (cultural or political areas), islands (sometimes grouped as archipelagoes), and the world. I suggest that a careful rethinking of the concept of archipelago might be a way of tracing complex relationships that transverse, crisscross, and entangle the supposedly unitary territories of states, areas, and islands and that make up the globalized world. In short, I propose to critically engage the leading territorial metaphors, to identify their heuristic geographies, and to elucidate the particular spatial heuristic of archipelagic thinking.

SOCIAL SCIENCES: SOVEREIGN TERRITORIES

Since their institutionalization in the nineteenth century, the social sciences have been premised upon notions of a spatially bounded unit: the sovereign territory, that is, the land and inhabitants belonging to or under the jurisdiction of a body politic, or state, conceived of as a country or nation. In all of these disciplines, the notion of the "social sphere" was enclosed by the political boundaries of states or their jurisdictions, such as towns, cities, provinces, territories, or colonies. The political predominance of the international state system, along with the expansion of national statistics in the nineteenth century, went hand in hand with the measurement and control of the territory and its corresponding subject populations.[1] Modern states were consolidated through the deployment of "political technologies" and "governmental rationalities." The first term refers to those theories and practices, in legal doctrine and cartography, that resulted in the demarcation of national territories and their internal geographic and cadastral surveys. The second term refers to the management of populations by means of policies informed by censuses and other statistical apparatuses.² The principal disciplines of the social sciences—sociology, economics, political science, geography, and demography—contributed to this effort. In particular, the social sciences were directed toward increasing social welfare, promoting economic growth, establishing stable political systems, and managing demographic and geographical resources. In the humanities, the premise of the state has also led to the demarcation of national differences in terms of tradition and identity, culture and history, language and literature.³ The heuristic orientation of all of these disciplines was directed at the problems of national unity, governance, and governmentality.

AREA STUDIES: REGIONS OF THE WORLD

The national state was not the only unit of interest. Emerging principally in the United States, "area studies" was institutionalized in the late 1940s, although its foundations had been laid down earlier. Area studies sought to define and delimit regions and apply interdisciplinary approaches to research problems. The underlying logic was that a region formed a complex whole that was unique, bounded, and could be distinguished from other regions by its sociocultural particularities. Julian Steward, perhaps the leading methodologist of area studies, wrote, "Area phenomena are interrelated in the context of a structured whole. The characteristics of the whole—the patterns of economic, social, religious, political, esthetic, and other special aspects of behavior—are determined by cultural heritage, but they are interrelated within the framework of particular societies. The unit of area study therefore must be a sociocultural whole."⁴

In his 1949 survey of area studies in the United States, Robert Hall found the following areas already defined and functioning in universities: Latin America, the Far East, the United States, and Russia. Area studies sought to promote "complete world coverage" based upon "universal social science laws."⁵ In contrast to Oriental studies, which was based in the humanities, area studies was rooted institutionally in the pragmatic, instrumental, and issue-oriented social sciences. The various disciplines—sociology, anthropology, political science, economics, geography, and so on—were expected to cooperate and produce interdisciplinary knowledge.⁶ Area studies promoted a concept of a differentiated whole: all the areas that constituted the world were divided into uniform, discrete, and contiguous regions. "Area" was understood, in ascending order of importance, as a natural landscape, a sociocultural homogeneity, and a structural-functional unit.⁷ Broadly speaking, area studies promoted modernization projects of economic development and state formation in the context of the Cold War struggle for influence in the "Third World." The area studies paradigm sought to divide the world into knowable, controllable chunks; from its inception its heuristic was interdisciplinary, instrumental, and hegemonic.

GLOBAL STUDIES: THE WHOLE WORLD

From its inception, then, the perspective of area studies was that of the whole world, not as a single unit but rather as discrete cultural configurations. However, the increasing mobility and connectedness of people, capital, commerce, technology, media, and ideology crosscut, superseded, and complicated the hermetic unity of national territories and the supposed sociocultural homogeneity of regions. During the last quarter of the twentieth century, advances in telecommunications and transportation increased the speed and scale of virtual and physical interconnectedness, which led to a compression of space and time. This spatial flatness and accelerated openness led in turn to deterritorialization as an inevitable, long-term process. Many of the conceptual referents were derived from theories of modernity, now rethought on a global scale. Studies of globalization revolved around questions of whether globalization signaled a transition to a "universalized modernity" and whether this suggested that the world is becoming a single space with a systemic, ordered unity. Global capitalism had extended the calculative rationality of territorial control to the population of the entire world.[8] The idea of globalization posited the world as one big, all-inclusive economic, ideological, and cultural unit.

According to Arjun Appadurai, "modernity," for decades understood as a national process, was now "at large," a much wider and more complex process that could not be contained by individual states. This "postnational" complexity arose from the global "disjunctures": overlapping, relatively independent flows of diasporas (people), cultures (media and ideologies), and economies (technology and money). Appadurai deployed the suffix "-scapes" in order to analyze these fluid, irregular movements: ethnoscapes, mediascapes, ideoscapes, technoscapes, and financescapes, respectively. By means of his central metaphor, he suggested that social actors "navigated" these "scapes" by means of social practices, including the "work of the imagination" in cultural spheres, on an intensely interactive global scale. Appadurai appealed to the open, boundless, and expansive metaphor of landscapes to describe these movements across global space.[9] In sum, the heuristic of global studies encompasses transnational projects of universal modernization.

ISLAND STUDIES: SMALL STATES AND TERRITORIES

In contrast to these large territorial units (states, regions, and the world), "island studies" began to explicitly conceptualize the complexity and uniqueness of small, delimited geographic spaces. Writing in the newly launched (2006) *Island Studies Journal*, Godfrey Baldacchino suggested that islands were distinctive locations: small, remote, and marked by a relatively closed compactness that made them natural laboratories for any number of disciplines, from anthropology to evolutionary biology. Indeed, he suggested that inter-disciplinary area studies might be a possible model for island studies.[10]

Despite the newness of the notion of "island studies," the island trope has a long history in European imagination and thought and is associated especially with exploration, conquest, and colonization. In European thought and colonial practice, islands were understood as naturally bounded properties that could become the sites of experimentation and innovation; they were synchronous and utopian, repeating and repeatable. Indeed, Europeans produced many innovations in the context of colonized islands. These innovations were wide-ranging: economics ("Plantations" and the Atlantic economy), anthropology (Malinowski, Radcliffe-Brown, and Sahlins), biology (Darwin and Wallace on evolutionary theory), philosophy (Rousseau's noble savage and More's *Utopia*), and literary production (*Robinson Crusoe, Treasure Island*, and their countless derivatives), etc.[11] Michelle Stephens has argued that the island trope, in this colonial context, frequently incorporated the pejorative notions of singularity and isolation, dependency and marginality, backwardness and provinciality.[12]

One of the most influential island tropes is the "repeating island," elaborated by Antonio Benítez-Rojo. In his study of Caribbean culture and literature, he argued that the Caribbean is constituted through a repeating plantation economy—the "Plantation"—and the consequent collision of races and cultures originating in the "subsoil" of Europe, Africa, and Asia. This collision produces polyrhythms, in both a literal and metaphorical sense, and a "certain kind" of performance: its poetics encompass a supersyncretic, improvisatory, carnivalesque aesthetic of pleasure.[13] The Caribbean is "chaotic," that is, its "processes, dynamics, and rhythms ... show themselves within the marginal, the regional, the incoherent, the heterogeneous, or, if you like, the unpredictable that coexists with us in our everyday world." These dynamic states repeat themselves, although paradoxically: no repetition is exactly the same but rather always "entails a difference." Finally, Benítez-Rojo argued that these repeating islands form a "meta-archipelago" that far transcend the Caribbean to become a global phenomenon.[14]

Benítez-Rojo's notion of the "repeating island" is an enthusiastic endorsement of Caribbean performance and its worldwide diaspora. For him, the island is not isolated; it is a metaphor for Caribbean culture that arises from multiple influences and, in turn, disperses its cultural style globally. What repeats and why is its influence worldwide? What repeats is an exploitative economic structure (the Plantation) that produces unequal interactions among different cultures, which finally leads (in chaotic, indeterminate ways) to the paradoxical cultural expressions in the Caribbean. Benítez-Rojo writes, "The Caribbean poem and novel are not only projects for ironizing a set of values taken as universal; they are, also, projects that communicate their own turbulence, their own clash, and their own void, the swirling black hole of social violence produced by the *encomienda* and the plantation, that is, their otherness, their peripheral asymmetry with regard to the West."[15]

In this argument, the repeating islands of the meta-archipelago are not related synchronically in space; rather they are analogous reiterations of the same conditions of peripherality and otherness. They do not change historically; rather they repeat. They do not form connections; rather they are comparable manifestations of the same dynamic. Even though each manifestation is unpredictably different, the underlying process is the same.[16] This dynamic originated in the Caribbean but it is no longer confined to this region due to the worldwide expansion of plantation-like exploitation and the diaspora of Caribbean peoples. In a flurry of disconnected references, Benítez-Rojo mentions Bombay, Gambia, Canton, Bali, Bristol, Bordeaux, Zuiderzee, Manhattan, and Portugal as all part of the meta-archipelago.[17]

In sum, the trope of the island is bound up historically with exploration, conquest, and colonization, in short, with empires. Even so, these very empires are both ever-present and yet undertheorized in island studies. Instead, recent appreciations of islands stress a heuristic of creative experimentation, discovery, innovation, and creation in natural, bounded, delimited, and controlled spaces that both repeat and are repeatable worldwide. Paradoxically, the trope of islands confounds and confuses the idea of the relational spaces of archipelagoes. The notion of unique, bounded spaces—repeatable or not—shuts off a detailed consideration of places constituted through connections with other islands, both near and far, and with continental territories, both national and imperial. In this vein, several authors have suggested that we move from the island, the classic metaphor of a closed system, to the archipelago, understood as an open system of relationships among islands, often in relation to continents. They argue that the metaphor of island is flawed precisely because it closes off conceptually the wider relationships among islands.[18] Let us now turn to the idea of archipelago not as repeating islands but rather as configurations of connected places.

ARCHIPELAGOES

These four geographical metaphors—territory, region, world, and island—suggest units that are demarcated and bounded, circumscribed and contained. In contrast to these metaphors, based on the premise of a unified geographic totality, the notion of archipelago suggests a way of focusing upon connections or networks dispersed throughout geographical spaces. Now, what is an archipelago? At the most basic empirical level in common parlance, an archipelago is simply a group of proximal islands considered as areas (such as the Caribbean) or states (such as Indonesia and the Philippines). Regarding the latter, Jay Batongbacal wrote that "archipelagic studies" has taken up the "issues concerning the impact of the archipelagic nature of the country [Philippines] and the neglect of the oceans as a subject of governance on the prevailing problems in environmental protection, the management of the economy, the preservation of national sovereignty, and the maintenance of national unity."[19] In this conception, the archipelago is simply another kind of unit: a national territory spread out over islands and the sea. Indeed, due in part to the United Nations Convention on the Law of the Sea (1982), the world's oceans and seas have been remapped and territorialized as the "exclusive economic zones" of states, whether continental, insular, or archipelagic.[20]

In contrast to the notion that islands or archipelagoes constitute discrete units, DeLoughrey has demonstrated the utility of a "tidalectic" approach, one that considers the relationships between land and sea, settlement and migration, indigeneity and displacement, nation and diaspora, in short, between "roots and routes" in the Caribbean and the Pacific.[21] Regarding the possible relationships between land and sea, Stratford and her colleagues have classified archipelagoes according to three possible topological relationships: island and sea; island and continent; and island and island.[22] First, the island-sea relationship suggests that the archipelago is a sea dotted with islands. This is what Epeli Hau'ofa calls the "islands in a far sea": small and remote "dry surfaces in a vast ocean far from the centres of power."[23] Here the emphasis is upon geopolitics and colonization, for example, as in Alfred Mahan's turn-of-the-century notion of "sea power," which was based upon a steam-powered navy, which in turn required safe, insular ports for provisioning, coal stations, and telecommunication hubs.[24] Second, the island-continent relationship refers to an archipelago of islands related to a dominant continent, in Stephens's terminology, a "continental archipelago": the connections among a continent and its contiguous islands differs from the oceanic archipelago of islands grouped in more open seas.[25] For example, Canada, Australia, and the United States encompass almost countless offshore islands that are formally part of the continentally based jurisdictions. Furthermore,

I should add that empires are often constituted by continental powers and their "imperial archipelagoes" that are neither geographically contiguous nor uniformly governed.[26] Spain, Portugal, France, Germany, Holland, and the United States colonized islands all over the world, and England, from its base on the island of Britain, also created an imperial archipelago.

Third, the island-island relationship, largely absent in scholarship, is an archipelago formed among lateral networks of islands.[27] This is what Hau'ofa calls "a sea of islands," which suggests a "holistic perspective in which things are seen in the totality of their relationships."[28] Pugh argues that lateral movements among islands themselves produce "creative transfigurations" of "material, cultural, and political practices," and that the trope of "metamorphosis" is more productive than those of repeating islands, center/periphery, or even mainland/island. This perspective of "island movements" is a welcome addition. However, archipelagic relationships are not necessarily as egalitarian and open as the idea of "island movements" envisions.[29] Indeed, the Caribbean is crosscut with metropolitan connections and imperial fissures that complicate and even obstruct the lateral relationships among the islands that constitute the wider archipelagic region.

Now, what do we mean by "relationship"? Let us turn to Édouard Glissant, whose *Poetics of Relation* is an exceptional combination of Deleuzian-influenced ontology, Hegelian-tinged history, sociology of the plantation, cultural theory, and literary analysis.[30] His central concept—Relation—refers to the historical, geographical, and cultural reality of archipelagoes. He writes, "The reality of archipelagos in the Caribbean or Pacific provides a natural illustration of the thought of Relation."[31] Throughout his text, he moves from the material and cultural relationships forged in the colonial contexts of the Caribbean to the poetics of Relation. He distinguishes relationship and Relation in the following way: "To the extent that our consciousness of Relation is total, that is, immediate and focusing directly upon the realizable totality of the world, when we speak of a poetics of Relation, we no longer need to add: relation between what and what? This is why the French word *Relation*, which functions somewhat like an intransitive verb, could not correspond, for example, to the English term *relationship*."[32]

Conceptually, then, Relation is related to, but different from, relationship. Relation partakes of flows and movements in which languages, cultural practices, and identities all influence and change one another through spontaneous and unimaginable creation. This dynamic process is chaotic because it is unpredictable and unstable; singularities that emerge at local levels may have far-reaching impact. These singularities are opaque rather than transparent. That is, they are irreducible to universal understanding, systematic classification, or neat typologies. Relation is, quite simply, the poetics arising from this *chaos-monde*, this chaos world in which cultural diversities are continuously brought into play and transformation.[33]

In contrast, relationships occur between specific things. A culture, for example, may be defined by its particular elements, the internal relationships of its components, or the external relationships that affect it from outside. These relationships may arise from domination and resistance, whether economic, cultural, or linguistic, and may be understood as social structures. The underlying processes creating structured relationships may be called "relation" (in lower case). Although Glissant does not explicitly define "relation" in this way, his implicit distinctions suggest it. For example, he writes that the "real subject" of his book is the analysis of the "entanglements of world-wide relation" insofar as they are related to the "poetics of Relation" (in upper case). Furthermore, Relation goes beyond the structures of relation: "The idea of relation does not limit Relation, nor does it fit outside it."[34] Sociology, anthropology, and the humanities study these relations (structured relationships) and create theoretical models to explain and understand them. Glissant critiques these disciplines as expressions of "ideological" or "theoretical" thought since they propose models or structures that are unable to follow the "uncertain paths" of the poetics of Relation, which are always open and conjectural and never conform to the stability of fixed patterns.[35] He writes, "Ideological thought (the need to analyze, understand, transform) invents new forms for itself and plays tricks with profusion: it projects itself into futurology, which also has no limits. It attempts, for example, to create a synthesis with likely applications from the sciences, which gradually leads into theories of model making. The models claim to base the matter of Relation in relationships; in other words, they claim to catch its movement in the act and then translate this in terms of dynamic or energized structures."[36]

However, this should not be understood as a complete rejection of the theoretical approaches of the social sciences or humanities. Indeed, Glissant appeals to a theoretical model to describe the "Plantation system" and its "structural principles": an enclosed social hierarchy, partially autarkic but actually highly dependent, with a technical mode of production based upon slavery.[37] Glissant does not reject the relevance of this structural model; rather he points out its limitations. He insists that the "multilingualism" that emerged in the plantations, described as a "*Baroque speech, inspired by all possible speech,*" was an unpredictable creation arising from a clash of cultures: "The place was closed, but the word derived from it remains open."[38] That is, the plantation was an oppressive structure, but from it Relation opened outward. Relation arose from the complex and chaotic dynamics of bringing things into local contact, which created diverse connections on an ever-grander scale, a *chaos-monde*, an "unmeasurable mixing" of languages and cultures that is both "unforeseeable and foretellable."[39]

This chaos-monde is foretellable in the sense that we can observe and even anticipate its occurrence, but the exact outcomes are singular, unforeseeable, and unpredictable.

According to Glissant, Relation emerges historically as the end result of imperial domination in the Caribbean. But what began in the Caribbean has now expanded throughout the globe; the chaos-monde is a *totalité-monde*, a world totality. Glissant describes a dialectical sequence of three moments. In the first moment, the European trajectories of voyaging, discovery, and conquest "link the places of the world into a whole made up of peripheries, which are listed in function of a Center."[40] The establishment of an Atlantic economy, of which the plantation was the central institution, brings "Others" of different racial and cultural backgrounds into violent contact.

The second moment is the movement from the periphery back to the center in which the European economy and culture are altered and defined in relation to Europe's empires. For Caribbean migrants, this was also the experience of exile. Finally, there comes a dialectical resolution, the third moment, in which Relation transcends the contradictions of colonial relations: not only does thought move from periphery to periphery, but as every periphery also becomes a center the "very notion of center and periphery" is abolished. In this process, the relations of imperial domination, in the first and second moments, resolve to Relation in the third. Glissant described the third dialectical moment: "What took place in the Caribbean, which could be summed up in the word *creolization*, approximates the idea of Relation for us as nearly as possible. It is not merely an encounter, a shock . . . , a *méstissage*, but a new and original dimension allowing each person to be there and elsewhere, rooted and open, lost in the mountains and free beneath the sea, in harmony and in errantry."[41]

For Glissant, this harmonious, creative movement—"errantry"—occurs in the final moment of the dialectic; it is a new trajectory that transcends the notions of center and periphery. Errantry results from new itineraries; it takes us from center to periphery, then back again from periphery to center, and also within peripheries, that is, in complex ways that complicate the categories of center and periphery. "The tale of errantry is the tale of Relation."[42] In this section, Relation appears as a dialectical supersession of relations of domination that result in mutual and egalitarian recognition. In other words, relations of domination produce the conditions for Relation. In true dialectical fashion, this final supersession abolishes the negative aspects sustaining the clash of cultures and conserves the positive that results in the resolution of contradiction. However, this scheme seems to be a ludic, pseudo-Hegelian dialectic. For Glissant, the final moment of the dialectic is not a synthesis, nor a self-consciousness, nor a transparent understanding, nor a coming to rest. Indeed, rather than transparency,

Glissant posits the "right to opacity," to be entirely singular and incommensurable while at the same time fully immersed in the whole world, the totalité-monde. Likewise, in his rendition, the final moment is not one of rest or completion. Rather, it gives way to errantry and the chaos-monde. Thus, Glissant subtly critiques and transforms the historical dialectic of patterned progress and internal logic. Instead, he posits an unpredictable and continuous dynamic without an a priori logic: "synthesis-genesis that never is complete."[43]

Nevertheless, the problem with this neat sequence of cleanly conceptualized moments is twofold. First, these three trajectories, laid out as a historical dialectic, are placed firmly within a temporal sequence rather than in a contemporaneous, synchronous, and spatial way. In this manner, the continuous and contemporary structuring of cultural hierarchies, economic inequalities, racial formations, and engendered differences are elided. Consequently, and this is the second point, the final moment, in which the violent encounter of imperial domination in the Caribbean dialectically gives way to Relation, is utopian. He writes, "Beyond the decisions made by power and domination, nobody knows how cultures are going to react in relation to one another nor which of their elements will be the dominant ones, or thought of as such. In this full-sense, all cultures are equal within Relation."[44]

This laudable declaration of equality cannot be realized simply through an elision of profound and continuous inequalities that continue to exist. I would suggest, to the contrary, that the history and actuality of empires and their archipelagoes is both a necessary point of departure and a continual referent, especially if the goal is to move toward egalitarian recognition and affirmation. That is, the worldwide structures and processes of relation do not lead effortlessly to Relation through a historical dialectic but rather the two are contemporaneous: relation is born of domination and violence, while Relation arises from resistance and affirmation. The project of archipelagic studies hopes to capture this dynamic: while it analyzes the worldwide entanglements of relation, its heuristic seeks Relation.

THE LOGIC OF ARCHIPELAGIC STUDIES

The concept of archipelago has a distinct methodological advantage, namely, that it facilitates the study of places connected by complex processes that traverse geographical spaces. Indeed, I would suggest that archipelagic studies might have its own "methodo-logic": an "archipe-logic."[45] Rather than a field defined by substantive studies of theoretical and empirical objects, archipelagic studies express ways of thinking *about, with,* and *from* archipelagoes.[46]

First, thinking *about* archipelagoes means to understand them, not simply as natural formations but rather as constituted places, islands brought together in complex historical and geographical configurations. This perspective seeks to overcome the time/space binary of the Enlightenment, which placed the temporal progress of civilizations as the primary focus for epistemology. Indeed, the modern fascination with progress through history led to the consideration of geography not in spatial terms but rather in terms of different levels in the development of civilization.[47] Instead, archipelagic studies would grant equal emphasis on time and space, history and geography. In this view, archipelagoes are not geographically static; rather they move and come into relation, much like the "moving islands" described by Vicente Diaz and J. Kēhaulani Kauanui for Pacific cultures.[48] Islands, then, are in flux: moving, changing, configuring, and reconfiguring as archipelagoes. They are not so much fixed terrains of state formation, unitary cultural areas, or hermetic isles; rather they are shifting, changing, negotiated relationships and connections arising from imperial rivalries and contestations, from domination and resistance, but also from cooperation and mutuality.

We are often much too literal when we speak of archipelagoes as constituted by proximate islands, because many archipelagic configurations are not precisely geographic. Rather, "proximity" is constructed or undone, assembled or disassembled. Imperial archipelagoes bring into relationship geographically dispersed islands under the dominion of empires. Imperial rivalries and dominions also divide and separate proximate islands, a frequent and well-known process in the Caribbean that also occurs in the Pacific. Guam, for example, is part of the Mariana Island chain but politically remains clearly distinct and relatively isolated from them. By considering the island relationships that transcend the limits of literal, geographic proximity, the notion of archipelago has a wider analytical use.

Second, thinking *with* the archipelago highlights the connections among material, cultural, and political practices that are spread out across islands and continents and are generated through the complex movements of capital and commerce, media and technology, ideas and ideology, and inventive, resourceful people. The islands that make up archipelagic networks may be understood, more abstractly, as nodes that are at once open and closed, at once isolated and connected, as both overdetermined globally and constituted locally, in sum, as relational places transcending contiguous geography.[49] Thus, "islandness" is often constituted through the establishment of colonies, possessions, and territories of all kinds, including islands, but also delimited as reservations, settlements, and enclaves. At any rate, "islandness" is constructed—historically, geographically, politically, economically, and ideationally—in terms of racialized and engendered projects of modernization, territorial expansion, and empire.

Furthermore, diasporic archipelagoes are configured through migratory movements to and from and habitations in all kinds of geographic places. Intracolonial diasporas from the colonized islands to the metropolis carry their islandness with them as they migrate back and forth. Since they are always linked to their archipelagic origin, easy assimilation to the colonizing nation is difficult and any construction of a national identity is often conflicted.[50] For example, Puerto Rican islanders often move to places on peninsulas (Orlando, Florida), on continents (Chicago), and in world cities (New York), where they form communities without losing their contact with Puerto Rico and without ever completely assimilating.[51] Moreover, if we push the metaphor slightly, colonial institutions, such as plantations, factories, schools, and barracks, often have the character of "islandness" and constitute institutional archipelagoes spread throughout colonies and connecting them to the metropolis. Paradoxically, then, the methodology of archipelagic studies would not be limited to strictly geographically defined islands. Rather than islands as such, archipelagic studies would stress instead the connections among places that form networks.

Finally, archipelagoes are places *from which* to think, write, and create; they are geosocial locations for the production of knowledge, not unlike "standpoint epistemology" (Harding) and "border thinking" (Mignolo).[52] Archipelagic thinking reaffirms that knowledge is situated socially (through gender, sexuality, race, and class) and geographically (through nations and borders, centers and peripheries, empires and colonies, islands and archipelagoes). However, unlike the "double consciousness" invoked by standpoint and border epistemology, archipelagic thinking is multiple and relational. It is multiple because it seeks to consider the simultaneous intersections of different social locations and, at the same time, of different geographical standpoints. In contrast to the universality of modern concepts, archipe-logics seek "Diversity": to understand all differences as co-constitutive and relational.[53]

In this way, archipelagic thinking contributes to the wider project of shifting the geography of reason, an initiative of the Caribbean Philosophical Association since its founding in 2003. This project seeks to go beyond the hegemonic horizons of Eurocentric reason and to "decolonialize" knowledge. It is premised on the argument that modernity, with all of its attendant philosophical, scientific, and literary concepts, was brought into being through colonialization, along with all of its forms of economic exploitation, racialized inequalities, and engendered hierarchies.[54] Likewise, we seek to contribute to the overcoming of the "forgetfulness of coloniality," to reveal the necessary connections between modernity and colonies, between any and all imperial projects and the development of nations and power, knowledge and epistemology, philosophy and ontology. This decolonial standpoint intervenes in the hierarchical unity of modernity and coloniality and seeks to upset its epistemological power in order to open up the possibility of overcoming its dominance.[55] Archipelagic thinking, then, aims to shift the geography of reason.

Writing *from* archipelagoes necessitates that we go beyond the strict adherence to the limits of academic disciplines and move explicitly toward comparative transdisciplinary inquiry, interpretation, and research. First, since archipelagoes encompass connections within a realm of differences, they suggest fields for comparison and contrast. Indeed, many archipelagic studies have been comparative in one way or another.[56] At the most basic level, archipelagoes suggest relations between islands and the sea, between islands and continents, and among islands. From this premise arise questions about how and why connected nodes (or islands) are similar and different. Furthermore, archipelagoes themselves may be subject to comparative analysis.[57] From this premise arise questions about similarities and differences among distinct archipelagic configurations. Second, archipelagic studies look toward transdisciplinary approaches that transverse and integrate, at a minimum, the social sciences and the humanities. Glissant's own work provides an example. He combined structural studies of plantations, the history of the Caribbean, philosophy, literary analysis, and poetry to create something new and integrated and yet outside any particular academic discipline. If we take "relation" to mean the study of entanglements of social structures, history, and geography, then we are clearly in the realm of the social sciences. If we take "Relation" to mean the recognition and affirmation of "Others" that leads to the creation of language and literature, music and dance, culture and imagination, then we are in the realm of the humanities. So, archipelagic studies propose precisely the transdisciplinary study of the worldwide entanglements of relation and the poetics of Relation.

CONCLUSION: ARCHIPELAGOES AND GEOGRAPHIES OF REASON

Each of these spatial metaphors—territory, area, world, island—encompasses particular geographical heuristics. The state is understood as a sovereign territory, a politically bounded space that social sciences both construct and study in the national interests of governance and governmentality. Area studies delimit cultural regions as realms of interest and influence and so divide up the world into regional blocks of international involvements and interventions; its heuristic is interdisciplinary, instrumental, and hegemonic. Recently, theories of globalization have imagined the entire world as an open, unitary space of economics and culture that transcends national boundaries due to the speed and reach of communications and transportation. Its heuristic is a continuation of modernization under supposedly new postnational and postcolonial conditions. In contrast to the grand scale of globalization, islands are often understood as small, relatively closed units. Island studies suggests the heuristic of laboratories that are controlled spaces of experimentation and innovation, distinct yet repeatable.

In contrast, archipe-logics seek to study roots, formed by place and habitation, and connected through routes, understood as complex relationships, and to map the historical trajectories of their geographic configuration. This allows us to describe the creation of discontinuous, but interconnected, places, which differ from the continuous, territorial spaces of the state, the unitary region of area studies, the isolated island, and the deterritorialized flatness of the global. The logic of archipelagic studies should allow us to trace relationships and map their dispersions in space and time. This logic would emphasize discontinuous connections rather than physical proximity, fluid movements across porous margins rather than delimited borders, and complex spatial networks rather than the oblique horizons of landscapes—in sum, moving islands rather than fixed geographic formations. In this view, archipelagoes are not natural phenomena but rather spatial and historical configurations assembled and reconfigured, shaped largely by imperial and postcolonial processes. The archipelagic metaphor also suggests different fields of comparison, both within and across archipelagoes. Thinking about, with, and from archipelagoes seeks to shift the geography of reason, to decolonialize theory and knowledge, and to overcome the forgetfulness of coloniality. Archipelagic thinking posits the historicity of geography, the unity of time and space, the connections of roots and routes, and the value of transdisciplinarity across the social sciences and humanities. Archipe-logics studies the structures of worldwide entanglements, shifts the geography of reason, and seeks the poetics of Relation. This is its heuristic.

NOTES

1. Immanuel Wallerstein, *Open the Social Sciences: Report of the Gulbenkian Commission of the Restructuring of the Social Sciences* (Stanford: Stanford University Press, 1996).

2. Stuart Elden, "How Should We Do the History of Territory?" *Territory, Politics, Governance* 1, no. 1 (2013): 5–20; Mitchel Dean, *Governmentality: Power and Rule in Modern Society*, 2nd ed. (London: Sage, 2010). These authors argue that "territory" and "population" are historical concepts that arise simultaneously with the creation of modern states.

3. Elizabeth DeLoughrey, *Routes and Roots: Navigating Caribbean and Pacific Island Literatures* (Honolulu: University of Hawai'i Press, 2009), 4–5.

4. Julian Steward, *Area Research, Theory, and Practice* (New York: Social Science Research Council, 1950), 151.

5. Robert Hall, *Area Studies: With Special Reference to Their Implications for Research in the Social Sciences* (New York: Social Science Research Council, 1949), 49, 82.

6. Biray Kolluoglu-Kirli, "From Orientalism to Area Studies," PMLA: *The New Centennial Review* 3, no. 3 (2003): 93–111.

7. Steward, *Area Research*, 54.

8. Barrie Axford, *Theories of Globalization* (Cambridge: Polity Press, 2013), 178 (published digitally by John Wiley & Sons and accessed November 2014 through ProQuest

Ebrary); Stuart Elden, "Missing the Point: Globalization, Deterritorialization and the Space of the World," *Transactions of the Institute of British Geographers*, New Series 30, no. 1 (2005): 8–19.

9. Arjun Appadurai, *Modernity at Large: Cultural Dimensions of Globalization* (Minneapolis: University of Minnesota Press, 1996).

10. Godfrey Baldacchino, "Islands, Island Studies, Island Studies Journal," *Island Studies Journal* 1, no. 1 (2006): 3–18.

11. Rod Edmond and Vanessa Smith, introduction to *Islands in History and Representation* (London: Routledge, 2003); DeLoughrey, *Routes and Roots*; Carmen Beatriz Llenín-Figueroa, "Imagined Islands: A Caribbean Tidalectics" (PhD diss., Duke University, 2012); Baldacchino, "Islands."

12. Michelle Stephens, "What Is an Island? Caribbean Studies and the Contemporary Visual Artist," *Small Axe* 41 (2013): 8–26.

13. Antonio Benítez-Rojo, *The Repeating Island: The Caribbean and the Postmodern Perspective*, trans. James Maraniss (Durham, NC: Duke University Press, 1992), 12–16, 19–21.

14. Benítez-Rojo, *Repeating Island*, 2–3.

15. Benítez-Rojo, *Repeating Island*, 27.

16. Likewise, Stephens argues that the "fractal-like pattern" of the repeating archipelago "is ruled by the logic of self-similarity rather than difference." Stephens, "What Is an Island," 16.

17. Benítez-Rojo, *Repeating Island*, 4.

18. Elaine Stratford, Godfrey Baldacchino, Elizabeth McMahon, Carol Farbotko, and Andrew Harwood, "Envisioning the Archipelago," *Island Studies Journal* 6, no. 2 (2011): 113–30; Jonathan Pugh, "Island Movements: Thinking with the Archipelago," *Island Studies Journal* 8, no. 1 (2013): 9–24; Stephens, "What Is an Island?"; Brian Russell Roberts and Michelle Stephens, "Archipelagic American Studies," *Journal of Transnational American Studies* 5, no. 1 (2013): 1–20.

19. Jay Batongbacal, ed., *Archipelagic Studies: Charting New Waters* (Quezon City: University of the Philippines Printery, 1998), 2. See also Dale Andrew, "Archipelagos and the Law of the Sea: Island Straits States or Island-Studded Sea Space?" *Marine Policy* 2, no. 1 (1978): 46–64.

20. DeLoughrey, *Routes and Roots*, 30–37.

21. DeLoughrey, *Routes and Roots*, 1–6.

22. Their stated goal is to "(re)inscribe the theoretical, metaphorical, real and empirical power and potential of the archipelago: of seas studded with islands; island chains; relations that may embrace equivalence, mutual relation and difference in signification"; Stratford et al., "Envisioning the Archipelago," 113.

23. Epeli Hau'ofa, "Our Sea of Islands," in *A New Oceania: Rediscovering Our Sea of Islands*, edited by Eric Waddell, Vijay Naidu, and Epeli Hau'ofa (Suva, Fiji: School of Social and Economic Development, University of the South Pacific, Suva, 1993), 7.

24. Alfred Thayer Mahan, *The Influence of Sea Power in History* (Boston: Little, Brown, and Company, 1890). Tomás Pérez Varela, "Puerto Rico en la agenda tecnológica de Estados Unidos 1890–1912: Telecomunicación global y colonialismo" (PhD diss., University of Puerto Rico, 2015).

25. Stephens, "What Is an Island?" 12–13.

26. Lanny Thompson, *Imperial Archipelago: Representation and Rule in the Insular Territories under U.S. Dominion after 1898* (Honolulu: University of Hawai'i Press, 2010).

27. Stratford et al., "Envisioning the Archipelago," 116–17.

28. Hau'ofa, "Our Sea of Islands," 7.

29. Pugh, "Island Movements," 9.

30. Headley argues convincingly that Glissant adapts the ontological vocabulary of Gilles Deleuze. See Clevis Headley, "Glissant's Existential Ontology of Difference," CLR *James Journal* 18, no. 1 (2012): 59–101. While Headley's discussion of "Relation" informs the following discussion, he does not distinguish this term from "relationship" or "relation."

31. Édouard Glissant, *Poetics of Relation*, translated by Betsy Wing (Ann Arbor: University of Michigan Press, 1997), 34. The following section incorporates many of the ideas expressed by J. Michael Dash in two essays, "Édouard Glissant: The Poetics of Risk," *Small Axe* 15, no. 3 (2011): 102–07; and "Homme Du Tout-Monde," *Caribbean Review of Books* 25 (January 2011), http://caribbeanreviewofbooks.com/crb-archive/25-january-2011/homme-du-tout-monde/, retrieved November 14, 2014. I am indebted to Professor Dash for suggestions to a previous draft.

32. Glissant, *Poetics*, 27.

33. Glissant, *Poetics*, 133–40, 189–94. Betsy Wing, the translator of *Poetics of Relation*, chose not to translate *chaos-monde*, which roughly refers to a chaos world, not a world of disarray or disorder. It is a neologism in French and is treated as such in the English translation. The same may be said of *totalité-monde*, which appears below; see "Translator's Introduction," xiv–xv.

34. Glissant, *Poetics*, 31, 185.

35. Glissant, *Poetics*, 169–70, 173.

36. Glissant, *Poetics*, 173.

37. Glissant, *Poetics*, 63–76.

38. Glissant, *Poetics*, 75, emphasis in the original.

39. Glissant, *Poetics*, 138.

40. Glissant, *Poetics*, 28.

41. Glissant, *Poetics*, 34. Although it is not entirely clear in this quote, Glissant distinguished "creolization" from *métissage*. The former referred to the process of infinite and unforeseeable cultural combinations, while the latter refers to a static hybrid, a synthesis of two pure forms. "Creolization" is consistent with "Relation," which is not limited to simply *métissage*. See Headley, "Glissant's Existential Ontology," 89–92.

42. Glissant, *Poetics*, 18.

43. Glissant, *Poetics*, 174, 189.

44. Glissant, *Poetics*, 163.

45. I am indebted to William Maxwell, who made a similar play on words in his informal comments to the panel on archipelagic American studies at the annual American Studies Association Convention, San Juan, Nov. 16, 2012.

46. This formulation synthesizes expressions from Édouard Glissant, *Tratado de todo-mundo*, translated by María Teresa Gallego Urrútia (Barcelona: El Cobre Edicio-

nes, 2006); Linda Martín Alcoff, "Mignolo's Epistemology of Coloniality," *CR: The New Centennial Review* 7, no. 3 (2007): 79–101; and Pugh, "Island Movements."

47. Walter Mignolo, *The Darker Side of Western Modernity: Global Futures, Decolonial Options* (Durham, NC: Duke University Press, 2011), chap. 5; and Johannes Fabian, *Time and the Other: How Anthropology Makes Its Object* (New York: Columbia University Press, 1983).

48. Vicente Diaz and J. Kēhaulani Kauanui, "Native Pacific Cultural Studies on the Edge," *Contemporary Pacific* 13, no. 2 (2001): 315–42.

49. Elaine Stratford, "Flows and Boundaries: Small Island Discourses and Challenges of Sustainability, Community and Local Environments," *Local Environment* 8, no. 5 (2003): 495.

50. Yolanda Martínez-San Miguel, *Coloniality of Diasporas: Rethinking Intra-Colonial Migrations in a Pan-Caribbean Context* (New York: Palgrave Macmillan, 2014).

51. Jorge Duany, *The Puerto Rican Nation on the Move: Identities on the Island and in the United States* (Chapel Hill: University of North Carolina Press, 2002).

52. Sandra Harding, *The Science Question in Feminism* (Ithaca, NY: Cornell University Press, 1986); and Walter Mignolo, *Local Histories / Global Designs: Coloniality, Subaltern Knowledges, and Border Thinking* (Princeton, NJ: Princeton University Press, 2000).

53. The term "Diversity" is from Glissant: "The Universal has toppled into, and is now jostled by, Diversity." He refers to Diversity as "concurrent diversities" and the "piling up of Relations." See Glissant, "The Unforeseeable Diversity of the Word," in *Beyond Dichotomies: Histories, Identities, Cultures, and the Challenge of Globalization*, edited by Elisabeth Mudimbe-Boyi (Albany: State University of New York Press, 2002), 287–98.

54. Lewis Gordon, "From the President of the Caribbean Philosophical Association," *Caribbean Studies* 33, no. 2 (2005): xv–xxii.

55. Nelson Maldonado-Torres, "Thinking through the Decolonial Turn: Post-Continental Interventions in Theory, Philosophy, and Critique—an Introduction," *Transmodernity: Journal of Peripheral Cultural Production of the Luso-Hispanic World* 1, no. 2 (2011): 1–15.

56. Martínez-San Miguel, *Coloniality of Diasporas*.

57. Tom Boellstorff, "From West Indies to East Indies: Archipelagic Interchanges," *Anthropological Forum* 16, no. 3 (2006): 229–40.

2 | IMAGINING THE ARCHIPELAGO

Elaine Stratford

AMONG WORKS BY US-AMERICAN PAINTERS on display in the National Gallery of Art in Washington, DC, few are coastal or island scenes; an exception is Childe Hassam's *Poppies, Isles of Shoals* (figure 2.1). This graceful work was painted in 1891 when Hassam and his wife Kathleen were visiting Maine and the island home of hotelier Levi Thaxter and his wife, renowned poet and writer Celia Thaxter. It was Celia who hosted visits in the fashion of a *salonnière*, and whose garden on Appledore was much admired.[1]

Poppies is vibrant, the scarlet hues of Thaxter's garden commanding attention before the gaze shifts from foreground to nearshore, horizon, and open sea. From Appledore's safe harbors, perched on the shelf of a mighty continental landmass, the imagination roams oceans and other lands, the poppies signifying the dreams of Hypnos of Greek myths, perhaps, or the deathliness of his brother Thanatos. Suggesting sacrifice, poppies are among the blooms that first appear in blasted battleground landscapes. John Ruskin referred to them as Heaven's burning coals, and both Thaxter and Hassam knew of this allusion.[2]

Hassam's painting, Thaxter's poppies, and the nine isles are an assemblage by which to imagine the United States of America *as* an archipelago formed in a crucible both deeply inventive and brutal—this despite an apparently overwhelming propensity to view American space in continental terms.[3] How to explain this inclination? Donald Meinig notes that by the end of the 1700s US-Americans were forging "a new nation . . . [in a] . . . restless, violent, creative way on a continental scale."[4] Examining one instance of that—the United States' purchase in 1803 of Louisiana from the French—Meinig suggests that this doubling of the federation's area confirmed the republic's destiny as a nation with natural boundaries as yet unfilled (figure 2.2).[5]

Diverse imperial impulses informed long-standing debates about those shifting boundaries: one the expansionist sort that "discerned 'the finger of na-

Figure 2.1. F. Childe Hassam (1859–1935), *Poppies, Isles of Shoals*, 1891. Oil on canvas, 19.75 × 24 in. Courtesy of the National Gallery of Art, Washington, DC. Gift of Margaret and Raymond Horowitz 1997.135.1.

ture' pointing out appropriate additions," and the other the conservative sort, whose advocates thought natural barriers signified imperatives to "fix a limit to national expansion."[6] Work to resolve such disputes likely fueled a durable—but not unassailable—fivefold ideology of liberal developmentalism that Emily Rosenberg describes as encompassing: belief in the United States' developmental experience as an ideal blueprint that should be replicated; trust in private free enterprise; the provision of free trade and investment; freedom of information and the support of culture (along particular and prescriptive lines despite liberty's guise); and general (if variable) acceptance that government activity could usefully protect private enterprise, stimulate growth, and regulate conduct.[7]

Figure 2.2. John Gast (1842–1896), *American Progress*, 1872. Oil on canvas, 12.75 × 16.75 in. Museum of the American West, Los Angeles, California.

Evidently, the expansive perspective largely prevailed. Witness President James Monroe's doctrine of 1823 pronouncing that further efforts by European powers to recolonize parts of the Americas would be viewed as hostile, highlighting US geopolitical approaches to external threats to internal (continental) security and the advent of new centers of regional and hemispheric (archipelagic) power.[8] Or consider President Theodore Roosevelt's description of the United States as ordained to bear the civilizing burden of intervention as an international police force.[9] In such declarations, one discerns the idea of Manifest Destiny and expressions of *Pax Americana* for which both transoceanic and transcontinental strategies were crucial. Those strategies were realized using conquest and annexation; genocide, enslavement, and rejection; immigration's embrace; innovative, aggressive, and uncompromising commitments to the free market; and near unswerving faith in specifically US notions of liberty and democracy. The paradox and point is that over time the US "heartland" has appeared to be thoroughly continental, its archipelagic tendrils seen to have use value to protect that core. In this regard, much has been made of the attacks of September 11, 2001; the continental United States had not been invaded since the War of 1812 with Great Britain, and there "had been nothing from outside that struck at the heart of the nation.... To have war brought home was an unusual experience for America, to have the mainland not only invaded but attacked from the skies ... [was] unique."[10]

What, then, might it mean to decenter US continentalism and imagine the United States' complex spatiality in archipelagic terms? The idea of the archipelago both implies and inscribes figurative and literal assemblages, mobilities, and multiplicities, opening possibilities for new ways of thinking,[11] not least along the fluid borders of island, archipelagic, oceanic, and hemispheric studies. New insights emerge from this thinking on the significance of island-studded seas, oceanscapes, and coastlines.

Metaphor has been important in such revivifying labors, but not unproblematically so.[12] One especially durable figure is the desert island, which Gilles Deleuze saw as marking a profound opposition between land and water.[13] This opposition fascinated him as an imaginary. It is, he wrote, a "pulling away, of being already separate, far from any continent, of being lost and alone—or it is dreaming of starting from scratch, recreating, beginning anew"?[14] Perhaps this is the repeating dream of a US archipelago? Either way, and lamenting the insertion of dulling continental imperatives upon this desert island imaginary, Deleuze turns to Daniel Defoe's *Robinson Crusoe* and decries the latter's vision of the world, which "resides exclusively in property.... The mythical recreation of the world from the deserted island gives way to the reconstitution of everyday bourgeois life from a reserve of capital.... And the providential function of God is to guarantee a return ... [aided by] Friday, docile towards work, happy to be a slave.... [Thus] Robinson Crusoe represents the best illustration of that thesis which affirms the close ties between capitalism and Protestantism."[15]

Alternatively, seeking to redress Western tendencies to "hydrophasia"—a forgetting of the sea—Margaret Cohen suggests that Crusoe "epitomizes experimentation at the limits, not a regression to a state of nature," and not the exemplification of the "paradigmatic *homo economicus*"; rather, he "is *homo viator*, man the traveler."[16] Thus, he is able to move freely and thus to profit.[17] Cohen links this unfettered movement and, one could infer, the *choice* to stop, conquer, and settle to Hugo Grotius's precept of *Mare Liberum*, the idea of the free sea. This precept was, itself, constitutive of extended notions of liberty that came to typify US liberal developmentalism, and which required that—in the grip of Hypnos and Thanatos—so many lost their dreams, freedom, and lives. Such paradox is not lost on Cohen, nor on Marcus Rediker, who draws deep insights from William Blake's poem *America, A Prophecy*, written in 1793. Blake, it appears, understood the global ramifications of the Age of Revolution as symptomatic of "earlier struggles from below and a circulation of subversive experience."[18] At least some of these struggles, and Blake's knowledge of them, were founded on partial understandings of America's "stateless, kingless, masterless, egalitarian tribes ... carried in sailors' yarns and written accounts back to Europe."[19] There, such narratives were to provoke modes of thinking that were decidedly utopian and revolutionary, if conveniently blind to race or gender, or the plight of Native Americans or other Indigenous peoples. Starkly, Rediker underscores the unassailable reality that the "violence of the Atlantic was planned at the highest levels and was in no way marginal or incidental. To the contrary, the violence was fundamental to and formative of the social and economic processes of Atlantic capitalism, and took four corresponding forms ... the violence of expropriation ... of the Middle Passage ... of exploitation ... [and] of repression."[20] How, then, to contemplate the *geographical imaginaries* that are the US archipelago—those taken-for-granted constructions through which particular spatial orderings are valorized and reified in ways both reasoned and felt, and which are powerfully implicated in processes of "worlding"? In case this idea seems ambiguous, US expansionism "must not be viewed as simply a great westward movement ... to fix claim to a thousand-mile territorial frontage on Pacific shores. Rather, it should be seen as a powerful outward movement, putting pressure on the borderlands to the north and south as well as thrusting westward, and ranging out to sea to place islands and coastlands near and far under commercial, cultural, demographic, and political influence."[21]

Below, drawing on scale as a heuristic, the question about such worlding processes motivates a rethinking of the United States of America in terms of *five modes of archipelagicity* that also constitute the five sections to follow. Scale's gestalt requires asking about relationships along the continuum inferred by the terms "local" and "global." Yet caution is required lest scale be afforded ontological status instead of being understood as "simultaneously metaphor, experience, event, moment, relation and process."[22] Thus, my account could start with—and subliminally privilege—the United States' continental and nearshore archipelagic elements and then move outward to ocean space, but such framing is neither impermeable nor immutable, and so is usefully unsettled.

My aim is to imagine the United States as an archipelago to unsettle overpowering discourses of continentalism and give shape to other and different ontologies, epistemes, and values. The point here is to avoid superimposing a continental telos upon US-affiliated islands that have partially constituted the broader archipelagic Americas, especially because such a telos might frame that broader space as existing to satisfy the needs of the continental United States. Offered instead is a reordering of how one might imagine both the idea of the archipelago and the United States per se.

ISLAND STATES AND ISTHMUSES

Certain geographical imaginaries constitute the most obvious elements of the US-affiliated subset of the archipelagic Americas: Hawai'i, Alaska and the Aleutians,[23] and the Panama Canal. The first of these, the former Sandwich Islands, were once among the most remote island groups in the world. By the 1850s, they had become the "new Pacific frontage of the United States ... linked, in some cases quite routinely" with Asia, the Pacific, Australasia, and South America.[24] In time, attracted to its shores were traders, whalers, missionaries, navies, diplomats, opportunists, and laborers, among them Japanese, Chinese, Koreans, Filipinos, Portuguese, Spaniards, Puerto Ricans, and African diasporic subjects. By the mid-1860s, the United States began work on a series of economic agreements and political maneuverings to enable the islands' absorption into the polity. As Meinig describes it, in the end the islands were formally appropriated swiftly after the United States' victory in the Philippines against the Spanish. "Within a few weeks . . . a joint resolution of annexation was passed by Congress and on July 7, 1898, was signed by President McKinley."[25] Hawai'i, of course, continues to be a major strategic post of the US archipelago, not least as headquarters of the United States' Pacific Fleet and Pacific Air Forces. Strong sovereignty and counter-sovereignty movements remain active, underscoring sustained tensions and differences.

Alaska's vast territory was initially too remote to be considered important to the United States' expansionist ambitions.[26] Then Spain ceded its holdings on the west coast of the continent, and it became imperative to hold at bay British North American / Canadian and Russian interests. Bought from the Russians in 1867, by 1912 there was compelling logic to declare Alaska an organized territory. The decision to further incorporate this remote domain into the fabric of the nation followed expansion into the Pacific: the annexation and eventual independence of the Philippines; the constitution of a strategic arc from San Francisco to Honolulu, Midway, Wake, and Guam; the consolidation of American Samoa; and the appraisal of the Aleutians and the harbor of Unalaska as the shortest route to Japan and China. The strategy to fully embrace Alaska was later confirmed by growing technological capacities enabling further exploitation of its immense resource base; threats from imperial Japan that were to accelerate dramatically during World War II; the onset of the Cold War and the Korean conflict; and endogenous desires and requests for statehood, granted—as in Hawai'i—in 1959.[27]

The Panama Canal is no longer directly in US control but remains within its ambit and arguably was a creation of certain US-Americans' worlding archipelagic imaginary. The advent of the canal and the politics of the isthmus are wrapped up in complex geopolitics involving Cuba, among other Caribbean, South American, and European players.[28] Cuba had transcendent interest for the United States, commanding maritime approaches to the Gulf of Mexico that bordered five states and the Mississippi delta, through which flowed vast quantities of US exports. It was a metonymic Gibraltar in geopolitical strategies coalescing around the idea of an American Mediterranean with two openings that would enable transoceanic routes to foster further expansion westward into the Pacific and consolidate influence in the Antilles and Atlantic sphere.[29] Yet, like Cuba, Panama was skirted around, claimed, occupied, and then "lost" by the United States.

Tracing such geopolitics by thinking of the United States as archipelagic adds weight to other scholarly labors that reveal the complex realities and imaginaries of the Caribbean, and US, interests in this complicated region.[30] Later, of course, in a reverse maneuver, the United States became to the Pacific islands what Europe had been to the Americas in colonial times. Here was another (westbound) *archipelagraph*, a term I deploy here to build on and improvise from Elizabeth DeLoughrey's ideas on archipelagraphy. In her original essay on these ideas, DeLoughrey argues that "no island is an isolated isle and that a system of archipelagraphy—that is, a historiography that considers chains of islands in fluctuating relationship to their surrounding seas, islands and continents—provides a more appropriate metaphor for reading island cultures."[31] Read differently, archipela*graphy* invites into existence the idea of archipelagraphs—drawings or maps or other such renderings of islands that may be mobilized as part of a geographical imaginary. Hence the power of an incessantly repeating figure of islands that involves shifting modes of geopolitical and economic organization.[32] In the terms offered by Antonio Benítez-Rojo, this kind of repetition stands in contrast to a "certain kind of way" of being—and is a hopeful and hoped for "desire to sublimate apocalypse and violence.[33]

"CONFETTI OF EMPIRE"

In collaborative work with coeditor Donald Pease and other American studies scholars in *Cultures of United States Imperialism*, Amy Kaplan constituted a research agenda to reveal "the multiple histories of continental and overseas expansion, conquest, conflict, and resistance which have shaped the cultures of the United States and the cultures of those it has dominated within and beyond its geopolitical boundaries."[34] Here, I am suggesting that imagining the United States as an archipelago reveals something else: that boundaries shift like imperial fortunes and tides; they blow in the wind and get taken up by currents like the "confetti of empire," a term I borrow and repurpose from Kate Marsh,[35] to describe the continental United States' population's general consciousness of their own government's planetary-archipelagic claims. Someone with a continental mindset might ask, who can keep track of each piece of confetti as it is strewn across a room, and who can keep track of the flecks of land claimed by the United States in the far seas and oceans?

As well as embracing Hawai'i, Alaska, and the Panama Canal in various geopolitical configurations, the US archipelago encircles the unincorporated organized territories of Guam, Puerto Rico, the Northern Marianas, and the US Virgin Islands, as well as the unincorporated unorganized territories of American Samoa, Baker, Howland, Jarvis, Wake; the Midway, Johnston, and Palmyra Atolls; and Kingman Reef. The US Department of the Interior defines each such territory as an *insular area*: a "jurisdiction that is neither a part of one of the several States nor a Federal district . . . [and] any commonwealth, freely associated state, possession or territory or Territory . . . [and it] may refer not only to a jurisdiction which is under United States sovereignty but also to one which is not."[36] The genesis of this category of territory—which could be held without ever being considered for membership of the Union—resides in the Guano Islands Acts. In 1856, the Senate and Congress enacted legislation "to authorize Protection to be given to Citizens of the United States who may discover deposites [*sic*] of Guano." Prolific on islands, guano was a key source of saltpetre, and islands that provided it and that were "not within the lawful jurisdiction of any other government, and not occupied by the citizens of any other government" could be peaceably possessed and claimed, as could islands furnishing other opportunities.[37] As an assemblage, an archipelagic formation, these island territories might be read as having been enrolled into the dreamscape of US expansionism to serve the military complex—small white dots barely noticed but symbolically and materially important.

In a different territorial grouping, Puerto Rico and the Northern Marianas are commonwealths—unincorporated organized territories self-governing under constitutions adopted by the areas' peoples, but where such status could be withdrawn by Congress, although not unilaterally. The Philippines, having been a US colony between 1898 and 1934, was itself a commonwealth until independence in 1946. Where insular territories are unincorporated, only "selected parts of the United States Constitution apply."[38] Where incorporated, a status given in perpetuity, insular territories enjoy full constitutional rights; where organized, the US Congress has enacted an organic act providing a bill of rights and (limited) self-government.

Puerto Rico and the Philippines, a present commonwealth and an ex-colony respectively, also exemplify the imperial volatilities of the geographical imaginaries with which we are dealing. In historical terms, for example, with the Louisiana Purchase in 1803 the United States gained "its first territorial frontage on the Gulf of Mexico."³⁹ Meinig notes that as the geopolitical implications of that expansion emerged, a "whole circuit of coasts—Florida, Cuba, Yucatan, Mexico, Texas—suddenly took on new meaning for Americans, and before long such places were . . . of compelling national interest."⁴⁰ Indeed, there was palpable concern that the region was "a broad and a dangerous archipelago" to be traversed if the United States was to span two ocean spheres. Thus, it was necessary to "bring the Bahamas, Jamaica, Hispaniola, and Puerto Rico into this new American view. . . . This was not a tranquil prospect."⁴¹

Nor was engagement with the Philippines peaceable. The United States took control of the colony in 1898 at the close of the Spanish-American War, and on signing the Paris Treaty Spain also relinquished Cuba, Puerto Rico, and Guam. For neither the first nor last time, there followed heated debate in the United States. On one side was the argument to curb the imperial-expansionist tendencies that were compromising the highest ideas of US liberty and democracy. On the other side was a contradictory—and ultimately victorious—argument to take full advantage of Manila's strategic position to pursue an expanded version of Manifest Destiny—the geographical imaginary of a US-Americanized world. By a margin of one vote, the United States annexed the islands and then faced Emilio Aguinaldo's resistance movement and bloody guerilla warfare ultimately involving 125,000 US troops, several thousands of whom died alongside an estimated 200,000 Filipinos.⁴²

In present times, significant tension still characterizes Puerto Rico's status as a territory, and ongoing struggles exist in the Philippines, which is signatory to all manner of bilateral agreements and "special relationship" provisions.⁴³ These "agreements" underscore the sustained and repeating patterns of archipelagic maneuverings that have typified US geopolitics.

LIMINAL ARCHIPELAGRAPHS—RENDERINGS OF THE UNITED STATES AS ISLAND SPACE

As noted above, Elizabeth DeLoughrey has argued persuasively for a "system of archipelagraphy."⁴⁴ Equally, continents might be so understood, and that might provide other ways to read their geographies, histories, and cultures, since it is not only on islands that we bear witness to the continually repeating "convergence of imperial, scientific, literary and anthropological discourses."⁴⁵ DeLoughrey has also suggested that the use of more complex geographical and aquatic metaphors to understand islands might free them from "their supposed isolation from continental metropoles."⁴⁶

Inverting this image, one might imagine how island spaces in the United States' ambit might free continents from their supposed solidity and apparent inviolability. This labor of imagining and remapping or refiguring is important conceptually, ethically, and politically: it enables the possibility of things being otherwise, which is important if one is to decenter US continentalism and imagine this complex space archipelagically, a task whose possibility is central to the thinking underpinning this chapter. Work on assemblage thinking by Ben Anderson and his colleagues is helpful in this regard.[47] They ask how various spatial forms and processes are "assembled, are held in place, and work in different ways to open up or close down possibilities."[48] They also question how those assemblages might have been otherwise composed, ordered, held together, and stabilized. Such questions point to diverse politics of assemblages—a process that "maps how powerful assemblages form and endure, thus loosening the deadening grip abstract categories hold over our sense of political possibility."[49]

In the geographical imaginary constituting the US archipelago, then, there are states, and territories, and other liminal spaces such as reefs and banks. Navassa, for example, is managed by the US Fisheries and Wildlife Service, but has been claimed by Haiti since 1801.[50] In turn, the United States claims and would enfold Bajo Nuevo Bank and Serranilla Bank were they not Colombian territories. Three especially noteworthy threshold spaces in the US archipelago are Guantánamo Bay in Cuba, Diego Garcia in the southern Indian Ocean, and Bikini Atoll in the Pacific. The very distribution of these "interests" illuminates the reach of the United States' worlding, and emphasizes repeating patterns of concern about securitization and imperatives to protect the heartland. In brief, Guantánamo Bay was leased to the United States in 1903 and remains both the focus of tensions between Cuba and the United States that have complex genealogies that continue to unfold to the present time, and the subject of significant international legal debate. One view is that "for as long as the United States withholds its consent to termination, it effectively exercises not only complete control and jurisdiction over the area, but effectively all the trappings of sovereignty ... [however] since the agreement provides for the 'continued ultimate sovereignty' of Cuba ... [the question that remains is] whether sovereignty or continued sovereignty can be trumped by virtue of a lease agreement that does not state a specific date of termination."[51] In turn, there is Diego Garcia, the largest island of the Chagos Archipelago, a British territory some 560 miles south of the Maldives. Leased by the US government, serving as a major military installation, and elemental in the United States' international security network, Diego Garcia appears as the progeny of Monroe and Roosevelt, among others. Its geopolitics is embroiled in charges of forced removal by the British of the Chagossians who settled the islands in the eighteenth century.[52]

Finally, on Bikini Atoll similar tactics of removal were used during the period after World War II when the United States was engaged in testing nuclear weapons. In a peculiar twist, the Marshall Islands' atoll is now managed by the

Bikinians and marketed as an extreme dive tourism experience, and while they remain "scattered ... and their atoll remains uninhabitable due to radioactive contamination, many hope to repatriate soon. ... [There] is still a stark contrast between Bikinian visions of the atoll as a homeland and the deserted isle mythology that underlies widely circulated representations of the atoll espoused by others."[53]

OCEAN SPACES

Thus far, I have pointed to a range of insights that derive from framing the United States archipelagically. Implicit in that discussion—and more than mise-en-scène—are vast ocean spaces constitutive of that very framing. In fact, under the United Nations Convention on the Law of the Sea (UNCLOS), only five sovereign states are explicitly considered archipelagic under the terms of the convention: Fiji, Indonesia, Papua New Guinea, the Bahamas, and the Philippines, which championed the archipelagic doctrine at various UN meetings on the law of the sea from 1958. That doctrine stipulates, "An archipelagic State is composed of groups of islands, with the waters within the baselines as internal waters."[54] Nevertheless, and although such resistance was finally mostly overcome, non-archipelagic maritime states initially battled such territorial claims, not least on the basis that they posed a threat to the "innocent passage" of commercial, fishing, and war vessels.[55]

The United States is, of course, a maritime state, yet it is the nation's insular areas and territories—and not just the length of its continental shelf—that give it one of the world's largest exclusive economic zones.[56] While observing the international legal codifications of the UNCLOS, the United States has not yet ratified the document, despite pressures, most recently from President Obama, that the Senate should act to do so.[57] According to Yann-Huei Song and Elias Blood-Patterson, the reasons to ratify are many, and include the capacity to have security over Arctic territorial claims—and to thus provide surety to investors—and to credibly influence geopolitical tensions in the South China Sea.[58] However, and despite strong bipartisan support, as many as thirty-four conservative members in the Senate continue to block ratification on the grounds that UNCLOS threatens the United States by privileging foreign obligations over "vigorous, unfettered sovereignty."[59] This ideological impetus is not new, and, as John Gillis has remarked, it was "from its mastery of the seas, not lands, that Europe experienced its first great economic boom. The wealth accumulated through its archipelagic empires of access would find its way back to the continent [and] ... would ultimately overturn the old order of things." Gillis notes, too, that by the late 1700s, land and sea boundaries had become more defined, and that during the 1800s, new nations such as the United States were focusing "their energies on their own interiors. . . .

[Indeed, the] rebellious North American settlers declared themselves to be 'continentals.'"[60]

At this juncture it will be useful, first, to heed Hester Blum's argument that the oceans should be central to considerations of movements, relations, and histories, especially at the global level. Blum suggests that this focus be used to shape new epistemologies "about surfaces, depths, and the extra-terrestrial dimensions of planetary resources and relations," to produce "new critical locations from which to investigate questions of affiliation, citizenship, economic exchange, mobility, rights, and sovereignty," and to enable "capacious possibilities for new forms of relationality through attention to the sea's properties, conditions, and shaping or eroding forces."[61]

Second, it will be important to accept invitations to undertake more critical work on islands, archipelagoes, and ocean spaces that have been proffered by scholars such as Elizabeth DeLoughrey. Certainly, her aforementioned work on archipelagraphy has highlighted "the ways in which centuries of transoceanic diaspora and settlement have rendered island spaces as vital and dynamic loci of cultural and material exchange. In fact, the sea is a vital component of island identity, and has contributed to the formation of a complex maritime imagination in historical, literary and cultural production."[62]

Finally, it will be useful to recall Philip Steinberg's prescient observations that the oceans will take on more and more in the way of significance in global governance, and that it will be crucial to understand the social construction of ocean space and its imbrication in new social orders, a project he has continued to refine in terms of its human and more-than-human assemblages, not least among them the seasteading movement.[63] This libertarian impulse and initiative has been described by the naval architect George Petrie in the following terms: "Who among us has not looked at the current dysfunctional state of political systems and wished, 'If only there were a deserted island where we could start over again.' The bad news is there are no deserted islands that are not claimed by a jurisdiction, so the only way to have one is to build your own."[64] While these expansionist ambitions may materialize first in continental coastal waters, it is clear that the commons are in the line of sight—a new frontier awaiting conquest, a kind of repeating island or fleeting meta-archipelago and geographical imaginary, of the kind that also gave effect to the spaces and Manifest Destiny that became the United States of America.[65]

CONTINENTAL COASTLINES AND NEAR-SHORE ISLANDS

Here, the coastline reinserts its significance as part of the assemblage that constitutes territorial waters, contiguous zones, exclusive economic zones, and international waters. It is at the edge of oceans and lands, with ambitions for both transoceanic and transcontinental worldings, and with awesomely transformative geographical imaginaries that our scalar investigations might end. But in the same way that an isle may seem like a closed loop, I now wish to consider those littoral/literal domains of the continental part of the US archipelago; that is, the east, west, and Gulf coastlines of what has traditionally been described as the US mainland.

Tim Ingold claims that lines are everywhere, observing that colonial-imperial impulses are not the "imposition of linearity upon a [putatively] non-linear world [that is implicitly Indigenous, pre-modern, and static], but the imposition of one kind of line on another [or multiple others]. It proceeds first by converting the paths along which life is lived into boundaries in which it is contained, and then by joining up these now enclosed communities, each confined to one spot, into vertically integrated assemblies. Living *along* is one thing; joining *up* is quite another."[66] Coastlines are classes of lines important to the impositions and attendant processes that Ingold refers to. One simply has to consider the definition of low watermark "baselines" in UNCLOS to understand the US National Oceanic and Atmospheric Administration defining them as "the mean of the lower low tides as depicted on the largest scale NOAA nautical charts" and describing them as "ambulatory and subject to changes as the coastline accretes and erodes."[67] This mutability, to me, is deeply if unwittingly reminiscent of discussions about the archipelagraph and a tidalectic view of islands, continents, the waters that delineate them, and the cultures, geographies, and histories with which they are entangled.[68]

It is not surprising, then, that Philip Steinberg argues that coasts are spaces by which to understand the links among maritime regions, and through which it is possible to unsettle the binary conceptualizations of land and water undergirding modern notions of state territoriality and given effect by lines.[69] Paul Carter, too, notes that coasts of imperial times past enabled the capacity to trace, enharbor, breach or insert, document, and claim. Indeed, Carter argues that coasts were both conditions and possible origins of colonialism. Coasts were metageographical because they were abstractions, "analogue[s] of the associative reasoning essential [to orderly progress and legitimation of colonialism].... To fulfill these intellectual ambitions, to become an image of reasoning, the coast itself had to be ... reconceptualized as a *coastline*."[70] Thus, as visual representations of prerogative, coastlines were (and remain) horizons of possibility, points joined together to delineate gaps and thresholds that might unify or bracket off.

In respect of this last marginalizing action—and the crushing reality that colonial "possibilities" were extraordinarily destructive—Brian Harley argues that to assert the absence of Indigenous engagements in the early cartographies and subsequent shaping of the Americas' coastlines (and then nearshore and deep interiors) is to perpetuate the "denial of coevalness."[71] His admonition underscores the subtle ways in which diverse forms of everyday resistance manifest[72] and remain current in any consideration of the US archipelago. This is because "the place that Native American studies occupies in the contemporary US academy is at best marginal."[73] Assuredly, the experiences of Native Americans are "foundational to the development of US society and its trademark democratic institutions.... The core project... is the redressive inquiry into how it came to be, and has continued to be, that Indians are marginal and largely invisible in their own land."[74] This project, of course, extends beyond the margins of the United States and doubtless it requires and attracts sustained, critical attention to others' histories and present circumstances.[75] This resonant point is made by Rediker when he observes of *America, A Prophecy* that "Blake looks from below, considering the actions of sailors, slaves, soldiers, prisoners, women and children, black and white, the whole human race. These actors shrunk the world ... as they expanded the human capacity to transform it."[76]

Nearshore islands are also in the embrace of the coastal continental part of the US archipelago. In a sweep extending thousands of miles, from the northeast border with Nova Scotia to the northwest border with British Columbia, one might randomly refer to Matinicus, Nantucket, Manhattan, Martha's Vineyard, Oak Island, the Isle of Palms, Hilton Head Island, Sugarloaf Key, Marco Island, Grand Isle, the Channel and Farallon Islands, and Whidbey Island. Such islands at least count for something in literal archipelagic reckonings. Yet in the interior of the United States and rarely—if ever—considered are hundreds of lacustrine and riverine islands such as Isle Royale in Lake Superior.[77] There, Ojibwa economic and cultural practices were supplanted by colonial forms of resource extraction and later by the national parks and international biosphere movements. Do such "specks" constitute an interiority to the US archipelago even as they disappear from view because they are not part of a salty outside, even though they are deeply entangled in all that seems exterior to them? Assuredly, the archipelago should not be rendered an empty signifier by too liberally attaching to it anything aquatic, insular, or having the appearance of an assemblage. But one wonders what an involution of this particular geographical imaginary might produce in terms of new topologies with which to think (about) varied spatial relations.

ISLE OF SHOALS REPRISE

So let this work end as it began by contemplating Childe Hassam's painting *Poppies, Isles of Shoals*, which constitutes a geographical imaginary—a spatial and political assemblage of the United States *as* an archipelago forged in a crucible simultaneously creative and destructive. There and again later the point was made that the United States is most often constituted as continental, and so it may be; but if so, its continental materiality is profoundly indebted to insular and archipelagic relations. Rereading Hassam's work in light of the five modes of archipelagicity that are outlined above, it is possible to see that each "inhabits" the canvas—but in ways neither linear nor straightforward. The United States' archipelagicity is not mobilized from interior to foreshore, and nearshore, then offshore, to horizons, and open oceans, nor is it mobilized in reverse. Rather it is perhaps an imbrication, a layered assemblage operating at multiple scales both temporal and spatial. Painterly conventions suggest that the gaze should settle initially upon the land, with its apparent surety of continental ideologies and mythologies. Yet, were one first to "join with" *Poppies* from the deck of the small yacht behind Babb's Rock, or from the line of the horizon, other imaginaries would surely propagate: fluid engagements such as Anderson and colleagues refer to when they posit that the politics of assemblages is a politics that invites new and different ways of thinking the world into existence.

NOTES

1. David Park Curry, *Childe Hassam: An Island Garden Revisited* (New York: W. W. Norton and Company, 1990), 14.

2. Norma H. Mandel, *Beyond the Garden Gate: The Life of Celia Laighton Thaxter* (Lebanon, NH: University Press of New England, 2004), 140; Ted Harrison, *Remembrance Today: Poppies, Grief, and Heroism* (London: Reaktion Books, 2013), 170–71.

3. Such propensities are repeatedly unsettled in Meinig's four-volume *The Shaping of America: A Geographical Perspective on 500 Years of History*. Assuredly, island groups are archipelagoes; so too continents and islands; "by taking the broadest possible geographical framework" we avoid essentializing distinctions between them; John R. Gillis, "Island Sojourns," *Geographical Review* 97, no. 2 (2007): 277. See also Edward K. Muller, "Book Review: 'The Shaping of America: A Geographical Perspective on 500 Years of History. Volume 4: Global America, 1915–2000,'" *Annals of the Association of American Geographers* 99, no. 4 (2009): 810–17.

4. Within the regions that have now become the eastern United States, the appellation "American" appeared in the mid-1760s and came to refer "to a vigorous movement, an elaborating set of arguments about the nature and existence of a particular polity and society, and a growing sense of identity among a people ready to claim a place among the other major peoples of the world. . . . In a single generation, American shifted in connotation and claim from 'colonial' to 'equal' to 'separate' to 'superior'"; Donald Meinig, *The Shaping of America: A Geographical Perspective on 500 Years of History* vol. 1, *Atlantic America, 1492–1800* (New Haven, CT: Yale University Press, 1986), 306, 418.

5. Ernest Renan, "What Is a Nation?" in *Nation and Narration*, ed. Homi K. Bhabha (London: Routledge, 1990): 8–22.

6. Donald W. Meinig, *The Shaping of America: A Geographical Perspective on 500 Years of History*, vol. 2, *Continental America 1800–1867* (New Haven, CT: Yale University Press, 1993).

7. Emily S. Rosenberg, *Spreading the American Dream: American Economic and Cultural Expansion, 1890–1945* (New York: Hill and Wang, 1982), 7.

8. Donald W. Meinig, *The Shaping of America: A Geographical Perspective on 500 Years of History*, vol. 3, *Transcontinental America, 1850–1915* (New Haven, CT: Yale University Press, 1998), 361ff; Jay Sexton, *The Monroe Doctrine: Empire and Nation in Nineteenth-Century America* (New York: Hill and Wang, 2011).

9. Barry J. Ryan, "Reasonable Force: The Emergence of Global Policing Power," *Review of International Studies* 39, no. 2 (2013): 435–57.

10. Richard Gray, *After the Fall: American Literature Since 9/11* (Chichester, UK: Wiley-Blackwell, 2011), 4.

11. Elaine Stratford, Godfrey Baldacchino, Elizabeth McMahon, Carol Farbotko, and Andrew Harwood, "Envisioning the Archipelago," *Island Studies Journal* 6, no. 2 (2011): 113–30. In terms of such multiplicities, the US archipelago is a powerful imaginary including railways and air travel, space travel and satellites, cables and networks, trade agreements and treaties, alliances and sanctions.

12. See, for example, Peter Hay, "A Phenomenology of Islands," *Island Studies Journal* 1, no. 1 (2006): 19–42; Philip Hayward, "Aquapelagos and Aquapelagic Assemblages," *Shima: International Journal of Research into Island Cultures* 6, no. 1 (2012): 1–11.

13. There is a "disconnect between the idealized sea of poststructuralist theorists and the actual sea encountered by those who engage it," and metaphors may be "pernicious when they detract attention from the actual work of construction ... that transpires to make a space what it is"; Philip E. Steinberg, "Of Other Seas: Metaphors and Materialities in Maritime Regions," *Atlantic Studies* 10, no. 2 (2013): 158.

14. Gilles Deleuze, *Desert Islands and Other Texts, 1953–1974* (Los Angeles: Semiotext(e) Foreign Agents Series, 2004), 10.

15. Deleuze, *Desert Islands*, 12.

16. Margaret Cohen, "Literary Studies and the Terraqueous Globe," *Publications of the Modern Language Association of America* 125, no. 3 (2010): 660; Cohen, "Literary Studies," 661.

17. Defoe's primary passion was for analysis of trade, a matter that did not escape Karl Marx in his own labor theory of value; Maximillian Novak, "Robinson Crusoe and Economic Utopia," *Kenyon Review* 25, no. 3 (1963): 474–90. Defoe wrote *General History of Trade* six years before *Robinson Crusoe*, and likely knew of Alexander Selkirk, a mariner returned to England after more than four years on the remote Juan Fernandez Islands, several hundred miles west of present-day Argentina's Santiago in the Pacific Ocean. By "isolating first his hero and then a small group of settlers and returning them to a state of nature, Defoe was attempting to [use Crusoe to] illustrate some of his most basic economic concepts ... a theory of invention, a theory of value and an economic theory of society"; Novak, "Robinson Crusoe," 474.

18. Marcus Rediker, "The Red Atlantic; or, 'a terrible blast swept over the heaving sea,'" in *Sea Changes: Historicizing the Ocean*, ed. Bernhard Klein and Gesa Mackenthun (New York: Routledge, 2004), 117.

19. Rediker, "Red Atlantic," 118.

20. Rediker, "Red Atlantic," 121.

21. Meinig, *Shaping of America*, 2:169.

22. Richard Howitt, "Scale and the Other: Levinas and Geography," *Geoforum* 33, no. 3 (2002): 306. On scale and ontological status, see Andrew Herod, *Scale* (Abingdon, UK: Routledge, 2010).

23. Barring the remote and westernmost Commander Islands, administered by Russia.

24. Meinig, *Shaping of America*, 2:164.

25. Meinig, *Shaping of America*, 3:367.

26. Meinig, *Shaping of America*, 3:374ff.

27. Donald W. Meinig, *Shaping of America: A Geographical Perspective on 500 Years of History*, vol. 4, *Global America, 1915–2000* (New Haven, CT: Yale University Press, 2004), 195–202.

28. Meinig, *Shaping of America*, 2:22–24. Alongside Hawai'i, Alaska, and Puerto Rico, Cuba and Panama consistently feature in each of Meinig's volumes. The importance of the agency of Indigenous, enslaved, and settler peoples, and of other colonizing powers, is apparent in his work. See Emily F. Davidson, "Among Spectators and Agents of History: Navigating through the Memory Sites of the Panama Canal," *Global South* 6, no. 2 (2013): 130–53; Thomas A. Hollihan, "The Public Controversy over the Panama Canal Treaties: An Analysis of American Foreign Policy Rhetoric," *Western Journal of Speech Communication* 50, no. 4 (1986): 368–87; Peter Hulme, "Writing on the Land: Cuba's Literary Geography," *Transactions of the Institute of British Geographers* 37, no. 3 (2012): 346–58.

29. With the United States' economic development being entangled with Europe's, President Lincoln's chief economic advisor, Henry Carey, lamented that all routes in the United States led to Liverpool; Meinig, *Shaping of America*, 2:557ff. Carey was an influential architect of the "American System" of political and economic philosophy intended to secure national self-sufficiency by protecting industry using tariffs, and subsidies, government investment in infrastructure, and by creating a national bank. These measures both required and constituted the sorts of expansionism that undergirds the US archipelago, and arguably has perpetuated others' dependency and underdevelopment.

30. See Hester Blum, "The Prospect of Oceanic Studies," *Publications of the Modern Language Association of America* 125, no. 3 (2010): 670–77; Elizabeth DeLoughrey, "'The litany of islands, The rosary of archipelagoes': Caribbean and Pacific Archipelagraphy," ARIEL: *A Review of International English Literature* 32, no. 1 (2001): 21–51; J. Brian Harley, "Rereading the Maps of the Columbian Encounter," *Annals of the Association of American Geographers* 82.3 (1992), 522–42.

31. DeLoughrey, "'The Litany of islands,'" 23.

32. Epeli Hau'ofa, "The Ocean in Us," *Contemporary Pacific* 10, no. 2 (1998): 391–410.

33. Antonio Benítez-Rojo, *The Repeating Island: The Caribbean and the Postmodern Perspective* (Durham, NC: Duke University Press, 1996), 12, 16.

34. Amy Kaplan, "'Left Alone with America': The Absence of Empire in the Study of American Culture," in *Cultures of United States Imperialism*, ed. Amy Kaplan and Donald E. Pease (Durham, NC: Duke University Press, 1993), 3.

35. Attributed to Napoleon Bonaparte, the idea of the *territoires d'outre-mer* as confetti of empire is expounded upon by Kate Marsh in *Narratives of the French Empire:*

Fiction, Nostalgia, and Imperial Rivalries 1784 to the Present (Lanham, MD: Lexington Books, 2013), 10ff.

36. See United States Department of the Interior, Office of Insular Affairs, *Definitions of Insular Area Political Organizations*, n.d., accessed June 2014, http://interior.gov/oia/islands/politicatypes.cfm.

37. "An Act to Authorize Protection to Be Given to Citizens of the United States Who May Discover Deposites [sic] of Guano," 34th Cong., 1st Sess. I, Ch. 164, 1855, 119, accessed December 2014, http://legisworks.org/sal/11/stats/STATUTE-11-Pg119.pdf.

38. United States Department of the Interior, *Definitions*.

39. Meinig, *Shaping of America*, 2:22.

40. Meinig, *Shaping of America*, 2:24.

41. Meinig, *Shaping of America*, 2:24.

42. Meinig, *Shaping of America*, 3:368ff.

43. See Rick Baldoz and César Ayala, "The Bordering of America: Colonialism and Citizenship in the Philippines and Puerto Rico," *Centro Journal*, 25, no. 1 (2013): 76–105; Julie Tuason, "The Ideology of Empire in National Geographic Magazine's Coverage of the Philippines, 1898–1908," *Geographical Review* 89, no. 1 (1999): 34–53.

44. DeLoughrey, "'Litany of islands,'" 23.

45. DeLoughrey, "'Litany of islands,'" 24.

46. DeLoughrey, "'Litany of islands,'" 40.

47. Ben Anderson, Matthew Kearnes, Colin McFarlane, and Dan Swanton, "On Assemblages and Geography," *Dialogues in Human Geography* 2, no. 2 (2012), 172.

48. Anderson et al., "Assemblages and Geography," 172.

49. Anderson et al., "Assemblages and Geography," 186.

50. Roy F. Nichols, "Navassa: A Forgotten Acquisition," *American Historical Review* 38, no. 3 (1933): 505–10.

51. Alfred de Zayas, "The Status of Guantánamo Bay and the Status of the Detainees," *UBC Law Review* 37 (2004): 290 and 292.

52. See Peter Harris, "Decolonising the Special Relationship: Diego Garcia, the Chagossians, and Anglo-American Relations," *Review of International Studies* 39, no. 3 (2013): 707–27. The presence of US military establishments around the globe is archipelagic, there being—for example—fourteen bases in Japanese Okinawa alone; Stephen R. Fischer, *A History of the Pacific Islands* (Houndmills, UK: Palgrave, 2002).

53. Jeffrey S. Davis, "Representing Place: 'Deserted Isles' and the Reproduction of Bikini Atoll," *Annals of the Association of American Geographers* 95, no. 3 (2005): 607. See also http://www.bikiniatoll.com/.

54. United Nations General Assembly, *United Nations Convention on the Law of the Sea, 1982*, accessed June 2014, http://www.un.org/Depts/los/convention_agreements/convention_overview_convention.htm. In particular, "The Convention . . . contains a new feature in international law, which is the regime for archipelagic States . . . [for which] the territorial sea is a 12-mile zone extending from a line drawn joining the outermost points of the outermost islands of the group that are in close proximity to each other. The waters between the islands are declared archipelagic waters, where ships of all States enjoy the right of innocent passage. In those waters, States may establish

sea lanes and air routes where all ships and aircraft enjoy the right of expeditious and unobstructed passage"; accessed June 2015, http://www.un.org/Depts/los/convention_agreements/convention_historical_perspective.htm#Historical Perspective.

55. Specifically: "In the face of overwhelming support from the international community . . . the maritime powers have finally accepted the principle on conditions specifying a maximum water to land ratio, the number of and maximum lengths of baselines, and the transit passage and overflight through and over archipelagic waters"; Jorges R. Coquia, "Development of the Archipelagic Doctrine as a Recognized Principle of International Law," *Philippine Law Journal* 58 (1983): 37.

56. The term "insular" was settled upon during President Taft's term in office from 1909 to 1913, and likely influenced by his earlier political dealings as governor-general of the Philippines from 1901 to 1904, or as secretary of war to which the Isthmus Canal Commission reported in 1904, or as instigator of the second occupation of Cuba in 1906; Meinig, *Shaping of America*, 3:373.

57. On May 28, 2014, the White House Office of the Press Secretary noted the following: "With respect to the Law of the Sea, the President made very clear that part of how the United States shows our own commitment to those rules and norms is by upholding them ourselves. And we act consistent with the Convention on the Law of the Sea, but it would send an important message for the Senate to ratify it, because that is the means by which we want to see disputes resolved. *So, again, we lead on behalf of an international order that can uphold peace and security both by what we do in regions like the Asia Pacific and on issues like trade and cyber and maritime, but we also have to lead on behalf of that international order through our own example.* And that's why we believe the Senate has long passed the time when they should have ratified the Law of the Sea"; President Barack Obama, "Background Conference Call on the President's Commencement Address at West Point," Briefing Room, Statements and Releases, May 28, 2014, accessed June 2014, http://www.whitehouse.gov/the-press-office/2014/05/28/background-conference-call-presidents-commencement-address-west-point; emphasis added.

58. Yann-Huei Song and Elias Blood-Patterson, "Likelihood of U.S. Becoming a Party to the Law of the Sea Convention during the 112th Congress," *Journal of Maritime Law and Commerce* 43, no. 4 (2012): 447–66.

59. Song and Blood-Patterson, "Becoming a Party," 465.

60. John R. Gillis, "Islands in the Making of an Atlantic Oceania, 1500–1800," in *Seascapes: Maritime Histories, Littoral Cultures, and Transoceanic Exchanges*, edited by Jerry H. Bentley, Renated Bridenthal, and Kären Wigen (Honolulu: University of Hawai'i Press, 2007), 33.

61. Hester Blum, "Introduction: Oceanic Studies," *Atlantic Studies* 10, no. 2 (2013): 151–52.

62. Elizabeth DeLoughrey, "Island Writing, Creole Cultures," in *The Cambridge History of Postcolonial Literature*, ed. Ato Quayson (Cambridge: Cambridge University Press, 2014): 802–32.

63. Philip E. Steinberg, *The Social Construction of the Ocean* (Cambridge: Cambridge University Press, 2001); Steinberg, "Of Other Seas"; Philip E. Steinberg, Eliza-

beth Nyman, and Mauro J. Caraccioli, "Atlas Swam: Freedom, Capital, and Floating Sovereignties in the Seasteading Vision," *Antipode* 44, no. 4 (2012): 1532–50.

64. George Petrie and Jon White, "The Call of the Sea," *New Scientist* 215, no. 2883 (2012): 26–27.

65. Benítez-Rojo, *Repeating Island*.

66. Tim Ingold, *Lines: A Brief History* (London: Routledge, 2007), 2–3; emphasis in the original.

67. National Oceanic and Atmospheric Administration, Office of General Counsel, "Maritime Zones and Boundaries," n.d., accessed December 2014, http://www.gc.noaa.gov/gcil_maritime.html.

68. Where the dialectical process involves thesis, antithesis, and synthesis, Kamau Brathwaite proposed tidalectics as a method to maintain openness to ongoing answers. In one of his poems about an elderly Caribbean woman sweeping sands from her front yard, he writes that he cannot fully understand the important ritual she was performing, but endlessly tries to:

> And then one morning I see her
> body silhouetting against the
> sparkling light that hits the
> Caribbean at that early dawn
> and it seems as if her feet,
> which all along I thought were
> walking on the sand ... were
> really ... walking on the wa-
> ter ... and she was tra
> velling across that middlepass
> age.

See Anna Reckin, "Tidalectic Lectures: Kamau Brathwaite's Prose/Poetry as Sound-Space," *Anthurium: A Caribbean Studies Journal* 1, no. 1 (2003): Article 5, accessed December 2014, http://scholarlyrepository.miami.edu/anthurium/vol1/iss1/5.

69. Philip E. Steinberg, "Lines of Division, Lines of Connection: Stewardship in the World Ocean," *Geographical Review* 89, no. 2 (1999): 254–64; Steinberg, "Of Other Seas," 163.

70. Paul Carter, "Dark with Excess of Bright: Mapping the Coastlines of Knowledge," in *Mappings*, ed. Denis Cosgrove (London: Reaktion, 1999), 125; emphasis in original.

71. Harley, "Rereading the Maps," 524.

72. James C. Scott, "Everyday Forms of Resistance," *Copenhagen Journal of Asian Studies* (July 1987): 33–62.

73. Patrick Wolfe, "The Settler Complex: An Introduction," *American Indian Culture and Research Journal* 37, no. 2 (2013): 4.

74. Wolfe, "The Settler Complex," 4. See Karl W. Butzer, "The Americas before and after 1492: An Introduction to Current Geographical Research," *Annals of the Association of American Geographers* 82, no. 3 (1992): 345–68.

75. Brad Coombes, Jay Johnson, and Richard Howitt, "Indigenous Geographies II: The Aspirational Spaces in Postcolonial Politics—Reconciliation, Belonging and Social Provision," *Progress in Human Geography* 37, no. 5 (2012): 691–700.

76. Rediker, "Red Atlantic," 116. See Paula Baker, "The Domestication of Politics: Women and American Political Society, 1780–1920," *American Historical Review* 89, no. 3 (1984): 620–47; Paul Blank, "The Pacific: A Mediterranean in the Making?" *Geographical Review* 89, no. 2 (1999): 265–77; William Kessen, "The American Child and Other Cultural Inventions," *American Psychologist* 34, no. 10 (1979): 815–20; and Nathaniel Millett, "Borderlands in the Atlantic World," *Atlantic Studies* 10, no. 2 (2013): 268–95.

77. United States National Park Service, "Isle Royale National Park," accessed June 2014, http://www.nps.gov/isro/index.htm.

PART II | ARCHIPELAGIC MAPPINGS AND META-GEOGRAPHIES

3　GUAM AND ARCHIPELAGIC AMERICAN STUDIES

Craig Santos Perez

THE LOST ISLAND

"Lost islands" arise from tales of untouched paradise or cannibalistic nightmares. These "imagined island topographies," along with the "ideological construction of anticipated island landfall,"[1] have played important roles in projecting and justifying colonial desire and imperial power across the terraqueous globe.

Destiny's Landfall is one such lost island in the western Pacific. The Natives, born from stone, were mythic navigators who *flew* aboard outrigger canoes. One day, a sea creature began eating the island. The women wove their hair into a net and sang songs to lure the beast. They cast their net and saved their home.[2]

As enchanted as Destiny's Landfall seems, *it actually exists*.[3] You can discover the 212-square-mile island on some maps. Look for a tiny dot at 13 degrees north latitude and 144 degrees east longitude. Look for "Guam, USA." In space, Guam is approximately 3,800 miles west of Hawai'i and 1,500 miles east of the Philippines and south of Japan. Many US-Americans have never heard of Guam because the island and its indigenous Chamorro population are considered too small and meaningless to be of any historical, political, cultural, or demographic significance.

Thus, I steer this essay into the "archipelagic" current of American studies as a productive way to more fully engage Guam and the emergent field of Guam studies.[4] In their article "Archipelagic American Studies and the Caribbean," Brian Russell Roberts and Michelle Stephens conceive of islands, continents, and oceans as archipelagic spaces of "cultural, epistemological, and political relationality."[5] Within archipelagic logic, "intermittent locales assume spatial forms that may be ordered in reference to racial, imperial, tectonic, or other cultural heuristics."[6] This envisions a "wider planetary archipelago (that is, the world's islands of the sea) in a truly decentered and unbounded, meta-archipelagic vision."[7] Archipelagic thinking has roots in Caribbean and Pacific studies, as Elizabeth DeLoughrey notes in *Routes and Roots: Navigating Caribbean and Pacific Island Literatures*. For example, she highlights Edward Kamau Brathwaite's idea of "tidalectics" as a "methodological tool that foregrounds how a dynamic model of geography can elucidate island history and cultural production, providing the framework for addressing the complex and shifting entanglement between sea and land, diaspora and indigeneity, and routes and roots."[8] Conceptualizing islands as part of a larger vastness contrasts colonial views of islands as isolated, small, and insignificant. In other words, *no island is an island* because islands exist in dynamic relationality to a larger archipelago and ocean.

Even as this essay largely maintains a focus on Guam, I argue that no island is an island because *any island is itself an archipelago*, or an "auto-archipelago." Guam is an auto-archipelago because it is constituted by multiple, interlinked, and changing identities, which are articulated and contested by various populations and interests vying for representational, historiographical, ideological, and political power. Understanding an island's multiversioned and multilayered self is essential to tracing the complexities of *intra*-island relations. This essay embodies an auto-archipelagic structure by viewing Guam simultaneously as a "lost island," a "strategic island," a "footnote island," a "moving island," an "archipelagic island," a "territorial island," and a "decolonial island." Mapping Guam through this complex archipelagic logic reveals Guam to be more than just a footnote to US-American empire and an intellectual footnote to the field of American studies. Guam is instead seen as an important source of Indigenous culture, history, literature, and scholarship, as well as a central node through which to analyze, understand, and critique the US empire. This shift foregrounds the structures and fissures of territoriality in the formation and ongoing articulation of empire, drawing attention to how territorialisms have indelibly shaped auto-, intra-, inter-, and transarchipelagic relations.

THE STRATEGIC ISLAND

In 1521, Magellan sailed around the Americas, made his way to the equator, and turned westward; after a few months, he made landfall on Guam, making it "the first inhabited island in the Pacific Ocean known to Europeans."[9] In the east-west expanse between Hawai'i and the Philippines, and the north-south expanse between Japan and Papua New Guinea, Guam is the only island with a deep, protected harbor and enough land for several airports. For the next five centuries, Guam's "strategic" location and topography made it "far more significant than islands much larger, much less isolated, and much better known."[10]

Spain claimed Guam and the Philippines in 1564, establishing its first colonies in the Pacific and Asia. In the following decades, galleons loaded with silver disembarked from Acapulco and reprovisioned off Guam before arriving in the Philippines to trade with Chinese merchants. When the galleons returned to Acapulco, the products traveled across the New World and the Atlantic to European markets. Spain mapped "a great circular loop around the Pacific north of the equator [with Guam as] a sure and useful landmark and stopover on the trans-Pacific trade route."[11] A century later, Spain established a Catholic mission, a military garrison, and a colonial government, which ruled Guam for two hundred years.[12]

Guam's destiny changed course after the Spanish-American War of 1898, when the United States acquired Guam, along with other former Spanish colonies. From 1898 to 1941, the US Navy administered Guam and established new laws, schools, hospitals, businesses, and roads.[13] During this time, Guam became a strategic location for army transports traveling among San Francisco, Hawai'i, and the Philippines.

In December 1941, Japan invaded Guam and defeated the US forces. During the occupation, Japanese authorities initiated several militarizing and civilizing projects to "eradicate forty years of American symbols, values, and, ultimately, [US] loyalty among the Chamorros."[14] Guam was renamed Omiya Jima (Great Shrine Island) and became a strategic base for Japan's imperial endeavor to create a "Co-Prosperity Sphere of Greater East Asia."[15]

On July 21, 1944, the US military invaded Guam, defeated the Japanese forces, and reclaimed the island. In 1950, an Organic Act granted US citizenship to the residents of Guam. Throughout the following decades, the US militarily refurbished Guam, making it one of the nation's most important military bases, which currently boasts one of the highest military enlistment rates per capita.[16] Because of its strategic location and topography, Guam has become one of the longest continuously colonized places in the world.

THE FOOTNOTE ISLAND

Guam lies west of the International Date Line and is a day ahead of any other US state or territory. In the 1970s, the Guam Visitors Bureau developed a slogan— "Guam, Where America's Day Begins"—to market it as the next major tourist destination in the Pacific after Hawai'i.[17] Even though the slogan started as a tourism ploy, you can now read the slogan on T-shirts; find it on websites, in advertising, and in articles; and hear it spoken during public events and political speeches. Ideologically, the slogan articulates Guam "not as a point of inequality or exploitation, but rather as a point of celebratory exceptionality." By repeating the slogan, Chamorros "embody America and claim to finally be a secure piece of it."[18]

In the poem "My Island Is One Big American Footnote," Chamorro poet and scholar Michael Lujan Bevacqua critiques the perception of Guam as a "footnote" to the US empire. The "main text" of Bevacqua's poem is only five words long: "Guam, Where America's Day Begins." Ironically, three footnotes are appended to the slogan, and the footnoted text inhabits *three entire pages*. The speaker in the footnotes describes Guam as a "small island of text [that] no one bothers to read or quote [because it is simply] conditional, contextual, so dependent on the [main] text."[19] By exposing the colonial relationship between the *footnote island* of Guam and the *main text* of the United States, Guam no longer signifies a celebratory footnote of US democracy; instead, Guam is "Where America's Empire Begins."[20] By highlighting the voice from the footnote island, Bevacqua reimagines the signifying power of Guam. In the final footnote, the speaker exclaims, "Release us to flutter beyond these American borders and margins! / Leave us to determine self-fully! A text of our own!"[21]

In Bevacqua's dissertation, "Chamorros, Ghosts, Non-Voting Delegates: GUAM! Where the Production of America's Sovereignty Begins," he critiques the perception of Guam as an intellectual footnote in American studies. Bevacqua notes how the Pacific has "gained relevance in [American studies], and become not just an interesting or exotic site on the map of American culture, but a necessary one in understanding how America has been produced over the past two centuries."[22] Despite these gains, the Pacific continues to be fantasized as "an object, an inactive supplementary fragment . . . a dependency, a dot on a map, the tip of a spear, something that does nothing more than signify the prowess and greatness of the United States."[23]

The metaphor of Guam as a "footnote" points to the subordination of island spaces to dominant continental spaces. An archipelagic framework resists this tendency because the "interlinking of island- and continent-spaces into a common planetary meta-archipelago asserts the parity of land-spaces regardless of magnitude."[24] In turn, continents are "reframed as islands that are constituent parts, rather than continental administrators, of the global meta-archipelago."[25] This reconceptualization places the Pacific Islands and Pacific Islanders "at the center of the analysis—their political sovereignty, their resistance, their voices, the ways in which they do not comfortably fit within the United States or the way it writes itself, the ways in which they remain beyond the ability to be incorporated or reduced to the strategic chess pieces or laboratory vessels."[26] Through his poetry and scholarship, Bevacqua decenters the main text of US-American power and releases Guam from its footnote status to highlight how "its banality, its geography, its coloniality, all intersect in particular ways, to constitute the United States, its power, its authority, its might, its sovereignty."[27]

THE MOVING ISLAND

In "Voyaging for Anti-Colonial Recovery: Austronesian Seafaring, Archipelagic Rethinking, and the Re-Mapping of Indigeneity," Vincente M. Diaz explains *etak*, or "moving islands," as a "technique for calculating distance traveled, or position at sea by triangulating the speed of the islands of departure and destination with that of a third reference island. This is accomplished, furthermore, by plotting these islands' courses in the celestial sky."[28] Another important seafaring technique is *pookof*, "the inventory of creatures indigenous to a given island, as well as their travel habits and behavior."[29] If you see a bird associated with a certain island, then you know that island is nearby—the island has figuratively expanded. By imagining islands moving and expanding, we can imagine that the canoe remains still.

From aboard the flagship journal *American Quarterly* we witness how Guam *moves* in and out of visibility, which is indicative of Guam's place in American studies. When Guam is sighted/cited, it is usually alongside its most common reference islands (Cuba, the Philippines, Puerto Rico, Hawai'i, and American Sāmoa); when Guam is not visible, we can still sense its *pookof* (military bases, Indigenous peoples, colonial law, and territories).

One of the first sightings of Guam was in the "American Calendar" of the fall issue of *American Quarterly* in 1960. Under the awards, fellowships, and prizes section, we get a glimpse of the United States' imperial archipelago: "Competition for Opportunity Fellowships are open to Negroes, Spanish-Americans, Chinese-Americans, Japanese Americans, American Indians, and to residents of Guam, Puerto Rico, Samoa, the Virgin Islands, the Appalachian and Ozark Mountain Areas, and the Trust Territories."[30] Guam is later mentioned in three articles in the 1970s that reference territories and military bases.[31]

Guam disappears throughout most of the 1980s and 1990s, until it is cited in an article in 1996 titled "Resituating American Studies in a Critical Internationalism," by Jane C. Desmond and Virginia R. Dominguez, which highlights "subaltern studies and postcolonial studies . . . both in terms of the relevance of the US to postcolonial conditions around the globe (for example, in Cuba, the Philippines, Guam), and to an analysis of the United States as a postcolony."[32] In Janice Radway's American Studies Association (ASA) presidential address in 1998, titled "What's in a Name?,"[33] Guam moves right alongside the flagship journal when Radway praises Diaz's "Pious Sites: Chamorro Culture between Spanish Colonialism and American Liberal Individualism"[34] as exemplary of the new American studies.

Even though Guam disappears over the next few years, it can be sensed from its pookof of indigeneity, empire, and territoriality. In "A Room of One's Own at the ASA: An Indigenous Provocation," Robert Warrior asserts that Indigenous studies can be "a provocative presence in American studies, challenging old and new orthodoxies and demanding attention to the still-present realities of the foundational history of this continent."[35] Amy Kaplan's presidential address of 2003, "Violent Belongings and the Question of Empire Today," examines the

Guantánamo Bay Naval Base as a "floating colony" that exists in the ambiguous political space "between the domestic and the foreign."[36] Notably, though unmentioned by Kaplan, Guam was considered a possible location for the detainees.[37] Shelley Fisher Fishkin's presidential address of 2004, "Crossroads of Cultures: The Transnational Turn in American Studies," emphasizes the "vexed and often violent places [of] legal borderlands," such as prisons, military bases, and territories because these places reveal the complex dimensions of empire and "disrupt celebratory nationalist narratives."[38]

Guam reappears when it is mentioned in a footnote in Henry Yu's article "Los Angeles and American Studies in a Pacific World of Migration" (2004), which speaks to how "scholarship focusing on imperialism and territorial expansion has placed areas such as the Southwest and overseas colonies such as Hawai'i and the Philippines at the center of U.S. history."[39] This scholarship provides a way of seeing the Pacific as a place with "its own history, not autonomous and separate from the United States, but integral and intersecting, blending local and global connections."[40] Similarly, Guam is sighted/cited alongside its reference islands in three different essays that focus on US territorial law in a special issue from 2005 titled *Legal Borderlands: Law and the Construction of American Borders*.[41] Guam disappears again for a few years until Lisa Kahaleole Hall, in her article "Strategies of Erasure: U.S. Colonialism and Native Hawaiian Feminism" (2008), mentions Guam alongside Hawai'i and American Sāmoa.[42] And even though Guam is not mentioned in the special issue in 2000, *Alternative Contact: Indigeneity, Globalism, and American Studies*, the issue turns toward the Pacific with essays about Hawai'i, Sāmoa, Aotearoa/New Zealand, and the Philippines.[43]

Two articles from 2012 mark a historic landfall. First, Jana K. Lipman's "'Give Us a Ship': The Vietnamese Repatriate Movement on Guam, 1975" details the repatriation struggles of Vietnamese refugees who were stationed on Guam after the Vietnam War.[44] Second, Keith L. Camacho's "Militarized Borders and Social Movements in the Mariana Islands" examines the Indigenous and labor rights discourse of activist groups in Guam and the Commonwealth of the Northern Mariana Islands in the contexts of militarization and settler colonialism.[45] After moving in and out of view for nearly twenty years, our destination island finally arrived.

The new homeport for *American Quarterly* is the American Studies Department at the University of Hawai'i at Mānoa. The theme for the special issue published in September 2015 was *Pacific Currents*. The issue focuses on the "intersections of American Studies and Native Pacific Cultural Studies, examining histories and social movements in which Pacific Islands and Islanders are central."[46] There are more than four hundred pages of scholarship on the Pacific. Two essays focus on Guam: "'No Walk in the Park': US Empire and the Radicalization of Civilian Military Labor in Guam, 1944–1962," by Alfred Peredo Flores, and "Militarization and Resistance from Guåhan: Protecting and Defending Pågat," by Tiara R. Na'puti and Michael Lujan Bevacqua. I also have a short essay, "Transterritorial Currents and the Imperial Terripelago," in the "Forum" section.[47] While American studies has slowly been turning toward Guam and other spaces of the United States' imperial archipelago, the move to Hawai'i anchors the field in the moving islands of the Pacific.

THE ARCHIPELAGIC ISLAND

Guam is the largest and southernmost island of a fifteen-island archipelago that extends across five hundred nautical miles in a north-to-south crescent. The northern islands are Rota, Aguijan, Tinian, Saipan, Farallon de Medinilla, Anatahan, Sarigan, Guguan, Alamagan, Pagan, Agrihan, Asuncion, Maug, and Farallon de Pajaros. Together, the islands constitute a total land area of nearly four hundred square miles. Chamorro peoples traveled in their canoes from "Austronesia" and first settled the archipelago four thousand years ago.

Magellan named the archipelago Islas de los Ladrones (Islands of the Thieves); later, the Catholic authorities renamed it Las Islas Marianas. After the Spanish-American War of 1898, the archipelago was partitioned: Guam became a US territory, while Spain sold the northern islands to Germany. In 1914, Japan seized the northern islands, forming the "new Japanese frontier in the equatorial Pacific."[48] The archipelago was reunited from 1941 to 1944, when Japan occupied Guam. After World War II, Guam once again became a US territory, and the northern islands became part of the United Nations Trust Territory of the Pacific Islands, administered by the United States until the 1970s, when the islands became the Commonwealth of the Northern Mariana Islands.

The separate political paths of the Mariana Islands has created a scholarly and "historiographical tendency to view histories of Guam and the Northern Marianas as seemingly separate and unrelated areas of study when, in fact, much contact and exchange occurs between the colonial, indigenous, and settler populations of these island groups."[49] An archipelagic perspective reconnects the archipelago to examine "the roots of these divisions as products of competing colonial histories, and to create, instead, inclusive venues for representing Chamorro cultural and political narratives of the past."[50] Resituating Guam within its own local archipelago would also elucidate the commonalities that territories and commonwealths have in their colonial association with the nation.

THE TERRITORIAL ISLAND

Even though the idea of the archipelago offers a "vision of bridged spaces rather than closed territorial boundaries,"[51] it is essential to foreground the history and processes of territorialism in the origins and ongoing formation of the US empire.

The word "territory" derives from the Latin *territorium*, meaning "land around a town, domain, district" (from *terra*, "land," and *-orium*, "place"). The specific US definition of territory as an organized, self-governing region dates to the turn of the eighteenth century. *Territorium* might also derive from *terrere*, meaning "to frighten"; thus, another meaning for *territorium* could be "a place from which people are warned off."[52] With these definitions in mind, I propose a new term, "terripelago," that combines *territorium* and *pélago*. Thinking with the terripelago, and taking a "transterritorial turn" in American studies, highlights the twinned phenomena of relationality and territoriality.[53]

In *Does the Constitution Follow the Flag? The Evolution of Territoriality in American Law*, Kal Raustiala describes "territoriality" as the organizing principle and central phenomenon of modern government, international law, and global empire.[54] Territoriality refers to "the organization and exercise of power over defined blocs of space. At the core of contemporary statehood is the idea ... that each sovereign state has its own discrete and exclusive territory. Under this view, legal rules and rights are generally seen as tied to territorial borders."[55] The establishment of the United States as a sovereign nation-state justified its acquisitions of new territories through the international doctrines of discovery and conquest, as well as through its ability to make treaties and purchase lands. In turn, the Northwest Ordinance of 1787 "not only set forth pattern of territorial development which exists even today but also stated the underlying principle of territorial evolution in U.S. law and tradition: that the goal of all territorial acquisition eventually was to be Statehood."[56] The Territorial Clause (Article IV, Section 3) of the US Constitution declared that Congress has the power to determine the laws of these territories and the rights conferred upon those inhabiting the territories. The Territorial Clause dealt mainly with already acquired, contiguous territories that would be incorporated as states in the federal union with full constitutional rights. However, when the United States expanded its territory into Indian lands and overseas areas, territoriality was no longer inviolate. Raustiala points to two ways the United States has pulled, stretched, and even broken the relationship between law, rights, and territory: "One occurs when domestic law extends beyond sovereign borders. This is commonly called *extraterritoriality*. The other ... takes place when domestic law is restricted to certain national territory; in other words, when different areas within a sovereign state have distinct legal regimes. [Raustiala] call[s] this *intraterritoriality*."[57] The US empire has continuously articulated new forms of territoriality for strategic military, economic, and political interests.

With the acquisition of discontiguous territories after the Spanish-American War of 1898, questions arose about whether or not these new territories should be automatically incorporated and granted citizenship and full constitutional rights. In other words, "Does the constitution follow the flag?" A series of Supreme Court cases (known as the Insular Cases), dating from 1901 to 1922, decided that full rights and citizenship did not automatically apply to the new territories but instead would be determined by the plenary power of Congress. A new political category was created: the "unincorporated territory." This curious kind of territory belonged to the United States but was not a fully incorporated part of the nation. Being trapped in the limbo between the domestic and the foreign has not only denied Guam the rights that other US citizens are granted but has also kept Guam from attaining decolonization, self-determination, and sovereignty.

In "Discontiguous States of America: The Paradox of Unincorporation in Craig Santos Perez's Poetics of Chamorro Guam," Paul Lai replaces "united" with "discontiguous" to map US-American imperial topography and highlight the paradoxical situation of reservations, offshore territories, and outlying states. According to Lai, the creation of the "unincorporated territory" suggests a "discontinuous logic of unity, one in which leaps of logic are necessary to create a semblance of wholeness."[58] Lai considers "discontinuities rather than connections" to note how the "complicated and contradictory layering of sovereignty, power, and cultural history in these discontiguous states calls for more analysis of alternative formations of America and American Studies."[59] Indeed, the United States is "the largest overseas territorial power in the world [governing] five areas (Puerto Rico, Virgin Islands, Guam, the Northern Marianas, and American Samoa) with a population of almost four million people and has special responsibilities for three additional areas (Federated States of Micronesia, the Marshall Islands, and Palau)."[60]

The United States not only territorializes land through a variety of territorial (il)logics but also territorializes oceans and waterways. As DeLoughrey maps in "Heavy Waters: Waste and Atlantic Modernity," the rise of the United States as a global naval power coincided with "an unprecedented era of global ocean governance and militarization."[61] After World War II, the United States "violated the freedom-of-the-seas doctrine by extending the littoral state to two hundred miles out to sea and then annexed Micronesia, an area as large as the North Atlantic. All told, this new ocean territorialism tripled the size of the United States."[62] Ocean territorialism increased internationally as well when the 1982 United Nations Convention on the Law of the Sea "catalyzed the most radical remapping of the globe in modern history, expanding all coastal nations through an exclusive economic zone of two hundred nautical miles. Roughly thirty-eight million square nautical miles of the global sea were enclosed by the state, a privatization of thirty-five percent of the world's ocean."[63] DeLoughrey points out that this new territorialism also controls submarine space in order to "protect the passage of nuclear submarines, sea-launched missiles, and maritime surveillance systems undergirded by thirty thousand miles of submarine cables."⁶⁴ Relatedly, Guam has been constituted as a "critical node" in the transpacific cable network for "U.S. military's establishment of Guam as a strategic space; private telecommunications companies' investment in Guam as an Asian hub; and the expansion of infrastructures that depend on and generate traffic for cables, including networks of sea transport, air transport, and migration."⁶⁵ Overall, the processes of extraterritoriality, intraterritoriality, and the accumulation of old and new marine and submarine territorialisms have transformed Guam, other islands, and the Pacific Ocean into a militarized space of empire.

THE DECOLONIAL ISLAND

Chamorros have continually struggled against colonialism and fought for decolonization, demilitarization, political sovereignty, environmental preservation, land reclamation, and cultural revitalization.⁶⁶ One way that Chamorros have articulated resistance is through poetry.

In 2006, the United States and Japan announced a major realignment of US military forces and operations in Guam. This "megabuildup" would include the construction of facilities to house and support the transfer of 8,600 marines and their 9,000 dependents from Okinawa to Guam. Additionally, the buildup would establish an Air and Missile Defense Task Force, a live firing range complex, and the creation of a deep-draft wharf for nuclear powered aircraft carriers. A "Draft Environmental Impact Statement" (DEIS) for the military buildup was released in 2009. This eleven-thousand-page document detailed how the military planned to build a live firing range complex around the ancient Chamorro village of Pågat, to replace hundreds of acres of jungle for permanent military facilities, and to rip out more than two million square feet of living coral reef to dredge a deep-draft wharf—all while producing at least eight tons of hazardous waste. Additionally, the increase in population would increase violence, crime, prostitution, and rape, and put an unsustainable stress on affordable housing, social services, education, health care, and utilities.⁶⁷

The public was given ninety days to read, interpret, and comment on the DEIS. Public hearings were held throughout the island, at which residents could comment on the buildup proposals. The first hearing was held on January 7, 2010, at Southern High School in the village of Santa Rita, which is in the southern part of Guam near the naval base. Chamorro poet Melvin Won Pat-Borja, who taught creative writing at Southern High School, performed a prose poem, "No Deal," for his public testimony.

The poem opens with a student asking a teacher, "Sir, what if we protest and unite as a people, and in the end they just do whatever they want?"⁶⁸ The teacher responds, "I understand that the federal government has done worse things and gotten away with it, like smallpox blankets, like nuclear testing in the Marshall Islands, like dropping bombs on Vieques, like holding the sovereign queen of Hawai'i at gunpoint to sign the annexation."[69] The teacher points to these transterritorial injustices to show that the United States has a history of simply ignoring Indigenous protests. Relatedly, the speaker points to how the United States even ignores the fact that Chamorros enlist in the military at high rates: "We are loyal servants fighting for your freedom of action. . . . We are so loyal that we enlist more sons and daughters into America's armed services to fight and die than anywhere else in the world. We have paid your ultimate sacrifice time and again."[70] Despite the display of loyalty and sacrifice, the teacher highlights the hypocrisy of living in an unincorporated territory: "The hands of your Presidents are drenched in the blood of our fallen—the same presidents that we are not allowed to vote for."[71] Borja's poem volcanically concludes, "Let the record show that in the face of oppression and injustice, the people of Guam refuse to live a life absent of liberty, that we refuse to accept anything less than justice, that we refuse to sell Guam to the highest bidder. And should we die fighting your war machine, let your history books show your children the struggle that we fought to find freedom in a country filled with hypocrisy. Let the record show that Guåhan stood up and said, Uncle Sam, sorry, but *No Deal.*"[72] Throughout Borja's passionate performance, audience members cheered loudly, sometimes muffling his recitation. As he spoke the last words, "No Deal," the room erupted.[73]

Another Chamorro poet and educator, Kisha Borja-Kicho'cho', testified at a hearing on January 9, 2010. She recited her poem, "Re-Occupation Day (aka 'Liberation Day')," which begins, "Every 21st of July, / the people of Guåhan march in their red, white, and blue, / thanking uncle sam and his men in uniform."[74] "Liberation Day" is an annual commemoration of the day the US military invaded Guam to "liberate" the island from Japanese occupation. The key theme of Liberation Day is Chamorro loyalty to the United States, and the actual event includes a parade down Guam's major road, Marine Corps Drive, with marching bands, floats, and games.[75]

Borja-Kicho'cho' questions the idea of liberation and loyalty by rearticulating July 21st as "Re-Occupation Day," suggesting that the return of the United States in 1944 was merely a continuation of the colonial occupation of Guam that began in 1898. She also rearticulates Chamorros not as loyal soldiers but as enslaved "by the SPAM-crazed golden arches / by drafts and recruitments / by 'the land of the free.'"[76] She names other injustices caused by the United States: "They took [Sumay] / and used it for their military. / They made us citizens / but denied us the vote. / They stole our language / and made us speak english."[77] The poem disrupts any celebratory narrative of US liberation that might be used to justify the military buildup.

While Won Pat-Borja's poem ends in resolute refusal, Borja-Kicho'cho's poem ends in a mournful tone. The penultimate line is written in Chamorro, and the last line in English: "I taotao-hu trabiha ti man libre. // My people are not free."[78] The voices of these poets transformed Guam into a decolonial island.

CONCLUSION

Since US foreign policy claimed the twenty-first century as "America's Pacific Century" and began negotiations for the Trans-Pacific Partnership and the further militarization and territorialization of the Asia-Pacific region,[79] it is crucial for American studies to follow the flag toward the Pacific Islands. As the "westernmost 'border' of the U.S. geopolitical imaginary,"[80] Guam and the Northern Mariana Islands could provocatively become where American studies begins. Indeed, Americanists might begin by navigating Chamorro studies, a scholarly movement that emphasizes Chamorro struggles for sovereignty, self-determination, demilitarization, and decolonization; highlights issues of colonialism, missionization, tourism, and militarism; and prioritizes Chamorro epistemologies, methodologies, cultural practices, languages, and ecologies. While centered in our ancestral archipelago, Chamorro studies also examines Chamorro migration, diasporas, and diasporic subjectivities.[81]

Archipelagic American studies offers a productive theoretical and methodological framework to engage Guam, Chamorro, and Pacific studies. It potentially recenters Guam in various articulations of a global meta-archipelago, resituates Guam within its own local archipelago, and reenvisions Guam as a complex auto-archipelago. Turning toward the archipelagic horizon also foregrounds the fluctuating processes of territorialization, including extraterritoriality, intraterritoriality, and the old and new terrestrial and marine territorialisms that have created and continue to shape the meta-terripelago of the US empire. When we understand that nearly every country in the world is currently involved in a territorial dispute over possession and control of borders, islands, waters, peoples, and lands, then we can denaturalize the false union of empire.[82] Lastly, by listening to the decolonial voices of Indigenous poets, we can remember that the ultimate destiny of any territorialized space can be rewritten and reimagined.

NOTES

1. Elizabeth DeLoughrey, "'The litany of islands, The rosary of archipelagoes': Caribbean and Pacific Archipelagraphy," *ARIEL: A Review of International English Literature* 32, no. 1 (January 2001): 31–32.

2. Bo Flood, *Marianas Island Legends: Myth and Magic* (Honolulu, HI: Bess Press, 2001).

3. Rodney F. Rogers, *Destiny's Landfall: A History of Guam* (Honolulu: University of Hawai'i Press, 1995).

4. See Nicholas Goetzfridt, *Guahan: A Bibliographic History* (Honolulu: University of Hawai'i Press, 2014).

5. Brian Russell Roberts and Michelle Stephens, "Archipelagic American Studies and the Caribbean," *Journal of Transnational American Studies* 5, no. 1 (2013): 15.

6. Roberts and Stephens, "Archipelagic American Studies," 14.

7. Roberts and Stephens, "Archipelagic American Studies," 13.

8. Elizabeth DeLoughrey, *Routes and Roots: Navigating Caribbean and Pacific Island Literatures* (Honolulu: University of Hawai'i Press, 2007), 2.

9. Rogers, *Destiny's Landfall*, 1.

10. Rogers, *Destiny's Landfall*, 1.

11. Rogers, *Destiny's Landfall*, 15.

12. See Francis X. Hezel, SJ, "From Conversion to Conquest: The Early Spanish Mission in the Marianas," *Journal of Pacific History* 17 (1982): 115–20; Francis X. Hezel, SJ, "From Conquest to Colonization: Spain in the Marianas, 1690–1740," *Journal of Pacific History* 23 (1988): 137–55; and Rainer F. Buschmann, Edward R. Slack Jr., and James B. Tueller, eds., *Navigating the Spanish Lake: The Pacific in the Iberian World, 1521–1898* (Honolulu: University of Hawai'i Press, 2014).

13. See Anne Perez Hattori, *Colonial Dis-Ease: US Navy Health Policies and the Chamorros of Guam, 1898–1941* (Honolulu: University of Hawai'i Press, 2004); Robert Anacletus Underwood, "American Education and the Acculturation of the Chamorros of Guam" (PhD diss., University of Southern California, 1987); Christine Taitano DeLisle, "Navy Wives / Native Lives: The Cultural and Historical Relations between Naval Wives and Chamorro Women in Guam, 1898–1945" (PhD diss., University of Michigan, 2008); Vicente Diaz, "Paved with Good Intentions . . . Roads, Citizenship and a Century of American Colonialism in Guam," paper presented at the Centennial of the Spanish American War Summer Seminar, Obermann Center for Advanced Study, University of Iowa, 1998.

14. Keith L. Camacho, *Cultures of Commemoration: The Politics of War, Memory, and History in the Mariana Islands* (Honolulu: University of Hawai'i Press, 2011), 44.

15. See Mark R. Peattie, *Nan'yō: The Rise and Fall of the Japanese in Micronesia, 1885–1945* (Honolulu: University of Hawai'i Press, 1988).

16. See Michael Lujan Bevacqua, "The Exceptional Life and Death of a Chamorro Soldier: Tracing the Militarization of Desire in Guam~~USA~~," in *Militarized Currents: Toward a Decolonized Future in Asia and the Pacific*, ed. Setsu Shigematsu and Keith L. Camacho, 33–62 (Minneapolis: University of Minnesota Press, 2010).

17. See Keith L. Camacho, "'Enframing I TaoTao Tano': Colonialism, Militarism, and Tourism in Twentieth-Century Guam" (master's thesis, University of Hawai'i, 1998).

18. Michael Lujan Bevacqua, "Chamorros, Ghosts, Non-Voting Delegates: GUAM! Where the Production of America's Sovereignty Begins" (PhD diss., University of California, San Diego, 2010), 2.

19. Michael Lujan Bevacqua, "My Island Is One Big American Footnote," in *The Space Between: Negotiating Culture, Place, and Identity in the Pacific*, ed. Marata Tamaira (Honolulu, HI: Center for Pacific Islands Studies, 2009), 120–22.

20. Michael Lujan Bevacqua, "Guam: Where America's Empire Begins," February 18, 2008, accessed May 15, 2014, http://minagahet.blogspot.com/ 2008/02/guam-where-americas-military-empire.html.

21. Bevacqua, "My Island," 122.

22. Bevacqua, "Chamorros, Ghosts," 66.

23. Bevacqua, "Chamorros, Ghosts," 3.

24. Roberts and Stephens, "Archipelagic American Studies," 13.

25. Roberts and Stephens, "Archipelagic American Studies," 14.

26. Bevacqua, "Chamorros, Ghosts," 78.

27. Bevacqua, "Chamorros, Ghosts," 8.

28. Vicente M. Diaz, "Voyaging for Anti-Colonial Recovery: Austronesian Seafaring, Archipelagic Rethinking, and the Re-Mapping of Indigeneity," *Pacific Asia Inquiry* 2, no. 1 (Fall 2011): 26.

29. Diaz, "Voyaging for Anti-Colonial Recovery," 27.

30. "American Calendar," *American Quarterly* 12, no. 3 (Autumn 1960): 434.

31. See William J. Schafer, "Beyond Bubblegum: Randy Newman and Harry Nilsson," *American Quarterly* 22, no. 3 (Autumn 1970): 742–60; H. H. Wubben, "American Prisoners of War in Korea: A Second Look at the 'Something New in History' Theme," *American Quarterly* 22, no. 1 (Spring 1970): 3–19; and Randall B. Woods, "Terrorism in the Age of Roosevelt: The Miss Stone Affair, 1901–1902," *American Quarterly* 31, no. 4 (Autumn 1979): 478–95.

32. Jane C. Desmond and Virginia R. Dominguez, "Resituating American Studies in a Critical Internationalism," *American Quarterly* 48, no. 3 (September 1996): 487.

33. Janice A. Radway, "What's in a Name? Presidential Address to the American Studies Association, 20 November 1998," *American Quarterly* 51, no. 1 (March 1999): 1–32.

34. Vicente M. Diaz, "Pious Sites: Chamorro Culture between Spanish Catholicism and American Liberal Individualism," in *Cultures of United States Imperialism*, ed. Amy Kaplan and Donald E. Pease, 312–39 (Durham, NC: Duke University Press, 1993).

35. Robert Allen Warrior, "A Room of One's Own at the ASA: An Indigenous Provocation," *American Quarterly* 55, no. 4 (December 2003): 686.

36. Amy Kaplan, "Violent Belongings and the Question of Empire," *American Quarterly* 56, no. 1 (March 2004): 7.

37. Karen J. Greenberg, *The Least Worst Place: How Guantanamo Became the World's Most Notorious Prison* (Oxford: Oxford University Press, 2009).

38. Shelley Fisher Fishkin, "Crossroads of Cultures: The Transnational Turn in American Studies," *American Quarterly* 57, no. 1 (March 2005): 17.

39. Henry Yu, "Los Angeles and American Studies in a Pacific World of Migration," *American Quarterly* 56, no. 3 (September 2004): 539.

40. Yu, "Los Angeles and American Studies," 539.

41. Christina Duffy Burnett, "The Edges of Empire and the Limits of Sovereignty: American Guano Islands," *American Quarterly* 57, no. 3 (September 2005): 779–803; Amy Kaplan, "Where Is Guantanamo?" *American Quarterly* 57, no. 3 (September 2005): 831–58; Linda K. Kerber, "Toward a History of Statelessness in America," *American Quarterly* 57, no. 3 (September 2005): 727–49.

42. Lisa Kahaleole Hall, "Strategies of Erasure: U.S. Colonialism and Native Hawaiian Feminism," *American Quarterly* 60, no. 2 (June 2008): 273–80.

43. Paul Lai and Lindsey Claire Smith, preface to "Alternative Contact: Indigeneity, Globalism, and American Studies," *American Quarterly* 62, no. 3 (September 2010): 407–36.

44. Jana K. Lipman, "'Give Us a Ship': The Vietnamese Repatriation Movement on Guam, 1975," *American Quarterly* 61, no. 1 (March 2012): 1–31.

45. Keith L. Camacho, "After 9/11: Militarized Borders and Social Movements in the Mariana Islands," *American Quarterly* 64, no. 4 (December 2012): 685–713.

46. The *American Quarterly* website, accessed May 27, 2014, archived page for the "Pacific Currents" issue call for papers: http://archive-org-2014.com/org/a/2014-06-23_4166313/.

47. Alfred Paredo Flores, "'No Walk in the Park': US Empire and the Racialization of Civilian Military Labor in Guam, 1944–1962," *American Quarterly* 67, no. 3 (September 2015): 813–35; Tiara R. Na'puti and Michael Lujan Bevacqua, "Militarization and Resistance from Guåhan: Protecting and Defending Pågat," *American Quarterly* 67, no. 3 (September 2015): 837–58; Craig Santos Perez, "Transterritorial Currents and the Imperial Terripelago," *American Quarterly* 67, no. 3 (September 2015): 619–24.

48. Peattie, *Nan'yō*, 16.

49. Camacho, *Cultures of Commemoration*, 3.

50. Camacho, *Cultures of Commemoration*, 3.

51. Camacho, *Cultures of Commemoration*, 14.

52. "Territory (n.)," *Online Etymology Dictionary*, accessed May 1, 2014, http://www.etymonline.com/index.php?term=territory.

53. For an expanded discussion of this topic, see Perez, "Transterritorial Currents."

54. Kal Raustiala, *Does the Constitution Follow the Flag? The Evolution of Territoriality in American Law* (New York: Oxford University Press, 2009).

55. Raustiala, *Does the Constitution Follow the Flag?*, 5.

56. Arnold H. Leibowitz, *Defining Status: A Comprehensive Analysis of United States Territorial Relations* (Netherlands: Martinus Nijhoff, 1989), 6.

57. Raustiala, *Does the Constitution Follow the Flag?*, 5.

58. Paul Lai, "Discontiguous States of America: The Paradox of Unincorporation in Craig Santos Perez's Poetics of Chamorro Guam," *Journal of Transnational American Studies* 3, no. 2 (2011): 3.

59. Lai, "Discontiguous States," 3.

60. Leibowitz, *Defining Status*, 3.

61. Elizabeth DeLoughrey, "Heavy Waters: Waste and Atlantic Modernity," PMLA 125, no. 3 (2010): 705.

62. DeLoughrey, "Heavy Waters," 705.

63. DeLoughrey, "Heavy Waters," 705.

64. DeLoughrey, "Heavy Waters," 705.

65. Nicole Starosielski, "Critical Nodes, Cultural Networks: Re-Mapping Guam's Cable Infrastructure," *Amerasia Journal* 37, no. 3 (2011): 19–20.

66. See Penelope Bordallo Hofschneider, *A Campaign for Political Rights on the Island of Guam, 1899–1950* (Saipan: CNMI Division of Historic Preservation, 2001); Laura Souder and Robert Underwood, eds., *Chamorro Self-Determination / I Direchon y Taotao* (Agana, Guam: Micronesian Area Research Center, 1987); Hope Alvarez Cristobal, "The Organization of People for Indigenous Rights: A Commitment towards Self-Determination," *Hinasso: Tinige' Put Chamorro, Insights: The Chamorro Identity* (Agana, Guam: Political Status Education Coordinating Committee, 1993); Michael P. Perez, "Contested Sites: Pacific Resistance in Guam to U.S. Empire," *Amerasia Journal* 27, no. 1 (2001): 97–115.

67. Gwen Kirk and Lisa Natividad, "Fortress Guam: Resistance to US Military Mega-Buildup," *Asia-Pacific Journal*, May 10, 2010, accessed April 15, 2014, http://japanfocus.org/-Gwyn-Kirk/3356.

68. Melvin Won Pat-Borja, "No Deal" (2010). Written version of poem provided via personal communication, 2012.

69. Won Pat-Borja, "No Deal."

70. Won Pat-Borja, "No Deal."

71. Won Pat-Borja, "No Deal."

72. Won Pat-Borja, "No Deal."

73. See Melvin Won Pat-Borja, "No Deal" (2010), accessed on Feb 23, 2012, http://www.youtube.com/ watch?v=YzmXU6u5CTE.

74. Kisha Borja-Kicho'cho', "Re-Occupation Day (aka Liberation Day)" (2010), accessed February 24, 2012, http://www.youtube.com/watch?v=Fi5yN9ehtZI. Written version of the poem provided via personal communication, 2012.

75. See Cecilia Taitano Perez, "Liberation Day: A Re-Telling," in *Kinalamten Pulitikat: Sinenten I Chamorro / Issues in Guam's Political Development: The Chamorro Perspective* (Agana, Guam: Political Status Education Coordinating Commission, 1996); Vicente Diaz, "Deliberating 'Liberation Day': Identity, History, Memory, and War in Guam," in *Perilous Memories: The Asia-Pacific War(s)*, ed. T. Fujitani et al. (Durham, NC: Duke University Press, 2001), 155–89; and Camacho, *Cultures of Commemoration*.

76. Borja-Kicho'cho', "Re-Occupation Day."

77. Borja-Kicho'cho', "Re-Occupation Day."

78. Borja-Kicho'cho', "Re-Occupation Day."

79. Lori Wallach, "A Stealth Attack on Democratic Governance," *American Prospect*, March 13, 2012, accessed April 2, 2012, http://prospect.org/article/stealth-attack-democratic-governance.

80. Camacho, "Militarized Borders," 686.

81. In addition to those already cited in this essay, Chamorro studies scholars include Julian Aguon, Jesi Lujan Bennett, Michael Clement, Vivian Dames, Alfred Flores, Evelyn Flores, Nicholas Goetzfridt, Kenneth Gofigan Kuper, Antoinette Charfauros McDaniel, Laurel A. Monnig, Leiana Naholowa'a, Tiara Na'puti, Lisa Natividad, Michael Perez, Sharlene Santos-Bamba, Faye Untalan, and James Viernes, to name a few.

82. See Annalisa Merelli, "Map: Every Country in the World Involved in a Territorial Dispute," *Atlantic*, March 20, 2014, accessed May 23, 2014, http://www.theatlantic.com/international/archive/2014/03/map-every-country-in-the-world-involved-in-a-territorial-dispute/284533/.

4 THE ARCHIPELAGIC BLACK GLOBAL IMAGINARY

Etsuko Taketani

WALTER WHITE'S PACIFIC ISLAND HOPPING

THIS ESSAY IS AN INVITATION to revisit a spatial paradigm shift that occurred in the 1940s United States, which imagined a break with the long-accepted Mercator projection—a shift that, I suggest, had a significant bearing on the African American planetary imaginary. Equator-based Mercator mapping, the standard projection for maritime navigation since the sixteenth century, is a resilient paradigm that continues to exert a profound influence on scholarly and popular perceptions of the world. Although it is not acknowledged as often as it should be, Paul Gilroy's influential "black Atlantic" framework (1993) is theorized within and against Mercator's Eurocentric codification of the modern world.[1] It fixes on the image of the sailing ship, evocative of the Middle Passage of the slave trade, as a "chronotope" (temporospatial frame) that is necessary to understand the experience of transnational black modernity.[2] Mercator's map, however, rapidly lost its narrative power during World War II. Instead, an innovative cartography adopting an aerial perspective—popularized by the cartographic artist Richard Edes Harrison and his "One World, One War" map (1941), drawn in an azimuthal projection centered on the North Pole—represented the United States' fresh world outlook.[3] It ushered in what Alan K. Henrikson has termed "air-age globalism."

Air-age globalism, according to Henrikson, emerged with the "surprise" air attack on the US naval base at Pearl Harbor—a target presumed to be impossible to attack because of distance—as a "primal event." The distance was conceptually even greater in the traditional Mercator map centered on the Greenwich meridian, which entailed the division of the Pacific, placing the two archipelagoes, Hawai'i and Japan, at the extreme left (west) and right (east) sides, respectively.[4] It is hardly coincidental that Harrison's "One World, One War" map, providing a salutary reminder of the Earth's sphericity and continuity, gained credence. It was appropriate to the modern age in which aviation created new realities of movement on the globe and, in World War II, meant the rise of airpower.

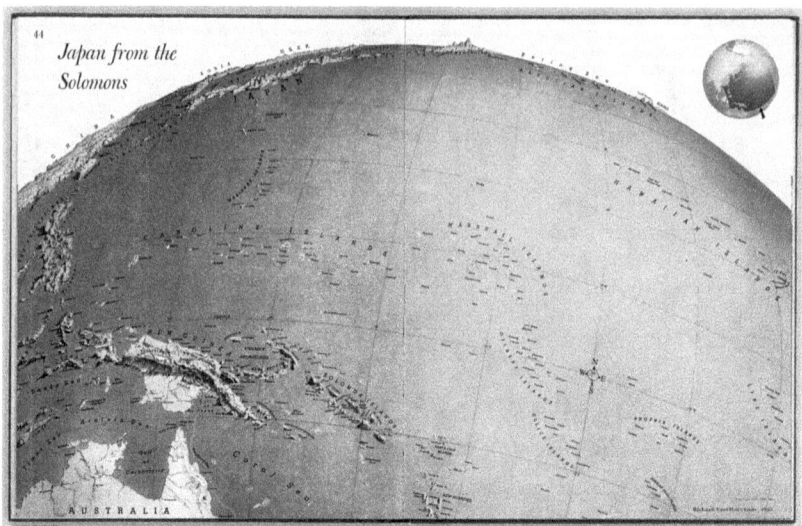

Figure 4.1. "Japan from the Solomons." From Richard Edes Harrison, *Look at the World: The FORTUNE Atlas for World Strategy* (New York: Alfred A. Knopf, 1944), 44–45. Used with permission of the Estate of Richard Edes Harrison.

Harrison's post-Mercator mapping not only brought into question hemispheres and continents, the basic global divisions that have long been taken for granted, but also closed up the strategic value of Pacific islands and thus shaped the conduct of the war. One of Harrison's signature stratospheric perspective maps, titled "Japan from Alaska," showed how the northern air route, via the Aleutian Islands, "cuts into the heart of the Japanese Empire."[5] Another of Harrison's maps, titled "Japan from the Solomons," brought home to the viewer from the air the relative adjacency and proximity of the Pacific Islands—depicted in Mercator's flat map as widely dispersed—to Asia, while restating the vast span of waters that challenged marine power (figure 4.1).[6] United States forces would use these and other Pacific islands for the military tactics of island hopping or leapfrogging, building airstrips and integrating the network of military operations with aircraft.

This essay asks what is enabled by a critical inquiry into such paradigm shifts. I consider this question by examining the air travels of Walter White, African American writer and executive secretary of the National Association for the Advancement of Colored People (NAACP), who navigated this changing spatial context in the 1940s. White's transatlantic flight to the European and North African theaters of World War II, which inspired his book *A Rising Wind* (1945), is reasonably well known. Less appreciated is the writer's historic journey as an accredited war correspondent in the Pacific theater, where he made a 36,000-mile, island-hopping tour, visiting, among other islands and atolls, Oahu, Johnston, Kwajalein, Guam, Saipan, Tinian, Leyte, New Guinea, Biak, Luzon, and Peleliu, and thus drawing a new literary geography of the Pacific.[7] Recent scholarship on black internationalism has adopted the "black Pacific" as a heuristic frame of reference—complementing Gilroy's black Atlantic—to reclaim Afro-Asian exchange.[8] With the focus on the Pacific Rim and Asian nations, this scholarly discourse, albeit unwittingly, erases from maps the many small islands and atolls within the Pacific that the US forces occupied to secure air control. White flew precisely in the network of such island-based air routes created by the wartime United States.

Four years after the end of World War II, White resumed his globe-trotting, joining a round-the-world tour sponsored by the public affairs program *America's Town Meeting of the Air*. White's black "Voice of America" was broadcast in a turbulent Asia to defend One World at a time when the Iron and Bamboo Curtains were being erected to divide the globe, and the United States was building a "defense perimeter" on a string of military bases on offshore islands—an inheritance from World War II—in the Pacific. In what follows, I examine the political geography of race charted by White's air travels in the 1940s, complicating our understanding of the African American planetary geography predicated on the two hemispheric/oceanic frames, the black Pacific, and the more prominent black Atlantic. Ultimately, this essay seeks to advance what I term "the archipelagic black global imaginary" produced by White as the air age shaped not only the conduct of the wars (World War II and the early Cold War) but also the structure and horizons of black experience. It is a mutually implicated vision of geography and processes of racialization that moved beyond a specifically "black" context as the United States, with its power increasingly rooted in interlinked island bases, evolved into an informal empire that was no longer hemispheric but now global in scale.

THE AERIAL (TRANSCONTINENTAL) ATLANTIC

In January 1944, armed with his press credentials as a *New York Post* war correspondent, Walter White boarded a Britain-bound aircraft of the US Army Air Transport Command (ATC) from Long Island's LaGuardia airfield.[9] This idea, according to White's own published account, *A Rising Wind*, took shape when he received a letter from an African American Red Cross worker in the British Isles. Although the letter had been subject to military censorship, from reading between the lines, White felt the urgent need to investigate "the transplanting of racial emotions and patterns from Mississippi to the Midlands," where US military installations were established with the arrival of black troops in England in May 1942.[10] White applied to the Department of War to secure the difficult permissions required to travel overseas.

White's three-and-a-half-month investigation of segregation and discrimination in the US armed forces resulted in his war report, *A Rising Wind*. As much as it is about the status of African American soldiers in the European and North African theaters, *A Rising Wind* is also about the emergent air-age globalism in the 1940s. Its opening pages present the spatial reorientation of travel brought by aviation. Having flown the Atlantic, via the island base of Newfoundland, to Ireland "in the space of a sound sleep" on an ATC Douglas C-54 Skymaster, White writes, "Though I had read often of others doing so, it was a jolt to have experienced the virtual demolition of time and space. And then I thought, why should I be surprised? In a sense, wasn't that what this whole trip was about?" White's tour was made possible by an ATC that had helped create the aerial Atlantic world, changing the temporospatial dimension of Mercator's maritime world plied by slave ships. White describes how aviation transformed planetary geography, reckoning distance not in miles but in hours, and embracing the United States' temporospatial proximity to England and Africa, and to its new neighbor half a globe away, India. He writes, "Now England was less than a score of hours from New York; India sixty hours instead of sixty days from Manhattan; Africa but little farther than England" (RW, 13).

A Rising Wind reveals how air-age globalism made "the Jim Crow on the go." The practices of racial segregation flew across the oceans and between continents, which had once been "material obstacles" (RW, 13), to follow the US military fighting for freedom and democracy. The footprints of Jim Crow were already visible in the British Isles at the time of White's arrival in January 1944. American Red Cross clubs in London separated black and white Americans, and the "off-limits" rule was applied outside London, whereby black troops were restricted to one town and whites to another. Britons were warned that African Americans "are not like your colonials" and "they will rape your women" (RW, 16).[11] The most egregious effect of the mobility of the Jim Crow was that it left in its wake black GIs fighting for freedom behind prison bars. White tells how the court-martial procedure was "used to break the spirit of Negro soldiers, particularly those who knew their rights and insisted upon exercising them." These black servicemen were "considered by some of the officers to be 'radicals' or 'troublemakers'" (RW, 24).

The ultimate irony is that in the Jim Crow economy of war, African American soldiers are produced and constituted as *abject*, and denied basic human rights that protected even white enemy prisoners of war. In Britain, a soldier from the US South told White of an incident in which Nazi prisoners of war were "fed in comfort in a restaurant" while wounded African American soldiers, en route to hospital, had to "go around to the back and eat in the kitchen"; and this was not an isolated episode (RW, 36, 126).[12] In North Africa, where White arrived after he left the European Theater of Operations of the United States Army, he saw an outfit of thousands of combat-trained black US soldiers reduced from combat to service status. These fighting men of color were given the task of unloading ships in Algeria after their arrival from the United States, despite the fact that "there were many Italian prisoners of war available for such manual labor," which crushed their morale (RW, 76). Illustrating how the great wartime migration of Jim Crow and its structural violence problematize the geography of freedom and bondage, *A Rising Wind* thus reads as a black version/vision of the aerial Atlantic world.

With the declassification of British government documents about White's tour, however, *A Rising Wind* begins to look different. London's foreign office files reveal that White initially planned a tour and a book—coupled together—both of global scope. His draft itinerary was to travel from the United States to "England and Ireland, and later to French Equatorial Africa, Liberia, Algeria, Morocco, Libya, Sicily and Nairobi." From there, he would proceed to "Iraq, Persia, Trans-Jordan, Syria, Russia, India and China," to write a book on "Global War in Terms of Race."[13] This grandiose idea of a global tour, conceived during the wartime State Department's restrictions on civilian international travel, was inspired by Wendell L. Willkie's journey around the world in forty-nine days on the bomber *Gulliver*. From August to October 1942, Willkie, the defeated Republican candidate for the presidency in 1940, made the 31,000-mile goodwill flight as a private citizen and special envoy of President Franklin D. Roosevelt. He circled the globe from the United States to the Caribbean, South America, Africa, the Middle East, the Soviet Union, and China, in the interest of United Nations solidarity and to demonstrate that "the Allies were in control of strategic air routes."[14] Willkie's best-selling memoir of the tour, *One World*, was published in 1943, embellished with a map charting the flight route of the *Gulliver*, which crossed the equator twice (figure 4.2). The map represented an aerial One World that the image of the airplane unified, expressing Willkie's belief that the world is one and that "freedom is an indivisible word."[15]

This air-age sensibility pervaded the wartime Roosevelt administration. From May to July 1944, Vice President Henry A. Wallace made a fifty-day, 27,000-mile goodwill tour to the Soviet Union and China on an ATC Skymaster with some of the airmen who crewed the *Gulliver*. The Wallace party followed the "Great Circle" flight course across the Bering Sea. Wallace included a polar-centered map in his travelogue, *Soviet Asia Mission* (1946), and called the route "a rainbow in the North Pacific."[16] Eleanor Roosevelt also undertook a goodwill flight south to Australia and New Zealand from August to September 1943. She traveled 25,000

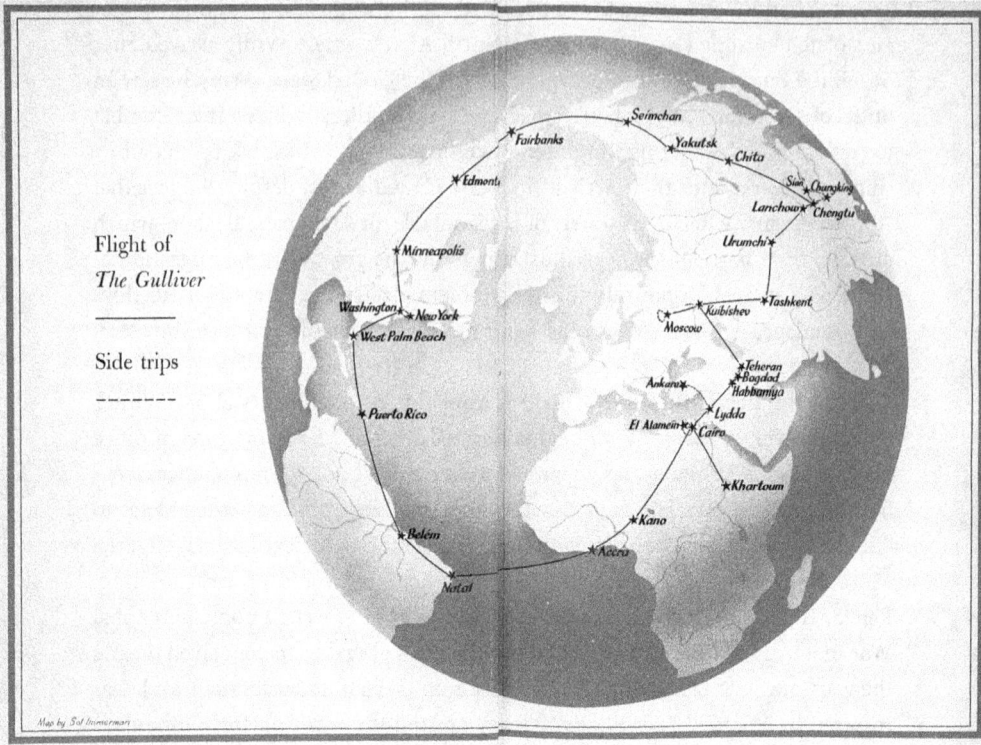

Figure 4.2. "Flight of *The Gulliver*." From Wendell L. Willkie, *One World* (New York: Simon and Schuster, 1943), front endpaper.

miles, making stops at the islands of Hawai'i, Christmas, Penrhyn, Bora Bora, Aitutaki, Tutuila, Samoa, Fiji, New Caledonia, Efate, Espiritu Santo, Guadalcanal, and Wallis, to visit US troops fighting against the Japanese in the Pacific.[17] The title of White's book, *A Rising Wind*, was taken from Eleanor Roosevelt's radio broadcast given on September 28, 1941, shortly before Pearl Harbor, in which she criticized the isolationists in peace camps for their misguided idea that "there is such a thing as separation and isolation for any individual country." She described World War II as the rise of a wind of freedom, saying, "A wind is rising throughout the world of free men everywhere, and they will not be kept in bondage."[18]

Given such emergent air-age globalism, I ask, what does it mean that White's tour plan never materialized and was kept in the classified documents of Great Britain? White was not welcomed by London's foreign office. Prior to his departure, White had spoken with British ambassador Viscount Halifax in Washington about his wish to visit British India and to interview some of the imprisoned

Indian nationalists, including Mohandas K. Gandhi and Jawaharlal Nehru.[19] As historian Thomas Hachey observes, White's travels considerably "concerned the British Government, and the confidential precautions . . . were undertaken, some of them in conjunction with American authorities, to insure that White's travels and investigations would not embarrass or prove troublesome to either Ally."[20]

Indeed, as we look closely at the flight route of the *Gulliver* on Willkie's map, we see that the bomber never landed in, nor flew over, India, one of the original signatories of the United Nations, and it reached China not through India but by what Willkie calls "the back door" of Siberia.[21] The end result was that the spatial imagery of an aerial One World that the *Gulliver* drew was curiously warping. Shortly before Willkie's departure, a crisis brewed over the "Quit India" movement launched by Gandhi and his followers in the Indian National Congress. Immediately, the Congress leaders were "put in prison, location undisclosed," because India's declaration of independence was a distraction for Britain's war effort against the Japanese in the South-East Asian theater.[22] India was thus omitted from the *Gulliver*'s itinerary, a decision reflecting Roosevelt's policy to strengthen British-US ties during the war and not to intervene in Britain's internal affairs.[23]

I would suggest that White intended his global tour and book, in tandem, to be an attempt to complete Willkie's unfinished One World for "indivisible freedom." Despite censorship, news about the government of India's mass incarceration and repressive measures percolated into the US press, including the government's use of whipping as a form of punishment, which may well have recalled the treatment of African Americans under slavery. As *Time* magazine reported, over sixty thousand Indians were jailed and at least 958 flogged during the first three months of the "Quit India" crisis, ironically symbolizing the "bondage" that lay at the heart of the United Nations.[24] Like his predecessor, however, White was not allowed to proceed to the Indian subcontinent. The British foreign office reasoned that, given that "Willkie, of whose world tour White's journey is reminiscent," was denied access to India, it would not be advisable for White to receive the facilities to reach India.[25] After spending six weeks in Britain, White had to abandon his flight plan to the subcontinent. He left the British Isles for North Africa in March, determining to visit India later via the Pacific.[26] This determination, as I shall discuss below, led to a shift in White's geographic imaginings to go beyond the aerial and transcontinental Atlantic and to break new ground in the archipelagic Pacific.

ISLAND HOPPING IN THE PACIFIC

In December 1944, White resumed his air travel from San Francisco, bound for Hawai'i. This jaunt constituted what would become his reattempting to circumnavigate the globe. Although British authorities warned, "He cannot expect to see Congress leaders while interned," he hoped to reach the Indian subcontinent by an air route from the Pacific. Officials in Whitehall learned of White's plan to "arrive in India from Chungking [China] about January 15, visiting first [the] Burma front, then Assam, Calcutta, Delhi, Bombay, Karachi, and thence to Moscow" from the British Information Services at the consulate general in New York.[27] London's foreign office sent a telegram to the South East Asia Command stating that though White was "European in appearance" with his blue eyes and fair skin, as an African American he "is a fervent apostle of the coloured races and is in fact gathering material for a book on 'Global War in Terms of Race Relations.' "[28]

The archives reveal that White's attempt was once again stonewalled. On January 17, 1945, two days after his intended date of arrival in India, White notified Lord Wavell, viceroy of India, in New Delhi, that he was delayed until February and would advise them of the exact date of his arrival from Australia.[29] On January 25, he requested travel orders from General Douglas MacArthur to fly from "Sydney to the China–Burma–India Theatre by whatever air route is available."[30] However, orders from MacArthur were never issued.

With the subcontinent of India closed, White ended up making a 36,000-mile flight over water studded with islands and atolls in the Pacific theater of World War II. He had been granted authority from the commander in chief of the US Pacific Fleet and Pacific Ocean Areas to travel from Pearl Harbor to Kwajalein, Saipan, Tinian, Guam, Anguar, Leyte, New Guinea, Bougainville, and Australia, with the Naval Air Transport Service (NATS) as an accredited representative of the *New York Post*.[31] United States forces adopted an island-hopping strategy by invading the Japanese-held Pacific Islands and building military bases to move all the way to the Japanese archipelago. This conduct of the war was shaped by the "mobility of imagination" that Harrison's post-Mercator mapping of the Pacific enabled.[32] During White's four months in the Pacific, these islands, networked by aircraft, served as bases to bring Tokyo and other Japanese cities under a massive load of incendiary bombs, which climaxed in the destruction of Hiroshima and Nagasaki by atomic bombs in August 1945. Atomic bombs were carried by Boeing B-29 Superfortress bombers from an airfield on the captured island of Tinian six and a half months after White's visit; these were to force Japan to surrender in response to what President Harry S. Truman called "a rain of ruin from the air."[33]

Unlike the transatlantic flight that inspired *A Rising Wind*, White's island hopping in the Pacific theater of World War II resulted in several fragmented pieces. Some remained unpublished because of military censorship, and White's autobiography, *A Man Called White* (1948), recalls how a story that he wrote for the *New York Post* about the black soldiers on Guam was suppressed. Jim Crow island-hopped with the US military, and White found instances of friction between white and black troops on Guam—fighting side by side against the Japanese—devolving into a "race riot" with casualties and death. White, a recipient of honorary doctorate degrees of law from Howard University and Atlanta University, played the role of defense counsel, representing forty-four black sailors charged with rioting. The naval board's decision was made after he left the island, with all of the men being sentenced to prison terms.[34] The US military's press policy also prohibited the material related to Japanese prisoners of war and Indigenous inhabitants of the islands captured by US forces. These prohibitions included "no photographs of identifiable Japanese military prisoners or disrobed prisoners," "no interviews with or quotations from prisoners," "no indication of interrogation of prisoners or use of material which could have been obtained only by interrogation," "no breakdown of prisoners taken (as Japanese, Koreans, Chamorros)," and "no indication of an expected favorable reaction to our occupation by inhabitants, prior to securing the objective."[35]

White's jaunt via NATS, circumscribing this proscribed subject matter, produced island-based writing that redraws the black Pacific. White's Pacific Island pieces, with their shift in focus away from the continentally oriented Pacific Rim, make legible the small islands within, each of which emerged differently as a theater of World War II. Asian countries on the Rim, Japan and the Philippines, do figure, but they emerge in their geographical form; that is, in their islandness. In this respect, White's black Pacific departs significantly from what Hsuan L. Hsu has termed the literary emergence of "the spatial dynamics of the 'American Pacific'" in Asian American and Pacific Islander literature, where Pacific Islands, Guam in particular, are produced as space vis-à-vis continental Asia and the continental United States, and are presented in a conflated or conflicted manner.[36] Isolated news articles that the island-hopping White wrote—those on Jim Crowed black GIs, Japanese prisoners of war, and Indigenous islanders that US forces "liberated" from the Japanese—were never incorporated into the totality of a volume (unlike his transcontinental Atlantic travel that resulted in *A Rising Wind*). Instead, they were given unequal treatment and scattered, with some remaining unpublished, thereby describing the "Global War in Terms of Race Relations" archipelagically.

Consider, for instance, "Navy Lt. George Ray Tweed, 'Hero' of the Japanese Occupation" (unpublished, circa October 1946) and "Jim Crow Goes to Japan" (January 9, 1946), both written for White's regular column in the black weekly *Chicago Defender*, not for the mainstream *New York Post*. In the former, White critically rewrites the then popular story of the Robinson Crusoe of Guam, George Ray Tweed. Tweed was a naval staff radioman who hid in the jungle for thirty-one months, refusing to surrender to the Japanese. Rescued by US forces that recaptured Guam, Tweed flew back to the United States in July 1944 with war correspondent Robert Sherrod to become a war hero. Tweed's "Robinson Crusoe life" was featured in *Life* magazine,[37] and the navy's documentary propaganda film, *Return to Guam* (1944), presented Tweed as "a Robinson Crusoe who stood up alone against the whole Japanese Empire." The film showed Tweed reporting how the Japanese occupation forces subjected the Chamorros, who were "happy" under the prewar US Naval government, to "slavery, misery, and death"—a report overlaid with images of victims, some of whom were decapitated. The film's closing scenes captured the US construction work of building airstrips, and its rolling credits included a memo from the US secretary of the Navy, James Forrestal, regarding the need for sufficient "apparatus and supply and shipping" to rebuild Guam into a forward deployment base against the enemy.[38]

Tweed's own account of the story, *Robinson Crusoe, USN* (1945), described how, for Guam Chamorros, the American Robinson Crusoe evolved into a symbol of hope that Uncle Sam would return. The book told how loyal Chamorro families helped Tweed to survive, and how the US Navy's rescue turned him from "a wild animal," hunted by the Japanese, into a "human again." Tweed also related the atrocities of the Japanese against the Chamorros in graphic detail, including descriptions of amputations and torture. According to Tweed's account, one victim was Father Jesus Baza Duenas, a Catholic priest of Chamorro ancestry who was "tortured . . . until he finally broke down" and revealed Tweed's hideout, betraying the secret of the confessional. The Japanese, infuriated that Duenas failed to "report . . . his knowledge earlier," killed him.[39]

The draft of White's *Defender* article, "Navy Lt. George Ray Tweed, 'Hero' of the Japanese Occupation," presents a Guamanian version of the Robinson Crusoe story. It describes Father Oscar Lujan Calvo, the only other Chamorro Catholic priest on the island, as a visible speaking subject to fracture the stateside narrative of freedom and bondage. White writes, "Father Calvo told me the story. His copperish brown face alternately smiling and tragically calm, he told me of how the Japanese had beheaded Father Duenas . . . because Father Duenas had refused to divulge Tweed's hiding place," thereby resisting, not succumbing to, Japanese colonial authority. Having invited White to the naval hospital, "the only building left standing by the sixteen inch guns and the bombs from U.S. Navy ships" that utterly devastated the island when they returned, Calvo told him of the Pacific Island battle in which Guam Chamorros had been caught. It was an aerial war in which the airplane and radio airwaves decided the game. On Japanese-occupied Guam, "men, women and children were dragooned" to work in the tropical heat and to construct airstrips for the Japanese with the recompense of meager food—rice and salt fish or dried fish—and the radioman was hunted because the Japanese "believed him to be sending short-wave information to the American forces about Japanese installations." It was indeed a "titanic task" on the part of the Chamorros to keep Tweed alive, as it endangered and sacrificed their own lives dearly.[40]

The racial lens of White's Pacific Island piece then zeroes in on this US Navy radioman–Chamorro relation, a bond of American loyalty. As White tells via Calvo, Tweed, "a white American," increasingly took for granted the service status of the Chamorros and demanded food, batteries, and "still other conveniences which cannot be mentioned in a family newspaper." Showing how Tweed's survival depended on Chamorro support and sacrifice, White wonders why the Chamorros did not rid themselves of the radioman by betraying his whereabouts, claiming that it "was inexplicable both to Father Calvo" and himself. He suggests that besides their "resistance" to the wartime Japanese colonial governance, there was a fight that "dark-skinned Guamanians" had "against the prejudices of some of the American marines, sailors and soldiers on Guam to retain their faith in America," but Tweed was "one American they could never forgive." Calvo averred that Tweed "would be shown what Guamanians thought of [him] if he ever dared return to that Pacific island."[41]

White's draft article closes with the return of Tweed to postwar Guam. In September 1946, Tweed, having been promoted in rank in the US Navy, revisited the Pacific island for the public presentation of a Chevrolet sedan, a gift from General Motors, to his most loyal friend on the island, Antonio Artero.[42] As White narrates, a group of Guamanians led by Calvo picketed "Navy Lt. George Ray Tweed, self-styled hero in his book, 'Robinson Cruso [sic], U.S.N.,'" thereby bringing it home to Tweed that "whatever he might be in the United States, he was no hero in Guam."[43] The *New York Times* (September 17, 1946) reported the news of this picket as a demonstration of Guamanians "expressing resentment over a statement" in Tweed's book that Father Duenas "had revealed his hiding place by disclosing the confessional secret of one of his benefactors."[44] White's *Defender* readers, however, might have interpreted their protest differently. As White clearly states, Guamanians picketed against the "return" of Tweed—a figure symbolic of the United States in general and of the US Navy in particular, whose survival and rule on their island depended on their loyalties to the United States, which meant their subordination, not their citizenship. Tweed gratefully brought a gift from the United States, but Calvo and other Guam Chamorros, White's black readers might have reasoned, would not receive any gifts since they did not accept their second-class status on their own island to support the naval colonial government. Against the backdrop of postwar US militarization of the island, this Chamorro gesture of protest speaks volumes. With the return of the US Naval government, their home island, devastated by a war that was not of their own making, was appropriated and reconstructed into a Pacific base.[45] By August 1945, the US plan of strategy for self-defense had run through Hawai'i,

Guam, the former Japanese-mandated islands in the three major archipelagoes of Micronesia—the Marshalls, the Carolines, and the Marianas—and the Philippines.[46] In the United States' postwar air-age geography, Guam was no longer an isolated, insular outpost "surrounded by hostile Japanese islands" but constituted part of the new Pacific network of US island-based air routes and bases.[47]

Perhaps the most revealing instance of White's archipelagic Pacific is "Jim Crow Goes to Japan," a *Defender* article that tells the story of the wartime Japanese-occupied islands and the postwar Japanese home islands—a chain that US forces hopped over to drive the enemy back. The article begins with a reference to Robert Sherrod, a war correspondent who flew back from the Pacific theater to the United States with George Tweed. White draws attention to Sherrod's battle reports on "the strange obsession with suicide of the Japanese" on the island of Saipan that the US forces invaded in June 1944, shortly prior to Guam. White cites a passage from Sherrod's dispatches in which he wrote about a Japanese "orgy of self-destruction" on the then Japanese-mandated Pacific island. When the invading US forces captured Saipan, Japanese "soldiers killed themselves with hand grenades," and civilian men and women threw themselves off cliffs at Marpi Point "after throwing their young children into the water" and "drowned themselves"—as if to reinforce the image of fanatic enemies who would never allow themselves to be taken prisoner. In Sherrod's view, it was entirely "incomprehensible to Americans."[48]

White, however, argues that "it isn't incomprehensible to those of us who have talked with Japanese prisoners of war, military and civilians" in US-operated Pacific Island camps. "Like virtually every other white writer about the war in the Pacific," writes White, "Mr. Sherrod, wise and sensitive though he is, misses almost totally one of the chief causes" for the Japanese act. He releases the stories of Japanese prisoners of war—a proscribed topic during the war—from their enforced silence and reveals that he was "permitted to talk in a P.O.W. camp on an island which at the time was not far from the front" with "a not unintelligent Japanese soldier" shortly after his capture.[49] An interpreter, most likely one of six thousand second-generation Japanese Americans (Nisei) who served in the Military Intelligence Service, accompanied White.[50] The appearance of White, who had blond hair and blue eyes and was wearing a US Army uniform, filled the prisoner with "stark terror." The prisoner's first comment was a question: why do you torture me, why don't you "kill me and get it over with"? White explained that American soldiers honored the Geneva Convention and that they would not kill him unless he attempted to escape. The prisoner was not convinced and argued that "they kill and lynch all colored people . . . and my skin is dark. We understand that all Japanese men who are captured will be cruelly put to death and all Japanese women raped by the Americans until they are dead!"[51]

Wartime anti-American propaganda in Japan converged with the materiality of US race prejudice to elicit suicide by Japanese soldiers and civilians who were captured or in danger of being captured. White, who was in direct contact with the dark-skinned enemy on a human and personal level, albeit restricted, as this took place behind barbed wire, then told the prisoner that he "was a Negro and that although [he] was in the Pacific as a war correspondent, [his] main job for more than twenty-five years had been [as] a worker in an American organization for defense of Negroes' rights"—namely, the NAACP. The Japanese POW was incredulous at the notion that he was an African American, not white as he appeared, but "he appeared to believe only partially the statement that any American, particularly any white American, ever did anything but hate and oppress Negroes and all other dark-skinned people." "Is there any wonder," White then asks his *Defender* readers, "that many Japanese chose death for themselves and [their] families?"[52]

If, like White, Richard Wright had been allowed to go to war as a correspondent, he might have interpreted Sherrod's battle reports about the Japanese jumping off cliffs in yet another way. In 1941, Wright had applied to the State Department for a passport to travel to China and the Soviet Union as a war reporter for the Associated Negro Press, but his application had been denied.[53] As Brian Russell Roberts argues, Wright, in *12 Million Black Voices* (published in the same year) "conceiv[ed] of African American subjectivity via the psychogeographical figure of the island."[54] Wright remarks, "The word 'Negro' . . . is not really a name at all nor a description, but a psychological island whose objective form is the most unanimous fiat in all American history." Surrounded by "the sea of white faces," this island is delimited by "steep cliffs" and "its rocky boundaries have remained unyielding to the waves of our hope that dash against it." Though we are islands, in the concluding section he goes on to say, "We are moving in all directions," and some are envisioning a larger island chain to go beyond insularity. He writes that there are some of "us who feel the need of the protection of a strong nation so keenly that we admire the harsh and imperialistic policies of Japan and ardently hope that the Japanese will assume the leadership of the 'darker races.'"[55] Had Wright been presented with White's image of the Japanese jumping off cliffs at Marpi Point on Japan's Pacific island, no longer strong but invaded by "white faces" with battle helmets, this image might have resonated with, and ineluctably redrawn, Wright's account of the psychological geography of twelve million African Americans.

The closing scene of White's "Jim Crow Goes to Japan" is a depiction of postwar Japan under US occupation, in which the emperor's surrender technically made all Japanese people prisoners. White had received a letter from a black GI of the US occupation forces stationed at the Japanese home islands. Just like the letter from the African American Red Cross worker in wartime Britain, it suggested that the US military and Jim Crow continued their work hand in hand around the globe. White writes, "If the reports coming from Japan since V-J Day are accurate, the Japanese must surely be all the more convinced that the fears of the prisoner of war I talked with are well-founded." The US occupation of Japan began with a policy of racial segregation in force, and white GIs instructed Japanese proprietors of restaurants and recreational and entertainment facilities "to admit no Negro soldiers." The Japanese, continues White, "are becoming more and more bewildered and apprehensive at the kicking about of American soldiers solely because of their skin color by other American soldiers who happen to be white."[56]

The end result of the air-age global war was not the world as one in which freedom was indivisible. Instead White's Pacific Island pieces reveal that the island-hopping United States transformed existing structures of freedom and bondage in a way that became a system of racialized social control. In US-occupied Japan, the color line between GIs and the Japanese was drawn in public transportation, restaurants, cafes, bars, hotels, and office buildings. Paradoxically, in the private realm of sexual conduct, though, the barrier (despite the enforced nonfraternization policy) proved porous, resulting in numerous "occupation babies," some of them "brown babies" born to black GIs and Japanese women, and thus setting processes of racial hybridization in motion.[57] During his Pacific jaunt, White continually observed, "The skin color of the natives [in the Pacific Islands] range[s] all the way from light brown to almost ebon hue." It was an indicator of century-old processes of migrations and diaspora racial formations across the ocean—processes that air-age globalism certainly accelerated in a manner that was entirely unpredictable.[58]

INSULAR IMAGINATION OF THE ATOMIC AGE

Four years later, in 1949, Walter White was among airborne globe-trotters participating in a round-the-world tour of *America's Town Meeting of the Air* (ATMA), a radio program of the American Broadcasting Company. The postwar United States was, to borrow from Charles Hurd, "no longer a country separated by broad oceans from Europe and Asia," and its "former vacuum of insulating space [had] been filled, literally, by air and airplanes."[59] The round-the-world program via Pan American World Airways (Pan Am) was a showcase in which the airwaves and the airplane were presented as the foundations of the postwar One World. The party flew across the Atlantic from New York for a transcontinental jaunt visiting world capitals—London, Paris, Berlin, Vienna, Rome, Ankara, Tel Aviv, Cairo, Karachi, and New Delhi—and then island-hopped in the Pacific from Manila to Tokyo to Honolulu, and returned to the United States. The Soviet

Union and China were conspicuously missing from the itinerary, indicating that the Iron and Bamboo Curtains were descending in Europe and Asia and closing off the airspace.

White participated in a Town Meeting broadcast from Karachi, Pakistan—a dominion born out of the partition of British India. White argued that the world had to go beyond Rudyard Kipling's credo that "East is East and West is West, and never the twain shall meet" because in the atomic age ushered in by Hiroshima and Nagasaki, the choices to be made were no longer East or West but One World or none. The splitting of an "atom," which literally means the division of the indivisible, had "dwarfed the world to pigmy size." If cracked, the world and freedom—indivisible like atoms—would be reduced to dust or to slavery; and, White said, "the split atom will never be joined together again." White told his audience in Pakistan and the United States, "Either we must achieve one world, or there will be no world for any of us."[60]

Having passed the halfway mark of the round-the-world tour in New Delhi, White met with Jawaharlal Nehru at long last. Nehru, an ex-prisoner of the British turned India's first prime minister, was bearing the burden of India's newly gained freedom, which included partition, the Indo-Pakistani War, and refugees, making the region volatile. White confronted the possibility that the chain of the One World could break, once again, in the subcontinent of India. In a dispatch that he sent to the *New York Herald Tribune* from Calcutta, he writes, "If Pandit Nehru and his government fall, India is lost [and] it is certain that the rest of Asia will drop like an overripe plum to the Communists."[61]

Departing the Indian subcontinent, White's subsequent flights consisted of a series of island-hopping tours in the Pacific. What became increasingly clear to White as he visited, or in some cases revisited, the Pacific Islands—the Philippines, British Hong Kong, Okinawa, US-occupied Japan, and Hawaiʻi—was that this island chain ultimately joined with San Francisco on the West Coast of the United States and constituted a new dividing line between East and West. The Soviet Union's power was expanding in Asia, marking its perimeter through a continentally grounded expansion. If "the collapse of China" sparked a chain reaction in "the rest of Asia," White predicted, "the Soviet Union would control all this section of the world up to and probably including the Philippines and possibly even Hawaii—a short bomber flight from our West Coast." From Calcutta, he also reported, "in Hong Kong . . . the British have moved hurriedly 70,000 troops into that outpost to make a last-ditch stand" against the Chinese Communist troops approaching from the continent.[62]

It was, finally, during the tour's stay in Tokyo on August 29, 1949, that the Soviet Union exploded its first atomic bomb in Kazakhstan, Central Asia. A political cartoon by Herblock (Herbert Block) in the *Washington Post* of September 24,

Figure 4.3. A Herblock cartoon, 1949. © The Herb Block Foundation.

published immediately after the release of the news from the White House, registered the American nation's shock. In the cartoon, Mr. Atom, an atomic bomb holding a crude sunshade (nuclear) umbrella with an American flag, is staring at a footprint, obviously not his, on a deserted island—a moment of discovering the end of America's atomic monopoly (figure 4.3). Reminiscent of the famous scene in Daniel Defoe's *Robinson Crusoe*, this image symbolized the extent to which the island became central to the post–World War II United States' sense of world power, and how the figure of an island functioned discursively and materially as an icon in the Cold War United States. It also reflected what US militarization of the Pacific Islands meant. In the post–World War II period, isolated islands and atolls became sites for a series of US nuclear tests, and the first atomic bomb dropped from a B-29 in a time of peace exploded on Bikini Atoll in the Marshall Islands in July 1946. The islands chosen for tests were "uninhabited" because the indigenous Pacific Islanders were forcibly removed.[63] On the island of Guam, where the US Robinson Crusoe hid and returned, the Fena area became a nuclear warheads storage site.[64] Former Japanese World War II caves—or dugouts made by the forced labor of Guamanians—were used as US fallout shelters, marked by the yellow-and-black trefoil sign. They are now a tourist attraction in Latte Stone Park (Senator Angel Leon Guerrero Santos Latte Memorial Park).

White traveled through an evolving geographic and political spatial context, in which the US projection of power increasingly routed through the archipelagic as opposed to the continental, chaining Western Europe (divided from the Eastern Bloc by the Iron Curtain) to insular nations in the Pacific (divided from continental Asia by the Bamboo Curtain) and thus linking the aerial and transcontinental Atlantic to the island-hopping Pacific. White flew in the global networks of ATC, NATS, and Pan Am, the symbol of the United States' domination in the air, and thereby approximated hegemonic ideologies implicit in air-age geography. However, as I have discussed in this essay, his globe-trotting jaunts were a series of attempts to route through the dark-skinned peoples, who were insulated from one another and confined as earthbound prisoners, to chart the planetary geography in which the world and freedom are indivisible. White's archipelagic black global imaginary did not just reshape the language of freedom and bondage in Mercator's maritime world, which was plied by slave ships and represented by separable hemispheres and continents. Launching from Mercator's flat world into a three-dimensional air-age spatial context, it significantly brings the mobility of imagination to bear in scholarship on black transnationalism and planetary migrations.

NOTES

1. Bill Ashcroft and Pal Ahluwalia, *Edward Said*, 2nd ed. (London: Routledge, 2009), 92.
2. Paul Gilroy, *The Black Atlantic: Modernity and Double Consciousness* (Cambridge, MA: Harvard University Press, 1993), 4.
3. The best summary treatment of Harrison's innovative maps in the 1940s is found in Susan Schulten, "Richard Edes Harrison and the Challenge to American Cartography," *Imago Mundi* 50 (1998): 174–88.
4. Alan K. Henrikson, "The Map as an 'Idea': The Role of Cartographic Imagery during the Second World War," *American Cartographer* 2, no. 1 (April 1975): 19–20.
5. Richard Edes Harrison, *Look at the World: The FORTUNE Atlas for World Strategy* (New York: Alfred A. Knopf, 1944), 42–43.
6. Harrison, *Look at the World*, 44–45; Schulten, "Richard Edes Harrison," 180.
7. Walter White, memo (a list of visited places and distance in miles), box 24, folder 222, Walter Francis White and Poppy Cannon White Papers, Yale Collection of American Literature, Beinecke Rare Book and Manuscript Library, Yale University, New Haven, CT (hereafter cited as White Papers).
8. See, for instance, George Lipsitz, "'Frantic to Join . . . the Japanese Army': Black Soldiers and Civilians Confront the Asia-Pacific War," in *Perilous Memories: The Asia-Pacific War(s)*, ed. T. Fujitani, Geoffrey M. White, and Lisa Yoneyama (Durham, NC: Duke University Press, 2001), 347–77; Andrew F. Jones and Nikhil Pal Singh,

eds., *The Afro-Asian Century*, special issue, *positions* 11, no. 1 (Spring 2003); Gerald Horne, *Race War: White Supremacy and the Japanese Attack on the British Empire* (New York: New York University Press, 2004); Bill V. Mullen, *Afro-Orientalism* (Minneapolis: University of Minnesota Press, 2004); and Etsuko Taketani, *The Black Pacific Narrative: Geographic Imaginings of Race and Empire between the World Wars* (Hanover, NH: Dartmouth College Press, 2014).

9. Walter White, diary, January 2, 1944, New York, box 24, folder 228, White Papers.

10. Walter White, *A Rising Wind* (Garden City, NY: Doubleday, Doran, 1945), 13. Further references will be cited parenthetically in the text as *RW*.

11. On African American soldiers in the British Isles, see Graham Smith, *When Jim Crow Met John Bull: Black American Soldiers in World War II Britain* (London: I. B. Tauris, 1987).

12. For an account of how the US government detained German POWs, see Arnold Krammer, *Nazi Prisoners of War in America* (1979; repr., Lanham, MD: Scarborough House, 1996).

13. Viscount Halifax (Washington) to Foreign Office, telegram, November 20, 1943; R. J. Cruikshank (Ministry of Information) to Nevile Butler (Foreign Office), January 18, 1944, FO 371/38609, National Archives, Kew.

14. Steve Neal, *Dark Horse: A Biography of Wendell Willkie* (Lawrence: University Press of Kansas, 1989), 233.

15. Wendell L. Willkie, *One World* (New York: Simon and Schuster, 1943), 188.

16. Henry A. Wallace, *Soviet Asia Mission* (New York: Reynal and Hitchcock, 1946), 26n.

17. Eleanor Roosevelt, *This I Remember* (New York: Harper and Brothers, 1949), 295–310.

18. "Mrs. Roosevelt Assails Bigots in Peace Camp: Opening Broadcast Series, She Asserts Isolationist Plan Would Destroy U.S.," *New York Herald Tribune*, September 29, 1941, 13.

19. Halifax to Foreign Office, November 20, 1943, FO 371/38609.

20. Thomas Hachey, "Walter White and the American Negro Soldier in World War II: A Diplomatic Dilemma for Britain," *Phylon* 39, no. 3 (1978): 242.

21. Willkie, *One World*, 111.

22. Manu Bhagavan, *India and the Quest for One World: The Peacemakers* (Basingstoke, UK: Palgrave Macmillan, 2013), 13.

23. On the *Gulliver*'s flight route change, see M. S. Venkataramani and B. K. Shrivastava, *Quit India: The American Response to the 1942 Struggle* (New Delhi: Vikas, 1979), 317–18.

24. "Foreign News: India," *Time*, March 8, 1943, 30.

25. Foreign Office to Viscount Halifax, telegram, November 27, 1943, FO 371/38609.

26. R. J. Cruikshank to Nevile Butler, February 10, 1944; R. J. Cruikshank to Angus Malcolm (Foreign Office), February 11, 1944, FO 371/38609.

27. Secretary of State for India to Government of India, telegram, December 13, 1944, FO371/38609.

28. Foreign Office to Supreme Allied Command, South East Asia, January 1, 1945, FO 371/38609.

29. Walter White to Lord Wavell, telegram, January 17, 1945, box 24, folder 224, White Papers.

30. Walter White to G. H. Q. P. R. O. (attn.: Major J. T. Balch), January 25, 1945, box 24, folder 224, White Papers.

31. Commander in Chief, US Pacific Fleet and Pacific Ocean Areas, to Walter White, travel authority, December 22, 1944, box 24, folder 222, White Papers.

32. Richard E. Harrison and Hans W. Weigert, "World View and Strategy," in *Compass of the World: A Symposium on Political Geography*, ed. Hans W. Weigert and Vilhjalmur Stefansson (New York: Macmillan, 1944), 77.

33. "Statement by the President Announcing the Use of the A-Bomb at Hiroshima, August 6, 1945," in *Public Papers of the Presidents of the United States: Harry S. Truman, Containing the Public Messages, Speeches, and Statements of the President, April 12 to December 31, 1945* (Washington, DC: Government Printing Office, 1961), 199.

34. Walter White, *A Man Called White: The Autobiography of Walter White* (1948; repr., Athens: University of Georgia Press, 1995), 277–86.

35. "Press Policy for Forthcoming Operations," August 30, 1944, box 24, folder 222, White Papers.

36. Hsuan L. Hsu, "Guåhan (Guam), Literary Emergence, and the American Pacific in *Homebase* and *from unincorporated territory*," *American Literary History* 24, no. 2 (Summer 2012): 282.

37. Robert Sherrod, "Two Years Alone on Jap-Held Guam: Hunted by the Enemy, George Tweed Lived in Caves until Navy Returned," *Life*, August 21, 1944, 41.

38. United States Navy, *Return to Guam*, film, produced by the Industrial Incentive Division of the Navy Department, 1944.

39. George R. Tweed, *Robinson Crusoe, USN* (1945; repr., Yardley, PA: Westholme, 2010), 244, 247, 259. For an analysis of the conflictual memories of the death of Father Duenas, see Keith L. Camacho, *Cultures of Commemoration: The Politics of War, Memory, and History in the Mariana Islands* (Honolulu: University of Hawai'i Press, 2011), 161–77.

40. Walter White, ["Navy Lt. George Ray Tweed, 'Hero' of the Japanese Occupation"], 1–2, group II, box A74, folder 2, Records of the National Association for the Advancement of Colored People, Manuscript Division, Library of Congress, Washington, DC (hereafter cited as NAACP Records).

41. White, "Navy Lt. George Ray Tweed," 1, 3.

42. Robert F. Rogers, *Destiny's Landfall: A History of Guam* (Honolulu: University of Hawai'i Press, 1995), 179.

43. White, "Navy Lt. George Ray Tweed," 3.

44. "Guam Hero Is Picketed for Accusing Priest of Telling Japanese Where He Hid for Years," *New York Times*, September 17, 1946, 9.

45. Roy E. James, "Military Government: Guam," *Far Eastern Survey* 15, no. 18 (Sept. 11, 1946): 273–77.

46. Earl S. Pomeroy, *Pacific Outpost: American Strategy in Guam and Micronesia* (1951; repr., New York: Russell and Russell, 1970), 174.

47. Rogers, *Destiny's Landfall*, 207.

48. Walter White, "People, Politics and Places: Jim Crow Goes to Japan," *Chicago Defender*, January 19, 1946, 16; see also the draft of the article, group II, box A74, folder 2, NAACP Records. White's sources are Robert Sherrod, "The Nature of the Enemy," *Time*, August 7, 1944, 27; and Robert Sherrod, *On to Westward: War in the Central Pacific* (New York: Duell, Sloan and Pearce, 1945), 144–50.

49. White, "People, Politics and Places," 16.

50. On Nisei interpreters, see James C. McNaughton, *Nisei Linguists: Japanese Americans in the Military Intelligence Service during World War II* (Washington, DC: Department of the Army, 2006).

51. White, "People, Politics and Places," 16. A study of Japanese civilian attitudes made on the island of Saipan using Nisei interpreters corroborates White's observation about Japanese POWs. The study reports that "the greatest deterrent to surrender appeared to be the belief that they would be tortured or killed"; Navy Department, Military Government Field Report No. 52, "Japanese Civilian Attitudes on Saipan," March 31, 1945, 2, Records of Office of War Information, RG 208, entry 378, box 444, National Archives and Records Administration, College Park, MD.

52. White, "People, Politics and Places," 16.

53. R. B. Shipley, Passport Division, to Richard Wright, June 24, 1941, box 107, folder 1645, Richard Wright Papers, Yale Collection of American Literature, Beinecke Rare Book and Manuscript Library, Yale University, New Haven, CT.

54. Brian Russell Roberts, "(Ex)Isles in the Harlem Renaissance: The Insular and Archipelagic Topographies of Wallace Thurman's *The Blacker the Berry*," *Arizona Quarterly* 67, no. 3 (Autumn 2011): 101.

55. Richard Wright, *12 Million Black Voices* (1941; repr., New York: Thunder's Mouth Press, 2002), 30–31, 143.

56. White, "People, Politics and Places," 16.

57. Yukiko Koshiro, "Race as International Identity? 'Miscegenation' in the U.S. Occupation of Japan and Beyond," *Amerikastudien / American Studies* 48, no. 1 (2003): 62–64.

58. Walter White, draft article for the *New York Post*, February 2, 1945, 1, box 24, folder 228, White Papers.

59. Charles Hurd, "World Airways," in Weigert and Stefansson, *Compass of the World*, 109.

60. *Town Meeting: Bulletin of America's Town Meeting of the Air* 15, no. 19 (September 6, 1949): 12, 19.

61. Walter White, "Empty Stomachs in India: Walter White Calls for U.S. Aid as Key to Saving Asia from Reds," *New York Herald Tribune*, September 18, 1949, section 2, 2.

62. White, "Empty Stomachs in India," section 2, 2.

63. For a useful discussion of the United States as an empire grounded in networks and islands, see Ruth Oldenziel, "Islands: The United States as a Networked Empire," in *Entangled Geographies: Empire and Technologies in the Global Cold War*, ed. Gabrielle Hecht (Cambridge, MA: MIT Press, 2011), 13–41.

64. Rogers, *Destiny's Landfall*, 215.

5 | IT TAKES AN
ARCHIPELAGO TO
COMPARE OTHERWISE

Susan Gillman

IN THE ANNALS OF THE INVENTION OF AMERICA, it is a little-known fact that the "Mediterranean of the West" was discovered by Jamaican nationalist W. Adolphe Roberts in New York City (to which he had emigrated in 1904) during the wartime decade of the 1940s. A journalist and novelist, Roberts coined the term in his pioneering study, *The Caribbean: Story of Our Sea of Destiny* (1940), a history of the Caribbean from Columbus to the present, with a chapter celebrating the revolutionary role of José Martí in "Cuba Libre." Roberts's book was written at roughly the same moment as another West Indian, C. L. R. James, then living abroad in England, produced his own, even more sweepingly revolutionary history of the Caribbean, *The Black Jacobins* (1938). Writing from the exile in which West Indians are said, invariably, to transcend their island identity, both the English-speaking white Jamaican and the black Trinidadian worked comparatively with a critical awareness of the other colonial languages and struggles of the Caribbean. But while James's transoceanic history of the Haitian Revolution (along with his writings on cricket and Melville, Marxism and world revolution) is well known, Roberts, a prolific writer for over sixty years in the United States and the Caribbean, and a prominent cultural figure in Jamaica after his permanent return in 1950, has been largely forgotten, "at best a marginal figure in the canonical postcolonial narrative of an independent Jamaica."[1]

To bring together these two artist-activists of the late twentieth-century Caribbean under the archipelagic auspices of the Mediterranean of the West is the aim of this essay. Through that oceanic lens, the Mediterranean opens out, seeming analogous to or roughly congruous with other archipelagic spaces worldwide, providing a multinodal map to the comparative histories of other nationalist figures in other anticolonial conflicts: not only Roberts and James but also the "fathers" of Cuban and Filipino independence, José Martí and José Rizal, rough counterparts working across space and time in the late nineteenth-century

Caribbean-Pacific outposts of the waning Spanish empire. To bring all four of them together is the archipelagic challenge of this essay.

During the long wartime decade of the late 1930s–'40s, when James could hear the booming of Franco's artillery and Stalin's firing squads, as he put it in the preface to the first edition of *Black Jacobins*, Roberts researched and wrote his history of the Caribbean *from* the Caribbean, in Peter Hulme's words, "the first historical expression of a pan-Caribbean historical consciousness."[2] Roberts remembers this moment in his 1962 autobiography in a chapter titled "1939," when "it came to me that I must write the history of the entire Caribbean, from the discovery by Christopher Columbus up to the present day."[3] It wasn't until 1963 that James himself traced a similar trajectory in the famous appendix to *Black Jacobins*, "From Toussaint L'Ouverture to Fidel Castro," where he brought the 1938 edition, and its prologue that opens with Columbus landing in the New World, up to his own present.[4] Meanwhile, back in the 1940s, Roberts followed the Caribbean book with a trilogy of novels that he called his New Orleans historical series: *Royal Street* (1944), *Brave Mardi Gras* (1946), and *Creole Dusk* (1948). Set in the 1840s, '60s, and '80s, respectively, the novels might also be called "mediterranean" in their oceanic account of a nineteenth-century creole family in New Orleans, using the city at the center of Roberts's "Mediterranean of the West" as a gateway to overlapping spaces and times of circulation of people and goods—across the Atlantic Ocean to Europe and Africa, and across the Gulf of Mexico to Havana, Port-au-Prince, and Panama. Finally, in 1949 Roberts brought his trilogy back home with *The Single Star*, a novel set in Jamaica and Cuba in the late 1890s during the Cuban war of independence, framed with an epigraph by José Martí: "The day will come when we shall place, on the strongest fort of our country, the flag of the single star." Roberts fuses Martí's Cuba as a revolutionary model with the future independence of Jamaica, much as, we will see, James does with the Haitian Revolution as a model for Castro's Cuba, itself in turn predicting the decolonization of the whole West Indies. Taken together, these space-times, both the setting and writing of both Roberts's and James's books, locate the comparative—transnational and translingual—histories I want to trace, ultimately linking the Caribbean and the Pacific as outposts of the Spanish Empire at its end and the so-called American Century at its beginning.[5]

Ground zero of *The Caribbean*, at the center of Roberts's introduction, titled "Mediterranean of the West," is a Mediterranean comparison. The map of the Caribbean, read not geographically and topographically but skewed impressionistically, produces "an imaginative parallel with the Mediterranean," which depends on "a distortion of the Americas": "America north of the Isthmus of Panama becomes an aggregate of Europe and the islands of the Mediterranean"; "Asia has vanished in the Atlantic ... precisely where the lost continent of Atlantis is thought to have been"; "tilt the map slightly upside down," and "the Lesser Antilles begin at Trinidad, which is Cypress . . . Puerto Rico is Crete, and Hispaniola a Greece torn from the mainland. . . . The multitudinous Cuban cays and the Isle of Pines are Sardinia and Corsica smashed to fragments." The net result of this extended, and violent, inverted parallel: "A more vivid fancy" plus "a little poetical license," and "the two seas, about of a size, and similarly placed between the continents of eastern and western hemispheres," "can be rated as counterparts, while the imperial implications take on a startling resemblance" (18). Landlocked seas for Roberts are contact zones, "magnets" for nations striving to dominate as a single, imperial hegemon "those inland oceans" (13). The imperial resemblance—"South America, to the Conquistadores, was the Dark Continent"—is summed up as "the conflict for power" that is both "the destiny of the sea" and "our sea of destiny" (19, 13).

For Roberts, the archipelagic logic produces a disjunctive parallel. "To match one world against the other," the Mediterranean, transposed from east to west, becomes a sea of interisland, hemispheric, and continental relations. "Between the Americas . . . lies our own Caribbean. Held in the embrace of two continents, the Caribbean is the key to both" (13). However odd it is to think about American continents, in the plural, the phrase "held in the embrace of" is unmistakably discomforting, pointing to an eroticism both promising and threatening. With all of this baggage, the point of the comparison turns out to be its reversal, our Caribbean overturning the Mediterranean model. The map that illustrates this chapter makes the point visually and graphically (figure 5.1). A map with inset, conventionally used to show scale, either overview or close-up of a section, is in this case cartographically nonconforming: the main map is labeled "Caribbean Proper" with a small inset, a minimap labeled "Mediterranean Sea." The "hemisphere with the older civilization" may start as the model, but under the pressure of the imaginative parallel, the Caribbean becomes the main event to the miniaturized Mediterranean.

Roberts's Mediterraneanized Caribbean, produced by hypothetical distortion and poetic license, reflects several degrees of archipelagic thinking. First, the very notion of the archipelago took historical form specifically in the Mediterranean, in the etymological root of the term *archipelago*, deriving from the Greek and referring to the Aegean Sea. Second, beyond the Mediterranean as originary root, the "archipelago principle" is portable, tracing routes through other geopolitical locations across time and space. Both Mediterranean roots and archipelagic routes enhance the possibilities for comparative work, charted by Roberts and others, notably the Martinican theorist Édouard Glissant, in terms that are markedly relational and overtly self-reflexive. Roberts tests the outer limits of his portable Mediterranean template as an archipelagic logic of

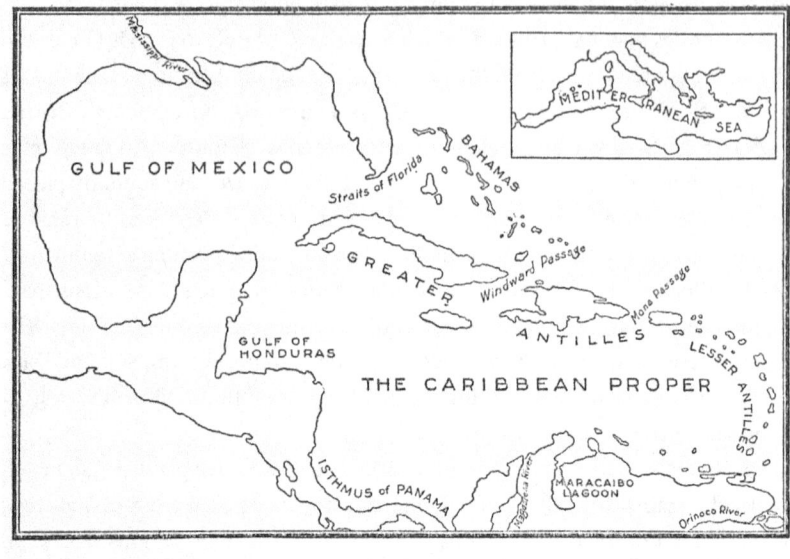

The Caribbean Area

Figure 5.1. "The Caribbean Area." From W. Adolphe Roberts, *The Caribbean* (Indianapolis: Bobbs-Merrill, 1940), 14.

the comparative, theorizing conjunctions and disjunctions between and among noncontiguous space-times, interisland, continental, hemispheric, and proposing speculative comparisons grounded in asymmetrical geohistories of imperial conflict. Glissant creates his "poetics of Relation" through an "Antillean imaginary" in which "each island is an opening," creating the conditions of possibility for an open-ended comparativism, attuned to the changing interrelations of space and time within physical and human geographies. If each island is an opening, then we can see, in defiance of timeless space, that the fate of all continents is to become archipelagoes. "*La pensée archipélique*," Glissant says in *Traité du Tout Monde* (Treatise of the Tout Monde) makes island space a traveling metaphor for openness: "Archipelagic thought, in its multiplicity, opens up these seas to us . . . ; the lands I inhabit become starbursts of archipelagoes." Third, as such, these definitions of the archipelagic speak to the limits of conventional comparative studies, the assumed disciplinary symmetries of two-country pairings or nation-language equations that so often underlie comparative history and literature. In the words of historian Harry Harootunian, the impulse to think through ever-larger singular, spatial units (the globe and empire dominate today, along with the planetary), which bring with them fixity, boundedness, and asynchrony, works against considerations of "the crucial spatiotemporal relationship" that must inform any comparative agenda. Harootunian's call for the reunion of time with space is nowhere better answered than by the logic of the archipelago as circuited through its Mediterranean roots and routes.[6]

Finally, my essay takes up the archipelagic challenge to bring together, unevenly (not divided into fourths or halves), four anticolonialists, exhibiting remarkable analogical relations paired with disjunctions that have stymied their previous comparison. They are case studies in resistant comparison, seemingly historically, politically, and culturally ready-made, but which have proved difficult to track: Martí and Rizal, the two great artist-activists writing in Spanish as founding fathers of the modern Cuban and Philippine nations during the twilight of the Spanish empire, and James and Roberts, writing as English-speaking West Indies nationalists a half-century later in the context of postwar decolonization. Despite "the near-simultaneity of the last nationalist insurrection in the New World (Cuba, 1895) and the first in Asia (the Philippines, 1896)," Martí and Rizal never met, nor is there direct evidence that they were aware of or influenced by one another; the gulf between Roberts and James is a function of both ideology and reputation, one forgotten, the other revered.[7]

In this case taking up the archipelagic challenge as a method of uneven comparativism requires thinking through a three-dimensional grid, so that comparisons are theorized through the idea of space-time, and language becomes a shuttle or conveyance for different space-times. Not least of the asymmetries among the four case studies is the relation of language to their colonial and national situation, English as the undisputed lingua franca of the British West Indies, and Spanish of Cuba, but not in the Philippines, where Tagalog (among other local languages) coexisted, first with Spanish and then with English. The "three great colonial languages of the Caribbean" all extend to the Pacific, where each language takes on different geopolitical functions in relation to its different imperial contexts.[8] As I will show, Spanish is both the "instrument of liberation" for Martí and a more ambiguous language of conspiracy for Rizal, French a Janus-faced language of revolution and counterrevolution for James and Roberts, and English, the omnipresent shadow, looming over all of these periods of colonial domination and resistance.[9] Taking the route of disjunctive comparison, I devote the greater part of the essay to the James/Roberts conjuncture and then move back in time, ending with a brief sketch of the nineteenth-century colonial language politics that join and separate Rizal/Martí.

JAMES/ROBERTS I

The long decade of the 1930s–'40s, Roberts's last in the United States before he returned to Jamaica in 1949, was for James a defining conjuncture he recognized in his 1938 preface to the first edition of *The Black Jacobins*. He locates his writing in the English suburb of Brighton, oceanically transposing the eighteenth-century history he tells of the Haitian Revolution, itself already transoceanic in multidirectional relation to the French Revolution, onto the then-coming decolonization of Africa; later in the appendix to the 1963 edition he would further extend this history of the present, asserting that "what took place in French San Domingo in 1792–1804 reappeared in Cuba in 1958. . . . Castro's revolution is of the twentieth century as much as Toussaint's was of the eighteenth. But despite the distance of over a century and a half, both are West Indian. . . . West Indians first became aware of themselves as a people in the Haitian Revolution."[10] James thus returns to his native land the series of oceanic transferences through which *The Black Jacobins*—in Robin Blackburn's apt formulation, "both the book and the historical force that it named"—always point elsewhere, an open-ended prophetic history. Each island is an opening, as Glissant says.[11]

It was amid the same fever and fret of the age, when Roberts—having left Jamaica and, as a US citizen with a public record as an outspoken advocate for self-government, was not permitted to return—produced his New Orleans trilogy. Roberts worked in 1940s New York for Jamaican nationalism, founding the Jamaica Progressive League, becoming a close friend of Norman Manley, Jamaica's first premier (credited as the architect of Jamaican independence in 1962), and reaching out to an international black community of New York Jamaicans. The debates over Jamaican nationalism—independent self-government or a larger transregional collectivity—are refracted in Roberts's New Orleans historical trilogy, in which he works through the ambiguities of his own position as a white Jamaican nationalist in New York whose poetry appeared in an anthology of Negro writing, a journalist-novelist-historian of the "Mediterranean of the West" in the context of US race relations and global decolonization.

The account of a Creole family fleeing the Haitian revolution—like so many of the Caribbean master class, going from Saint-Domingue to Cuba and the United States—Roberts's novels follow the triumphs and tragedies (mostly the latter) across three generations of Creole protagonists, artist-intellectuals like Roberts, embroiled in nationalist schemes with transnational, multilingual, and crossracial underpinnings. In turn, if we take a little of Roberts's license and extend the trilogy (1944–48) with two bookends, *The Caribbean* (1940) and *The Single Star: A Novel of Cuba in the '90s* (1949), then from this wide-angle view, Jamaica, the focus of Roberts's political work, is part of a larger region with a shared geography and history, not a part of England or a European appendage but rather Caribbean—and the Caribbean was American, in the broadest sense of the word.

Both James and Roberts thus archipelagically transpose the emerging independence struggles of the 1930s–'40s world, opening onto different times and places. But they ultimately take very different positions from within similar locations: the "small" island spaces of Jamaica and Trinidad, both English-speaking colonies of the British Empire, approached archipelagically, give way to other locations and vocations, the James/Roberts political writing and organizing from voluntary exile in England and the United States. The language question, specifically the relation of English to French, turns out to be an unexpected key to the anticolonial routes of this odd couple.

JAMES/ROBERTS II: JAMES'S FRENCH

Questions about James and language are generally approached via his relation to English, the colonial language of Shakespeare and Thackeray, that James, among "those few of us who got an education," was able to navigate. As part of that colonial education, he also learned French at Queens Royal College, and his knowledge of French, it turned out, provides a key to his work during his six-year stay in England, from 1932 to 1938. Crossing the channel for multiple research trips to examine the French archives of the Haitian Revolution, James later recalled that librarians were amazed that this black Trinidadian was fluent in French; in another of James's linguistic encounters, Anna Grimshaw reports how audiences he addressed in "imperial Britain" (where there were very few black people at the time, most concentrated in London) rarely knew where the West Indies were situated, and many people, believing him to be African, commented on his remarkable facility with the English language. But, as he usually responded, it would have been much more remarkable had he not been fluent in the language he had known since birth. "I have sometimes wished that I had a native language," he said in a 1971 speech on his seventieth birthday, "but I find English good enough to go on with for the time being."[12]

English proved less than good enough, though, when it came to James's "reading everything" he could on the Haitian Revolution. Aside from a few books by British writers during the 1850s (such as J. R. Beard's "little biography" of Toussaint in 1855), he was disappointed to find no books of "serious historical value" in colonial Trinidad. James remembered his reaction on reading one recent "very bad" biography of Toussaint, Percy Waxman's *The Black Napoleon*: "What the goddam hell is this? . . . I was tired of hearing that the West Indians were oppressed, that we were black and miserable, that we had been brought from Africa, and that we were living there and that we were being exploited."[13]

In the heavily annotated bibliography to *Black Jacobins*, James codified his critical assessments of the available scholarship in both English and French. He indicts the "brazenness of these imperialist historians" writing "the official French account" of Saint-Domingue, separating them from the main body of the "French historical school of the French Revolution . . . one of the greatest of Western civilisation"; the English sources James lambasts without exception. Both in England and the United States, the studies are categorically "of little value, for the writers, particularly in England, usually try to be what is known as 'fair to both sides.'" The historian who thus does not accept that in a revolution "excesses are normal" does not accept the revolution and, James concludes, "therefore cannot write its history" (385). The "Special Bibliography" thus provides the platform for a comprehensive revisionist survey of works on the Haitian Revolution, written from the eighteenth century up to the present, divided by subject matter and time (e.g., "The French Colonial Trade," "San Domingo before the Revolution"), runs the gamut from a Haitian historian, "an enthusiastic admirer of Toussaint but exceptionally fair," to Pamphile de Lacroix's 1819 *Mémoires pour servir à l'Histoire de la révolution de Saint-Domingue*, "biased in favour of the French" yet "indispensable" and "fully deserves its reputation" (*BJ*, 382, 381). From his blanket dismissal of the English-language studies of Haiti to his nuanced continuum of French writers, all working in the imperial language but in different genres and periods, with different biases and sympathies, to different ends, it is no wonder that James was misestimated at the time by reviewers critical of his failure to tap primary sources—and, later, underestimated by himself for his failure to seek slave sources. The bibliography, however, speaks for itself, setting straight the record on the histories of Haiti: thumbs down for those written originally in English, thumbs up for those in French.

The pragmatic question of available English translations thus underlies the whole historiographical manifesto, the multiple acts of translating, both marked and unmarked, that constitute *The Black Jacobins*.[14] The extended passages, for example, that James takes—translates—from Pamphile de Lacroix's *Mémoires* are only intermittently footnoted. His own shorthand "San Domingo," which he uses rather than the French Saint-Domingue and sometimes produces what sounds like a misnomer (French San Domingo), initiates another pattern of strategic mistranslation: the persistence of incomplete, inconsistent, or imperfect translations, such as "French San Domingo," that are only partially acknowledged *as* translations, or transparent translations, such as many quotations from the sources that are made silently. In another variation on the theme of half-spoken or transparent translation, we know that while Marx is evoked, his name is omitted in the celebrated case of "great men make history," the line in the preface to the 1963 edition noted by Scott and others.[15] However we might read the significance of these anomalies, what they all have in common is a will to open-ended and unfinished translation as yet another manifestation of the speculative history James is writing, in which the space-time of the Haitian Revolution prefigures and actually becomes African decolonization, while Haiti simultaneously becomes Cuba and all of the West Indies.

Paired with James's Haiti, Roberts's Mediterranean of the West makes the Caribbean into another of these island-openings, a trans-spatiotemporal and translingual series of open-ended revolutionary imperial locations. But Roberts maps a hypothetical southern empire for slavery, a "Creole republic," in the words of one of his protagonists ("a champion of the theory that Louisiana could attach herself to all the lands on the Gulf of Mexico and the Caribbean that France had once possessed"; *Brave Mardi Gras*, 17), "the Southern dream of a Caribbean empire," a lost past and unrealized future.[16] French-English is the major scene of conflict, with Spanish as colonial past and possible revolutionary future.

JAMES/ROBERTS III: ROBERTS'S FRENCH

The global anticolonial politics of the 1930s and 1940s, when Roberts did his research and writing in Jamaica and New Orleans, are refracted in the historical series that starts with *The Caribbean* and ends with *Single Star*, circuiting through "old New Orleans" in the aftermath of the Haitian Revolution, to Haiti and Santo Domingo (1844) during the Dominican struggle for independence, to Panama and the French canal project under De Lesseps (late 1880s), and finally full circle to Jamaica by way of Cuba and the war for independence from Spain (1898). In the place and time of both the setting and the writing of these texts, the competing liberation struggles—some nationalist and multiracial but not anticolonial, some anticolonial but not antiracist—are shadowed by the threat of US-Americanization, encoded in the changing street names of New Orleans. The first of the three New Orleans novels, *Royal Street* opens as "the anglicizing of street names was becoming common usage." The hero, Creole intellectual Victor Olivier, mocks English pronunciation ("The American tongue stumbles over our speech") but concludes, "There are more American tongues than French in New Orleans, and in this little matter they are likely to have their way. Already, outside the Vieux Carre, they post the names officially as *streets* not *rues*."[17] By the time of the second novel, set in the 1860s, the next-generation Creole representative of the Olivier clan regrets "yielding to the American influence again by accepting Royal Street as the right name," reminding himself and us that "since Louisiana was about to secede, national sentiment required a . . . return to the forms specified by Bienville when the city was founded."[18] The final, inevitable decline in Creole fortunes is registered in the third novel's silent capitulation to the English Royal Street, mirrored by the fate of Tchoupitoulas Street, "the old riverbank trail of the Indians and afterward the chief road [of] the French and Spanish colonizers," now a dreary waterfront street.[19] All of this is a subliminal comparative history in the sense that it refracts through the United States of the 1840–'80s the situation of Jamaica in the 1940s, as socioeconomic and political, racial and national issues of self-determination remained to be resolved.

Beyond the urban geography of New Orleans, the Creole expansionist map, read upside down, like Roberts's "Mediterranean of the West," also traces a larger circuit of anticolonial revolution in the pre–Civil War dream of "territory southward, in the West Indies, Mexico and Central America . . . , Texas and similar republics formed by adventurers on the neglected outskirts of the former Spanish Empire" and its postwar version, the ex-Confederate exodus "to Mexico or some Latin-American country, to take up land, . . . or enlist as soldiers of fortune."[20] As a hypothetical map of a US Creole republic, a world not yet come, the novels link space to time and language, creating the kind of open-ended comparative and translational imaginary that James produces with *The Black Jacobins* (the book and the force it names) and that Glissant associates with islands as openings.

Concluding this speculative mapping of hemispheric imperial and national conflicts is the revolutionary location that proved, with Haiti, most significant for West Indian nationalism, both Roberts's and James's: Cuba of 1898 for Roberts, Castro's Cuba for James. Roberts says in his autobiography (in a chapter titled "The Shaping of a Nation," on the late 1940s in New Orleans) that he had promised himself for years to write a historical novel about the Cuban War of Independence (*Single Star*, written 1948–49), and that a research trip to Cuba ("I retraced the route followed by the US expeditionary force . . . to San Juan Hill in 1898") clarified how and why turn-of-the-century Cuba finally provided the model closest to his aspirations for Jamaican independence.[21] "Jamaicans were Caribbean by temperament," he explains, addressing the question of Jamaican self-government versus federation. "In the long run we would react more like Cubans than like Englishmen or West Africans."[22] Bearing this out, the novel moves from Jamaica to Cuba, at the moment of the deaths of the revolutionary heroes José Martí, "the Apostle," and Antonio Macéo, "the Bronze Titan," where the Jamaican protagonist Stephen Lloyd (son of disillusioned ex-Confederate southerners) assumes multiple noms de guerre (e.g., Captain Dixie, Esteban Yo-eed), and serves in the Cuban army against Spain; the novel culminates with the US invasion of the island

and the raising not of the Cuban flag of the single star but of the Stars and Stripes of the United States.[23]

Roberts's Cuba thus speaks to Jamaican conceptions of race, political leadership, and the anticolonial project in an age of transition between empires. The novel's antagonists are both imperial Europe ("the empires that once shared the region, with only a few colonies left") and the United States (Teddy Roosevelt leads the Rough Riders up San Juan Hill as we hear Cuban/Jamaican fears that "American intervention would rid us of Spain . . . but we might only be exchanging masters").[24] The novel's historical heroes are also Jamaica's: Martí and Macéo, both of whom appeal to "every type of Cuban, white or colored," are associated with "the great Bolívar," resisting earlier Spanish attempts "to strangle liberty in America."[25] The novel's fictional hero, Stephen-Esteban, has a "linguistic flexibility" (fluent in several languages, he learned French at McGill University and quickly picks up Spanish in Cuba) in accordance with the novel's transregional and translational sensibility.[26] He calls his horse "Arawak, the name of the aboriginal tribe Columbus had found in Jamaica"; his English name, "translated" into the "Spanish form" by the Cuban female guerilla leader Inés (*La Estrella*) Carmona, is Esteban Yo-eed.[27]

Most striking of the novel's names and nomenclature is the protagonist's Mediterraneanizing speculation: "Think of the whole expanse of water bounded by eastern Cuba, Haiti and Jamaica as a little sea within the Caribbean. On certain old maps it is called the Jamaica Sea, and it merits a name of its own no less than the Aegean and the Tyrrhenian Seas in the Mediterranean. This is our region's womb of history."[28] Echoing a similar moment in *The Caribbean* ("the potent womb, our sea of destiny, the Mediterranean of the West"[29]), this is the novel's geohistorical vision of the Caribbean as a whole, a hypothetical Jamaica Sea connecting Caribbean concerns of 1898 and 1949. The figure of the Caribbean-as-womb itself has a long history, suggesting a special geostructural, sexualized affinity with that archipelagic region, notably captured in "The Kiss of the Oceans" postcard, a souvenir issued for the Panama-Pacific International Exposition in San Francisco in 1915, with the image of two female faces, their mouths about to meet, superimposed on a hemispheric map of the Americas right at the isthmus, the place of the "Meeting of the Atlantic and Pacific," where the Caribbean islands form a ring around the neck of one of the faces (figure 5.2). "Held in the embrace of two continents, the Caribbean is the key to both": Roberts's geographical fantasy draws on the bodily metaphors of these sorts of allegorical maps, forcing the common structures of geography into relation with seemingly disparate regional histories, such as Caribbean and Mediterranean, or even the Pacific Islands.[30]

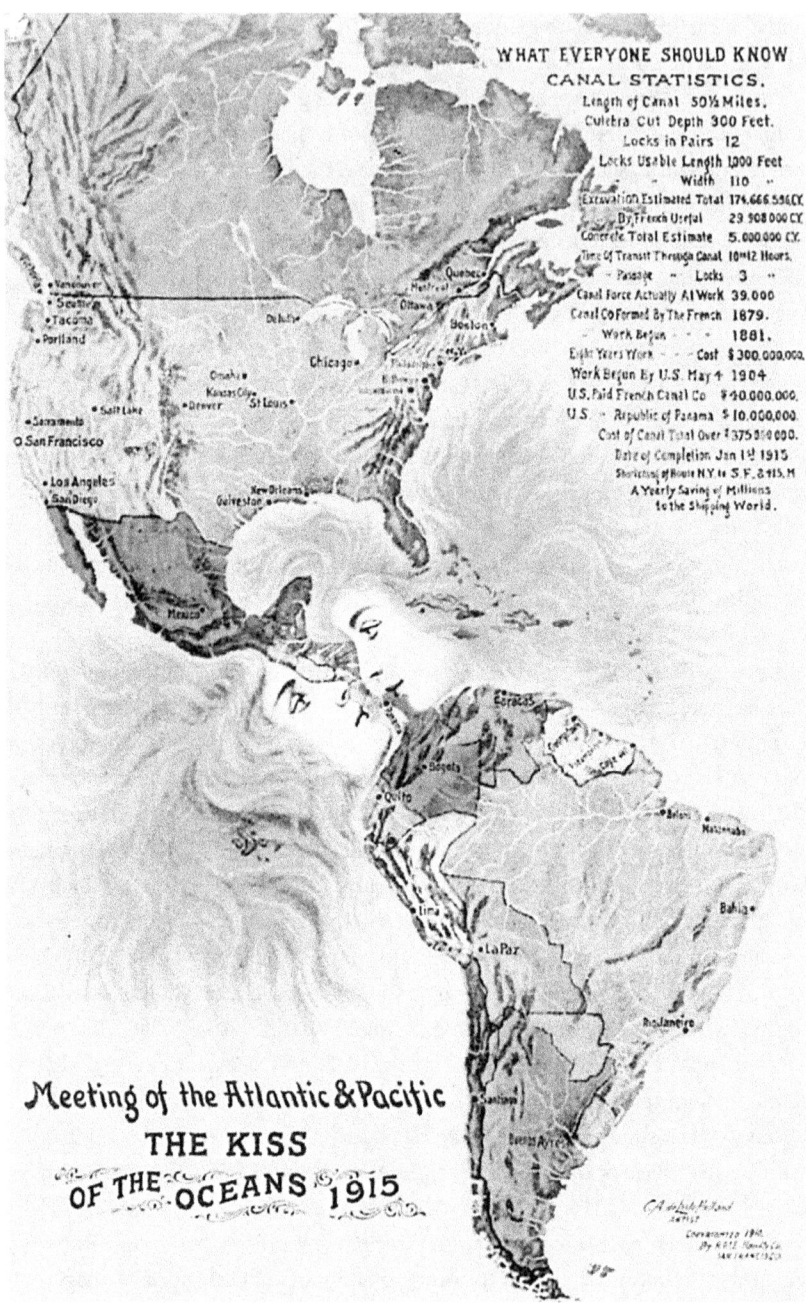

Figure 5.2. "Meeting of the Atlantic & Pacific: The Kiss of the Oceans, 1915." Souvenir postcard for the Panama-Pacific International Exposition in San Francisco, 1915.

MARTÍ/RIZAL: SOME SPECULATIVE CONCLUSIONS

Let me conclude with another hypothetical: José Martí and José Rizal at the Atlantic and Pacific ends, geographic and temporal, of the Spanish empire. Martí and Rizal are linked by as many possible parallels (their premature deaths, barely a year apart, at a transitional moment in their respective national struggles for independence from Spain and the looming neocolonial threat, foreseen by both writers, from the United States) as differences (in their personal and political histories as well as in the Cuban and Filipino colonial situations, especially in relation to the imperial metropole).[31] Nonetheless, it is hard to find the comparative space/time framework adequate to this particular global landscape of the late nineteenth century. In *The Spectre of Comparisons*, Benedict Anderson goes so far as to characterize the Philippines of the 1890s as the "westernmost part of Latin America" where "an early (for Asia) and late (for Latin America) uprising" took place and was soon crushed. John Blanco, also placing the Philippines within the Americas, argues that with the onset of English as the imperial language after 1898, "barely a generation after Rizal's death, Filipinos had already forgotten they were once part of Latin America."[32] The language question is key: Rizal yokes different Spanishes (Castilian, South American, Cuban, and even English-accented) to speak with ambiguous agency of nationalist conspiracy, while Martí invokes the translator's visibility in his activist philosophy of translation as intercultural rewriting, neither simply fidelity nor betrayal, on a continuum in Spanish and English.

Rizal presents a recognized problem as the celebrated Filipino national novelist writing in late nineteenth-century Spanish rather than Tagalog (a regional language spoken around Manila that became the basis for modern Filipino today). Few Filipinos could read Spanish then, when it was the language reserved for colonial authorities and educated *ilustrados* ("enlightened ones"), or now, when Filipino (standardized Tagalog) and English are the two national languages of the Philippines. So the two great Filipino national novels are written in the imperial language, mirroring rather than challenging, some would say, the hegemony of Spanish control. This line of argument—writing in Spanish, Rizal paradoxically chose a language that few Filipinos could read—points to a critical question about the role of language in the imperial archipelago. As a result of colonial policy dictating the use of local languages by Spanish clergy to facilitate conversion (thereby, as Vicente Rafael argues, embedding in the Catholic Church the structure of colonial rule), Tagalog (and to a lesser extent other regional vernaculars) was preserved in a way that distinguishes the Philippines from other Spanish colonies. Further, Rafael argues for the ambiguous agency of language, the use of Castilian Spanish by Filipino nationalists within the vernacular tradition, to tap the "promise of the foreign."[33]

Rizal works with and through these contradictions most starkly in *El filibusterismo: Novela filipina* (1891) rather than the better-known *Noli me Tangere* (1887) to which it is the nominal sequel (the subtitle in Spanish being *Continuación del Noli me Tangere*). Though written in Spanish, the *Fili* is "remarkably heteroglossic,"[34] using local slang and everyday Tagalog, with some paraphrases in Spanish that indicate Rizal's intended European audience,[35] as well as untranslated French, German, and Tagalog. The novel's mysterious protagonist, the jeweler Simoun, identified accidentally, early in the novel, as the new identity of the supposedly murdered Crisóstomo Ibarra, anti-Spanish hero of the *Noli*, confesses that he has come to Manila to aggravate colonial exploitation and thereby foster revolution. Alternately associated with various imperial locations and racial terms, American and European—he is called "mestizo" (8), "mulato Americano" (11), "Americano" (12), "indio inglés" (a British Indian) (11), "portugés" (64), and, in the English, "yankee" (8)—Simoun is said to have spent time in North America and to have come from Cuba, some believe to exert influence over the Manila authorities about the teaching of Spanish: "Your books are in Spanish [*castellano*, in the source text], and the teaching is not in that language" (18). And indeed, the main subplot is the failed student campaign to establish a Spanish-language academy. The novel mirrors its language politics in the unsettled and unsettling disguises of the protagonist.[36]

The multiple identities of Simoun have been read as Rizal's invocation of a New World Americas anticolonial nationalism to stand in for the as-yet unrealized Filipino project; as disguises reflected in his affected, ostentatiously bad Tagalog and excellent Spanish, spoken, though, it is said, with "un acento raro, mexcla de inglés y Americano del Sur" (a strange accent, a mix of English and South American; 5); and as his double role, a nominal outsider able to traverse the various levels of colonial society and move up and down the linguistic hierarchy.[37] All of these readings, put together, would point to what I see as the novel's use of Spanish against itself, a Spanish internally divided, both *el español* and *el castellano*, and externally multiplied, both Castilian and *americano*, meaning the hemispheric Americas, as well as *la América del Norte*. Spanish is at once the "inaugural language of globalization"[38] and the more local language of empire.

Put another way, Anderson remarks that Filipino anticolonial activists were faced with a tough choice not available in most of the Spanish Empire: "to reject Spanish or spread it."[39] Caught between these alternatives, Rizal fashions his own way out by going way in. Spanish becomes Rizal's ambiguous language of conspiracy, the nitroglycerine bomb hidden in the jeweled pomegranate-shaped lamp that Simoun plots and fails to detonate at the novel's climax. The failed conspiracy of the *Fili*, repeating the ruined revolutionary dreams of the *Noli*, is the key to Rizal's untimely vision, his "proleptic" if not prophetic fiction,[40] set in a future not yet come, shadowed by a past not yet completed: the extension across the transatlantic and transpacific worlds to the Philippines of Simón Bolívar's American revolutions against the Spanish Empire. It takes uncompleted revolution elsewhere, Anderson argues, in other times and places, whether the nineteenth-century Bolívar legacy of the Americas or the anarchist eruptions in 1880s Europe, to represent both an open-ended and an imminent Filipino future.

Here is where Anderson, famous first as a theorist of nationalism and second of comparison, may well be an unrecognized theorist of archipelagoes, given his training in Southeast Asia and his focus on Rizal's Philippines. The prospect for "a proper comparative approach,"[41] occasioned by Anderson's work on Rizal in both *Spectres of Comparison* (1998) and *Under Three Flags* (2005), is routed first through Anderson's investment in archipelagic regions, allowing him to see the Philippines as a broken-off bit of Latin America, and second through the way he theorizes comparison as a form of translation. With a little help from Rizal, the "spectre," as opposed to the earlier (mis)translated "demon," of comparison, Anderson's self-corrected translation of Rizal's "el demonio de la comparaciones" becomes what we might call the archipelagic comparative, defined by hauntings and ghostly double visions, generated by the island openings out at the opposite ends, spatially and temporally, of the Spanish Empire.

In contrast to Rizal's Spanish versus Spanish, Martí overtakes and takes over English, the language of the America that is not ours, by translating it into Spanish. As a translator writing in the late 1880s in New York for a Spanish-speaking audience in the United States and throughout the Caribbean and Latin America, Martí is known for choosing Helen Hunt Jackson's *Ramona* (1887), one of his favorite books in English, to translate and publish at his own expense in 1888—during his longtime exile from his native Cuba in New York City, where he also wrote his most famous essay, "Nuestra América" (Our America) in 1891. His introduction to the translation, itself titled *Ramona: Novela Americana*, provides a sense of his philosophy as a translator that will also serve as the sense of an ending for my essay.

Translation, in Martí's hands, is an intercultural dialogue and Cuban intellectual tradition—in the words of Cuban poet and critic Carmen Suarez Léon, a process of heterogeneous rewriting, producing original poetic language through adaptation to the cultural referents of his Spanish-speaking readers. Put another way, Martí rejects what Lawrence Venuti calls the translator's invisibility. When Martí called his *Ramona* "otra *Cabaña*" (another *Uncle Tom's Cabin*), speaking out in favor of the Indians as "la Beecher" did for the Negroes, he signaled that it is more than a literal translation; rather it is a *transculturation* (anticipating Cuban anthropologist Fernando Ortiz's term from the 1940s), the product of more than one author, belonging to more than a single national literary tradition, that elevates the role of translation to active participant in, rather than mere footnote to, the production of literary and cultural meaning. If Martí's view of translation is capacious—"traducer es transpensar" (to translate is to think through/across), he wrote—Martí's *Ramona: Novela Americana* is then less a novel translated from English to Spanish than a novel transculturated, to use Ortiz's term for the multidirectional relations, colony-to-metropole, core-to-periphery, of the contact zone (in effect anticipating a concept that Ortiz would not develop until 1947) from the United States back to its origins in Latin America.[42]

Translating this novel into Spanish, Martí went further in the direction of speculative comparison, as befits a translator who deals regularly with issues of linguistic and cultural (un)translatability, going so far as to imagine Jackson's *Ramona* as "perhaps our novel." His introduction repeatedly presents *Ramona* as "nuestra novela": "As [Como] Ticknor wrote the history of Spanish literature," Martí even speculates, toward the end of the introduction, "Helen Hunt Jackson, with more fire and knowledge, has perhaps written in *Ramona* our novel."[43] When Martí presented us with his transculturated *Ramona*, he was looking both backward and forward, anticipating a view of the contact zone that would not emerge until the new waves of decolonization in the late 1940s. This is the very moment that the archipelago principle appeared, innovated by thinkers including those in the Mediterranean of the West. Extending further, it takes an archipelago to put together the Caribbean and Southeast Asia, Latin America and Asia, as oceans, land masses, continents, and islands are all folded into the logic of the archipelago. Together, these products of a complex set of space-time shifts and transferences, aka "Mediterraneanizing," narrate alternative and speculative histories of the archipelagic Americas.

NOTES

1. Edmundo O'Gorman, *The Invention of America, an Inquiry into the Historical Nature of the New World and the Meaning of Its History* (Bloomington: Indiana University Press, 1961). On West Indians and exile, see Paul Buhle, *C. L. R. James: The Artist as Revolutionary* (London: Verso, 1988), 63; on Roberts as a marginal figure, see W. Adolphe Roberts, *These Many Years: An Autobiography*, ed. with intro. by Peter Hulme (Kingston, Jamaica: University of West Indies Press and National Library of Jamaica, 2015), xiv; Adolphe Roberts, *The Caribbean: Our Sea of Destiny* (Indianapolis: Bobbs-Merrill, 1940).

2. Roberts, *These Many Years*, xv.

3. Roberts, *These Many Years*, 283.

4. C. L. R. James, *The Black Jacobins: Toussaint L'Ouverture and the San Domingo Revolution*, 2nd ed., rev. (New York: Vintage/Random House, 1963), x, 256 (references, hereafter abbreviated BJ, cited parenthetically in text).

5. W. Adolphe Roberts, *Royal Street: A Novel of Old New Orleans* (Indianapolis: Bobbs-Merrill, 1944); W. Adolphe Roberts, *Brave Mardi Gras: A New Orleans Novel of the '60s* (Indianapolis: Bobbs-Merrill, 1946); W. Adolphe Roberts, *Creole Dusk: A New Orleans Novel of the '80s* (Indianapolis: Bobbs-Merrill, 1948); W. Adolphe Roberts, *The Single Star: A Novel of Cuba in the '90s* (Indianapolis: Bobbs-Merrill, 1949).

6. On the "archipelago principle" (traced to the era of postwar decolonization with the 1955 Bandung Conference and the West Indian Federation) and Glissant's "Antillean imaginary," see Brian Russell Roberts and Michelle Stephens, "Archipelagic American Studies and the Caribbean," *Journal of Transnational American Studies* 5, no. 1 (2013): 13–14; Édouard Glissant, *Traité du Tout Monde* (Paris: Gallimard, 1997), 31, 43; Harry Harootunian, "Some Thoughts on Comparability and the Space-Time Problem," *boundary 2* 32, no. 20 (Summer 2005): 24.

7. Benedict Anderson, *Under Three Flags: Anarchism and the Anti-Colonial Imagination* (London: Verso, 2005), 2.

8. Roberto Fernández Retamar, "Caliban: Notes Toward a Discussion of Culture in Our America," in *Caliban and Other Essays*, trans. Edward Baker (Minneapolis: University of Minnesota Press, 1989), 13.

9. Leopoldo Zea, *Latinoamérica en la encrucijada de lahistoria* (Mexico: Universidad Nacional Autónoma de México, 1981), 175.

10. James, *Black Jacobins*, 391–92.

11. Robin Blackburn, "The Black Jacobins and New World Slavery," in *C. L. R. James: His Intellectual Legacies*, ed. Selwyn R. Cudjoe and William E. Cain (Amherst: University of Massachusetts Press, 1995), 83; C. L. R. James, *The Future in the Present: Selected Writings* (London: Allison and Busby, 1977).

12. For "those few of us who got an education," see "The Old World and the New," in C. L. R. James, *At the Rendezvous of Victory: Selected Writings* (London: Allison and Busby, 1984), 205; Boris Souveraine, *Stalin: A Critical Survey of Bolshevism*, trans. C. L. R. James (New York: Longmans, Green, 1939); on "English good enough," see James, *Rendezvous*, 202.

13. See the interview with James in MARHO, ed., *Visions of History* (Manchester University Press, 1984), 267; and the interview with Stuart Hall, "Breaking Bread with History: C. L. R. James and *The Black Jacobins*: Stuart Hall interviewed by Bill Schwarz," *History Workshop Journal* 46 (1998): 21.

14. David Scott is one of a handful of critics who read the text, the 1938 and 1963 editions, as a series of changing "translations" in response to different historical moments, both of themselves and of the Haitian Revolution itself. See Scott, *Conscripts of Modernity: The Tragedy of Colonial Enlightenment* (Durham, NC: Duke University Press, 2004); Kara M. Rabitt, "C. L. R. James's Figuring of Toussaint Louverture: A Reassessment of C. L. R. James's Interpretation," in Cudjoe and Cain, *C. L. R. James: His Intellectual Legacies*, 118–35.

15. On this passage, see Brett St. Louis, *Rethinking Race, Politics, and Poetics: C. L. R. James' Critique of Modernity* (London: Routledge, 2007), 64.

16. The title of Robert May's classic work, *The Southern Dream of a Caribbean Empire, 1854–61* (Baton Rouge: Louisiana State University Press, 1973), quoted and elaborated in Matthew Pratt Guterl, *American Mediterranean: Southern Slaveholders in the Age of Emancipation* (Cambridge, MA: Harvard University Press, 2008), 27.

17. Roberts, *Royal Street*, 12–13.
18. Roberts, *Brave Mardi Gras*, 13–14.
19. Roberts, *Creole Dusk*, 323.
20. Roberts, *Royal Street*, 48; Roberts, *Brave Mardi Gras*, 274.
21. Roberts, *These Many Years*, 170.
22. Roberts, *These Many Years*, 169.
23. Roberts, *Single Star*, 109–10.
24. Roberts, *Single Star*, 89.
25. Roberts, *Single Star*, 40.
26. On "linguistic flexibility," see Faith Smith, "Between Stephen Lloyd and Esteban Yo-eed: Locating Jamaica through Cuba, *Journal of French and Francophone Philosophy / Revue de la philosophie française et de la langue française* 20, no. 1 (2012): 22–38, 34.
27. Roberts, *Single Star*, 229, 57.
28. Roberts, *Single Star*, 85.
29. Roberts, *Caribbean*, 19.
30. On *Single Star* in the context of Cuba and its Caribbean connections, see Peter Hulme, *Cuba's Wild East: A Literary Geography of Oriente* (Liverpool: Liverpool University Press, 2011), 260–67.
31. On the relations of Cuba and the Philippines to the metropole in terms of language, legal system, and insurrectionary tradition, see Anderson, *Under Three Flags*, 131, 141.
32. Benedict Anderson, *The Spectre of Comparisons: Nationalism, Southeast Asia, and the World* (London: Verso, 1998), 6; John D. Blanco, "Bastards of the Unfinished Revolution: Bolívar's Ismael and Rizal's Martí at the Turn of the Twentieth Century," *Radical History Review* 89 (2004): 102; see also John D. Blanco, *Frontier Constitutions: Christianity and Colonial Empire in the Nineteenth-Century Philippines* (Berkeley: University of California Press, 2009); Adam Lifshey, "The Literary Alterities of Philippine Nationalism in José Rizal's *El filibusterismo*," PMLA 123, no. 5 (2008): 1436; see also Adam Lifshey, *The Magellan Fallacy: Globalization and the Emergence of Asian and African Literature in Spanish* (Ann Arbor: University of Michigan Press, 2012).
33. Vicente L. Rafael, *The Promise of the Foreign: Nationalism and the Technics of Translation in the Spanish Philippines* (Durham, NC: Duke University Press, 2005).
34. Rafael, *Promise of the Foreign*, 54.
35. Anderson, *Under Three Flags*, 37.
36. José Rizal, *El filibusterismo, novela filipina*, trans. María Soledad Lacson-Locsin (Manila: Bookmark, 1997).
37. Lifshey, "Literary Alterities of Philippine Nationalism"; Anderson, *Under Three Flags*, 112; Rafael, *Promise of the Foreign*, 55.
38. Lifshey, *Magellan Fallacy*, 3.

39. Anderson, *Under Three Flags*, 88.
40. Anderson, *Under Three Flags*, 31, 121.
41. Harootunian, "Some Thoughts on Comparability," 36.
42. Carmen Suarez Leon, *La alegría de traducer* (Havana: Ciencias Sociales, 2007); prologue to Helen Hunt Jackson, *Ramona: Novela Americana*, in José Martí, *Obras Completas*, vol. 24 (Havana: Editorial Nacional de Cuba, 1965), 199; Lawrence Venuti, *The Translator's Invisibility: A History of Translation*, 2nd ed. (New York: Routledge, 2008); Fernando Ortiz, *Cuban Counterpoint: Tobacco and Sugar*, trans. Harriet de Onís (Durham, NC: Duke University Press, 1995); on *traducir es transpensar*, see Fernández Retamar, "On Ramona by Helen Hunt Jackson and José Martí," in *Mélanges à la Mémoire d'André Joucla-Ruau*, vol. 2 (Provence: Editions de l'Université de Provence, 1978), 699–705.
43. Martí, *Obras Completas*, 24:204.

PART III | EMPIRES AND ARCHIPELAGOES

6 | COLONIAL AND MEXICAN ARCHIPELAGOES

REIMAGINING COLONIAL CARIBBEAN STUDIES

Yolanda Martínez-San Miguel

THIS ESSAY REFLECTS ON THE INTERSECTION of colonial and imperial studies by focusing on the Caribbean archipelago as a geopolitical and historical unit. Historicizing the archipelago as an enduring frame and geographical unit permits us to redefine Caribbean studies by establishing connections with different regions that share similar colonial/imperial contexts, such as the Philippines, the Canary Islands, the Azores islands, and Hawai'i, among many others. A specific focus on colonial-archipelagic regions can lead to illuminating analyses of how clusters of islands tend to be conceived through administrative structures and symbolic imaginaries that are different from the sovereign and continental paradigms prevalent in many area studies frameworks.

In defining archipelagoes as systems of islands and the seas that connect them, my work draws upon the field of island studies but does not coincide fully with its main queries. By focusing on countries and regions that are mostly insular in their geography and geopolitical organization, island studies analysis has centered on "the constitution of 'islandness' and its possible or plausible influence and impact on ecology, human/species behavior and any of the areas handled by the traditional subject uni-disciplines (such as archaeology, economics or literature), subject multi-disciplines (such as political economy or biogeography) or policy foci/issues (such as governance, social capital, waste disposal, language extinction or sustainable tourism)."[1] More recently, another line of inquiry within island studies has focused on archipelagic connections among islands, as well as among islands and continental regions.[2] Furthering this trajectory, my definition of the archipelago moves toward integrating the study of seemingly disparate island chains (and their corresponding networks of ports, fortifications, plantations, and cities, as well as their social, cultural, and productive systems) to complicate our conceptualization of the Caribbean in conversation with other regions that share a similar set of conditions.

The notion of the archipelago is not new to Caribbean studies. The Caribbean has been conceived of as a system of islands encompassing a collective identity (as in "the Antilles" or the "Federation of the West Indies"), or a common political experience defined by fragmentation and the lack of a simple notion or order (such as the "imperial frontier" proposed by Juan Bosch).[3] Some countries include more than one island as a single national unit (such as Trinidad and Tobago).[4] The Tainos created chiefdoms in the Caribbean that established networks of trade and exchange with more than one island, and on occasions linked islands with territories in *tierra firme*.[5] So even in Indigenous articulations of space, archipelagoes (and not necessarily the individual islands) functioned as fluid units of thought, knowledge, or identification. Modes of archipelagic thinking have further unfolded in the works of foundational Caribbean scholars and thinkers.[6]

My scholarship aims to expand upon the work of the foundational scholars and thinkers who have revived understandings of the Caribbean as a system of islands, complementing this foundational work by bringing it into dialogue with more recent studies that refer to the region vis-à-vis an "imperial archipelago" or an "inter-Atlantic paradigm" of colonization.[7] In these studies, the framework of the archipelago is used to analyze how geographical conditions had an effect on the historical process of imperial incorporation of certain regions from the sixteenth through nineteenth centuries (as in the case of the Canary Islands, the Caribbean, and the Philippines). Lanny Thompson, for instance, has reflected on how the United States produced distinct discourses to assimilate colonial-insular others.[8] Other cultural critics and historians have advanced studies in which they link several US insular possessions, including the important connection of the Philippines and Cuba during the second half of the nineteenth century.[9] Additionally, Elizabeth M. DeLoughrey has conducted comparative studies of the literatures produced in the Pacific and Caribbean islands by tracing points of contact (which tend to inform apprehensions of commonalities as well as differences) that have constituted the insular and archipelagic imaginaries in these two regions.[10]

Cultural approaches to archipelagic and Caribbean studies can interrogate the meaning of the archipelago in the *symbolic* articulation of a broader conceptualization of the Caribbean. Clearly, much is to be gained from such single-island-oriented works as Antonio S. Pedreira's reflections on Puerto Rico in his 1934 book *Insularismo* and Jamaica Kincaid's reflections on Antigua in *A Small Place* (1988).[11] Nevertheless, Caribbean studies needs to move beyond the single-island insular model as a central framework precisely because the paradigm does not allow us to focus on the several ways in which archipelagoes, and not solitary islands, have functioned as the unit of analysis that facilitated the conception of certain colonial regions.

Following important work by Elaine Stratford and Jonathan Pugh that showcases the advantages of the archipelagic rather than the insular frame,[12] our definitions of the Caribbean need to include not only its islands and archipelagoes but also their specific historico-political relationship with colonialism. This is especially true in the regions of the Caribbean that experienced what I have discussed elsewhere as *extended colonialism,* which "began in the sixteenth and seventeenth centuries and lasted until the twentieth century (and sometimes until today), and [which] frequently includes the coexistence of more than one colonial system (Spanish and French in Martinique; Spanish and US-American in Cuba, Puerto Rico, and the Philippines; Spanish, French, and English in many islands of the Anglo-Caribbean)."[13] Many regions that have experienced more than one colonial regime over an extended period of time are also conceived of as systems of insular spaces that are distinguished from sovereign continental spaces.[14] As a result, colonial archipelagoes tend to exhibit what many consider as "unique status arrangements with much larger national or supra-national bodies."[15] I argue that these atypical relationships with sovereignty and nationalism are a legacy of their unusual condition as overseas imperial possessions.[16] In the following discussion, an example from a corpus of maps produced by European cartographers (in which the Caribbean is represented as the Mexican Archipelago) allows a meditation on how imperial and colonial archipelagoes were imagined in the competitive multi-imperial context of the seventeenth and eighteenth centuries, during the transition from the European mercantile era into a global capitalist world-system.[17] Subsequently, fast-forwarding to the present-day postcolonial Caribbean, a short story by Tiphanie Yanique, a Brooklyn-based Caribbean writer from the US Virgin Islands, provides an example of how this archipelagic colonial imaginary is transformed into a *decolonial archipelago* in the early twenty-first century. These case studies permit new reflections on the implications and utility of rethinking the Caribbean using the notion of the colonial archipelago.

ARCHIPIÉLAGO DE MEXICO:
"A BLUEPRINT FOR COLONISATION"

> The symbolic dimension of maps also links them to other texts. Modern cartographers usually regard their maps as factual statements written in the language of mathematics, but they are always metaphors or symbols of the world.
>
> J. B. HARLEY, "Texts and Contexts in the
> Interpretation of Early Maps"

Maps are dense historical and symbolical documents that can enhance our study of colonialism, postcolonialism, and decoloniality in the Caribbean. Especially illuminating on these questions is the foundational work of J. B. Harley quoted in the epigrah to this section, which unlocks the symbolic, metaphorical, and fictional dimensions of maps, and opens these texts for close readings of their intentions, functions, and perspectives.[18] According to Harley, maps are both historical and cultural documents, and they should be read simultaneously through the information they emphasize and the information they deemphasize or silence.[19] Harley proposes maps as a system of communication that is as complex as a language, and he uses literary criticism to define the cartographic "discourse" that is at the core of his influential essay "Maps, Knowledge, and Power."[20] Another crucial element for reflecting on the Caribbean as a colonial-archipelagic system is the meticulous analysis of the links between cartography and European colonialism as it unfolded in the Americas and more specifically in the Caribbean.[21] Ricardo Padrón's concept of "cartographic literature" is useful here, as a framework originally deployed in approaching iconographic and discursive representations of space in maps, historical *relaciones*, and literary texts related to Early Modern Spain's conceptions of its empire.[22] Expanding the ambit of cartographic literature's utility as a framework, I take up cartographic and literary representations of the Caribbean from the 1650s to the present to recover the historical and ideological motives that have helped articulate early modern and contemporary symbolic representations of these archipelagic possessions.

Especially germane to this project is a small corpus of maps produced by European cartographers between 1650 and 1750 in which the Caribbean is conceived of as the "Mexican Archipelago."[23] This is the time period in which France and England waged what Patricia Mohammed describes as a "war of maps," a series of conflicts during which "maps were used by competing European powers to claim territory in the New World."[24] As an example of this set of geographical representations of imperial archipelagoes, a map designed in 1689 serves as the point of departure for reflecting on how the Caribbean was constituted as a "colonial archipelago" by the competing European countries that were trying to expand their control of overseas territories in the Americas (figure 6.1). In this map, the entire Caribbean is identified as "Arcipelago del Mexico." In this same book, Vincenzo Coronelli also depicts some of the individual islands (such as Cuba, Hispaniola, and Jamaica) as part of the Mexican Archipelago, so the term encompasses both the islands and the sea that surrounds them.[25] What is important about this particular set of maps is that the designation of the archipelago is constituted visually and geopolitically as a distinct unit that identifies the imperial relationship between the metropolitan centers and the overseas possessions that are conceived of as a network of islands.

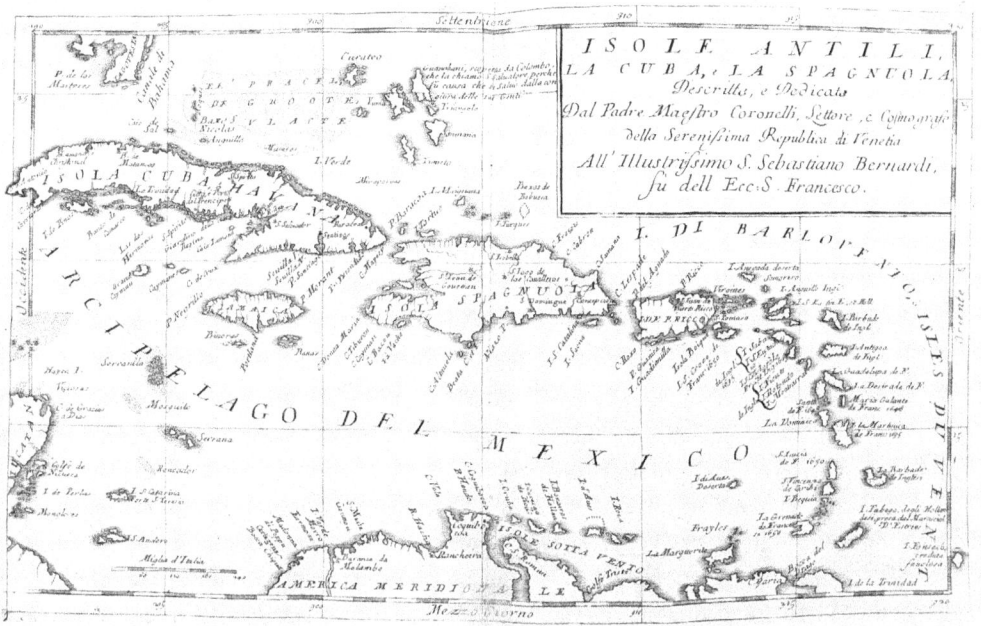

Figure 6.1. "Isole Antili, La Cuba e la Spagnuola." From Vincenzo Coronelli, *Citta, Fortezze, Isole e Porti Principali dell'Europa* (Venice: Domenico Padouani, 1689). Reproduction courtesy of the Newberry Library, Chicago. Call # Ayer 135.C8 1689, Plate 95.

Aside from the several maps in which the region is represented as the "Mexican sea" and the islands as the "Mexican archipelago," there are verbal references from roughly the same time period in which an archipelagic Mexico is presented as common knowledge. This is the case in Herman Moll's *A System of Geography; or, A New and Accurate Description of the Earth*:

I. ANTILLES *ISLANDS.*
After having made a distinct Description of the several Parts of the Continent of Northern *America*, together with some of the principal Islands that lye over against them; it is requisite in like manner to describe the sixth and last Part of the same *America*, that is to say, the Islands of the *Archipelago of Mexico*. They are all in general call'd by divers Geographers *Antillae*, q. d. *Ante Insulae*, i.e., *The Fore-Islands*, by reason to their Situation before the Gulph of *Mexico*, and in regard that they first come in sight to those that sail from *Europe*, or *Africa*, before the Coast of *New Spain*: Others only understand by that Name, the four greater Islands, *viz. Cuba, Jamaica, Hispaniola,*

COLONIAL AND MEXICAN ARCHIPELAGOES | 159

and *Porto Rico*; to which some add the *Caribbee-Isles*. But we shall here take the Term *Antilles* in its largest Signification, comprehending all the Islands which appear between *Florida*, a Part of Northern *America*, on the North; and *Terra Firma*, a Province of Southern *America*, on the South.[26]

Moll's description of the Caribbean is significant, because the Antilles are represented as a specific region that was in fact the first point of contact and entrance to the Americas. Moll conceived of the Antilles as a system, and in this passage the idea of the archipelago functions as a working category to refer to the collection of islands located between North and South America. This conceptualization of the Antilles also echoes the early sixteenth-century etymology of archipelago as "chief sea."[27] In this case, however, Moll is referring to the Mexican region, and perhaps even comparing the Mexican Gulf with the Aegean Sea, and the Mexican Archipelago's islands to the Aegean Islands.

This reference to archipelagic Mexico becomes so common that it is even included in the definition of the word "archipelago" in Louis Moreri's *Le Grand Dictionaire Historique* from 1707, although it is used to define the Gulf of Mexico instead of the islands themselves: "ARCHIPELAGUE DE MEXIQUE, est proprement le golfe de Mèxique, où il a de plusieurs Isles" (The Archipelago of Mexico is properly the Gulf of Mexico, where there are many islands).[28] This dictionary entry is telling, because in it the Caribbean islands become invisible to privilege their location in the Gulf of Mexico, associating them more with the Viceroyalty of New Spain than with a specific region within the Spanish Empire. Finally, in the nineteenth century, we encounter again the term in *Le Dictionnaire Phraséologique Royal: Anglais-Français* (1853), now conflating the definitions of "island" and "West Indies": "ÎLE, s. f. island. Les îles, West Indies, the islands of the archipelago of Mexico."[29] In this context, "the Caribbean archipelago" has become a synonym for "the West Indies" and "the Caribbean," as overseas colonial territories of different European countries. Yet my main interest in this geographical description grows out of two central questions. First, why is the Caribbean conceived of as an administrative, political, and even economic dependency of Mexico? Second, why is the concept of the archipelago (both as a system of islands, ports, and centers of production and as the sea that connects them) significant in this particular context?

The answer to the first question requires a contextualization that must take place across several administrative, economic, and political strata. First we need to review the administrative structure of the Spanish Empire in the Americas. In Spain, the King administered the American possessions, while the Casa de Contratación (founded in 1503) regulated commerce and the exchange of resources and goods, and the navigational routes.[30] The Consejo de Indias (founded in 1524) was in charge of the legal and political administration of the colonies and appointed imperial functionaries. In the Americas, the highest administrative units were the viceroyalties (of New Spain, 1535; Peru, 1543; Nueva Granada, 1717; and de la Plata, 1776), followed by the regional *audiencias* (such as Santo Domingo) and the local *capitanías generales* (Santo Domingo, 1535; the Philippines, 1574; Puerto Rico, 1580; Cuba, 1607; Guatemala, 1609; and Yucatán, 1617). In this structure, what we now think of as the Caribbean clearly fell under the administrative purview of the Viceroyalty of New Spain. Yet it is important to note that the insular Caribbean, or archipelagic Mexico, was the first colonial post of the Spanish Empire. Furthermore, the administrative boundaries between the viceroyalties and the audiencias were not clearly defined. The audiencias generales were in charge of the legal administration of the region and reported directly to the King of Spain, and as such Santo Domingo had an ambiguous administrative place as the site of the first court of the Spanish Crown in the Americas. Since the president of the Audiencia de Santo Domingo was also the general captain, this colonial functionary had broad powers and autonomy to administer the Spanish possessions in the Caribbean.[31]

To complicate matters even more, Cuba was the point of departure of the original expedition to what would later become the Viceroyalty of New Spain, and it continued to be a strategic port for several navigational routes of the Spanish Empire, so its location within the power structure of the imperial administration was ambiguous, to say the least. Perhaps the most important navigational route was the *flota* system, which became particularly relevant during the seventeenth and eighteenth centuries, at the height of the imperial competition for American possessions through piracy and contraband. The flota system was used between 1566 and 1790, and it was a convoy system used to protect vessels transporting silver, gold, agricultural products, and exotic or expensive goods to and from the few authorized ports for conducting official business between the Pacific, the New World, and Spain. The treasure fleets sailed the following two main routes: the most important one, the "Flota de Indias," departed from the Casa de Contratación in Seville and stopped in continental ports located in Veracruz, Portobelo, and Cartagena and reconvened in Havana before returning to Spain.[32] A secondary route was the "Galeón de Manila," the commercial route that connected Europe with the coveted Orient between 1565 and 1815, to bring silver from the Americas to the Pacific, and to transport silk, exotic spices, and other products from China following a route via Manila, Acapulco, Veracruz, the Caribbean-Canary Islands, and Europe. Goods coming from Manila reached Acapulco and were transported overland to Veracruz, where they joined the "Flota de Indias" to return to Spain. In the context of these commercial routes, the competition and alternative centrality between the Viceroyalty of New Spain and Havana becomes evident.³³ At the same time, the routes of these two flota systems connected a series of colonial archipelagoes that were administered through the Viceroyalty of New Spain.

Financially speaking, however, the Viceroyalty of New Spain functioned as the royal coffers, de facto constituting New Spain as the economic center of the Spanish Empire that allowed the proper administration of the Pacific and Atlantic possessions. New Spain had a strategic location for the Manila Galleons. The Viceroyalty of New Spain was also the administrative center of the *situado mexicano*, a subsidy sent by the Crown to Puerto Rico and the Philippines, which was also used to build the defensive fort system in the insular and continental Caribbean between 1587 and the nineteenth century (that included Cuba, Hispaniola, Puerto Rico, Cartagena, Venezuela, Panama, and Veracruz).³⁴

In this context, the maps produced by these European cartographers basically refer to the centrality of New Spain viceroyalty for the financial administration of the insular territories, at the historical juncture in which the European imperial competition taking place in the region would balkanize the Mexican archipelago into the political, cultural, and linguistic divisions that we still know today in the Caribbean. This imperial-administrative structure, centered in New Spain, actually complicates and enriches more recent conceptualizations such as Greater Mexico, defined by Américo Paredes as "all the areas inhabited by people of a Mexican culture—not only within the present limits of the republic of Mexico but in the United States as well—in a cultural rather than a political sense."³⁵ In both cases, New Spain/Mexico serves as a mediating instance or active border between metropolitan centers (Spain/the United States) and colonial peripheries. José David Saldívar's recent and compelling work on Greater Mexico also reminds us of Mexico's Asian-Pacific routes and showcases the more contemporary centrality of archipelagoes in the Mexican and Chicano/Mexican American cultural imaginaries.³⁶

This financial centrality of the Viceroyalty of New Spain, which eventually translated into an administrative and political dominance, was already prefigured in Bernardo de Balbuena's famous poem "La grandeza mexicana" (1603).³⁷ In a collaborative close reading of this poem, Barbara Fuchs and I have elsewhere argued that "in the *Grandeza Mexicana*, Balbuena produces a new imaginary that displaces the center of the Spanish empire to the viceroyalty of New Spain by conceiving the city of Mexico as a center of operations that links Asian and European markets."³⁸ Gunder Frank argues that the Manila Galleons mobilized the first truly global commercial circuit, and in that context New Spain functioned as what Fuchs and I have called a "colonial metropolis."³⁹ Therefore, by referring to the Caribbean as the Mexican Archipelago, these European cartographers were recognizing the de facto financial and commercial prevalence of New Spain over the military and the navigational importance of the capitanías generales of Cuba and Santo Domingo.

Yet a second question still remains unanswered: why is "archipelago" the meaningful category to refer to these colonial overseas possessions? An answer to this question emerges from a handful of colonial texts in which the Caribbean functions as the central spatial referent. The imperial/colonial archipelago has functioned as a central motif for narratives produced in and about the Caribbean from the colonial period to the present. For example, although Columbus thought he was arriving at another archipelago (Cipango/Japan),[40] the truth is that his "discovery" of the Americas was mediated first by the geopolitical nature of the Caribbean archipelago as a network of islands that literally displaced and postponed the much-desired route to the orient.

The archipelago as a potential system of territories or a frontier is an important motif in many colonial texts. One has only to remember the detailed descriptions included by Bartolomé de Las Casas of the "destruction" and "depopulation" of the Indies, in which islands were more vulnerable to the brutal decimation of the Indigenous populations than the possessions in the tierra firme. The reiteration of such a destructive model is so frequent in the text that Las Casas creates a template that is applied to many insular possessions in the Americas:

> THE ISLANDS OF PUERTO RICO AND JAMAICA
>
> In 1509, the Spanish, with the same purpose in mind as they had when they landed on Hispaniola, found their way to the two verdant islands of Puerto Rico and Jamaica, both of them lands flowing in milk and honey. Here they perpetrated the same outrages and committed the same crimes as before, devising yet further refinements of cruelty, murdering the native people, burning and roasting them alive, throwing them to wild dogs and then oppressing, tormenting and plaguing them with toil down the mines and elsewhere, and so once again killing off these poor innocents to such effect that where the native population of the two islands was certainly over six hundred thousand (and I personally reckon it at more than a million) fewer than two hundred survive on each of the two islands, all the others having perished without ever learning the truths of the Christian religion and without the benefit of the Sacraments.[41]

In some cases this same geopolitical motive has even allowed authors to produce archipelagic narratives in which the imbrication of islands and characters is more central than the articulation of one particular imperial or national identity, as is the case in Samuel Champlain's *Narrative of a Voyage to the West Indies and Mexico in the Years 1599–1602*.[42] Champlain traveled to the West Indies to access information that was otherwise out of reach for Frenchmen. His narration links the Caribbean region with New Spain, and the journey is represented in a crescendo that culminates with his hyperbolic and superlative description of the richness of the city of Mechique.[43] Evidently, the Caribbean islands and ports are not as rich as the Mexican Viceroyalty, yet in these peripheral regions Champlain finds harbors in which English and French merchants can exchange goods as part of a global market that takes place outside the mercantile controls of the Spanish Empire. Furthermore, in his narrative archipelagoes function as a navigational constellation or network that makes possible the journey between Europe and New Spain:

> Leaving the Canary Islands, we passed by the Gulf of Las Damas, having the wind astern, so that in two months and six days after our departure from St. Lucar, we got sight of an island named La Deseade, which is the first island that pilots *must necessarily recognize* in going to all the other islands and ports of the Indies.
>
> . . .
>
> We were four months at the Havanna, and leaving it with the whole fleet of the Indies, which had assembled there from all parts, we proceeded to pass the channel of Bahan (Bahama), which is the passage of consequence, *and which must necessarily be passed in returning from the Indies*.
>
> . . .
>
> Four days after passing Bermuda we had such a great tempest, that the whole of our armament was more than six days without being able to keep together. After the six days had passed, the weather becoming finer and the sea more tranquil, we all reassembled, and had the wind favourable till we perceived the Açores. . . . All vessels returning from the Indies *must of necessity approach the said islands of Açores to take their observations*, otherwise, they could not with surety finish their route.[44]

So archipelagoes morph in Champlain's narrative from a geopolitical category into a navigational and discursive structure that connects Europe and the Americas. At the same time archipelagoes become part of the narrative to represent the vulnerabilities of the colonizing and exploitative models applied by the Spaniards (Las Casas, Champlain), or function as a repetitive scenario that displaces and postpones the arrival to the coveted Orient (Columbus) or the superlative richness of New Spain (Champlain). Finally, if we establish a dialogue between the map analyzed at the beginning of this section and the colonial narratives just reviewed, archipelagoes seem to index the tension between imperial economies (Spain, the Viceroyalty of New Spain) and colonial borders (the Canary Islands, the insular Caribbean, and the Philippines).

"OUR NEW POSSESSIONS":
THE DECOLONIAL ARCHIPELAGO AS A POETIC

The legacies and transformations of the imperial/colonial archipelago can be traced in more recent decolonial Caribbean imaginaries. This is the case in the work of contemporary writer Tiphanie Yanique, who originates from an archipelago that is currently one of the unincorporated territories of the United States. Although Yanique seems to write from a context very different from that of the Mexican Archipelago (not the Hispanophone but Anglophone, not colonial but present-day, and not in relation to an Old World empire but in relation to the US empire), her work's treatment of the US Virgin Islands positions it well to be read vis-à-vis the framework of a colonial archipelago. Although at first the connection between Yanique's work and the colonial-era maps and texts could seem tenuous, the Mexican archipelagic imaginary remains an important reference. Tiphanie Yanique is a diasporic Caribbean writer, born in the US Virgin Islands and currently residing in Brooklyn, New York. Her short story, "The Bridge Stories: A Short Collection," traces the archipelagic as a poetic and a creative response to the historical and political legacies of extended colonialism as they are particularly inflected and experimented with in the insular Caribbean.

The US Virgin Islands were controlled by Spain, England, Holland, and France before becoming a Danish possession (and were hence known as the Danish West Indies) at the end of the seventeenth century. Saint Croix was not originally part of the archipelago owned by Denmark until it was purchased from France in 1733. Beginning in 1867, the United States attempted to acquire the islands, first as part of the secretary of state William Henry Seward's plan of "peaceful territorial expansion," and later in an attempt to secure a route to the Panama Canal, and to keep the islands from German control during World War I.[45] Finally, the United States purchased the archipelago from Denmark in 1917 for the total price of $25 million. The islands were first administered by the US Navy (1917–31) and in 1932 were transferred to the Department of Interior. Initially, residents of these islands were considered US nationals but not US citizens, but in 1927 Congress granted US citizenship to anyone born in the islands after 1917. The Organic Act of 1954 currently defines these islands as an organized unincorporated territory of the United States, adding them to the list of US insular possessions with an ambiguous status. Island residents have elected their own governors since 1970. In 1993 the residents attempted to hold a status referendum (in which participants voted for US territorial status, integration with the United States, or independence), but less than 30 percent of the inhabitants of the islands participated, so results were not considered valid.[46] In 2009 the Fifth Constitutional Convention proposed a constitution for the islands that was rejected by US Congress in 2010. This colonial archipelago is the immediate setting of the short story by Yanique that performs an archipelagic poetic.

"The Bridge Stories: A Short Collection" is structured as a series of vignettes depicting stories of the lives of several characters who exist within a system of bridges built by a local US Virgin Island artist to connect the entire Caribbean. Inspired by and building upon Enmanuel Martínez's analysis of the links among Yanique's anthology, her short stories, and an archipelagic form of writing,[47] my reading focuses on the ways in which the narrator creates a constellation or a historical, spatial, and geographic network characteristic of the Caribbean archipelago to produce a narrative imbrication of brief plots in which a small group of characters relate at multiple levels. I argue that in this case, the archipelagic functions simultaneously as a geographical category, metaphor, and structuring motif for the short story.

The story takes place in Saint Croix on the night of July 3, when Virgin Islanders celebrate the 1848 abolition of slavery on their islands, and the eve before the celebration of Independence Day in the United States. This specific temporal juncture is telling, since it references extended colonialism in the region by invoking simultaneously black emancipation under Danish rule and independence under US dominion. The first vignette begins with the story of an artist that makes bridges, and who one day decides to make his project more monumental:

> There was a bridge maker. He made bridges that people put in their earlobes and around their fingers. Tiny little bridges . . .
>
> His living family insisted that he leave a real legacy. He was famous for small things. They wanted him to be known for big things. So he built a real bridge. Paid for by the Yankees—not to honor his memory, but really for their own convenience. . . . Huge and stretching from Guyana—the place in the world most south—to Miami—the place in the world most north. Before allowing the public to walk on the bridge he gathered all his family onto it for a picture. But the bridge was built like his others, the only way he knew how, delicate and pretty but not able to bear weight.
>
> When the picture flashed—a big, beautiful, blinding light—the bridge fell apart. And not only in that spot but in places all over the Caribbean, so the many families who had gathered to take pictures (without express permission) also went into the ocean.[48]

In this passage the bridges built by the artist link the insular and continental Caribbean in a new postcolonial context financed by US interest. In this context, the archipelago emerges as a constellation of insular and continental territories rearticulated by a neoimperial gaze. Yet it is also redefined as a decolonial archipelago by the multifocal narrative perspective of the short story, as well as by the artistic project of the bridges that connect all of the islands. This network of bridges might be read as the progeny of the colonial Mexican Archipelago in the context of Paredes's and Saldívar's work on Greater Mexico. It might also be read as an afterimage of the Caribbean confederation in the nineteenth-century Spanish Caribbean, or of the West Indian Federation of the 1950s–1960s Anglo-Caribbean. Yet the bridges must also refer to neocolonial and transnational archipelagoes of the twenty-first century. The collapse of the whole system marks the crisis or end of a particular model of imperial geopolitical organization, and it hints at symbolic and cultural connectivities that can reconstruct the fragmented archipelago in a different way that goes beyond continental or unitary definitions of identity as nationhood.

The subsequent vignettes tell the history of some of the other characters who are at the bridges when the system collapses. Each story seems totally independent, but intersects in subtle ways with the previous and/or succeeding vignette(s). The second vignette, for example, is the story of Margo, a native of Dominica, originally from a Pentecostal family, who converts to Islam in order to marry her husband Rashaad and follows him to Saint Croix. Years later, their relationship is in crisis and Margo leaves her family to return to Dominica. On July 3, Margo has decided to return home to reunite with Rashaad. Waiting for her husband, Margo decides to walk to the bridge. There she thinks she sees her husband with another woman in a vessel; heartbroken, she decides to jump from the bridge just before the entire system collapses.

The third vignette narrates the family crisis between Salli and Toni and their son Pete. Toni is a fisherman who is confronting the economic crisis of the fishing industry precipitated by the building of the bridge system. Salli decides to leave Toni for another man, and confesses to her son Pete that Toni is not his real father. On July 3, the day before Pete moves to the United States to study at a Catholic school, father and son try to mend their relationship by spending the day fishing together. At the end of the day, Pete sees Margo jumping from the bridge and loses his life trying to save her.

The fourth vignette is the story of Guadeloupe, a Puerto Rican–born woman whose family has migrated to Saint Croix,[49] and who has decided to compete in the Miss Emancipation pageant to win the love of Juan Diego. Guadeloupe represents several palimpsestic references to the marginality of the Caribbean in the Spanish colonial imaginary. On one hand, Guadeloupe and Juan Diego's names refer us to the myth of origin of the Mexican national cult to the Virgin of Guadeloupe. While the Mexico–Puerto Rico reference revives the colonial Mexican Archipelago that I have analyzed earlier, in the context of this story the Mexican archipelagic connection indexes the many layers of coloniality that inform intra-Caribbean relations. On the other hand, Guadeloupe's fear of losing Juan Diego's love is completely unfounded. Her plan to recover Juan Diego's love is also fragile, since winning the title of Miss Emancipation confronts her with the internal racial divisions between light-skinned Spanish Caribbeans and dark-skinned West Indians. Guadeloupe realizes that she is too white to embody black emancipation in the Anglo-Caribbean, and is unable to escape a sense of dislocation. It is then that she decides to run to the bridge. There, she sees Margo, Toni, and Pete: "There was a black sack figure crossing the bridge too. There were two figures in a boat just below. It was late, dark. The moon was high and crescented. She wanted to be on top of that moon. She wanted it at her feet—like a boat to get her across anything. *She was such a frigging drama queen. She couldn't know what she had in common with these three figures.* But she felt she had to choose one set or the other."[50] Just before the bridge system collapses, Guadeloupe realizes that she can become the human bridge that links this constellation of personal stories. Yet she is totally incapable of understanding all of the nuances and complexities of her own intuition. This is precisely the moment in which all of the bridges fall, and the narratives end.

The archipelagic framework functions to articulate this story at various levels. First, the archipelago is literally where the action of the story takes place, but Yanique seems to be proposing another definition of the archipelago that transcends the Caribbean region. All of the characters of these vignettes coincide in Saint Croix, but their routes also link the island with Dominica, countries in Africa and Asia, the United States, Puerto Rico, and many other locations in the Caribbean. At the same time, the archipelago is a referent to the manner in which each character is linked in a network of meanings and misunderstandings provoked by the juxtaposition of story lines. At the structural level, the story is divided into insular narratives that do not seem to work together even though they are totally intertwined. The connections between characters are fragile, temporary, and even illusory. The moment in which a master narrative can congeal is announced, but never happens. Yet this story is not about the failure of the archipelagic narrative.

At a macrostructural or political level, the archipelago is also the metaphor that articulates this network of bridges that fails. Perhaps the story is referencing here the historical fragility of the Caribbean confederation, but most likely the archipelagic refers here to the delicate transnational and global diasporic networks that connect the colonial and postcolonial Caribbean of the present with the metropolitan nodes in the first world. In the narrative mode proposed by Yanique, the decolonial archipelago is simultaneously a centripetal and centrifugal force that produces meaning and nonsense, transparency and opacity. It is precisely through this ambivalent gesture that "The Bridge Stories" consolidates an alternative theorization of the archipelagic that transcends the colonial legacies of archipelagic Mexico. This alternative archipelagic poetic is built through an intuition that what ultimately connects the insular overseas possessions are precisely the immense differences that coexist within a fascinating network of places located beyond the organizing impulses of the imperial, the national, or the continental.

CONCLUSION: FROM THE IMPERIAL TO THE DECOLONIAL ARCHIPELAGO

In the two examples discussed here, the Caribbean is on one hand an imperial/colonial archipelago that is imagined from the top by European cartographers and Spanish functionaries in the seventeenth and eighteenth centuries, and on the other hand it is a decolonial archipelago, reimagined from below as a cultural and historical constellation or network of communities and individuals. In each case, the network of islands and communities linked by imperial and neocolonial structures reconstitutes itself as a system of meaning that goes beyond the original politico-administrative organization of the archipelago. The archipelago, then, becomes a unit of geographical meaning capable of reconnecting the Caribbean with other systems of islands that have been imagined and reimagined as colonial archipelagoes or overseas possessions of European and US-American empires. These two examples are an invitation to reflect on the utility of archipelagoes in studying the specificity of the political and historical experiences of insular regions that are simultaneously marginal and central in the imperial and global imaginaries. This focus on the comparative study of imperial, colonial, and decolonial archipelagoes reconnects the Caribbean with other regions that share similar experiences, allowing us to interrogate the disciplinary and intellectual frameworks of area studies and national literatures and cultures. Perhaps this is another way in which we can reinflect a critical engagement of early modern and contemporary globalizations. Within this mode of thought, archipelagoes are no longer distant overseas possessions but are now transformed into clusters of islands with anomalous political states that defy the normativity of national and transnational imaginaries.

NOTES

1. Godfrey Baldacchino, "Islands, Island Studies and Island Studies Journal," *Island Studies Journal* 1, no. 1 (2006): 9.

2. Elaine Stratford et al., "Envisioning the Archipelago," *Island Studies Journal* 6, no. 2 (2011): 113–30; Jonathan Pugh, "Island Movements: Thinking with the Archipelago," *Island Studies Journal* 8, no. 1 (2013): 9–24.

3. Juan Bosch, *De Cristóbal Colón a Fidel Castro: El Caribe frontera imperial* (Santo Domingo, Dominican Republic: Editora Alfa y Omega, 1981).

4. Many Caribbeanists question the definition of the region as being mostly insular, yet I do not conceive of archipelagoes as exclusively insular; rather, they may include continents.

5. William Keegan and Morgan D. Maclachlan, "The Evolution of Avunculocal Chiefdoms: A Reconstruction of Taino Kinship and Politics," *American Anthropologist* 91, no. 3 (1989): 613–30.

6. Antonio Benítez-Rojo, *The Repeating Island* (Durham, NC: Duke University Press, 1996); Édouard Glissant, *Traité du Tout-monde* (Paris: Gallimard, 1997).

7. See Javier Morillo Alicea, "Uncharted Landscapes of 'Latin America': The Philippines in the Spanish Imperial Archipelago," in *Interpreting Spanish Colonialism: Empires, Nations, and Legend* (Albuquerque: University of New Mexico Press, 2005), 25–53; and Lanny Thompson, *Imperial Archipelago: Representation and Rule in the Insular Territories under U.S. Dominion after 1898* (Honolulu: University of Hawai'i Press, 2010); Anthony Stevens-Arroyo, "The Inter-Atlantic Paradigm: The Failure of Spanish Medieval Colonization of the Canary and Caribbean Islands," *Comparative Studies in Society and History* 35, no. 3 (1993): 515–43.

8. Thompson, *Imperial Archipelago*.

9. See Vicente Rafael, *The Promise of the Foreign: Nationalism and the Technics of Translation in the Spanish Philippines* (Durham, NC: Duke University Press, 2005); John Blanco, *Frontier Constitutions: Christianity and Colonial Empire in the Nineteenth-Century Philippines* (Berkeley: University of California Press, 2009); and Koichi Hagimoto, *Between Empires: Martí, Rizal, and the Intercolonial Alliance* (New York: Palgrave, 2013).

10. See Elizabeth M. DeLoughrey, *Roots and Routes: Navigating Caribbean and Pacific Island Literatures* (Honolulu: University of Hawai'i Press, 2010).

11. Antonio S. Pedreira, in a book-long essay that attempts to answer the question of Puerto Rican national identity in the 1930s, reflects on the colonial condition of the island and argues that the country's *insularismo* (isolation/islandism) explains its lack of a sovereign state and a clear historico-political projection; Antonio S. Pedreira, *Insularismo: Ensayos de interpretación puertorriqueña* (1934; reprint, Río Piedras, Puerto Rico: Editorial Edil, 1992). In *A Small Place* (New York: Farrar, Straus, and Giroux, 1988), Jamaica Kincaid meditates on the psychodynamics of writing from a small island located within the Caribbean archipelago.

12. See Stratford et al., "Envisoning the Archipelago"; and Pugh, "Island Movements."

13. Yolanda Martínez-San Miguel, *Coloniality of Diasporas: Rethinking Intra-colonial Migrations in a Pan Caribbean Context* (New York: Palgrave, 2014), 6.

14. Stratford, "Envisoning the Archipelago."

15. Baldacchino, "Islands, Island Studies," 3.

16. For a study of the problematic relationship between sovereignty and Caribbean state formations, see Yarimar Bonilla, "Nonsovereign Futures? French Caribbean Politics in the Wake of Disenchantment," in *Caribbean Sovereignty, Democracy, and Development in an Age of Globalization*, ed. Linden Lewis (New York: Routledge, 2012), 208–27.

17. Immanuel Wallerstein, "The Rise and Future Demise of the World Capitalist System: Concepts for Comparative Analysis," *Comparative Studies in Society and History* 16, no. 4 (1974): 387–415.

18. J. B. Harley, *The New Nature of Maps: Essays in the History of Cartography* (Baltimore, MD: Johns Hopkins University Press, 2001), 37. I take the quoted phrase in the section title from Patricia Mohammed, *Imaging the Caribbean: Culture and Visual Translation* (Oxford: Macmillan, 2009), 72.

19. Harley, *Nature of Maps*, 45.

20. Harley, *Nature of Maps*, 54–55.

21. See Harley, *Nature of Maps*; Barbara E. Mundy, *The Mapping of New Spain* (Chicago: University of Chicago Press, 1996); and Ricardo Padrón, *The Spacious Word: Cartography, Literature, and Empire in Early Modern Spain* (Chicago: University of Chicago Press, 2004); see Mohammed, *Imaging the Caribbean*; and Santa Arias, "Rethinking Space: An Outsider's View of the Spatial Turn," *GeoJournal* 75, no. 1 (2010): 29–41.

22. Padrón, *Spacious Word*, 45.

23. Spaniards conceived of their political, commercial, and navigational maps as secret documents for internal consumption until the early eighteenth century; Mohammed, *Imaging the Caribbean*, 62, 67; Harley, *Nature of Maps*, 59. This is why I am analyzing how Spanish and other European possessions were imagined and represented by non-Spanish cartographers. This division is not as clear-cut as it seems, since some non-Spanish European cartographers were also in the service of the King of Spain.

24. Mohammed, *Imaging the Caribbean*, 67.

25. Vincenzo Coronelli (1650–1718) was a Franciscan monk born in Venice who was a well-known cartographer, cosmographer, and publisher. In the late 1680s he was invited to Paris to build globes for Louis XIV, King of France. Later in life he held the position of cosmographer of Venice. For more information, see James Lawrence Fuchs, "Vincenzo Coronelli and the Organization of Knowledge: The Twilight of Seventeenth-Century Encyclopedism" (PhD diss., University of Chicago, 1983).

26. Herman Moll, *A System of Geography; or, A New and Accurate Description of the Earth*, vol. 2 (London: Timothy Childe, 1701), 183.

27. "Chief sea," *Oxford English Dictionary* online, last modified December 2014, http://www.oed.com/.

28. Louis Moreri, *Le Grand Dictionaire Historique* (Paris: Chez Denisse Mariette, 1707).

29. J. Ch. Tarver, *Le Dictionnaire Phraséologique Royal: Anglais-Français* (London: Dualu & Co., 1853).

30. The *Casa de Contratación* oversaw exploratory missions and housed documents of discovery as secret documents. One such document was the "Padrón Real," a master world map that was kept up to date by trained cartographers; Harley, *Nature of Maps*, 93.

31. James Lockhart and Stuart B. Schwartz, *Early Latin America* (New York: Cambridge University Press, 1989), 102–6.

32. On the routes of the flota system, see Curtis Nettels, "England and the Spanish-American Trade, 1680–1715," *Journal of Modern History* 3, no. 1 (1931): 1–32; and Timothy R. Walton, *The Spanish Treasure Fleets* (Sarasota, FL: Pineapple, 1994).

33. For more information on the Manila Galleons, see William Schurtz, *The Manila Galleon* (New York: E. P. Dutton, 1959); Katharine Bjork, "The Link that Kept the Philippines Spanish: Mexican Merchant Interests and the Manila Trade, 1571–1815," *Journal of World History* 9, no. 1 (1998): 25–50; and Dennis O. Flynn and Arturo Giráldez, "Born with a 'Silver Spoon': The Origin of World Trade in 1571," *Journal of World History* 6, no. 2 (1995): 201–21.

34. Luis González Vales, "El situado mexicano y la financiación de las fortificaciones de San Juan de Puerto Rico," Oficina de Servicios Legislativos de Puerto Rico, accessed January 4, 2016, edicionesdigitales.info/biblioteca/situadomexicano.pdf.

35. Américo Paredes, *A Texas-Mexican Cancionero* (Urbana: University of Illinois Press, 1976), xiv. This concept is also central in José Limón, *American Encounters: Greater México, the United States, and the Erotics of Culture* (Boston: Beacon Press, 1998); and José David Saldívar, *Trans-Americanity: Subaltern Modernities, Global Coloniality, and the Cultures of Greater Mexico* (Durham, NC: Duke University Press, 2012).

36. Saldívar, *Trans-Americanity*, 123–51.

37. Bernado Balbuena, *La grandeza mexicana y Compendio apologético en alabanza de la poesía* (Mexico: Porrúa Balbuena, 1971).

38. Barbara Fuchs and Yolanda Martínez-San Miguel, "'La grandeza mexicana' de Balbuena y el imaginario de una 'metrópolis colonial,'" *Revista Iberoamericana* 75, no. 228 (2009): 677. My translation.

39. Gunder Frank, *ReOrient: Global Economy in the Asian Age* (Berkeley: University of California Press, 1998); Fuchs and Martínez-San Miguel, "La grandeza mexicana," 677–78.

40. Columbus wrote, "I should like to depart today for the island of Colba, which I believe according to the indications of its size and riches given us by these people must be Chipangu"; Christopher Columbus, *The Four Voyages* (New York: Penguin, 1969), 72 (entry for Tuesday October 23). Columbus mentions Cipango in his entry for October 6 as well (page 50).

41. Bartolomé de Las Casas, *A Short Account of the Destruction of the Indies* (New York: Penguin, 1992), 26.

42. Samuel Champlain (1574–1635) was a French navigator, cartographer, geographer, chronicler, explorer, colonizer, and diplomat. He is a well-known historical figure in Canada, as he made the first map of the coast, was the founder of Quebec City, and is known as the "consolidator of the French colonies in The New World." His *Brief Discours des Choses plus remarquables que Sammuel Champlain de Brouage a reconneues aux Indes Occidentalles au voiage qu'il en a faict en icettes en l'année 1599 et en l'année 1601, comme ensuite* was not published in French until 1870, and the first English publication took place in 1859. See C. T. Ritchie and Samuel Champlain, "Samuel de Champlain," *Encyclopedia Britannica* online, last modified November 2, 2014, accessed December 27, 2014, http://www.britannica.com/EBchecked/topic/105187/Samuel-de-Champlain.

43. Samuel Champlain, *Narrative of a Voyage to the West Indies and Mexico, 1599–1602* (London: Printed for the Hakluyt Society, 1859), 21–40.

44. Champlain, *Narrative of a Voyage*, 6, 45, 48; my emphasis.

45. "Purchase of the United States Virgin Islands, 1917," US Department of State Archive, January 20, 2001, to January 20, 2009, accessed January 4, 2016, http://2001-2009.state.gov/r/pa/ho/time/wwi/107293.htm. For more information about the history of the US Virgin Islands, particularly their relation to the United States, see William W. Boyer, *America's Virgin Islands: A History of Human Rights and Wrongs* (Durham, NC: Carolina Academic Press, 2010); and Isaac Dookhan, *A History of the Virgin Islands of the United States* (Epping: Caribbean Universities Press for the College of the Virgin Islands, 1974).

46. Malik Sekou, "The Failure of the Political Status Process in the U.S. Virgin Islands," paper presented at the 19th Annual Conference of the Caribbean Studies Association, Mérida, Mexico, May 23–27, 1994.

47. Enmanuel Martínez, "Archipelagic Content and Form in Tiphanie Yanique's 'The Bridge Stories: A Short Collection.'" I thank Martínez for sharing this unpublished work with me in 2013.

48. Tiphanie Yanique, *How to Escape a Leper Colony* (Minneapolis, MN: Graywolf Press, 2010), 15.

49. For a study of Puerto Rican migrations to Saint Croix, see Nadja Ríos Villarini and Mirerza González Vélez, "Oral Histories of Bilingual Education Teachers from the Puerto Rican Diaspora in St. Croix: Exploring Ideological Tensions Inside and Outside the Classroom," *Sargasso* 2 (2009–10): 35–49; and Mirerza González-Vélez, "Mapping Points of Origin in the Transnational Caribbean: The Foundational Narrative of the Puerto Rican Pioneer Family in the Virgin Islands," *Revista Umbral* 8 (April 2014): 46–63.

50. Yanique, *How to Escape,* 29; my emphasis.

7 | INVISIBLE ISLANDS

REMAPPING THE TRANSPACIFIC ARCHIPELAGO OF US EMPIRE IN CARLOS BULOSAN'S *AMERICA IS IN THE HEART*

Joseph Keith

> The world is an island.
> MACARIO, in Carlos Bulosan,
> *America Is in the Heart*, 1946

EARLY ON IN CARLOS BULOSAN'S NOVEL *America Is in the Heart* (1946), the young protagonist, Carlos, falls ill from overworking on his family's farm in the Philippines. His brother, Macario, comes to visit him and, at Carlos's request, retrieves a book to read to him at his bedside. The book he chooses to read is *Robinson Crusoe*.

> He started reading the story of a man named Robinson Crusoe who had been shipwrecked in some unknown sea and drifted to a little island far away. My brother patiently explained the struggle of this ingenious man who had lived alone for years in inclement weathers and had survived loneliness and returned safely to his native land.
>
> I was fascinated by the bearded man, and a strong desire grew in me to see his island.[1]

His brother goes on to explain the story's significance for Carlos and invites him to see himself reflected in the tale: "You must remember the good example of Robinson Crusoe.... Someday you may be left alone somewhere in the world and you will have to depend on your own ingenuity.... Maybe you will be thrown upon some unknown island someday with nothing to protect you except your hands and your mind" (32). As it turns out, Carlos does reflect back several times upon Crusoe over the course of the novel. As he recounts his subsequent journey as a migrant laborer to the United States, chronicling the hardships and racist abuse he suffers in the Alaskan canneries and Californian agricultural fields, he comes increasingly to identify with Crusoe's isolating experience as an island castaway. "I remembered Robinson Crusoe, and compared him with my fate," he thinks near the end of the novel, and then concludes that the only difference is that his own "lostness" is more acute, because he is "lonely among men" on the "far away" and "unknown island" upon which he finds himself a castaway—namely, "America" (252).

I want to begin this essay by taking up the unusual but deeply suggestive identification that Carlos—*and* the novel—establish between his "voyage in" (to borrow Edward Said's phrase)[2] from the Philippines to the United States and *Robinson Crusoe*'s infamous "voyage out" from the metropole of England to a lonely and "little island far away." Certainly, Defoe's novel is one of the canonical narratives of the colonial imagination. It is also, relatedly, one of the foundational works in establishing the repertoire of meanings and representations of islands within the history of continental and Western thought. Briefly put, it depicts the Western male subject cast away from the mainland of European civilization, who is accidentally washed ashore on a deserted and decidedly isolated island. He is there transformed from survivor into colonizer as he slowly gains possession of the remote, undeveloped, and uninhabited space of the island on which he finds himself.

This representation of the distant island upon which the European castaway finds, and refashions, himself helped inspire an entire island genre of European and US literary, philosophical, and artistic works that became enormously popular during the eighteenth and nineteenth centuries. As Elizabeth DeLoughrey points out, *Robinson Crusoe* was reprinted six times in its first year of publication, and over five hundred "desert island" stories, or "Robinsonades," were published in England alone between 1788 and 1910. As she further points out, this tradition of representations and discourses on islands, which *Robinson Crusoe* helped found, is also deeply embedded in the history and practice of empire. Broadly speaking, it articulated a representational grammar of island boundedness, isolation, and atemporality that in turn helped to rationalize and legitimate European and US colonial and imperial domination. "The self made man who accidentally colonizes a desert island," summarizes DeLoughrey, "has been a powerful and repeated trope of empire building."[3]

Returning to *America Is in the Heart,* I argue that in mapping the tale of *Robinson Crusoe* onto his journey from the islands of the Philippines to the United States, Carlos inverts the narrative and, in turn, undercuts its underlying spatial assumptions—spatial assumptions that have at once helped legitimate and obfuscate the imperial connection between the "mainland" of US-America and the "islands" of the Philippines. More specifically, in recasting the United States as the "unknown island," Bulosan's novel overturns one of the dominant US geographical imaginaries regarding immigration—namely, the vision of a continental vastness linking an ostensibly boundless spatial mobility to a correspondingly limitless social mobility. *America Is in the Heart* animates instead a submerged historical landscape disavowed and displaced by the exceptionalism—and *continental* exceptionalism—of the United States.[4] Ultimately, Bulosan's novel remaps the colonial insular imaginary (à la Crusoe) to chart a US subaltern geography—an insular topography of racialized and "unincorporated" subjects and spaces stretching across the borders of the national terrain to an island empire in the Philippines.

AN ARCHIPELAGIC BILDUNGSROMAN

America Is in the Heart parallels *Robinson Crusoe* in a number of significant ways. Like Defoe's novel, *America Is in the Heart* portrays a man stranded far away from home, traumatically separated from the world he knows. More specifically, Carlos, like Crusoe, is able to turn the struggle for survival into self-renewal; that is, like Crusoe, Carlos's isolation enables his progress to self-reliance and self-understanding. Put in different terms, both novels are fundamentally invested in linking the experience of the "island castaway" to the project of *Bildung*: to the education and formation of the self.

But it is also in comparing their respective projects of Bildung that we might more fully glean the stakes of Bulosan's geographic and geopolitical remapping of Defoe's island castaway tale. On one hand, *Robinson Crusoe* provides one of *the* paradigmatic Bildung representations of the autonomous individual whose heroic and solitary adventures lead to a personal development that eventually reaffirms the values of the society from which he has been cast away, but which awaits his reintegration. In particular, Crusoe's literary education—namely his daily reading of the Bible from among the books of his salvaged library—leads him to discover for himself the necessity of the ethical ideas and religious values of the social order left behind, which he re-creates and reaffirms on his isolated island domain.[5]

America Is in the Heart, on the other hand, while appropriating the formal and thematic criterion of the bildungsroman, resists this logic of synthesis. Indeed, Carlos's "Robinsonade" narrative of self-formation and education—forged out of the fragments of books and resources available to him—emerges explicitly out of and animates the contradictions and *limits* of the social order: a social order that has *relegated* him to the status of "castaway." In turn, his developing self-understanding leads him to reimagine his "far away island" not as a space where the principles and institutions of the larger social order of the nation (in this case "America") are reaffirmed and reconstructed—as did Crusoe—but rather as a space where they are challenged and, ultimately, undermined.

But if *America Is in the Heart*'s insular imaginary reveals the idealized Bildung of the United States and US immigration as stunted—as leading not to integration but to exclusion and isolation—the novel still represents a bildungsroman, albeit an alternative one. Specifically, it uses the figure of the island not only to critique but also to reroute the bildungsroman's logic of incorporation and synthesis into an alternative political, literary, and geographic form that does not take the nation as the ultimate endpoint of the genre. Out of the failed promise of the US-American bildungsroman, the narrator fashions a bildungsroman that transforms his exclusion (his self-defined position as a *castaway*) into a standpoint from which to integrate himself into a nonnational, ever-widening, and ultimately what I define as an "archipelagic" form of community and cosmopolitanism—from the "island" of an ethnic immigrant enclave within the United States to a multiracial archipelago of global migrants laboring at the limits of citizenship.

Ultimately, then, the alternative bildungsroman fashioned by *America Is in the Heart* produces a profoundly dialectical vision of the archipelagic. On one hand, the archipelagic in *America Is in the Heart* signifies a decidedly *repressive* political and social geography. It depicts a series of disconnected "islands" of racialized exclusion that together map a critical countercartography to the "continental" US-American national landscape and its ideals. On the other hand, this insular imaginary also becomes a generative source for the narrator, and the novel, to imagine an alternative political form of community and belonging beyond the nation—namely, a heterogeneous archipelago of racialized nonnational subjects: a stateless subaltern counterpublic of "islands" and "island castaways" spanning the transpacific shadows of US empire.

Finally, in mapping this transpacific imperial archipelago I hope to speak to and build upon a growing scholarly effort to theorize the transpacific as an emergent field of study. Recent works, such as Janet Hoskins and Viet Thanh Nguyen's *Transpacific Studies*, have set out to decenter the continental political, historical, and epistemic hegemony of the United States—and Asia—in framing the region. They have attempted instead to critically remap the "transpacific world" via the insular networks and histories of exploitation and resistance—from colonialism to our neoliberal present—that those "continental" empires and logics have at once engendered and disavowed. This includes an effort, Hoskins and Nguyen write, "to reimagine what Europeans called the Pacific, from the points of view of those who live in the islands and the ocean."[6] In recasting "America" as merely one island among many across an imperial archipelago of Pacific islands, Bulosan's insular imaginary, and the archipelagic more generally, might provide, in the end, a generative analytic and model for this form of "transpacific" heuristic.

ISLAND MOVEMENTS AND CONTINENTAL IMMOBILITIES

In keeping with the tradition of the bildungsroman, *America Is in the Heart* is structured upon the theme of movement. Indeed one might say it is fixated on it. From its very outset, as we follow the dissolution of Carlos's family's ownership of their land that sends each of the four sons off in different directions (three to the United States), to the novel's very final scene, where Carlos sets off once again across California, *America Is in the Heart* chronicles, almost obsessively, the place name of each and every town through which the narrator passes. Within the seven-page chapter 23, for example, we read, "I went to Pismo Beach"; "I went to Seattle to wait for the fishing season in Alaska"; "I took another train to Sacramento"; "I took a bus for San Bernardino"; "I took a train for San Diego"; "I took a ferry boat to Coronado"; "I went to Walnut Grove"; "I went to Stockton"; "I became restless and went to the bus station and bought a ticket to San Luis Obispo" (174–80). The novel details over a hundred places through and to which the narrator travels, a staggering number that, as Sau-ling Cynthia Wong notes, produces a chaotic narrative of "directionless" movement that is "impossible to chart" and that undermines any coherent development for the story of Carlos's life.[7]

Building on Wong's argument, I want to place this pattern of constant movement that defies mapping into critical dialogue with the bildungsroman tradition and its underlying spatial ideals. Franco Moretti, for one, argues that movement and mobility is a dominant theme of the bildungsroman, with the journey being the most common narrative metaphor for youth. Modernity disrupted what he calls the "socialization of 'old' youth," or what we might equally deem status society, unleashing an alienating but exhilarating multiplication of possibilities: "In dismantling the continuity between generations... the new and destabilizing forces of capitalism impose a hitherto unknown *mobility*. But it is also a yearned for exploration, since the selfsame process gives rise to unexpected hopes, thereby generating an *interiority* not only fuller than before, but also perennially... dissatisfied and restless." This principle of "restlessness" finds its material sign in the bildungsroman tradition in space and through narratives of spatial mobility. The multiplication of possibilities, in other words, finds its analogue in the multiplication of places.[8]

It is not hard to see how this ethos of movement and mobility can be transposed to the US context; indeed it closely adheres to one of the very founding geographic imaginaries of "America." As far back as the Puritan "errand into the wilderness," American exceptionalism has been defined, in no small measure, through the intertwined terms of spatial and social mobility. North America's untamed continental expanse presents the unprecedented opportunity to "adventure into a new land" to begin life anew and, through hard work and struggle, the possibility of a seemingly limitless social mobility. In this regard, it seems that few places would offer a more inviting home for the bildungsroman than "America." Certainly this perception of the wide-open continent (or frontier, or wilderness, or road)—and the opportunity it implies—has been one of the most persistent if variegated principles of US literature and literary studies.

In one sense, Carlos's youthful journey is consistent with this spatial ideology of movement, attesting to the novel's close adherence to the thematic criterion of the genre. The first third of the book chronicles the pressure of a "growing industrialism" that leads to the dismantling of the family's farm and to a "hitherto unknown mobility" for Carlos and his brothers. And it is also a mobility linked to an internal restlessness. Carlos confesses, for example, "Then it came to me that my life was too small to float the vessels of my desires" (65). At the same time, Carlos's "directionless" journey radically complicates the correspondence between spatial and social mobility. Or rather, it reveals how that correspondence is fundamentally redefined when the territory of that journey is stretched beyond the "mainland" of the United States to encompass the transpacific geography and subjects of US-America's island empire.

Indeed, this redefinition is articulated by Carlos's very legal status as a Filipino. Prior to the Tydings-McDuffie Act in 1934, which granted commonwealth status to the Philippines and established a ten-year transition to full independence, Filipinos occupied an ambiguous national position in the United States. They were colonial wards or "US nationals"—an innovative legal category established by the Supreme Court in 1901 that emerged out of the "Insular Cases" in which Puerto Rico and the Philippines were defined as "unincorporated territories" (the High Court used the famous phrase "foreign to the United States in a domestic sense").[9] This designation meant that the United States could not restrict Filipino immigration, since as US nationals Filipinos were journeying within the territory of the United States rather than moving to a different country as putative foreigners. At the same time, Filipinos were denied the possibility of citizenship. Until 1946, with the establishment of an independent Philippines, Filipinos in the United States thus inhabited what E. San Juan Jr. has termed "a limbo of indeterminacy" marked by empire.[10] More specifically, this indeterminate insular condition bore within it the particular contradictory pattern of a *US-American* empire that dare not speak its name.

In terms of the bildungsroman, Carlos and his companions were thus at once *integrated into* what has been conceived of as the continental US mainland, but also at the same time *officially excluded* from its general patterns of social mobility and from the promise of settlement and reconciliation between individuals and the social order that is so central to the ideological aims of the genre. Their anomalous national status, in other words, excludes Carlos and his fellow Filipino companions from the promise of Bildung represented by national narratives of America and American immigration. They are denied the promise of mobility as a form of becoming and of the "development" from "youthful" estrangement into the "maturity" of US citizenship and belonging.

Instead, the narrator's journey is criminalized. As Carlos observes, "I came to know afterward that in many ways it was a crime to be a Filipino in California" (121). Carlos's travels do not follow the pattern of incorporation and settlement but rather come to represent a fragmented and disorienting *fugitive* movement that the narrator continually describes as a form of flight. "Never stop moving," is the last advice his brother Luciano gives him before he leaves (88). Carlos then describes his arrival as "the beginning of my life in America, the beginning of a long flight that carried me down the years" (101). Later he wonders if his "life would always be one long flight from fear" (128). Repeatedly, this imposed pattern of flight disrupts every effort Carlos makes to settle down or to provide a direction to his movement. Various forms of state and civic violence (police officers, hired thugs, railway detectives, employers, etc.) continually set him "on the run" to some new town, or, as he describes it, on a journey "to nowhere" (111).

In the end, Carlos's fragmented and directionless pattern of movement is reinforced until it becomes the dominant pattern of his life and, by extension, the narrative. It is a form of horizontal mobility deprived of any possibility of progress or upward mobility, and in fact bears witness to its antithesis. In other words, the narrator's constant mobility is a marker of his *im*mobility. As such, the narrative of mobility within *America Is in the Heart* undermines—as opposed to underwrites—the story of Carlos's self-formation. And rather than marking a multiplicity of possibilities, the succession of places to which the narrator's journey takes him across the "wide-open territory" of the United States demarcates the confining limits of his migrant world—a world that in being "impossible to chart" ultimately disorders the geographical and ideological patterns of US-America's continental exceptionalism, animating instead, as we will see, a very different material and discursive landscape.

ISLANDS OF DESPAIR

Carlos describes one of the places typical of those in which he finds himself during his "flight" within the United States and which come to constitute and delimit his migrant world: "It was a noisy and tragic street, where suicides and murders were a daily occurrence, but it was the only place in the city where we could find a room. There was no other district where we were allowed to reside, and even when we tried to escape from it, we were driven back to this *narrow island of despair*" (134; my italics). It is striking that the narrator uses the word "island" here—as he does throughout the novel—to describe these "vice districts," these segregated migrant communities marked by criminal and sexual violence from which he cannot "escape." On one hand, it serves to evoke the isolation and enforced exclusion of these social spaces and communities. Indeed, as islands within the nation, these spaces embody, geographically, the same paradoxical status as that of Carlos and his fellow Filipinos. Both are at once inside the nation but also deemed unassimilable to it, embodying forms of "deviance" that require vigilant exclusion. It is a geographic imaginary that animates, as such, the uneven incorporation of racialized subjects into the putative mainland of US-American citizenship and maps an anomalous topography of insular spaces that constitutes (or deconstitutes) the continental United States—a cartography of segregation and immobility in sharp contradiction to the inclusive national landscape of American pluralism and the "wide-open" spaces of American social mobility.

The image of a "narrow island of despair" also brings us back to Robinson Crusoe, who named his own narrow island the "Island of Despair."[11] In linking these segregated and racialized enclaves in the domestic United States with the "faraway island" of Crusoe's exile, Bulosan at once reproduces *Robinson Crusoe*'s representational grammar on islands (as spaces of isolation, boundedness, and immobility) but subversively overturns the imperial logics and practices to which those meanings have been dedicated. As already suggested, Defoe's novel produced a repertoire of meanings about islands that was founded on casting the island as the radical and constitutive other of continents. In the US-American context, as Brian Russell Roberts and Michelle Stephens have pointed out, this discursive distinction between islands and continents has taken acute form within the historical logics and legacies of US empire. "Continental exceptionalism," they write, "certainly underwrote the US's late nineteenth-century investment in taking under its care what it framed as numerous small islands of the Caribbean and Pacific that were not capable of protecting themselves.... A long-running formal distinction between small islands and the large continent has framed the continent as the massive and natural source of the US's drive toward hemispheric and planetary dominance."[12]

In recasting these domestic national spaces—à la Crusoe—as "islands of despair," *America Is in the Heart* undercuts the very distinction between continent and island and, in turn, undermines continental exceptionalist assumptions about insularity. Indeed, Carlos's depiction evokes a crucial *correspondence* between these unincorporated spaces and subjects *within* the United States and those "unincorporated" spaces or territories *outside* the nation—namely the Philippines. In the end, these narrow islands of despair suggest a transnational geography of "insular cases"—an archipelago of islands extending beyond the nation's perimeters, linking together these domestic spaces of exclusion with the colonial history and island spaces of the Philippines. It is a subaltern geography of the United States that maps the interconnectedness between the seemingly domestic politics of racial difference with the foreign policy of empire—a social and political landscape rendered structurally invisible by the nation-state and occluded by the exceptionalism (and continental exceptionalism) of US-America.

Finally, in Carlos's evocation of his increasing social, political, and epistemological isolation in the United States, the figure of the island is used to map a narrative of *under*development. At the outset of the novel, for instance, while the narrator sits with his brothers in the Philippines, he declares, "I know that if there was one redeeming quality in our poverty, it was this *boundless* affinity for each other, this humanity that grew in each of us, as *boundless as this green earth*" (10; my italics). The narrator thus casts the islands of the Philippines not as an isolated and confined geographic, political, and social space (topographical assumptions historically ascribed to the insular) but instead as the source of a decidedly expansive, indeed *cosmopolitan*, fraternal or peasant solidarity, that is, a cosmopolitanism as "boundless as this green earth." The novel, in turn, chronicles the narrator's disassembling from this island boundlessness into an ever-more atomized sense of self and disidentification as he migrates to the continental United States, a condition that once again finds its analogue—and partial cause—in the confined insular geographic spaces of US-America. "Perhaps it was this narrowing of our life into an island, into a filthy segment of American society, that had driven Filipinos like Doro inward, hating everyone and despising all positive urgencies toward freedom" (121). In the end, if the canonical bildungsroman narrates a logic of development in which the particular and youthful individual "matures" or integrates into the broader social order and its ostensibly universal ideals, *America Is in the Heart* inverts that narrative. Carlos moves from a boundless universalism *"inward"* into a narrowing particular—a movement cast not as one from island to continent (nor the inverse), but instead as a journey across two starkly different political and social forms of insularity.

In turn, if this experience of "flight" to, and across, the continental United States produces a narrative of antidevelopment (from a "boundless" universalism to a "narrowing" particular), the narrative's structuring principle remains illegible to the narrator for much of the novel. He is unable to make sense of or to establish connections between the various "islands"—spaces, people, and episodes—of his deracinated life: "I was in flight away from an unknown terror that seemed to follow me everywhere" (119). Later, he thinks, "I needed some kind of order to guide me in the confusion that reigned over my life" (265). As he encounters other itinerants riding the rails he can only "wonder what I had in common with them beside the fact that we were all on the road rolling to unknown destinations" (119). And in thinking of his life, he finally admits, "It was a planless life, hopeless, and without direction. I was merely living from day to day: *yesterday* seemed long ago and *tomorrow* was too far away. It was *today* that I lived for aimlessly, this hour—this moment" (169). Carlos is unable to organize his life into any explanatory order or continuity because his experiences remain illegible to the interpretive structure of the US-American bildungsroman. As such, the narrative itself becomes a series of "narrow island[s] of despair" as every effort to map a narrative of continuity or progress disrupts into discontinuous episodes of hopelessness and incoherence. And thus in order quite literally to make sense of his life, Carlos must give up this form of education (or Bildung) and adopt another—namely, one capable of rendering the connections between the isolated "islands" of his life, that is, an archipelagic, literary, and political form.

READING ARCHIPELAGOES AND CONSTELLATIONS

This brings us back to one final parallel with Robinson Crusoe, or rather to his reading, which plays such a central role in his self-formation—in his project of Bildung. Reading and books supply both island castaways with an archival substitute for society, an alternative literary means for developing their personality and ethical consciousness. For Crusoe, daily reading from the Bible serves, among other things, as a mode of socialization that activates—and assimilates him to—the ethical and religious ideals of the larger European social order that ostensibly remain latent within him even on his decidedly uncivilized island space. Carlos, however, creates a curriculum out of the books available to him that undermines the traditional paradigm of education as a path to self-development and national inclusion. Instead literature and reading provide him with an alternative conceptual and ethical framework to the nation—one through which he can begin to understand connections between his own "island" position as a noncitizen migrant laborer and other political struggles and spaces both within the United States and in the world.

In other words, learning to read, and ultimately write, generates a different type of journey from the episodic and fragmentary pattern that characterizes Carlos's physical journey. Books and reading lead to a series of intellectual awakenings that Carlos chronicles over the course of the novel. "I was beginning to understand," Carlos describes, "what was going on around me, and the darkness that had covered my present life was lifting" (71). Carlos is careful to chronicle his encounter with various authors (e.g., Richard Wright, Walt Whitman, Mikhail Sholokhov, Yone Noguchi, Daniel Defoe, and many others) and what he learns from each (from Whitman, the dream of multiracial equality;

from Sholokhov, insight into the "collective faith of a people"; from Noguchi, a role model of another Asian-born migrant laborer turned revolutionary writer, etc.; 245). In the end, Carlos's literary education provides him a form of comparative knowledge through which he begins to see himself reflected in multiple political contexts, enabling him to imagine forms of identification that facilitate a broader and ultimately *cosmopolitan* perspective that transcends existing geographic and national borders and that, in turn, renders legible connections, communities, and ways of knowing excluded from and obfuscated by the nation and its continental ideal. "I discovered," Carlos declares, "that one writer led to another: that they were all moved by the same social force. . . . So from day to day I read, and reading widened my mental horizon, creating a spiritual kinship with other men who had pondered over the miseries of their countries. . . . I, too, reacted to my time. I promised myself that I would read ten thousand books when I got well. I plunged into books, boring through the earth's core, leveling all seas and oceans, swimming in the constellations" (246). While the "antidevelopment" of Carlos's migrant journey of flight forced him "inward" into social, geographic, and epistemological isolation, here reading enables Carlos to map an alternative narrative of development in which the study of one writer leads to another, engendering an ever-"widening" *imaginative* awareness of his relationship to a global network of disparate struggles. In fact, he provides here a suggestive archipelagic counterimage to that of isolated "narrow islands of despair" in his evocation of the disparate stars across the night sky organized in coherent formations of constellations.

In the end, Carlos's literary education engenders a model of self-formation that challenges the assumption of a unitary and essentially solitary heroic development in the traditional bildungsroman model. Instead, *America Is in the Heart* fashions an alternative model of Bildung founded on a principle of what we might call "spatialization" (the image the novel invokes most frequently and admiringly, as it does in the passage above, being that of "boundlessness"). That is, Carlos's education and development is marked or defined by his ability to establish "widening" identifications that dissolve the borders between himself, his situation, and his story and those of others (e.g., "I felt a great urge to identify myself with the social awakening of my people"; 139). Carlos's self-formation is thus defined, in the last instance, less by his ability to reassemble the story of his *personal* development than by his ability, ultimately, to *de*personalize himself and his story. Put differently, *America Is in the Heart*'s narrative of development is based on the move from a personal to an impersonal voice—from an individual to a collective experience (Fredric Jameson has termed this type of literary narrative of transformation from an individual to collective voice a form of "counterautobiography").[13]

This counterautobiographical trajectory from an individual to a collective experience brings us not only forward but also back, in many regards, to the Philippines. As already suggested, the early part of the novel provides glimmers of other—collective—forms of life existing in the Philippines (i.e., forms of "boundless affinity"). These other modes of living are, in turn, depicted as eroding in the face of a superimposed US-American modernity driving toward greater individualism—a narrative of "development" that culminates with Carlos's enforced individualism and isolation as he moves to and within the United States. Thus while the collective ethos of Carlos's alternative model of Bildung emerges from, and is a rejection of, the individualistic "insular" life he is forced to live within modern "America," it is also a return to and retooling of (now within a radical labor movement context) a collective ethos he locates in the peasant life of the Philippines archipelago, as an alternative to that US-American insular modernity.

In the end, this ethos of collective development poses, at once, a challenge to the form of the nation (in suggesting alternative modes and topographies of collectivity) and also, correspondingly, to the form and logic of the bildungsroman. Rather than a centering of bourgeois subjectivity through the emergence and assimilation of the individual protagonist (as in the canonical case of *Robinson Crusoe*), *America Is in the Heart* refigures the genre, forging an alternative bildungsroman born out of Carlos's insular "castaway" status that maps a decentering of the narrator's subjectivity across an ever-widening community (or "constellation") of social commitments. It is an archipelagic cosmopolitanism—one not contained by narratives of US citizenship and belonging—that is capable of rendering and linking together politically, epistemologically, and aesthetically those "narrow islands of despair" both inside and outside the nation.

AMERICA'S ARCHIPELAGO

But who, more precisely, constitutes this archipelagic community? Near the end of the novel, Carlos and his brother Macario meet to discuss strategies for developing a Filipino labor movement. In one of several such instances in the novel, Macario reframes this political task as part of a much broader discursive project to recover a usable tradition of Americanism. The effort leads to a melodramatic reaffirmation of his belief in "America" as a yet unfulfilled emancipatory project: "America," he declares, is "not a land of one race or one class . . . [but a] prophecy of a new society of men" (189). But then Macario concludes by declaring his commitment to an alternate community and a much darker "prophecy" of America: "America is also the nameless foreigner, the homeless refugee, the hungry boy begging for a job and the black boy dangling on a tree. America is the illiterate immigrant who is ashamed that the world of books and intellectual opportunities is closed to him. We are all that nameless foreigner, that homeless refugee, that hungry boy, that illiterate immigrant and that lynched black body. All of us, from the first Adams to the last Filipino, native born or alien, educated or illiterate—*We are America!*" (189). It is hard not to hear beneath this language a haunted countervoice to the immigrant narrative of the United States ("Give me your tired, your poor, your huddled masses . . ."). But rather than a liberatory national narrative of integration, Macario's vision testifies to a violent tradition of exclusion at the "heart" of "America." It is significant in this regard that the "also" drops out of the equation: it moves from "America is *also*" in the first sentence to the final "We are America." The final switch suggests that while Macario's declaration serves to affirm his commitment to "America," it also, more poignantly, reveals how these figures represent not historical aberrations but structural necessities in the very construction of "America." It exposes, in other words, how US-America's inclusive ideal has relied upon a long tradition of structured and violent exclusion that has served as its seemingly inevitable historical accomplice. (This is captured saliently in Macario's inclusion of the "last Filipino" within the "we" of America, a gesture that subtly but critically suggests the "insular case" of the Philippines and the corresponding exclusionary status of Filipinos as US nationals but never citizens.)

Macario's final emphatic declaration of "We are America" is thus not merely a call for the incorporation of these subaltern figures into a more inclusive "America" but a call as well for making them the bearers and definition *of* America. As such, Macario's embrace of "America" is a profoundly dialectical one, as is the novel's. In claiming "America" from this standpoint of exclusion, Macario at once identifies America with his emancipatory ideals but also makes those American ideals bear the experiences of precisely those subjects and geographies of racial, class, and colonial subalternity that have served as the United States' necessary externality. Thus in making "America" his own, Macario's definition of it cannot be integrated within its existing political and territorial horizons but requires its remapping.

Put slightly differently, Macario redeploys the language of "America" to define not the national community but its disavowed counterpoint—a heterogeneous subaltern community of racialized nonnational subjects laboring in the shadows of the United States. It is, to reinvoke *Robinson Crusoe*, a community of "castaways"—that is, one increasingly composed of regional and global migrants "voyaging in" from the world's "periphery" to narrow islands of despair in the "metropole." It is, as such, an "American" community consistent with the unique formation of capital and of empire represented by the United States during the twentieth century—one in which racialized exclusion from citizenship and national belonging, and not simply class consciousness, will define their political and economic identities. Neither citizens nor the proletariat, these "castaways" constitute instead a multiracial stateless subaltern counterpublic in the shadows of a global twentieth-century economic and political order increasingly dominated by the United States. And it is this community at the representational limits of the nation—and the novel—that Bulosan moves from the periphery into the central vantage point from which to remap "America" into the world. It is a remapping that reorders the American landscape, rendering a displaced and disavowed social and political topography—an archipelago of nonnational subjects and spaces that traverses the borders of the United States and thus dismantles the opposition between inclusion and exclusion, and between continent and island, upon which the nation has depended for its ideological and territorial coherence.

In animating what we might define as an insular vision of a transnational America, Bulosan's subaltern counterpublic of "castaways" suggests another "castaway" community—namely, those whom C. L. R. James would famously define only a few years later, in 1952, as the "mariners, renegades, and castaways" of the modern and postmodern world. Written during his imprisonment as an undesirable alien on Ellis Island in the early Cold War, James's rereading and reimagining of Melville's *Moby Dick* represents, according to Donald Pease, an axiomatic expression of transnational American studies.[14] What is worth noting in this context, however, is how central the figure of the *island* was to James's—as it was to Bulosan's—transnational vision (something captured in the very figure of the castaway). Indeed, the island is central for James both as a critical vantage point (i.e., his island prison) and in defining the terms of this subaltern counterpublic of "mariners, renegades, and castaways." "They came from all over the world," he writes, "were islanders from places like the Azores and the Shetland Islands. Nearly all on Ahab's ship were islanders."[15] Thus if James's "mariners, renegades, and castaways" represent a foundational model for a new transnational American studies (as do the island "castaways" of Bulosan, I would argue), then we might recognize the crucial though largely uncommented role of the insular not only in the formation of these stateless subaltern counterpublics but also, in turn, in the very constitution of the field imaginary of transnational American studies.

THE BOUNDLESSNESS OF THE "AMERICAN" FRONTIER

Let me turn finally to the closing image of *America Is in the Heart* and its enigmatic, and much debated, final embrace of "America." It is the morning after his brother Macario has left to join the army (following the Japanese invasion of the

Philippines during World War II), and Carlos sets off for yet another journey, this time up to the cannery workers in Portland:

> I looked out of the bus window. I wanted to shout good-bye to the Filipino pea pickers in the fields who stopped working when the bus came into view. How many times in the past had I done just that? They looked toward the highway and raised their hands. One of them, who looked like my brother Amado, took off his hat. The wind played in his hair. There was a sweet fragrance in the air.
>
> Then I heard the bells ringing from the hills—like the bells that had tolled in the church tower when I had left Binalonan. I glanced out of the window again to look at the broad land I dreamed so much about, only to discover with astonishment that the American earth was like a huge heart unfolding warmly to receive me. I felt it spreading through my being, warming me with its glowing reality. (326)

The declaration of "the American earth" spreading warmly through his being, especially coming as it does at the very end of the novel, has served as perhaps the defining moment for so many critics to either celebrate or castigate Bulosan's novel as a reaffirmation of the US-American immigrant story of assimilation. But if we resituate this passage—this embrace of "America"—within an archipelagic frame, it reveals, perhaps, a far more unsettled and unsettling perfect union.

In one sense, this climactic image of Carlos seeing the "*broad* land" he had always dreamed of, and of the "*boundless* American earth" like a "*huge* heart unfolding warmly"—integrating individuals and dissolving borders as it spreads—appears to reproduce a rhetoric of US-American continental exceptionalism. That is, it reiterates an ideology about the vast scale and, in turn, possibility inscribed within the "boundless" American landscape that so much of the novel had appeared to put into question. But crucially, what actually triggers the "astonishing" epiphany, wherein the American earth suddenly and sublimely transforms into a huge unfolding heart, are the sounds of bells, "like the bells that had tolled in the church tower when I had left Binalonan." These sounds function not just as a moment of nostalgia but rather also perform a metonymic function, in effect collapsing the boundaries between the two spaces, and thus transforming the "American earth" into a postnational archipelagic space, extending beyond the boundaries of the nation's perimeters to incorporate the colonial space of the Philippines.

In other words, the blurring of borders between Carlos and the American earth—once again a climactic bildungsroman image of integration between the individual and "America"—actually coincides with the collapsing of borders between America and the Philippines. As such, this postnational space actually draws to the surface and renders legible the underside of American "boundlessness." That is, while the boundlessness of America invokes a narrative and logic of US-American continental exceptionalism and imperial expansion, that very boundlessness also carries within it the potential to destabilize its own borders and to produce new forms of collectivity and identity that overflow these borders. Amy Kaplan has referred to this capacity of imperialism to produce the terms of its own unraveling as the "anarchy" of empire, though we might also think, more specifically in this context, of Antonio Benítez-Rojo's related notion of the "chaos" of the repeating island. That is, the scene traces a repetition of the islands of the Philippines within the United States that chaotically disrupts and unravels the binary established between US-America and the Philippines; between metropole and colony; and between continent and island.[16]

Thus Carlos's final embrace of "America" does not just mark an end to his foreign estrangement but also makes America foreign to itself: it brings the political geography of empire and migrant labor into the very "heart" of a postnational America. In turn, the image of a "boundless affinity," which Carlos uses to represent the form of global belonging (as "boundless as this green earth") to which his alternative literary and aesthetic education leads him to aspire and in which his bildungsroman culminates, does not merely affirm or critique "America" but rather suggests a kind of archipelagic universalism transvalued from *within* US-American imperial and capitalist expansion itself, in its capacity for unraveling boundaries between nations, peoples, and those "narrow islands of despair" both within and outside the nation.

Finally, it is worth considering, in this context, the final conversation that Carlos and Macario have on the eve of Macario's departure, in which they discuss, one last time, *Robinson Crusoe*. Macario's reading of the text has now subtly but profoundly shifted from the novel's beginning. "He laughed when he recalled the story of *Robinson Crusoe*. 'The whole world is an island,' he said again remembering. 'We are cast upon the sea of life hoping to land somewhere in the world. *But there is only one island, and it is in the heart*'" (323). Here, ultimately, the image of the island no longer signifies isolation or boundedness but has taken on a cosmopolitan, indeed planetary, scale and figuration. It has come to define an alternative, global form of becoming and belonging. In this respect, Macario's final rereading of *Robinson Crusoe* mirrors the larger project of *America Is in the Heart* as a whole, namely, to find in the figure of the island a form for imagining alternative geographic imaginaries for thinking of and belonging in this world beyond nations and continents.

NOTES

1. Carlos Bulosan, *America Is in the Heart* (1946; repr., Seattle: University of Washington Press, 1976), 32.
2. Edward Said, *Culture and Imperialism* (New York: Vintage, 1994), 239–62.
3. Elizabeth M. DeLoughrey, *Routes and Roots: Navigating Caribbean and Pacific Island Literatures* (Honolulu: University of Hawai'i Press, 2007), 12–13. See also Elizabeth DeLoughrey, "'The litany of islands, The rosary of archipelagoes': Caribbean and Pacific Archipelagraphy," *ARIEL: A Review of International English Literature* 32, no. 1 (2001): 21–61.
4. For a discussion of "continental exceptionalism," see Brian Russell Roberts and Michelle Stephens, "Archipelagic American Studies and the Caribbean," *Journal of Transnational American Studies* 5, no. 1 (2013): 5–10. See also Martin W. Lewis and Kären Wigan, *The Myth of Continents: A Critique of Metageography* (Berkeley: University of California Press, 1997).
5. Crusoe's salvaged library consists of "Books of Navigation . . . three very good Bibles . . . some *Portugeze* Books also, and among them two or three Popish Prayer-Books, and several other Books, all which I carefully secur'd." Daniel Defoe, *Robinson Crusoe: A Norton Critical Edition,* 2nd ed., ed. Michael Shinagel (New York: W. W. Norton, 1994), 48.
6. Janet Hoskins and Viet Thanh Nguyen, *Transpacific Studies: Framing an Emerging Field* (Honolulu: University of Hawai'i Press, 2014), 9.
7. Sua-ling Cynthia Wong, *Reading Asian American Literature: From Necessity to Extravagance* (Princeton, NJ: Princeton University Press, 1993), 134–35.
8. Franco Moretti, *The Way of the World* (London: Verso, 1987), 4.
9. Quoted in Christina Duffy Burnett and Burke Marshall, eds., *Foreign in a Domestic Sense: Puerto Rico, American Expansion, and the Constitution* (Durham, NC: Duke University Press, 2001), 5. For a discussion of this category, see Mae Ngai's *Impossible Subjects: Illegal Aliens and the Making of Modern America* (Princeton, NJ: Princeton University Press, 2004), 96–126; see also Amy Kaplan, *The Anarchy of Empire in the Making of U.S. Culture* (Cambridge, MA: Harvard University Press, 2002), 1–12.
10. Epifanio San Juan Jr., *The Philippine Temptation: Dialectics of Philippines-U.S. Literary Relations* (Philadelphia, PA: Temple University Press, 1996), 133.
11. Defoe, *Robinson Crusoe*, 60.
12. Roberts and Stephens, "Archipelagic American Studies," 8.
13. Fredric Jameson, "On Literary and Cultural Import-Substitution in the Third World: The Case of the Testimonio," *Margins* 1 (spring 1991): 11–34.
14. Donald Pease, "C. L. R. James, *Moby Dick*, and the Emergence of Transnational American Studies," *Arizona Quarterly* 56, no. 3 (2000): 93–123.
15. C. L. R. James, *Mariners, Renegades, and Castaways: The Story of Herman Melville and the World We Live In* (Hanover, NH: University Press of New England, 2001), 18.
16. Kaplan, *Anarchy of Empire*, 12–15.

8   "MYTH OF THE CONTINENTS"

AMERICAN VULNERABILITIES AND "RUM AND COCA-COLA"

Nicole A. Waligora-Davis

IN 1945 THE ANDREWS SISTERS dominated the US Billboard charts, holding captive three of the top four slots with their immensely popular "Rum and Coca-Cola," "Don't Fence Me In," and "Ac-Cent-Tchu-Ate the Positive."[1] "Rum and Coca-Cola," a calypso tune, transfixed US-Americans, settling in at the top slot for ten straight weeks. This seemingly US hit traveled the world by virtue of radio waves and record players, and by way of the Andrews themselves, who routinely performed the song during an eight-week United Service Organization (USO) tour for US soldiers stationed abroad. "Rum and Coca-Cola" quickly became, in the words of the Andrews, "the national anthem of the GI camps."[2] What was for these singers pithy shorthand capturing the popularity of this song ("national anthem") is as well a telling caption of the history of US-Caribbean relations from World War II to the civil rights movement, and arguably beyond. The circulation of this song, the copyright infringement cases pursued (in 1945–48), and the social histories marshaled in its lyrics, provide an entry point for understanding US militarization in the West Indies and its reciprocal social, political, economic, and cultural effects. Differently torqued, the history and metahistory embedded in this song place under suspicion state narratives of US continentalism and reveal how the Caribbean, to cite a 1941 article by Trinidadian historian Eric Williams, is in fact "*de jure* as well as *de facto* 'our sea' in the American use of the term."[3] The history of US-Trinidadian relations during World War II thickens our perception of island-continent interrelations, and worries a tradition of American continentalism that narrowly reads islands as isolated, peripheral, and ancillary.

"Rum and Coca-Cola," originally written and performed in 1943 by Trinidadian Rupert Westmore Grant (stage name Lord Invader), who transposed his lyrics onto Lionel Belasco's early twentieth-century tune "L'année passé," was created for a Trinidadian calypso tent show and immediately published and copyrighted in a Trinidadian World War II song catalogue, *Victory Calypsoes 1943 Souvenir Collection*. An instant island sensation, this calypso was summarily stolen by visiting USO entertainer Morey Amsterdam, who revised a few lines, quickly secured a US copyright, and licensed Invader's song to US performers. The lyrics and legal history of Invader's/Belasco's composition place in relief a politics of (unlawful and gratuitous) consumption that defines a long history of US policy and practice in the Caribbean. The range of counterclaims Amsterdam employed to defuse the plaintiff's infringement claim—involving obscenity protection, public domain, laches, and improper copyright transfer—mirror the proprietary (US-American) colonial politics that understood the West Indies, its peoples, and its resources as possessions, as extensions of the United States' own backyard.[4] For Invader, however, the lyrics accurately measured encounters between US-Americans and Trinidadians on the island: each stanza detailed the social effects of thousands of US troops arriving and being stationed in Trinidad following US acquisition of ninety-nine-year land leases to build bases in 1941 on six British colonial possessions in the Caribbean. This arrangement benefited both countries: a war-embattled England gained desperately needed ships for its navy, and the United States gained a wider sweep of protection in the Western Hemisphere. Trading fifty over-age destroyers for these lease rights, President Franklin Delano Roosevelt's exchange guaranteed unmitigated access to these islands in what a US-based perspective has often viewed as "America's lake"—their land, waterways, and airspace—and deepened US influence over the economic and social policy of these countries at the very moment when US rhetoric advocating democracy and self-determination for colonial territories and dependencies was at a fever pitch.

The circulation and social history of Invader's stolen calypso do more than place in relief US militarization efforts and long-standing practices and commitments to empire building in the Antilles; they also focalize a turn in US geopolitics and national defense strategy away from isolationism and toward an understanding of the world as a global theater of potential threat against US safety and interests. Roosevelt's base agreement materializes this geopolitical turn and underscores the fiction belying continentalism—continents *are* vulnerable. By reading archipelagically we gain a nuanced understanding of continent/island relations that dispels, by reversing, the myth of which space is vulnerable (continent) and which facilitates expansion (island archipelago). In its shared status as calypso and national anthem for US military service personnel, "Rum and Coca-Cola" manifests and historicizes the effects of this signal turning point in US foreign policy practice.

"DANGEROUSLY VULNERABLE"

Traveling aboard the presidential train on September 30, 1940, Franklin Delano Roosevelt offered a bit of continental US-American history to reporters assembled for a press conference engaging domestic and foreign policy. Reading from the draft of a speech on the base treaty that he later shared with Congress, Roosevelt equated the national security value of US militarization in the West Indies to the Louisiana Purchase of 1803. "This is the most important action in the reinforcement of our national defense that has taken place since the Louisiana Purchase," Roosevelt boasted. He continued, "The value to the Western Hemisphere of these outposts of Security is beyond calculation. . . . They are essential to the protection of the Panama Canal, Central America, the Northern portion of South America, The Antilles, Canada, Mexico, and our own Eastern and Gulf Seaboards."[5]

This trope of the benevolent US protector of the Western Hemisphere, couched also in Roosevelt's geographical litany, does little to mask a proprietary imperative fueled by a long history of US dependency on the West Indies—not least on its labor, its raw materials, its land, and its waterways. The trade of fifty World War I destroyers for unmitigated access to Bermuda, the Bahamas, Jamaica, Saint Lucia, Trinidad, Antigua, and British Guiana betrayed the widening gulf between the stated democratic claims of the republic and its expanding empire.[6] The United States signaled its concerns over the welfare of peoples in the archipelago in the formation of the Anglo-American Caribbean Commission (later Caribbean Commission) and its auxiliary Caribbean Research Council and West Indian Conference—all part and parcel of a larger US security project. Roosevelt's justification for US militarization in the Caribbean as an act of defense that was "an inalienable prerogative of a sovereign state"[7] casts the rhetoric of inter-American cooperation that marked official diplomatic correspondence in ways that his comparative reference to the Louisiana Purchase tellingly intimates.

In a boisterous tongue, FDR continued his train-car lesson on US-American history, candidly discussing how the Louisiana Territory served as the linchpin for the difference between a United States whose borders ended with the Mississippi and a nation that could extend "clear up to Montana."[8] By FDR's estimate, the territory covered by the Louisiana Purchase "is one-third of the whole of the United States."[9] Though separated by more than one hundred years, each of these acquisitions (one on the continent, and one in the Caribbean) reveals the real or perceived risk mobilizing US landgrabs that effectively (if even only temporarily in the case of the Caribbean) transformed US geopolitical borders. Addressing the Academy of Political Science in 1941, Rear Admiral Clark Howell

Woodward, the United States Navy commandant of the Third Naval District, celebrated the scale of "this far-flung outer line": Roosevelt's imperial bargain produced "a new defense curtain of steel stretching 4500 miles from Newfoundland on the north to British Guiana on the south, and screening America's east coast."[10] Woodward's "far-flung outer line" speaks to the geographical breadth the United States gained through the base agreement; it marks the incorporation of the extraterritorial, the Caribbean, into US terrain. The Churchill-Roosevelt deal resuscitated proprietary imperatives that governed US geopolitical expansion from the earliest moments of our national formation in the late eighteenth century to Manifest Destiny in the nineteenth century onward to the Monroe Doctrine, the Roosevelt Corollary, the Good Neighbor Policy, and the Act of Havana in the twentieth century.[11] "Destroyers for Bases" further formalized ambitions already evident in multinational treaties such as the Act of Havana (1940), an agreement that the *Chicago Defender*'s Metz Lochard insisted "provides for unceremonious seizure of European possessions in the Western Hemisphere" by the United States should it feel threatened. For Lochard, the Havana Act was little more than a veiled campaign to "loot weaker states" packaged as "continental solidarity."[12]

Lochard's geographical shorthand for complex inter-American geopolitics—"continental solidarity"—offers plain speech and transparency to a set of US-American foreign diplomacy maneuvers that were anything but benign, and nothing short of deeply self-interested. The ninety-nine-year naval base lease transformed long-standing threats made by the United States against the incursion of foreign powers in the Atlantic into ever more real possibilities, fueled congressional and popular debates over acquiring the West Indies, and rendered the archipelago "America's lake." In this way, the Roosevelt-Churchill contract emblematizes a continentalist logic and the (racialized) imperial designs governing this discourse. The British West Indies' subsumption within the geopolitical boundaries of the United States made possible by this arrangement bears out the teleology of continentalist politics. Roosevelt's assertion of the "inalienable prerogative of a sovereign state" to justify appropriating these islands poignantly signals the ways in which continentalist thought, according to Brian Russell Roberts and Michelle Stephens, relies on two contradictory readings of islands—"bounded" on the one hand, and ideally suited for expansion on the other.[13] Calling to task the epistemological effects of an anti-insular rhetoric shaping American studies since the late twentieth century, Roberts and Stephens write,

> On the one hand, much of anti-insular sentiment is the effect of a discourse with a fundamentally *continental* logic, pitting a continental and cosmopolitan universalism against more island-bound creole forms, and thereby ratio-

nalizing Euro-American domination of island spaces. Yet continental logic's construction of island-space as quintessentially *bounded* also has evoked the island in terms particularly useful to imperial nationalism and the politics of sovereignty. As land masses whose most salient attribute lies precisely in their boundedness, islands have been key in utopian visions of national sovereignty. Thus, even as the island's insularity has been enduringly framed in a negative way within traditions dedicated to rationalizing continental superiority and imperial expansion, the insularity of island spaces has nonetheless emerged as persistently useful to the project of imaging the self-enclosed national space.[14]

For critics such as Vincent Byas, the expanded US military presence in the Caribbean brokered through the base compact discomfitingly reflected the "steady march of necessitated conquest,"[15] a conquest driven by the vulnerability of an underprotected US Atlantic coast and the Panama Canal—gates to key transcontinental waterways for transporting goods and resources vital to the US economy and national security that ranged from sugar to oil to bauxite and copper.[16] For Rear Admiral Woodward, it was not simply that this US "acquisition" promised to increase "our east coast security by at least 75 per cent," but that *"without them our security plans would have remained dangerously vulnerable."*[17]

In the spring of 1940, a year before the base accord was complete, FDR repeatedly addressed the flawed logic of a continental defense strategy for a nation occupying a world in which aviation, naval, and missile technology had effectively shrunk the globe. In radio-broadcast fireside chats to the nation, speeches before Congress, and lectures to professional societies and universities FDR outlined the hazards of subscribing to "some form of mystic immunity" based on "a false teaching of geography," of continuing to believe "that we could maintain our physical safety by retiring within our continental boundaries."[18] For FDR, isolationist ideology and its concomitant continental-defense approach to national security read like a perverse dream that promised to transform the United States into the quintessential mark of vulnerability—an island:

> Some indeed still hold to the now somewhat obvious delusion that we of the United States can safely permit the United States to become a lone island, a lone island in a world dominated by the philosophy of force. Such an island may be the dream of those who still talk and vote as isolationists. Such an island represents to me and to the overwhelming majority of Americans today a helpless nightmare of a people without freedom—the nightmare of a people lodged in prison, handcuffed, hungry, and fed through the bars from day to day by the contemptuous, unpitying masters of other continents.[19]

Innovations across multiple fields, including warfare, paradigmatically shifted the discourse and enactment of foreign policy precisely because "the basic geographical foundations of our national security" had now been radically and irrevocably altered; US security vulnerabilities had exponentially increased.[20] Roosevelt's comparison of an imperiled continental United States to an "island" strikingly rehearses the aporias and anachronisms of continentalism: drawn to its conclusion, US continentalism's logical fallacy argues that islands, unlike continents, are vulnerable (largely because of their presumed isolation and small size). But here it is the continental United States reimagined as an "island" that is at risk, and it is a chain of islands in the Antilles that promises this endangered continent protective cover.

This new defense strategy, anchored to geopolitics rather than scaled to continental sweep, unmoored and disarmed what political geographer Hans Weigert referred to as the "central strategy" of US foreign policy's continental defense up to this point, encapsulated in a certain geopolitical terrain and vision—"'the western hemisphere.'" Weigert penned,

> At one time President Roosevelt used to speak of "this hemisphere" or of "the western hemisphere" as if it were a clear regional concept permitting us to define geographically how far this country would go in defending and stabilizing its security zone.... Now, in the age of the B-36 and the atomic bomb, few can believe that the zone of North American security is that which was accepted, almost as a law of nature, ever since the Monroe Doctrine warned "Hands off the western hemisphere." *What is the western hemisphere? Where are its frontiers?*[21]

By 1959, J. A. Lukas's "The American Imperial Disease" described "an American world empire involving continents and an overwhelming network of American military bases abroad."[22] Within the ambit of a "shrunken globe," or the new global arrangement that Martin Luther King, Jr., described as "geographical togetherness" driven by scientific and technological innovation, "domestic" and "national" were ill-afforded parochialisms.[23] If national security had become contingent on the presence (and continued proliferation) of military bases around the globe, if it required a recalibration of the Western Hemisphere and its frontiers, then during World War II Trinidad became one of the most critical borders of this new US-American frontier.

Eleven years after Roosevelt requested a world map to show reporters the newly leased islands forming US-America's putatively protective curtain of steel, film director Vincent Sherman similarly employed cartography to remind US audiences of the central security role Trinidad played in US defense. Sherman's

Figure 8.1. Max Fabian, Franz Huebling, and a German arms buyer discuss how a newly fashioned ballistic missile launched from the West Indies places the continental United States at risk. Film still from *An Affair in Trinidad*, directed by Vincent Sherman. © 1952, renewed 1980 Columbia Pictures Industries, Inc. All Rights Reserved. Courtesy of Columbia Pictures.

An Affair in Trinidad (1952) illustrates the ways in which the Caribbean (even after World War II) haunted a US-American political and cultural unconscious as a potential site of vulnerability: here the archipelago figures as a site for Cold War espionage and a potential launchpad for wide-ranging nuclear assaults targeting the continental United States. *An Affair* tracks a widowed US expatriate coerced by a British Crown Inspector, Smythe, into spying on a family friend and known "saboteur for the enemy," Max Fabian. "We have reason to believe," worries Smythe, "that [Fabian] is engaged in activities that threaten our security."[24] But as the figure of a dead US-American's body dredged from a harbor in Port of Spain in the opening scene already intimates, it is not the United Kingdom but rather the United States that remains dangerously vulnerable.

In the film's final revelation of the saboteur's exploits, audiences watch an enraptured German arms buyer staring with bated breath at a world map broken by penciled lines marking the potential trajectory of a newly designed set of long-range ballistic missiles launched from Trinidad and engineered by Fabian's scientist-for-hire, Dr. Franz Huebling (figure 8.1). Reveling in his achievement,

Huebling translates the effects and efficiency of his bomb: "With launching bases in the Caribbean, there is not a vital area in the United States that is not within striking distance."[25] This map reenvisions, from a US perspective, the archipelagic net of defense needed on the surrounding islands to protect the continent. Indeed, both map and film uncannily rearticulate the very security concerns Roosevelt expressed regarding the Caribbean in the late 1930s and early 1940s: "The islands ring the Panama Canal. The occupation of any one of them by a possible enemy of American democracy would be a dagger pointed at the heart of this nation."[26] Speaking to a Congressional joint session in May 1940, Roosevelt warned, "If Bermuda fell into hostile hands, it is a matter of less than three hours for modern bombers to reach our shores."[27] Trinidad became the buckle in what war pundits and military experts alternately labeled the "safety belt" or "steel ring"—a "neutrality zone" composed of the British and French West Indies that cordoned off the Americas from foreign enemies.[28]

The presence of US military personnel stationed in the West Indies correlated with an increased cultural preoccupation with these island spaces, a preoccupation that translated into the production of numerous Hollywood and naval films and television shows, travel guides, adventure and mystery novels, island ethnographies, and a "calypso craze."[29] For some the Caribbean would come to represent a particular kind of American lifestyle, one that was easy to procure—direct Pan-American flights nicknamed "milk runs" for their convenience and affordability following postwar air travel and airport expansions, the seven-day calypso diet, and listening to "Miss Calypso" (Maya Angelou) recordings—and durable and pleasurable, such as owning an iconic Packard Caribbean sedan (1953–56).[30] Collectively and singly, these cultural objects, fetishes, and obsessions evince a cultivated political and cultural attitude toward the West Indies that militated against black antiracist and anticolonialist politics in both the United States and the Caribbean.

STOLEN (NATIONAL) ANTHEMS

Most visitors to the lovely island of Trinidad, have one pet question:

What is Calypso? Well ... the name by which the folk lore songs of the natives is designated is really and truly no Calypso at all. The real name for this form of song ... is 'Kalluso.' As to its meaning and origin, we can come to no other conclusion, but that it is lost in antiquity. The songs portray every aspect of local life and have lately even embraced international affairs.

MOHAMED KHAN

A 1951 article on calypso in Paul Robeson's *Freedom* newspaper opens with a verbal sweep that rehearses popular characterizations of this musical form.[31] It is a list evocative of the racialized vocabulary Hortense Spillers christened our "American Grammar": "'Exotic!' 'Charming!' 'Delightfully primitive!' 'Full of native simplicity!' 'So colorful!'"[32] The recurrence of these and similar colloquialisms for a musical tradition rooted in slavery whose form calypsonians define as Trinidadian "folklore," as "a style of singing, putting current events in the form of song,"[33] attests to the depoliticization that shaped a US reappropriation, commodification, and commercialization of this Trinidadian expressive tradition. *Freedom* describes a genre driven by political satire that in its taking to task the deleterious effects of British colonialism on its subjects led to the routine jailing of its performers and frequent censorship or banning of songs altogether "by the Colonial Secretary as 'subversive' or detrimental to the government." The first half of the twentieth century saw the passage of ever more regulatory legislation to curb the radical tenets of black nationalism and militantism that leaked into calypso: license requirements for tent shows, police surveillance over these performances, and state conflation of calypsonians with political propaganda. These shifts highlighted colonial administrators' anxious relation to the genre and its performers.[34] Yet the US calypso craze typically attributed to the 1950s—but that arguably, in fact, finds the trace of its beginnings much earlier with the Andrews Sisters' best-selling rendition of "Rum and Coca-Cola" or calypso covers by Ella Fitzgerald, Nat King Cole, or Louis Armstrong—neutered the discourse of resistance, the (decolonial) politics of opposition, that was calypso's idiom. Stripped of its "sharp topical comment and political satire," this craze left in its stead a "deliberately distorted . . . shell of its real self."[35]

Yet in analogy to the rhizomatic quality of calypso itself, I want to return to where this essay began—with a stolen anthem. The Andrews Sisters' designation of "Rum and Coca-Cola" as "the national anthem of the GI camps" was hardly the innocent bluster of performers; the song was a mainstay in their USO program and, as made clear by the court records in the copyright infringement suits brought by Mohamed H. Khan, Rupert Westmore Grant (Lord Invader), and Lionel Belasco against Leo Feist Incorporated, Paul Baron, and Morey Amsterdam, Invader's composition was regularly sung and adapted by US soldiers based in Trinidad.[36] In what could have been the hook for an entirely different tune, the three US soldiers who testified in *Khan vs. Feist* each reported that they "heard it almost everywhere."[37] And by 1945 hundreds of thousands of US-American listeners also heard this US billboard hit everywhere, thanks to Amsterdam's theft and the Andrews Sisters' subsequent recording and performances of the stolen calypso. The troupe's reference to "Rum and Coca-Cola" as a "national anthem" speaks to a problem of attunement, an audic dissonance that holds deeper implications for how we understand the (neo)colonial strands that inhere within the geopolitics of continentalism. This problem of attunement is announced in the radically different *hearing* that the label of a US national anthem affixed to "Rum and Coca Cola" makes poignantly evident. Simply, what does it mean when a cultural history of colonialism focused on the socioeconomic implications, violence, and sexual exploitation of a US military occupation becomes a celebrated anthem? What kind of signifying rupture occurs when the lyrics and rhythms of radical Afro-diasporic political consciousness are mistaken for a patriotic US-American tune? How does this reattunement operate as a neocolonial intervention against what Fred Moten pointedly characterizes as the arrhythmic postcolonial groove that *is* calypso?[38]

Perhaps it is best to return *again* to the beginning.

"The Calypso singer," insisted Mohamed H. Khan in his trial testimony, "is the mouthpiece of the inarticulate masses, and his power to determine public opinion is simply tremendous."[39] As "the mouthpiece" for his people singing a genre others described as "Trinidad's living newspaper,"[40] Invader's lyrics capture the complicated social and sexual relations produced by the presence of a US military force on an island where poverty affected so many, and where local Trinidadian wages registered like tin against the buying power of the US dollar. Here, figures are telling. Not unlike the wage economy in Panama that signaled the vast gap between US-Americans and Central Americans as the difference between gold or silver employees,[41] in Trinidad the salaries of white laborers were calculated in dollars per hour while Trinidadian rates remained scaled in coins. Documenting Trinidad's new foreign (i.e., US-American) labor pool, *Life* tabulated, "Mechanics earn from $54 to $82 for a 48-hour week; truck drivers, $464; carpenters and supervisors, $150; with time and a half for overtime. The native laborer earns an average of 92 cents a day, roughly 30 cents above the local prevailing wage, and thinks he's in clover."[42] Invader's "Rum and Coca-Cola" appropriates a nineteenth-century cultural slang as a catchphrase to caption the effects US military occupation had on the island's socioeconomic terrain, a phrase he later used as the title for a subsequent calypso in 1946: "Yankee dollar."[43]

The pay differential was not just a source of inter-racial conflict; it also affected intraracial relations between black GIs and local black men and women of the island. Sexual liaisons among black GIs and Trinidadian women were common and frequently transactional. Through these transactions, women gained access to money, resources, goods, and social spaces—capital—that located them precariously in relation to Trinidadian males, now often unable to successfully compete for their affections.[44] Invader's "Rum and Coca-Cola" captures the perspective of the spurned Trinidadian male in its lyrical indictment of an exploitive sexual politics driven by the United States' own colonial hierarchy of compensation that had devastating effects on local domestic arrangements: in thinly veiled language Invader describes a social economy transformed by the buying power of the US dollar wherein Trinidadian women engage and traffic in sexual liaisons with US GIs and contractors precisely because these arrangements prove socially and/or financially lucrative. A former major based in the Army Air Force in Trinidad, twenty-nine-year-old Seamus Nunan, testified in 1947, in *Khan vs. Feist,* that Invader's verses described the perceptible shift in local sexual politics effected by the presence of US troops: "Well, before the American soldiers came to Trinidad the native girls used to go out with the boys, natives; but after the American or Yankee soldiers came to Trinidad the girls found out by going out with the Americans they would spend more money on them."[45] Indeed, it was precisely because Invader's verses describe the "conduct of Trinidad women and American soldiers in a cheap and vulgar way" that Leo Feist Incorporated cited as part of its defense against copyright infringement that the "inherently salacious, immoral and lewd" nature of the song rendered it ineligible for copyright protection.[46] According to Invader, even the sanctity of the marriage bed fails to hold when measured against the shimmer of US money as young brides readily abandon their Trinidadian husbands for minted US soldiers. Here the calypso's titular commodity—"Rum and Coca-Cola"—consumed by GIs and Trinidadian women alike, stands as a placeholder for the Trinidadian women who become the purchased sexual object of Yankee consumption, the interethnic sexual liaisons that ensue, and the circulation of US dollars and popularity of US goods within Trinidad's economy.

Irrespective of whether these sexual liaisons among Trinidadian women and American men were legally "immoral" (i.e., prostitution), the coupled power and privilege marshaled in the Yankee dollar altered social relations, and in the frequent reports of altercations and even a riot, at times it did so violently.[47] "As is usual with the American soldier in a foreign country," chastened a former Trinidad Base Command officer, "they showed utter disrespect for the women whom they seemed to first regard as being there for their pleasure only."[48] The army's official history of the Trinidad sector acknowledged the recurring petitions directed to the commanding general by abandoned Trinidadian men "appealing to him for help and complaining about the soldiers taking away their girl friends" just as it recognized the ways in which the salary differential between local men and black US GIs affected Trinidadian sexual politics. It was acknowledged that the 99th Coast Artillery, a black military unit, "mixed quite freely with the blacks of all levels, and since, as American soldiers, they received much more money than the local men, they appealed more to the female element. The male civilians, on the other hand, resented the fact that these men had so much money to spend on entertainment, placing them out of competition."[49] Invader's 1946 sequel to "Rum and Coca-Cola," tellingly titled "Yankee Dollar" and sung with a lyrical lilt that belies its sobering message, rehearsed this familiar complaint: "She don't want no native fella, / So she told me plainly, / She love Yankee money, / And she said . . . Don't bother / If you know you ain't got the Yankee dollar."[50]

With only faint gestures toward the complex sexual and social politics marring US military and Trinidadian relations, US listeners hearing the Andrews Sisters' rendition would have been as unaware of the national histories and idioms that Lord Invader insists are the work of calypso as the singing troupe were admittedly uninterested in the lyrics themselves: "The rhythm . . . attracted the Andrews Sisters to 'Rum and Coca-Cola,'" confessed Maxine Andrews. "We never thought of the lyric . . . it was cute, but we didn't think of what it meant; but at that time, nobody else would think of it either, because we weren't as morally open as we are today and so, a lot of stuff—really, no excuses—just went over our heads."[51] The salacious content that Leo Feist Incorporated argued in court militated against any possibility of copyright protection would become under Amsterdam's hand sanitized lyrics whose descriptions of beaches and fun were more befitting of travel brochures than a calypso authored during the US militarization of the island.[52] Now, rather than being sung from the perspective of a jilted Trinidadian, the lyrics are rewritten to assume the perspective of a stateside US soldier helpfully orienting another (less knowledgeable) soldier before his potential deployment to Trinidad. Here not only the pleasures of listening to Calypso music are promised but the women that Invader insists are engaging in prostitution are skillfully recast as beach vendors selling rum and Coca-Cola to presumably thirsty US-American men. And while sexual innuendo remains present in the Andrews' rendition, particularly in the trope of dancing Native women who make every day feel like a celebration to the United States' uniformed men, it stops short with the proverbial kiss shared on a holiday and is a far cry from the cuckolding that occurs in Lord Invader's rendition. But this innuendo is, nonetheless, so slight that Khan's courtroom testimony best captures the Andrews' distortion: "The verses were sung about the same, but in view of the words comprised on the Decca record," he argued, "it seems they were *accents* of harmony with the syllables."[53]

Naming the flaw in the Andrews' rendition of Invader's song—"*accents* of harmony"—Khan fingers a dissonance manifested when an (originary) enunciative context is erased. With turns of phrase as subtly damaging as their performance was catchy, the Andrews' rendition reenvisions Trinidad as an outpost of empire such that the altered narrative perspective between the two versions—Invader's rejected Trinidadian male lover and the Andrews' cosmopolitan American male solider—meaningfully torques the signifying effect of a pronoun as seemingly simple and benign as the word "they." For Invader, the word "they" names the United States as an interloper and locates this singer, his experiences, and this island as the enunciative site—anchoring and central—to the geopolitical history shared. Here the United States, despite its military hegemony and in spite of its continental scale, is peripheral to the needs and daily living of this island's people. The Andrews' version of the song, however, privileges an imperializing US lens that renders Trinidad and its people ancillary. Insomuch as "they" in the Andrews' tune signifies Trinidadians, it reorients the focus away from the island's local communities and toward a United States cast as colonial metropole with this island its concomitant "backyard." Moreover, the singing troupe's singular investment in the geographical position of Trinidad relative to the United States as an island to the south reads as more than an attentiveness to geospatial specificity but also as a measure of the imputed moral distance between these two nation-states and the anticipated moral decline of US troops visiting the isle. So too, the references to US money do double time as geographical/cultural markers and as colonial codes freighted with the logic and entailments of superiority that are the kith and kin of imperialism.

ERASURE

Between December 1944 and February 1945, Leo Feist Incorporated printed a series of advertisements in *Variety Magazine*, the *New York Inquirer*, and a trade journal celebrating the commercial success of the Andrews Sisters' single (figure 8.2).[54] In one ad, a caricatured Jeri Sullavan stands beside a towering stack of sheet music firmly grasping a microphone that literally (and fallaciously) stakes her as being among the song's originators (her name frequently appeared on records minted, advertisements circulated, and sheet music sold for the calypso). Fraud aside, this ad captures the financial and, notably, *the political stakes* of appropriating authorship over this calypso. To read this ad or consume its listed product is to participate in the sale of a wholly US commodity, one disconnected, if not absolutely divorced, from the seat of its actual production—Trinidad. Rather, to listen to or purchase Amsterdam's musical score or Decca's "Rum and Coca-Cola" is to invite Jeri Sullavan or, more likely, the famous Andrews troubadours into your home. Zealously boasting the popularity of this song ("Most spectacular song success of the music business!" and "300,000 copies—first print order without a single radio plug!!"),[55] Feist's ad erases any trace of calypso as an archipelagic American cultural form of the Caribbean and instead fashions "Rum and Coca-Cola" as a continentally based US-American product by anchoring its inception and circulation to US female performers. Designating these US-Americans as composers and implying, as the ad does, that Jeri Sullavan "introduced" "Rum and Coca-Cola" at a popular New York nightclub, erases the enunciative context of this song. This effacement bears epistemological consequences: to undo, negate, or efface the enunciative context,

Figure 8.2. Advertisement appearing in *Weekly Variety*, January 17, 1945, 39. Variety © Variety Media, LLC.

particularly in relation to Antillean expressive cultural traditions in which geography conveys history and politics, is to defuse the signifying possibilities of these very cultural artifacts.

Simply, it is precisely because "Rum and Coca-Cola" circulated in USO performances around the world as an Andrews Sisters' jingle that GIs stationed outside the Caribbean basin would designate it as a "national" (read "US") anthem. This disarticulation of the political deafened audiences to Invader's critique of US militarization, and further populated a US cultural seedbed that flourished well into the 1950s calypso craze. This practiced disarticulation of political dissent that underlies US-American appropriations of Caribbean expressive forms is indicative of the very parochialism that US continentalist thought has ascribed to island nations. The irony here should not go understated. The very insularity credited to islands exposes a larger US national parochialism and ethnoracial chauvinism that permits a kind of sonic and semantic distortion—an out-of-tuneness—that willfully mishears and productively translates histories in service of larger geopolitical and economic imperatives of the US nation-state. The promotion and circulation of this song as a US ("national") anthem *conscripts* "Rum and Coca-Cola" for the cultural work of a US national project: it both negates the song's provenance and sidles past the "dangerous vulnerability" that precipitated US militarization on these islands. The *necessary* erasing of the Trinidadian relationship (to this song and to US security and economic interests) in order to successfully promote and popularize this calypso for US audiences parallels the *necessary* erasing of discourses of US vulnerability that warranted the presence of military bases in the Caribbean. In this way, the colonizing impulse signaled by the copyright theft of this tune discomfitingly echoes and reinforces the imperializing gestures, discourses, and practices that would come to mark and mar the US military presence on these islands.

Despite this history of cultural appropriation, we do well to remember that Invader's "Rum and Coca-Cola" *is* an anthem for Trinidad that bears the national idioms intrinsic to calypso. And in remembering the political dissonance and dissent underwriting Invader's anticolonial testimony, we might also remember that just as islands are far from peripheral to the geopolitical and economic interests of the United States, so too the supremacy of continents is nothing short of a myth. Along these lines, and recalling hemispheric American studies' valorization of José Martí's term *nuestra América* ("our America") as a means of looking toward a non-US-centric object of study within American studies,[56] I would riff on Eric Williams's deployment of the term "our sea" (quoted in this essay's introduction) to gesture toward a new American map in which seas may be American and yet not appurtenances of the United States, in which continental Americanism is recognized for what it is (mythic), and in which Americanist critical thought transitions toward postcontinental visions. On this map, Martí's "our America" overlaps with Williams's "our sea," undoing the epistemological and material frameworks that have attempted to efface our seas and our islands. On this map, we see in high relief the scattered and yet coherent American archipelagoes that have constituted the archipelagic Americas.

NOTES

1. "Best Sellers," *New York Times*, February 25, 1945, X5. The Andrews Sisters were accompanied by Bing Crosby in "Don't Fence Me In" and "Ac-Cent-Tchu-Ate the Positive."

2. "Andrews Sisters Back; Wonder How They're Going to Work for 'Ordinary Civilians,'" *New York Times*, August 21, 1945, 17.

3. Eric Williams, "Impact of the International Crisis upon the Negro in the Caribbean," *Journal of Negro Education* 10, no. 3 (July 1941): 540–41.

4. "Laches" is a technical legal term referring to a specific kind of defense involving equity issues in which the defendant is arguing (in this case) that the plaintiff filed their claim for damages too late. Each of the items in between the em dashes was a form of "defense" that the defendant mounted to counter the plaintiffs' copyright infringement claim.

5. Franklin Delano Roosevelt, "The Six Hundred and Seventy-Seventh Press Conference: On Board President's Train En Route to Washington, D.C. September 3, 1940," in *The Public Papers and Addresses of Franklin D. Roosevelt: With a Special Introduction and Explanatory Notes by President Roosevelt,* 1940 vol., *War and Aid to Democracies* (New York: Macmillan Company, 1941), 378.

6. Kelly Miller, "U.S. Grabbing for West Indies Shows Tendency of America to Sway from Democracy," *Chicago Defender,* December 2, 1939, 15.

7. Roosevelt, "Press Conference," 377–78.

8. Roosevelt, "Press Conference," 380.

9. Roosevelt, "Press Conference," 381.

10. Clark Howell Woodward, "Naval Strength," *Proceedings of the Academy of Political Science,* 19, no. 2 (January 1941): 26–27.

11. Brian Russell Roberts and Michelle Stephens compellingly trace the long history of continentalist thought undergirding these rationales for domestic and extraterritorial expansion beginning in the seventeenth century. They write, "The notion of continental primacy has had a long-running history in American thought. As historian James D. Drake has convincingly illustrated, North American colonists and US citizens of the seventeenth and eighteenth centuries developed a sense that their entitlement to national sovereignty was a logical corollary of North America's continental vastness, which was putatively superior to the insular smallness of England and the islands of the British Caribbean. . . . In the American context, a long-running formal distinction between small islands and the large continent has framed the continent as the massive and natural source of the US's drive toward hemispheric and planetary dominance"; Brian Russell Roberts and Michelle Stephens, "Archipelagic American Studies and the Caribbean," *Journal of Transnational American Studies* 5, no. 1 (2013): 8.

12. Metz T. P. Lochard, "West Indians Oppose Grab of Islands: Pan American Defense Plans Stirs Natives; Plead at Confab," *Chicago Defender,* August 10, 1940, 1.

13. Roberts and Stephens, "Archipelagic American Studies," 4.

14. Roberts and Stephens, "Archipelagic American Studies," 4.

15. Vincent W. Byas, "Whither Martinque?" *Phylon* 3, no. 3 (3rd qtr. 1942): 282–83.

16. The Guianas were a principal supplier of the bauxite used to fabricate the aluminum needed for US war-plane manufacturing. Likewise nearly fifteen thousand West Indians immigrated to the United States in 1943 to offset labor shortages caused by the war. Robert A. Johnston, 1st Lieutenant, Infantry, *History of the Trinidad Sector and Base Command, Vol. 1, Narrative Part One,* Historical Manuscript File, Office of the Chief of Military History, Special Staff US Army, 1946, 18; S. Burns Weston, "The Caribbean: Laboratory for Colonial Policy," *Antioch Review* 3, no. 3 (Autumn, 1944), 377. See also Christina J. Hostetter, "Sugar Allies: How Hershey and Coca-Cola Used Government Contracts and Sugar Exemptions to Elude Sugar Rationing Regulations" (master's thesis, University of Maryland, 2004); "West Indies Recommended for 'Strategic Materials,'" *New York Amsterdam Star-News,* June 20, 1942, 2; and Philip Bell, "Colonialism as a Problem in American Foreign Policy," *World Politics* 5, no. 1 (October 1952): 86–109.

17. Woodward, "Naval Strength," 28; emphasis added.

18. Franklin Delano Roosevelt, "Radio Address before the Eighth Pan American Scientific Congress," "At This Time When the World Is Threatened," and "We Will Extend to the Opponents of Force the Material Resources of this Nation," in *Public Papers of Franklin D. Roosevelt*, 186–87, 231, 261.

19. Roosevelt, "At This Time," 261.

20. Hans W. Weigert, "Strategic Bases and Collective Security," *Foreign Affairs* 25, no. 2 (January 1947): 251.

21. Weigert, "Strategic Bases," 251; emphasis added.

22. J. A. Lukas, "The American Imperial Disease," *American Scholar* 28, no. 2 (Spring 1959): 142.

23. Martin Luther King Jr., "Facing the Challenge of a New Age," *Phylon* 49, nos. 3/4 (Autumn–Winter, [1957] 2001), 286.

24. *An Affair in Trinidad*, DVD, directed by Vincent Sherman (1952; Culver City, CA: Sony Pictures, 2008).

25. *An Affair in Trinidad*, DVD, 1952.

26. Quoted in Reginald Pierrepointe, "West Indians in U.S. Back Roosevelt Stand," *New York Amsterdam News*, September 23, 1939, 5.

27. Quoted in Reginald Pierrepointe, "War Brings West Indies into Limelight: FDR's Speech Is Significant: Sees Islands as Possible Air Base for Raids on United States," *New York Amsterdam News*, May 25, 1940, 5.

28. Reginald Pierrepointe, "U.S. Maps Plan to Safeguard West Indies: U.S. Vows to Protect Western Hemisphere," *New York Amsterdam News*, October 14, 1939, 1; Johnston, *History of the Trinidad Sector*, 20–21; James C. Shoultz, Jr., Captain, CMP, *History of the Trinidad Sector and Base Command, Vol. II, Narrative Part Two*, Historical Manuscript File, Office of the Chief of Military History, Special Staff US Army, 1947, 131–32; A. M. Wendell Malliet, "W. Indians Should Oppose Imperialism: Must Be Alert to U.S. and British War Deals," *New York Amsterdam News*, February 27, 1945, 1.

29. See *Dirty Gertie from Harlem U.S.A., Island in the Sun, High Wind in Jamaica, Calypso Heat Wave, Calypso Joe, Bop Girl Goes Calypso*; Melville Herskovits's and Frances Herskovits's *Trinidad Village* (New York, NY: Alfred A. Knopf, 1947); John W. Vandercook's *Murder in Trinidad: A Case in the Career of Bertram Lynch, P.C.B.* (Garden City, NY: Doubleday, Doran & Co). Zora Neale Hurston, Harry Belafonte, William Grant Still, Alan Lomax, and Blind Blake cashed in on a US fascination with music from these islands.

30. Eunice Telfer Juckett, "Island Hopping in the West Indies: Network of Airlines Now Makes Extended Tour a Practical Reality," *New York Times*, October 26, 1952, XX3; Marilyn Kaytor, "Behind the Scenes—The Calypso Diet," *Look* 21, no. 15 (July 23, 1957): 47–48.

31. This section's epigraph is taken from Mohamed H. Khan vs. Leo Feist, Inc., et al., 165 F. 2d 188 (2d Cir. 1947), 63–64.

32. Hortense Spillers, "Mama's Baby / Papa's Maybe: An American Grammar Book," *Diacritics* 17, no. 2 (Summer, 1987): 64–81; "Calypso Songs Use Biting Satire to Criticize Colonial Rule," *Freedom* 1 (February 2, 1951), 6. My thanks to Cedric Tolliver for sharing this article from *Freedom* with me.

33. Testimony of Rupert Westmore Grant / Lord Invader, Transcript of Record at 75, Khan vs. Feist et al., 165 F. 2d 188 (2d Cir. 1947) (No. 20694).

34. "Calypso Songs," 6; Jocelyne Guilbault, *Governing Sound: The Cultural Politics of Trinidad's Carnival Musics* (Chicago: University of Chicago Press, 2007), 47. See also Gordon Rohlehr, *Calypso and Society in Pre-Independence Trinidad* (Port of Spain, Trinidad: G. Rohlehr, 1990).

35. "Calypso Songs," 6.

36. Transcript of Record at 131, Khan vs. Feist et al., 165 F. 2d 188 (2d Cir. 1947) (No. 20694).

37. Transcript of Record at 131, 136, 141, Khan vs. Feist et al., 165 F. 2d 188 (2d Cir. 1947) (No. 20694). Invader signed over exclusive rights "to the publication, distribution, sale, and use" of "Rum and Coca-Cola" to Khan, a Trinidadian entertainment promoter.

38. Speaking of Charles Mingus's disdain for the calypsonian music of free jazz musician Ornette Coleman, Fred Moten queries, "How does Mingus register, and how is he disrupted by, an arrhythmia that is driven by and towards the postcolonial?"; Fred Moten, "The New International of Rhythmic Feel/ings," unpublished manuscript, copy in author's possession, 17.

39. Transcript of Record at 63–64, Khan vs. Feist et al., 165 F. 2d 188 (2d Cir. 1947) (No. 20694).

40. Quoted in Donald Hill, *Calypso: Early Carnival Music in Trinidad* (Gainesville: University Press of Florida, 1993), 105.

41. In the Panama Canal Zone, West Indians were paid in silver while their American counterparts received gold. This differential produced its own shorthand for distinguishing labor communities now summarily labeled either "gold or silver employees"; John Biesanz, "Race Relations in the Canal Zone," *Phylon* 11, no. 1 (1950), 23.

42. Trevor L. Christie, "Yankees in Trinidad," *Life* 11, no. 20 (November 17, 1941): 20.

43. The use of the term "Yankee dollar" in the lyrics borrows from decades of international usage referring to the US dollar. An example of such usage is a traditional sailing song referenced in Charles Nordhoff's *Nine Years a Sailor: Being Sketches of Personal Experience in the United States Naval Service, the American and British Merchant Marine, and the Whaling Service* (Cincinnati, OH: Moore, Wilstach, Keys, 1857), 41.

44. Harvey Neptune, "Manly Rivalries and Mopsies: Gender, Nationality, and Sexuality in United States–Occupied Trinidad," *Radical History Review* 87 (2003): 78–95.

45. Transcript of Record at 128, Khan vs. Feist et al., 165 F. 2d 188 (2d Cir. 1947) (No. 20694).

46. Khan vs. Feist et al., 165 F. 2d 188 WL (2d Cir. December 20, 1947), 1; Transcript of Record at 10–11, Khan vs. Feist et al., 165 F. 2d 188 (2d Cir. 1947) (No. 20694).

47. United States contractors who arrived on the island were not always respectful of local law, nor necessarily willing to abandon the discriminatory race practices of US Jim Crow. James C. Shoultz, Jr. Captain, CMP, *History of the Trinidad Sector and Base Command*, James C. Shoultz, Jr. Captain, CMP, *History of the Trinidad Sector and Base Command, Vol. 5, International Relations*, Historical Manuscript File, Office of the Chief of Military History, Special Staff US Army, 1947, 131. The army's official

newspaper, *Trinidad News Tips*, circulated strategies for the "fostering of better relations" and managing an antiwhite sentiment among Trinidadians; Shoultz, *History of the Trinidad Sector*, 5:135. In April 1943 a riot ensued between black GIs and local Trinidadian men triggered by the percolating hostilities brewed through these shifting social relations, that lead to the brutal beating of civilians, injuries to innocent bystanders and local police, and property damage; Shoultz, *History of the Trinidad Sector*, 5:143. See also Harvey Neptune, *Caliban and the Yankees: Trinidad and the United States Occupation* (Chapel Hill: University of North Carolina Press, 2007), and "Manly Rivalries."

48. Quoted in Shoultz, *History of the Trinidad Sector*, 5:132.

49. Shoultz, *History of the Trinidad Sector*, 5:142.

50. Lord Invader, *Yankee Dollar, Lord Invader Calypso in New York: The Asch Recordings, 1946–1961*, track 10, compact disc, © 1946; 2000 Smithsonian Folkways Recordings, used by permission of Haka Taka Music (BMI).

51. Quoted in John Sforza, *Swing It! The Andrews Sisters Story* (Lexington: University Press of Kentucky, 2004), 76.

52. United States copyright protection excludes works deemed salacious; an exclusion that the defendants in Invader's infringement case readily attempted to exercise in their defense against the calypsonian's ownership claims by asserting that references to Yankees giving local women higher compensation for services rendered were thinly veiled references to solicitation. Transcript of Record at 128–19, Khan vs. Feist et al., 165 F. 2d 188 (2d Cir. 1947) (No. 20694).

53. Transcript of Record at 35, emphasis mine, Khan vs. Feist et al., 165 F. 2d 188 (2d Cir. 1947) (No. 20694).

54. Transcript of Record at 50, Khan vs. Feist et al., 165 F. 2d 188 (2d Cir. 1947) (No. 20694).

55. "Rum and Coca-Cola" advertisement, *Variety Magazine*, January 17, 1945, 39.

56. See Jeffrey Belnap and Raúl Fernández, eds., *José Martí's "Our America": From National to Hemispheric Cultural Studies* (Durham, NC: Duke University Press, 1998).

PART IV | **ISLANDS OF RESISTANCE**

9 | "SHADES OF PARADISE"

John Carlos Rowe | CRAIG SANTOS PEREZ'S TRANSPACIFIC VOYAGES

say we can cross

any body

of water if we believe in

our own breath—

CRAIG SANTOS PEREZ,
from unincorporated territory [saina], 2010

THE DEVELOPMENT OF TRANSPACIFIC STUDIES in contestation with approaches identified with the "Pacific Rim" has called special attention to sovereignty movements in the Pacific and the variety of peoples, cultures, and languages previously overlooked in our rush to connect East Asia and the United States. Looking directly at specific Pacific communities is certainly one distinctive feature of transpacific studies, but the very metaphor of sight seems contradicted by the critical term itself. Movement is registered optically in interrupted bursts, such as in the cinematic illusion created by twenty-four frames per second. But the issue of how to represent the "trans" in the "Pacific" is rendered even more problematic when we consider the multiple crossings involved for anyone who has lived in this vast region defined by ceaseless, complex, and contradictory passages.[1] Just how transpacific studies fits into a more broadly conceived "archipelagic American studies" depends crucially on theorizing how we "see" these multiple movements in the enormous Pacific region.

An older approach to "Pacific Islanders" attempted to challenge the Pacific Rim by insisting on specific objects of study within the Pacific. But as theoretically valid as such an approach seemed, it could not deal adequately with the movement of the peoples within the Pacific region, even those who had never traveled beyond their island homes. European, US, and Japanese colonialism in the Pacific produced political, economic, social, cultural, linguistic, environmental, and biological dislocations for most inhabitants, constituting massive diasporas at home and abroad. In diaspora studies, we do not write enough about domestic diasporas, in which people are forced from their homes by a wide variety of means: land theft and "removal," genocide, and the radical redefinition of where and how they live. Theorists of "settler colonialism," such as Patrick Wolfe and Lorenzo Veracini, contend that the settlers' purpose is to remove Indigenous peoples by violence and guile to occupy their territory.[2] Yet another purpose, perhaps more intentional than we often realize, is the production of cognitive dissonance that makes everyday life virtually impossible for an Indigenous person caught between familiar and suddenly imposed foreign epistemologies and languages.[3]

Forced to acquire new psychic, linguistic, economic, political, and cultural knowledge and the methods to translate or negotiate these different domains, the individual is profoundly alienated, often experiencing everyday life as social death.[4] The situation is compounded further by family and kinship relations in which individuals adapt unevenly to these colonial and postcolonial circumstances. Add to these factors the habitus of foreigners, including imported laborers, merchants (both resident and traveling), military personnel, and tourists. Postcolonial sovereignty movements have often assumed rigorous "nativist" positions that challenge the colonial traces still active in these different groups and planted deeply in the land and its history. Chinese laborers imported by the Spanish to the Philippines worked industriously to produce export goods for Spanish markets. As tools of Spanish imperialism, who competed with Indigenous workers and were themselves exploited, these Chinese nonetheless left their influences on the colonial and postcolonial Philippines.[5] In her criticism of how US educators in the Philippines combined Christian and US nationalist values to "convert" Filipinos to US politics and culture after the Spanish-American War, Susan K. Harris concludes, "American Protestant culture could not be exported" to the Philippines.[6] But the hybrid culture and economy in the Philippines of the twenty-first century suggests that the US sphere of influence has had a profound effect on all aspects of life.[7]

In a similar fashion, colonial economic and cultural forces motivate emigration on a scale and degree that is often indistinguishable from diaspora. With the post–World War II closure of the US naval bases in American Samoa, Samoans working for the US military immigrated to the United States, especially California, where they often found work with the US Navy and in related defense industries. By 2009, more people of Samoan descent lived in the United States (approximately 180,000) than in American Samoa (approximately 179,000). Legally "American nationals" (not "US citizens") in American Samoa, an unincorporated territory, Samoans could travel freely to Hawai'i and the rest of the United States in quest of work and could easily qualify for citizenship "stateside."[8] This emigration of American Samoans to Hawai'i and the West Coast is an unrecognized form of diaspora. The same might be said of dislocations caused by the radical degradation of the environment of many island communities, usually by colonial military powers using both the land and the sea for nuclear and other testing, and the dumping of toxic and related industrial waste. Although the removal of the inhabitants of the Pikinni Atoll (Republic of the Marshall Islands) before the United States' post–World War II nuclear testing has received considerable attention, there are many other examples of significant populations across the Pacific being forced to either move from their homes or suffer extreme biological injury by colonial military damage to the environment.[9]

These are just some of the reasons why sovereignty movements across the Pacific have faced such complex questions about inclusion and exclusion in the proposed or established nations. The Hawaiian sovereignty movement (in Hawaiian, *ke ea Hawai'i*) continues to debate how "Hawaiian nationals" will be determined if Hawaiian sovereignty should ever be achieved.[10] Legal definitions of affiliation are difficult to establish, given the complexities and multiple affiliations of most residents in a state such as Hawai'i, thanks in large part to colonialism and the various often-contradictory programs of assimilation and citizenship "rights." The circumstances in such an "unincorporated territory" as American Samoa are even more complicated, when we consider that two members of the same native Samoan family might well be separated legally, as "American national" and "US citizen," and may live as far apart as Pago Pago, American Samoa, and Long Beach, California.

"Native" or "Indigenous" identity is thus extraordinarily difficult to determine in many Pacific Island communities, encouraging "blood quantum" approaches that have virtually reinstated imperial racial categories for many Native Americans and Hawaiians.[11] Confronted by legal demands from both the US government and sovereignty movements for precise identification of one's affiliation, many people have abandoned political positions of any sort. In these circumstances, literature and other cultural work can do a great deal to provide the historical, rhetorical, linguistic, and cultural contexts to support different identifications with a "homeland" and thereby help galvanize new political solidarity otherwise difficult to achieve in fractured postcolonial situations. We usually understand that literature does this cultural work formally by means of response dynamics that attract diverse readers by providing them with a range of choices within a well-articulated field of possibilities.

In these complicated historical and intellectual contexts, then, I understand the paradigm of archipelagic American studies to include not only the specific island communities of the Pacific, Caribbean, Atlantic, Mediterranean, and Indian Oceans with specific importance for the Americas, but also to mean a methodology that is "archipelagic," working in some rhizomatic way resembling the "nomadology" theorized by Gilles Deleuze and Félix Guattari.[12] In the transpacific region, many Indigenous people living under the shadow of multiple colonial occupations and effects understand intimately the political and existential schizophrenia of capitalism and imperialism. What links these people with others around the globe is not necessarily their "insular" conditions but their *alienation* from power, rights, and representation. Thus transpacific studies and archipelagic American studies ought to share interests in how relations among disparate Indigenous, ethnically marginalized, and otherwise colonized peoples can be established as part of the work of decolonization. In short, the goals are not simply to create contexts for representing discrete and previously minoritized peoples across the island worlds covered by these new fields but also to find points of contact and interrelation that avoid the imperial frameworks and yet respect the cultural, linguistic, and regional differences of these many different regions.

This archipelagic methodology is more than merely a scholarly approach; it is also an alternative ontology for peoples who have experienced the multiple occupations of colonial powers. In *Routes and Roots,* Elizabeth M. DeLoughrey describes her own archipelagic methodology as relying on a "paradigm of rooted routes, of a mobile, flexible, and voyaging subject who is not physically or culturally circumscribed by the terrestrial boundaries of island space."[13] The effort to think beyond "terrestrial boundaries" also involves epistemological and ontological acts, not just scholarly methods, in order for one to become a "voyaging subject" capable of imagining the mobile lives of island people. Deleuze and Guattari's "rhizome" is a deeply European and in the end terrestrial concept, but it provides a useful analogy for those of us educated in this tradition to begin to think outside it and to approach an "archipelagic" mode without having lived the oceanic flow integral to island lives.

I want to be cautious not to connect too easily the island worlds of peoples living in very different regions, but there are certain repetitions in the colonial world system that render many Indigenous peoples as "Indians," "savages," "cannibals," and "primitives" in order to exploit their lives and lands. Antonio Benítez-Rojo opens *The Repeating Island: The Caribbean and the Postmodern Perspective* by noting how beneath the different "colonial experiences and languages" of the nations "'of the Caribbean basin,'" they nonetheless "share certain undeniable features."[14] To be sure, Benítez-Rojo's Caribbean has endured diverse but structurally similar imperial occupations in its modern history, so these repetitions are a bit clearer than they might be across the Pacific, where Asian, European, and US colonial occupations have often clashed in military, economic, political, and cultural ways with lasting influences on the Indigenous peoples of this enormous region. But Benítez-Rojo's idea of "the repeating island" still has relevance for understanding what has occurred in the multiple transgressions, many still under way, by the colonial world system in the transpacific region.

Craig Santos Perez's work as a Chamorro teacher, scholar, poet, and activist provides an exceptionally clear example of how archipelagic American studies encourages cultural specificity and yet works "nomadically" to connect with other peoples and through a wide range of disciplines. Perez's work is also characterized by its strategic repetitions of words, phrases, and places, often to indicate how buried Chamorro history is by the colonial world system's appropriative power. In rare cases, such repetitions work against the colonial grain, affirming a new power of self-determination and representation. I will focus on Perez's remarkable series of poems in his three volumes, *from unincoporated territory [hacha]* (2008), *from unincorporated territory [saina]* (2010), and *from unincorporated territory [guma']* (2014). Written in English, Chamorro, Spanish, and Japanese, and combining documentary materials with mythic, literary, and family stories, the three volumes constitute an ongoing series in the writer's effort to provide that cultural representation for the people of Guam (Guåhan) I consider a precondition for their political sovereignty and decolonization.[15] Of course, no single writer can perform this work on his or her own, but it is also true that new political and intellectual conditions may enable otherwise unrecognized writers and artists to intervene in politically significant ways.

Craig Santos Perez is a Chamorro creative writer and associate professor of English at the University of Hawai'i at Mānoa, where he teaches Pacific literature and creative writing. He completed his PhD in comparative ethnic studies at the University of California, Berkeley (2015); he earned his bachelor's degree at the University of Redlands (2002) and his masters of fine arts in creative writing from the University of San Francisco (2006). Winner of a Ford Foundation Predoctoral Fellowship and a Eugene Cota-Robles Fellowship, Perez has the credentials of one of our top scholars in ethnic studies.[16] His poetry draws centrally on Chamorro culture and language while indicting the destructive effects of Spanish, Japanese, and US colonial occupations of Guam. Yet that bare description does not express adequately Perez's ability to represent the deep investments in both the Native and colonial history of Guam that define virtually everyone connected with the island. His poetic project complements his scholarly and activist work for a decolonized, sovereign Guåhan, but Perez never allows anyone, least of all himself as the poet, to escape complicity with the imperialism that has so profoundly changed the island and its oceanic environment.

His series *from unincorporated territory* borrows widely from Chamorro, Euro-American, Spanish, Japanese, and other Pacific Island cultures. Polylingual, allusive, citational, and typographically avant-garde, the poetry reminds the reader of such modern experimentalists as Ezra Pound, T. S. Eliot, Charles Olson, and e. e. cummings while constantly stressing how their poetry is profoundly tied to Western imperialism. Early in the third volume, *[guma']*, for example, Perez begins one poem, "*ginen* ta(la)ya," with an epigraph from Pound's infamous radio broadcasts from Italy during World War II, in which Pound proposes to negotiate peace with the Japanese in the Pacific by trading Guam for "*the 300 best Noh dramas.*"[17] Pound's poetic persona, Hugh Selwyn Mauberley, ends his poetic journey as "an hedonist," shipwrecked on a "coracle of Pacific voyaging," in a modernist fantasy of wanderlust that has nothing to do with the realities of the Pacific.[18] A latter-day Odysseus or Elpenor, Mauberley ought to have been stranded on some Aegean island. Nevertheless, the avant-garde poetry of Pound and other Euro-American modernists also inspires Perez, especially as he adapts its radical free verse to his transpacific interests. James Joyce famously begins *Finnegans Wake* in the middle of a sentence—"river run past Eve and Adam's . . ."—and Perez's series, *from unincorporated territory*, begins with a lower-case preposition specifically noting the derivative status of his work. Perez is able both to criticize and repurpose his sources in ways that connect his anticolonial intentions with his sense of historical responsibility. For Perez, we decolonize effectively when we remember the persistence of colonial forces in our politics and culture.[19]

In one of the repeated sections of the poem, "*from* all with ocean views," for example, Perez weaves together quotations from tourism advertisements and promotional literature published by the Guam Visitor's Bureau to create poems critical of the romantic idea of the Pacific paradise such commercialism promotes. On the one hand, Guam offers the tourist

        'airline by airline'
'costs falling'
    . . . 'a dream   itinerary'[20]

On the other hand, the educated traveler may share with the Native residents of Guåhan

              'the failed myth
           of healing waters'
      'will the trendy new | pilgrimage | tattoo hell on our
                       skins'
    (*[saina]*, 37)

In each instance, these poems are followed by what appears to be a prose footnote, printed in less visible grey-toned type, drawn from news stories that belie the clichés of the tourist industry:

> **guahan is** being briefed by federal officials from us department of homeland security on new guam-cnmi visa waiver program will allow visitors from hong kong but not from china or russia primarily concerned illegal immigrants or asylum-seekers will enter us along with security issues of military buildup government of guam banking on visa waivers for china and russia to drive declining tourism arrivals
>
> ([*saina*], 37)

Tourism arrivals in Guam have, of course, declined in large part thanks to the enormous environmental damage caused by the US military presence on the island. One of five unincorporated US territories with its own civilian government, Guam remains one of the largest US military possessions in what Chalmers Johnson has termed the US "empire of bases."[21] Since the US defeat of the Japanese on July 21, 1944, "Liberation Day," Guam has become the home port to the US Pacific fleet, and its political status since the Organic Act of Guam in 1950 defines it as an "unincorporated organized territory," a mere euphemism for its previous identity as a US "possession" or colony (*[saina]*, 42–43). Like the Marshall decision of the US Supreme Court in 1823 that defined Native American tribes within the geopolitical United States as "domestic dependent nations," the legal ambiguity of "unincorporated organized territory" intentionally obscures the imperial theft of land, people, and resources. As the major employer on the island, the US Navy controls the lives of the entire population; not surprisingly, a large percentage of the Chamorro people serve in the US military, thanks to both vigorous recruitment efforts by all branches of the US armed forces and the military culture shared by many Chamorro families living both on Guam and in the United States.

The US Navy's colonization of Guam has also had devastating effects on the island's terrestrial and marine resources. The widely publicized invasion of Guam by the brown tree snake (*Boiga irregularis*), a mildly venomous arboreal rear-fanged colubrid, occurred sometime between 1945 and 1952, undoubtedly the unintended consequence of naval transport through Guam from the snake's native habitat in northern and eastern Australia, New Guinea, and numerous islands of Indonesia. An aggressive predator that has done serious damage to the native birds, forest vertebrates, and other wildlife of Guam, the brown tree snake has also caused regular power outages in residential and commercial buildings and injury to humans, especially children.[22] But the invasion of Guam by the brown tree snake is just one of the countless biohazards introduced by the US military, including irreparable damage to coral reefs, toxic dumping on land and in the surrounding sea, and the destruction of ecosystems by military construction.

Although I cite other sources to document US military imperialism in Guam, I could have cited exclusively Perez's three volumes of poetry. One of his six repeated titles for individual poems in *[saina]* is "*from* Organic Acts," which includes portions of the Organic Act of Guam (1950), specifically "*Executive Order No. 10178 Oct. 30, 1950, 15 F. R. 7313,*" which is included in *[saina]* (31–33). Like Muriel Rukeyser's inclusion in *The Book of the Dead* (1938) of the Congressional testimony in the Union Carbide mining scandal at Gauley Bridge, West Virginia, Perez includes documentary materials in an avant-garde poem to demonstrate that the discursive complexity in the poem is a political consequence of imperialism, rather than a testament to the poet's genius.[23] The mere list of the acreage of the island claimed by the US government for its military activities in the Organic Act gives particularity to the fact that 75 percent of the island is owned by the US government and includes many of the island's "undersea lands." Reading the legal language of the Organic Act, which nominally granted Guam a civilian government while claiming most of the island for the US Navy, we recognize the fantastic aspect of the imperial imaginary. What we merely read is *lived* everyday by the civilian population of the island.

Of course, the US military colonization of Guam is just the most recent stage in the long history of Guam's occupation by Spain, Japan, and the United States. Ferdinand Magellan landed on Guam in 1521, and a century later Spain established a formal colony on the island, sending Padre San Vitores to head the Catholic mission and its proselytizing efforts among the Chamorros. Guam was a regular port for Spain's "Manila Galleons," which crossed the Pacific annually for two centuries as part of Spain's commercial exploitation of its larger colony in the Philippines.[24] The Spanish ceded Guam to the United States at the conclusion of the Spanish-American War in 1898, formally transforming Guam into a US "possession" with the Treaty of Paris.[25]

The Japanese occupation of Guam from 1941 to 1944 began just hours after the December 7, 1941, attack on Pearl Harbor, when on December 8 the Japanese bombed Guam and initiated a reign of terror that included forced labor, torture, beheadings, and rape as they turned the island into a virtual prison colony to support their war in the Pacific. Forced to "bow" to the Japanese sentries and wear identifying badges in Japanese like POWs, Chamorro workers are compelled to "build the airstrip in Barrigada" and "machine gun encampments" (*[guma']*, 33). But "Liberation Day" merely subjects the Chamorros to new forms of imperial domination by the US state, often with consequences as violent. In *[guma']*, Perez records the obituaries of Pacific Islanders killed in Iraq and Afghanistan during the Second Gulf War between 2004 and 2007, crossing out the official death announcement and placing it in grey but leaving the name of the person untouched (*[guma']*, 32–36), as in the following example:

> [U.S. Army Spc]. Jonathan Pangelinan Santos, a former Santa Rita resident, was killed in Iraq, when his vehicle hit a land mine. He was 22] (*[guma']*, 32)

Perez also uses this technique of crossing out official discourse in the other volumes in the series, adopting a typography employed by poststructuralists such as Jacques Derrida to indicate what might be *sous rature,* or "under erasure," yet permitting the cancelled text to be read.[26]

I cite this particular example because Perez focuses on Jonathan Pangelinan Santos's life and military death in the sixth of his seven-part series "Surviving Our Fallen: Chamorros, Militarism, Religiosity, and 9/11."[27] Perez does not merely "delete" the military accounts of Pacific Islanders killed in our recent wars but he also protests the ways they were recruited into the US military as well as the loss of their lives in yet another misguided imperial war. Perez suggests that we should not repudiate Jonathan Pangelinan Santos's military service and death in Iraq but instead challenge it as part of a broader activism that includes remembering how other colonized people have been used to fight our imperial wars. His protest is not simply an individual act but also part of the Community Writers Collective he has helped organize at the University of Hawai'i at Mānoa, whose first act was to compose "protest-poetry" to demonstrate against a meeting of the Asia-Pacific Economic Cooperation (APEC) held on the campus. The Asia-Pacific Economic Cooperation is a forum of twenty-one Pacific Rim nations that meet annually to promote "free trade" and mutual cooperation. The cooperation has been one of the leading advocates of the much-protested Trans-Pacific Partnership (TPP), an economic agreement that critics contend will have devastating economic consequences for small economies, just as the North American Free Trade Agreement has diminished the pay, benefits, and rights of workers on both sides of the US-Mexico border.[28]

Like the three volumes in *from unincorporated territory,* Perez's other writings in print, on websites, and in "protest-poems" at traditional political demonstrations refer to each other, often repeating the same key stories and historical facts. Such repetition is necessary, because the history of imperialism, especially in the transpacific region, has produced such discursive and intellectual confusion as to be nearly unreadable. Add to this situation the traditional neglect of the Pacific—its people, terrestrial and marine life, and diverse languages and traditions—and the reader understands Perez's strategy of reiterating key issues in order allow them to emerge from the white noise of neoimperialism. For Perez, then, repetition becomes a technique of emphasis in his effort to penetrate the distracting screen discourses that occlude the realities of island lives.

The center of his work is the traditional literary effort to represent how ordinary human beings struggle to negotiate the large political and historical forces of imperialism. In *[guma']*, Perez quotes at length from Chamorro writer Helen Perez's "Bittersweet Memories," recalling "her childhood growing up in 1960s Virginia, where her military father was stationed" (*[guma']*, 17). Helen Perez recalls her mother telling her when she was a child that Guam is "in the Pacific Ocean, and it's a tiny dot on the map, so find the Philippine Islands first because it's not far from there," but when asked by her teacher to show the class where she is from, Helen scans a map of the Pacific, finds the Philippine Islands, but still can't find Guam: "'I looked at my teacher and said, 'Please help me find Guam'" (*[guma']*, 17–18). Trying to put Guam on the map isn't as easy as it seems, both Perezes remind us, because the colonial maps worked to write over Indigenous landscapes, languages, locales, and peoples with their own imposed topographies. As Walter Mignolo has argued, decolonial efforts must address how cartography has played a crucial part in the colonization of space.[29]

The lower-case preposition *"from"* (or the Chamorro *"ginen"*) in the titles of these volumes and in the titles of the individual poems suggests the derivative and historically enmeshed situation of the Chamorros. But the Chamorro words in the titles all suggest origins Perez hopes to recall *through* that imperial dissonance, rather than *beyond* or apart from it. *Hacha* is the Chamorro word for the numeral "one," and thus an appropriate title for the new beginning announced in the first volume of the series.[30] *Saina* is the Chamorro word for "parents elders spirits ancestors," as Perez defines it in *[saina]* (15). "Saina" was the name given by the builders to the first modern Chamorro sailing outrigger canoe (or Sakman) with its lateen sail, built between 2007 and 2008. *Guma* is the Chamorro word for the traditional Chamorro chiefs' houses built on the *latte* or stone columns on Guam and in the Northern Marianas, but it is, of course, also an anagram for "Guam" itself.

Sakmans, which were destroyed by seventeenth-century Spanish colonists in the Chamorro-Spanish Wars (1671–98), were known to be "the fastest sailing vessels in the world" (*[saina]*, 14). Forbidden by Spanish authorities to sail the ocean, the Chamorros had forgotten "how to build and sail" the craft by the mid-nineteenth century (*[saina]*, 14). Following plans drawn in the mid-eighteenth century by an Englishman, George Anson, of a Sakman captured and disassembled on a British ship, Chamorros working under "the guidance of master navigator and canoe builder" Manny Sikau from Polowat in the Federated States of Micronesia built the modern Sakman and in 2009 sailed it to Luta in the Northern Marianas (*[saina]*, 15). Like Perez's own work in the series *from unincorporated territory,* his teaching and scholarship on Pacific literatures and cultures, and his organization of such groups as the Community Writers Collective and small presses such as Ala Press, the collaborative work of the Pacific Island builders of a modern Sakman depends on a community forged in anticolonial struggle, intent on reclaiming Indigenous traditions but also drawing on colonial archives.

Perez encourages us to think of the Sakman as a complex text, in keeping with the metapoetic sources that influence his form and style, but it is also worth recalling that the Sakman is a sailing vessel, not a book. Buried as we so often are in archives, we may lose sight of the fact that seafaring people represent themselves best in their ships and boats. Thus the disappearance of traditional sailing vessels such as the Sakman is often even more distressing than the loss of a legendary story. Several important scholars of transpacific and archipelagic studies recognize the importance of rebuilding not just specific island heritages but also the practical tools that shape their histories, including seafaring craft. Elizabeth DeLoughrey thanks the New Zealanders who helped her learn what Maori seafaring was like by sailing on a reproduction of a traditional Maori vessel.[31] Like Perez, Vicente Diaz considers the recovery of traditional seafaring vessels and navigational practices to be integral parts of anticolonial work.[32]

The title *[hacha]* relies on a similarly intertextual story, the most detailed version of which comes in *[saina]*, where Perez recalls how his grandmother has forgotten that "hacha" is the Chamorro word for "one":

> grandma counts in spanish—when she read my first book she asked what does 'hacha' mean?—i said hacha means 'one'—she looked surprised, asked in what language?—in chamorro, i said—she replied: i speak chamorro all my life and i never heard that word, one is uno in chamorro—no grandma, that's spanish—she looked confused—hacha, hacha, she repeated, feeling the sound in her mouth—maybe you mean 'hatsa' she said, hatsa means 'to hit'—uno is one I never heard of hacha—(*[saina]*, 59)

A few lines later, Perez writes, "*In spanish 'hacha' would mean a large candle, torch, or ax—the gachai, a Chamorro traditional stone-tipped adze used to cut and carve wood, is said to sail from the spanish word 'hacha'*" (*[saina]*, 59). Perez's metaphor that the Chamorro term "sails" from the Spanish word acknowledges linguistic crossings produced by colonial occupation, but the verb also reminds us of the Spanish ban on Chamorro sailing, an activity essential to Chamorro economy and community. And yet the very tool the Chamorros might have used to cut the wood for the Sakman outrigger canoes may have developed philologically from a Spanish word.

Perez is not endorsing postcolonial hybridity as so many postcolonial theorists, such as Gloria Anzaldúa and Homi Bhabha, did in the 1980s and 1990s. Like Walter Mignolo, Perez understands hybridity as an inevitable effect of colonial production, but as far as the Chamorros are concerned, there is no precolonial Chamorro cultural reality in which contemporary Chamorro people can live.[33] To be sure, the factual and cultural history of the Chamorros can and should be recovered, and Perez contributes to that work in his various activities as poet, scholar-teacher, editor, publisher, blogger, and political activist. At the center of [saina] is his profound love for his aging and ailing grandmother, whose survival of Japanese occupation, US military colonization, and her own diaspora to the United States testify to the strength and adaptability of Chamorros. She has forgotten that "hacha" is Chamorro for "one," not the Spanish "uno," but she had traveled to Japan to learn Japanese before the Japanese occupation, as Perez's mother narrates in [saina]:

> "the people are all hiding
> in the caves *she says*
> we didn't hide in the caves
> and when the soldiers came to the farm to take the food
> they saw that she spoke Japanese and they only took the food
> ([saina], 96)

More importantly, the grandmother uses her language skills to foster Chamorro community during life-threatening military occupation:

> "speaks
> chamorro japanese english spanish
> so she could translate
> the radio and read the newspapers to them
> and she always makes a huge pot of soup
> for everyone
> ([saina], 103)

Devoutly Catholic, confusing Spanish and Chamorro, carrying within her body disease likely tied to the environmental damage caused by the US military in Guam (perhaps even in California), the grandmother is nonetheless a heroic figure if not precisely a role model for Perez. Toward the end of [saina], he writes,

> i say "saina" and i know i am not between two languages—not between fluency and fluency—not a simple switch—i say "saina"—heat along converging diverging linguistic boundaries—i write "saina"—seamount, island—within torrents of english—i am not between two languages—one language controls me and the other is a lost ocean—wavelength, wavebreak—not code, but compositions of history, story, genealogy, sound, change, meaning, practices—i say "saina" and it weaves the air i write "saina" and it roots i read "saina" envelops ([*saina*], 111)

The poetic invocation of the Chamorro word for one's ancestry—parents, elders, ancestors—is the performance of a Chamorro community in the present, rather than a nostalgic recollection of a lost homeland or "a lost ocean." Rather, for Perez the "lost ocean" functions as a decolonial space or place within ongoing neoimperial incursions and violence, which Perez enacts through his "compositions of history, story, genealogy, sound, change, meaning, practices." The "lost ocean" is also the ocean destroyed by environmental damage, so that decolonial work must include its reconstruction. Some of this recovery work is poetic and textual, insofar as Perez views his poetic space as an effort to visualize the ocean that differs from terrestrial maps and maritime charts.[34]

Perez's third volume, *[guma'],* suggests that by recalling the history of the precolonial Chamorro chiefs' houses, the poet and reader might "build" new homes on venerable Chamorro foundations. But the Chamorro dwelling or "homeland" in the twenty-first century looks very different from its predecessor. Perez knows it is unlikely that the anticolonial struggle of Chamorro activists will decolonize Guam and restore it as Guåhan, in part because more than half of the Indigenous population of the island now lives in Hawai'i and the continental United States. He also acknowledges that Chamorro will not be revived as a living language for most descendants of the island's Native population. There is also no longer any "singularity" to the political affiliations of indigenous Chamorros, given the strong ties of the majority with the US military and a significant minority working actively to decolonize the Pacific, as well as other global sites. In part, Perez imagines his own books as the "homes" where Chamorro culture survives, although I think this metaphor of a "house of fiction" tells only part of the story.

Perez argues against postcolonial hybridity as much as he rejects the glib universals endorsed by some postmodern writers. He is "not between two languages" (or even more, as his grandmother tried to negotiate Chamorro, Japanese, and Spanish) because he understands how English "controls" him in its dominant imperial power. Calling English into question as one tool of US militarism in the Pacific, Perez also authorizes Chamorro as a "native language" that better expresses living *within* the Pacific, that "lost ocean," understood as a living space within, rather than against, the legacies of empire. But Chamorro is just one among several different languages spoken across the Pacific, among postcolonial activists, and in the discourse of anti-imperialist critique. Many of these are Native languages well worth preserving, not only for their expressive values in literary works but also because many are discourses of opposition and critique, like the "protest-poetry" of Perez and his collective, and the more conventional political demonstrations in which bodies gathered together "speak" to power.

In *[guma']*, during his recitation of the obituaries of the Pacific Islanders killed in the Second Gulf War and Afghanistan, Perez provides an instructive endnote:

—I am indebted to Keith Camacho, Michael Lujan Bevacqua, Vince Diaz, Lisa Natividad, Gwen Kirk, and David Hanlon for their scholarship on Liberation Day, Chamorro soldiers, the history and religiosity of militarization on Guåhan, and war claims legislation in Micronesia. I am indebted to Victoria Leon-Guerrero for her article "The War Reparations Saga: Why Guam's Survivors Still Await Justice," posted on the website Guam War Survivor Story. I am also indebted to the scholarship of H. D. K. Herman on the War in the Pacific National Park. (*[guma']*, 87)

Unlike T. S. Eliot's mockery of scholarship in his endnotes to *The Waste Land* (1922), Perez's endnote provides a testament to the leading anti-imperialist scholars of the Pacific, who in turn have been influenced by the general criticism of US imperialism by scholars over the past three decades and antiwar work by activists, scholars, and public intellectuals from the Vietnam War to the present. Perez makes it clear in all of his writings that his family's move from Guam to California was a "removal," recalling the forced march of the Cherokee on the Trail of Tears and other Native American diasporas throughout US history. In *[guma']*, an early prose poem, "*ginen* (sub)aerial roots," summarizes the key dates in the diaspora of the Chamorros in the modern period. From the 1890s, when a thousand Chamorros "lived in Honolulu and California as part of the whaling industry" (39) to 2010, when "more of [us] chamorros live off-island than on-island" (40), Perez chants within these dates: "*removed from,*" stressing the forcible displacement of Chamorros by US imperialism.

Even though Perez celebrates his return to Guåhan to give a reading in the year he turned thirty, thus dividing his life evenly into the fifteen years he spent growing up on the island and the next fifteen years he spent going to school in California, he identifies himself as a diasporic writer. As a scholar-teacher-activist in Hawai'i, deeply influenced by his undergraduate education at the University of Redlands, his masters of fine arts in creative writing at the University of San Francisco, and his PhD work in ethnic studies at the University of California, Berkeley, he knows the protocols of diaspora studies, the traditions of critical theory, and the literary canons of Anglo-American modernism. Quoting Charles Olson and Muriel Rukeyser in *[saina]*, Perez also criticizes these Anglo-American moderns (*[saina]*, 63, 113). Citing the Tongan writer and social anthropologist Epeli Hau'ofa (1939–2009), Perez explains why Olson's concept of "projective verse," with its effort to put the poet "in the open," "doesn't entirely translate into my own cultural experience" (63). In contrast with "a perspective based on imperial desires to see only extant land surfaces, only the closed insular island," Epeli Hau'ofa "draws our attention to an oceania, préoceania, and transoceania surrounding islands, below the waves, and in the sky—a deeper geography and mythology" (*[saina]*, 63). Indeed, the title of Hau'ofa's volume of essays, *We Are the Ocean* (2008), seems to better express Perez's understanding of poetic ontology than Olson's late modernist ideas.[35]

This "oceanic" epistemology has been a distinctive characteristic of a new geography committed to theorizing experience beyond terrestrial and "continental" models. Martin Lewis and Kären Wigen have made a compelling case for this approach in *The Myth of Continents* (1997), whose criticism of traditional geography and cartography continues to influence cultural critics as well as new geographers.[36] Although most of their book focuses on the Atlantic world, both geographers are specialists in the Pacific region. Their knowledge of the Pacific may well provide just the sort of "oceanic" perspective needed to challenge Eurocentric myths of the Atlantic world. Just as scholars of transnational American studies have struggled to define an alternative to US neoimperialism's integral role in one-way globalization by developing terms such as "planetary," "postpostcolonial," and "postnational," the advocates of "oceanic" and "archipelagic," rather than "continental," thinking imagine a utopian concept that acknowledges their own diasporic conditions without the possibility of a return "home."

Learning to live and survive in these oceanic conditions need not be the experience of the castaway, feeling "adrift" from one's origins. Imperialism has alienated us, threatened to drown us beneath its overwhelming tide. But there are other ways to navigate the oceans and recognize their archipelagoes. Perez argues eloquently for a Chamorro "home" aboard that Sakman built in 2007 by the Traditions About Seafaring Islands (TASI) group, founded in 1992, committed to "revive and perpetuate navigational practices, from canoe building to the reading of winds, waves, stars, and currents *with [our] entire breath*" (*[guma']*, 39). In 2012, Traditions About Our Seafaring Ancestry (TASA) "began building a canoe house" in Guåhan, naming the house "Guma' Latte Marianas" to recall those traditional Chamorro houses built on latte columns (39).

These collaborative efforts are important for reviving Chamorro social and cultural practices, and they do so in late-modern, neocolonial circumstances. Whereas the metaphor of the "voyage" has for so long been invoked by poets to align their work with the boldness and daring of the imperial conqueror, such as Walt Whitman's "Passage to India" (1871) and Hart Crane's "Voyages" (1926) and *The Bridge* (1930), Perez offers his poetry, teaching, activism, cultural recovery, and multimedia fluency and performance as islands connected by an ocean that is his very life and being. Influenced by avant-garde modernists, Perez has constructed his multiple identities as an assemblage. For Duchamp and other modernists, their materials were drawn from modernist technology and repurposed for critical functions. Perez uses instead the islands and oceans themselves, both as they have been polluted by imperialism and as they have sustained life. His work is thus postdiasporic, insofar as it attempts to overturn the idea of forced removal while remaining attentive to a material history of human suffering and natural damage.

Perez avoids the nostalgia for a "lost home" that structures the work of so many other colonized and postcolonial peoples for whom the recovery of past homelands is clearly impossible. Instead, he understands his own work as poet, teacher, activist, and scholar to decolonize not through "erasure" but by "excerpting" a poetic "ocean," as he puts it: "I imagine the blank page as an excerpted ocean filled with vast currents, islands of voices, and profound depths. I imagine the poem forming as a map of this excerpted ocean, tracing the topographies of story, memory, genealogy, and culture. So creating the visual vocabulary of my work is a process of both drafting these word maps and navigating their currents."[37] In this poetic ocean, we do not escape even in our imaginations the traces of imperial pollution, but such damage becomes readable, even *visible*, in relation to the other stories still being told. The reader's experience, then, is postdiasporic, a return not to a lost homeland as much as a recognition of the historical ocean that reader must navigate. In this "excerpted," textualized ocean of poetry we find our bond less through essential ethnic identity or forgotten tribal kinship than in our shared commitment to understand these "word maps." *Beyond* diaspora is the utopia of people of different backgrounds, interests, competencies, and modes of expression living together, sharing their space, using their hands and feet to keep that Sakman flying on the wings and waves of a new history.

NOTES

1. See John Carlos Rowe, "Transpacific Studies and the Cultures of U.S. Imperialism," in *Transpacific Studies,* ed. Janet Hoskins and Viet Nguyen (Honolulu: University of Hawai'i Press, 2014), 134–50.

2. Patrick Wolfe, *Settler Colonialism and the Transformation of Anthropology: The Politics and Poetics of an Ethnographic Event* (London: Cassell, 1999); Lorenzo Veracini, *Settler Colonialism: A Theoretical Overview* (Houndmills, UK: Palgrave Macmillan, 2010).

3. Jodi Byrd, *The Transit of Empire: Indigenous Critiques of Colonialism* (Minneapolis: University of Minnesota Press, 2011), 3–5, uses the term "cacophony" to represent the epistemic chaos experienced by Indigenous peoples in the history of colonialism.

4. Orlando Patterson, *Slavery and Social Death: A Comparative Study* (Cambridge, MA: Harvard University Press, 1982), 25.

5. Edgar Wickberg, "The Chinese Mestizo in Philippine History," *Journal of Southeast Asian History* 5, no. 1 (March 1964): 68–72.

6. Susan K. Harris, *God's Arbiters: Americans and the Philippines, 1898–1902* (New York: Oxford University Press, 2011), 125.

7. Dylan Rodriguez, *Suspended Apocalypse: White Supremacy, Genocide, and the Filipino Condition* (Minneapolis: University of Minnesota Press, 2009), 98–105.

8. Tupuola Terry Tavila, "Following Census, PM Says: 'Have More Children,'" *Samoa News*, August 9, 2012. Accessed Sept. 21, 2016. www.samoanews.com/node/5104.

9. On ecological damage and human injury and death from the atomic testing on Pikinni Atoll in the Marshall Islands, see Rowe, "Transpacific Studies," 145.

10. J. Kēhaulani Kauanui, *Hawaiian Blood: Colonialism and the Politics of Sovereignty and Indigeneity* (Durham, NC: Duke University Press, 2008), 37–66.

11. Byrd, *Transit of Empire*, 154–55.

12. Gilles Deleuze and Félix Guattari, *A Thousand Plateaus: Capitalism and Schizophrenia,* trans. Brian Massumi (Minneapolis: University of Minnesota Press, 1987), 315–423.

13. Elizabeth DeLoughrey, *Routes and Roots: Navigating Caribbean and Pacific Island Literatures* (Honolulu: University of Hawai'i Press, 2009), 3.

14. Antonio Benítez-Rojo, *The Repeating Island: The Caribbean and the Postmodern Perspective,* trans. James E. Martinez (Durham, NC: Duke University Press, 1996), 1.

15. The civilian government of Guam decided in 2010 to change the name of the island to "Guåhan," the Chamorro verb meaning "we have," arguing that "Guam" is an imperial name for the island. I will use "Guam" in contexts of imperial domination and "Guåhan" in specific decolonial and sovereignty contexts.

16. For a more detailed and instructive professional biography, see "About," Craig Santos Perez website. Accessed Sept. 22, 2016. http://craigsantosperez.wordpress.com/about-2/.

17. Craig Santos Perez, *from unincorporated territory [guma']* (Richmond, CA: Omnidawn Publishing, 2014), 21. Further references in the text as *[guma']*.

18. Ezra Pound, *Hugh Selwyn Mauberley,* in *Selected Poems of Ezra Pound* (New York: New Directions, 1973), 47.

19. See Craig Santos Perez's discussion of his use of "from" in his series *"from unincorporated territory,"* in "Craig Santos Perez: The Poetics of Mapping Diaspora, Navigating Culture, and Being From (Part 1)," April 15, 2011, Doveglion Press website. Accessed Oct. 15, 2016. http://www.doveglion.com/2011/04/craig-santos-perez-the-poetics-of-mapping-diaspora-navigating-culture-and-being-from-part-1/.

20. Craig Santos Perez, *from unincorporated territory [saina]* (Richmond, CA: Omnidawn Publishing, 2010), 37. Further references in the text as *[saina]*.

21. Chalmers Johnson, *The Sorrows of Empire: Militarism, Secrecy, and the End of the Republic* (New York: Henry Holt, 2004), 151–86.

22. "Brown Tree Snake," *Guampedia*, accessed Sept. 22, 2016. http://www.guampedia.com/brown-treesnake/.

23. John Carlos Rowe, *The New American Studies* (Minneapolis: University of Minnesota Press, 2002), 135–49.

24. Henry Kamen, *Empire: How Spain Became a World Power, 1492–1763* (New York: HarperCollins, 2003), 198.

25. Vicente Diaz, *Repositioning the Missionary: Rewriting the Histories of Colonialism, Native Catholicism, and Indigeneity in Guam* (Honolulu: University of Hawai'i Press, 2010), 35–36.

26. Jacques Derrida, *Of Grammatology*, trans. Gayatri Spivak (Baltimore, MD: Johns Hopkins University Press, 1967), 60. Derrida adapted the hermeneutic procedure of "placing" a term "under erasure" from Martin Heidegger, who had argued as early as the 1920s in *Sein und Zeit* (1923) that a word's denotative meaning could not convey its connotative complexity, much less its historical variations. Derrida uses "erasure" as a deconstructive procedure that challenges conventional meaning while allowing that convention to remain visible. Perez further elaborates this Eurocentric philosophical idea by applying it with special force to official pronouncements, such as military obituaries, congressional acts, and even his own testimony at the United Nations, in order to stress the inadequacy of discourse under ideological control.

27. Craig Santos Perez, "Surviving Our Fallen: Chamorros, Militarism, Religiosity, and 9/11 (Part 6)," Sept. 17, 2011, *Craig Santos Perez* website. Accessed Oct. 15, 2016. https://craigsantosperez.wordpress.com/2011/09/17/surviving-our-fallen-chamorros-militarism-religiosity-and-911-part-6/. See "The Community Writers Collective: An Initiative," Craig Santos Perez website, October 17, 2011, http://craigsantosperez.wordpress.com/2011/10/17/the-community-writers-collective-an-initiative/http://craigsantosperez.wordpress.com/2011/10/17/the-community-writers-collective-an-initiative/.

28. See, for example, the endorsement of TPP by the APEC Secretariat, "APEC and Trans-Pacific Partnership Mutually Useful: Research," APEC website. Accessed Sept. 22, 2016. http://www.apec.org/Press/News-Releases/2011/1025_TPP.aspx.

29. Walter Mignolo, *The Darker Side of the Renaissance: Literacy, Territoriality, and Colonization*, 2nd ed. (Ann Arbor: University of Michigan Press, 2003), 259.

30. Craig Santos Perez, *from unincoporated territory [hacha]* (San Diego: Tinfish Press, 2008). Further references in the text as *[hacha]*.

31. DeLoughrey, *Routes and Roots*, vii.

32. Vicente M. Diaz, "Voyaging for Anti-Colonial Recovery: Austronesian Seafaring, Archipelagic Rethinking, and the Re-Mapping of Indigeneity," *Pacific Asia Inquiry* 2, no. 1 (2011): 21–32.

33. Walter Mignolo, *Local Histories / Global Designs: Coloniality, Subaltern Knowledges, and Border Thinking* (Princeton, NJ: Princeton University Press, 2000), 170.

34. "The Page Transformed: A Conversation with Craig Santos Perez," *Lantern Review* blog, March 12, 2010. Accessed Oct. 15, 2016. http://www.lanternreview.com/blog/2010/03/12/the-page-transformed-a-conversation-with-craig-santos-perez/.

35. Epeli Hau'ofa, *We Are the Ocean: Selected Works* (Honolulu: University of Hawai'i Press, 2008), 5.

36. Martin Lewis and Kären Wigen, *The Myth of Continents: A Critique of Metageography* (Berkeley: University of California Press, 1997).

37. "The Page Transformed."

10 | INSUBORDINATE ISLANDS AND COASTAL CHAOS

Cherene Sherrard-Johnson

PAULINE HOPKINS'S LITERARY LAND/SEASCAPES

> The dangerous and dreaded island, or rather islands, of Bermuda... called commonly The Devils Islands... are feared and avoided of all sea travelers alive, above any other place in the world.
>
> WILLIAM STRACHEY

THIS ESSAY RESPONDS TO TWO intersecting questions: Why does Pauline E. Hopkins choose to open her two novels *Contending Forces: A Romance Illustrative of Negro Life North and South* (1900) and *Winona: A Tale of Negro Life in the South and the Southwest* (1902) on islands? What is it specifically about an island's geography that makes its land and seascapes specifically useful to Hopkins's highly wrought, historicized fiction? I suggest that her use of islands and coastal territories as interracial, transnational geographies to stage her serialized, post–Civil War narratives of passing and slavery evinces what Brian Russell Roberts terms the "revolutionary topography" of the island landscape in contrast to more rigid, continental conceptions of national identity.[1] Opening her novels on islands—*Winona* commences on an unnamed archipelago near Grand Island on the US-Canada border and *Contending Forces* begins in Bermuda—allows Hopkins to deploy an array of island tropologies; she alternatively imagines islands as utopic paradises and as hotbeds of revolutionary ideology and contagion in order to demarcate the multiple insurgencies enabled by the island's topography and the mutable, national identification of its human and nonhuman inhabitants. By imagining islands as archipelagic circuits including coastal communities, Hopkins goes against the grain of dominant island tropes that imagine the bounded geography of the island as a "distinct territory" that is "naturally" politically unified.[2] Rather than conceiving of islands as organically sovereign spaces, Hopkins extends her archipelagic understanding of US transnationalism to include the continental coast.

Starting off in island space and on island time enables Hopkins to recycle imperial and utopic tropes of the island as paradise, while simultaneously evincing a black circum-Caribbean sensibility of insurgency via the Haitian Revolution. "Haiti," in its coalescence of Indigenous and fugitive insurrection, surfaces in Hopkins's writing as an infectious revolutionary spirit that traverses land and sea, just as it haunts the permeable, national literature of the United States. Hopkins invokes Haiti—part of a bounded island (Hispaniola) containing two sovereign nations with a contested, dynamic, bloody, border—as she narrates microhistories of other revolts (such as John Brown's skirmishes and raids).³ She augments her revisionist reveries through the intertextual relationship of her fiction to the biographical profiles of heroic Haitian revolutionaries such as Toussaint L'Ouverture featured in the *Colored American Magazine*, which she edited from 1900 to 1904. Though unnamed in the island openings, Haiti is everywhere present as a "parallax zone": "a place that has no spatial or corporeal proximity, but rather, an unsettling interplay between near and far."⁴ Existing as a "specter of [alternative] democracy," and in light of Dessalines's massacre, a warning for its slaveholding neighbors, Haiti is an ever-present shadow island, the successful example within an archipelagic history of revolts.⁵ As Michael Drexler asserts, "No event captures the contradictions of new world history more than the Haitian Revolution."⁶ Indeed, early African American periodicals frequently ran biographical portraits of the revolution's leaders and serialized stories, such as *Theresa—A Haytien Tale*.⁷ Like Haiti, Hopkins's islands have the potential to be both insurgent and counterrevolutionary as ever-changing political landscapes alter the islands and their inhabitants: the British abolition of slavery in the case of Bermuda, and the passing of the fugitive slave law, which slave catchers invoke to remand Winona and her foster brother Judah from the independent sovereignty of their island to the slave state of Missouri. Such forays suggest there is a specifically insubordinate sensibility endemic to island/archipelagic space and temporality.

The dual natures of Hopkins's island prologues, which contain both insurgent and reactionary island tropes, play off against each other and the continental narratives that follow. This sense of duality necessarily marks the hybrid, multiracial bodies of the protagonists who circulate along the archipelagic circuits of the Atlantic and the interior. The island locale in *Winona* occasions a provocative model of alternative indigeneity: an Afro-Native identity possible only in "neutral" waters with flexible national and temporal boundaries. In *Contending Forces*, the Bermudian stage reveals the contradictions of British abolitionism; the false idea of the benevolent slaveholder and the contaminating adherence of Creoleness that follows ultimately transmutes a mixed-race identity onto the body of Grace Montfort, the slaveholder's wife. In addition to foregrounding the island openings of these novels, I spotlight scenes in which characters of indeterminate or questionable multiethnic heritage travel across waterscapes provoking national anxiety that both threatens and consolidates US identity at key moments in the long nineteenth century.

Although Pauline Hopkins is thought of as a quintessential New England writer, it bears remembering that the state of Massachusetts includes its own archipelago of coastal islands, including Cape Cod, and the farther afield islands of Martha's Vineyard and Nantucket, which exist in a conjunctive, yet distinctive, relationship to the US continent. Hopkins may also have had personal ties to Bermuda and embedded her own familial history within the Montforts' horrific tale. Far-reaching in their locales and genre reconceptualizations, her textual innovations mark her as an early pioneer of speculative and diasporic fiction. In addition to her status as the "single most productive black woman writer at the turn of the century," several key features of her writing are worth highlighting: her experimentations with genre, such as the dime novel, the western, romance, and science fiction; her simultaneous use and promotion of popular fiction for African Americans as inseparable from her political aims; her revisionist historiography, which includes the insertion of women into the historical record and stresses that rape is a crime equally heinous as lynching—one of the main "contending forces" facing turn-of-the-century post–emancipation era blacks.[8]

Applying fundamental and emergent frameworks arising from island and archipelagic studies, I propose that Pauline Hopkins uses the island-opening in two significant ways. First, these island prologues function as exemplars of hybrid ethnic and ecological harmony, a representative strategy derived in part from imperialist tropes of the island paradise in contrast to the chaos of continental strife. Her experiments with genre, specifically the romance and adventure story, as well as the western and speculative sci-fi/fantasy elements, work in concert with aspects of the desert-island narrative. Yet a submerged, almost too subtle, layer of resistance in Hopkins's island ecology allows her to effect a resistant turn in what might be otherwise read as purely reactionary. Second, the methodologies and inquiries of archipelagic studies reveal the entwined definitions of indigeneity and nationhood concentrated in her opening scenes. For Hopkins, the island serves as synecdoche for a utopic nation, while being simultaneously illustrative of the porosity of national boundaries composed of archipelagic ties, as in the relationship between Bermuda and the Carolina coast in *Contending Forces*, or the unnamed desert isle floating between Canada and the state of New York featured in *Winona*. The island preludes set in motion the expansive continental narratives that follow.

My analysis of Hopkins's invocation of island discourse as part of an archipelagic understanding of US transnational identity is further illuminated if we approach her island openings as occurring in what Paul Giles describes as "parallax zones," spaces similar to Mary Louise Pratt's "contact zones" of imperial encounters and reciprocal (if frequently inequitable) exchange.[9] As Roberts discusses in his adaptation of Giles to Zora Neale Hurston's "engagement with island-space," parallax zones exist in relation to one another via their common relation to a third zone (e.g., though geographically distant from each other, the United States and Australia attain a parallax relation to one another through their common colonial connections to Britain).[10] Or, as I am discussing here, Hopkins's islands, though appearing within different literary texts, attain parallax relation to one another through their common description and representation through diction steeped in island tropologies and genre manipulations. Growing out of his reliance on the notion of parallax zones, Roberts uses the term "archipelagic diaspora" to describe how, "in contrast to imperial, racial, and religious modes of theorizing the planet, archipelagic diaspora creates a sense of planetary connectivity not by identitarian heuristics or imperial superimposition but by connection, via unanticipated formal recognitions, across perceived ontological difference."[11] This apt definition also illuminates Hopkins's understanding of geographic connectivity in which a bounded US nation and a permeable circum-Caribbean come together through the hybrid space of the floating island; however, my application diverges somewhat to privilege what I perceive in Hopkins's writings as an elastic circuit that is simultaneously porous, recursive, and forward-looking. Hopkins's archipelagic diaspora is also always materially linked to the sea via maritime routes of travel as well as what Edward Kamau Brathwaite terms a submarine unity shared by islands that can be "both autonomous and geographically, politically and culturally connected to their island neighbors,"[12] and, I would add, coastal communities. *Contending Forces* creates a parallax zone that links Cape Hatteras to Bermuda, which is closer to the continental United States than it is to islands initially part of the Bermudian colony.

Mapping Hopkins's island spaces reveals that rather than a full dispersal, the submarine unity of her archipelagic diaspora is held in suspension in an elastic circuit that contracts and extends in an undulating fashion. The island-opening in *Contending Forces* situates the prefatory action and the reader in the "plantation zone" of the global South.[13] Hopkins's land/seascapes exist as archipelagic formations. They participate in the economy and ecology of the "southscape,"[14] but also extend in the form of circum-Caribbean circuits that link islands to coasts, cultivate porous national boundaries, creole identities, and alternative indigeneity. Not everything is relayed through the circuit, as certain idyllic forms—"benevolent" slavery (*Contending Forces*) or Indigenous kinship ties

(*Winona*)—become unsustainable off island, while other practices (such as "the one-drop rule") and objects (such as the whipping post and the canoe) travel through a transnational and transcultural space between.

Hopkins's positing of an unnamed freshwater island in the North American interior in *Winona* expands on Édouard Glissant's invitation (to consider that "each island is an opening"[15]), asking readers to think beyond the insularity of continental discourse *within* the continent itself. In this variation on a southerly, circum-Caribbean archipelagic diaspora, the island prelude privileges a northern, prenational submarine unity that links the continent to Indigenous ecologies on Hopkins's unnamed, fugitive isle of refuge, and its nationally affiliated (though not uncontested) adjacent islands and coast. *Winona*'s grafting of the Robinsonade and other tropologies of the "Antillean imaginary" inform this interrogation of Hopkins's land/seascapes as submarine structures that act upon and within the continental, essentially restaging contact zones in intermediary spaces where land and water (salt and fresh) collide and coalesce, becoming neither solid nor liquid but both, and providing a chaotic theater for key moments of textual action.

DEVILISH ISLANDS AND SUBMERGED RESISTANCE

In the opening chapter of *Contending Forces*, "A Retrospect of the Past," Hopkins appears to intentionally misquote *The Tempest*:

> and thus Shakespeare's magic island of Prospero and Miranda has become indeed, to the traveler:
>
> > "The spot of earth uncurst,
> > To show how all things were created first."[16]

With these few sentences Hopkins manages to chaotically evoke the origins, mythology, and assembly of fantastical associations with her chosen setting of Bermuda. Though prefaced with Shakespearean allusion, these lines are drawn from Edward Waller's epic poem "The Battle of the Summer Islands" (1645). In fact, the only direct reference to Bermuda in *The Tempest* occurs in act 1, scene 2: "Thou called'st me up at midnight to fetch dew / From the still-vexed Bermudas."[17] Famous for shipwrecks caused by its dangerous reef system, Bermuda became known as the Devil Island. In fact, Bermuda is a *constellation* of islands resembling the archipelagoes of the Pacific. Hans Hannau writes that Bermuda is like "visiting a South Sea island in the North Atlantic," as it "is not one but about 138 islands."[18] In reading Hopkins's deployment of island tropology and geography, it is vital to keep in mind Elizabeth DeLoughrey's observation that "no island is an isolated isle and that a system of archipelagraphy, that is a historiography that considers chains of islands in a fluctuating relationship to their surrounding seas, islands and continents—provides a more appropriate metaphor for reading island cultures."[19] Viewing Bermuda's "vexed" colonial history within an archipelagic structure explains how despite its unusual position in the North Atlantic apart from the other islands that formed British holdings in the Caribbean, such as Antigua, its proximity to the continental United States—Bermudians ran the blockades during both the Revolutionary and Civil Wars—made the island a key player in international and national conflicts. The mythology surrounding its establishment as a colony intrinsically links it to the earliest English settlements in the Atlantic and along the North American coast. In 1609, the *Sea Venture,* captained by Sir George Somers, was sailing from Plymouth to Jamestown when a "dreadfull storme and hideous began to blow."[20] However, Bermuda's resistant ecological features did little to discourage settlement as the shipwrecked survivors who made landfall became the first colonists of the "Somers," or Summer, Islands. The wreck story written by William Strachey—secretary-elect of Virginia—was widely circulated in England and is believed to have inspired *The Tempest*.[21]

Hopkins's conflation of Waller's epic with her Shakespearean invocation powerfully reinforces her fictive treatment of Bermuda as an allotopia whose potential insurgency is overlaid with Edenic imagery; much of the tension in this section arises from the fact that her romantic, florid language is tied specifically to Bermuda's material history and importance as a colony. *The Tempest* reference is more than an imaginative association; it is part and parcel of the nautical disaster that led to the island's settlement. Hopkins's decision to open her novel in Bermuda gains significance for its material particularity as well as its mythic representativeness. The coexistence of the metaphoric and the material in maritime studies is evident in the frequent citation of poet Derek Walcott's evocative maxim "the sea is history."[22] In contrast, Hester Blum significantly asserts that the "sea is not a metaphor" and grounds island and oceanic studies in a practice that is attentive to the "material conditions and praxis of the maritime world."[23] Viewed through these multiple frames, Bermuda becomes vital to Hopkins not only because of its connection to *The Tempest* and Tempest-inspired literature, but also because it plays a crucial role in British abolitionist discourse. More importantly, while the island's devilish ecology initially thwarts the colonists' imperial endeavors, the eventual settlement and subsequent transformation of the island to a brutal plantocracy in turn *bedevils* the enslaved. These opposing narratives of Bermuda, as a resistant archipelago ultimately subdued and mythologized in colonial memory on one hand, and as a site of horrific enslavement on the other, encircle Hopkins's occasionally imperialist, yet potentially insurgent, archipelagic diaspora.

Bermuda's pernicious history was made infamous by the circulation and publication of *The History of Mary Prince, A West Indian Slave* (1831), which describes via amanuensis the harrowing and brutal tales of the author's enslavement. Prince's portrait of Bermuda's slavocracy refutes accounts of the island's supposed leniency, a perception ironically also perpetuated by Hopkins. Prince's story begins with a sense of place: she "was born at Brackish-Pond, in Bermuda, on a farm," the daughter of enslaved parents. Her narrative has much in common with African American slave narratives, including early separation from parents and siblings, the childhood realization of one's subordinate position, and numerous incidents of slaveholders' brutality to their slaves and family members. Such indiscriminately violent behavior, Prince argues, results when "English people . . . go to the West Indies," where "they forget God and all feeling of shame."[24] Above all, she bears witness: "it is my duty to relate . . . I have been a slave—I have felt what a slave feels, and I know what a slave knows; and I would have all the good people in England to know it too, that they may break our chains, and set us free."[25]

Prince's narrative proves that early colonizers and enslaved occupants clearly understood the Bermuda islands as an archipelago with close ties to other island clusters. She describes how she is sent to "Turk's Island" (now the Turks and the Caicos) on a four-week journey. Bermudian explorers encountered Turk's Island in 1668; they immediately built salt ponds on the desert island and it became a mainstay of the economy, effectively expanding the colonial archipelago by one thousand miles until 1801, when it was annexed under protest to the Bahamian colony. Upon arrival at Turk's Island, Mary is sold to the owner of the salt ponds. She describes the labor and toil in devastating detail:

> I was given a half barrel and a shovel, and had to stand up to my knees in the water, from four o'clock in the morning till nine, when we were given some Indian corn boiled in water . . . [we] worked through the heat of the day; the sun flaming upon our heads like fire, and raising salt blisters in those parts which were not completely covered. Our feet and legs, from standing in the salt water for so many hours, soon became full of dreadful boils, which eat down in some cases to the very bone, afflicting the sufferers with great torment. . . . We then shovelled [sic] up the salt in large heaps, and went down to the sea, where we washed the pickle from our limbs, and cleaned the barrows and shovels from the salt.[26]

I have quoted from this scene at length to underscore the physical cost resulting from human manipulation of the island environment that coexists with the promotion of the Caribbean island as a respite from the metropole, ideal for settlement. The salt pans on "Salt Cay" are the only remaining markers of a transformed environment that literally "pickled" human laborers. Prince's amanuensis asserts in the prologue that "the spirit and character of slavery are everywhere the same," be it in "the cane culture of Mauritius and Jamaica" or the salt flats of Turk's Island.[27] Thus, Prince's focus on the particularity of her enslaved experience on Bermuda and Turk's Island becomes part of the accessible discourse of the repeating island.[28]

Given Hopkins's widespread knowledge and historiographical efforts in the *Colored American Magazine*, it is certainly possible that she may have encountered Prince's narrative. Yet her fictive account of the conditions of slavery in Bermuda is a striking departure from Prince's, at first appearing to share an uneasy resemblance to later incongruent accounts included in promotional travel guides that admit revolts were "repressed with unspeakable cruelty" but maintain "there was mutual dependence and affection between whites and their black servants."[29] Mary Prince chillingly recounts being passed from "one butcher to another": "Mr D has often stripped me naked, hung me up by the wrist, and beat me with the cow-skin, with his own hand, till my body was raw with gashes. Yet there was nothing very remarkable in this; for it might serve as a sample of the common usage of the slave on that horrible island."[30] Prince uses the whipping post and salt flats scenes to protest slavocracy's enslavement, subjugation, and transformation of the black body into a commodity and island ecology into profit and suffering-producing networks. Her spare account serves as a template for Hopkins's extended exposition on the spectacle of Grace Montfort's ordeal at the close of the novel's historical prologue, an act of spectacular violence that Prince relays as merely commonplace in her experience of slavery in Bermuda. In ironic contrast to Prince's account, Hopkins's Bermuda is set as a counterpoint to the continental United States: she claims that "slavery never reached its lowest depths on this beautiful island" and portrays English "restraint" in opposition to the "ferocious acts of brutality so commonly practiced by the Spaniards."[31] In the interest of extending her concept of the nation and showcasing the vileness of US slavery, Hopkins leaves the brutality of Bermudian slavery unchallenged; instead, she focuses on how "African blood had become diluted from amalgamation with the higher race"—a sardonic illustration that limiting corporal punishment does not promote sexual restraint. What *does* get smuggled onto the continent is the iconic instrument of torture, the whipping post, a Creolized identity that challenges whiteness-based US citizenship claims, and the shadow of another "still-vexed" island. Operating as another intertextual node, Haiti follows as dual specter of interracial carnage and emancipatory revolt alongside Bermuda's entangled history as a "devilish island" in transatlantic literary culture and a site of horrors in British abolitionist discourse.

PAULINE HOPKINS'S CIRCUM-CARIBBEAN ANCESTRAL PROLOGUE

Reading *Contending Forces*, this quintessential New England tale, through its island-opening and in the context of an archipelagic and global South framework, reveals a multigenerational narrative that records the ruthlessness of slavocracy and the need for redemption and redress, which spans from the antebellum South to the postbellum North. But also, by beginning, as I have already indicated, in Bermuda, it extends across the circum-Caribbean.[32] The facts of the prologue are plain: in order to maintain his enslaved property when faced with the gradual emancipation of slavery in the British colonies, Charles Montfort makes the fateful decision to relocate his household to North Carolina.

Hopkins depicts Bermuda as an Edenic garden about to be forced into violent upheaval: "Bermuda's fifteen square miles of area lays six hundred miles from the nearest American coast. Delightful is this land, formed from coral reefs, flat and fertile, which to the eye appears but a pinpoint upon the ocean's broad bosom, one of 'a thousand islands in a tropic sea.'"[33] Thus this epic tale of consanguinity and amalgamation begins in meta-archipelagic space that connects the landscape and slaveholding practices of Bermuda to "the shores of Pamlico Sound" (a mere six hundred miles away in North Carolina), where the Montforts later disembark on the "rickety wharf" with their human and nonhuman cargo.[34] Hopkins's penchant for recursive, revisionist historiography is deftly deployed as she recounts a history of Bermuda that stands at the interstice between the time and space of Haitian revolution and British emancipation: "In the winter of 1790, when these important changes in the life of the Negro in the West Indies were pending, many planters were following the course of the events with great anxiety."[35] In contrast to the "magic island" they have left behind, on the continent the Montforts encounter a "phantasmagoric landscape" haunted by the sorrow songs of slaves unloading the barges in the harbor.[36]

Before Montfort departs, two enticing island scenes tempt him to stay in "this land of love and beauty." First, a market scene where

> a crowd of slaves were enjoying the time of idleness. Men were dancing with men, and women with women, to the strange monotonous music of drums without tune, relics of the tom-tom in the wild African life which haunted them in dreamland. Still, there was pleasure for even a cultivated musical ear in the peculiar variation of the rhythm. . . . Over there, waterfalls fell in the sunlight in silvery waves; parti-colored butterflies of vivid coloring, and humming-birds flashed through the air with electrical radiance.

"Where, my son," said the clergyman, indicating the landscape with a wave of his hand, "will you find a scene more beautiful than this?"[37]

Then, on the eve of his departure, Montfort contemplates the bay, "contrast[ing] it with the comparative barrenness of the new spot he had chose. The water was alive with marine creatures; the sea aflame. The air was full of light-giving insects, incessantly moving, which illumined the darkness and gave life to every inanimate object."[38] These exotic scenes of island life with its fecund and sensual imagery are indicative of Hopkins's "suddenly sensual" and "highly wrought" language.[39] The contemplated bay is literally "aflame" with the "nighttime phosphorescences" Antonio Benítez-Rojo identifies as part of the character of an archipelago.[40] The prior scene unfolds like a lush watercolor with multiple depths and dimensions overpopulated by visual and aural stimuli. This Technicolor island idyll, where African retentions (presumably West African drum rhythms) are permitted and practiced with relish by primitivist subjects with "gleaming teeth" "dancing" with idle abandon, is unsettling. The chaotic land/seascape represented in these scenes appears to be at odds with Hopkins's faintly ironic portrayal of slaveholding Bermuda as "intensely British," "the Gibraltar of the Atlantic." On one hand she establishes Bermuda and England—sites where the air "is too pure for any slave to breathe"—as moral and cultural exemplars, superior due to their abolition of slavery prior to the United States. Yet on the other hand, she condemns Montfort's unwillingness to relinquish his property "without recompense" and his paternalistic intention to free his slaves and reward them with land only *after* "settling" elsewhere and "without impoverishing himself."[41]

The presence of such profound contradictory elements in Hopkins's fictions illustrates how "claims to nationalism can never be made in a simple manner, but must be located at the circuitous intersection of an American and African identity."[42] Hopkins's simultaneous resistance to and manifestation of imperialist desires makes it difficult to rationalize her florid, romanticized portrait of Bermuda in *Contending Forces* and the unnamed desert isle on the US-Canada borderlands/borderwaters in *Winona*. The Bermudian bishop entreats Montfort to see the colonized nation through "imperial eyes,"[43] thus revealing "the inextricable intermingling of nationalist and transnationalist visions" in black Atlantic discourse.[44] Despite the bishop's warning that the maternal guidance and "liberty of England is not found" "out there" "point[ing] in the direction of the bay," Montfort is undeterred and relocates his family to New Bern, North Carolina. The foretold "barrenness" is not the only ominous sign of their arrival on the shores of the Pamlico Sound. A harbor scene opens the next chapter: "A motley crowd of slaves, overseers, owners of vessels and a phantasmagoric landscape" is set in stunning contrast to Bermuda's "temperate climate," "fragrant cedars and fruitful tamarinds," "limpid rivers," and "balmy fragrance and freshness of the air."[45] This contrasting tableau refutes the idyllic beauty of the island to emphasize the chaos of the slavocracy that has traveled the circum-Caribbean to the coast.

From the "motley" coastal assembly two strangers, Bill Sampson and Hank Davis, emerge (just as two similarly low-class interlopers will later assess Judah and Winona) to debate the prudence of Montfort's arrival: "The 'Island Queen' from Bermudy. Planter named Montfort on her. He's movin' his niggers here to Caroliny; gittin' too hot for him back thar." Bill indicates "thar" "with a backward jerk of his thumb in the supposed direction of Bermuda."[46] Just as Haiti is too close for comfort to New Orleans, trade routes keep Bermuda in close proximity to the Carolina coast through the circulation of raw and refined goods. In this way, Hopkins shrinks the distance (only 568 miles) between the coastal Carolinas, their islands, and Bermuda, rendering it as circum-Caribbean space, a South that is local and global, through two hand gestures: the bishop's wave "out here" to the bay meets Bill's backward thumb jerk, establishing a multilayered, complex circuit that belies the simplicity of their gesticulations.

This archipelagic circuit provides the conditions that enable Grace Montfort to be read within the visually evocative iconographic tradition of the mulatta despite her ostensibly British Bermudian birth, nullifying her claims to whiteness and voiding legitimacy of her marriage within the auspices of the Church of England. The narrator describes Grace as "a dream of beauty even among beautiful women. . . . Her complexion was creamy in its whiteness, of the tint of the camellia; her hair, a rich golden brown, fell in rippling masses far below the waist line; brown eyes, large and soft as those seen in the fawn; heavy black eyebrows marking a high white forehead, and features as clearly cut as a cameo, completed a most lovely type of Southern beauty."[47]

In addition to embodying the hybrid physiognomy and imagery associated with antebellum mulatta figures (namely, alluring, exotic dark eyes and an excessively creamy and/or tinted complexion that marks its whiteness as artificial), this passage also depicts Montfort as a Caribbean mermaid.[48] Who else but a siren has hair falling in rippling masses to her waist and induces irrational lust in men? Anson Pollock, the architect of the Montforts' demise, declared himself "maddened by [Grace's] beauty" "from the first moment he saw her aboard the 'Island Queen.'"[49] Though in Bermuda Grace Montfort was mistress and social equal within her husband's circle, once she disembarks, her exotic island beauty is immediately cast as "Southern" and suspicious. If Haiti's revolutionary blackness can flow across (and under) the water through national boundaries, the creolization process can also be viewed as a "blackening" that can render one radically transgressive or, as in the case of Grace Montfort, radically vulnerable.

Moreover, as the mermaid iconography attests, Montfort is also questionably quasi-human. Worse, with her "fawn"-colored eyes, she is infantilized quarry. Her "cameo"-cut features reference a popular upper-class jewelry item engraved with a classical, feminine profile and accentuate her "sharp," or "Anglo," attributes while simultaneously connoting the commodification of conch shells "found on the Southern coast of America, and also on the coast of the West India Islands, and commonly known as the "*black conch* . . . ,'" from which shell cameos were carved in the mid-nineteenth century.[50] Grace's body, with its layers of maritime overtones, is also a type of vessel, imprinted, or *cut*, with the history of institutionalized, interracial sexual assault.

After declaring that Hank had "never seed sich a booty in [his] life" (note how the dialect permits a threefold objectification of Montfort's body as a commodity; she literally becomes pirate "booty" available for distribution), Bill "meditatively" replies, "Strikes me, Hank, thet thet ar female's got a black streak in her somewhar," "thar's too much cream in the face and too little blud seen under the skin for a genooine white 'ooman.'"[51] The excessive creaminess of Grace's complexion, and the presumed squeamishness attributed to the British about claiming their mixed-race children, immediately calls into question her racial identity, thus rendering the Montforts foreign and therefore vulnerable in this coastal community. At the close of this conversation, the narrator intervenes from the future, reminding readers of the "flotsam and jetsam left from the wreck of the Civil War" and inviting us to rejoice that the "poisonous and bitter" "fruit of slavery" no longer exists. Using maritime diction to connect the relics of slavery's oppression, imagining Civil War as a *ship* "wreck," these opening chapters establish the flotsam and jetsam that linger through the subsequent narrative of Reconstruction.[52]

Grace Montfort's visually white body is rendered questionable the moment she disembarks the ship from Bermuda; the taint of Creolization, of a foreignness that is nevertheless close, flows across national boundaries and adheres to her flesh. The "motley crowd of rough white men and ignorant slaves" speculate about the excessive "cream" of her flesh and the opacity of the "blud seen under the skin" through creolized bifocals. Caribbean otherness, read within the context of US black/white binaries, marks and renders her body violable, and through association her husband also becomes suspect. Rather than reading Charles Montfort's refusal to manumit his slaves according to British law as evidence of shared affinity with his continental cousins in New Bern, "the friendly relations of the neighbors turned to coldness and reserve" as rumors spread that he intended to free his slaves. This seditious talk, along with his wife's purported African ancestry, "spread abroad like wildfire."[53] These suspicions become the basis for Montfort's murder by Anson Pollock, who has long coveted his wife's "booty" and property. With her husband dead, Pollock, together with Davis and Sampson, subjects Grace to a viciously eroticized whipping.

Just as Fred Moten in *In the Break* refuses to look away or remain deaf to Aunt Hester's scream and brutalization, I posit the infamous, masochistic scene at the start of Hopkins's novel as a pornographic tableau that registers both visually and aurally.[54] Unwilling to rely on her own visually charged diction, Hopkins includes an illustration as frontispiece behind her author photo and opposite the title page indicating that this precise image haunts her tale of "displacement and diaspora" (figure 10.1).[55] The spectral depiction contrasts the whiteness of Montfort's body with a darkening pastoral landscape. Her aggressors' serpentine whip hovers over her inert, horizontal body and a pool of dark blood is visible near her head. This illustration, together with highly sexualized diction, is a sharp counter to the idyllic island scenes of the Montforts' native Bermuda. The "snaky leather thong" is literally revealed as the evil concealed by paradise as it visits "its rapid, vengeful descent" upon Grace's "tender white back."[56]

The graphic nature of this "scene of subjection," to borrow from Saidiya Hartman, traffics in a global appetite for spectacular tableaux of racial and sexual violence.[57] Similar to the visual and aural assault of Douglass's rendering of Aunt Hester's whipping, Hopkins's fictive revisitation of Douglass's "primal scene" (and echoes of Mary Prince's testimony) prompts early black feminist critics to read Grace Monfort's whipping as a figurative rape.[58] Hazel Carby's assertion that "the institutionalized rape of black women has never been as powerful a symbol of black oppression as the spectacle of lynching" may factor into why Hopkins depicts Montfort's violation so explicitly.[59] The echoes of Aunt Hester's shriek can be heard in both the whistle of the whip, the rawhide's phallic, "mathematical precision," and the ritardando of Montfort's "shriek, a stifled sob, a long-drawn quivering sigh."[60] Thus the sonic memory of this brutal encounter reverberates alongside the "pool" of "blood" that concludes Hopkins's equally "terrible spectacle."[61]

Hopkins's staging of this intertextual scene on the continent transmutes whiteness into blackness with a crucial prop, the whipping post (figure 10.2), which surfaces as the Montforts' undeclared ancestral baggage. In Bermuda, the lingering and commemorated remnants of whipping posts and other instruments of torture validate Prince's and other oral histories of island abuse that counter the trope of the island as paradise. Although Prince and Hopkins have different agendas—Prince protests Atlantic slavery and the rendering of the black body into a commodity, while Hopkins's postemancipation narrative manipulates historical memory to trouble national and racialized boundaries by complicating the status of the white, Creolized body—they align in these paradigmatic scenes

HE CUT THE ROPES THAT BOUND HER, AND SHE SANK UPON THE GROUND AGAIN. (See page 69.)

Figure 10.1. "He cut the ropes that bound her, and she sank upon the ground again." Image opposite the title page of Pauline Hopkins's *Contending Forces* (Boston, MA: The Colored Co-Operation Publishing Co., 1900).

Figure 10.2. Replica of whipping post in the historic town of St. George, Bermuda. Photo by Cherene Sherrard-Johnson.

of torture. As the sinister artifact travels across time and space, the dehumanizing implications of bodily subjugation adhere to it, allowing the post to manifest and reinforce each author's intent. Revealed as a nonhuman traveler of the archipelagic diasporic circuit, this object plays a cameo role in retracting the Montforts' whiteness and exposing the mixed-race black female body as available for subjugation. This is a subjugation only hinted at in Hopkins's seemingly benign rendering of Bermudian slavery in the island prologue that activates the parallax zone linking the United States to a broader circum-Caribbean space. In addition to blackening the Montforts via a Creolized Caribbean connection that complicates US-American nationalist claims based on whiteness by accentuating black ancestry, the intertextually smuggled whipping post recursively unravels Hopkins's Edenic allotopia, revealing it to be illusory, or "no place." After her viciously brutal assault, Grace Montfort returns to the sea: "The waters of the Pamlico Sound tell of sweet oblivion for the broken-hearted found within their soft embrace."[62] Recalling Montfort's association as a mixed-race siren, her drowning not only recapitulates the fate of Hans Christian Andersen's *Little Mermaid* (1837), who dissolves into sea foam after her disappointing sojourn on land, it also follows the trajectory of the antebellum tragic mulatta popularized by William Wells Brown's *Clotel* (1853), who in seeking to escape from her pursuers "sunk forever beneath the waves of the [Potomac] river."[63]

The mark of Creolization and its fraught juxtaposition of respectability and exoticism will recur later in the novel among the black female community of New England, where protagonist Sappho Clark's beauty is immediately identified as foreign: "thar ain't nothing like that growed outside o' Looseyannie"; Sarah Anne names Sappho's physiognomy as indigenous to the ethnic, cultural, and natural ecosystem of southern Louisiana, indicating that even as the novel leaves the coastal chaos of the Carolinas, Hopkins extends her circum-Caribbean land/seascape to include New Orleans.[64] As Davis observes, "The Gulf of Mexico and the Caribbean Sea form waterways of connection and flow with the bayous and rigolettes of the southern Louisiana coast." [65] New Orleans is a mere twelve hundred miles from Haiti, but in the transnational imaginary that distance shrinks so that Haiti is in intimate proximity to the continent, like Bermuda, just "over there," part of the southscape that flows across national and temporal boundaries, a spectral presence of insurgent, transnational blackness that nevertheless inhabits a particular territory and has material effects. The territories and waterways that constitute the global South (or at least the streams of exchange I follow from the Caribbean and along the Atlantic Coast) illustrate that seditious, infectious ideas can be carried like human and nonhuman cargo across the water to port cities, and while these aquatic connections can be chaotic, they are also opportunities to foreground the connectivity Hopkins carries into her larger narrative of resistance and redemption.

INDIGENOUS ROMANCE: HOPKINS'S DESERT-ISLAND ADVENTURE

Placing the oceanic prologue from *Contending Forces* in conversation with *Winona*'s island-opening illuminates Hopkins's awareness and intention of locating an Indigenous relationship between "settlers" such as White Eagle and the fugitive *marronnage* of subjects such as Winona and her foster brother. Following DeLoughrey's application of Brathewaite's "tidalectics" to interlink Caribbean discourse and the Pacific Islands, I trace Hopkins's deployment of "an alter/native historiography" that centers women's stories to create a "feminized vision of history" that destabilizes continental politics that avoid the global implications of black diasporic identity and view island constituencies/geographies as insular.[66] The tidalectic archipelagraphy evident in the textual circuits of *Contending Forces* shifts in *Winona*'s island-opening to a freshwater lake where Hopkins's archipelagic diaspora inventively foregrounds questions of indigeneity and belonging in a revisionist multigenre epic that manifests a transnational connectivity between the United States and Canada. In *Winona*'s archipelagic framework, tidalectics functions as a reading practice that challenges "rigid claims of ethnic nationalism," a model that does not "romanticize indigeneity nor pathologize diaspora."[67] Hopkins unsettles such intentions primarily because she so often links her historicized romances with other popular genres, such as the adventure narrative, fantasy, mystery, and the western. At times, she appears to reinforce the very problematic tensions the methodological frameworks I have linked together were intended to dispel; at others, Hopkins's examination of these tensions, entangled and contradictory as they might appear, also generates a *productive* chaos as her purposeful genre innovations offer layered, alternative visions to the continentality of the nation.

The other island tropology Hopkins repurposes to her "Western" novel is the Robinsonade. Critics such as Alisha Knight read *Winona* as a bildungsroman reflective of Hopkins's desire to replicate the US-American success novel; others have focused on the novel as a tale of heroism and masculinity "muddied by issues of Native American removal and westward expansion."[68] I focus singularly on the first installment—the initial three chapters of the serial novel that take place on an unnamed desert island. The desert-island genre is a form of adventure novel popularized by Daniel Defoe's *Robinson Crusoe*. In addition to its mass appeal, the genre was "central to the indoctrination of young British boys into the emerging ideologies of masculine British nationalism and colonialism."[69] Many critics have identified *Winona* as Hopkins's Western adventure story, focusing on the novel's dramatization of John Brown's massacre at Pottawatomie Creek in 1854 and its critique of the Kansas-Nebraska Act nullifying the Missouri Compromise; none, however, has noted the particular significance of the island-opening to Hopkins's repurposing of popular masculinist genres to her political and aesthetic aims. White Eagle, clearly a Crusoe figure, is introduced and ushered off stage in the first pages of the serial, providing the context but not the central theme of the story. His absence allows Hopkins to recast the children as castaways, thus setting in motion her sweeping continental narrative.

The opening paragraph of the serial novel immediately locates readers in a liminal space, floating on a canoe suspended between the United States and Canada on a figurative boundary that is simultaneously artificial, natural, and flexible:

> Crossing the Niagara river in a direct line, the Canadian shore lies not more than eight miles from Buffalo, New York, and in the early 50's small bands of Indians were still familiar figures on both the American and Canadian borders. Many strange tales of romantic happenings in this mixed community of Anglo-Saxons, Indians, and Negroes might be told similar to the one I am about to relate, and the world stand aghast and try in vain to find the

dividing line supposed to be a natural barrier between the white and the dark-skinned race.[70]

Several aspects of Hopkins's island locale resonate with historical accounts regarding Grand Island, situated in the Niagara River near Niagara Falls. The Seneca used Ga-We-Not (Great Island) as a hunting preserve before it became the contested terrain of several ethnic and national disputes. Possession of Grand Island transferred from Iroquois, Erie, Seneca, French, and English hands before its final incorporation as part of New York when purchased in 1815 for one thousand dollars.[71] The specific and contested Indigenous and national identity of Grand Island and its adjacent islands become part of the archipelagic representation of the imagined refuge of Judah and Winona.

Hopkins maps the specific geography of Grand Island onto her imagined isle, while manipulating the temporality of her locale. Time thus becomes recursive and retrospective (recall that the title of *Contending Forces*' first chapter is "A Retrospect of the Past"); such recursiveness is inextricable from the sense of allotopia present in Hopkins's rendering of the island settings in both texts. The island scenarios thus occur in "island time," which I am positing here as a spatial and temporal construct that draws productively on Wai Chee Dimock's broadening model of a "deep time" that extends beyond the continental newness of the United States and follows the crisscrossing threads that weave their way through the US-American and, more generally, archipelagic American literary traditions. My reading of Hopkins is a knot on one of those transnational threads, linking fresh- and saltwater islands to their continental referents through an archipelagic structure that exists even in the interior. Set against the scope of deep time, the insularity of the island coexists with the temporal and spatial openness of Glissant's "Antillean imaginary" of islands as openings.[72] In *Winona*'s prologue, island time is less about revolutionary sensibility than it is about inserting an Indigenous temporality underneath nation time, though the acts of disruption that occur on the island do foreshadow the national upheaval of the coming civil war. "Island time" takes seriously Marjorie Perloff's somewhat flippant, yet persistent, reference to desert island insularity as a necessary conduit for slow reading.[73] I contend that "island time" in *Winona* also manifests a political *urgency* evident in the episodic structure that allows Hopkins to manipulate time and space in ways that further a revisionist historiography that imagines the continent presettlement. Her invocation of *Hiawatha* is another recursive tool: the nostalgic epic establishes her protagonists' Indigenous identity; however, the novel ultimately renders their Native claims incompatible with US national assertions of identity.

The very next scene provides a narrative consistent with romanticized stories of first contact drawn in part from iconographic representations of native peoples as noble savages:

> On the sandy beach Indian squaws sat in the sun with their gaudy blankets wrapped around them in spite of the heat, watching the steamers upon the lakes, the constant traffic of the canal boats, their beaded wares spread temptingly upon the firm white sand to catch the fancy of the free-handed sailor or visitor. Upon the bosom of Lake Erie floated a canoe. . . . The occupants were fishing; presently the canoe headed for an island lying close in the shadow of Grand Island, about a mile from it. The lad who handled the paddle so skillfully might have been mistaken for an Indian at first glance, for his lithe brown body lacked nothing of the suppleness and grace which constant exercise in the open air alone imparts. He wore moccasins and his dress otherwise was that of a young brave, save for feathers and paint . . . as the sunlight gleamed upon his bare head it revealed the curly crispy hair of a Negro.

Even as she envisions the Robinsonade in a new setting, Hopkins finds prelapsarian imagery useful to her larger project of revisionist American historiography, which includes a reorientation of Afro-Native kinship ties. Also in the canoe is a girl with "two long plaits of sunny hair" but no other obvious racial designation. DeLoughrey argues that the canoe (whose English name is a transliteration from an original Arawak cognate) functions as a vessel of history vital to the "historical genealogy" of the Caribbean and Pacific archipelagoes.[74] The canoe's occupants, two children named Judah and Winona, similarly embody a multiethnic, transnational history. They are the foundlings of White Eagle, a white man "gone native," "adopted" by the "Senaca [sic] Indians" after he saves the life of the chief Red Eagle.[75] They live with their benefactor on a "small island in the lake" (Lake Erie) with a mixed-race, "half-breed" woman named Nokomis, who serves as housekeeper. Winona is the daughter of an escaped slave, an unnamed "well-educated mulatress" whom White Eagle married in Canada under English law.[76] Hopkins's Indigenous island imaginary enables a family unit based on a shared cultural history that is not dependent on blood as a direct counter to personhood or nationalist claims based solely on whiteness.[77]

Black representation of the type of Indigenous iconography found in the aforementioned scenes was far from uncommon in early African American literature and art. Dorri Beam and Lois Brown both observe that Hopkins draws the names of her characters from Henry Wadsworth Longfellow's popular *The Song of Hiawatha* (1855).[78] Longfellow's epic poem is central to US-American mythology regarding settlers' claims to inhabiting the New World; its persistence in nineteenth-century art and literary culture is symbolic of the recursive tendency of "colonial powers [to] fetishize what they have effectively destroyed."[79] African American artists and writers, such as Afro-Native sculptor Edmonia Lewis, were similarly enamored with the trope of the "vanishing Indian" promoted by Longfellow.[80] Placed in the complex context of African American literary representations of Native figures, Hopkins's deployment of Indian iconography in *Winona* is ambivalent to say the least, yet it is consistent with her tendency to intertwine imperialist sensibilities with her critique of racialized policies. Once again, she unites reactionary and insurrectionary tropes, in this case of the "Native," to stress the porosity of the nation's hybrid ethnic ecology.

As in Hopkins's Bermuda, Edenic overtones and outrageous natural beauty overwhelm the deliberately unnamed island space. Winona and Judah play and sing amid wild turkeys and partridges, picking flowers and generally enjoying their innocent prelapsarian state, insulated from the politics of nations and continents—until their idyll is interrupted by two white interlocutors in a scene that reproduces both Grace Montfort's racial coding and the violence of first contact between white and Native peoples, even if in this case the "natives" are passing. Two strangers approach the island by boat during a hunting excursion: "They came on rapidly, and in a moment the occupants stood on the beach before the surprised children. They were white men, garbed in hunter's dress. They seemed surprised to see the girl and boy on an apparently uninhabited island."[81] Mutual surprise turns swiftly to calculation on the part of the intruders, who quickly determine and assert their rights to capitalize on both the island and its occupants. Hopkins inserts the Robinsonade trope (and *Sea Venture* origin story) of accidental colonization into an American frontier context. A brief conversation with the children determines that the island is "not a part of the Canadian shore." "It's just an island," responds Judah. This line of inquiry quickly moves the island from unnamed, unowned land to unclaimed, and therefore available, property, which includes human and nonhuman inhabitants. Judah is deemed a "likely nigger," and Winona, though racially indeterminate to one of the men, is "no puzzle to" the other, who declares she is "a nigger, too." When the children are asked to clarify their racial identity—"Then you're Indians?"— Judah responds in the affirmative. Unfortunately, his "crisp" and "wool[ly] head," along with Winona's inability to claim the paternal whiteness of her absent father, render both children chattel under the law and custom of the United States.[82] Like any canny colonials, the strangers deliberately export their racial hierarchies, nullifying any Indigenous sovereignty of the desert island.

This restaging of the landfall of first contact demonstrates how much issues of sovereignty, boundaries, and cartography, bound up with racialized taxonomies of identification, are at the forefront of Hopkins's texts. The strangers temporarily return to "civilization" only to come back, murder White Eagle, and remand his children into slavery in Missouri, despite the temporary interference of an enamored Englishman who happens to be passing by and endeavors to help his "island protégés." In a replay of the Montfort seizure, the British Maxwell is dumbfounded to learn that the children were claimed under "the new act for the rendition of fugitive slaves jes' passed by Congress." In response to his incredulity and protest that such seizure was illegal because "both were born free," he is told that "the child follows the condition of the mother."[83] Maxwell is then drawn into the adventure story, and later subjected to a brutal experience of US-American oppression, via his romantic attraction to Winona. The interracial love triangle established in the island-opening foreshadows an ending that indicates "the failure of the American nation to provide a home for Hopkins's mixed-race characters."[84]

To underscore Winona's nonviability in the United States, Hopkins consistently identifies Winona with the Indian Pipe, an indigenous flower with the curious property that it lacks chlorophyll or pigmentation, that she situates on the unnamed isle.[85] The flower's appearance communicates delicacy, sensuality, Indian lore, and indigeneity. All are characteristics associated with Winona's "beautiful chiseled features, the olive complexion with a hint of pink like that which suffused the fragile flowers."[86] Beam argues that the Indian Pipe represents Winona's awakening sexuality: Hopkins's florid style of language is not excessive or arbitrary but is part of a carefully embedded strategy for inserting moments of interiority, spirituality, and erotic individuality within the script of uplift narrative.[87] Building from Beam, I contend that Hopkins grafts the Indian pipe onto Winona's body to emphasize their shared indigeneity to the fictive island, a nativity that renders both Winona and the flowers incapable of flourishing within the national boundaries of the continental United States. The Indian pipe's lack of chlorophyll renders it translucent (a translucence that Grace Montfort's skin lacks), but it also creates a curious effect: the petals "turn black as soon as you touch them."[88] The racialized gaze of outsiders, which falls both on Grace and Winona in turn, is an act of looking that becomes a kind of blackening touch.

Hopkins's use of island and archipelagic space in *Winona* also prefigures island references in later African American texts; the floral arousal in the Indian pipe scenes (Winona's first encounter with the "gauzy" "pink stems" causes her to "drop upon her knees in silent ecstacy [sic]") anticipates Janie's often discussed sexual awakening beneath the pear trees in Zora Neale Hurston's *Their Eyes Were Watching God* (1937) and complements her gestures toward island space. Winona's eroticized encounter with the island's Indian pipes foreshadows a later scene on the continent when she secretes herself away, propelled by "some impulse of the wild things among whom she had lived" on the island.

On a "divan of dried moss," she "lay in a sweet stupor until forced to arouse herself."[89] Given the specifically sexual dangers surrounding attractive, mixed-race, black women, moments of private erotic pleasure and interiority are rare and often violently disrupted. Similarly, in *Their Eyes*, it is just after Janie's sexual awakening that her grandmother ("Nanny") insists on a forced marriage to break the chain of sexual violence she believes is unavoidable in the continental United States. Roberts notes that Nanny's reference to "some place way off in de ocean where de black man is in power" marks Hurston's "engagements with island-space."[90] Nanny's verbal gesture to an island space with inverted power relations is likely a reference to the Haitian revolution, but its nonspecificity, like the multiple gestures "over there" in Hopkins's texts, also communicates that such an island exists only as a utopic fantasy, or, as in the case of *Winona*, cannot be found contiguous to the continental United States. But how do we reconcile Grace Montfort's hyperbolic pain with Winona's stolen, florid pleasure in the midst of a revolt? Instead of a brutalizing whipping post, pleasure is smuggled onto the continent in the form of wild, indigenous flora that temporarily enables Winona's individual resistance to the overwhelming conscription of enslaved black female identity that condemns Montfort. Here Hopkins's island-opening fosters a "water- and land-evoked connectivity" in which the Indian pipes, the unnamed island, Niagara Falls, hunters, Indians, and Winona's and Judah's fluctuating national and ethnic status are suspended in a productive chaos.[91] This is a chaos that prefigures the coming war, and the insurrectionary resistance perpetuated by John Brown and the Free-Soilers, whose continental narrative Winona, Judah, and Maxwell are all swept into.

Unlike *Contending Forces*, *Winona*'s characters do return to their desert isle; however, it is no longer a viable habitation but a nostalgic stopover on their way to exile in England, the only place Winona can claim her noble heritage. As Aunt Vinnie relates, "Dar's dat gal, she's got black blood nuff in her to put her on de block in this fersaken country, but *over dar* she's a lady with de top crus' of de crus'." Once again, Hopkins establishes England as a sanctuary, yet Aunt Vinnie uses Winona's story as a warning that the absurdity of US racial distinctions cannot continue; every time she repeats the tale to her white and black neighbors she concludes with "a short sermon on the fate of her race," ending prophetically that "somethin's gwine happen" over *here*.[92]

More than simply reading Hopkins as an early diasporic African American author, I see her directly engaging Atlantic and maritime discourse to advance her revisionist historical fictions. In *Contending Forces*, the Bermudian ship that conveys the Montforts to their doom also portends the "wreck" of the coming Civil War; *Winona*'s island-opening shifts the adventurer's spyglass away from the single, white, working-class male to an Afro-Native duo that embody the contradictions and contestations of US national identity and citizenship claims. Hopkins's island openings activate spatial-temporal circuits residing in island tropes; these linguistic and nonverbal gestures mark her diaspora as part of an archipelagic Atlantic tradition illustrating that frameworks deriving from archipelagic analyses have much to offer the continental study of US-American and, more specifically, African American literature. They are applicable to contemporary authors such as Toni Morrison, as well as to slave and travel narratives that constitute the earliest examples of black Atlantic literature, including those written by Olaudah Equiano, Nancy Prince, and Mary Seacole. In focusing on Hopkins's island openings, I extend an open invitation to landlocked scholars to reread other quintessentially African American narratives on island time, within the diverse framework of scholarship resulting from archipelagic, oceanic, and hemispheric American studies. Such forays enhance our understandings of alternative concepts of nationality, citizenship, and submarine categories of unification.

NOTES

Epigraph: William Strachey, "From A True Reportory of the Wreck and Redemption of Sir Thomas Gates [1625]," in *The Bedford Companion to Shakespeare: An Introduction with Documents*, ed. Russ McDonald, 2nd ed. (Boston: Bedford/St. Martin's), 181.

1. Brian Russell Roberts, "Abolitionist Archipelago: Pre- and Post-Emancipation Islands of Slavery and Emancipation," *Atlantic Studies* 8, no. 2 (2011): 234.

2. Philip E. Steinberg, "Insularity, Sovereignty and Statehood: The Representations of Islands on Portolan Charts and the Construction of the Territorial State," *Geografiska Annaler: Series B, Human Geography* 87, no. 4 (2005): 253.

3. "Island time" signifies and reorients what Wai Chee Dimock calls "deep time," a concept with a long view of history that interrogates the "shorthand" of American literature by working to understand its place in global culture. My term also signifies the more colloquial use of "island time," as a slower, or extended pace, like slow reading; Dimock, *Through Other Continents: American Literature across Deep Time* (Princeton, NJ: Princeton University Press, 2006), 3.

4. Paul Giles, "Antipodean American Literature: Franklin, Twain, and the Sphere of Subalternity," *American Literary History* 20, nos. 1–2 (2008): 23.

5. I borrow this phrase from Ivy Wilson's identification of "politically nonmaterial elements of democracy in the antebellum United States" as "specters" or "shadows"; Wilson, *Specters of Democracy: Blackness and the Aesthetics of Politics in the Antebellum U.S.* (New York: Oxford University Press, 2011), 3.

6. Michael Drexler, introduction to *The Secret History, or the Horrors of St. Domingo and Laura*, by Leonora Sansay (Peterborough, Can.: Broadview Press, 2007), 12.

7. Lois Brown, *Pauline Elizabeth Hopkins: Black Daughter of the Revolution* (Chapel Hill: University of North Carolina Press, 2008), 297.

8. Richard Yarborough, introduction to *Contending Forces*, by Pauline Hopkins (New York: Oxford University Press, 1988), xxviii; hereafter cited as CF.

9. Giles, "Antipodean American Literature," 23.

10. Brian Russell Roberts, "Archipelagic Diaspora, Geographical Form, and Hurston's *Their Eyes Were Watching God*," *American Literature* 85, no. 1 (March 2013): 125.

11. Roberts, "Archipelagic Diaspora," 125.

12. Edward Kamau Brathwaite, *Contradictory Omens: Cultural Diversity and Integration in the Caribbean* (Mona, Jamaica: Savcou Publications, 1974), 64.

13. My understanding of the plantation zone is similar to Monique Allewaert's designation of "a place that is tropical (or subtropical) and whose economy and political structures are shaped by the plantation form"; Allewaert, *Ariel's Ecology: Plantations, Personhood, and Colonialism in the American Tropics* (Minneapolis: University of Minnesota Press, 2014), 30. However, I diverge from Allewaert's usage of the term to examine alternate versions of personhood connecting plant life, humans, and nonhuman beings, to orient the term toward island slavocracies *beyond* the tropics.

14. Thadious Davis identifies the "southscape" as a formulation that attends to the South as a social, political, cultural, and economic construct; Davis, *Southscapes: Geographies of Race, Region, and Literature* (Chapel Hill: University of North Carolina Press, 2011), 2.

15. Quoted in Brian Russell Roberts and Michelle Stephens, "Archipelagic American Studies and the Caribbean," *Journal of Transnational American Studies* 5, no. 1 (2013): 14.

16. Pauline E. Hopkins, *Contending Forces: A Romance Illustrative of Negro Life North and South*, ed. Henry Louis Gates, Jr. (1900; repr. New York: Oxford University Press, 1988), 22.

17. William Shakespeare, *The Tempest*, act 1, scene 2 (London: Arden Shakespeare, 2001), 165.

18. Hans W. Hannau, *The Bermuda Isles in Full Color* (London: Macmillan Press, 1994), 5.

19. Elizabeth DeLoughrey, "'The litany of islands, The rosary of archipelagoes': Caribbean and Pacific Archipelagraphy," ARIEL: *A Review of International English Literature* 32, no. 1 (2001): 23.

20. Hannau, *Bermuda Isles*, 9.

21. The significance of the wreck of the *Sea Venture* cannot be overstated. In addition to its literary influence, it is fundamental to the rise of capitalism in the maritime Atlantic. As Peter Linebaugh and Marcus Rediker argue, "Within the story of the *Sea-Venture* and its people lies a larger story about the rise of capitalism and the beginning of a new epoch in human history"; Linebaugh and Rediker, *The Many-Headed Hydra: Sailors, Slaves, Commoners, and the Hidden History of the Revolutionary Atlantic* (Boston: Beacon, 2000), 15.

22. Derek Walcott, "The Sea Is History," in *Selected Poems* (New York: Farrar, Straus, Girroux, 2007), 137.

23. Hester Blum, "The Prospect of Oceanic Studies," PMLA 125, no. 3 (2010): 670.

24. Mary Prince, *The History of Mary Prince, A West Indian Slave, Related by Herself, with a Supplement by the Editor*, 3rd ed. (London: F. Westley and A. H. Davis, 1831), 22, 23, accessed Sept. 30, 2016, http://docsouth.unc.edu/neh/prince/prince.html.

25. Prince, *History*, 11.

26. Prince, *History*, 10.

27. Prince, *History*, 38.

28. Antonio Benítez-Rojo coins the trope of the repeating island as a way of positing the "sociocultural fluidity that the Caribbean archipelago presents, with its historiographic turbulence and its ethnological and linguistic clamor"; Antonio Benítez-Rojo, *The Repeating Island: The Caribbean and the Postmodern Perspective*, 2nd ed., trans. James E. Maraniss (Durham, NC: Duke University Press, 1996), 4.

29. Hannau, *Bermuda Isles*, 15.

30. Prince, *History*, 10.

31. Hopkins, CF, 22–23.

32. There is extensive criticism of the novel as a multigenerational tale of trial and triumph. *Contending Forces* is widely considered Hopkins's masterpiece. For criticism on the novel in its entirety, see Lois Brown, *Pauline Elizabeth Hopkins: Black Daughter of the Revolution* (Chapel Hill, NC: University of North Carolina Press, 2008), 221.

33. Hopkins, CF, 20–21.

34. Hopkins, CF, 40.

35. The Haitian Revolution concluded with Jean-Jacques Dessalines's proclamation of 1804. Slavery was abolished in the British colonies in 1833.

36. Hopkins, CF, 21, 32.

37. Hopkins, CF, 26.

38. Hopkins, CF, 30.

39. Characteristics of Hopkins's style that Dorri Beam identifies in her reading of *Winona* are also applicable to *Contending Forces*. See Dorri Beam, *Style, Gender, and Fantasy in Nineteenth-Century American Women's Writing* (Cambridge: Cambridge University Press, 2010), 135.

40. Benítez-Rojo, *Repeating Island*, 2.

41. Beam, *Style, Gender, and Fantasy*, 21, 17. British planters were belatedly compensated for the confiscation of their "property"; the enslaved were gradually manumitted and denied reparations. The issue of reparations for the enslaved continues to be raised in British and US courts.

42. Yogita Goyal, *Romance, Diaspora, and Black Atlantic Literature* (Cambridge: Cambridge University Press, 2010), 54.

43. Mary Louise Pratt, *Imperial Eyes: Travel Writing and Transculturation* (London: Routledge, 1992).

44. Rather than reading *Of One Blood* as pan-African or Ethiopianist, as several critics do who position it as the ur-diaspora novel, Goyal suggests that Hopkins's "turn to Africa" is imperialist in nature; Goyal, *Romance*, 6.

45. Hopkins, CF, 21. The idea of Bermuda as an island where "winter never comes" would become an essential part of the island's promotion as a "coral chip of England"; Hannau, *Bermuda Isles*, 5. It should also be noted that New Bern, part of the coastal communities that compose the Pamlico National Seashore, is not actually as barren as Hopkins depicts.

46. Hopkins, CF, 35.

47. Hopkins, CF, 40.

48. Elsewhere I have posited the development of the iconography of the mulatta in the mid-nineteenth century through a shared grammar of racial representation; Cherene

Sherrard-Johnson, *Portraits of the New Negro Woman: Visual and Literary Culture in the Harlem Renaissance* (New Brunswick, NJ: Rutgers University Press, 2007), but here I look to an earlier codex to understand the features identified by seaside spectators taken up by Teresa Zacknodnik, *The Mulatta and the Politics of Race* (Jackson: University Press of Mississippi, 2014); and Eva Allegra Raimon, *The "Tragic Mulatta" Revisited: Race and Nationalism in Nineteenth-Century Antislavery Fiction* (New Brunswick, NJ: Rutgers University Press, 2004).

49. Hopkins, CF, 50.

50. "Cameo Cutting," *Appleton's Mechanics' Magazine and Engineers' Journal* 1, no. 5 (1851): 303.

51. Hopkins, CF, 41.

52. Hopkins, CF, 42.

53. Hopkins, CF, 41, 45.

54. Fred Moten, *In the Break: The Aesthetics of the Black Radical Tradition* (Minneapolis: University of Minnesota Press, 2003), 24.

55. Brown, *Pauline Elizabeth Hopkins*, 221.

56. Hopkins, CF, 69.

57. Saidiya Hartman, *Scenes of Subjection: Terror, Slavery, and Self-Making in Nineteenth-Century America* (New York: Oxford University Press, 1997).

58. Moten, *In the Break*, 3.

59. Hazel Carby, *Reconstructing Womanhood: The Emergence of the Afro-American Woman Novelist* (New York: Oxford, 1987), 39.

60. Hopkins, CF, 69.

61. Hopkins, CF, 69; Frederick Douglass, *Narrative of the Life of Frederick Douglass* (Oxford: Oxford University Press, 1999), 18.

62. Hopkins, CF, 71.

63. William Wells Brown, *Clotel; or, the President's Daughter: A Narrative of Slavery in the United States* (London: Partridge and Oakley, 1853), 218.

64. Hopkins, CF, 107.

65. Davis, *Southscapes*, 206.

66. Elizabeth M. DeLoughrey, *Routes and Roots: Navigating Caribbean and Pacific Island Literatures* (Honolulu: University of Hawai'i Press, 2007), 2.

67. DeLoughrey, *Routes and Roots*, xi.

68. Brown, *Pauline Elizabeth Hopkins*, 368.

69. DeLoughrey, "'Litany of islands,'" 22.

70. Pauline Hopkins, *Winona; A Tale of Negro Life in the South and Southwest*, 1902, in *The Magazine Novels of Pauline Hopkins* (New York: Oxford University Press, 1988), 287.

71. Frances M. Yensan, *The History of Grand Island*, http://isledegrande.com/gihist.htm.

72. Quoted in Roberts and Stephens, "Archipelagic American Studies," 14.

73. When Perloff asks "Where else but on a desert island can this luxury become reality?" she acknowledges both the continued resurgence of the Robinsonade and that her slow reading process is enabled by first-world privilege. Her island is an easy chair in a library on the Upper West Side; her "adventure" involves making sense of a paratext accessible only through persistent rereading without the constraints of academic

speech or imposition; Marjorie Perloff, "Removing the Eggshells: Rereading Wittgenstein on a Desert Island," *Genre* 33 (Fall/Winter 2000), 276.

74. DeLoughrey, *Routes and Roots*, 21–22.

75. Hopkins, *Winona*, 287–89.

76. Hopkins, *Winona*, 290.

77. Brit Rusert asserts that "Afro-Native America" offered a counterdiscourse "of kinship that did not always privilege biological kinship" "but [depends] on a shared plight—a shared history of racial violence, removal, containment, and subjugation by the United States"; Rusert, "Types of Mankind: Visualizing Kinship in Afro-Native America," *Common-Place: The Journal of Early American Life* 13, no. 1 (October 2012), http://www.common-place-archives.org/vol-13/no-01/tales/.

78. The name Winona comes from Hiawatha's mother, Wenonah, and his grandmother, Nokomis; Beam, *Style, Gender, and Fantasy*, 166. Recent scholarship has fixated on Hopkins's extensive recycling of other texts. JoAnn Pavletich's research reveals that several passages appearing in *Winona* closely resemble sections of Mary Hartwell Catherwood's *The White Islander* (New York: The Century Co., 1893). For further examinations of the source texts integrated by Hopkins see JoAnn Pavletich, "... we are going to take that right": Power and Plagiarism in Pauline Hopkins's *Winona*," *The College Language Association Journal*, 59.2 (December 2015), 115–30, and Geoffrey Sanborn, "The Wind of Words: Plagiarism and Intertextuality in *Of One Blood*," *J19: The Journal of Nineteenth-Century Americanists* 3, no. 1 (2015): 67–87.

79. DeLoughrey, *Routes and Roots*, 30.

80. Other examples of stories romanticizing Indian removal include James Fenimore Cooper's *The Last of the Mohicans* and other of Longfellow's works, such as *Evangeline: A Tale of Acadie* (1847). See also Kirsten Pai Buick, *Child of the Fire: Mary Edmonia Lewis and the Problem of Art History's Black and Indian Subject* (Durham, NC: Duke University Press, 2010), 79.

81. Hopkins, *Winona*, 294.

82. Hopkins, *Winona*, 294–95.

83. Hopkins, *Winona*, 314, 315.

84. See Goyal's assessment of *Of One Blood*'s prototypical tragic mulatta resolution; Goyal, *Romance*, 29.

85. Chlorophyll is a green pigment that allows plans to absorb energy from light; it is a critical molecule in the process of photosynthesis.

86. Hopkins, *Winona*, 290.

87. Beam, *Style, Gender, and Fantasy*, 165.

88. Hopkins, *Winona*, 292.

89. Hopkins, *Winona*, 376.

90. Hurston, *Their Eyes*, 14; Roberts, "Archipelagic Diaspora," 125.

91. Roberts, "Archipelagic Diaspora," 125.

92. Hopkins, *Winona*, 436, 437. My italics.

11 "WE ARE NOT AMERICAN"

COMPETING RHETORICAL ARCHIPELAGOES IN HAWAIʻI

Brandy Nālani McDougall

IN HER 1993 SPEECH FOR THE OVERTHROW of the Hawaiian Kingdom centennial at ʻIolani Palace, Haunani-Kay Trask addressed fellow Hawaiians with an upturned fist: "We are not American. We are not American. We are not American. Say it in your heart. Say it in your sleep. We are not American. We will die as Hawaiians. We will never be Americans."[1] Following four generations of intense US-Americanization, militarization, and tourism in Hawaiʻi, Trask's words shocked many. She continued, "The Americans, my people, are our enemies and you must understand that. . . . They took our land, they imprisoned our queen, they banned our language, they forcibly made us a colony of the United States."[2] Trask's rhetoric relied upon a tradition of a unified Hawaiian archipelago, ka pae ʻāina Hawaiʻi, which was and remains separate geographically, culturally, and politically from the United States. In positing Hawaiians as distinct from US-Americans, Trask implied the continued cultural sovereignty of Hawaiians, even without internationally recognized political sovereignty. Positing US-Americans as "enemies" further solidifies her invocation of a unified Hawaiian archipelagic identity exclusive of and despite US colonialism.

While there is much that can be discussed of Trask's speech, I share the above excerpts because they challenge the US-American "rhetorical archipelago" that reinforces Hawaiʻi as part of the United States, while reinforcing the "rhetorical archipelago" of Hawaiʻi as a continuing lāhui (nation, people). I offer the term "rhetorical archipelago" as a means to examine the rhetorical symbology and other exigencies that determine the unified yet negotiable relationality and borders of the archipelago. I argue that because archipelagic unification is always vulnerable and in flux, the rhetorical archipelago is subject to and mediated by domestic and foreign relations of power that are themselves vulnerable and in flux and depend on the inclusion and exclusion that unification provides. Moreover, as the rhetorical archipelago is bound by the politics of a place, the particulars of its unification exigencies are often complicated by competing rhetorics of unification that may use the same symbology to achieve and maintain Indigenous and colonial communion, as is the case within Hawaiʻi.

The archipelago is useful for challenging the rigidity and omnipresence of colonial situations. Elizabeth DeLoughrey's "system of archipelagraphy," for example, centers "a historiography that considers chains of islands in fluctuating relationship to their surrounding seas, islands, and continents."[3] With these "fluctuating relationships" in mind, I examine Kamehameha I's unification of ka pae ʻāina o Hawaiʻi (the Hawaiian archipelago), as well as how genealogy, the Hawaiian flag, and Kamehameha I have been leveraged to reaffirm the rhetorical archipelagoes of the Hawaiian Kingdom and the United States. I conclude briefly with recent discussions focused on Hawaiian independence to argue that the Hawaiian rhetorical archipelago continues to destabilize the fixity of US colonial incorporation.

UNIFICATION AND KAMEHAMEHA I'S RHETORICAL PAE ʻĀINA

In his series "Ka Moolelo Hawaii Kahiko" in *Ka Naʻi Aupuni* in 1906, Joseph Poepoe describes Ka Pae Moku o Hawaiʻi (also, the Hawaiian archipelago) as stretching twelve hundred miles "mai ka Piko mai o Wakea, oia hoi ka Poai-Waena" (from the navel of Wākea, or the Poai-Waena [equatorial circle]). He notes that ancestral traditions name as many as twelve islands that "e nee lalani like ana" (have been emerging linearly) from the east to the west and lists them: Hawaiʻi, Maui, Kahoʻolawe, Lānaʻi, Molokini, Molokaʻi, Oʻahu, Kauaʻi, Niʻihau, Lehua, Kaʻula, and Nihoa.[4]

None of the constitutions of the Hawaiian Kingdom is as specific, using only "Hawaiian Islands" to describe its territory. United States colonial documents such as the failed Annexation Treaty (1897) and the Newlands Resolution (1898) follow with the same ambiguity. The Organic Act of 1900, which incorporated Hawaiʻi as a US territory, however, defines the archipelago as consisting of "Hawaii, Maui, Oahu, Kauai, Molokai, Lanai, Niihau, Kahoolawe, Molokini, Lehua, Kaula, Nihoa, Necker, Laysan, Gardiner, Lisiansky, Ocean, French Frigates Shoal, Palmyra, Brooks Shoal, Pearl and Hermes Reef, Gambia Shoal and Dowsett and Maro Reef,"[5] noticeably proceeding from Hawaiian to foreign names and encompassing a much larger territory than the one Poepoe outlines.[6] Together, these colonial documents appear to permanently fix the Hawaiian archipelago not only as a part of the United States, but also as encompassing more land and ocean territory than previous Hawaiian Kingdom perceptions.

Though the *Oxford English Dictionary* traces the etymology of "archipelago" to the Italian *arcipélago*, with *arci-* meaning "chief" or "principal" and *-pélago* meaning "deep," "abyss," or "pool," referring to the Aegean Sea, the contemporary meaning is "any sea, or sheet of water, in which there are numerous islands; [or]

a group of islands." This shift indicates how the term "archipelago" has come to be applied outside of its original context and with an emphasis on multiple islands in proximity,[7] naturalizing the grouping of islands as inevitable and static. The Hawaiian term for archipelago, *pae ʻāina* or *pae moku* in ʻōlelo Hawaiʻi (the Hawaiian language), stands in strong contrast. *Pae* means to "cluster, row, or group"; it can also mean "to land, disembark, or come ashore." *ʻĀina*, or "that which feeds," is the word for land, while *moku* means "district, island, or islet" or "to be cut or severed, divided." Both terms are used interchangeably and conceive of multiple lands as interconnected;[8] however, they also imply active human and state intervention in the creation of an archipelago, as opposed to a naturalized grouping of lands because of geographical proximity. In this way, the unification possibilities of an archipelago, just as the unification possibilities of an island or continent, are multiple, shifting, and dependent on the benefits and rhetoric of unification.

By 1810, Kamehameha achieved unification of ka pae ʻāina Hawaiʻi after a nearly twenty-five-year campaign.[9] While he had conquered the islands under his rule politically, their unification was not necessarily stabilized culturally. Being of their own separate kingdoms and aliʻi (rulers), the people of each island had their own histories, as well as their own locational cultures and traditions. Kamehameha's government needed rhetorical symbols of unification that offered a shared history and lived experience. He found these symbols in the moʻokūʻauhau (genealogy) of Papahānaumoku and Wākea and in the Hae Hawaiʻi (the Hawaiian flag). These projects, which helped to reinforce a shared affinity among the islands, enabled the shift from individual island kingdoms into a unified archipelagic political configuration and polity that is still in place today.

Papahānaumoku (Papa) is often seen as the Hawaiian Earth Mother, and Wākea, as the Hawaiian Sky Father. The name Papahānaumoku credits Papa with giving birth to many of the Hawaiian Islands through her union with Wākea. It is unclear how popular Papahānaumoku and Wākea were in the collective memory of the people at the time of Kamehameha's ascension to power, especially in comparison to the ancestral aliʻi of each island kingdom. They were certainly well known, however, throughout the islands, through various moʻolelo, or (hi)stories. Valuing a common rhetorical archipelago, Kamehameha appointed an elder aliʻi, Kaleikuahulu[10] of Hawaiʻi island, to teach his knowledge of moʻokūʻauhau to the aliʻi under him. One of the oli moʻokūʻauhau (genealogy chants) he taught them details the parentage of each of the Hawaiian Islands as well as the temporary separation of Papa and Wākea, when both create islands separately.[11] Hawaiʻi, Mauiloa (Maui), Kahoʻolawe, Kauaʻi, and Niʻihau are born from Papa by Wākea; Lānaʻi is born from Kaula by Wākea; Molokaʻi is born from Hina by Wākea; and Oʻahu is born from Papa by Lua. The oli also relates the births of several generations of aliʻi, in addition to the creation of various kapu, or degrees of sacredness, conferred to aliʻi. Another famous chant of similar theme composed by Pakui, a kahuna (priest and scholar) of Molokai, also circulated throughout the newly formed kingdom at this time. David Chang surmises that Pakui, a junior member of Kamehameha's court, must have known Kaleikuahulu and perhaps even worked closely with him. He concludes that both composers must have "draw[n] upon historical and genealogical sources that would have enjoyed legitimacy" and were "in accord with older songs and stories" in order for the oli to be so broadly accepted among the populace; thus, "the relations between islands they describe were not merely inventions in the service of Kamehameha's ascendancy," but historically grounded compositions rhetorically designed to support archipelagic unification.[12]

Though Kaleikuahulu's chant, like other oli moʻokūʻauhau, relates the history of aliʻi, the makaʻāinana (literally the "people that attend the land," or commoners) could identify with the births of their home (is)lands to which they were spiritually, culturally, and genealogically connected and further see how their islands were joined to each other as a unified whole. Thus, less than twenty years after Kamehameha's death, the Hawaiian scholars who wrote *Ka Mooolelo Hawaiʻi* in 1838 credit Papa and Wākea as "na kupuna mua o ko Hawaii nei lahui kanaka, na kanaka a me naʻlii" (the first ancestors of the Hawaiian nation's people, the commoners and the aliʻi).[13] David Malo confirms Papa and Wākea are "presumably the earliest progenitors of the Hawaiian race," while Kepelino also recognizes them as the ancestors of all Kānaka, naming sixty-six generations of chiefs "born from the loins of Wakea and Papa, . . . [who] became the people of Hawaiʻi."[14]

Abraham Fornander notes that moʻolelo of Papa birthing islands was very popular during the time of Kamehameha,[15] because, as I suggest, it articulated a shared history and common ancestry between islands, which was necessary as Kamehameha maintained unification. Though there are no known records indicating that Kamehameha used the moʻokūʻauhau of Papa and Wākea to favorably campaign for continued unification under his rule, his charging of Kaleikuahulu, and perhaps Pakui, to share this and other moʻokūʻauhau with aliʻi and kahuna, his penchant for strategic management of aliʻi and ʻāina, and the resulting popularity of Papa and Wākea during his reign point to the strong possibility of their being part of Kamehameha's rhetorical archipelago.

Another symbol of unification Kamehameha employed also served to express political sovereignty within the international arena: the Hae Hawaiʻi. While there are competing moʻolelo of the Hae Hawaiʻi's origination,[16] most agree that the first version of the flag was created sometime between 1806 and 1816 under Kamehameha's direction. By 1816, Kamehameha had forged a relatively stable unified archipelago through diplomacy and an emphasis on common ancestry. His unified kingdom, however, was undergoing great change as it entered globalized trade and faced the ongoing threat of foreign imperialism. He took measures to ensure the sovereignty of his newly unified kingdom by creating a national flag that would be recognized by other nations of the world.

Jonathan Pugh uses the term "metamorphosis" to describe "how island movements adapt, transfigure and transform their inheritances into original form" beyond mere mimicry.[17] Thus, though most scholars note the influence of the British, US, and French national flags in the Hae Hawai'i, Patrick Ka'ano'i shares that what is perceived as the "great jack" represents the ālia; the two crossed spears with an upright spear in the center symbolize the māmakakaua, the warrior class; and the puela, a long tapa strip, is used as a marker or banner. Additionally, "the color white represents spirituality; the color red represents the blood of all men or the people of Hawaii; [and] the blue represents continuity as such is the color of the heavens and the sea where it never ends."[18] Embodying this symbolism, the Hae Hawai'i unified the archipelago under the Hawaiian Kingdom, emphasizing common cultural values. As an internationally recognized symbol of sovereignty among an archipelago of nations, the Hae also enabled Hawai'i to enter global trade and negotiate and secure treaties with other countries. From 1846 to 1887, Hawai'i negotiated treaties with eighteen major nations, including the United States, France, and Great Britain, all of whom recognized Hawai'i's independence.[19] As a metamorphosis, the Hae served as an emblem of protection that helped to reinforce the sovereignty and unity of Kamehameha's rhetorical archipelago among nations.

THE HAWAIIAN KINGDOM'S RHETORICAL ARCHIPELAGO

Kamehameha I's rhetorical archipelago was so successful that kingdom-era Hawaiian epistemologies continued to be mobilized to view the interlinkings rather than separations of the islands. While there were several rhetorical symbols of continued archipelagic unification, mo'okū'auhau, the Hae Hawai'i, and Kamehameha I (even after his death in 1819) provide prime examples of how the rhetorical archipelago in the Hawaiian Kingdom continued.

The Kamehameha dynasty lasted over sixty years in Hawai'i (1810–72), enduring several dramatic social, cultural, and political shifts. Despite this, the authority of Kamehameha I's children and grandchildren was never challenged by a competing line of ali'i. Even after the end of Kamehameha's dynasty, succeeding monarchs competed for the throne by demonstrating proximity to his lineage. As rhetorical archipelagoes themselves, genealogies and the act of genealogizing are demonstrations and exercises in relationality. The Hawaiian Kingdom was bound as a lāhui by moʻokūʻauhau, which also served as the national histories of the people. Moʻokūʻauhau, therefore, were used to leverage that relationality and assert and maintain claims to rule.

Jonathan Osorio stresses that "for Hawaiians, the king was not an office of the government; he was the symbol of the Hawaiian people, the bodily link to divine ancestors and the greatness of the Conqueror [Kamehameha]."[20] The successive monarchs, William Charles Lunalilo and David Kalākaua, did not have the benefit of being direct descendants and needed to demonstrate their claims. In the campaign for king against Kalākaua, Lunalilo won largely because of his close lineage to Kamehameha I (as his grandnephew) in 1873. Following Lunalilo's death in 1874, however, Kalākaua was a candidate once again, now running against the Dowager Queen Emma, a descendant of Kamehameha I's brother Keliʻimaikaʻi, and widow of Kamehameha IV. Thus, though Kalākaua was elected as Hawaiʻi's monarch by the legislative vote, Queen Emma held the popular vote due, in part, to her Kamehameha lineage.

Kalākaua could not claim as close a link with the Kamehameha line, so he chose to reinforce his succession to the throne by demonstrating his descent from Keaweʻīkekahialiʻiokamoku (an ancestor of Kamehameha I) through the Kumulipo, an oli moʻokūʻauhau detailing the creation of the universe and humankind. He also created and funded a Board of Genealogy; revived the Hale Nauā, a royal Hawaiian society dedicated to the sciences, cultural arts, and genealogies; and published the Kumulipo.[21] By emphasizing the importance of moʻokūʻauhau as well as by demonstrating his rank, Kalākaua was able to establish his own dynasty.

Despite his dedication to researching and preserving moʻokūʻauhau and asserting his own genealogical claim to the throne, Kalākaua needed to further assuage Emma's supporters and forge political unity among his people; one way he did this was by honoring Kamehameha I. In 1878, the legislature appropriated ten thousand dollars for a Kamehameha statue, and Kalākaua commissioned a bronze sculpture (figure 11.1). Walter Murray Gibson, a supporter of Kalākaua's who was in the House of Representatives, argued for funding the statue by extolling the greatness of Kamehameha: "What is the most notable event, and character, . . . in this century, for Hawaiians to commemorate: What else but the consolidation of the archipelago by the hero Kamehameha? The warrior chief of Kohala towers far above any other one of his race in all Oceanica [sic]."[22] Glenn Wharton suggests that "the Kamehameha sculpture was yet another way to promote the Native monarchy,"[23] as the sculpture of the warrior king invoked a surge of aloha ʻāina (patriotism, love for the land) among Hawaiians for their unified kingdom.

Figure 11.1. Kamehameha statue standing today in front of Aliʻiōlani Hale, a building named for Kamehameha V, currently housing the Hawaiʻi State Supreme Court and formerly serving as the seat of government of the Hawaiian Kingdom. Photo by Cristo Vlahos, 2011. Available at https://commons.wikimedia.org/wiki/File:King_Kamehameha_Statue.JPG. Creative Commons License (CC BY-SA 3.0), https://creativecommons.org/licenses/by-sa/3.0/.

The statue was commissioned that year, in 1878; however, it was not completed until 1880, after US-American Thomas Gould completed the sculpture in Florence, Italy, and it was bronzed in Paris, France. The choice of sculptor and the choice of bronze for the statue illustrate Hawaiʻi's presence within an archipelago of nations within which there were cross-cultural exchanges. Both decisions intended to honor Kamehameha using recognizably European customs and displays of national wealth to perhaps further demonstrate Hawaiʻi's rightful place as an equal among other independent nations. Due to complications, the statue did not arrive in Honolulu until 1883. Still, it was welcomed "with honor guard and great ceremony, . . . carried by horse team to Aliʻiōlani Hale, on King Street, where King Kalakaua unveiled it while the Royal Hawaiian Band played 'Hawaiʻi Ponoʻī,' "[24] Hawaiʻi's national anthem, which Kalākaua wrote in 1874. With a lavish and celebratory display, Kamehameha I was honored as the founder of the Hawaiian Kingdom and as a symbol of the strength of its unification, and Kalākaua was able to demonstrate his intention to follow in Kamehameha's footsteps.

Aside from moʻokūʻauhau and Kamehameha I, the Hae Hawaiʻi also continued to be a powerful symbol in the Hawaiian Kingdom's rhetorical archipelago. In 1845, the flag was standardized with eight stripes to represent the eight main islands, and was rearranged in the reverse order of colors previously used. The stripes were reversed to commemorate the restoration of Hawaiʻi's sovereignty by British admiral Richard Thomas on July 31, 1843, after the Paulet Affair.²⁵ During the five-month occupation, the British naval officer Lord George Paulet ordered all of the Hawaiian flags to be burned. Upon the restoration of Hawai'i's sovereignty, Kamehameha III raised the Hae again and coined what became the motto of the Hawaiian Kingdom: "Ua mau ke ea o ka 'āina i ka pono" (The sovereignty of the land is perpetuated in righteousness), declaring July 31 Lā Ho'iho'i Ea, Sovereignty Restoration Day. Hawai'i was recognized through treaties as independent and was formally welcomed into the archipelago of nations by Britain, France, and the United States later that same year. And the Hae Hawai'i stood even more strongly for Hawai'i's enduring independence.

In 1856, during the reign of Kamehameha IV, the newspaper *Ka Hae Hawaii* was started and represented the government as the official newspaper of Ka Papa Hoonaauao (the Department of Public Instruction). On the first page of the first issue of *Ka Hae Hawaii*, the editor, J. Pula (Fuller), shared the purpose behind the creation of *Ka Hae Hawaii*:

> Ua kau ka Hae o kakou. Eia ke kapalili mai la. . . . Eia ke ano o keia Hae: ke kahea nei i ka poe aloha ia Hawaii nei, e kokua mai ma na mea e holo mua i keia aupuni uuku ma kahi kiekie a me ka hanohano iwaena o na aina o ka honua nei. . . . He pepa keia e kokua ana i na 'lii a me na makaainana.

> This Hae of ours has been established with much anticipation. . . . Here is the point of this Hae: to address the people who love Hawai'i nei, those who will help move this small kingdom forward into a place of prominence and honor among the countries of the world. . . . This is a paper that is going to help the ali'i and the maka'āinana.²⁶

Ka Hae Hawaii ran for six years and is evidence of how the Hae Hawai'i was seen and used by the kingdom as a rhetorical symbol uniting all classes of Hawaiians. It published its final issue on December 25, 1861.

Ka Nupepa Kuokoa, edited by H. M. Wini (Whitney), was established earlier that year and was seen as similar in scope. After *Ka Hae Hawaii*'s last issue, *Kuokoa* published an issue on January 1, 1862, featuring the Hae Hawai'i in full color, an industrious feat virtually unheard of at the time (figure 11.2).²⁷ Under the flag, the caption read, "Ka Hae Nani o Hawaii, E mau kona welo ana" (The Beautiful Flag of Hawai'i, May she always wave.) The accompanying article explained that the editors did this "no ke koiia ana mai e ko makou aloha nui i ko kakou Moi, a me ka Moiwahine, a me ka Haku o Hawaii, ka laua keiki, a me ko Aupuni hoi o kakou. He mea mau ke aloha o na Makaainana i ka Hae o ko lakou

Figure 11.2. Black-and-white reproduction of *Ka Nupepa Kuokoa*'s January 1, 1862, full-color rendering of the Hae Hawai'i.

aina, a i ko lakou wa e ike ai ia ia e welo ana, e hoopiha mai no paha ia i ka naau me ka olioli" ([because they were] compelled by our great love for our King, and the Queen, and the Prince of Hawai'i, their child, and for our Kingdom. The people [maka'āinana] love the flag of their country, and when they see it waving, their hearts should be filled with delight).[28] The innovation of printing the flag in full-color was praised as exemplary of "ke akamai o kanaka maoli" (the intelligence of Kānaka Maoli), who can do anything "like me na ili keokeo" (those with white skin can do).[29]

An oli of fifty-four lines honoring the Hae Hawai'i was included only in the Hawaiian version. Aside from praising its beauty and recounting the loss and restoration of sovereignty, the oli also underscored archipelagic unification in the lines "E welo oe ma Hawaii nae Niihau e hoomalu pu / Malalo iho o kou mau eheu" (You wave from Hawai'i to Ni'ihau to protect [our islands] completely / Under your wings).[30] This issue of *Kuokoa* highlighted the ongoing use of the Hae Hawaii as a rhetorical symbol of archipelagic unity and sovereignty, but it also demonstrated that the Hae was seen as a symbol of protection, enduring independence, and aloha 'āina after 1843.

THE REPUBLIC-TERRITORY-STATE OF HAWAI'I'S RHETORICAL ARCHIPELAGO

During the five years following the kingdom's illegal overthrow by US citizens and business interests in 1893,[31] the Hae Hawai'i was used as the national flag by both the Provisional Government of Hawai'i and the Republic of Hawai'i, though it also continued to be used to represent independence by Hawaiian patriots. Aside from the anti-annexation petitions and an attempted armed rebellion, Kānaka patriots resisted and demonstrated their aloha 'āina through various displays of the Hae Hawai'i, including hatbands, koa wood shields with the Hawaiian coat of arms and crossed flags, and Hawaiian flag quilts.[32] The Hawaiian flag quilts in particular became almost synonymous with the Hae Hawai'i, and often included royal symbols such as the kahili (Hawaiian royal standards), the crown, and the coat of arms along with the words "Ku'u Hae Aloha" or "Ku'u Hae Hawai'i," both meaning "My Beloved Hawaiian Flag." As such, "Hawaiian Flag quilts could simultaneously glorify and celebrate the Hawaiian nation's sovereignty expressed through its political symbols, convey expressions of loyalty to the independent Hawaiian nation and Hawaiian monarchy, and communicate Hawaiians' resistance to foreign political domination."[33] Mo'olelo abound of Hawaiian flag quilts being secured under bed canopies so people could sleep under the flag and thus sleep under the sovereignty and love of country it represented.[34] Today, Hawaiian flag quilts, along with the Hae Hawai'i itself, continue to be cherished family possessions because of their political significance.

The Hae Hawai'i is still a part of both Hawaiian and US rhetorical archipelagoes, as it is now the state flag of Hawai'i, a colonial appropriation that seeks to transform Hawai'i from existing within an archipelago of nations to existing within an archipelago of US states. The purported fixity of statehood proved compelling enough for even the United Nations to remove Hawai'i from its list of non–self-governing territories in need of decolonization in 1959. Despite the flag's cooptation, and the four generations of intensive US-Americanization Hawaiians experienced since the end of the Hawaiian Kingdom, the flag's meaning did not change for Hawaiian patriots, who shared mo'olelo of the flag and its rhetorical symbolism of sovereignty with successive generations. Thus, the Hae Hawai'i is still flown and displayed (often inverted as an international signal of distress) by patriots to represent the ongoing sovereignty of Hawai'i amid US occupation. As Bryan Kamaoli Kuwada writes, we "must remind the State that Hae Hawai'i is our pua hanohano, our lei, our child."[35]

Similarly, Kamehameha I has also been appropriated as a symbol by the state of Hawai'i and the United States. In 1969, ten years after statehood, a new bronze statue of Kamehameha was cast from a mold of the original in Honolulu. Made

Figure 11.3. Replica of the original Kamehameha statue, standing today in Emancipation Hall in the Capitol Visitor Center, Washington, DC. Photo by RadioFan, 2009. Available at https://en.wikipedia.org/wiki/File:Kamehameha_capitol.JPG. Creative Commons License (CC BY-SA 3.0), https://creativecommons.org/licenses/by-sa/3.0/.

to be an exact replica, it was gifted by the state of Hawai'i to the US Capitol's National Statuary Hall, where it stood among other statues reinforcing an archipelago of states. Ironically, the statue was too heavy and in 2008 was moved to Emancipation Hall in the Capitol Visitor Center, where it could perhaps be seen needing emancipation from the United States. On June 11, Kamehameha Day, the only official holiday "of royal origin to survive" in Hawai'i or in any US state,[36] the DC Kamehameha statue is draped in lei, just like those in Hawai'i.

The Capitol website describes the statue as having a "spear in his left hand symboliz[ing] the ability to defend oneself and one's nation; it is also a reminder that Kamehameha ended the wars among the Hawaiian people. His right hand is extended in a gesture of aloha, the traditional spirit of friendly greeting."[37] The statue's inclusion in the Capitol collection, along with this description of Kamehameha's pose, belies the history of the kingdom's struggle to retain internationally recognized sovereignty amid US occupation. Though the spear Kamehameha holds "symbolizes the ability to defend oneself and one's nation," no mention is made of any struggle, especially insofar as the United States is implicated. Moreover, Kamehameha is depicted as a peacemaker, overlooking his prominence as a warrior king. The description of his right hand "extended in a gesture of aloha" problematically conveys a sense of welcoming hospitality. Because of the location of this particular statue in the Capitol, the description and pose imply that Hawai'i welcomed annexation to the United States (figure 11.3).

Figure 11.4. Coin image from the US Mint.

Similar rhetoric can be seen in the Hawai'i quarter design as part of the US Mint's fifty-state quarters program. In 2007, the design titled "Hawai'i—Diverse but Unified" was chosen via a public opinion poll on the Hawai'i governor's website.[38] The design on the reverse side of the quarter features the motto the state of Hawai'i appropriated from the kingdom, and Kamehameha I stretching his hand toward the eight main Hawaiian Islands, belying US control of a much more expansive Hawaiian archipelago. The quarter went into circulation on November 3, 2008.[39] Though clearly Hawaiian, the images and text signify belonging to the United States by virtue of the quarter's status as US currency (figure 11.4).

Newspaper coverage of the quarter design largely reflected the US-American rhetorical archipelago, with Kamehameha used to symbolize both Hawai'i's unity and Hawai'i's place within an archipelago of states. Then-governor Linda Lingle emphasized that "although there are many islands, [the quarter shows] we're united as a state."[40] In the same article, local design commissioner Gregory Hunt explained, "The chosen coin is about reminding people that Hawai'i is part of America. Sometimes people forget that we are part of the United States.... Visitors to the Islands say, 'You know, back in the states,' and we remind them, 'You mean, back on the Mainland.'"[41] While Hunt recognizes the sense of disunity between Hawai'i and the United States, he insists on this unification, while also reifying notions of continental supremacy (using "Mainland" to refer to the continental United States). As Brian Russell Roberts and Michelle Stephens assert, "The continent [has been framed] as the massive and natural source of the US's drive toward hemispheric and planetary dominance."[42] In appropriating Kamehameha's image, the US-American rhetorical archipelago affirms the inevitability of its continental imperialism, while borrowing from and corrupting

Kamehameha's conceptualization and realization of a united and independent Hawai'i.

The Papahānaumokuākea National Monument provides an example of how moʻokūʻauhau have been appropriated to further colonial control in Hawai'i and the Pacific. The Papahānaumokuākea Marine National Monument was formed in 2006 and originally encompassed 139,797 square miles, the first and largest maritime monument of its kind. Despite previous establishments of reserves and refuges in the area, the monument purports to "provide a higher level of protection" than previous designations.[43] The name Papahānaumokuākea is described as "commemorat[ing] the union of two Hawaiian ancestors—Papahānaumoku and Wākea—who gave rise to the Hawaiian Archipelago, the taro plant, and the Hawaiian people."[44] The meaning of Papahānaumokuākea, however, misrepresents the monument as reflecting Hawaiian perceptions of the archipelago, when various versions of the Papa-Wākea moʻokūʻauhau do not include several of these islands originally, and only two of the monument's islands are known to have Hawaiian cultural sites (Nihoa and Mokumanamana). Furthermore, though access may be granted to "support or advance the perpetuation of traditional knowledge and ancestral connections of Native Hawaiians to the Northwestern Hawaiian Islands,"[45] Kānaka must apply for a permit and outline how their activities may be considered "Native Hawaiian practices" according to federal standards. Kanaka cultural sites are purported to be preserved and protocols observed, though without regular visits granted to Kanaka practitioners, it is unclear how this care is maintained according to Hawaiian cultural standards (figure 11.5).

Using Papahānaumokuākea as a name for the monument connotes a sense of colonial innocence and deep history in the Pacific that naturalizes US control of an expansive oceanic territory, even as it may signal Indigenous cultural sensitivity to some. Three other Pacific Ocean monuments closely followed Papahānaumokuākea: the Pacific Remote Islands National Monument, Marianas Trench Marine National Monument, and the Rose Atoll Marine National Monument. Papahānaumokuākea was expanded in August 26, 2016 through a proclamation signed by President Barack Obama to 582,578 square miles—over four times its original size.[46] This follows his September 25, 2014 expansion of the Pacific Remote Islands National Monument from 86,888 square miles to approximately 370,000 square miles, and joins the 96,714 square mile Marianas Trench National Monument and the 13,436 square mile Rose Atoll National Monument, enabling US control of the region to increase to 1,062,728 square miles. Some Pacific activists see the creation of this and other Pacific monuments as "blue-washing," using the guise of conservationism to conceal

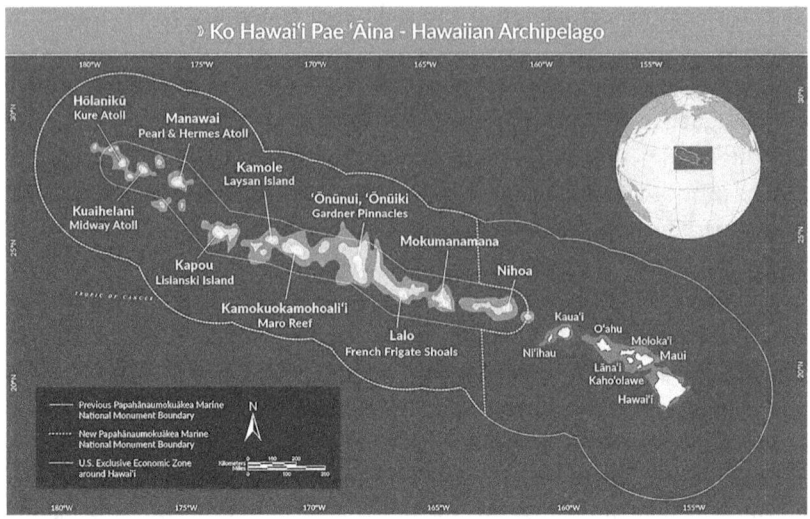

Figure 11.5. Map of the expanded "Ko Pae 'Āina Hawai'i (The Hawaiian Archipelago)" as rendered and claimed by the United States in 2016, featuring the latest boundaries of the Papahānaumokuākea Marine National Monument in relation to Hawai'i. Map courtesy of the National Oceanic and Atmospheric Administration.

militarization,[47] as military bases are suspiciously allowed within these monuments, as well as to support the Trans-Pacific Partnership trade agreement.

CONCLUSION: RETURNING TO THE LĀHUI OF LAND AND SKY

The rhetorical archipelago, as it is now used by the state of Hawai'i and the United States, continues to reinforce a naturalization of the Hawaiian archipelago as part of the US-American imperial archipelago. Colonial appropriation functions to claim and establish a somewhat harmonious relationality, one that belies a history of colonial violence and genealogies of Indigenous governance and resistance, as well as the international illegality of an occupied nation. Thinking with the rhetorical archipelago urges us to interrogate the rhetorics of unification; as it is applied within colonial contexts, it further urges us to question how rhetorics of unification are created and leveraged in the ongoing dispossession of Indigenous peoples, whether continental or insular. As has been suggested by Elaine Stratford, "thinking with the archipelago" allows for "multiple emancipatory narratives that enunciate exceptions to colonizing grammars of empire that rendered islands remote, isolated and backward."[48] By examining how rhetorical symbols and productions are used to reinforce the boundaries of the US-American archipelago, we may continue to dismantle various colonizing logics and envision true "ea"—liberty, freedom, and sovereignty.

In Hawai'i, some of the very rhetorical symbols that were mobilized to reinforce the unification and sovereignty of the Hawaiian Kingdom have been used by the United States to reinforce and obscure its colonial occupation of Hawai'i and to assimilate Hawaiians into the US-American polity. Together, these symbols, whose original meanings have been distorted through a "process of de-contextualization and re-contextualization,"[49] portray Hawai'i as a unified archipelago under a naturalized US-American colonial rule, with Hawaiians as US citizens instead of Hawaiian nationals. This semblance of assimilation and colonial erasure through the appropriation of symbology has depended largely on the silencing of Indigenous voice, language, and agency, though it must be understood that this silencing has never been completely successful. Since archipelagic unification is always vulnerable and in flux, the Hawaiian rhetorical archipelago remains, retaining its archipelagraphy of original meanings that continue to be reclaimed and used. In this way, Hawai'i's sovereignty has never been extinguished; rather, it has been replenished with every defiant reconnection with our ancestors and the history of our lāhui.

On the page following the dedication of *From a Native Daughter*, a page usually left blank, Haunani-Kay Trask offers her own mo'okū'auhau, with the following explanation reaffirming a nationalist Hawaiian rhetorical archipelago: "Despite American political and territorial control of Hawai'i since 1898, Hawaiians are not Americans. . . . We are the children of Papa—earth mother—and Wākea—sky father—who created the sacred lands of Hawai'i nei. From these lands came the taro, and from the taro, the Hawaiian people. . . . Who we are is determined by our connection to our lands and to our families."[50] Our descent from Papahānaumoku and Wākea connects us genealogically to our islands and the 'āina that continues to feed us in body, mind, and spirit, while also forming our filial responsibility to mālama 'āina (care for the land), and enacts our claims to lands and sovereignty. Connections to being US-American are comparatively superficial and reflect an ever-weakening rhetorical stronghold as Hawaiian independence gains stronger momentum within the Hawaiian sovereignty movement.

Over two decades since Trask's famous speech at 'Iolani Palace, many Hawaiians still identify emphatically as Hawaiians, not Americans, as seen in various responses to proposals for "federal recognition," which is a legal status that would not confer recognized Hawaiian independence from the United States but instead would have the US federal government officially recognize the existence of a Native Hawaiian governing entity analogous to the Native American tribes of the forty-nine continental US states.[51] Several versions of the Native

Hawaiian Government Reorganization Act, commonly known as the Akaka Bill, have been introduced in Congress since 2000, but all have failed for various reasons. This process took a turn in 2004, when Kau Inoa, a Hawaiian Civic Club–led initiative, began a registry of Native Hawaiians who would be part of a Hawaiian governing entity. While Kau Inoa failed to register the majority of Hawaiians (roughly 27 percent of 401,000), their effort was later taken up again in 2011, when former Hawaiʻi governor Neil Abercrombie signed Act 195. Act 195 provided state recognition and funded an initiative called Kanaʻiolowalu to complete a "roll" of the Native Hawaiian population. Those already registered with Kau Inoa were reregistered with Kanaʻiolowalu. To date, Kanaʻiolowalu has also failed to register the majority of Hawaiians (roughly 22 percent of 560,000) and has been closed to any new registrations since 2015. An independent organization, Naʻi Aupuni (its name a rhetorical reference to the unified kingdom under Kamehameha), funded by the Office of Hawaiian Affairs (OHA), however, proceeded to assemble delegates anyway, using the Kanaʻiolowalu roll to constitute the citizenry of a Hawaiian governing entity. Over the course of just four weeks, 125 self-nominated Hawaiian delegates convened to create and adopt a reorganized governing document or constitution in February 2016.[52] While the delegates identified as representing an array of governance views and the constitution was worded so as to be open to the pursuit of independence, the constitution's process and timing closely aligns with recent efforts toward a federally recognized Hawaiian governing entity.

These actions coincide with the Department of the Interior's (DOI) Advance Notice of Proposed Rulemaking (ANPRM) process, which was composed of a series of public meetings in June–July 2014 about special administrative rules that would allow the DOI to facilitate federal recognition. The hearings overwhelmingly demonstrated that most speakers opposed federal recognition and supported having Hawaiʻi's independence restored. Despite the outcome of the streamed hearings (from which all testimonies were also transcribed), the DOI reported in September 2015 that the hearings generated testimony from "more than 5,000 members of the public, and they overwhelmingly favored creating a pathway for re-establishing a formal government-to-government relationship." Hence, the DOI announced a proposal in 2015 to create an administrative procedure and criterion that the Secretary of the Interior would apply if the Native Hawaiian community forms a unified government that then seeks a formal government-to-government relationship with the United States.[53] The report does not give an exact account of the testimony submitted, but given that five thousand constitutes less than one percent of the Hawaiian population, and not all of the five thousand members of the public were Native Hawaiian nor were in support of the government-government relationship proposed, the statement cannot represent Native Hawaiian opinion in good faith. Delivering on its word, in August 2016, the DOI published a final rule establishing an "administrative process for reestablishing a formal government-to-government relationship with the Native Hawaiian community to more effectively implement the special political and trust relationship that Congress established between that community and the United States." The rule states that "Congress already federally acknowledged or recognized the Native Hawaiian community by establishing a special political and trust relationship through over 150 enactments" and that this "unique special political and trust relationship exists even though Native Hawaiians have not had an organized government since the overthrow of the Kingdom of Hawaii in 1893."[54] As such, the issue of federal recognition and, thus, Hawai'i's belonging within/to the US-American rhetorical archipelago is a foregone conclusion as far as the US is concerned; rather, the only issue at stake is how "the Native Hawaiian community" may form a governing entity to fully realize this nation-within-a-nation relationship. While it appears that federal recognition, like annexation, and like statehood, are also being forced upon us, our Hawaiian rhetorical archipelago continues to define who we are as Hawaiians, and the kuleana (privilege and responsibility) to our 'āina as an ancestor and our aloha 'āina endures. As Kahu Lyons Naone of Maui testified during the hearings,

> America, like Canada and like Australia, it's only an idea.... You see all these people here, they work the land; they are part of the land. The land is their kupuna.... We are the descendants of our ancestors and we are the ancestors of our children right here, which means you have a kuleana. This is about kuleana. We just cannot give up. We just cannot give up.[55]

NOTES

1. Haunani-Kay Trask, "Speeches for the Centennial of the Overthrow, 'Iolani Palace 1993," in *Huihui: Navigating Art and Literature in the Pacific*, ed. Jeffrey Carroll, Brandy Nālani McDougall, and Georganne Nordstrom (Honolulu: University of Hawai'i Press, 2014), 99.

2. Trask, "Speeches," 100.

3. Elizabeth DeLoughrey, "'The litany of islands, The rosary of archipelagoes': Caribbean and Pacific Archipelagraphy," ARIEL: *A Review of International English Literature* 32, no. 1 (January 2001): 26.

4. J. M. Poepoe, "Ka Moolelo Hawaii Kahiko," *Ka Na'i Aupuni* (HI), February 2, 1906.

5. "Territory of Hawaii," *Organic Act: An Act to Provide a Government for the Territory of Hawaii*, accessed November 11, 2014, http://www.hawaii-nation.org/organic.html.

6. The other northwestern islands are currently part of the Papahānaumokuākea Marine National Monument (discussed later in this chapter).

7. "Archipelago," *Oxford English Dictionary* online, accessed November 11, 2014, http://www.oed.com/view/Entry/10387?redirectedFrom=archipelago#eid.

8. In "Ka Moolelo Hawaii Kahiko," Poepoe writes that the terms are interchangeable, though he chooses to primarily use the term "Pae Moku": "A o lakou apau, ua lahuiia malalo o ka inoa ka Pae Moku o Hawaii, a i ole, ka Pae Aina o Hawaii" (And all of the [islands], they were gathered under the name ka Pae Moku o Hawai'i, or Ka Pae 'Āina o Hawai'i), *Ka Na'i Aupuni* (HI), February 2, 1906. The term *paeaina* or *pae aina*, however, seems to have been more commonly used throughout the nineteenth-century Hawaiian-language newspapers.

9. For a comprehensive history, see Samuel Kamakau's series "Ka Moolelo o Kamehameha I" in *Ka Nupepa Kuokoa*, October 20, 1866–January 9, 1869; the translation of Samuel Kamakau's historical writings, *Ruling Chiefs of Hawai'i* (Honolulu, HI: Kamehameha Schools Press, 1992); and Joseph Poepoe's series "He Moolelo no Kamehameha Ka Na'i: Aupuni o Hawaii," in *Ka Na'i Aupuni*, November 27, 1905–November 16, 1906.

10. Abraham Fornander, *Ancient History of the Hawaiian People to the Time of Kamehameha I* (Honolulu, HI: Mutual Publishing, 1996), 360.

11. Fornander, *Ancient History*, 360. Unfortunately, the original Hawaiian version of the oli was lost. According to Fornander, it was not among Lorrin Andrews's papers, where he found the English translation.

12. David A. Chang, *The World and All the Things Upon It* (Minneapolis, MN: University of Minnesota Press, 2016), 12–13.

13. David Malo et al., *Ka Mooolelo Hawaii*, ed. Sheldon Dibble (1838; repr., Honolulu: Hawaiian Historical Society, 2005), 32. All English translations are my own unless otherwise stated.

14. David Malo, *Mo'olelo Hawai'i* [Hawaiian Antiquities], trans. Nathaniel B. Emerson (Honolulu, HI: Bishop Museum, 1898), 5; I use the terms "Kanaka" and "Hawaiian" to mean the Indigenous people of Hawai'i, although in some instances I use "Hawaiian" to describe a nationality (as opposed to an ethnicity), because Hawai'i was internationally recognized as a sovereign country before it was forcibly annexed by the United States in 1898. Other terms used by scholars include "Kanaka," "Kanaka 'Ōiwi," "Kanaka Maoli," and "Native Hawaiian." "Kānaka" with a macron indicates the plural form, whereas the term without a macron indicates the singular; Kepelino, *Traditions of Hawai'i*, trans. Martha Beckwith (1932; repr., Honolulu, HI: Bishop Museum Press, 2007), 190.

15. Fornander, *Ancient History*, 12.

16. Colleen Hanai, "Hae Hawaii," *Hawai'i Historical Review* (October 1963): 94.

17. Jonathan Pugh, "Island Movements: Thinking with the Archipelago," *Island Studies Journal* 8, no. 1 (2013): 10.

18. Patrick Ka'ano'i, "Oli ka Hae," *Royal Hawaiian Guard*, accessed July 23, 2014, http://royalhawaiianguard.weebly.com/oli-ka-hae.html.

19. Keanu Sai, "International Treaties," *Hawaiian Kingdom*, accessed November 12, 2014, http://www.hawaiiankingdom.org/treaties.shtml.

20. Jonathan Kay Kamakawiwo'ole Osorio, *Dismembering Lāhui: A History of the Hawaiian Nation to 1887* (Honolulu: University of Hawai'i Press, 2002), 150.

21. Noenoe Silva, *Aloha Betrayed: Native Hawaiian Resistance to American Colonialism* (Durham, NC: Duke University Press, 2004), 105.

22. Walter Murray Gibson, quoted in Glenn Wharton, *The Painted King: Art, Activism, and Authenticity in Hawai'i* (Honolulu: University of Hawai'i Press, 2012), 19.

23. Wharton, *Painted King*, 18.

24. Helen G. Chapin, "The Kamehameha Statues," *Hawaiian Historical Society*, accessed July 23, 2014, https://www.hawaiianhistory.org/time-capsules/land/the-kamehameha-statues/.

25. Howard M. Ballou, "The Reversal of the Hawaiian Flag," *Papers of the Hawaiian Historical Society* 12 (1905): 5–6. Ballou quotes Gilman, who quotes John Papa 'Ī'ī as the source for reversal of the colors, though Ballou is doubtful. Marie Alohalani Brown, the leading scholar and biographer of John Papa 'Ī'ī, however, validates the likelihood of 'Ī'ī sharing this information with Gilman because Ī'ī hosted Gilman in his home for a period during the Paulet Affair. Personal Communication with Marie Alohalani Brown, June 14, 2014.

26. Ballou, "The Reversal of the Hawaiian Flag," 5–6.

27. It is likely that the full-color printing of the Hae Hawai'i was also an example of kaona (veiled meaning) to underscore Kuokoa's succeeding Ka Hae Hawaii.

28. "Ka Hae Nani o Hawaii, E mau kona welo ana," *Ka Nupepa Kuokoa* (HI), January 1, 1862. Though the article was printed in both Hawaiian and English, the English version was not a direct translation; thus, I chose to translate the Hawaiian version myself.

29. "Ka Hae Nani o Hawaii."

30. "Ka Hae Nani o Hawaii."

31. For a more detailed account of this history, see Noenoe Silva's *Aloha Betrayed*.

32. Bernice Pi'ilani Irwin, *I Knew Queen Lili'uokalani* (1960; repr., Honolulu: Native Books, 2000), 46.

33. Joyce D. Hammond, "Hawaiian Flag Quilts: Multivalent Symbols of a Hawaiian Quilt Tradition," *Hawaiian Journal of History* 27 (1993): 6.

34. Hammond, "Hawaiian Flag Quilts," 8.

35. Bryan Kamaoli Kuwada, "E Mau nō Kou Welo 'ana: The Appropriation of the Hawaiian Flag," *'Ōiwi: A Native Hawaiian Journal* 4 (2009): 30.

36. Robert C. Schmitt, "Holidays in Hawai'i," *Hawaiian Journal of History* 29 (1995): 143.

37. "Kamehameha I," *Architect of the Capitol*, last modified January 14, 2014, http://www.aoc.gov/capitol-hill/national-statuary-hall-collection/kamehameha-i.

38. "State quarter design features Kamehameha," *Honolulu Advertiser* (HI), April 24, 2007.

39. P. Solomon Banda, "Hawaii Commemorative Coin, the Final State Quarter, Struck at Denver Mint," *Honolulu Advertiser* (HI), October 14, 2008.

40. Banda, "Hawaii Commemorative Coin."

41. Banda, "Hawaii Commemorative Coin."

42. Brian Russell Roberts and Michelle Stephens, "Archipelagic American Studies and the Caribbean," *Journal of Transnational American Studies* 5, no. 1 (2013): 8.

43. National Ocean Service, Office of National Marine Sanctuaries, National Oceanic and Atmospheric Administration, "Papahānaumokuākea Marine National Monument," accessed October 10, 2016, http://www.papahanaumokuakea.gov.

44. "Papahānaumokuākea Marine National Monument," National Ocean Service.

45. "Papahānaumokuākea Marine National Monument," National Ocean Service. Ibid.

46. National Ocean Service, "President announces expansion of Papahānaumokuākea," accessed October 10, 2016, http://www.papahanaumokuakea.gov/news/expansion_announcement.html.

47. Craig Santos Perez, "Blue-Washing the Colonization and Militarization of Our Ocean," *Hawaii Independent* (HI), June 26, 2014.

48. Elaine Stratford, "The Idea of the Archipelago: Contemplating Island Relations," *Island Studies Journal* 8, no. 1 (2013): 4.

49. Kuwada, "E Mau nō Kou Welo ʻana," 22.

50. Haunani-Kay Trask, *From a Native Daughter* (Honolulu: University of Hawaiʻi, 1993), n.p.

51. See Amy E. Den Ouden and Jean M. O'Brien, *Recognition, Sovereignty Struggles, and Indigenous Rights in the United States* (Chapel Hill: University of North Carolina Press, 2013), for a history of recognition, a focus on recent legal and cultural processes, and an examination of contemporary recognition struggles throughout the United States. Specifically in this anthology, J. Kēhaulani Kauanui's chapter "Precarious Positions: Native Hawaiians and US Federal Recognition" examines the question of federal recognition as it has persisted in Hawaiʻi since 2000 with the Akaka Bill (311–36).

52. "Naʻi Aupuni List of 154 Participants for February ʻAha," *Naʻi Aupuni*, accessed January 19, 2016, http://www.naiaupuni.org/docs/NaiAupuniListOf154Participants-010616.pdf.

53. Office of the Secretary, US Department of the Interior, "Interior Proposes Path for Re-Establishing Government-to-Government Relationship with Native Hawaiian Community," September 30, 2015, accessed January 19, 2016, https://www.doi.gov/pressreleases/interior-department-proposes-pathway-re-establishing-government-government.

54. US Department of the Interior, 4334–63 "Procedures for Reestablishing a Formal Government-to-Government Relationship with the Native Hawaiian Community," September 23, 2016, accessed October 10, 2016, https://www.doi.gov/sites/doi.gov/files/uploads/final_rule_43_cfr_part_50_pathway_for_reestablishing_a_formal_government_to_government_relationship_with_the_native_hawaiian_community.pdf, 2–3.

55. US Department of the Interior, transcript of "Public Meeting Regarding Whether the Federal Government Should Reestablish a Government-to-Government Relationship with the Native Hawaiian Community," Lahaina, Maui, July 7, 2014, accessed November 21, 2014, https://www.doi.gov/sites/doi.gov/files/uploads/King-Kamehameha-III-Lahaina-Maui-070714.pdf.

PART V | **ECOLOGIES OF RELATION**

12 PERFORMING ARCHIPELAGIC IDENTITIES IN BILL REID, ROBERT SULLIVAN, AND SYAMAN RAPONGAN

Hsinya Huang

IT IS PRIMARILY FOR THOSE ANCHORED to the alleged sublimity of the continent that insularity equals imprisonment. But instead of small islands in the remote sea, Pacific writer Epeli Hau'ofa reenvisions the Pacific/Oceania as a sea of islands that has given rise to traditional Indigenous ways of life unique to the region, and expressed through outstanding cultural landscapes and seascapes and in the intangible heritage of traditions, knowledge, and stories. In the spirit of Hau'ofa's vision of islands not as isolated but as opening onto vast oceanic worlds, this chapter foregrounds (alter)Native models of reckoning space, place, and time that both require an active and participatory engagement with the Pacific seascapes and invoke a planetary consciousness. Drawing on Native North American Haida artist Bill Reid's piece *The Spirit of Haida Gwaii, the Black Canoe,* Aotearoan (New Zealand) poet Robert Sullivan's *Star Waka,* and Pongso no Tau writer Syaman Rapongan's *Eyes of the Sky* as anchor texts, I demonstrate how Indigenous cultural production from the Pacific, both visual and versal, decontinentalizes American studies through the powerful metaphor of the canoe navigating across the pathway of the sea.

Bill Reid is based on the islands of Haida Gwaii, eighty kilometers off the coast of British Columbia. Meanwhile, Robert Sullivan is of Maori origin, and Syaman Rapongan is from Austronesian Taiwan. Each of these writers evidences multiple kinds of Pacific connection and commonality, as multiple kinds of Indigenous canoes travel across the Pacific. In these visual arts and literary writings, nonhuman beings such as whales, flying fish, and amphibians, and artistic objects such as canoes literally travel across an Indigenous Pacific. These beings, objects, and canoes detail complex cosmological genealogies at both the macro and micro scale of multispecies relationships, opening up a prospect greater than the continent and connecting the sea and sky with human and nonhuman souls. With these genealogies in mind, all three artists envision a large Oceania, an archipelagic region in the Pacific; all renativize islands into a countercontinental site aligned with Oceania. Through multiple kinds of Pacific connections and commonalities among North America, Aotearoa, and Austronesian Taiwan, this comparative study opens up Pacific pathways and their islands as a set of routes and locations for an archipelagic American studies.

I employ "the Pacific" as a contact zone to examine the shifting relationship between land and sea and, in so doing, I weave Pacific connections by stressing island temporalities and topographies to counteract the logic of US continental exceptionalism. The Pacific is the largest oceanic divide on Earth. In recent years, issues around global capitalism, national identity, the sense of community, and the ecology of the Pacific region have sparked intriguing and provocative discussions. Research along these lines celebrates the networking and coalitional activities of various groups of people in the Pacific, and highlights the circulation of ideas and cultures that I believe to be crucial to an archipelagic turn in American studies. Comparing Indigenous writers from the Pacific Islands, this study offers an oceanic perspective to balance continental ways of thinking, and supplements or challenges transnational approaches to imperialism, indigeneity, and ecology. The Pacific emerges as "a world of people connected to each other" through narratives and objects of Oceanic connection and ecology: as Hau'ofa puts it, "The sea is our pathway to each other and to everyone else, the sea is our endless saga, the sea is our most powerful metaphor, the ocean is in us."[1] The stories and images of the survival and revival of traditional seafaring practices provide an Indigenously ordered, anticolonial, and anticontinental praxis. They map and remap the uncharted spaces of the Pacific Islands. The canoes navigate a course that is not overdetermined by the trajectories of imperialism and colonialism from land and the continents. They traverse a Pacific independent of colonial demarcations and in this way sustain a paradigm of trans-indigeneity, of rooted routes, of a mobile, flexible, and voyaging subject who is not physically or culturally circumscribed by terrestrial boundaries.

Indeed, much exciting work in recent years has demonstrated how global identities have been shaped and transformed by seascapes and islands. Antonio Benítez-Rojo, for instance, coins the term "repeating island" to advance the image of the Caribbean islands not as a localized subset but rather as a planetary continuum, "an island that proliferates endlessly, . . . founding and refounding ethnological materials."[2] The islands repeat, proliferate, and multiply and in this way interlock world cultures, for the history of the Caribbean islands bespeaks the circulation of civilizations across the waters and should be regarded as a "useful model for understanding the new globalized culture."[3] Islands as the spaces that intersect land and sea must be recognized as a formal geographical key to interpreting and comprehending global cultures and civilizations. They are not simply metaphors, such as those in John Donne's signature sentence "no man is an island" or in Gilles Deleuze's conceptualization of "desert islands."[4] Islands involve everyday physical realities and have provoked human imagination or have even been a "co-measure of humankind itself."[5] For, islands are cradles of flora and fauna, which have "co-enabled, geologically and biologically, the very Earth we know"; as Steven Roger Fischer puts it, "from fabled Atlantis to . . . modern Manhattan, from Taiwan to Tahiti, islands have fascinated and empowered, inspired and enriched, delighted and rescued."[6]

PACIFIC ISLANDS ON THE MOVE

Contemporary discourse on islands has slanted toward the Caribbean and the Atlantic, the primary site of Western/Euro-American expansion since the early colonial period. Martinican writer Édouard Glissant's "Poetics of Relation," for example, revolves around the Caribbean as key to world culture.[7] Furthermore, Elizabeth DeLoughrey investigates the "routes and roots" of both the Caribbean and the Pacific experiences by building on Barbadian writer Edward Brathwaite's idea of "tidalectics" from Caribbean cultural discourse, while Jace Weaver's global Indigenous studies emerges from the "Red Atlantic."[8] This West-oriented scholarship runs the risk of ignoring the fact that the Pacific accommodates perhaps the richest assemblage of islands and archipelagoes. It is true that the traumatic nature and colonial situation of Caribbean island experiences deserve close scrutiny in the postcolonial era, and have provided invaluable lessons regarding world culture.[9] But in terms of self-reproducing and self-generating impulses as well as language and cultural resistance, the geographical reality of the Pacific Islands, or Oceania in its concrete and particular materiality, may serve to complement and profoundly enrich the Atlantic-oriented discourse on islands. The interwoven relationship among the islands demonstrates enormous desire to be connected, to enter into relations with one another, and to destabilize the myth of island isolation. In comparison with the Atlantic, the Pacific has produced folds and fluidity and inspired imagination that may shape a more optimistic view of island worlds.[10] It is from the Pacific perspective that islands appear to take on a new configuration, a promising vision of interconnectedness and resilience in the face of contemporary environmental peril. To borrow Walter Benjamin's terminology, the islands resemble a "constellation," which in a precise and evocative fashion expresses a new way to look at these islands as interrelation rather than in sequence.[11]

Specifically, Hau'ofa substitutes the name "Oceania" for the "Pacific" to recall a culturally and politically empowering legacy of travels and interconnectedness in the face of the Pacific colonial and postcolonial histories. As Vicente M. Diaz and J. Kēhaulani Kauanui pinpoint, the colonial, "belittling economically and geographically deterministic view of Oceania overlooks historical processes and forms of 'world enlargement' carried out by island peoples that make nonsense of national and economic boundaries and zones that mark colonial legacies and postcolonial relationships."[12] Hau'ofa conceives of "a sea of islands" as a vision whereby Pacific peoples look beyond the limits of the land as home; they look to the surrounding ocean, the underwater realm, and the sky above. He replaces the "belittling" colonial agenda that defines the islands as small, remote, and isolated dots—and its inhabitants as fixed—with a powerful "Oceania" shaped by the long conduit of travel from island to island, first by canoe and later by aircraft. For Hau'ofa, as for cultural studies critic and historian James Clifford, travel in sea space represents empowering ways of understanding world civilization, especially as related to "native culture" of the Pacific.[13] In his classic essay "Our Sea of Islands," Epeli Hau'ofa reminds us that contrary to modernist imaginaries of our world as a scattering of tiny, isolated, remote islands, Oceania is better understood as a sea of islands whose watery domain is a pathway that connects rather than isolates us.

Likewise, in his article "Moving Islands of Sovereignty," Vicente Diaz examines a very long history of Indigenous geo- and oceanographic dispersal, or an Indigenous time/space forged through maritime travel. In so doing, he argues for a distinct tradition of the Pacific Islanders' sovereignty grounded on their experiences and techniques of navigation. The navigating techniques of the Pacific Islanders involve reckoning the distance traveled and one's location at sea by calculating the rate at which one's island of departure moves away from the traveling canoe and the rate at which a second reference island moves along another prescribed star course. The cosmos, stars, and seascapes actively participate in the seafaring process while the canoe becomes the center of the universe, investigating its environment in flux. By these well-crafted canoes and with sophisticated maritime technologies and knowledge, the Pacific Islanders settled roughly two-thirds of the globe's southern oceanic hemisphere, a dispersal that began about eight thousand years ago.[14]

The canoes and related technologies of navigating the Pacific have been featured in the *Manawa: Pacific Heartbeat* exhibit and catalogue, connecting the Maori and Northwest North America Coast Indians as well as their artistic practices. Held in 2006 at the Spirit Wrestler Gallery in Vancouver, Canada, *Manawa: Pacific Heartbeat* involved two art-making cultures reaching out across the Pacific to exhibit together. Their art weaves Pacific connections by stressing island temporalities and topographies, counteracting the logic of US "continental exceptionalism."[15] Both cultures have built large ocean-going canoes (in Maori, *waka*), and, as part of their everyday practices, these canoes were used for fishing, trade, commerce, and visiting relatives on neighboring islands. Now, they weave the aesthetic connections of the Pacific Islands as they are exhibited jointly to represent "Pacific heartbeat." One of the stories accompanying the artifacts, originating from the oral history of Indigenous people from the Pacific Northwest Coast, relates to the contact made in ancient times between the Maori and the Northwest Coast:

> Three Maori in a large ocean waka followed the powerful trade winds that flow at different times northward and southward connecting New Zealand and North America and landed at this northern village. Here they remained for three years waiting for the winds to reverse. In preparing for the return journey, they joined local carvers in building two Nuu-chah-nulth/Hesquiat-style canoes. At the time of departure, they were presented with three wives—and assuming that they arrived home safely, it is likely that family ties exist between the two nations.[16]

According to the tradition preserved in this oral narrative, blood ties spread across the Pacific as the islanders traveled by canoe. Both cultures are linked through common ancestry, living histories, and ancient and present-day art forms. By spirit, the canoes are the extensions of both cultures reaching out to include diverse genetic codes and thus civilizations that are conveyed through these codes. In his red cedar sculpture, Maori artist Joe David represents a superhero of the Maori with his supernatural canoe. In the carving, the (super)human and his canoe are "one and the same, joyfully flying in out and through one adventure after another, transforming himself and all around him at will."[17]

The canoe in the Pacific has many names: in Maori, it is *waka moana*, literally "canoe of the ocean," which had sailed across the ocean for more than eight thousand years before Euro-Americans arrived; in Fiji, it is called *camakau*; in the Marshall Islands, it is named *waan aelon kein* or *walap*; in Tonga, it becomes *tongiaki* or *kalia*; in Samoa, *taumalua* or *alia*; in the Cook Islands, *vaka taurua*; in Kiribati, *baurua*; in a Taiwan Aboriginal language it is *Pongso no Tau, Mi tatala*, literally "assembled boat."[18] The names of the canoe permeate the stories of the Pacific Islands as the vessel traverses the ocean. Nowadays, the vessel is created as a reflection on the cultural commonalities of the Pacific and as a symbol of traditional values that exist among the islanders—there is close affinity among Maori of New Zealand, other Polynesian peoples, and the First Nations peoples of the Northwest Coast of North America. As Nigel Reading and Gary Wyatt put it in describing one of the artifacts, the *Ipu Ika* (Fish Vessel), in the *Manawa: Pacific Heartbeat* exhibit, the canoe is "a connecting heartbeat," representing "a genetic imprint," which "determines who is Polynesian, who is Maori," as well as the First Nations Peoples of the Pacific Northwest: "We are many cultures, but through our genetic links we are one people of the waka (canoes), intrepid sailors and master navigators, Polynesian peoples who spanned the vast reaches of the Te Moananui a Kiwa [the Pacific Ocean]."[19] The canoe iconizes the connectivity among Maori, other Polynesian peoples, and the First Nations peoples of the Pacific Northwest Coast. It underscores a shared history of Native science and navigation; it also highlights the values of hospitality, reciprocity, and the power of the personal, the communal, the human, and the nonhuman—all conflated in the islanders' cosmology. It is an important tie to the islanders' ancestry, and it is from the canoe that individual beings, islands, and threads are woven into mutual interconnectivity. It serves as the container of cultural memories and Native science of the Pacific. In the canoe, Pacific indigeneity embodies latitudes of knowledge that can be alien to the land-based Native Americans. The Pacific canoe traverses imperial mappings and defines Indigenous identities as the result of ancient and ongoing processes of making, trading, moving, and migrating across water. It forms a network among multiple dimensions, interlocking history and modernity; the individual, the tribe, and the universe; and nature and human civilization.

BILL REID'S *BLACK CANOE* AND THE INDIGENOUS ART OF THE PACIFIC

Bill Reid's famous sculpture *The Spirit of Haida Gwaii, the Black Canoe* represents the prototype of the vessel in the Pacific Northwest of the Americas (figure 12.1). Featuring the ecological metaphor of a lifeboat during the great flood, *The Spirit of Haida Gwaii* includes forms of life that have managed to survive in their respective environments over time, throughout history, that is, in geological time beyond the human span. The boat carries more than human beings—there are the raven (the traditional trickster of Haida mythology), the eagle, the bear, the beaver, the wolf, the frog, the mouse woman, the dogfish woman, the ancient reluctant conscript, and the chief, some on the watch, and others urgently paddling. The chief is situated at the focal point of the sculpture, wearing the Haida cloak and woven spruce root hat and holding a tall staff carved with the bear, the raven, and the killer whale. Crowded with humans and other mammals, birds, and amphibians, Reid's *Black Canoe* makes explicit the importance of interspecies relationship in sustaining human survival.

The Indigenous heritage of the Haida Gwaii region in the Pacific Northwest is evidenced in Reid's carving. First, the diversity and interdependence of the canoe's passengers represent the natural environment on which the Haida rely for their survival. The artist's imagination centers on a restored continuum of human and nonhuman beings in ecological peril, and retrieves a multispecies eco-aesthetics rooted in Indigenous stories and myths of the Pacific. The Pacific Ocean remains a site of cobelonging and cohistory across the species boundaries. *The Spirit of*

Figure 12.1. Bill Reid, *The Spirit of Haida Gwaii, the Black Canoe*, 1991. Located outside the Canadian Embassy in Washington, DC. Photo by Bengt Oberger. Available at https://commons.wikimedia.org/wiki/File:Bill_Reid_Haida_Gail_01.jpg. GNU Free Documentation License.

Haida Gwaii exemplifies the ocean planet as the contested site of ecological crisis and opportunity. There seems to be nowhere to escape to and yet, in facing the flood, the Haida demonstrate the sophisticated mating of "organic grace and patience with technological audacity and skill" of navigation: as Robert Bringhurst poetically puts it in interpreting Reid's art, "It is an ocean-going canoe"—"a steerable leaf, coaxed stroke by stroke by hand from the grain of a prehistoric tree, propelled now stroke by stroke through shifting wind and current into whatever future still remains."[20] The ancient moving canoe, made of "a prehistoric tree," is transformed into the *Black Canoe*, an artistic piece that will carry the Haida into future generations and, like the wind and current of the ocean, become what still remains. Beneath the art lie the deeper worlds of the Haida Gwaii people: the land, the ocean, and the creatures that inhabit them—all of these form an interconnected web of coexistence and interlocking stories. The sense of community reaches out not only to similar people in the seas but to nonhuman species, generating a widening circle of associations. The canoe is where a multispecies world emerges, representing a radical alterity to reveal the discontent of modern civilization, which privileges the story of human progress away from other nonhuman species. The Haida world is one in which reciprocal relations are always involved.

Besides, as *The Spirit of Haida Gwaii* demonstrates, the world of the Haida Gwaii archipelago, previously known to its inhabitants as "The Islands at the Boundary of the World," and recently as "The Islands of the People," is mutable, delicate, and yet self-repairing.[21] The *Black Canoe* provides an (alter)Native model of resilience in the face of flooding as well as an ethics and aesthetics of environmental adaptation, whereby the world would be more justly constructed. The mythology from the Indigenous Pacific, like "the forests and streams, beaches and reefs it was born in, has been heavily mistreated," and yet, like the land and the water, it is "nevertheless alive."[22] The resilience of ecosystems and multispecies worlds in *The Spirit of Haida Gwaii* is to be extended to human adaptation and in this way transform ecological peril into the equilibrium of the islands' social-ecological systems and mythologies.

As Robert Bringhurst details each of the occupants of Reid's *Black Canoe*,[23] we finally spot the whale as the uppermost figure in the canoe. At the top of the staff, the whale is the visible form of the gods. It is the killer whale, which the Indigenous peoples of the Pacific Northwest Coast have honored throughout their history, art, spirituality, and religion. The ancient Haida regarded killer whales as the most powerful animals in the ocean, the custodians of the sea and a benefactor of humans. Haida mythology tells of killer whales living in houses and towns under the sea, as the rulers of the underwater realm. According to these myths, they took on human form when submerged, and humans who drowned went to live with them.[24] Through the whale, the multiple boundaries between different worlds—between the human and the nonhuman, between the water and the sky, between history and prehistory, between the Northern and Southern Hemispheres—are blurred. Indeed, symbolic of the kinship between humans and fishes, the whale is the medium that bridges the divides between land and sea, human and nonhuman, trespassing human, rational dichotomies. The lifeboat not only bears the ecological, cultural, and tribal treasures of prehistorical genes and memories but also, surfing with the whale, whose image is carved into the top of the chief's staff in the *Black Canoe*, undertakes the voyage to survive the flood. This voyage is an outward-turning mission of "survivance" (to borrow Gerald Vizenor's term), as Bringhurst brilliantly says, "from the almost vanished nation to the reigning power of the hemisphere; and an exploratory vessel, sailing an unknown course through unknown seas. Beings looking for other beings to speak to, feast with, trade with, perhaps to intermarry with, not for a place to plant a flag."[25] By comparison, one notes the founding myth of Paikea, who rode a whale to Aotearoa and became the ancestor of the Maori people. The ancient whale taught the Maori to navigate the Pacific and brought them from Hawaiki to the islands in the southwest, "to the reigning power" of the other hemisphere. The voyage was not for colonialism, not "to plant a flag," but to interact, exchange, connect, and traffic with other ocean peoples and to produce offspring that would populate the islands.[26]

Let us now go back to the *Manawa: Pacific Heartbeat* exhibit and a relevant sculpture at the center of its catalogue, created by the Maori artist Fred Graham and titled *Whakamutunga (Metamorphosis)*. Chadwick Allen elaborates on this piece at length in his project to propose a trans-Indigenous methodology.[27] Graham's sculpture is composed of a three-dimensional figure of a diving whale, carved from New Zealand prehistoric kauri trees and set against a two-dimensional background of a horizon that divides the ocean into two hemispheres. The upper end of the diving whale (the tail and fins) is carved and decorated in a distinctly Northwest Coast–style known as formline, while the lower end (the head) is carved and decorated in a distinctly Maori style of interlocking spirals.[28] The primary color of the sculpture is black, typical of Northwest Coast design, as exemplified in Reid's *Black Canoe* piece. Red is applied as a secondary color not only to emphasize the formline in the whale's tail and fins but also to highlight the whale's tongue in the spirals of the head, an important feature of Maori carving. The piece then becomes a contact site where the Pacific Northwest Coast meets the Maori through art. The horizon line, representing the equator of the globe, opens up a geographical contact zone between the sky and the ocean, and between the Northern and Southern Hemisphere. This contact zone simultaneously carries cultural significance and serves as the zone of transformation (metamorphosis) in the figure of the whale, where its Northwest Coast body intersects its Maori head. The conflation of both arts has a realistic coordinate, as Graham explains in his statement included in the catalogue:

> The whale is a frequent traveller between the Northern and Southern Hemispheres. In my sculpture, as the whale crosses the equator it changes both in shape and in body design, from Northwest Coast Indian to Maori. Day changes to night. The visits of the whales "down under" remind me of the visits of Northwest Coast Indian artists to *Aotearoa*, where they become one of us: *tangata whenua*—people of the land. In 1992, [the Northwest Coast artist] George David stayed with my wife, Norma, and me. Earlier this year, his brother [the artist] Joe David stayed with us for a few days. He drew the Northwest Coast design for me, and I hope my sculpture does his drawing justice.[29]

From Reid's black canoe to Graham's whale of metamorphosis there appear Indigenous signs traveling across locations, between the First Nations peoples of the Pacific Northwest Coast and the Maori. As Chadwick Allen puts it, a sense of trans-Indigenous aesthetics "revives to inscribe difference as Indigenous signs travel through time and space, appreciated, interpreted, understood in Indigenous (though not necessarily *original*) terms."[30] This comment links back to the idea, inspired by Reid, of recognizing the Indigenous afterlives of Indigenous signs in travel. As Reid puts it in his poem "Out of the Silence," first published in 1971, "When we look at a particular work / . . . / and see the shape of it, / we are only looking at its afterlife. / Its real life is the movement / by which it got to be that shape."[31] It is this "afterlife" that contemporary viewers of these works experience, as Indigenous signs of Pacific travel across space, language, and culture.

ROBERT SULLIVAN'S *STAR WAKA*

Robert Sullivan's *Star Waka* also represents the "afterlife" of Indigenous signs merging art with words. There are three sections in this volume of poetry, indicated by three different numbering systems, from Roman to Arabic to "waka" numbers, symbolizing the progression of human civilization from the Greco-Roman and the Western to the Pacific era. In the initial "Note," the poet identifies his threads in terms of the star-waka-ocean continuum: "Each poem must have a star, a waka or the ocean."[32] Oceanic voyaging becomes the context in which Sullivan imagines the emergence of island- and sea-based historical processes and cultural identities. In this process, three worlds intertwine, corresponding to his three key terms: "star," the celestial body; "waka," the extension of human self through art and technology; and "the ocean," including animals, plants, and plankton of the underwater: as the poet puts it, "it is subject to the laws of nature,"[33] erasing the divides between the human and the nonhuman.

Waka navigates across the ocean through the guidance of the stars. In its title, the poet indicates the Oceanic systems of star navigation—stars provide guidance for waka, calling up the celestial and cosmological association of traditional seafaring practices:

> Star hangs on ears of night, defining light.
> .... The bottom line
> For us to know where to go—star points
> ....
> System is always there for waka.
> Star rises and falls with night.
> So guidance system attached.
> In ancient days navigators sent waka between.
> Now, our speakers send us on waka.[34]

Waka serves not only as a vehicle of navigation but also as a container and medium of memories and words. Waka is the core of the myth making but also the contemporary recreation of myth in words. Literally waka is a canoe, and yet in contemporary time waka is also a poetic waka, a word canoe, a vehicle for transmitting the ancient tradition. The explicit definition of "waka" appears in poem "xvii: Some definitions and a note on orthography": "in English the waka / is a canoe / but the ancestral waka / were as large / as the European barks / of the eighteenth century explorers."[35] Sullivan defines "waka" with reference to the size of the colonial vessels, and yet this Native science of waka making and navigating took place much earlier than the European counterpart:

> In ancient days navigators sent waka between.
> Now, our speakers send us on waka. Their memories,
> Memory of people in us, invite, spirit,
> Compel us aboard, to home government, to centre.[36]

As Chris Prentice insightfully puts it, waka evokes the Pacific ancestry, recollecting the voyaging journeys between the Polynesian islands as well as the migration and settlement of Maori from the mythic Polynesian homeland of Hawaiki in Aotearoa.[37] In this sense, the migratory waka is the vehicle "for the reproduction and transmission" of the collective cultural memory and identity.[38] Sullivan's collection itself is a "poetic waka," or a kind of "word canoe," that retains the seafaring practices and traditions of the Indigenous Pacific people that survived European colonialism. Toward the end of the collection, the poet addresses the stars: "And you stars, the ancestors."[39] The cosmological intersects with the genealogical: the family line is extended to incorporate the celestial beings. Waka links the past with the contemporary, the human with the nonhuman. Waka represents Oceanic ancestry in name and form, binding Maori people into Oceanic solidarity. The Oceanic descendants will pass on the waka tradition and communicate the values they inherit from their ancestors, which allow them "to navigate *our* [their] history down lines."[40] In using the possessive collective pronoun "our," Sullivan retrieves transoceanic relations through a collective "we"—those relations that animate the "ocean planet," bring the living into presence, and revitalize the dead into life. The genealogical "lines" include not only the human but also celestial bodies and sea creatures, from the upper, middle, and lower lays of the universe, all integral to the Maori cosmos of life. Altogether they form a genealogy, which Chadwick Allen deploys as Maori *whakapapa*. "Whakapapa" is a preeminent trope of Maori cosmology and covers the descent of all living things: "everything in the universe has a whakapapa," "a system of names and a set or coordinates—for the analysis of one's rightful place in the universe."[41] "Whakapapa" therefore defines the deep structure of the Maori "lines," which spring from their collective unconscious/memories and resurge in the modern world to rectify the conflicting colonial "written record":

> I have only waka floating beneath the stars,
> at night and in the day, directed by swells,
>
> whose crews are sustained not by seabirds
> or fish, but by memory—some in conflict
>
> with the written record.[42]

island is
pue (circular)

no-man

island is
pue (circular)

whale

island is
pue (circular)

Robert

carved shaped loved floating totara

Figure 12.2. Robert Sullivan, "53." From *Star Waka* (Auckland, New Zealand: Auckland University Press, 1999), 58. Used with permission of Auckland University Press.

By piecing together the ancestral intelligence of a more-than-eight-thousand-year mission of navigating the ocean, Sullivan revitalizes the cells/genetic codes of the Maori "lines," in which lie references to waka. His poetry identifies methods of navigation and knowledge of stars, currents, and wind, specifically the method of "moving islands" as a "sovereign act," to borrow Vicente M. Diaz's terminology. In one of Sullivan's visual poems, number "53," Sullivan demonstrates the Oceanic/Polynesian concept and technique of "moving islands," a primary knowledge system of Oceanic navigation that involves islands and seascapes and sets them all in motion (figure 12.2). There are fourteen words in the poem, composed into ten lines and arranged into three circular "islands" and four horizontal lines, presumably entities floating on the sea. This figurative mapping visually includes three islands and four entities—"no-man," "whale," "Robert," and "carved shaped loved floating totara."[43] "No-man" indicates the anti-anthropocentric idea in the Indigenous cosmology, while "whale" evokes the multispecies connectivity between human and whale as continuum—or rather, whale being part of the ancestral tradition and lineage of the Maori, as the famous movie *The Whale Rider* has shown—the Maori ancestor Paikea traveled and settled in New Zealand on the back of a whale. The totara is a tree native to New Zealand used in the making and carving of waka. Robert, the poet, is positioned atop a board of waka, watching the world from a sea-level perspective.[44]

The three circular "islands" feature the most significant message directly related to the technique of Polynesian navigation, namely, that of the "moving island." In his article "Moving Islands of Sovereignty," Diaz explains the concept and technique of "moving islands" in detail. In Polynesian language, *etak*, "moving islands," is the technique for calculating distance traveled or "position at sea" by triangulating the speed of one's islands of departure and destination with that of a third reference island. Sullivan enacts the ancient technique of "moving island" in his "word canoe" by structuring the poetic lines into three circular islands. To put it plainly, the navigator gets on waka and follows the stars in the direction of his destination island. As the island of departure recedes from view, he also pays attention to a third island as it appears to move along another prescribed star course. Waka is conceived as stationary beneath the star points, whose position is also regarded as fixed. The ocean flows past and actively participates in the navigation. The island astern recedes while the destination island comes nearer and the reference island moves backward beneath the navigating stars until it comes abaft and then farther behind. As a navigator, literally and figuratively, Robert or the poet revisions the ancient technique into words and in so doing performs his insular identity as archipelagic by plotting his navigating course in relation to the islands, stars, and sea creatures. He refers to the stars, the celestial sky, as a veritable map for the world below, hence the significance of vertical relations between the human and the sky in Oceanic navigation. He touches on flora and fauna, and also land and seamarks, which constitute a horizontal map of the navigating route. Interweaving the vertical and horizontal maps, the "moving island" technique represents the Pacific Islanders' Indigenous way of conceptualizing space in order to fix one's place. It was a critical technological development that permitted Polynesians to traverse over three-fourths of the globe long before Europeans ventured into the Pacific.[45]

SYAMAN RAPONGAN'S *EYES OF THE SKY*

Drawing on a similar geographical imaginary, Rapongan's work on Oceania in the Northeast Pacific likewise envisions an archipelagic region, reshaping Taiwan as space linked to Austronesian/Polynesian/Oceanic modes of language, space, body, and culture. Taiwan has long been recognized as the origin of the Austronesian culture and language. The rich culture of the ocean and islands deterritorializes the arbitrary and hegemonic boundaries of colonialism. As Rapongan depicts an Oceanic perception of place and space, and as he reframes the ocean into an immense formation, Pongso no Tau becomes part of the interconnected islanders' heritage of Oceania.[46] Rapongan's Tau ancestors used to move freely in the Pacific Ocean, following the migratory route of the flying fish that was subject to the flow of the Kuroshio/Black Current. This north-flowing current on the west side of the North Pacific drives the flying fish migration, which, in turn, shapes and reshapes the migratory route of the island Indigenes. Because of the annual/regular movement among the islands, the islanders conceive of an extensive, communal body of solidarity following the pathway of the current. As Rapongan's people feed on the flying fish and center their rituals and calendars on the movement of the fish, both humans and fish traverse the Pacific, deterritorializing the ocean. The flying fish return every year, inspiring the islanders' will to survive and serving as fountainhead of their fighting spirit. The fish—indeed, the very waves—carry memories of Tau ancestors.

Rapongan questions the idea of the nation's territorial sovereignty, configuring lines of mobility and escape: like "the dense schools of flying fish," the diverse island inhabitants cross over and pass over the ocean, following the natural rhythm of the Black Current. This act of border crossing characterizes Syaman Rapongan's tribal Indigenes as it does the inhabitants of other Pacific islands. Like Sullivan's Maori ancestors, the Tau cultivate forests and plant trees (*Mi mowamowa*), leaving the lands to their offspring as an invaluable inheritance. Forest timber is harvested from the interior mountains for their traditional boats, and the wood selected and ranked as appropriate for building decorative (*Mivatek*) and nondecorative boats. Using their adroit boat-building skills (*Mi tatala*) and incorporating their rudimentary knowledge of waves, the Tau produce streamlined carriers of traditional beauty. They anticipate that their boats will become good friends to the fish. The *Mi tatala*, like *waka* in Maori's vocabulary, bespeaks a symbolic order of the Tau's intimate relationship with the ocean. Their assembled boats become the medium for significant connections between the Tau, the sea, and their blood relations in the sea.

Rapongan's recent work *Eyes of the Sky* opens with the significance of the navigating boat: "Boat—a tool of my journey on the sea and also my second oceanic ancestor,"[47] calling up an explicit connection to Sullivan's conceptualization of *waka* as Maori ancestry. Like *Star Waka*, *Eyes of the Sky* centers on the stars, too, as its title features: "The eyes of the sky were extraordinarily bright, turning the sea at night into luminous waves, flickering with the watery movements of the sea surface."[48] In the Tau community, fish hunting means dealing with the ever-changing ocean; the unpredictability of the sea contributed to the Tau male-centered fishing family, including boat building and boat sailing. Rapongan's father, upon his return to his home island after graduating from the university in 1991, built a traditional plank boat for him to celebrate his return and settlement. It was a gift he had craved for a long time. Rapongan enlivens this memory and designates the return as a reconversion into his tribal tradition of seafaring and sea-savoring practices:

> The plank boat my father made was about four meters long; the width of the rowers' seats in the middle was merely eighty-five centimeters. It rocked all the time when floating on the sea, and there were only about twenty centimeters between the edge of the boat and the sea. Fortunately, as a member of the tribe, I had always heard many stories so I managed to adapt myself very quickly to the sea. After all, I am the descendant of a sailing family; the stories are encoded in my blood.[49]

The poet revitalizes the seafaring stories passed down by his (fore)fathers. The skills and techniques of navigating the ocean are encoded genetically in the blood. He describes how as he made the first voyage in his life by sailing the plank boat, the "eyes of the sky and the clear firmament caught [his] attention" and "the flow of waves and the fish-hunting ceremonies were the powers that motivated and excited beginners."[50] That night, he kept traveling on the sea on a journey of his own, out of an innate craving. As if predestined to make such a journey, on the dark sea, he pointed to the sky with his index finger, to a bright star that was "the eye of [his] soul and from which [his] romantic dream originated."[51]

Rapongan's writing shows a close affinity to the Native literature of the transpacific Indigenous communities. He writes of the Taus' genealogy, which, like whakapapa in Maori tradition, includes humankind along with what is underwater and in the sky to forge a vision of the cosmos. In one of the stories, Rapongan's mother formulates a planetary framework interfusing the self, the ocean, and the heaven/sky, resembling the complex cosmological genealogies at both the macro- and microscale of multispecies relationship, which the Maori waka and Tau boats detail: "The sky has many eyes, Mom told me, and one of them is my sky-eye that will keep illuminating my way until I die. If I have great strength of life or work hard to catch fish, my sky-eye will be very bright. Thinking of my Mom's words made me feel much relieved to cruise on the sea with the whale, and I felt lucky to be chosen by him. Wow!"[52]

"Eyes of the sky" in the Tau language means the stars. Reminiscent of Sullivan's guiding *light* and guiding *ancestors*, Rapongan's "eyes of the sky" provide a sense of direction for the poet, who was first initiated into the ocean by a whale in a dream before his father brought to him the material gift of the plank boat. His "sky-eye" becomes his mind's eye, transmitting power, knowledge, and trust through his bloodlines. In the dream, the whale, named Bawong, took the child on his back and continued to swim underwater. The event took place in May, during the Tau fishing season (which lasts from February to June), when many large predatory fish swam beneath the schools of flying fish. Bawong taught the child the names of the large fish, one by one—tuna, yellow fin tuna, *ulua* (jackfish), blue fin trevally, barracuda, dolphin fish, black marlin, and swordfish[53]—opening up his view to a world of multispecies dynamics under the water. In the communion among the human, the whale, and the stars, the child traversed the biosphere and became whale-human. The young boy witnessed the saturation of human nature by other natures, marveled at the ocean energy and dynamics, and said emphatically, "May my soul be strong."[54] The journey into the interconnected world of the ocean climaxes in an ecodynamic spectacle:

> Hundreds of thousands of flying fish leapt out of the sea, flying and dashing forward.... More fish jumped into my boat! Wow, wow! I was hit by thirty or forty flying fish.... Wow! This was a hunting-feeding ceremony of large predatory fish, and that was the flight of scared fish. Also there was the fleeting wave-cloud that I was lucky enough to witness on my first voyage out. Wow, I cried out to myself hearty words of good fortune and amazement. Hundreds of thousands of flying fish leapt out of the sea once, twice, and for a third time, and then the sea and flying fish all became perfectly silent and peaceful. The wild and magnificent spectacles are left only to the natural men who fish with primitive tools.[55]

Creatures previously appearing as food for humans have been pressed into the foreground alongside humans as creative agents and active participants. Rapongan's text can be qualified as not merely an encyclopedia of the Pacific fish but also as a biography or, rather, an auto-ethnography of these sea creatures. The fish become epic heroes of a battle in water while the human, standing in the line of the extended, multispecies Tau family, witnesses the epic event and becomes amazed and enlightened. The fishermen do not have active agency in catching fish; in the Tau cosmology, the flying fish offer themselves to the human as a seasonal ritual when predatory fish chase them. It is only in this particular season that Tau fishermen go out to sea to fish. By the end of the flying fish season, the tribal people then follow the natural rhythm and switch to coral reef fishing, waiting for the flying fish to return along with the north-flowing Black Current.[56] The Black Current transports warm, tropical water, which sustains the microbes and coral reefs, thus bringing a variety of marine organisms that migrate in the eddies as they live out their lives. Interweaving humans, stars, and other creatures and organisms in the sea currents, Rapongan bases his narrative on Tau traditional ecological knowledge to formulate a network spanning the ocean.

Rapongan draws our attention to the interconnectedness beneath the waves and in the sky, hence describing a deeper geography and mythology. His poetics is an ecologically interconnected, planetary, and renativized counterconversion to islands and other seascapes. The fish inspire the Tau boat building. The Tau build their boats by modeling *Panowang* (the hull of a ship) on the body of the jackfish to ensure the craft can cut through currents while retaining the primordial aesthetics.[57] This does not just bespeak the ocean-sailing tactics of the Tau people. Syaman Rapongan depicts the boat as a carrier and container of Tau civilization and bases his poetics on his renewed awareness of Native and natural knowledge, which emerges from the nonhuman multispecies communities of the Pacific Ocean.

CODA

The Pacific artists and poets radically rename the biocommunity from an oceanic/nonhuman viewpoint in which the regenerative energy of primordial planetary belonging can lead the islanders to become born-again Natives of the ocean. Their poetics and imagination surrounding islands and canoes retrieve the shared history of Indigenous Pacific peoples and their complex historical relationships to the waters and to cosmic beings. Together they significantly shape a discourse that would counteract contemporary land-based and continent-oriented scholarship of American and Native studies.

As the planet's largest unit of demarcated waters, and necessary to sustaining life and well-being, the Pacific Ocean could become the means of envisioning ecological and Indigenous solidarity, if compellingly framed in terms that elicit consent and inspire an imagination of cobelonging and care. Islands are not to be belittled. They are both aesthetically pleasing and intensely practical. Even more significantly, they form "our sea of islands," the immensity of a sea body without confines, as Hau'ofa puts it.[58] Reid, Sullivan, and Rapongan reflect on the oceanic Indigenous cultural milieu and ways of life to address the nature of islands from the past to the future, to achieve a better understanding of the uniqueness, connections, cultures, ethics, technologies, and sustainability for the many possible futures of islands. In this vision, places such as Haida Gwaii, Pongso no Tau, and Aotearoa become central rather than peripheral. The ancestors of the "ocean peoples" have lived in the Pacific for over eight thousand years. Their view of their world as "a sea of islands" is a holistic perspective in which things are seen in the totality of their relationships,[59] where Oceania becomes a collective body. The interwoven relationship among these islands demonstrates enormous desire to be connected, to enter into relations with one another, and to destabilize the myth of island isolation. It is hoped that the cultural urgency of the Pacific Indigenous people will shift our angle of reference and, as it does so, open up a less instrumentalist vision of space and place, time, and history. This is a vision in which we could imagine more equitable comparisons and networks, and in which places such as Haida Gwaii, Pongso no Tau, and Aotearoa offer valuable lessons as to how we can see ourselves as oceanic citizens as much as earth dwellers.

NOTES

1. Epeli Hau'ofa, *We Are the Ocean: Selected Works* (Honolulu: University of Hawai'i Press, 2008), 50, 58.

2. Antonio Benítez-Rojo, *The Repeating Island: The Caribbean and the Postmodern Perspective, 2nd ed.* (Durham, NC: Duke University Press, 1996), 9.

3. Brian Russell Roberts, "Archipelagic Diaspora, Geographical Form, and Hurston's *Their Eyes Were Watching God*," *American Literature* 85, no. 1 (2013): 123.

4. Gilles Deleuze, *Desert Islands and Other Texts*, ed. David Lapoujade, trans. Mike Taormina (New York: Semiotext[e], 2004).

5. Steven Roger Fischer, *Islands: From Atlantis to Zanzibar* (London: Reaktion Books, 2012), 6.

6. Fischer, *Islands*, 6.

7. Édouard Glissant, *Poetics of Relation*, trans. Betsy Wing (Ann Arbor: University of Michigan Press, 1997), 5–9, 11.

8. See Edward Brathwaite, *Contradictory Omens: Cultural Diversity and Integration in the Caribbean* (1974; repr., Mona, Jamaica: Savacou, 1977); Elizabeth M. DeLoughrey, *Routes and Roots: Navigating Caribbean and Pacific Island Literatures* (Honolulu: University of Hawai'i Press, 2007); Jace Weaver, *The Red Atlantic: American Indigenes and the Making of the Modern World, 1000–1927* (Chapel Hill: University of North Carolina Press, 2014).

9. Celia Britton, *Édouard Glissant and Postcolonial Theory* (Charlottesville: University of Virginia Press, 1999), 40.

10. See Rob Wilson, *Be Always Converting, Be Always Converted: An American Poetics* (Cambridge, MA: Harvard University Press, 2009); Rob Wilson, "Toward an Ecopoetics of Oceania: Worlding the Asia-Pacific Region as Space-Time Ecumene," paper presented at the Anthropological Futures Conference, Taiwan, Institute of Ethnology, Academia Sinica, June 12–13, 2010; Rob Wilson, "Oceania as Peril and Promise: Toward Theorizing a Worlded Vision of Trans-Pacific Ecopoetics," lecture given at "Oceania Archives and Transnational American Studies," Hong Kong University, June 4–6, 2012; Michelle Keown, *Postcolonial Pacific Writing: Representations of the Body* (New York: Routledge, 2005); Michelle Keown, *Pacific Islands Writing: The Postcolonial Literatures of Aotearoa/New Zealand and Oceania* (New York: Oxford University Press, 2007); Hau'ofa, *We Are the Ocean*; Vicente M. Diaz, "Moving Islands of Sovereignty" (unpublished essay provided to the author through personal correspondence).

11. Walter Benjamin, *The Arcades Project*, trans. Howard Eiland and Kevin McLaughlin (1982; repr., Cambridge, MA: Harvard University Press, 1999).

12. Vicente M. Diaz and J. Kēhaulani Kauanui, "Native Pacific Cultural Studies on the Edge," *Contemporary Pacific* 13, no. 2 (Fall 2001): 317.

13. Hau'ofa, *We Are the Ocean*, 27–40; James Clifford, *Routes: Travel and Translation in the Late Twentieth Century* (Cambridge, MA: Harvard University Press, 1997); James

Clifford and George E. Marcus, eds., *Writing Culture: The Poetics and Politics of Ethnography* (Berkeley: University of California Press, 1986).

14. These Pacific Islanders were Austronesian seafarers. Linguistically, the Austronesian family stretches eastward to Madagascar, east of the African continent, and travels across the Indian Ocean to occur in some coastal vernaculars in South Asia, northward to Aboriginal Taiwan in East Asia (which has been viewed as the "cradle" of Austronesian languages), to the southern reaches of Aotearoa (New Zealand), and eastward to Rapa Nui (Easter Island). Micronesians and Polynesians owe most of their genetic and cultural makeup to Austronesian ancestors. See Diaz, "Moving Islands"; Fischer, *Islands,* 11–12. See also Peter Bellwood, "The Austronesian Dispersal and the Origin of Languages," *Scientific American* 265, no. 1 (1991): 88–96.

15. Brian Russell Roberts and Michelle Stephens, "Archipelagic American Studies and the Caribbean," *Journal of Transnational American Studies* 5, no. 1 (2013): 5–8.

16. The story was told to the Nuu-chah-nulth/Hesquiat artist Tim Paul by his grandfather, quoted in Nigel Reading and Gary Wyatt, *Manawa—Pacific Heartbeat: A Celebration of Contemporary Maori and Northwest Coast Art* (Seattle: University of Washington Press, 2006), 31.

17. Reading and Wyatt, *Manawa,* 97.

18. Jon Tikivanotau M. Jonassen, "Double-Hulled Canoes, Navel Connections, and Sacred Pigs in the Large Ocean Island State: Chants, Songs, and Narratives Encountered in the Pacific," presented at and listed in the program book for the 2012 International Austronesian Conference: Weaving Waves' Writings—Memories, Stories, and Spiritual Resonance in Oceania, held in Taiwan, November 27–28, 2012, 72–73.

19. Reading and Wyatt, *Manawa,* 103.

20. Robert Bringhurst, *The Black Canoe: Bill Reid and the Spirit of Haida Gwaii* (Vancouver, BC: Douglas & McIntyre, 1991), 13.

21. For the names of the archipelago, see Joel Barry Martineau, "Islands at the Boundary of the World: Changing Representations of Haida Gwaii, 1774–2001" (PhD diss., University of British Columbia, 2002).

22. Bringhurst, *Black Canoe,* 8.

23. Martineau, "Islands," 49–60.

24. Daniel Francis and Gil Hewlett, *Operation Orca: Springer, Luna, and the Struggle to Save West Coast Killer Whales* (Madeira Park, BC: Harbour Publishing, 2007), 115–20.

25. Bringhurst, *Black Canoe,* 76.

26. For detail of the myths and contemporary literature surrounding whales in the transpacific context, see Hsinya Huang, "Toward Trans-Pacific Ecopoetics: Three Indigenous Texts," *Comparative Literature Studies* 50, no. 1 (2013): 120–47.

27. See Chadwick Allen, "A Transnational Native American Studies? Why Not Studies That Are Trans-Indigenous?," special forum on "Charting Transnational Native American Studies: Aesthetics, Politics, and Identity," *Journal of Transnational American Studies* 4, no. 1 (2012): 1–22; Chadwick Allen, *Trans-Indigenous: Methodologies for Global Native Literary Studies* (Twin Cities: University of Minnesota Press, 2012), xi–xxxiv.

28. See Allen, "Transnational Native American Studies?"
29. Reading and Wyatt, *Manawa*, 105.
30. Allen, "Transnational Native American Studies?," 2.
31. Bill Reid, *Solitary Raven: The Essential Writings of Bill Reid* (Vancouver, BC: Douglas & McIntyre, 2009), 99.
32. Robert Sullivan, *Star Waka* (Auckland, NZ: Auckland University Press, 1999), xiii. Portions of the reading of *Star Waka* and *Eyes of the Sky* are drawn from my "Re-visioning Pacific Seascapes in Robert Sullivan's *Star Waka* and Syaman Rapongan's *Eyes of the Sky*," in *Landscape, Seascape, and the Eco-Spatial Imagination*, ed. Simon C. Estok, I-Chun Wang, and Jonathan White (London: Routledge, 2016), 179–96; and my "Toward Trans-Pacific Ecopoetics: Three Indigenous Texts," *Comparative Literature Studies* 50, no. 1 (2013): 120–47.
33. Sullivan, *Star Waka*, xiii.
34. Sullivan, *Star Waka*, 3.
35. Sullivan, *Star Waka*, 21.
36. Sullivan, *Star Waka*, 3.
37. Chris Prentice, "'A Knife through Time': Robert Sullivan's *Star Waka* and the Politics and Poetics of Cultural Difference," ARIEL 37, nos. 2–3 (2006): 116.
38. Prentice, "Knife through Time," 122.
39. Sullivan, *Star Waka*, 112.
40. Sullivan, *Star Waka*, 17.
41. Chadwick Allen, *Blood Narrative: Indigenous Identity in American Indian and Maori Literary and Activist Texts* (Durham, NC: Duke University Press, 2002), 131.
42. Sullivan, *Star Waka*, 70.
43. Sullivan, *Star Waka*, 58.
44. Sullivan, *Star Waka*, 58.
45. See Diaz, "Moving Islands of Sovereignty."
46. Pongso no Tau literally means "the island of the original people," which is also known as the island of Lanyu or Orchid Island. It is the home island of the Tau people, located forty kilometers southeast of Taiwan, where men and women continue to live a life close to their oceanic tradition, which is part of the larger Austronesian culture. Taiwan is considered the origin of the Austronesian family, and while Han Chinese, who began to immigrate to Taiwan in the 1600s, constitute over 90 percent of the population of Taiwan, it is through the mediation of Pongso no Tau that Taiwan can be reshaped as a space linked to Austronesian/Polynesian/Oceanic modes of language, space, body, and culture. See Murray A. Rubinstein, *Taiwan: A New History* (New York: Routledge, 2014).
47. Syaman Rapongan, *Tekong de yanqing* 天空的眼睛 [Eyes of the sky] (Taipei, Taiwan: Linking Books, 2012), 1; English translations from Rapongan are by my assistant, Roy Wu.
48. Rapongan, *Tekong de yanqing*, v.
49. Rapongan, *Tekong de yanqing*, xv.
50. Rapongan, *Tekong de yanqing*, 15.
51. Rapongan, *Tekong de yanqing*, xv.
52. Rapongan, *Tekong de yanqing*, xiii.

53. Rapongan, *Tekong de yanqing*, ix–x.
54. Rapongan, *Tekong de yanqing*, x.
55. Rapongan, *Tekong de yanqing*, xvi.
56. Rapongan, *Tekong de yanqing*, 30. The Tau calendar divides the year into three seasons, determined by the activities and life circles of the flying fish: *rayon*, the flying fish season (from March to early July), when men go out to the sea to catch the flying fish; *teiteika*, the end of the flying fish season; and *amyan*, the winter season, when men wait for the flying fish to return. Most of the flying fish caught during the highlight season are smoked and preserved as food sources for the rest of the year. For filmic reference to the Tau flying fish tradition, see "Yami Flying Fish Festival and Traditional Boats," accessed Oct. 16, 2016: https://www.youtube.com/watch?v=IMlIV4yeW1c and "Orchid Island Land of the Flying Fish," accessed Oct. 16, 2016: https://www.youtube.com/watch?v=O-pqNoPv4TM, on YouTube. In the Oscar-winning film *Life of Pi*, director Ang Lee took inspiration from the Tau flying fish culture to build a spectacular episode of flying fish raining down upon the starving Pi.
57. Rapongan, *Tekong de yanqing*, 8.
58. Hau'ofa, *We Are the Ocean*, 35.
59. Hau'ofa, *We Are the Ocean*, 31.

13 | ARCHIPELAGIC TRASH

DESPISED FORMS IN THE
CULTURAL HISTORY OF THE
Ramón E. Soto-Crespo | AMERICAS

"THIS PIECE OF ENGLISH TRASH," exclaims Jacob Clarke in British Guianese writer Edgar Mittelholzer's novel *Kaywana Blood* (1958), referring to his daughter-in-law, a bar maid from London whose presence threatens to undo decades of family scheming to preserve the colored branch of the van Groenwegel family.[1] Written between 1952 and 1960, the Kaywana saga chronicles the history of Guyana by way of the history of the van Groenwegels and the emergence of a large white underclass in the Caribbean. "Only a white skin and nothing else," Jacob claims, and we wonder what has shifted in Caribbean culture that leads Jacob to express such contempt for pasty white skin.[2] In Mittelholzer's Kaywana saga, white skin becomes a signifier in trouble since it stops referring exclusively to upper-class whiteness and instead begins to signify an emerging devaluation of whiteness. Circum-Atlantic fiction after World War II marks the entry of white trash into Caribbean literary history.

Whereas in the antebellum United States white trash was predominantly considered the result of bad genes, this conjecture started to change in the mid-twentieth century, when it was speculated that white trash was the result of poor education.[3] Unlike those explanations, however, postwar Caribbean fiction introduces an account of white trash that understands it as resulting from an individual's economic downfall, that is to say, as a result of a loss of capital or decapitalization. As Mittelholzer's example above illustrates, the transatlantic passage of an English poor white subject to the Americas also entails the cultural passage from poor white to white trash. In the Caribbean, one is not born white trash, but rather one becomes white trash. Circum-Atlantic postwar fiction shows the poor white subject and the suddenly decapitalized white subject mutating into definitively white trash subjects, with a set of new connotations.

In the plantocracy, where whiteness had symbolized wealth, progress, and status, by the 1950s white skin was rapidly losing its luster. "I can afford to ignore such trash," claims Dirk, the last Kaywana patriarch, in reference to a member of the growing white trash population whose existence threatens to upend the colony's traditional hierarchy.[4] Mittelholzer's *Children of Kaywana* (1952), the first novel in the trilogy, marks the moment of emergence of this trash subjectivity and, relatedly, of an emerging genre of "trash fictions" in the Caribbean. Trash fiction as a popular literary form also comes to stand as the vehicle for representing an increasingly despised (white) population. *Kaywana*'s sequels reiterate and expand this turning point in Caribbean culture. Mittelholzer's saga thus writes into Caribbean literature a shift that has taken place in culture, a shift in both the understanding and the representation of a certain type of whiteness. How do we make sense of this work of postwar fiction that features the transformation of a white Caribbean subject into a white trash menace? In the Spanish Caribbean and Latin America, white trash does not exist; its presence is found only in postwar Anglophone Caribbean literature.[5] But even though that is the case, there is no adequate critical framework for understanding the location of Mittelholzer's work and its ilk in the vast archive of Caribbean trash fiction.

I want to suggest that we can make sense of the archipelagic emergence of trash fictions in terms of an archive, an archipelagic archive, accumulating a diversity of trash subjects.[6] Spurred by the renewed interest in William Faulkner's works in the late 1940s, circum-Atlantic plantation family sagas exploit the boundaries of race, gender, sexuality, and social decorum. Scandalous and popular, but despised by most critics for their lack of structural sophistication, these postwar plantation trash fictions introduce a literary convergence in which narrative forms deemed facile become venues for the representations of despised entities such as the white trash subject.[7] The archive of trash in the circum-Atlantic collects those entities that no longer govern the colonial states or the new national literary canons. White trash in this context points to a white subjectivity dislocated—one that lacks the means to rule, command, or organize cultural value. This collection of (white, trash) subjects gathers itself together in modes of political belonging that differ from the hegemonic nationalist narratives shaping circum-Atlantic discourse at midcentury.

It is as such that I argue that white trash fictions reflect forms of political belonging different from the governing metaphors of nationalist narratives. I examine the postwar boom in Caribbean trash fiction as specifically an archive of archipelagic trash. This archipelagic archive's organizing principle is the circum-Atlantic trash subject. Forming a large archipelago of island sagas, this archive of trash forms covers a region made of separate yet connected spaces. Collecting types of subjectivities and literary types that are deviant with respect to national or continental archives, this archipelagic archive of trash fictions preserves the refuse, detritus, by-products, and wild imaginative contributions of the postwar period that include alternative modes of political belonging. Because it generally does not ask us to examine governing national entities but rather invites us to consider assemblages of material ejected from national entities, the archipelagic frame *uncovers* archives we don't expect precisely because they cross boundaries of genre, geography, and linguistics. This essay focuses on postwar literary plantation family sagas, a subgenre within a larger circum-Atlantic archive of trash forms that includes historical, political, pornographic, literary, and ethnographic texts. A nonfictional example from this archive is H. Gordon Andrews's "'White Trash' in the Antilles" (1934), which remains one of the most overlooked sociohistorical accounts of white trash in the Caribbean. The archipelagic frame allows us to see a multigenre, multifield archive of trash forms that we simply would not apprehend if we were to approach circum-Atlantic literary works through a nationalist or continental lens.

In the postwar circum-Atlantic boom of trash forms, we encounter a strong bond between the more canonical archipelago of fiction and trash fiction's position as an unnoticed collection of literary works. In this vast corner of the archive we find the fiction of writers who today are barely remembered: Jan Carew, Ashley Carter, Nancy Cato, Elizabeth Boatwright Coker, Lonnie Coleman, Herbert de Lisser, Julie Ellis, Rupert Gilchrist, Raymond Giles, Alice Walworth Graham, Shirley Ann Grau, John Hearne, Eleanor Heckert, Lance Horner, George McNeill, Edgar Mittelholzer, Christopher Nicole, Ada Quayle, Kyle Onstott, and Richard Tresillian. These literary works vary in quality and scope, some consisting of a single multigenerational novel and others of a multivolume family saga. The sagas discussed in this essay—Kaywana, Haggard, and Amyot—offer representative samples of the vast archive of trash plantation family sagas that emerged in the postwar circum-Atlantic. Others—such as the Beulah Land plantation saga, the Blackoaks plantation series, the Chane plantation series, the Wyndward saga, the Georgians series, the Golden Stud series, the Jalna series, the Royal series, the Sabrehill plantation saga, and the Windhaven plantation saga—would provide over one hundred examples of innovation in the conventions shaping the plantation family saga narrative form. This flux in novelistic forms can also be found in the hundreds of plantation novels that did not evolve into multivolume series. Together these trashy fictions bring to light a submerged path in literary forms from Mittelholzer to Jean Rhys, and, concurrently, make evident a white trash presence in the circum-Atlantic. These works form not only a vast archive, a massive literary heap, containing hundreds of specimens of despised forms, but also a vast archipelago of trash sagas extending across the circum-Atlantic.

ARCHIPELAGOES OF TRASH: MORETTI AND CIRCUM-ATLANTIC FICTION

In order to make sense of this archipelago of trash, I draw on some concepts developed by novel theorist Franco Moretti in two books. In *Distant Reading* (2013), Moretti proposes that we consider literary traditions as archipelagic rather than national. To illustrate his point, Moretti contends that there is no such thing as a singular European literature but rather "*an archipelago of distinct yet close national cultures, where styles and stories moved quickly and frequently, undergoing all sorts of metamorphoses.*"[8] "In the European archipelago," he explains, space is important because a literary form requires "a space discontinuous enough" in which to reproduce itself.[9] The archipelago is an ideal framework for understanding the connection between literary evolution, morphological change, and vast geographic areas. The archipelagic formation provides the critical elements of discontinuity and relatedness that enable the evolution of the literary form—"a space discontinuous enough to allow the simultaneous exploration of widely different paths."[10] Moretti's archipelagic viewpoint places national traditions in a nonnationalist frame, given that archipelagoes are formed by those elements that exceed narrow local interests. That is to say, archipelagic formations introduce a diversification of paths and multiple routes to follow. In Moretti's method, literary archipelagoes are supranational forms that skip over unity for the sake of a diversified type of relatedness. The circum-Atlantic archipelago of trash exerts pressure on Moretti's archipelagic model by decontinentalizing the space of its novelistic production: archipelagoes of trash are not only deeply antinationalist but also fundamentally noncontinental. Whereas Moretti's archipelagoes of fiction elucidate a European canon, archipelagoes of trash illuminate works ejected by newly formed literary canons. In privileging the spaces in between continents, these archipelagoes of trash emphasize islands and travel crossings.

I would like to connect these fictional archipelagoes to what, in *Graphs, Maps, Trees* (2005), Moretti describes as lesser literary works that function as the "protagonists of the middle layers of literary history."[11] Written for fast consumption, these middling works were often regarded as "monstrous" because they exploited lowbrow themes and suffered from a lack of formal and aesthetic development. I want to argue that postwar archipelagic trash fiction should be understood, following Moretti, as a forgotten stream feeding the river of literary forms. Put differently, I am examining in this essay an archipelagic "middle layer." Archipelagic middle layers are composed of a network of noncanonical texts whose mobility, circulation, and morphological innovations take place unobstructed. By understanding the movements of these lesser works as a stream that flows into the canon and outward from the canon, my essay tracks down an unseemly constellation of works as an unofficial archive. The middle layer as an organizing principle allows the identification and recognition of these plantation family sagas as part of an archipelagic archive of trash forms. This organizing principle captures the dynamic circulation of trash fictions by making us aware of their outward movement as scattered and floating discarded residue, as flotsam and jetsam.[12] But it also alerts us to their inward movement into the stream of literary forms, influencing, reflecting, and integrating into literature new social phenomena and new subjectivities. As is the case with all such extensive archives, the white trash subjectivity that emerges from it is diverse and conflicted.

In this context, we can begin to appreciate how these knockoff novels function as a petri dish of literary forms. The archipelagoes of trash fiction develop their own peculiar set of narrative conventions, thus innovating a peculiar subset of literary forms without reverting to either the social realism of the previous decades or the literary modernism of the early twentieth century. Moretti's viewpoint allows us to see that what develops in the "middle layers" of literary history is not a dialectical coming together of Western narrative form and a generic local raw material.[13] Rather, what these examples illustrate, Moretti would argue, is the emergence of weird novelistic forms that combine a tripartite set of elements: the Western form, the raw material, and the local form (an archipelagic perspective that adds new connotations to the foreign form). Poor white (a foreign form) in the West Indian context of plantation economy (raw material) acquires a new nuance by adding decapitalization to its narrative (white trash). This supplementary nuance is then carried across national borders, thus complicating the other meanings of white trash where it had been understood as emerging from social class background. In this case, white trash in the US South, such as it appears in the works of William Faulkner, becomes entangled in a global Southern context in which white trash acquired a new definition. As such, these trash fictions map the circulation patterns that literature and its subjects take across geographical and national borders.

Trash subjectivity flourished in the Caribbean plantation narratives of the postwar period as part of a paperback revolution in book publishing that followed the demise of Great Depression–style pulp publications. Designed for mass consumption, these novelistic forms allowed the emergence of unexpected elements, such as what I am calling the archipelagic white trash subject. Considered by many as trashy aesthetic forms, these paperback fictions were crucial in popularizing white trash subjectivity in the circum-Atlantic region. Publishing houses such as Dell, Fawcett Crest, Arrow Books, and Signet expanded their inventory of plantation family sagas and accelerated the pace of innovations in forms of white trash subjectivity. According to Paul Talbot, this boom in plantation fiction was a market response to the demand for works dealing with the history of slavery. This subgenre's primary readership were the increasingly more educated African American communities residing in the northeastern United States. As Talbot explains, *Mandingo* was so successful in this context that historian Earl Conrad of the Associated Negro Press called it "the most sensational, yet the truest book I have ever read."[14] African American writer Richard Wright was "so impressed" with *Mandingo* that he "convinced a contact in France to publish a French translation."[15] Before Alex Haley's classic saga *Roots* (1976), postwar plantation fiction filled the gap in the history of slavery. Here I navigate this stream of trashy novelistic forms in an effort to identify the various types of trash—aesthetic, sexual, racial, and generic—that its overflowing waters bring to quench the thirst of the postwar marketplace. With this framework in mind, I want to address the postwar archipelago of plantation family sagas as a literary subgenre that shows accelerated levels of mutation during the period from 1950 to 1983.

Cultural critics such as Doris Sommer and Benedict Anderson have shown how literature became a key component in the foundation of modern nations.[16] However, this adjudication of national value originated from the formation of literary canons. Departing from this critical consensus, my essay shows that the emergence of white trash subjectivity in postwar literary works gives shape to an *antifoundational* model (against Sommer's and Anderson's national-foundational models) of political belonging. I argue that this archipelago of trash forms successfully exploits the story of decapitalized whiteness. In this particular stream, decapitalized whiteness and a cluster of other narrative themes—miscegenation, slave breeding, male-male desire, and nonnormative sex—contest the national and continental ideologies dominating the postwar circum-Atlantic world. Archipelagic narratives of trash are important not just for their representations of a historical moment after the end of slavery but also for their role in enabling literary masterpieces to emerge—such as Jean Rhys's *Wide Sargasso Sea* (1966). This essay proposes that archipelagic postwar works of trash set the path for a postfoundational understanding of belonging that finds its best depiction in *Wide Sargasso Sea*. Their postnational, postfoundational imaginative model of belonging inverts the myth of the Sargasso Sea by transforming it from a historical source of dread into an inspiring modernist model of future cohabitation.

A SARGASSO-LIKE ARCHIPELAGO OF WHITE COCKROACHES

The publication of *Wide Sargasso Sea* coincided with the spread of decolonization movements worldwide but especially in the Caribbean. Mittelholzer's Guyana attained its independence from Britain in 1966. His Kaywana saga provides an imaginary narrative rendition of this historical event, marking a shift from the end of Caribbean whiteness to the emergence of the Caribbean white trash subject. In *Wide Sargasso Sea*, Rhys captures the consciousness of a white Caribbean subjectivity that finds itself displaced and essentially homeless. Rhys's novel makes clear that trash subjectivity marks the moment in history when a white colonial subject is displaced by a newly created white trash subjectivity. Her narrative offers an account of how a White West Indian subject becomes a "white cockroach."[17]

In mid-twentieth-century Caribbean literature, the key idea of "the People" forming a newly decolonized nation was challenged by an archipelagic network of trash subjects scattered throughout the circum-Atlantic. Where nineteenth-century historical novels placed their faith in enlightenment ideas of rational temperance and cultural equality, these postwar family sagas projected their doubts about civil society by positioning trash subjects as key narrative elements. Glimpses of this strategic repositioning are apparent in *Wide Sargasso Sea*, specifically in Rhys's rewriting of mad Bertha, a key character in *Jane Eyre* (1847). Early in the novel, Rhys uses an equivalent of Caribbean trash subjectivity to describe mad Bertha as Antoinette Mason. Her term "white cockroach" marks the political change that took place in postemancipation Jamaica. Rhys makes clear that the British Parliament's decision to create a new subjectivity in the West Indies, a free Negro subject, begets another subjectivity, the suddenly impoverished white planter, whom she refers to as the white cockroach. Historian David Lambert explains the structural conundrum of British whiteness during this transitional period in imperial history: "The controversy over slavery was fundamentally bound up with the contested articulation of white colonial identities between colony and metropole."[18] British emancipation triggered a political and economic realignment in which trash subjectivity emerged to complicate the abolitionists' rosy picture of postslave society.

Wide Sargasso Sea, far from being the first exemplar of this thematic twist in mid-twentieth-century Caribbean literature, is instead one of its culminating points. In Rhys's novel we see a successful use of the motifs developed in postwar plantation family sagas set in the Americas that had been popularized for European and US readers. Rhys reproduces these popular themes in the context of an intervention in the British literary canon by recasting them in a modernist style. Yet, what *Wide Sargasso Sea* has in common with this trend in Caribbean popular fiction is that it makes explicit the political dimensions already developed in postwar plantation fiction. Rhys's white cockroach subjectivity is constructed in terms of politics. She thus shares the critical perspective toward the newly decolonized territories that had become common in Caribbean fiction during the mid-twentieth century. Postwar plantation family sagas had set the terrain for Rhys's literary innovations.

Rhys's connection with the West Indian fiction boom in postwar Britain and the development of a plantation family saga genre in the Americas remains largely uninterrogated in literary history. Rhys provides the metaphor of the Sargasso Sea to capture the politics that informed her narrative world of white cockroaches. Postwar plantation narratives pave the way for Rhys's novel by furnishing it with the political vision of what I would call a Sargasso political structure. The Emancipation Act, ratified by the British Parliament in 1834, was in fact a first step in the abandonment of the West Indies as a primary area of imperial interest, England's attention having turned to the East Indies. This shift in metropolitan interest compounded a sense of despair on the part of white Creoles by throwing their peculiar political/racial/class position into relief.

Consider, for instance, the story that Antoinette Mason tells on the very first page of the novel—a brief tale of Mr. Luttrell's devaluation. Confronted with his dramatic loss of capital as a result of slave emancipation, Mr. Luttrell decides to join the detritus of the Sargasso Sea instead of becoming a white cockroach.

> Another day I heard her talking to Mr Luttrell, our neighbour and her only friend. "Of course they have their own misfortunes. Still waiting for this compensation the English promised when the Emancipation Act was passed. Some will wait for a long time."
>
> How could she know that Mr Luttrell would be the first who grew tired of waiting? One calm evening he shot his dog, swam out to sea and was gone for always.[19]

At first glance Mr. Luttrell's death can be construed as suicide, but I propose that we interpret this tale differently: as a de facto white trashed subject, Mr. Luttrell embraces the warm waters of the Sargasso Sea and becomes part of its floating detritus. His body merges with other forms of trash that float in the circular currents of a circum-Atlantic ocean. The Sargasso Sea is a living archipelago of unanchored trash forms. Setting the novel's tone from the start, this brief account points to the Sargasso Sea, hovering just above the Caribbean (Sea) in the middle of the North Atlantic Ocean, as a vital political metaphor (see figure 13.1).

The novel's title becomes emblematic of an odd Caribbean form of belonging lurking at the edge of worldwide decolonial movements. Consider the fact that the Sargasso Sea has been described as "a sailor's graveyard," "a desert of the sea," "a place of forgotten winds."[20] It is said that the *Sargassum*, as a free floating alga, remains in the open ocean for its entire life cycle and does not need roots to hold fast for attachment; for the plants that reach the calm of the Sargasso Sea there is virtual immortality.[21] This alga collects all sorts of detritus and trash from various ocean currents (see figure 13.2).

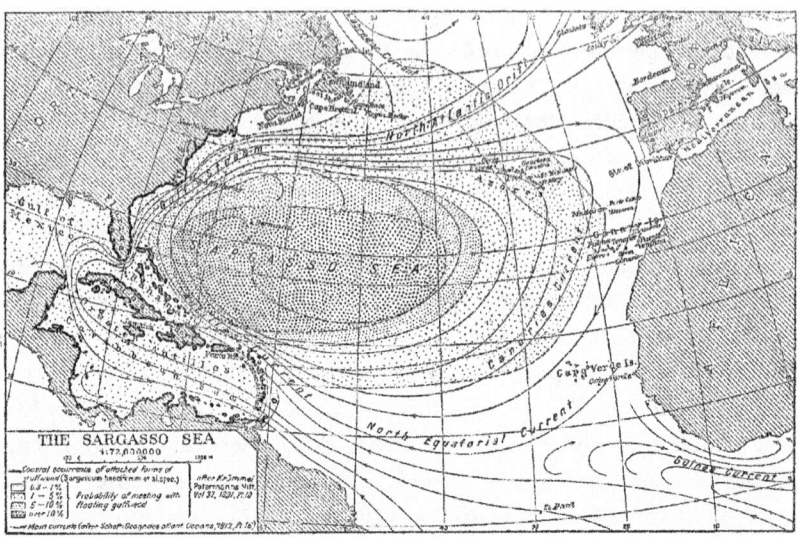

Figure 13.1. Map situating the Sargasso Sea among currents of the North Atlantic Gyre, including the North Equatorial Current, the Antilles Current, the Gulf Stream, the North Atlantic Drift, and the Canaries Current. From William H. Babcock, *Legendary Islands of the Atlantic: A Study in Medieval Geography* (New York: American Geographical Society, 1922), 28.

As a living garbage heap, the Sargasso Sea gathers rejected pieces from multiple shores to create an unattached living arrangement. Inspired by its uniqueness, the modernist tradition has used the image of the Sargasso Sea as a metaphor. In his "Portrait d'une Femme" (which begins "Your mind and you are our Sargasso Sea"), Ezra Pound uses the Sargasso Sea as a metaphor for a feminine mind that collects but fails to synthesize bric-a-brac into true art.[22] Pound seeks to differentiate his modernism from a feminized trash aesthetic for which the Sargasso Sea is the emblem.

Hovering between the continental Americas, the archipelagic Americas, Africa, and Europe, the Sargasso Sea is the earth's only sea without a land boundary. A sea without coastlines, it lies beyond the jurisdiction of any country. This metaphor for the political cohabitation of trashy subjectivities runs counter to the decolonization movements and their nationalist agendas. But it seems consistent with assessments by historians such as Gordon K. Lewis, who in *The Growth of the Modern West Indies* (1968) emphasizes what he calls the region's "anomalous decentralization."[23]

In a postcolonial Caribbean, postwar trash fiction replaces nation building—as literature's historical role in helping consolidate newly emerging nations in the

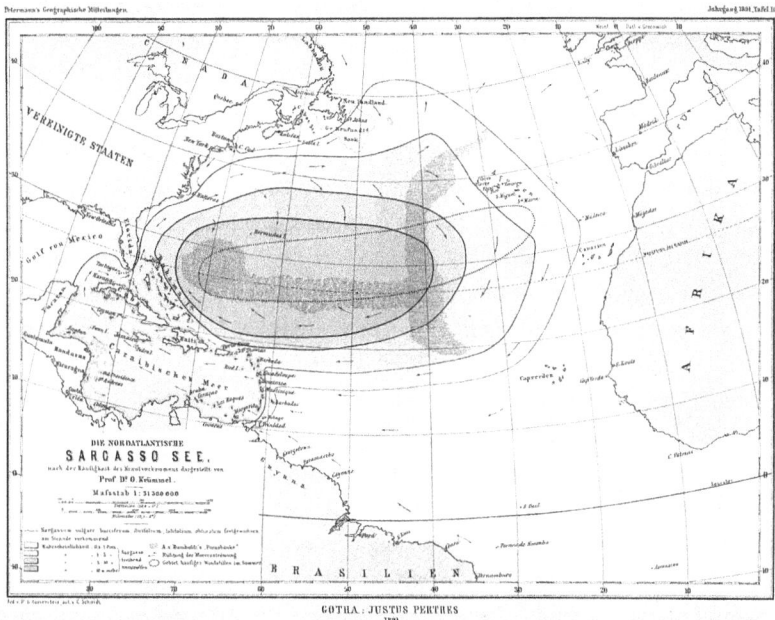

Figure 13.2. German publisher Justus Perthes's *Sargasso See*, 1891, by O. Krümmel. Map image courtesy of the National Oceanic and Atmospheric Administration.

Americas—for a Sargasso political model. The constitutional myth of the nation is replaced by an antinationalist vision. The imagined myth of a Sargasso-like political construct, an oceanic commons, takes us beyond previous academic models for understanding the role of literature in the construction of nationhood. Postwar archipelagic trash fiction represents a challenge to critical models such as the imagined communities of nationalism espoused by Benedict Anderson, the foundational fictions of nineteenth-century Latin American liberalism explained by Doris Sommer, and the national allegories of magical realism delineated by Fredric Jameson.[24] At stake in this study is the archipelagic imaginative world of Caribbean white trash subjects, the boldness of their Sargasso-like political vision, and the farsightedness stemming from their unprecedented decapitalized condition.

THE POSTWAR EMERGENCE OF WHITE COCKROACHES

Mittelholzer wrote the Kaywana family saga with the assistance of a Guggenheim fellowship for creative writing, the first West Indian writer to be honored with this award. For Victor Chang, one of the few critics who has engaged Mittelholzer's work, the Kaywana trilogy revealed not only "formidable powers of invention, historical reconstruction, and psychological insight," but also "the most sensational and explicit treatment of the darker side of sexuality."[25] In Kaywana, he argued, one could find "incest, rape, flagellation, mutilation, castration, adultery and the furthest reaches of masochistic behavior."[26] Chang explains that, influenced by his love for detective fiction, Mittelholzer's works were considered "far from normal."[27] His twenty-two novels, travel book, autobiography, poems, short stories, plays, essays, and sketches provide a wide range of representations of abnormality and eccentricity.[28] Branded as a producer of literary pornography rather than of West Indian literature, Mittelholzer remains an underexamined writer, his literary contributions to a trash Caribbean aesthetics largely unknown.[29]

Hendrickje, the protagonist of the first Kaywana novel, embodies the trash subjectivity that runs in the van Groenwegel's family name. Not only does she whip her husband into submission, destroy his art, and lock him in a room, she also convinces her grandchildren to kill their own mother (her daughter-in-law). Determined to live up to the standards of Kaywana's bad blood in her, she beds the best-endowed African slaves in her plantation, thus treating sex as a natural nuisance that the slaves must satisfy for her. All types of African men pass between her sheets: Mandingo, Royal Hausa, and so on. Yet not with any of these do we see the level of cruelty that we witness in Hendrickje's treatment of slaves. Not only does she work her slaves to death, she also buries alive those who are old and feeble, especially those who have fallen ill. The slaves are forced to use their last breaths to dig their own graves. In *Women Writing the West Indies* (2004), Evelyn O'Callahan identifies several types of plantation mistresses, such as the "white witch," the ministering angel, the drudge, and the pampered degenerate.[30] Hendrickje is a perfect example of a cross between a "white witch" and a pampered degenerate. This last type, the pampered degenerate, would be the most successful type in the trash fiction plantation genre, due to the sexploitation potential of miscegenation.

Introducing the white trash type into Caribbean literature with his Kaywana saga, Mittelholzer astutely builds on the white witch literary type that had been canonized by Herbert de Lisser in his best-selling novel *The White Witch of Rose Hall* (1929). Mittelholzer combines this literary type from the Caribbean historical imagination with the new economic reality of postcolonialism. What he captures is a historical juncture where capital and whiteness had transformed into empty shells of their former selves. With independence, investment capital in the Caribbean nations had shifted from commonwealth grants to long-term international loans in order to pay for national modernization projects. If independence brought with it a new economy based on debt, this new economic reality echoed the sudden indebtedness of white planters in the aftermath of emancipation, when their human capital vanished overnight into an unprofitable human condition. In this new world of negative investment, decapitalized whiteness transforms itself into white trash, and thus adds one more type of devalued entity to the accumulation of specters that makes up circum-Atlantic cultural history. The capitalization of whiteness that reached its heights in the eighteenth and nineteenth centuries becomes suddenly divested in the postemancipation Caribbean, and this process is captured in Mittelholzer's Caribbean trash fiction.

It is in the context of multiple and unconventional understandings of white trash that we can appreciate the first speech act by an archipelagic white trash subject, which takes place in Mittelholzer's novel *Children of Kaywana*. When Hendrickje van Groenwegel, the protagonist, calls her effeminate homosexual son Cornelis "a piece of trash," her utterance establishes Cornelis as the first white trash historical subject and consequently founds a literary type.[31] This abrupt characterization initiates the stream of trash subjects at the heart of an emergent novelistic form in the Caribbean. Hendrickje and her son are both trashy subjects who mark the beginning of a powerful stream of trashy novelistic forms.

Advertised on its front cover as "a savage novel of slave rebellion—of untamed sex and unspeakable violence," *Children* delivers more than it promises. It should not surprise us that a slew of plantation novels would base their potential success in the fiction market by presenting themselves as akin to *Children* in quality and theme. For instance, the cover page of Jan Carew's *Black Midas* (1958) reads, "If you liked *Children of Kaywana* we recommend *Black Midas* with confidence."[32] Mittelholzer's novel created a new literary space for the writing of the white trash subject in the Caribbean, a space that would be widened by knockoffs of the plantation family sagas in the Caribbean and across the hemisphere. Mittelholzer's *Children* marks the beginning of an archipelago of plantation family sagas that would extend from the Caribbean to the broader Americas, and from there, to the globe.

CIRCUM-ATLANTIC TRASH FICTION: CHRISTOPHER NICOLE'S GLOBAL ARCHIPELAGOES

Also emerging from British Guiana, Christopher Nicole's Caribbean plantation sagas affirm whiteness while embracing a white trash subjectivity. Harking back to Mittelholzer's Kaywana saga, Nicole's Amyot saga takes us closer to the US border, where a white trash subject not only establishes an island plantation but also claims ultimate sovereignty from British, US, or any other national political system. Set at the fringes of national and international jurisdictions, the imagined cay is located within the borderwaters of all "normalized" circum-Atlantic political models. In this particular geopolitical location, the island plantation becomes a unique territory where trash is sovereign.

"A Black Slave's Trash" is the phrase that Nicole uses to describe Catherine Amyot, the heroine of his first Amyot volume.[33] Composed of *Amyot's Cay* (1964), *Blood Amyot* (1964), and *The Amyot Crime* (1965), the Amyot saga narrates the multigenerational process through which Catherine and her descendants take control of an island north of Nassau, Bahamas. Known as Amyot's Cay, the island plantation has secured its fortune by illegal means, including shipwrecking, gunrunning, and bootlegging. In humorous fashion, Nicole characterizes his female protagonist as follows: "She killed as many as she loved, and those have not been counted."[34]

Amyot's Cay's most important contribution consists in its description of a political transformation that threatened to normalize Providence town into a royal colony at the time of British imperial expansion in the Americas. Written in 1964, but set in the middle of the seventeenth century, Nicole's novel attempts to grasp the early stages of colonization and imperial rule in the peripheries of European empires in the New World. It is this geographical location on the periphery that allows Catherine to devise a separate society in Amyot's Cay, one distinct from other societies developing in Nassau, the colonies that would become the United States, and the British Empire. In Amyot's Cay, to be a black slave's trash was neither norm nor anomaly. Catherine Amyot crosses all boundaries by being not only white trash but also a black slave lover. As in Mittelholzer's Kaywana saga, the Amyot saga describes its protagonist Catherine as belonging in flesh and spirit to a black slave not her own. It is this particular social arrangement that becomes crucial in the development of a sense of local independence from dominant structures of imperial power.

Having acquired a reputation as a "haven for the homeless," Amyot's Cay had "accumulated the refuse of two continents and spewed them forth again as privateers."[35] A "haunt of witches and devils, a place to be shunned," Amyot's Cay represents the ultimate anti-imperial bastion against the Spanish, French, and English empires; accordingly, Nicole describes the island as a "sore on the map of the world."[36] It is precisely this status as the world's sore that enables the novel to give us an unexpected angle on the larger story of imperial global expansion. As a "sore whose stench reached even to Whitehall,"[37] Amyot's Cay opens a geographical location that is perceived as a danger to maritime trade. The cay, located near the Sargasso Sea, is pictured here as accumulating the human trash released by all continents that make up the circum-Atlantic region.

The Amyot saga marks the beginnings of the Caribbean plantation family sagas' global expansion, particularly in Nicole's criticism of emerging nationalisms in recently decolonized Caribbean countries. His works criticize the institutions that shape the newly formed governments with their demarcated local and international jurisdictions: "The Amyots had lived in these islands before there had been a governor or an assembly. They had been pirates and wreckers; one of their ancestors had stepped from the gallows in old Fort Nassau, not a mile from her father's house. Even after the suppression of piracy they had continued to defy both law and custom from their reef-protected islet."[38] Undoubtedly, Nicole deploys white trash subjectivity to contest the narratives of cultural and political belonging produced to consolidate newly formed nation-states. At this historical juncture, white trash subjectivity represents a distinct historical reality but also an ideological departure from conventional forms of national belonging.

Nicole's Haggard saga, which appeared in 1980–82 after the Amyot saga, is a series of novels narrating the archipelagic crossings of the Barbadian planter John Haggard. The Haggard saga continues the examination of trash subjects by discussing the white indentured labor from England to the West Indies but also by unsettling the white Creole location in the circum-Atlantic. Considered "uncouth colonials," white Creole subjects were advised to travel to England to be polished as fully white subjects.[39] Thus, perceived to be underbred and what Matt Wray calls "not quite white," the white Creoles were nothing but "foreigners" on English soil.[40] In Haggard, we find a view of the West Indies as "a breeding ground for piracy and every ill known to mankind."[41] Uncouth and belonging neither to the island of Barbados nor the British Isles, the protagonist John Haggard belongs instead to the trashy themes of lust that reign supreme in Nicole's circum-Atlantic novels. The Haggard chronicles tell the tale of the circulation of white trash to the West Indies: "Their clothes were in rags, even at a distance of thirty feet he could smell them, and their faces wore at once the pallor and the misery of people without hope."[42] One trader explains to Haggard the trade of devalued white flesh: "They're not for sale. Indenture. Ten pounds a piece for a ten-year term. What they smell like is immaterial."[43] But beyond the "grime and the stench" of decapitalized whiteness, the saga also tells the tale of sexual trash: "how his heart swelled in tune with his penis," "the gentle caress of Byron's fingers sliding over my cock," and sexual penetration in the "most unnatural fashion . . . caring not where he made his entry."[44] From gangbangs to spread-eagle penetrations, from peppered nipples to fingering lesbians, the sagas portray a world that is fundamentally fractured, discontinuous yet connected.[45] The archipelago of trash introduces us to a seductive world where subjects are less than respectable and are totally bewitched by lust. Nicole summarizes the seductive character of this archipelagic middle layer by having his main character confess, "I'm bewitched . . . but I don't want ever to be normal again."[46]

The Amyot and Haggard sagas, although voluminous, are just a drop in the bucket of Nicole's hyperproductive output of trash family sagas. These first two sagas were accompanied by eighteen others of greater narrative length: the Caribee of the Hiltons saga, the Haggard Chronicle saga, the China series, the Sun of Japan series, the Black Majesty saga, the McGann saga, the Kenya series, the Murdoch Mackinder saga, the Pearl of the Orient series, the Sword of India series, the Dawson saga, the Bloody Sun series, the Russian saga, the Arms Trade series, the Berkeley Townsend series, the Jessica Jones saga, the Anna Fehrbarch saga, and the Jane Elizabeth Digby saga. Consisting of an average of five to eight novels each, these sagas amount to an enormous production. More extensive sagas were written under Nicole's various pseudonyms: Peter Grange, Andrew York, Robin Cade, Mark Logan, Alison York, Leslie Arlen, C. R. Nicholson, Daniel Adams, Simon McKay, Caroline Gray, and Alan Savage. From the Caribbean as its primary setting, Nicole's narratives expand to encompass larger geographical regions. The narratives spread north and south, east and west, to include the United States, Europe, Africa, India, China, Japan, and Russia. This geographical expansion also involves a chronological broadening by setting some sagas in the world of Roman and Greek antiquity (the Eleanor of Aquitaine, Ottoman, Moghul, Queen of the Night, and Queen of Lions sagas), and in the spectral world of the beyond in supernatural narratives (the Helier L'Eree trilogy). Collectively, Nicole's works form a worldwide archipelagic archive, which in turn contains the multivolume archipelagoes of its sagas, containing in turn a multiplicity of trash subjects. Ever multiplying, ever refracting, Nicole's imagination spares no geographical, chronological, or parallel region. For Nicole's sagas, our planet is not enough.

In *Modern Epic* (1996), Moretti argued that the Western epic aims to encompass the globe by bringing together a vast array of "independent elements"; highly inclusive, the epic represents a "form in continuous growth," he contends.[47] In the context of Nicole's oeuvre, we see the infinite aggregate of a novelistic form that has spread globally. Not exactly an epic but a sprawling novelistic innovation, Nicole's plantation sagas distribute Caribbean attributes to all corners of the visible and invisible world. If Mittelholzer developed his narratives within the geographical horizon of the Caribbean, Nicole's productivity pushed the limits of the genre to the limits of the globe. No longer encompassed by the Western epic, the planet has been enveloped under a global archipelago of trash fiction.

CONCLUSION

Postwar narratives of trash extend visibility to those elements that are ruinous for nineteenth-century political liberalism, and especially its central ideal of national unity. In a sense, the emergence of a trash subject triggers a repositioning of literary fiction in culture. Trash subjectivity marks the moment in history when a white colonial subject is displaced by a newly created white trash subjectivity; this newly emerging form in turn dislocates the assumed role that literary fiction had coveted since the beginning of the nineteenth century. Let me say then that, contrary to the foundational role that Doris Sommer attributes to nineteenth-century historical romances as imagined national foundations, these twentieth-century postwar family sagas instead illuminate antifoundational elements. In modifying a new breed of family sagas, these postwar writers reexamine the conditions that link literature to the state and politics to literary form. If nineteenth-century Latin American romance novels represented narrative strategies by the *letrado* class to disseminate via fiction the idea of a unified nation, then my research suggests that at a similar historical juncture during the 1950s, when newly independent nations sought to forge decolonized national identities by imagining a union of different class, ethnic, and racial elements, postwar trash fictions circulated narratives of unsettled foundations. Instead of representing the essence of a future national destiny, these narratives captured in literary form the emergence of a new trash subjectivity. Thus, where Sommer examines how historical fiction became more effective than experiments in constitutionality by enabling newly formed national citizens to imagine a viable political entity,[48] archipelagic white trash family sagas show what creeps out from under the demise of the nineteenth-century plantation complex.

If, in these particular postwar plantation narratives, the past has been invoked raw, rawness should not be mistaken as truthfulness. Rather, rawness is due to an intensification that has taken place in which elements from the past have found correspondences with a critical present. In this case, those elements that had remained out of sight in accounts of the Caribbean plantation system—such as sexual and racial violence, physical brutality, and signs of queer degeneracy—find themselves recognized in the postwar archipelago of themes organizing these texts. The past, heightened and realigned, shapes these plantation narratives. Far from resembling a Jamesonian "national allegory," or an Andersonian "imagined community," these postwar trash fictions propose models of cohabitation that are fundamentally unanchored and antifoundational. From archipelagic family sagas to a Sargasso political model, we have traced a literary history of repetition and replication but also of innovation and mutation that tells a different story than the one found in canonical literary histories. The middle layers of literary history produce an unconventional account—one that is archipelagic, circulatory, and worth telling. The postwar archive of plantation family sagas offers not only a collection of trash novels but also a political vision put forth by decapitalized circum-Atlantic white subjects. As such, these works are not foundational fictions but an archipelago of despised novelistic forms.

NOTES

I would like to thank the volume editors for their careful reading and helpful suggestions. I especially want to thank Tim Dean for his enthusiasm and feedback on this essay.

1. Edgar Mittelholzer, *Kaywana Blood* (1958; repr., London: Secker and Warburg, 1960), 391.

2. Mittelholzer, *Kaywana Blood*, 391.

3. Matt Wray explains that poor education is the framework that has been used to understand the conditions of the white poor in the United States in the middle decades of the twentieth century; Matt Wray, *Not Quite White: White Trash and the Boundaries of Whiteness* (Durham, NC: Duke University Press, 2006).

4. Mittelholzer, *Kaywana Blood*, 274.

5. Space constraints prevent me from expanding on the limited presence of the *petit Blanc*, "poor white," in Francophone Caribbean literature. Suffice it to say that the petit Blanc's location in Haitian society, for instance, was one of being equally despised by both the white planter class and the African slaves. For more on the petit Blanc in Haiti, see Léon François Hoffman, "Haitian Sensibility," in *A History of Literature in the Caribbean*, vol. 1 *Hispanic and Francophone Regions*, ed. Albert James Arnold, Julio Rodríguez-Luis, and J. Michael Dash (Amsterdam: John Benjamins, 1994), 372.

6. The "arkhi" of archipelago is not identical to the "arkhe" of archive. Whereas "arkhi" means "chief" (and "pelago" means "sea"), the "arkhe" of "archive" refers to "government." Yet "chief" and "government" are related words, cousins we may say, in the structures of cataloguing, mapping, and identifying cultural forms. See "archipelago," *Oxford Dictionaries*, accessed July 28, 2014, http://www.oxforddictionaries.com/us/definition/american_english/archipelago, and "archive," *Oxford Dictionaries*, accessed July 28, 2014, http://www.oxforddictionaries.com/us/definition/american_english/archive.

7. My use of "facile" here stems from Pierre Bourdieu's account of aesthetic value in which he explains that facile forms arouse "distaste" and "disgust" because they are "simple, and therefore shallow . . . easily decoded and culturally 'undemanding' "; Pierre Bourdieu, *Distinction: A Social Critique of the Judgement of Taste*, trans. Richard Nice (Cambridge, MA: Harvard University Press, 1984), 486. I expand on this at great length in the introduction to my in-progress book *Hemispheric Trash: Despised Forms in the Cultural History of the Americas*.

8. Franco Moretti, *Distant Reading* (London: Verso, 2013), 1. Original italics.

9. Moretti, *Distant Reading*, 18.

10. Moretti, *Distant Reading*, 18.

11. Franco Moretti, *Graphs, Maps, Trees* (London: Verso, 2005), 14.

12. I thank Michelle Stephens and especially Brian Roberts for suggesting the concepts of flotsam and jetsam.

13. See Fredric Jameson, *The Antinomies of Realism* (London: Verso, 2013), 11.

14. Quoted in Paul Talbot, *Mondo Mandingo: The Falconhurst Books and Films* (New York: iUniverse, 2009), 19.

15. Talbot, *Mondo Mandingo*, 27.

16. Doris Sommer, *Foundational Fictions: The National Romances of Latin America* (Berkeley: University of California Press, 1993); and Benedict Anderson, *Imagined Communities: Reflections on the Origins and Spread of Nationalism* (London: Verso, 1983).

17. Jean Rhys, *Wide Sargasso Sea* (1966; repr., New York: W. W. Norton, 1982), 23.

18. David Lambert, *White Creole Culture, Politics, and Identity during the Age of Abolition* (New York: Cambridge University Press, 2005), 5.

19. Rhys, *Wide Sargasso Sea*, 17.

20. Rachel L. Carson, "The Sargasso Sea," in *Wide Sargasso Sea: Backgrounds, Criticism*, ed. Judith L. Raiskin, Norton Critical Editions (New York: W. W. Norton, 1999), 118.

21. Carson, "Sargasso Sea," 118.

22. Ezra Pound, "Portrait d'une Femme," in *Ripostes* (London: Stephen, Swift, and Co., 1912), 17.

23. Gordon K. Lewis, *The Growth of the Modern West Indies* (London: Macgibbon & Kee, 1968), 47.

24. Fredric Jameson, "Third-World Literature in the Era of Multinational Capitalism," *Social Text* 15 (1986): 65–88.

25. Victor L. Chang, "Edgar Mittelholzer: Guyana's Greatest Novelist (1909–1965)," blog, March 6, 2006, http://edgarmittelholzer.blogspot.com/2006/03/victor-l.html.

26. Chang, "Edgar Mittelholzer."

27. Chang, "Edgar Mittelholzer."

28. Chang, "Edgar Mittelholzer."

29. One of the few journal issues devoted to Anglophone Caribbean popular culture, *Small Axe* released a special issue on *The Caribbean Popular* (no. 9 published in 2001), paradoxically ignoring the vast production of popular fiction Caribbean trashy novels of the 1950s.

30. Evelyn O'Callahan, *Women Writing the West Indies, 1804–1939: "A Hot Place, Belonging to Us"* (London: Routledge, 2004), 26.

31. Edgar Mittelholzer, *Children of Kaywana* (1952; repr., New York: Bantam, 1976), 304.

32. Jan Carew, *Black Midas* (1958; repr., London: Ace Books, 1960), cover page.

33. Christopher Nicole, *Amyot's Cay* (1964; repr., New York: Bantam, 1974), frontispiece.

34. Nicole, *Amyot's Cay*, 2.

35. Nicole, *Amyot's Cay*, 59, 7.

36. Nicole, *Amyot's Cay*, 7, 59.

37. Nicole, *Amyot's Cay*, 59.

38. Christopher Nicole, *Blood Amyot* (1964; repr., New York: Bantam, 1974), 5–6.

39. Christopher Nicole, *Haggard* (New York: Signet, 1980), 116.

40. Wray, *Not Quite White*, 41; Nicole, *Haggard*, 215.

41. Nicole, *Haggard*, 111.

42. Nicole, *Haggard*, 24.

43. Nicole, *Haggard*, 24–25.

44. Nicole, *Haggard*, 26, 302, 221.

45. Nicole, *Haggard*, 33, 36.

46. Nicole, *Haggard*, 48.

47. Franco Moretti, *Modern Epic: The World System from Goethe to Garcia Marquez* (London: Verso, 1996), 96.

48. Sommer, *Foundational Fictions*, 12, 26.

14 | THE GREAT PACIFIC GARBAGE PATCH AS METAPHOR

THE (AMERICAN) PACIFIC YOU CAN'T SEE

Alice Te Punga Somerville

> I will never be lost for I am a seed sown at Rangiatea [originary Pacific home].
>
> Traditional Māori proverb
>
> Every piece of plastic ever made still exists.
>
> Common saying about plastic pollution

IT'S OUT THERE, FLOATING AROUND THE PACIFIC: bigger than Texas and with roots not on the ocean floor but in the disposable lives of other people. No, not people whose lives are deemed disposable but people whose lives are based on disposability. It turns out that small bits of trash, discarded by those whose position is marked by what they have the luxury to throw away as much as by what they keep, do not merely dissolve in an endlessly diluting sea but have, alas, been shaped by the currents and tidal pulls of the ocean into a large stretch of rather concentrated plastic debris. Marine life is gently suffocated, and the ocean water that has felt impossibly and excitingly vast to continental folks has started to reveal secrets it has whispered to islanders for a very long time. The great Pacific garbage patch feels like something from a movie, but, frustratingly, it cannot be captured on film. Actually, it is so filmy it cannot be captured. Unlike biodegradable matter, plastic released into the ocean is not endlessly broken down to the point of effective disappearance but instead structurally disintegrates into tiny "microplastic" fragments that are mostly invisible (or only partially visible) but certainly have enough bulk and presence to affect the surrounding environment.

The garbage patch in the North Pacific is the result of plastic matter being dumped into the ocean and then being moved in the regular system of tides and currents that produce gigantic circular "gyres" to which the plastic debris (broken down into parts, then particles) is shifted and within which it eventually circulates.[1] Like the Pacific region, the garbage patch is both under the control and beyond the control of several nations—not just one—but the dominant supplier of plastic to the patch is America and American-controlled industry, and the dominant language used to talk about the patch—the dominant referent—is American. The garbage patch has frequently been compared to Texas, although since 2008 this comparison has been revised in many publications to "twice the size of America," and even in its name it is described by the American English terms "garbage" and "trash" (as in the "Pacific trash vortex"[2]) rather than by terms used in other Englishes, such as "rubbish" or "litter."

This chapter proposes that the uncountable nonbiodegradable debris that floats in the North Pacific known as the "great Pacific garbage patch" could serve as a productive—if contingent—metaphor for the long-standing, diverse, irreversible, and invisible/suffocating relationship between the United States, the idea of America, and the Pacific.[3] The Pacific is out of (American) sight in two distinct ways: the size of Pacific human presence in the United States with which most continental US-Americans are familiar is too negligible to "count" in most analyses, and Pacific spatial presence in the United States (specific Pacific sites under US political control) is overwhelmingly ignored with the exception of occasional representations of Hawai'i inelegantly squeezed alongside a similarly out-of-scale Alaska on media weather maps. To take one example of what this Pacific invisibility looks like in a scholarly context, Harvard-based historian David Armitage opens a book review in the *Times Literary Supplement* in December 2013 with the words "The Pacific has long been the hole at the heart of world history,"[4] a comment about Pacific absence that foregrounds the broader context in which such a claim can be made without expecting to be countered or ridiculed for being, well, ridiculous. Armitage's short sentence renders the Pacific ready (again) for exploration, ownership, first encounters; as if these things had not already happened over and over for five hundred years. (Indeed, the Pacific has been producing Indigenous historians for millennia and Indigenous historians with Western academic training for at least a century.) More blunt, of course, in another realm is then-US Secretary of State Henry Kissinger's famous comment in the context of US weapons testing in Micronesia: "There are only 90,000 people out there. Who gives a damn?"[5] The ensuing discussion, then, is an examination of this double invisibility, and asks how we might conceptualize presence in a context that feels (perhaps *looks*) rather more like absence. Specifically, in this chapter I contemplate whether the great Pacific garbage patch might offer a metaphor for thinking in new ways—archipelagic ways—about apparently invisible presence and the multiple kinds of connection between America and the Pacific.

AN ACCIDENTAL ARCHIPELAGO: A GREAT PACIFIC METAPHOR?

What happens when we decide to think about America through the structure and networks of the archipelago rather than (or perhaps as well as) the continent? While many scholars have moved through continentalism, then island focus, before taking up the idea that archipelagoes might provide a geographic unit of analysis that foregrounds networks and interconnectedness in a way that helps in thinking not only about "island" regions but about continental configurations as well, many other scholars have a different starting point. Two of the dominant "island" regions of the world—the Caribbean and the Pacific[6]—have produced scholars and artists who begin "at home" with the island in an expansive, perhaps even always already archipelagic, sense. When the island is a starting point, it does not need to first be an anticontinent, and so the step from the bounded island to the entangled archipelago is unnecessary;[7] islands are already experienced and understood as having multiple connections to other land and liquid spaces. In the Caribbean, most expressions of the archipelago focus on the meeting of Africa and Europe, and while there is sometimes a gesture toward Indigenous presence, this tends to be merely incorporative.[8] One could argue that the Pacific contributes to American studies a stubborn (and important) *non*metaphoric argument that America is archipelagic, because Pacific studies makes visible Pacific archipelagoes such as Hawai'i and the Marianas, and perhaps the Philippines (historically/militarily), that are part of the United States of America on the basis of geography and political spread.

"They say we are many things," wrote Native Hawaiian thinker John Dominis Holt in 1964, "but what do we think of ourselves?"[9] In the Pacific, islands, archipelagoes, and the ocean are configured not only by continental or diasporic types but also by people Indigenous to those spaces. Surely the most widely read (or at least widely cited[10]) Pacific scholar in the context of island/archipelagic studies is the Tongan intellectual Epeli Hau'ofa, with his famous articulation of an Indigenous view of the region as our "sea of islands" rather than the colonially imagined "islands in a far sea."[11] Pacific people have stories to tell about American presence in the region and Pacific presence in America. Metaphors involving navigation are widely engaged to describe the various ways Pacific people (and non-Pacific people, and states) have moved, and continue to move, around our region and beyond. The history of our collective ancestral navigation—an unparalleled feat in which the ancestors of all Indigenous Pacific people deliberately explored and spread across a region that covers a third of the earth's surface—provides us with a narrative: mobility is who we are rather than a departure from who we are. Navigation provides a way to imagine purpose, strategies, and methods of ongoing movement. Although our many Indigenous Pacific concepts, such as navigation, are sufficiently supple and complex to account for our diverse present realities, surely they do not preclude us from drawing on new metaphors too.

Despite the number of "actual" archipelagoes in the Pacific region, however, and despite the rich potential of thinking about Pacific diasporic sites as archipelagic (alongside, for example, thinking about them as transnational or regional, or merely as islands), the archipelago at the center of this chapter is one of my own invention. Or at least, it's a "manufactured" archipelago, to use Jonathan Pugh's suggestive term, by which he refers to "wind turbine arrays, island military bases, and moving islands that create dynamic archipelagoes, like fleets of military vessels or oil tankers."[12] Certainly it is one of human invention, albeit accidental. Like any archipelago, the great Pacific garbage patch is made up of constituent parts whose medium both of connection and disconnection is the ocean. Like any archipelago, there are general currents and tides that affect the whole larger entity as a kind of complex system, but there are also extremely diverse experiences and entities within that system. Also like many archipelagoes, the garbage patch was first seen by outsiders as a series of small bounded items that floated separately in the sea; it was on further and wider examination that the extent of the networked relationship between various parts was discerned, and as the system became visible, so too did much smaller parts that were not seen—and certainly not appreciated as active mobile parts of the system with an effect on the whole environment—until there was a desire to imagine they might be there.

In 1993 captain Charles Moore sailed from Hawai'i to California and noticed that all kinds of trash surrounded his vessel. Not a day went by, he realized, without the sight of plastic. Upon arriving on land he initiated research into the extent to which the Pacific Ocean was becoming clogged by cast-offs. At first he responded to the presence of visible trash, but it soon became clear that invisible trash was also present: a follow-up trip included scientific sampling that suggested as much as a six-to-one ratio of plastic to zooplankton by weight.[13] The great Pacific garbage patch has a devastating impact on marine life, and, because humans are more dependent on marine life than continental societies have tended to admit or consider, it has a "flow-on" effect for human life too. The plastic particles of the garbage patch choke seabirds, fish, sea mammals, and shellfish; they also coat living coral and other grounded organisms. Furthermore, these same particles act as a suspension in the ocean, altering the usual transparency of the water to the point of blocking sunlight in part or completely. Of course, the Pacific Ocean is not affected only by the microscopic plastic particles; these also work in concert with overfishing, radiation (for decades this has come primarily from weapons testing in Polynesia and Micronesia but more recently from the Fukushima nuclear plant crisis in Japan), other kinds of pollution, and climate change.

It is possible that thinking about the great Pacific garbage patch archipelagically gives us new insights into the garbage patch itself; hopefully it will also give us insights into the notion of the archipelago. What I am asking in this chapter is whether and how the archipelagic form of the garbage patch enables us to notice the relationships among apparently discrete units that turn out to be part of a larger system when you look at them in a certain way or from a certain distance. Despite Hester Blum's claim that "the sea is not a metaphor" and her call for "oceanic studies . . . to be more invested in the uses, and problems, of what is literal in the face of the sea's abyss of representation,"[14] it does not seem unreasonable to imagine that the "literal" of the sea—in this case, a specific aspect of its pollution—might also act metaphorically. This chapter offers one example of what Philip Steinberg, in his response to Blum, described as "thinking with the ocean in order to enhance our understanding of—and visions for—the world at large."[15] Also following from Steinberg, perhaps the garbage patch is, in turn, one way (perhaps, echoing Blum, one "literal" way) in which ocean regions might be understood as an "assemblage." All metaphors involve a tenor and vehicle.[16] The tenor—the main focus—in this instance is the relationship between the Pacific and America, especially as that relationship is articulated and evidenced by diverse forms of Pacific presence in America. The vehicle here is the great Pacific garbage patch; I am proposing that there is something in the nature or structure of an almost unimaginable stretch of plastic debris in the North Pacific that can, or perhaps might, convey something of the relationship between the Pacific and America, especially in relation to how we think about visibility/invisibility. What richness might be found in this metaphor? Jennifer Gabrys writes about the Pacific garbage patch as a "sink" in the specific sense of being an "indeterminate hybrid . . . of waste, technology, ecology, humans, and non-humans."[17] Gabrys argues that "sinks do not necessarily settle into a global-local dichotomy; they, instead, reveal a complex set of natural-cultural processes always in the making."[18] In the garbage patch we find things that tie the Pacific and America together: proximity, movement, disposability, invisibility, history, excess, destruction, reconfiguration, giant multimodal currents, and their life-changing effects on marine as well as human life.

Certainly this is an inappropriate metaphor. There is something distasteful about comparing any group of people or any place to rubbish or debris; in the context of the Pacific, soaked as it is by five centuries of European and US-American colonial imaginaries of the region as marked by contamination, barbarism, savagery, and even purity, such a comparison is downright alarming. Perhaps the garbage patch would be an ideal vehicle for a discussion of imperialism in the

Pacific, but to use such a deeply and irredeemably negative metaphor for Pacific people seems to add rather than take away from such colonial views. In the context of the belittling of migrant and Indigenous communities through metaphors of disease and contamination, describing our own people as pollutants is beyond problematic. Indigenous people in the Pacific—including those in the continental United States as well as those all around the region—are descended from divine genealogies, and count scientists, diplomats, politicians, warriors, agriculturalists, navigators, and artists among their ancestors. Surely it is the height of rudeness—and worse—to suggest that such people are trash.

And yet, there is something appealing about a metaphor that gives us a way to think about the difference between invisibility and absence. At some point, there is value in attempting these kinds of interrogations as long as we acknowledge the risks involved. In the context of (colonial) discourses about cultural integrity dissolving, rupturing, and being "lost," a metaphor of impossible degeneration feels a little exciting. Finally, to push a little harder on the idea of the great Pacific garbage patch as debris shed into the ocean from land, much of the scholarship that engages the ever-shifting relationship between land and sea falls back on the assumption that the land is always at risk of danger from the sea (erosion, flood, tsunami) rather than the other way around. This reinforces the sanctity of land (usually continental land) and its vulnerability to the ocean, and in turn quietly affirms that the ocean is the place where danger and risk are located. In our garbage patch we find an inversion. Rather than solid land being vulnerable to water, water—the ocean—is vulnerable to the breaking off of matter (solidness, nonliquid, a product of land) from land into the sea.

INVISIBLE: FROM SEA TO SHINING SEA

Describing the problem of imagining the scope of the garbage patch, the *National Geographic* website intones, "We have no way to measure this unseen litter."[19] In the United States, too, the measurement of invisible Pacific populations proves tricky because the bulky weight of continentalism complicates any conversation about the ongoing interactions between the Pacific and America. Narratives about Pacific presence in the United States, and about US-American presence in the Pacific, need first to contend with how the United States understands its continental self (or, perhaps, understands itself as continental) and how this is inextricable from specific reference to the sea as its natural border.[20] How do we talk about this nation that has for so long understood itself as continental and yet which has decidedly watery fringes along two long shores?[21] One major challenge to the landlocked version of the Americas has come from scholars whose work on the Atlantic triangle trade extends and complicates rather than affirms specific national borders. The Atlantic Ocean, a sea that had been framed as a space of nothingness—a border between "here" and "there"—has become rather more accurately and hauntingly reconfigured as a particularly dense space of somethingness. Just as thousands upon thousands of people could not have cruelly tumbled from ships into a mere border, however thickly inscribed, the nations involved in the trade did not themselves operate in bordered ways. Easterly boundaries of the Americas became less sharp as they oozed into the ocean between the former homes of African and European citizens.

The phrase "from sea to shining sea" that provides the second part of the heading for this section is the triumphant final line, as US-American readers of this volume probably already recognize, of the popular patriotic song "America the Beautiful." "From sea to shining sea" identifies and reinforces the imagined territorial limits of the nation, drawing on natural boundaries between ocean and land in order to naturalize certain national borders.[22] Clearly, it is less complicated to produce and normalize national territory geographically rather than historically. In the US-American case, longitudinal boundaries feel more certain than latitudinal boundaries with Mexico and Canada, which, again, require a turn to the historical in order to explain the exact position of the borders. The division between land and sea is so deeply understood as a natural border in European and Euro-American culture[23] that, just as Vasco Núñez de Balboa claimed "the sea and all the lands it washed upon" for Spain when he climbed a hill in Panama and became the first European to see the Pacific, in "America the Beautiful" the sea operates as an empty border space—an absence—between presence (land) and other presence (other land). When US-Americans sing "America" they really mean "the United States." Similarly, when they sing "from sea to shining sea" they do not actually mean the sea; they mean all of the things between the Atlantic and the Pacific. Between the two seas you find "America," and so it follows that the sea—and everything in it—is "not-America." Or does it?

The naturalization of "sea" as national boundary makes invisible the extent to which "America! America!" (really "The USA! The USA!") deliberately extends its control of territory beyond, through, and over "sea," and significantly this articulation of "America" stretched from "sea to shining sea" at the very moment the United States expanded in new and apparently irreversible ways into the sea itself. The year of the original composition of "America the Beautiful" was the year that US-America's boundaries crept, through the illegal overthrow of the Hawaiian monarchy, 2,500 miles "into" the "shining sea." The lyrics of the song were originally penned in 1893 by Katherine Lee Bates in the form of a poem of four stanzas titled "Pikes Peak."[24] Impressed by her recent journey through a significant stretch of the continental United States, including time spent at the World's Columbian Exposition in Chicago, Bates stood on Pikes Peak (a major summit in the Rockies) and felt compelled to compose a poem that both celebrated her view of the nation and looked hopefully toward a future. In the first publication of the poem in 1895, the final stanza read, "America! America! / God shed His grace on thee / Till nobler men keep once again / Thy whiter jubilee."[25] In the contemporary moment, we might feel a bit awkward at the racial overtones of a final vision of future whiteness, a concept that was both popularized and extended by the "White City" at the center of the Columbian Exposition. Quite apart from present sensibilities around equating whiteness with purity, however, this line also felt unsatisfactory in the context of the original readership of the poem; the suggestion of the possibility of future improvement was seen to undermine those readers (or, later, singers) actually reading (or singing) the line.

Over time the poem was rewritten and the phrase "from sea to shining sea," which had not appeared in the original version at all, cropped up at the end of the second and eighth stanzas in a version from 1904 and was retained in the same positions in the widely known version from 1913.[26] By the time the version of the poem in 1904 introduced the phrase "from sea to shining sea," Hawai'i had moved through a short phase as a republic under the control of US-American individuals and had been annexed to the United States in 1898,[27] the same year "America the Beautiful" also extended its imperial control over the Philippines and Guam (and Puerto Rico) as spoils of the Spanish-American War. Just as Elizabeth McMahon observes "the coincidence of John Donne's pronouncement that 'no man is an island' in 1623 being the same year the British claimed their first island colony in the Caribbean,"[28] so Bates "coinciden[tally]" composed her poem, which in a later revision would naturalize the US nation-state by imagining the continent through terms usually reserved for islands—bounded by water, with a perfect correspondence of political and geographic territory—the same year the United States claimed its first island colony in the Pacific. The reach of subsequent US expansion can be found all around the Pacific region, in the circulation histories of various islands and island groups that have had a wide variety of relationships with the United States (territories, dependencies, Pacific war sites, entities with Compacts of Free Association, states, possessions, military installations, and so on). Consequently, the ongoing impact of that reach can be found in the circulation histories—the presence—of Pacific people all around the United States of America: in its territories, its states, and its military forces on foreign soil.[29]

FOREIGN: FLOTSAM, JETSAM, AND SPILL

When Captain Moore first "discovered" the Pacific garbage patch, the fact of its existence was already a matter of history. Debris in the Pacific Ocean both marks and stands in for a series of historical moments in which an original item was produced, discarded, became debris, and traveled to the part of the sea in which is it presently found. Looking at the remnants of a plastic bottle floating on the crest of a wave is not solely about the moment of looking and floating but is also (perhaps mostly) about the circumstances that led to it. Considering the relationship between the Pacific and America, we find ourselves, like Moore, in the middle of a contemporary moment that is itself a sign of diverse historical activities. Brian Russell Roberts and Michelle Stephens articulate the promise of recognizing the historical dimension of an archipelagic configuration ("historicizing the insular will uncover other meanings and understandings of the shifting human experiences with island spaces"), while Stacy Alaimo suggests genealogy rather than history as a useful frame: "The human is held, but not held up, by invisible genealogies and a maelstrom of often imperceptible substances that disclose connections between humans and the sea."[30] In the case of our accidental archipelago, we find that Pacific presence in America is not produced in the moment of encounter with that presence but has been produced by imperial relationships between various nations—including the United States—in and around the region for centuries. The 1.2 million Native Hawaiians and other Pacific Islanders (NH&OPI) enumerated in the 2010 US national census are not merely proof of a present situation but by definition stand in for, well, as many as 1.2 million histories—or genealogies—of connection between America and the Pacific.

If the garbage patch provides a metaphor that might enable new thinking about Pacific presence in America, it is worth taking a step further and considering the various nonmarine items that make up the Pacific garbage patch. Marine law provides specific terminology for foreign objects found in the sea: flotsam, consisting of any items or parts of boats floating or washed up on land after the wreckage of a ship; and jetsam, consisting of the specific items deliberately discarded from a vessel, especially in order to lighten the load and avoid sinking. The great Pacific garbage patch is made up partly of these but also of litter that spills into the ocean directly from specific landmasses (continents, yes, but also archipelagoes such as Japan). Although the various constituents of the patch are pulled apart and pushed together by a diverse range of processes (sunlight, winds, waves, weather patterns) until they are all part of the same ever-enlarging entity, these three sources of trash (the deliberately discarded, the result of wrecks, and the overflow of waste) suggest a structure for prying apart, reflecting on, and historicizing three quite different ways in which the Pacific and America interact.

The category of jetsam draws our attention to the histories (and ongoing acts) of US imperial expansion into Pacific spaces that have been deliberately discarded or made invisible in order for the good ship America to stay afloat.[31] Pacific presence in the United States is not merely or solely diasporic, after all.

Humans move, but so do national boundaries. About half of NH&OPI identify as Native Hawaiian, and around another one-quarter are made up of Indigenous Pacific communities in other sites (Guam and American Sāmoa) for whom presence in US-America is the result of moving borders rather than moving people. So, approximately three-quarters of the Pacific presence in the United States has come about as a result of the opposite interaction: US presence in the Pacific. It is important to note at this point that acknowledging US *presence* (including presence enforced by maps, borders, and inhabitation) is not at all the same as acknowledging or affirming that US presence in the Pacific is a fixed or even final predicament. Long-standing, complex, and convincing claims about the legal and moral illegitimacy of US presence in Hawai'i, for example, are not undermined by an attempt to trace this presence; Haunani-Kay Trask among others has plainly articulated that Hawai'i is "not American."[32] Hopefully the literally and conceptually fluid nature of US claims on the Pacific that are highlighted by this chapter help draw attention to the contingent and incomplete nature of US-American claims in the region.

The concept of flotsam makes visible the Pacific presence in US-America that comes about as a result of wrecks: weapons testing, military activity, and exploitative resource extraction. For the United States, relative proximity is one of the key attractions of the Pacific: in some militarized terms, Pacific proximity to Asia is advantageous; in others, such as weapons testing and tourism, the value of the Pacific lies in its distance from "reality" (read: the portion of the United States of America that sits between sea and shining sea). Diasporic Pacific presence in the United States[33] is partly a result of migrations away from (economically, climactically, legally) inhospitable homes as well as toward (economic, medical, religious, educational) opportunities. We might consider here the high rates of Micronesian and American Samoan eastward-facing migration, including those people displaced or disadvantaged by US military, economic, and political activities. While wrecks can be single, sudden, and spectacular events, they can also be brought about by much slower processes of decline and the gentle taking-on of water: the imposition and violence of capitalist economic systems, the shifting of cultural values and expectations, tides that were supposed to return two-way migrants but never did. While Hau'ofa's configuration of Oceania needs no repeating in the context of this collection on archipelagic American studies, it is worth noticing the connection he draws in his most famous essay between a complex network-centered articulation of the region and Pacific presence in the United States, including an exemplar of what he calls "world enlargement": a Tongan man based in California who moves in and out of US-America as he regularly circulates around the region between Tonga, Fiji, California, and Hawai'i.

Of course, there is an overlap between the flotsam and jetsam described here: some diasporic Pacific presence is in non-Pacific parts of the United States, but a great deal is within the American Pacific itself. The mobility and presence of Pacific people through the American Pacific is much more complex and fascinating than a mere "islands versus continent" migration story. Chamorros from Saipan are in Guam, while Chamorros from Guam are in Hawai'i, where they find themselves alongside not only Hawaiians but also American Samoans. An outsider view might simply see Pacific people in their home region of the Pacific, but this mobility between, and presence in, other Pacific places is underpinned and made possible by currents of US imperialism. More broadly around the region, the largest and oldest Pacific diasporas are found in other Pacific places. Through direct New Zealand and US imperialism in the region, there are large non-Indigenous (mostly Polynesian) communities in Aotearoa (New Zealand) and Hawai'i; Mormon religious migration from many of the region's islands has been the basis for building a large and diverse Pacific community in Hawai'i; as a result of "blackbirding" (forced labor migration), Melanesian communities and descendants are in the central Pacific nations of Fiji and Sāmoa; and because of environmental devastation and military weapons testing, Micronesian people have moved elsewhere in Micronesia (especially Guam[34]), to Hawai'i, and, in the case of the i-Kiribati from Banaba, to Fiji.

Finally, "spill." The overflow of waste that is both evidence and requirement of gross capitalist commodification and exploitation reminds us of the ways in which economic and environmental factors produce various forms of Pacific migration and Pacific presence—around the American Pacific, beyond the American Pacific, and to the American continent. Although different plastic items might have diverse pathways into the garbage patch, they are ultimately affected by the same process of being broken down into component particles and then swept into the same gigantic gyre. This brings to mind the wide range of circumstances that lead to Pacific presence in the United States (and US presence in the Pacific), and yet the strikingly similar experiences and frames imposed on Pacific communities. The larger Pacific populations (the 75 percent of NH&OPIs who are Hawaiian, "Guamanian," or American Samoan) are present in the United States for reasons that can be explained by most people familiar with US imperialism. How the other 25 percent got to the United States is a much more complicated tangle of stories. Some are from communities who satisfy our criteria for flotsam and jetsam, and some practice mobility for reasons that are less connected to US forces (or expected US forces) than we might assume. To take the example of Fijians in the United States, the size of the community doubled between 2000 and 2011. It is tempting to assume that this can be accounted for by the economic reasons for US migration that shape the experiences of many populations that have the United States as a diasporic destination. However, just as debris enters the ocean from a vast range of sources and for diverse reasons, it seems an economic explanation is only partial here. In 2000, Fiji's fourth coup since 1987 engendered another rapid departure from the country, and internally the coup was followed by tricky economic and political circumstances that led to an increased desire on the part of many Fijians to migrate to any one of a number of diasporic destinations. In the context of this numerically tiny diaspora, the United States as a diasporic site is decidedly *un*exceptionalist: it is merely one Fijian diasporic site alongside New Zealand, Australia, the United Kingdom, Canada, Dubai, Europe and others. The notion of "spill" emphasizes the impact of systems regardless of whether they are deliberately designed to incorporate specific items: the current that produced the garbage patch originally created another, more positive, archipelago—a concentration of plankton and other organisms.[35]

SUBSTANTIAL PRESENCE

We can easily imagine the effects—and the danger—of the presence of larger items of plastic on, for example, turtles mistaking floating plastic bags for jellyfish and fatally ingesting them for lunch. The impact of microplastic on coral, tiny oceanic organisms, or the breathing parts of living fish is not so easy to visualize precisely because such tiny physical presences are beyond direct comparison with most other things in our experience. A turtle and plastic bag, or a dead albatross chick with a belly full of plastic bottle caps, are visible and envisionable, but—like DNA, atoms, and bacteria—we can struggle to conceptualize miniscule shreds of plastic as long as they remain out of sight. The great Pacific garbage patch is difficult to think about because it is simultaneously immense and tiny. Its spread across a large stretch of the ocean and the sheer range and number of items that have contributed to its production mean it is larger than the territorial boundaries of most nation-states and thereby poses the idea that there might be forces that operate beyond and outside national boundaries. At the same time, because of its existence beyond the usual human senses (it is too small to be seen or even touched, and much of it floats beneath the surface of the ocean), it is almost otherworldly in its presence, that is, perhaps more ghostly than corporeal.

Likewise, Pacific presence in the United States is insufficiently bulky to be visible in any meaningful numerical way. Pacific demographic presence in US-America is numerically microscopic and US political (imperial) presence in the Pacific is persistently minimized. The problem with this numerical smallness in relation to people, and the accompanying amnesia in relation to place, is that in the American national context, numbers matter. Even (or especially) the language of diversity is mathematical: in the United States there are minorities, and numbers (as metaphor—"minority"—as well as statistics) are the arbiter not only of presence but also of significance.[36] Even after a dramatic increase in the NH&OPI population between the 2000 and 2010 censuses, by 2010 Pacific bodily presence in the United States still made up only 0.4 percent of the national community. You have to know exactly where to go if you want to walk down the street and bump into someone from the Pacific; most Americans live their entire lives without speaking to a single Pacific person, and most American studies scholars will complete their careers without reading or engaging with a Pacific scholar. The United States has presence in the Pacific, and Pacific people are present in the United States, sure, but is that presence substantial?

For migrants and other noncitizens, in order to determine the degree of one's relationship to the United States (in the context of taxes or visa applications), one must satisfy a "substantial presence test" that measures the number of days an individual's body is situated inside US political borders in any given year. The "test" identifies not just whether an individual is "present" but whether that presence is "substantial." For the purposes of the test, presence becomes "substantial" through time. The unit of measure is days (268 days would be more substantial than 14 days); and these days become less substantial each year (they are worth half as much each year as time passes, so that 268 days in 2014 would be "worth" 134 days when calculated in 2015). The relationship between place and time is thus directly manipulated by the US government in order to understand its relationship with a specific noncitizen, and the relationship is configured in a way that space (US territory) is fixed, whereas time (the number of possible days in any year, and the "value" of those days over time) is the variable. Presence, then, from the point of view of the state, is not enough by itself: that presence needs to be substantial; the presence needs substance.

We find in the pollution of the seas a breach of law and morality that is imperceptible or perhaps inarticulable because it feels too invisible to be significant, but we also find the immense power of incredibly small things—plastic particles, yes, but also small populations. If the great Pacific garbage patch tells us anything, it tells us that tiny particles still have heft, and even a tiny fragment can tell us not only about itself but also about broader configurations—tides and wind patterns—by which all kinds of particles are moved. My own community provides an example of how incredibly small any Pacific community might be in the United States: just shy of 2,000 individuals claimed to be Māori in the 2010 census. To borrow a concept from a Sherman Alexie poem, if the 1.2 million NH&OPI people in the 2010 census were bundled into one city, the city would be the size of Dallas, Texas.[37] And if all of the Māori people were gathered together, we would fill up the large apartment building at the end of the street I used to live on in Honolulu. As well as our numerical smallness, however,

Māori are legally untraceable in the United States. Although we are culturally a Pacific community (the Polynesian community Indigenous to Aotearoa/ New Zealand), nationally we are part of a settler nation whose passports we (or most of us) carry. Unlike Tongans from Tonga or Solomon Islanders from the Solomon Islands, Māori never show up reliably on any census outside New Zealand because our citizenship and nationality are obscured by our own occupying settler state. While this unreliability between citizenship and community is also true for Tongans who carry Fijian or US passports, or ni-Vanuatu who carry New Zealand passports, on US census forms Māori is not recordable as a "race" category and so remains unincorporated in the size of the NH&OPI population. Instead, Māori is an "ethnicity" category, and so even when the NH&OPI numbers are more specifically crunched for people who are seeking information about the specific communities indicated on census forms, unlike a Fijian with a New Zealand passport who can identify herself or himself as racially Fijian regardless of citizenship, Māori are unable to be listed under NH&OPI and are thereby quietly removed from the region to which we belong.[38] Our Pacificness is untraceable because our particular form of Pacificness remains, in the US, unraceable.

Māori presence in the United States is largely the result of economic and religious migration. Economic migration from New Zealand is different from that from any other place in the Pacific region: although Māori are least likely to benefit from its advantages, New Zealand is at least on the face of it a first-world country. Bluntly, economic migration to the United States is, although not exclusively, more likely to be undertaken to benefit from advanced educational, creative, and professional opportunities for individuals and their immediate family groups.[39] Religious migration is a rather more central player in the case of Māori migration to the United States than it is to other places. The immense and long-standing popularity of the Church of Jesus Christ of Latter-Day Saints (Mormons) in parts of New Zealand has translated into a multigenerational Māori community in traditional Mormon sites (Hawai'i, Utah) and thereabouts (California, Nevada, Arizona). It is worth noting that because Mormons have had particular strength in specific tribal areas of New Zealand, the Māori community in the United States is disproportionately made up of people from particular northern and eastern tribes.

To trace the movement of this tiny diaspora in the context of the academy, there is over a century of (usually short-term) educational migration by Māori individuals who have studied and worked in the United States, from Maui Pomare, who studied medicine in Michigan (1895–1900); Hamuera Te Punga, who trained as a Lutheran minister in Illinois (1906–12); and Te Rangihiroa, who worked at (and eventually headed) the Bishop Museum in Hawai'i from the 1930s until his passing in 1951 and spent much of that time on the graduate faculty of the Anthropology Department at Yale University after a successful two years spent teaching there. Later in the twentieth century, Ngapare Hopa taught anthropology for seventeen years at California State University after receiving her doctorate from Oxford; a number of Māori scholars have taught at BYU-Hawai'i (including Vernice Wineera, who was also the first Māori woman to publish a collection of poetry in English) and the University of Hawai'i; writer Paula Morris taught creative writing at Tulane; and through the Fulbright program and other diverse pathways many other Māori people have been a part of the US academy. How might we determine the "substantial presence" of this tiny group of individuals? It would be difficult to make a strong argument for a visible Māori contribution to the broader US academy, but perhaps the garbage patch reminds us that origins are as important as destinations. Many of the journalistic accounts about the garbage patch make a point of talking about the seemingly random range of origins for bits of plastic that have been swept alongside one another. For US-America, Māori are invisible and rightly so: the United States owes us no duty of care as a result of past or ongoing imperial actions (or no more than it does to any community, and certainly less than it does to many), and our demographic presence is barely atomic. For Māori, the story might be different. We recall Pomare's training as one of the first Māori medical doctors regardless of how light his impact might be on any US-American archive. We can identify the tiny shreds and particulates that to most naked eyes are invisible, and build from them not just a story of presence but one of substance.

ALL THAT MOUNTAIN BENEATH

The promise of the archipelago is that the island is no longer an isolate; the limitations of continentalism, and the limitation of equating insularity with parochialism, are important interventions into conversations in American studies and on the Americas more generally. John Gillis, writing about islands, suggests that they "are defined by water,"[40] and certainly my hope is that one day the United States—and American studies—will realize that, at least from certain ways of looking, they are not dryly suspended between "sea [and] shining sea" but are "defined by water" too. Yet for people Indigenous to the Pacific no such promise—the promise of the networked island—is necessary because it is already understood. Reflecting on her experience of spending most of her adult life in Hawai'i, Vernice Wineera writes,

> this island
> is the tip of an underwater volcano
> so large it is disorienting
> imagining all that mountain beneath.[41]

The island is configured not as a bounded or small site but as a part of something "disorienting[ly]" large. Insularity, for Wineera, is impossibly expansive and inspires not only a sense of awe but also "imagin[ation]." Another foundational Pacific poet, Albert Wendt, also turned to the place of imagination in his articulation of a decolonized Pacific: "Only the imagination in free flight can hope—if not to contain her—to grasp some of her shape, plumage, and pain."[42]

This chapter has itself been an act of imagination. Thinking about the Pacific is always about scale, and perhaps imagination is a place—or mode—in which it is possible to try to hold together the microscopic with the regional. I have tried to imagine the great Pacific garbage patch as an archipelago, and have attempted to suggest that this could be a metaphor for Pacific presence in the United States that is simultaneously so vast (covering one-third of the earth's surface) and so tiny (statistically minimal *and* historically marginalized) that Pacific communities remain out of (US-American) sight. At the heart of this chapter's fundamental question is the relationship between visibility and presence. How do we imagine the bulk, heft, or weight of something we cannot see? Whether the garbage patch as a metaphor is timely, clever, edgy, or innovative is less important than the insights it can provide. What does this metaphor enable us to know? What does it make possible? What space does it clear for us to notice/discuss that we have not had until now? Ultimately, this has been an attempt to deliberately trace the ways in which different currents and tides appear to work together—if you step back far enough—to sweep specific debris, including humans, into unanticipated patterns of connection even where those patterns seem invisible to the naked eye.

NOTES

1. In this chapter I focus on the garbage patch known as the North Pacific Gyre; there are other smaller gyres in the Pacific as well as in the Atlantic.

2. "Marine Pollution," *National Geographic* online, accessed February 9, 2014. http://ocean.nationalgeographic.com/ocean/critical-issues-marine-pollution/.

3. Here, and at other points throughout this chapter, I am using the terms "America" and "the United States" to signify two different entities: the first is the imagined community produced through a long and diverse series of predominantly US-American imaginings; the second is the politically defined nation-state.

4. David Armitage, "From Guano to Guantánamo," *The Times Literary Supplement*, 5775. December 6, 2013: 10–11.

5. Quoted in David Vine, *Island of Shame: The Secret History of the U.S. Military Base on Diego Garcia* (Princeton, NJ: Princeton University Press, 2009), 164.

6. Although these are certainly not the only island regions in the world, they are dominant in island studies and in popular imaginaries of island places.

7. Nor should they be considered "mini-continents," as argued in John R. Gillis, "Not Continents in Miniature: Islands as Ecotones," *Island Studies Journal* 9, no. 1 (2014): 155–66.

8. Rather than acknowledging Indigenous presence as an identifiable community or experience, much Caribbean work assumes or even produces Indigenous absence; sometimes there is recognition of ongoing cultural, spiritual, or ritual presence, but this is usually incorporated as an ancestral rather than relational presence. Work by scholars such as José Barreiro challenges this denial of ongoing Indigenous Caribbean presence.

9. John Dominis Holt, *On Being Hawaiian* (1964; repr., Honolulu, HI: Ku Pa'a, 1995).

10. Unfortunately, many scholars who are active in the field of island studies do not engage with much Pacific scholarly work. People active in the field of Pacific studies would readily suggest adding to citations of Hau'ofa's work an engagement with the work of scholars such as Albert Wendt, Vicente Diaz, Teresia Teaiwa, and David Gegeo (among many others).

11. Epeli Hau'ofa, "Our Sea of Islands," in *A New Oceania: Rediscovering Our Sea of Islands*, ed. Eric Waddell, Vijay Naidu, and Epeli Hau'ofa (Suva, Fiji: University of the South Pacific, 1993), 7.

12. Jonathan Pugh, "Island Movements: Thinking with the Archipelago," *Island Studies Journal* 8, no. 1 (2013): 12.

13. This story of discovery is recounted in many places, including Jocelyn Kaiser, "The Dirt on Ocean Garbage Patches," *Science*, June 18, 2012, 1506. Moore has authored a book, *Plastic Ocean: How a Sea Captain's Chance Discovery Launched a Determined Quest to Save the Oceans* (New York: Avery, 2011). His TED talk "Seas of Plastic" summarizes much of his perspective on the issue: http://www.ted.com/talks/capt_charles_moore_on_the_seas_of_plastic.

14. Hester Blum, "The Prospect of Oceanic Studies," *PMLA* 125, no. 3 (2010): 670.

15. Philip E. Steinberg, "Of Other Seas: Metaphors and Materialities in Maritime Regions," *Atlantic Studies* 10, no. 2 (2013): 157.

16. Also known as ground and figure, target and source.

17. Jennifer Gabrys, "Sink: The Dirt of Systems," *Environment and Planning D: Society and Space* 27 (2009): 667.

18. Gabrys, "Sink," 668.

19. "Digging into the Great Pacific Garbage Patch," *IES Goya English Blog*, November 7, 2013, http://iesgoyaenglishblog.blogspot.com/2013/11/digging-into-great-pacific-garbage-patch.html (taken from *National Geographic Education,* http://education.nationalgeographic.org/encyclopedia/great-pacific-garbage-patch/).

20. It needs also to contend with US-America's widely held assumption that its people, like the sun, come first from the East (Europe, Africa) rather than from the place itself (the Indigenous Americas) or the West (the Pacific, Asia). This assumption requires a rather large leap of the imagination over acres and acres of history, including the complex and ongoing Indigenous, Pacific, and Asian presence throughout the entire stretch of US-American history.

21. This reframing on longitudinal grounds (Atlantic, Pacific) has, of course, also been accompanied by a great deal of rethinking of US-America in latitudinal terms: the Canadian and Mexican borders. I also want to note that the reconfiguration of the triangle trade is not strictly speaking a US-American frame as much as a project engaging the Americas, considering the presence of the Caribbean (as well as Canada) in that configuration.

22. A Pacific (or Pacific studies) reader of this essay may or may not recognize the line "from sea to shining sea" but will certainly at this point be thinking about the pressure Hauʻofa places on us to decolonize our thinking about the relationship between land and sea in the first place.

23. I am reluctant to describe this as "American" or even "continental" thinking. Many Indigenous nations from the American continents articulate and practice specific relationships with the ocean that do not easily map onto this division.

24. For background information on Katherine Lee Bates, see Paul G. Pierpaoli, Jr., "Bates, Katherine Lee," in *Encyclopedia of the Spanish-American and Philippine-American Wars*, vol. 1 (Santa Barbara, CA: ABC-CLIO, 2009), 47–48; and Lawrence Buell, *Writing for an Endangered World: Literature, Culture, and Environment in the U.S. and Beyond* (Cambridge, MA: Harvard University Press, 2003), 9–12.

25. Katherine Lee Bates, "America," *American Kitchen Magazine* (July 1897): 151.

26. Interestingly, the sea had been mentioned in the first version: "God shed His grace on thee / Till souls wax fair as earth and air / And music-hearted sea." But here it worked as an essential element, along with "earth" and "air," rather than as an articulation of the boundaries of US territory (Bates, "America"). See Peter Gardella, *American Civil Religion: What Americans Hold Sacred* (New York: Oxford University Press, 2013), 221.

27. This happened despite widespread anti-annexation activity, including a petition signed by over 21,000 Hawaiians who actively opposed annexation to the United States. Noenoe Silva's work has been instrumental in recovering this aspect of Hawaiian history in *Aloha Betrayed: Native Hawaiian Resistance to American Colonialism* (Durham, NC: Duke University Press, 2004).

28. Elizabeth McMahon, "Archipelagic Space and the Uncertain Future of National Literatures," *JASAL: Journal of the Association for the Study of Australian Literature* 13, no. 2 (2013): n.p. A further "coincidence" would be the declaration by historian Frederick Jackson Turner of the end of the US-American frontier in—you guessed it—1893.

29. For a range of reasons, Pacific people are highly overrepresented in the US military as a proportion of the national community.

30. Brian Russell Roberts and Michelle Stephens, "Archipelagic American Studies and the Caribbean," *Journal of Transnational American Studies* 5, no. 1 (2013): 4. Stacy Alaimo, "States of Suspension: Trans-Corporeality at Sea," *Interdisciplinary Studies in Literature and Environment* 19, no. 3 (2012): 478.

31. For a key example, see Teresia Teaiwa, "bikinis and other s/pacific n/oceans," *Contemporary Pacific* 6, no. 1 (1994): 87–109.

32. Haunani-Kay Trask, "Speeches for the Centennial of the Overthrow, ʻIolani Palace 1993," in *Huihui: Navigating Art and Literature in the Pacific*, ed. Jeffrey Carroll, Brandy Nālani McDougall, and Georganne Nordstrom (Honolulu: University of Hawaiʻi Press, 2014), 99.

33. As opposed to Indigenous Pacific presence, for example, Hawaiian people in Hawaiʻi, or Chamorros from Guam in Guam, etc.

34. And, as a result of the Melanesian laborers brought to work in Australia's sugar industry, in Northern Australia. Lola Quan Bautista's work on migrants in Guam from

other Micronesian states includes scholarship as well as a film, *Breadfruit and Open Spaces*.

35. Susan Dautel, "Transoceanic Trash: International and United States Strategies for the Great Pacific Garbage Patch," *Golden Gate University Environmental Law Journal* 3, no. 1 (2009): 181–208.

36. This suggests one reason for US-American struggles in thinking about indigeneity. Although any definition of indigeneity focuses on firstness rather than proportion of contemporary national community, Indigenous bodies in the United States are persistently racialized (American Indians are a "minority" group) and, as a consequence, are framed by an accounting rather than a genealogical system.

37. This idea comes from a Sherman Alexie poem in which he proposes a similar imaginary project for American Indians: "There are only two million Indians in the country. We would all fit into one medium-sized city. Someone should look into it"; Sherman Alexie, "The Unauthorized Autobiography of Me," in *One Stick Song* (Brooklyn, NY: Hanging Loose Press, 2000), 22.

38. The demographer Tahu Kukutai has undertaken research into how Māori appear in various census categories. I am grateful to her for sharing some of her data for the purposes of my proceeding with this part of the project.

39. New Zealand citizens emigrating strictly for labor and "standard of living" opportunities are more likely to move to nearby Australia, motherland UK, or elsewhere in the Commonwealth, such as Canada; partly this is because of the comparative ease of immigration in these places, partly to follow well-worn diasporic tracks, and partly because things feel more culturally familiar around the British Commonwealth.

40. John Gillis, "Not Continents in Miniature," 155.

41. Vernice Wineera, "This Island," in *Into the Luminous Tide* (Provo, UT: Brigham Young University, 2009), 4.

42. Albert Wendt, "Towards a New Oceania," *Mana* 1, no. 1 (1976): 49.

PART VI | **INSULAR IMAGINARIES**

15 | THE TROPICS OF JOSEPHINE

SPACE, TIME, AND HYBRID MOVEMENTS

Matthew Pratt Guterl

> There is no world, there are only islands.
>
> JACQUES DERRIDA,
> *The Beast and the Sovereign*, 2011

JOSEPHINE BAKER HAD A THING FOR ISLANDS. She invoked them in her music and embodied them—in all their variety—in dozens of unique performances. In doing so, she costumed and presented herself as a fixture of the oceanic colonial world, of those places where people and power came together outside of the metropole and outside of the nation-state. Repeatedly and over the long course of her life, she returned to islands, to waterfronts, to the edge of the land and of national territory, offering herself up as the personification of the tropics, positioning herself as the antidote to conventional modern life. Early on, she performed as Fatou, the archetype of Indochina in the French imagination, or wore a banana skirt and danced topless as a generic type of "African." Later, she played the role of the Near Eastern odalisque, draped in jewels and colorful silks. In film, song, and dance, she performed as generically Haitian, Indonesian, and West Indian. She gestured to a Caribbean origin story, and deployed a pan-American attitude toward music and family. And in her last act, after her adoptive family was created, she settled them along a river's edge far from Paris, a drifting reminder of the significance of flow, of passage, of movement in her assemblage, a reminder—as well—that she was never, truly and completely, a creature of the modern cityscape or nation-state.

Here, looking closely at two of her films from the late 1920s and early 1930s, I want to offer Baker's interest in islands and archipelagoes as an intentional disruption—a disruption, that is, of the hegemony of nation time and imperial time. By invoking these concepts, I am referring to the idea of shared temporal status, mediated by the state, a shared status that is constitutive of power and that makes the state's official work possible. And by "space," to follow, I am referring to the related sense that nations and empires are coupled, like similarly colored spaces on a map of the world, unified as a singularity. Attending to official time and imperial space, one can see power in formal action, but one can also see where and how power's actions are troubled in those temporal and spatial zones that fall outside of what is official, and outside of what is orchestrated to serve the state's interests.[1]

Time and space are the first building blocks of nation and empire. This simple summary—derivative, in some sense, of Benedict Anderson's classic text *Imagined Communities*—has been taken up recently by Susan Gillman, who has suggested that time and space should be objects of analysis in transnational American studies, and that oceanic spaces should be disentangled from a simple list of geographical labels, which she dismisses as "anachronistic, modern inventions."[2] Gillman encourages scholars to attend to language and to translation more specifically, so that "space, time, and language" can trouble our sense of history and literature, so typically bound to land and to the nation.[3] Following Gillman, then, what interests me about Baker's filmic efforts is that they dwell on the emergence, within the age of empire, of things and places and times that fall in that aforementioned *outside*. Outside, that is, of "anachronistic, modern" notions of nation and empire.

To say that these sites fall outside of time and space, as it was built and maintained by nation and empire, is also to recognize that a part of what Baker was attempting to do was to span the gaps without eliminating them altogether. "There is no world, there are only islands," writes Jacques Derrida, in the midst of an exegesis on sovereignty and loneliness.[4] Within Baker's filmic oeuvre, this effort to bridge colony and empire is showcased through her sympathetic loneliness, a mighty and powerful trope, invariably expressed by Baker's creole characters, each standing on the outside rim of empire, none of them wanting to assimilate, all of them isolated from France, and yet all of them composed against stereotype as global and cosmopolitan.[5] Each film includes a potential romance that fails, a failure that reestablishes differences of time and space, and a heartbroken heroine pining for her man. Reading that repeating loneliness, then, gives us the clearest sense of Baker's critique, and her lifelong desire for affiliation and community and belonging without erasure of the very things that made her, as she saw them, unique and desirable, those things that fell *outside*.[6] Though she is much beloved for her comedic timing, then, it is her melodramatic turn toward loneliness that spotlights her political point, and that draws our eye to islands.

LA SIRÉNE

After growing up poor and black in early twentieth-century Saint Louis, Josephine Baker fled first for Manhattan and then for Paris, where she quickly became a global superstar. By the time she was twenty, she was an icon of primitivism and sexuality, dancing on the Paris stage and starring in several films. When she was thirty, she was a friendly metaphor for the distant French colonies, unevenly related to the metropolitan core, a reference to the islands, to the tropics, to anywhere marginal.[7] Between these two decades, she underwent an extraordinary transformation, shifting away from her personal history as an African American expatriate to become a French citizen and, in many ways, the representation of French Empire. This rather remarkable switch—a sort of translation, as Gillman might put it, of her subjectivity into continental terms—accompanied the production of her movies, which is a part of what makes them so fascinating. They enabled her to become French, but also to keep the nation at bay.

Of course, Baker's idealization of decentered, "tropical" space and time is hardly unique. Performance artists from around the world, and perhaps especially those in the Caribbean and the Pacific, have embodied the "island" in a thousand different ways, calling attention to the complicated political work of insistent smiles, grass skirts, and swaying rhythms. There is a long history of taking these same iconic representations, rooted in colonialism, and transforming them into subversions—satirical or otherwise—of the normal order of things. And Baker is a part of this long history, an exemplar and not a standalone figure. What makes Baker so useful in a volume like this, though, is that she has for so very long been held up as a special case, as a powerful signifier with a rich, celebrity biography. As a direct consequence of her fame, her meditations on cosmopolitanism and civilization—her sense of the creative potential of islands—circulate as if they were somehow special. To think of her, instead, as a touchstone for a broader pattern of critique is to recognize that there were deeper historical changes that lay behind her life's story.

Baker's very first film was *La siréne des tropiques*, released in 1927. The title, of course, was a play on the Homeric idea that dangerous monsters, in the guise of alluring women with dreamy voices, would lure sailors and travelers with their song into the deadly shoreline of some remote island. *La siréne* departed from this mythic formula, at least somewhat, in several ways. Baker played Papitou, an indigene of mixed ancestry, a sympathetic creature of the "repeating" tropics, who was hardly a femme fatale.[8] Indeed, she was the much-adored centerpiece of the film, presented as a sweet, innocent, wide-eyed young girl. Additionally, in this case, Papitou is drawn away from her island, lured to Paris by a would-be lover, and accidentally finds herself on stage before an enthusiastic audience. In *La siréne*, then, it is the white lover who is the siren, and Papitou is the potential victim, with Paris representing those threatening shoals.

Papitou, of course, is not of France. She comes from *outside*. Monte Puebla, her home, is a tropical island, or perhaps a port city in the colonial world, or perhaps some trading entrepôt. It is hard to locate, and even harder to understand, but it certainly is not a threatening or dangerous landscape. If it was once a primordial place, empire had made it safe, and now all manner of men and women could come and go with hardly a concern. Wherever it is, though, it is certainly somewhere far from the heart of empire, someplace out of temporal and political sync with the modern world. Wherever it is, the place is marked by brownness and blackness, the color and shades of its earth, its material conditions, and its people. Paris, in contrast, is a city of straight lines and machined cuts, of steel and stone, of stark whites and deep blacks. Papitou's house, a reflection of Monte Puebla, is adorned with the abandoned material remnants of colonialism, and her wardrobe is a pastiche of old and out-of-date styles. If the very name of the place—along with the names of the people, such as Alvarez and Diego—hints at a Hispanophone past, the presence of so much French materiality, and so many Frenchmen and women, suggests an old colony now reoriented to a new metropole.

This representation of the oceanic colonial world is confusing. Baker's Monte Puebla is not a cauldron of proletarian sentiment and racial organization, but neither is it a site of explicit racial domination, nor a simple extension of the white metropole. White, black, and brown come together in public and in private, and chiefly around forms of leisure and entertainment and intimacy. The systematized racial organization of labor seems absent, or not yet fully realized— Andre, the engineer dispatched to the territory, is there to scout out some newly acquired land, so in truth the potential of the place is decidedly unsettled. With a future that is uncertain, it seems rather like a proverbial third space, not yet brutally exploitative nor fully incorporated into the empire, a space both inside and outside of empire, a still-indeterminate switching point, rich with contradiction and full of new and unique formations.

The plot of the film is a fairly straightforward metaphor for colonialism. Andre, an engineer, is sent abroad by a more powerful man because he is a rival in a lovers' triangle. Upon landing in Monte Puebla, he meets Papitou on the uneven ground of this once-and-future colony, and the two become close—not quite friends, not yet lovers. When Andre returns to Paris, Papitou secretly follows him. Once in France, her heart is broken when her beloved engineer reveals that he loves another woman, but she becomes an accidental star of the stage, and is the toast of the town as a consequence. In the end, she is Andre's salvation, secretly dispatching his chief rival—that more powerful man, a titled Marquis—and preserving his reason for living: a white Frenchwoman.

To establish Monte Puebla as temporally and physically distant, the film includes a long scene in which Papitou, following her love, sneaks on board an ocean liner and is transported—and transformed—by the very waterways this volume examines. The scene begins in the terminal, where Papitou attempts to get a ticket. In a throng of white passengers dressed in contemporary fashions, her stark white dress and elaborate headdress is neither "primitive" nor "modern." She misses the significance of the queue, causing chaos, and uses her posterior to push back against the line of conformist flapper types. And after all the excitement, in the end she cannot afford the ticket. So she decides, instead, to swim to the ship, entering through the industrial bowels, with the help of a white merchant sailor who lowers down a bucket and pulls her up and in through the window.

Once on board, she tries to hide and falls into a coal chute. Her white dress—already wet from the swim—becomes black, as does her brown skin. Dazed and exhausted, Papitou wanders the ship, still looking for a hiding place, until she encounters a wealthy passenger who nearly faints at the sight of this out-of-place—but still recognizable—"black" body. Elusive and fleet of foot, Papitou ducks into a flour bin in the ship's kitchen, a quick-thinking act that whitens her body. A calamitous chase ensues, with the entire ship's company questing for Papitou, who periodically appears as a flour-drenched presence in flight. Her white footprints eventually lead the ship's crew and guests to a fabulously appointed washroom, where she has stripped down and decided to take a bath. Jubilantly and innocently, she scrubs and sings at the same time, as a full complement of crew and guests take it all in.

One could make much of this scene. The overlays of blackface on top of pastiche, and whiteface on top of blackface, suggests, for instance, that the bath reveals the "true" Papitou, the one hidden beneath the racial masks she is forced, by her circumstances, to wear. And the role of the ship's proletarian innards (its coal chutes and kitchens and merchant seamen) highlights class formation, the means through which Papitou is, by her very "nature," partially excluded from the very idea of a working class. She is hoisted aboard, after all, but then chased down. These class-inflected locations—kitchens and coal chutes—may help to disguise her, but only the gilded suite with a deluxe bath can "reveal" her inner self. But I am most struck, in the end, by the location of this entire exegesis on race and class and place: on board a ship, in transit, moving from Monte Puebla to Paris. And by the way the scene itself suggests that Papitou's racial position emerges directly from the transoceanic transit. Papitou can find her way to Paris, but she cannot be schooled in the ways of France, and cannot be reduced (as Baker might have it) to blackness, which represents absolute difference, or whiteness, which represents assimilation. In one sweeping scene, she dons a host of masks, only to strip them all away at the end, revealing the creole cosmopolitan body, right before the film cuts to Paris.[9]

There is something about this ship, and its role in articulating official time and space—and what is outside—that deserves a little more scrutiny. Elizabeth

DeLoughrey, elaborating on the role of ships as miniature extensions of the nation-state and empire in the literature of colonialism, suggests that their appearance in narratives akin to Robinson Crusoe marks the end of a period of exploration and accumulation. Vast oceangoing vessels exist, in her framing of this genre, to "transport [the] human and material resources [of the island or colony] to the metropole," and also to shift metropolitan populations to regions of the world that might—were it not for the conflation of ship and nation—seem too distant for settlement. Baker, though, seems intent on presenting the ocean liner as decidedly more chaotic, as an extension of the uncontrollable, unpredictable, disorganized empire in the midst of a dramatic return to the metropole.[10]

DeLoughrey continues to note that, as time went on, and as the interests of empire shifted from settlement to management, the ship also became a metaphor of distance, establishing the island as remote and white populations in the tropics as distinct from their metropolitan betters.[11] Thinking, again, of Susan Gillman's provocations, though, we might say that Baker's disorderly clutter and her transgressive embarkation mark the possibility of simultaneously operative or even interchangeable spatial and temporal singularities. Indeed, the film screws around with time and space quite provocatively. We never really know where we are. And, except for when we are in Paris, we often do not know *when* we are. Still, we know that Monte Puebla exists in a different locality because of the usual markings: the riding of burros in the tropics contrasted with the futurist automobiles of Paris, or the dense, unkempt jungle juxtaposed with the manicured parks and gardens of the city. Likewise, abandoned Victoriana scattered in Monte Puebla didactically reinforce this simple, but powerful, confusion of time, space, and power, so that Monte Puebla—a land without flags but with obvious, formal colonial undertones—seems well outside of the simultaneities and histories of the nation-state and, perhaps, of colonialism itself.

ZOUZOU

By the time she appeared in *Zouzou*—released in 1934, several years after *La siréne des tropiques*—Baker had become a legitimate movie star, the most famous woman of color of the modern age, recognizable around the world, and admired, in many communities, for her outsized reputation and her outspoken refusal to live in the segregated spaces of the United States. By the mid-1930s, she had completed her translation from "African American exile" to the Francophone "Queen of the Colonies," a title she briefly held in 1931 for l'Exposition coloniale. She was living in a prestigious suburb of France, presenting herself as still wild, still outside, but now also recognizably French. The role of Zouzou was meant to be a capstone for Baker's nouvelle fame and celebrity.

Zouzou, we learn early on, is a child of the islands—in the abstract. Born and raised in a circus as an object of intrigue (she is presented with a white half-brother as a complementary curiosity, a freakish set of relations), she grows up to be a simple, sweet young woman, with a natural gift of song and dance. When her brother, Jean, gets a job at a theatre, Zouzou shows up and takes advantage of a stray spotlight to shadow dance on the stage. The producers of a show-in-the-making, who have lost their star, see the shadow dancing and are so entranced by her playful spirit that they hire Zouzou on the spot. And so the little girl raised as a freak, rooted in a world of interchangeable islands and displayed in the circus, grows up to be the star of a musical review and an object of intense spectatorship. Jean, the half-brother, is her supposed love interest, but he seems (like all of Baker's suitors) disinterested. At the close of the film, having lost him, Zouzou sings sadly of life in a gilded cage, of life as an object of white fascination. And she envisions the opposite of that life as a faraway thing, as a life that circulates between islands, a life that is outside of official and historical time.

The mysteries of islands are everywhere in *Zouzou*. At the start of the film, Zouzou and Jean are presented to the circus-going public as ten-year-old twins, born on a Polynesian island to the same mother. Their contrasting skin tones are the source of their freakishness. "They're not like us," Papa Mele, the ringmaster and their titular father, shouts to his audience. "Don't try to understand. Mysteries aren't meant to be understood." Their parents—"a Chinese woman and an Indian," he insists—did not want them, which is how they ended up on display in a French circus. Young Jean and young Zouzou are presented as self-evidently different, and the audience is meant to see their differences in tone as irreconcilable, and then, to explain that dissonance, Papa Mele gestures to the "Polynesian island."

Papa Mele's untrustworthy narration of these origins suggests, with a wink to the audience, that Jean and Zouzou are not related at all, and that their status as half-brother and -sister is a fiction of the show. The film cleverly refuses to specify the exact location of Zouzou's birth. "Your little Creole is cute. Where is she from?" the adult Jean's friends ask later, after the fictive brother and sister are reunited. "Martinique," he replies, matter-of-factly, with barely a glance at Zouzou. But this contrasts with Papa Mele's "Polynesian" origin story, and the contrast is never resolved. Such a contradiction does something more—or something different—than reinscribe coloniality, or render it as a flat, unchanging same. Indeed, it makes the prospective love affair between Zouzou and Jean possible. And, once more, because the film is a vehicle for Baker's superstardom, the film's representation of "creole" is anything but pejorative, since Zouzou (like Papitou) is the sympathetic heroine of the film.

Papa Mele is himself also a cipher for the islands. Like Diego in *La sirène des tropiques*, his origin is unknown, and he never claims to be—nor denies being—Zouzou's father. Her own "Polynesian" or "Martiniquan" heritage, and his last name—with its Hawaiian connotations, meaning, literally, "merry"—is coupled with his honorific title, "Papa," to transform him into a friendly, kindly parent, but with a global, cosmopolitan twist, with a gesture, perhaps, to the "Papa Legba" famously at the center of Haitian voodoo practice. The embodiment of the social universe that produced Zouzou, he is without a fixed origin or identity. And he is, the film suggests, to be treasured as such.

Zouzou's uncharted heritage is not necessarily central to the plot. As usual, the film is a series of set pieces designed to show Baker's range as a performer. Like *La sirène des tropiques*, though, *Zouzou* emphasizes Baker's friendship with members of the working class—with a singing troupe of white laundresses, for instance. Slyly, it rewrites the life of Josephine Baker, transforming her from a savvy businesswoman born in the ghetto who planned her way to fame, into the innocent embodiment of the tropics, whose inner qualities naturalized her route to fame. There is a biographical point to be made here about the role of these films in establishing Baker as something other than what she was, in recreating her as a fixture of the colonies, or of reminding her French fan base that she could manifest her exoticism in diverse textures. And they correspond, tellingly, to a moment in her life when she was focused on becoming French without losing some precious something else that made her desirable and interesting.

Not until the very close of the film do we get a sense of what *Zouzou*—and Zouzou—is meant to signify. There, in her triumphant performance, Zouzou is suspended in a giant birdcage, wearing a plumed, feathered costume. Her breasts are covered by small, feathered tufts, and she is barefoot, an elemental creature lifted right out of Shakespeare's *Midsummer Night's Dream*. At her feet—and outside of the gilded prison—a dozen or so white figures stand mutely, their arms held aloft in celebration. In celebration of Zouzou, of course, the titular character who, by the end of the film, is the star of her own show. The scene itself is the capstone of the young woman's extraordinary ascent from the simple life of a poor washerwoman to the glorious life of a celebrity. Zouzou's grand finale is marred by her obvious melancholy. She swings slowly, languidly, and sings sadly. She grips the bars of the cage, her eyes focused not on the interior space, or even on the throng gathered outside, but on some distant, elusive, difficult-to-see object. She sings, as we shall see below, of life elsewhere, and of islands as a creole third space—both evocative and outside of a future Third World.

But that scene is not the absolute ending of the film. Only when the show (and the song) is truly over does the triumphant music begin. And then, with a dazzling smile, Zouzou opens the door to the cage and jumps into the attentive arms of a troupe of male dancers, who catch her gracefully and then return her to the floor in an upright, standing position, all to more applause. The graceful "creole" from Martinique, or Polynesia, or somewhere in the mixed-up waterways and archipelagic spaces of the oceanic French Empire, has translated, right in front of her, her nostalgia for the past into a successful present, with white bodies doing her bidding, filling her pockets, and providing financial profit.

There is much to be made of this scene, too. Like the ship's transfer to the metropole in *La siréne des tropiques,* the final scene in *Zouzou* is rich with metaphor. There is the interplay of the white bodies on stage—in this case, adulatory and responsive—and the symbolic significance of the tropical body in the cage. There is Baker's gentle performance of a woman simultaneously trapped and spotlighted by fame, a performance that—as the film stresses—would have been understood by anyone watching in France as powerfully autobiographical. There is, once more, the melancholy close of a plot in which Baker, once again, fails to win the heart of her white lover.

But what interests me most—here and now in this essay and in this collection—is the song that Zouzou sings as she sits there, rocking back and forth, looking far into the distance. She sings of Haiti, of the island republic in the Caribbean—home, once more, to Papa Legba. "You are my only paradise," she trills, describing the island as a "beautiful blue country," marked by "big horizons" and "beautiful forests." Zouzou does not sing of Haiti in 1934—the Haiti, that is, that had been under US military authority since 1914, and that was only slowly inching toward independence under the "Good Neighbor" policy proposed by the recently elected Franklin Delano Roosevelt. The occupation of *that* Haiti had galvanized political opposition, especially among African American and Afro-Caribbean activists. It had also given the United States its first taste for modernization as ideology and practice.[12] But Zouzou does not reference her present, except, perhaps, elliptically, when she notes that even "the most beautiful cage is a prison." A benevolent extension of US empire—even one meant to shore up the country's infrastructure and finances and prevent further destabilization—was still, in the end, empire. Nor does Zouzou sing of the Haiti of the historical record—the Haiti of Toussaint L'Ouverture, the Haiti that haunted the dreams of slaveholders, the Haiti that was so dangerously, powerfully rebellious.

Instead, she sings of Haiti as an idyll of sorts, as a symbol of something outside of the black countermodern once illuminated by Paul Gilroy.[13] Something not formally politicized, in the ways of organizations or institutions committed to social justice, but, instead, something inspirational, affective, even existential. She describes, in short, an elusive space and time, neither black nor white, neither modern nor primitive, and found only in the waterways and transit hubs and island way stations of the world. This projection of "Haiti" as an idealized, temporally dislocated space mimics the earlier representation of Monte Puebla as somewhere and sometime outside of empire. Neither site can be synchronized with Paris in any real way, and both can be explicitly referenced only in the metropole when Baker is onstage, where time and space are always disrupted by performance.

For Baker, these repeated gestures to the outside spaces of *La siréne des tropiques* and *Zouzou* established the singer and dancer as the embodiment of cosmopolitanism, as a woman whose celebrity transgressed more than any one racial category or identity. They made her a repeating island, in a way, turning her body into something that was always slightly out of sync with modern Paris. They cemented her fame, and also—in a way—outlined a new self-narration, one in which Baker's US-American roots were replaced with something more resonant in France, and something she appears to have felt was more powerful and productive. And they dramatized, through a representation of an unrequited romance and an opportunity lost, a relationship between colony and metropole that was, Baker thought, less troublesome than complete subjugation or assimilation. In both *Zouzou* and *La Sirene*, Baker loses the man she loves but gains superstardom. But, in the end, the loneliness of her characters was a consequence of their metropolitan foolishness, and the audience's sympathies were meant to lie with her, and not with France. The men were recognizably fools, so she ends each film as an outsider, but one that the audience is meant to adore.

Through all of this, Baker offered a unique vision of the role of such places in global politics. She distinguished herself from simplistic, stereotyped fetishes of island primitivism, featuring weird fantasies of long-isolated tribes and unassimilable clans, and the presumption of great backwardness, emphasizing, instead, that such places were important wellsprings of creativity, and that cosmopolitanism was distinct from what was then called "civilization." She proposes that the most interesting thing about the modern world was not what was primitive—a fetish we recognize as primitivism—but what was liminal, or mobile, or outside. But she also decoupled her performances from the radical circuits of transnational migrants, the sorts of hemispheric and transnational social and political movements that were increasingly common in the age of Marcus Garvey, of negritude, and of anticolonialism. She might travel with the stevedores and laundresses and electricians who peopled her films, but she was not ever one of them. Their issues were not, in the end, hers. If she offered up islands—and especially port cities—as generative crucibles of mixture and political seedbeds for a more cosmopolitan future, she nevertheless imagined this future in terms that departed from those who advocated, as Garvey had, a black modern to counter the white Atlantic.[14]

And this is why Josephine Baker—who reimagined herself as a citizen of the world and a fixture of the island—both is and is not easy to make sense of. In her celebration of the most commercially appealing aspects of the colonial periphery, she would seem to be a part of empire's iconography. There is a reason that so many white hands applauded her performances or imagined her as a global sexpot. But there is also, as scholars of performance studies have taught us, a deeper sort of politics in play on stage, especially when the world is starkly uneven.[15] Hidden in plain sight is a lesson for anyone who conceives of political work as simply a matter of organizational labor and movement culture. On stage, surrounded by an adoring audience, Baker presented what she imagined was the hybrid potential of islands in the global South to a largely white audience of empire builders, and asked them to imagine a different future, in which the white lover—a feature of her filmic career—accepted his lover on something closer to her terms.

No singer or songwriter of the early twentieth century was more closely associated with the aesthetics of the "tropics." And Baker performed this aesthetics in ways that routinely drew on islands and archipelagoes as positive, generative spaces, linked to an expanding worldview and a patchwork racial genealogy. In all of her imaginative work, then, Baker reminds us of the power of these politically fecund spaces, these port cities and island communities, these places of transfer and exchange, places of imperial consolidation and confusion. And it is this latter notion—this idea of the island as a chaotic, generative space, producing something new and exciting that cannot be contained or controlled by the metropole—that identifies the distinctive tropics of Josephine. She repeatedly invoked an island persona, drawing attention away from metropolitan cities and toward archipelagic spaces—colonies, ports, islands—created in the crucible of imperial circuits. And, again, by making herself the centerpiece of the story, and by cultivating the sympathy of her audience, she created an affective alternative to empire's commitment to white supremacy and patriarchy.

CONCLUSION

Josephine Baker had a sense of a counterbeat that took her far, far away from the modern metropolis. A generation of scholars has taken up the work of Paul Gilroy's *The Black Atlantic* to trouble what was once, on the one hand, an uncritical celebration of white literary and cultural production in the "world cities" of yore, and, on the other hand, a politically potent embrace of blackness as a constant, unchanging opposite. Gilroy's proposition—written against the backdrop of cultural imperialism and emergent Afro-centrism—was that the cities of the modern Atlantic world (chiefly New York and London, in his account) constituted a singularity, knit together by commerce and migration and empire, and also that the culture emergent from this singularity included a counterbeat, a subversive alternative ripe with revolutionary promise. It was this counterbeat—from Ralph Ellison to Richard Wright to Langston Hughes—that Gilroy termed "the black Atlantic."[16]

Baker's islands and archipelagoes—those featured in her performances—are arranged without easy hierarchy or too much distinction, which is precisely why almost any "island" can do the same work. Her transit to and from the metropole of Paris does not produce a counterbeat so much as it proposes a black antimodern, a space outside of empire and nation, even on board a ship. Islands and archipelagoes and the waterways that bind them and separate them from the metropole, Zouzou and Papitou remind us, are also bridges and circuits, metaphorically or materially, to empires, to continents, and to other islands. In a featureless ocean, they provide the certainty of solid ground for travelers, and a containment of culture and experience. Courtesy of winds and currents and shipping lanes, they catch the drifting detritus of empire—cast overboard, or discarded at port—on their sandy beaches. But they are temporally and spatially troublesome.

This "trouble" is worth taking seriously. It has become a cliché of recent scholarly work to suggest that Josephine Baker was a radical or transgressive figure, a hero of the black Atlantic countermodern, though it is also true that in most of this literature she is also an obscure object—seeming less modern, perhaps, than her masculine contemporaries—and is deployed generally as context.[17] Some of this oversight is understandable, given her unusual politics and her refusal, generally, to attach herself to any of the competing political philosophies of the moment, or to organize a literary salon, or to build up transatlantic institutions. In the context of stern-faced movements spanning continents, Baker's comedy—striking against the backdrop of so much political seriousness—makes her seem, at best, like an outlier in our histories of the struggle for freedom from colonialism and segregation, or—as Elizabeth Ezra once smartly put it—like a "part of the décor" of modern empire.[18] Focusing on her playful mischief with time and space gives us a better sense of her significance. Her idiosyncratic politics emphasized the dynamic hybridity located not in those major cityscapes of the first world but in the islands and port cities where empire's penetration of the global South unwittingly produced new and unexpected cultural and racial formations. She routinely positioned islands and archipelagoes—and all manner of abstract, liminal, "tropical" spaces and temporalities—as somehow a part of the black Atlantic and also somehow rather different from it. She offered a creole cosmopolitanism that was a mash-up of coloniality and modernity, a mash-up that is hard to locate in a timeline that posits, as Gilroy's black Atlantic does, colonialism as a feature of the past and modernity as an indicator of the present.[19]

Scholarly fields such as American studies are now bigger than the continental boundaries of the United States, emphasizing the transnational and the diasporic.[20] But within the transnational, "postexceptionalist" American studies,[21] a stress on landlocked structures and metropolitan coordinates—points of departure and arrival—continues to dominate the field, to say nothing of the way that more traditional and still powerful disciplines are continually focused on cityscapes and land masses. What is missing is an emphasis on what is outside, on what Brian Russell Roberts and Michelle Stephens have called "the materiality of the island-as-stage."[22] It is not enough to look outside of the state, or to emphasize the contingency of the borders of the nation, or to just look transnationally outward. One needs, as well, to think of American studies as a heuristic and not as a topical designation. In focusing on those spaces and practices not bound to the nation or to empire, we can push our method offshore, away from the continent, away from a territorially centered American studies, even if still (for many of us) with one foot on the continent, looking out into the deep blue sea. We can shift it away from the overwhelming emphasis on points of articulation and nodes of a network that are, almost invariably, metropolitan and continental and joined, materially or otherwise, to the United States.

A focus on those spaces adrift and in circulation and beyond the official domain can challenge us to think differently about the way that islands and archipelagoes and the waterways that connect them can constitute a certain kind of mobile, imprecise time and space. Such a focus takes, as a given, that the nation-state needs to be decentered, that our objects of study should—when and where they dwell on the global or the hemispheric—make contributions to scholarly literatures well beyond the United States, to the histories and critiques, that is, of other continents, nations, regions, and localities, and still further to as-yet-unconceptualized geospatial ways of understanding. Along these lines, the archipelagic frame suggests that such contributions should not be to *other* national or imperial literatures, either, but should point toward entirely new fields and subfields of study. It challenges us, as well, to see the labels and place names on the conventional map as convenient political truths that do not accurately represent the full historical record. Doing all of this does not just mean that we should reinterpret the familiar but also that we should make better sense of the strange, of the distant, of the seemingly obscure, and of those things that fall outside.

NOTES

1. I am specifically thinking here of Homi K. Bhabha's argument about temporality and the nation, in "Dissemination: Time, Narrative, and the Margins of the Modern Nation," in Homi K. Bhabha, *The Location of Culture* (New York: Routledge, 1994), 139–70.

2. Benedict Anderson, *Imagined Communities: Reflections on the Origins and Spread of Nationalism* (London: Verso, 1983); Susan Gillman, "Oceans of Longue Durées," PMLA 127, no. 2 (March 2012): 330.

3. Gillman, "Oceans of Longue Durées," 331.

4. Jacques Derrida, *The Beast and the Sovereign*, vol. 2, trans. Geoffrey Bennington (Chicago: University of Chicago Press, 2011), 9.

5. For more on the abridgement of "creole" and "cosmopolitan," historically constructed as oppositional categories, see Françoise Lionnet, "Cosmopolitan or Creole Lives? Globalized Oceans and Insular Identities," *Profession* (2011): 23–43.

6. In referring to repetition here and elsewhere in this essay, I am playing with the notion of orderly disorder expressed in Antonio Benítez-Rojo, *The Repeating Island: The Caribbean and the Postmodern Perspective*, 2nd ed., trans. James E. Maraniss (Durham, NC: Duke University Press, 1996).

7. For three generally excellent biographies, each with a different take, see Jean-Claude Baker, *Josephine: The Hungry Heart* (New York: Cooper Square Press, 1993); Lynn Haney, *Naked at the Feast: The Biography of Josephine Baker* (London: Dodd Mead, 1981); Bennetta Jules-Rossette, *Josephine Baker in Art and in Life: The Icon and the Image* (Urbana: University of Illinois Press, 2007). More synthetically, see Phyllis Rose, *Jazz Cleopatra: Josephine Baker in Her Time* (New York: Vintage 1989). Other biographies include Ean Wood, *The Josephine Baker Story* (London: Sanctuary, 2000); and Stephen Papich, *Remembering Josephine: A Biography of Josephine Baker* (Indianapolis, IN: Bobbs-Merrill 1976).

8. Departing from standard editorial practice in this volume, the term "indigene" remains uncapitalized here because it does not refer to an Indigenous identity but to a European or Euro-American construction of a "native" identity that does not necessarily hinge on indigeneity but rather hinges on non-whiteness, whether or not that non-whiteness is specifically Indigenous.

9. For a very different interpretation, see Phil Powrie and Éric Rebillaird, "Josephine Baker and Pierre Batcheff in *La Siréne des tropiques*," *Studies in French Cinema* 8, no. 3 (2008): 245–64.

10. Elizabeth M. DeLoughrey, *Routes and Roots: Navigating Caribbean and Pacific Island Literatures* (Honolulu: University of Hawai'i Press, 2007), 14–15.

11. DeLoughrey, *Routes and Roots*, 14–15.

12. On the occupation of Haiti, see Mary Renda, *Taking Haiti: Military Occupation and the Culture of U.S. Imperialism* (Chapel Hill: University of North Carolina Press, 2001); and Hans Schmidt, *The United States Occupation of Haiti, 1915–1934* (New Brunswick, NJ: Rutgers University Press, 1971).

13. On Gilroy and the countermodern, see Paul Gilroy, *The Black Atlantic: Modernity and Double Consciousness* (Cambridge, MA: Harvard University Press, 1993), 1–5.

14. On the black Atlantic of the 1920s, see especially Michelle Ann Stephens, *Black Empire: The Masculine Global Imaginary of Caribbean Intellectuals in the United States, 1914–1962* (Durham, NC: Duke University Press, 2005), Part 1.

15. I am thinking here of José Esteban Muñoz, *Cruising Utopia: The Then and There of Queer Futurity* (New York, NY: NYU Press, 2009); and Daphne Brooks, *Bodies of*

Dissent: Spectacular Performances of Race and Freedom, 1850–1910 (Durham, NC: Duke University Press, 2006).

16. Gilroy, *Black Atlantic*.

17. Brent Hayes Edwards, *The Practice of Diaspora: Literature, Translation, and the Rise of Black Internationalism* (Cambridge, MA: Harvard University Press, 2003); Michelle M. Wright, *Becoming Black: Creating Identity in the African Diaspora* (Durham, NC: Duke University Press, 2004); James T. Campbell, *Middle Passages: African American Journeys to Africa, 1787–2005* (New York: Penguin, 2006); Kwame Anthony Appiah, *Cosmopolitanism: Ethics in a World of Strangers* (New York: W. W. Norton, 2007).

18. Elizabeth Ezra, *Colonial Unconscious: Race and Culture in Interwar France* (Ithaca, NY: Cornell University Press, 2000), 98.

19. Thanks to the editors of this volume for pointing out the mash-up quality of interactions between coloniality and modernity.

20. For work in this vein, see Micol Seigel, *Uneven Encounters: Making Race and Nation in Brazil and the United States* (Durham, NC: Duke University Press, 2008); Martha Hodes, *The Sea Captain's Wife: A True Story of Love, Race, and War in the Nineteenth Century* (New York: W. W. Norton, 2006); Kirstin Silva Gruesz, *Ambassadors of Culture: The Transamerican Origins of Latino Writing* (Chapel Hill: University of North Carolina Press, 2002); Kevin K. Gaines, *American Africans in Ghana: Black Expatriates in the Civil Rights Era* (Chapel Hill: University of North Carolina Press, 2006); Mary Dudziak, *Cold War Civil Rights: Race and the Image of American Democracy* (Princeton, NJ: Princeton University Press, 2000); Brenda Gayle Plummer, ed., *Window on Freedom: Race, Civil Rights, and Foreign Affairs, 1945–1988* (Chapel Hill: University of North Carolina Press, 2003); Penny Von Eschen, *Race against Empire: Black Americans and Anti-Colonialism* (Ithaca, NY: Cornell University Press, 1997); Penny Von Eschen, *Satchmo Blows Up the World: Jazz Ambassadors Play the Cold War* (Cambridge, MA: Harvard University Press, 2005); Adam McKeown, *Chinese Migration Networks and Cultural Change: Peru, Chicago, Hawaii* (Chicago: University of Chicago Press, 2001); Matthew Frye Jacobson, *Special Sorrows: The Diasporic Imagination of Irish, Polish, and Jewish Immigrants in the United States* (Cambridge, MA: Harvard University Press, 2001).

21. On "postexceptionalist" American studies, see Donald Pease, "Re-Thinking 'American Studies after US Exceptionalism,'" *American Literary History* 21, no. 1 (2009): 19.

22. Brian Russell Roberts and Michelle Stephens, "Archipelagic American Studies and the Caribbean," *Journal of Transnational American Studies* 5, no. 1 (2013): 2.

16 | **THE STRANGER BY THE SHORE**

J. Michael Dash | THE ARCHIPELIZATION OF CALIBAN IN ANTILLEAN THEATRE

THE BURNING BEACH

> Thinking thought usually amounts to withdrawing into a dimensionless place in which the idea of thought alone persists. But thought in reality spaces itself into the world.
>
> ÉDOUARD GLISSANT, *Poetics of Relation*

As Édouard Glissant's work has become better known and more widely circulated, it has been identified with certain abstract concepts such as *Relation, toutmonde, opacity,* and *creolization*. What these abstract concepts invariably mask is Glissant's central and unceasing concern with how we might inhabit the world poetically or how we might renounce territorial claims in earthly dwelling. Consequently, more so than his abstract formulations, the frequently invoked idea of being born or precipitated into the world (*naitre au monde*) allows us insight into this project of inhabiting the earth differently. In pursuing this ideal, Glissant arguably took from his teacher, Gaston Bachelard, the concept of poetic thought: a way of thinking positioned outside of systems of knowledge and intentionality. Furthermore, poetic thought opened up new, liberatory dream spaces as opposed to mapped or geometric space. This is why the archipelago has become Glissant's quintessential concept of dwelling in the world. Transgressive and insurrectionist in nature, thought sited in archipelagic space destabilizes categories of near and far, subjective and objective, inside and outside. This essay examines the impact of archipelagic thought on nativist ways of dwelling and claims of sovereignty by comparing two plays from the French Antilles, Aimé Césaire's *A Tempest* and Édouard Glissant's *Monsieur Toussaint*, together with the Benin playwright José Pliya's haunting but largely unknown play *Nous étions assis sur le rivage du monde* (We were sitting on the shoreline of the world).

It would not be an overstatement to say that the Glissantian imaginary is shaped by the conflict between two antagonistic ideas: on one hand, the problem of placeless thought or conceptual transparency, and on the other, thought as matter in all its material specificity. In the section of *Treatise of the Tout-Monde* titled "Ecrire" (Writing), Glissant asserts that "abstraction" and "idealization" should be banished and replaced by an emphatically referential concreteness. "It is the very matter of all places, their minute and infinite detail and the energized pulling together of their particularities which must be placed in complicity with those of all places."[1] Writing, always challenged by the world's proliferating opacity, needs to be profoundly materialist. Words can neither represent nor illuminate and are to be treated as if they were matter. When he declares, "I build my language out of rocks," he expects to be taken seriously.[2] Glissant, therefore, reserves his highest praise for those artists who resist the representational real, that is, the real as something primarily to be represented—abstractly, ideally, symbolically. For instance, he bestows that particular honor on Pierre Reverdy by calling him "a visionary of the concrete." Indeed, Glissant's essay on Reverdy in *The Poetic Intention* goes to the heart of the question of a materialist poetics. He writes, "Neither realist nor mystic, since here you can be a visionary without being a mystic, Reverdy is a purveyor of the concrete. But how to accomplish this form of art that 'is an eminently terrestrial thing?' You cannot without coming up against the obstacle, the unending torment, which is also the only weapon: the word. How does Reverdy, stubbornly tied to the concrete, make use of this abstraction, the word? He *densified* the word."[3] Reverdy is positioned as the opposite of Stéphane Mallarmé, who dedicated his creative energies to producing, as Glissant put it, "the world as book, the Book as world. His heroism within confinement is a way of celebrating a desired, dreamt-of totality within the absolute of the word."[4] Reverdy, however, by creating poetic equivalents of the real, becomes an exemplary densifier of the word, an "ascetic of the concrete." Glissant writes, "Having escaped the temple of books (And all these great ideas no longer move; they sleep, or are dead) man rediscovers there, outside, the immanence of things which calls out to and includes him."[5]

It is not merely that Glissant's thought is marked by a particularizing spatial dynamic but that his view of poetic space was uncertain, tortured, constantly drawn outward to ever-receding horizons. In particular, it is the shoreline that epitomizes tortured or, as Glissant later put it, "trembling" space and the challenges of poetic dwelling. As he puts it in *The Poetic Intention*, "Our space is marine, which both limits and opens. The island presumes other islands. The Antilles."[6] Here, Glissant cleverly plays on the meaning of the word "antilles" as specifically the French overseas departments, and "antilles" that etymologically suggests islands that come before, or islands whose contours cannot be fixed without knowing what is yet to come. As Glissant himself put it, "*antillanité* . . . represents quite simply the will to rally together and diffract the Ante-islands confirming us in ourselves and joining us to an elsewhere."[7] By emphasizing the promise of newness and unpredictability, Glissant challenges reductionist ideas of Caribbean space, whether the dominated space of the colonial past or the reterritorialized space of nationalist politics. Max Hantel puts it succinctly: "The politics of reduction to scale has little interest for Glissant because it does not create anything new, it does not harness the kernel of unpredictability through which a revolutionary consciousness becomes possible."[8] Consequently, it is unbounded, ungrounded island space that haunts the Glissantian imaginary, in particular, the mysterious frontiers represented by its unstable, untamed coastline.

The quintessential space of revolutionary becoming for Glissant is what he terms "the burning beach." This beach represents an extreme state of consciousness, which, constantly threatened by the crashing waves, becomes the primal space of poetic creation. This elemental space, where earth, fire, air, and water converge, returns obsessively in Glissant's works and marks a clear continuity between his earliest book of essays, *Sun of Consciousness* (1956), the later *Poetics of Relation* (1990), and one of his last theoretical texts, *A New Region in the World* (2006). The pattern is established from his first essays in *Sun of Consciousness*, in which he enigmatically declares, "I finally write close to the Sea, in my burning house, on the volcanic sand."[9] The precarious burning house in this liminal zone is the space of poetic dwelling and is explicitly named and acquires greater force in Glissant's later work, *Poetics of Relation*. The site where the shore mutely confronts the explosive forces of the ocean is the beach at Lamentin, in the south of Martinique, facing the marine monolith Diamond Rock. The volcanic black-sand beach that confronts the roaring chaos of the crashing waves of the ocean is the space of poetic birth in the world. In "The Black Beach" Glissant admits, "The movement of the beach, this rhythmic rhetoric of a shore, do not seem to me gratuitous. They weave a circularity that draws me in."[10] There is no possibility of turning "the immanence of things which calls out to and includes him" into language since the "page"/*plage* is itself a scrambled script "where morne meets beach, where the motifs are intertwined in a single vegetation, like words of the page."[11] By the time we get to *A New Region in the World*, the beach at Lamentin has become the space of the densified word. From the outset, he speaks of "this striking of a baroque and difficult and grainy wave, its surging motion relayed like the weaving together of a text" as if the waves were leaving undecipherable rough drafts on the blank page/plage. All around the rocks become exclamation points and question marks.[12]

In this threshold space, with its inextricable ever-changing script, Glissant described in *Poetics of Relation* an isolated figure, who for the purposes of this essay is as much a wordless Caliban as a maroon who is drawn (back) to the sea. Endlessly, silently walking, this enigmatic, opaque wanderer who refuses speech is a palpable emanation of this unpredictable landscape, the mute incarnation of an inscrutable connectivity, in Glissant's words, an "echo-monde." The ghostly walker is the incarnation of an archipelagic consciousness and inhabits this heterotopic space poetically. Neither he nor the ground is territorialized in any way. The marine horizon has ensured that there would be no "terre-mere" but a "terre-mer," not a mother*land* but a marine habitat, neither land nor sea, that propels the subject into the "chaos-monde," that roaring global (dis)order in which everything imaginable exists in a glorious cacophony. Sea and land are intertwined in a new nonterritorial geography of image and desire: "The naked ships navigate the savannas, the sugar cane sprouts in the heart of the waves."[13] In this context, insularity takes on another meaning. Ordinarily, insularity is treated as a form of isolation, a neurotic reaction to place. However, in the Caribbean each island embodies openness. It is only those who are tied to old ideas of empire and the continental mass who see insularity as confining. Antillean identity is grounded on the ever-shifting, unpredictable shoreline, constantly being acted on by heartland and horizon, by the inward pull of opaque interiors and the outward tug of the archipelagic space. Glissant confesses, "I have always imagined that these depths navigate a path beneath the sea in the west and the ocean in the east and that, though we are separated, each in our own Plantation, the now green balls and chains have rolled beneath from one island to the next, weaving shared rivers that we shall open up when it is our time and where we shall take our boats. From where I stand I see Saint Lucia on the horizon. Thus, step by step, calling up the expanse, I am able to realize this seabow [*arc-en-mer*]."[14]

Indeed, Glissant foresaw in archipelagic space a paradigm for global interactive space. In his *Treatise on the Tout-Monde* (1997) he envisaged a world in which "continents, those intolerant landmasses focused on a single truth . . . become archipelagoes of regions. Regions of the world become islands, isthmuses, peninsulas, lands thrusting out, mixing and connecting and yet continuing to exist."[15] Continental mass and grounded certitude were destined to be increasingly fissured into archipelagic configurations. In such configurations, specific sites would now be connected through networks that had nothing to do with territorial boundaries. Thought itself, Glissant speculated, was already becoming less systematic and more fluid. He devotes a chapter of his last book of essays, *Philosophy of Relation* (2009), to *la pensée archipélique*. Here he not so much opposes two forms of thought, the archipelagic and the continental, but juxtaposes them:

> Archipelagic thought, thought as probing, as intuitive impulse, which can be juxtaposed with continental thought, which would be primarily systematic. Continental thinking allows our minds to rush forward audaciously, but we feel then that we see the world as a whole, or what matters or in a flash, as if

grasped by some sort of system.... Archipelagic thought allows us to know, rocks in rivers, the smallest ones, rocks and rivers.[16]

Interestingly, Glissant does not oppose the two ways of knowing. Rather, the archipelagic is always prey to the continental just as the former undermines the latter. To oppose the two would be to betray archipelagic thought. Later in this work, Glissant contrasts the words "imagination" and "imaginaire" in order to demonstrate what a totalizing knowledge of the world would be as opposed to an intuitive sense of the tout-monde that was only possible through the imaginary. In a 2002 interview with François Noudelmann, Glissant seems to be suggesting that archipelagic thought is just that, a form of consciousness that does not seek control or domination and that harkens back to the walker, or *erreur*, on the black, burning beach and the ideal of poetic dwelling. "There is a new way of thinking because the form of the archipelago, as you say, does not lead to the notion of territory. The notion of territory is a continental notion.... One of the characteristics of the archipelago is that you can travel through its entirety and at some point find yourself in some part of this archipelago without being in the entire archipelago, without being troubled by this. Whereas with continental thinking, if you are in any part, the whole persists in your mind."[17] Archipelagic dwelling is a way of inhabiting global space poetically, that is, without "the whole persisting in your mind." This poetic imaginary is akin to that of the "echo-monde" that is in tune with the submarine forces that are constantly at work inventing island archipelagoes and fissuring continents archipelagically. The onlooker and the dweller on the black sand beach are not, however, the same. For the former there is always the struggle between the urge to imagine the whole, to think continentally, and the need to yield to reality's turbulent multiplicities, to feel archipelagically.

THE FATAL SHORE

> The fact is that Caliban, as the locus of encounters and conflicts, has become a symbol. Above and beyond Shakespeare's savage cannibal, a real dynamic is at play—a dynamic constituted by conflicts and encounters.
> ÉDOUARD GLISSANT, *Caribbean Discourse*

While the tendency is to read Aimé Césaire's plays circumstantially (that is, in terms of historico-political contexts), it could be argued that Césaire's theatre is essentially about how you occupy, dwell in, or build on postcolonial space. Such a reading of Césaire's plays allows us to link in an unprecedented way two plays from the French West Indies written in the 1960s: Césaire's *Une Tempête* (1969) and Glissant's *Monsieur Toussaint* (1961). Two critical biographies of Aimé

Césaire by Romuald Fonkoua and Gregson Davis suggest that Césaire's last play, *Une Tempête*, bears out Glissant's observation in the epigraph that the figure of Caliban has transcended its Shakespearean origins and has become a locus of conflict and contradiction in the Antillean imaginary. Both biographies indirectly point to ways in which *A Tempest* may have been misread in the past and the need to rethink Césaire's final theatrical project almost as the key to all of his dramatic works. Fonkoua seems to want to extract Césaire's text from a narrowly postcolonial approach, and Davis challenges a rigidly referential interpretation of the play.

Postcolonial theory questioned the universal validity of certain canonically enshrined texts and advocated an unmasking and rewriting of these texts counterdiscursively. Césaire's play would then seem to be a perfect example of the dismantling of Shakespeare's canonical text. Fonkoua, however, suggests this may not be the case. He quotes Césaire's observation that however the project may have begun, "Once I had finished working on it, I realized that there was not much of Shakespeare left."[18] So, in Césaire's *Une Tempête*, the original is not dismantled. It disappears. The disappearance of the original script is perhaps indicated from the outset by the *meneur de jeu*, or animator, of the role-playing. This is theatre as play, literally a game in which the actors are invited to choose masks and to perform a collective psychodrama in which mere traces of a script remain.

Davis also focuses on the performative and improvisatory aspect of Césaire's play when he states, "In an often quoted metaphor Césaire has referred to . . . *Une Tempête* as the third 'panel' (*volet*) in a larger 'triptych' of which the other two are *Christophe* and *Saison*. Apparently he conceived these three plays, at least, initially, as reflecting major sectors of the black world (Africa, The Caribbean and the USA). This neat triangular articulation is nonetheless misleading."[19] Davis's point is that the play should not be read as an allegory of a specifically African American racial drama. He goes on, "To be sure, the marks of the black power movement in the continental USA of the 1960s are prominent in the drama in the form of slogans (such as 'freedom Now' or 'Uhuru'); but the action of the play takes place on an island that distinctly recalls the Caribbean."[20] Such an observation invites us to see this play set on a tropical island as a collective Antillean psychodrama of insularity. As opposed to the Glissantian shoreline as a site of poetic dwelling, Césaire's "fatal shore" tragically grounds the loss of the dream of territorial sovereignty and the will to power that accompanies it. Again, the meneur de jeu offers a clue. When distributing the roles at the start of the play, he expresses surprise at who chooses which mask. This is a play in which repressed desires surface in apparently surprising places. For instance, he says of the actor who chooses the Caliban mask, "You want Caliban? Well, that's revealing!"[21]

Added to the unlikely Caliban is an equally surprising would-be Prospero who apparently unmasks his own secret desires. "You, Prospero? Why not? He has reserves of willpower [*volontes de puissance*] he's not even aware of himself."[22] The English translation does not adequately convey the Nietzchean will to power of the original. The desire for domination is not an attribute exclusive to a white colonial mentality but an urge that lurks among the powerless who are only too eager to assume the mask of Prospero. The meneur de jeu's final instruction, "ad lib" (*a volonte*), seems to further encourage the actors to feel free to play out their concealed fantasies or give vent to their repressions.[23]

One could argue that from the outset Césaire has used the creative imagination to dramatize and unmask the repressed colonial subject. For context, Césaire's landmark 1939 poem *Cahier d'un retour au pays natal* is only superficially about exile and homecoming. Its internal drama is concerned with a series of aborted returns from a state of self-delusion to a state of self-acceptance, which perhaps is the true meaning of the neologism "negritude." The poetic subject inhabits various incarnations of a rebellious Caliban. Visions of empowerment are invariably followed by moments of disillusion and self-doubt. This frenzy of self-interrogation culminates in the well-known confession of cowardice in the tramcar as the insecure subject publicly dissociates himself from the figure of the deformed black victim facing him. Relentless self-scrutiny now leads to self-knowledge as he literally throws overboard past delusions of grandeur and vengeance so that a true return can take place. The poem ends with the subject resisting the lure of drowning in the *grand trou noir*—the seething underside of the colonial unconscious—and finding a space he can inhabit.[24] Césaire's poetic itinerary arguably leads inexorably to the dominant image of his book of poems from 1982, *moi, laminaire . . .* (I, laminaria . . .). In a storm-tossed sea the *laminaire*, or seaweed, does not prevail but modestly and tenaciously endures in its marine habitat. Stripped of rhetoric, ideology disavowed, the once visionary poetic figure desperately clings to its bare marginal site.[25] Similarly, at the end of *A Tempest*, the principal figures, Caliban and Prospero, having each survived the storm of the play, are caught up in a psychic storm engendered by competing claims to sovereignty over Antillean island space. The seaweed can draw on the resources of its marine environment. In the play it is only Ariel who has this capacity to evoke poetically or musically a world of precarious ebb and flow: "The waves make a waterline / nothing is, all is becoming . . . there, at the waterline / as the sea swells within us." Prospero and Caliban, however, struggle futilely over dominating their island world. Prospero is horrified at the disorder of this space, its "unclean nature" and invasive wild beasts. Caliban's cries for freedom are ultimately drowned out by the cryptic sounds of the island. "In the distance, above the sound of the surf and the chirping of birds, we hear snatches of Caliban's song."[26]

The circumstances of the drama of self-revelation in Césaire's first poem in 1939 and those of his final play in 1969 are radically different. In three decades the historicopolitical framework had changed radically. The emancipatory hopes of anticolonial ideology had given way to the disillusion of postrevolutionary politics. The distance between the utopian vision of 1939 and the postcolonial predicament of 1969 is indicated by the liberated cry at the end of the *Cahier* as opposed to the "snatches of song," the barely audible cry of "Freedom," at the end of *A Tempest*. Freedom is fished from the "black hole" in 1939 as opposed to being drowned by crashing waves and birdsong in 1969. The volcanic release promised in Césaire's early poem never comes to pass, as the script of romantic resistance cannot be imposed on the unscripted shoreline that in *A Tempest* lacks the archipelagic frame. The mockingly lucid meneur du jeu at the beginning of *A Tempest* senses the need for a collective unmasking in his black cast. By extension, Césaire himself may have felt the need for therapeutic psychodrama to provide some release for the damaged psyches of fellow Antilleans.

Ultimately, the play may hark back to what Elizabeth DeLoughrey calls the trope of "the isolated isle," which brings out in the characters the need to possess and dominate.[27] The black actor playing Caliban harbors secret desires of reclaiming lost territory, of reestablishing his aboriginal identity as Native and Indigenous. This means that the performance of Caliban is knowingly filled with irony in the Césairean text. Césaire's Caliban is demanding sovereignty and laying claim to his birthright at the end of *A Tempest*, but most claims to an Indigenous identity by Caribbean people are necessarily spurious. It could well be argued that Césaire is demonstrating through the performance of this character, tellingly located on the shoreline, the inadequacies of this desire to territorialize identity and even the limits of a nationalist ideology. In Césaire's play Caliban is Prospero's black mirror image. The line that the meneur du jeu utters when a certain unlikely actor takes the Prospero mask equally applies to Caliban. Both have the same will to power that is not aware of itself. Ultimately psychodrama is about bringing about self-awareness, and pairing Prospero and Caliban at the end allows each to see the absurdity of the other's desperate will to power. Glissant almost seems to be referring to this confrontation between tragic insularity and the sense of possibility of an affective, rhizomed consciousness when he laments the violence that comes with a nativist "ecological mysticism": "As for the Antilles, for example, there is a lot of discussion concerning the legitimacy of land 'possession.' According to the mysterious laws of rootedness (of filiation) the only 'possessors' of the archipelago would be the Caribs or their predecessors, who have been exterminated. . . . Once that had happened,

Antillean soil could not become a territory but, rather, rhizomed land. Indeed Martinican soil does not belong as a rooted absolute either to the descendants of deported slaves or to the bekes or to the Hindus or to the mulattoes."[28] This observation is particularly relevant to the Antillean assertion of Indigenous legitimacy through the figure of Caliban. Caliban is a nativist fantasy in Césaire's psychodrama, and it is not coincidental that he winds up on the shoreline, which is continuously eroded and reshaped by the action of the waves, a space, to use Glissant's terms, that is "rhizomed land." The Glissantian shoreline is porous and unstable and not connected exclusively to Martinican territory but also rhizomatically to both an internal landscape and a marine horizon. These rhizomatic flows explode the fixed spatial frame of Caliban's beach. The politics of Glissant's burning beach are therefore not in Caliban's lone cry of resistance but in the enigmatic wandering of the silent stranger whose very opacity is the source of a revolutionary openness.

Glissant's observations uncannily resonate in José Pliya's one-act play of 2004, "Nous etions assis sur le rivage du monde" (We were sitting on the shoreline of the world), which stages a violent encounter between a man and a woman with a beach as their arena. Pliya arguably is responding to the end of Césaire's *A Tempest* and has read the psychodrama as a kind of postcolonial tragedy, and the island as a tropical purgatory. For him, Césaire's play has more in common with Jean Paul Sartre's *Huis clos* than with Shakespeare's *Tempest*. Pliya's trapped characters are not identified racially, and feed off each other's anxieties. They are screens onto which the public can project racial interpretations. The seemingly overwrought man on the shore claims the beach as his kingdom. He denies that it is the world's shoreline and claims absolute ownership of the beach and so will not allow the female stranger to pollute it with her presence. When the woman tells him he has no right to claim the beach as his own and that she grew up on this strip of land, he retorts, "You have the wrong island. You have the wrong beach.... You are in my home, on my land, under my law."[29] Pliya, as an African dramatist living in Martinique in 2004, stages violently the tragic dimension of the claims to an Indigenous legitimacy that brought Césaire's earlier play to a close. His male protagonist is a xenophobic Caliban who is ensnared in a violent conflict in which the right of ownership is vengefully asserted. Pliya uses the beach to stage an impassioned critique of the kind of tragic exclusion that was an integral part of Caliban's dream. More importantly for our purposes, Pliya's character is an agoraphobic Antillean Caliban who cannot see beyond the shoreline. As Édouard Glissant put it, "The Martinican is an Antillean blind to his true antilleanness. He cannot even see Saint Lucia and Dominica whose outlines are on the horizon in the south and north of the country. He sees with eyes other than his own."[30] As we earlier saw in Max Hantel's observation, a reductionist politics was of little interest to Glissant, who felt decolonization really meant a remapping of consciousness. The real tragedy of departmentalization (via the French overseas departments) was that it paralyzed the Antillean collective imagination, leaving it stranded in a fraught relationship with Europe instead of opening it to new, liberating postcolonial trajectories.

AN ARCHIPELAGO IN THE JURAS

> The absent man who walks exhausts no territory; he sets roots only in the sacred of the air and evanescence, in a pure refusal that changes nothing in the world.
>
> ÉDOUARD GLISSANT, *Poetics of Relation*

Édouard Glissant's play *Monsieur Toussaint* is not so much historical drama as a relational epic that secularizes gods and sets heroes adrift. In one of his last references to the play's protagonist, Glissant refers to Toussaint not as a founding father but as an errant ghost who escapes control or definition.[31] The play, which dramatizes Toussaint's final days in prison in the Juras, can be read as an examination of open versus closed insularity as the prison cell becomes a liberating heterotopic space instead of the dystopic open-air prison of Caliban's shore. Césaire evoked Toussaint as imprisoned in white(ness) in his poem in 1939, whereas Glissant's play turns on exploding Toussaint's prison cell. An archetypal drama of displacement is being enacted in the Jura Mountains as a liberatory poetics is drawn from the abduction and imprisonment of the revolutionary leader. The cell in the Juras, which is likened at times to the belly of the slave ship, becomes a space of beginning from which the debased, uprooted subject is projected into the world. The prison cell cum slave ship's hold is not a site of racial tragedy, nor is the doomed hero crying out to be avenged. The dungeon in the Fort de Joux represents a primordial abyss, a traumatic (middle) passage where dead and living, past and present, commune, and Toussaint is a variation of the ghostly figure on the burning beach, an "echo-monde," who is attuned to the ocean's roar of voices in his head.

Glissant was in Martinique at the same time Césaire's play was published, and he devoted much time in his Institut Martiniquais d'Etudes to investigating what he saw as the morbid passivity of Martinican society and the use of theatre as a form of collective psychotherapy. Césaire would probably have agreed with Glissant's view of the Martinican unconscious in that Glissant too used a modified Jungian approach to analyze what he called the nightmare of successful colonization in Martinique. In the section of *Caribbean Discourse* titled "Inconscient, Identite, Methodes" [Unconscious, Identity, Methods], Glissant defines what he means by a "collective unconscious": "We believe in the repercussion of socio-historical circumstances not only on beliefs, customs, ideologies . . . but also on the creation of certain shared impulses which could be called the collective unconscious of a collectivity. . . . What I call the Martinican collective unconscious is certainly not constituted by the traces of universal archetypes, but the negative result of certain inconclusive shared experiences and consequently of degraded relationship with our surroundings."[32] For Glissant, Martinicans, having chosen to deny their archipelagic reality, were blind to their own "antilleanness." It was Martinicans' paradoxical combination of smugness and frustration that led to an inability to act collectively. The two main sources of repression were their estrangement in space and time: the short-circuiting of the real country and the absence of collective memory.

It was through experimental theatre that Glissant's group of researchers at his Institut Martiniquais d'Etudes sought a therapeutic response to the problems in the Martinican psyche. In the section of *Caribbean Discourse* titled "Theater, Consciousness of the People" [Théatre, conscience du peuple], which first appeared in the journal *Acoma* in the early 1970s, Glissant explained theatre's potential for bringing about social change. Theatre was to him a vehicle that allowed a collectivity to become self-aware: "Theatre is the act through which the collective consciousness sees itself and consequently transcends itself."[33] Under normal circumstances there would be a "harmonious" transition for a community from its folkloric phase, or popular culture, to its self-consciousness as a people. As far as Martinique was concerned, this process never happened, as departmentalization short-circuited a process of maturation toward an archipelagic imaginary. Whereas for some departmentalization meant a loss of national sovereignty, for Glissant it prevented the development of an archipelagic self-consciousness. Consequently, the Antillean inhabits a no-man's land because "he dimly senses that he lacks in his real space-time a fundamental dimension, which is a Caribbean relationality. Rather than the unilateral link with a metropolis, he needs an ever multiplying relation with Caribbean diversity."[34] Without an archipelagic imaginary, Glissant believes, Antilleans cannot be born into the world. The shoreline then is not a tragic dead end but a site of epic possibilities where self-consciousness is a recognition of archipelagic openness.

To attain the stage of "theatralization," Glissant prescribes in the final part of this interrogation of drama-as-therapy not just a politically committed theatre but also a particular form of tragic theatre. It is as if in the face of the failure of anticolonial politics a new set of imaginative possibilities needs to be deployed. Glissant takes up this question in the concluding note to "Theater, Consciousness of the People" through the figure of the sacrificial hero in tragic drama, "a hero who takes unto himself the destiny of a community. Our drama is that we have collectively denied then forgotten the hero who is our real history who undertook resistance on our behalf: the maroon. This historical erasure engenders the absence of the tragic."[35] Césaire was similarly drawn to the tragic form, and his three plays could well be categorized as tragedies: the demiurgic tragedy of Haiti, the postcolonial tragedy of the Congo, and the tragedy of the unrealized nation. If this is the case, the protagonists King Christophe and President Lumumba are avatars of the forgotten rebel "who takes unto himself the destiny of the community." Hence, all three of the plays discussed in this chapter are profoundly Martinican in their desire to respond to what Glissant calls "the absence of the tragic" and to restore the expiatory figure of sacrificial negation.[36] Tragedy, however, verges on farce in *A Tempest*, as Caliban, alone at the end on a precarious strip of sand, is screaming for freedom and sovereignty for no one but himself. You could say that Glissant takes Césaire's Caliban stranded on the shore and reinvents him as an archipelagic maroon.

The frustrated Calibanesque cry of freedom at the end of Césaire's play establishes a revealing link between *A Tempest* and Glissant's *Monsieur Toussaint*, whose last words also scream for freedom. Glissant's Toussaint is imagined not in terms of Caliban's demands for redress and the right to territory but as a maroon precipitated into an unknown time-space. As Glissant puts it, "Toussaint Louverture is a kind of maroon [marronneur], of the same kind, I was going to say race, as the most obscure and misunderstood of the maroons of Fonds-Massacre in Martinique."[37] In the play Glissant does not try to explain Toussaint. As he says of the ghostly stranger by the shore, "It doesn't feel right to have to represent someone so rigorously adrift, so I won't try to describe him."[38] Rather, as Glissant would put it, he "densifies" the protagonist so that he becomes less and less easily understood, transparent, and incomprehensibly "thick" in poetic associations. Consequently, *Monsieur Toussaint* is not a tragedy of the expiatory hero but a modern relational epic that unleashes an archipelagic chain of different kinds of *marroneurs*. If the epic is traditionally associated with power and victory, Glissant imagines the relational epic as a counternarrative of errancy and disorder. Toussaint, who never founded a sovereign state, is a relational hero who is forced to dwell in a terra incognita of inexhaustible ever-multiplying relations. As presented in the play, the cell is a paradoxically unbounded, liminal space that carries memories of other places and times. The prisoner's very opacity allows him to be linked to the primordial (Calibanesque) maroon Macaia, the guerrilla tactician Makandal, and even the jailer Manuel, the Italian peasant from the Piedmont who, once Toussaint's military uniform is removed, recognizes in the prisoner someone who is a peasant like himself. Because Toussaint is so paradoxically and inscrutably linked to Haiti, a nation he neither envisaged nor knew, he can become a border-crossing symbol of freedom. Glissant's protagonist transcends the sacrificial hero that Martinique's lack of tragedy does not allow, and his vision of freedom is also different from Césaire's Caliban. Caliban in Césaire's play is concerned with individual freedom, which is very distinct from the *liberté générale*, or freedom for all, that Glissant's main character frequently invokes. Toussaint's final words are tellingly shouted in Martinican creole: "Man le la libete pou Sin-Doming!" (I want freedom for Saint-Domingue!),[39] and not the Haitian *moin vle*. Glissant's Toussaint voices the collective act that would be needed to change Martinique and that in the case of Saint-Domingue led to the emergence of the Haitian people.

In Toussaint's absence, Jean-Jacques Dessalines goes on to found the Haitian nation, but Glissant's Toussaint is not interested in what Hantel calls "the politics of reduction." He refuses the ancestral past and the martyrdom of the present, as well as Haiti's revolutionary nationalism. Indeed it is precisely the loss of territoriality that opens Glissant's marronneur to poetic dwelling or archipelagic thought. The prison in the Juras has been transformed into the "burning beach" as Glissant's Toussaint yields to the ocean's roar. Through the figure of Toussaint, Glissant is suggesting the need for new models, a new spatial poetics for the Antillean postcolony. In the first act, Toussaint refuses the invitation of the dead to return to the world of the sacred, to "paths unknown to the living." He shouts, "Leave me alone! I am starting my work all over. I will cross the seas again in the other direction."[40] He wrests himself free of the continental, in this case the ancestral African past, to commit himself to the crossing of ever-multiplying middle passages. By heading west, he is heading for future islands for which the Fort de Joux becomes another link in an archipelagic field. Toussaint, the marronneur, can therefore, like the walker on the black sand beach, create new paths whose pattern or direction elude us. He does not so much break free from his Alpine prison as transform terror into promise, heading west, toward the ever-receding horizon, following the archipelagic vision of the rainbow's marine arc. Césaire's Caliban, however, wedded to an imagined and now irrelevant past, remains imprisoned in his island with an open sea and sky.

NOTES

1. Édouard Glissant, *Traite du Tout-Monde* (Paris: Gallimard, 1997), 120.
2. Édouard Glissant, *L'intention poétique* (Paris: Gallimard, 1997), 49.
3. Glissant, *L'intention poétique*, 75.
4. Édouard Glissant, *Poetics of Relation*, trans. Betsy Wing (Ann Arbor: University of Michigan Press, 1997), 25.
5. Glissant, *L'intention poétique*, 76.
6. Glissant, *L'intention poétique*, 152.
7. Glissant, *Poetics of Relation*, 196.
8. Max Hantel, "Rhizomes and the Space of Translation: On Edouard Glissant's Spiral Retelling," *Small Axe* 17, no. 3 42 (2013): 110.

9. Édouard Glissant, *Soleil de la conscience* (Paris: Seuil, 1956), 43.
10. Glissant, *Poetics of Relation*, 122.
11. Glissant, *Poetics of Relation*, 207.
12. Édouard Glissant, *Une nouvelle région du monde* (Paris: Gallimard, 2006), 11.
13. Édouard Glissant, *La cohée du Lamentin* (Paris: Gallimard, 2005), 137.
14. Glissant, *Poetics of Relation*, 206.
15. Glissant, *Traite du Tout-Monde*, 181.
16. Édouard Glissant, *Philosophie de la Relation* (Paris: Gallimard, 2009), 45.
17. François Noudelmann, "Entretien avec Édouard Glissant: La relation, imprédictible et sans morale," *Rue Descartes* 37 (September 2002): 78.
18. Romouald Fonkoua, *Aimé Césaire* (Paris: Perrin, 2010), 339. Césaire seemed unaware when composing *A Tempest* in 1968 that there was literary precedent for using Shakespeare's play to deal with problems of colonialism. George Lamming used the figure of Caliban in his *Pleasures of Exile* (1950) and even cited Césaire. Césaire would no doubt have been aware of Octave Mannoni's study *Psychologie de la colonisation* (1950), which used Prospero and Caliban as central metaphors, and of Frantz Fanon's response in *Black Skin, White Masks* (1952).
19. Gregson Davis, *Aimé Césaire* (Cambridge: Cambridge University Press, 1997), 156. To further reinforce Davis's argument, Césaire claimed his early radio play *Et les chiens se taisent* (1956) was the crucible from which all his theatre was derived. In that case, Caliban in *A Tempest* was to be seen as a way of revisiting the figure of the rebel of the 1956 play.
20. Davis, *Aimé Césaire*, 157.
21. Aimé Césaire, *A Tempest*, trans. Richard Miller (New York: TCG Translations, 2002), 7.
22. Césaire, *Tempest*, 7. It is very tempting to read Césaire's psychodrama in Fanonian terms. Prospero, the colonizer, would then become the organizing principle of Caliban's, the colonized, imaginary. Caliban is therefore unable to free himself of Prospero, and his cry for liberty at the end is more a scream of frustration than of defiance.
23. Césaire, *Tempest*, 9.
24. Aimé Césaire, *Cahier d'un retour au pays natal* (Paris: Presence Africaine, 1956), 91.
25. Aimé Césaire, *Moi, laminaire* (Paris: Editions du Seuil, 1982).
26. Césaire, *Tempest*, 66.
27. Elizabeth DeLoughrey, "'The litany of islands, The rosary of archipelagoes': Caribbean and Pacific Archipelagraphy," *Ariel* 32, no. 1 (2001): 21–25.
28. Glissant, *Poetics of Relation*, 146.
29. Jose Pliya, *Les Effracteurs suivi de Nous étions assis sur le rivage du monde* (Paris: Collection des Quatre Vents, 2004), 81.
30. Édouard Glissant, *Le discours antillais* (Paris: Gallimard, 1997), 494.
31. Glissant, *La cohée du Lamentin*, 242. Toussaint is evoked as a specter wandering at will under the ramparts of the Fort de Joux.
32. Glissant, *Le discours antillais*, 493.
33. Glissant, *Le discours antillais*, 685.

34. Glissant, *Le discours antillais*, 479.
35. Glissant, *Le discours antillais*, 716–17.
36. Glissant, *Le discours antillais*, 716.
37. Glissant, *Le discours antillais*, 233.
38. Glissant, *Poetics of Relation*, 122.
39. Édouard Glissant, *Monsieur Toussaint*, trans. J. Michael Dash with the author (Boulder, CO: Lynne Rienner, 2005), 121.
40. Glissant, *Monsieur Toussaint*, 48.

PART VII | MIGRATING IDENTITIES, MOVING BORDERS

17 THE GOVERNORS-GENERAL

CARIBBEAN CANADIAN AND PACIFIC NEW ZEALAND SUCCESS STORIES

Birte Blascheck & Teresia Teaiwa

BARACK OBAMA CAPTURED the world's imagination in 2009 by becoming the first African American president of the United States. Yet when in 2005 Michaëlle Jean became the first governor-general of Canada of African-Haitian/Caribbean origin, and when in 2006 Anand Satyanand became the first governor-general of New Zealand of Indo-Fijian/Pacific descent, "the world" barely noticed. Why do some minority successes gain more global attention than others? Historic firsts in the United States are trumpeted in global media, while firsts in other parts of the world might pass by without receiving any attention at all. There are obvious economic and geopolitical reasons for such imbalance in the construction and circulation of news. We therefore read the effort to articulate an archipelagic American studies as a critique of such US-centrism. Through examining the complex narratives of these former governors-general, this essay seeks to broaden our understanding of minority achievement beyond the celebritization of political leadership.

The Commonwealth is an association of former British colonies bound by agreed principles of exchange and cooperation. Not all former British colonies are members of the Commonwealth; some opt out, while others are ejected or suspended for not conforming to governing principles. Decolonization in the British Empire historically took one of two constitutional paths: complete republican independence, or a form of political independence that was combined with the retention of a ceremonial but nevertheless constitutional role for the British monarch as head of state. The United States is a former British colony that took the first option and has not been a member of the Commonwealth. In countries that took the latter option, membership is secured by the constitutionally mandated role of the governor-general, who then serves as proxy for the British monarch. The position, therefore, is as close as a citizen can get to royal status in Canada and New Zealand without inheriting such a rank or marrying into the British monarchy.

The Caribbean Sea is located between North and South America, and the Pacific Ocean covers a third of the earth's surface. Yet based on the hegemonic aspirations of outsiders, the Caribbean and Pacific archipelagoes have been portrayed repeatedly as "small" and "cut-off" from modernity. Such "imagined geographies" have been contested through postcolonial discourses, but they continue to influence contemporary images. Interestingly, Canada and New Zealand have also been beset by problems of perception. As the second-biggest country in the world after Russia, Canada is still overshadowed by its economically and politically stronger neighbor, the United States; and New Zealand has a similar relationship across the Tasman Sea with Australia.[1] Unlike Canada, however, which is geographically disparate from the Caribbean, New Zealand's islands are part of the Pacific. As a Caribbean Canadian and a Pacific New Zealander respectively, Jean and Satyanand were thus complexly positioned between depictions of their archipelagic diasporas and those of their nations.

Descendants of Caribbean migrants in Canada and of Pacific migrants in New Zealand trace their ancestry to individual or multiple islands. As members of "small island" communities in their diverse nation-states, they increasingly develop a consciousness of their archipelagic collectivity vis-à-vis continental identities such as the African, Asian, or European diasporas. As we compare and analyze the phenomena of Caribbean Canadians and Pacific New Zealanders as "archipelagic diasporas within nations,"[2] we also take into account Canada's transatlantic and New Zealand's transpacific histories of colonialism. Celebritizations of individual success stories attract various forms of attachment within mass consumer societies. Our focus on the governors-general examines how this relates to diaspora, nation, and youth.

Based on analyses of media reports, Jean's speeches, an interview with Satyanand, and discussions with young Caribbean Canadians and Pacific New Zealanders, we investigate the meanings of Jean's and Satyanand's success stories for the next generation. The essay draws attention to Jean's and Satyanand's distinct trajectories as members of "twice diasporized" and "small island" communities, and the discourses of indigeneity, biculturalism, and multiculturalism that shape the politics of their respective nation-states. We thus use archipelagic American studies as a relational approach that bridges island and continental spaces,[3] which reveals minority and majority positions that are fixed neither to size nor location but demonstrates interconnected power relationships.

ARCHIPELAGIC DIASPORAS WITHIN NATIONS

Indigenous histories, colonial transformations, and more recent forces of globalization have shaped the Caribbean and Pacific islands.[4] After successive waves of settlement, the populations of both archipelagoes represent rich mixtures of cultures.⁵ Contradicting the fabricated colonial image of island isolation, the Caribbean Sea and the Pacific Ocean in fact functioned as mediums for dynamic histories of encounter, exchange, and wide-ranging relationships between islanders and outsiders. Caribbean and Pacific peoples' identities thus need to be understood through a more fluid notion, in which maritime contexts form the development of a collective consciousness. Ties of "kinship" through shared histories and cultures unite these diverse archipelagoes within themselves and across their diasporas.⁶ Yet as "small island" populations, Caribbean and Pacific peoples also struggle in global environments that continue to privilege size, so they have by necessity established strategic alliances in the form of economic, political, and cultural organizations.⁷ Whereas Caribbean peoples are usually understood as "diasporic," tracing their hybrid pre-Caribbean heritage mainly to Africa, Asia, and Europe, most Pacific peoples understand themselves to be "indigenous" to the Pacific, even if some might not use this term.⁸ However, Pacific peoples who are not Māori are indisputably diasporic in New Zealand, while most Caribbean peoples in Canada are, to draw on Stuart Hall, "twice diasporized."⁹

The Canadian census tends to enumerate Caribbean Canadians under single-island nationalities or other diasporas, and does not provide an explicit category for Caribbean identities. There are approximately 36 million people living in Canada, and more than 500,000 are of Caribbean origin.¹⁰ While there have been longer presences, most Caribbean peoples migrated to Canada between the 1960s and 1970s, when Canada reformed its immigration laws to accommodate labor shortages. The majority came from the Anglophone islands, mainly Jamaica, followed by Trinidad and Tobago, and Guyana.¹¹ Some also moved from Britain and the United States.¹² The majority of Caribbean Canadians settled in the province of Ontario, especially in Toronto. Haitians settled mainly in the province of Quebec, which favors Francophone immigrants.¹³ A much smaller number of people came from the Hispanophone islands of Cuba and the Dominican Republic, France's overseas departments Guadeloupe and Martinique, and the Netherlands' Antilles. The annual Caribana carnival held in Toronto portrays the spectrum of Caribbean Canadian expressivities. But because of the predominance of African-Caribbean and Jamaican heritage, there is a tendency in Canada to equate Caribbean Canadians with these two characteristics; Jamaica stands for all Caribbean islands, and the Caribbean is a "pseudonym for blackness."¹⁴ Belying such quick glosses, children of Caribbean migrants who were either born or raised in Canada are frequently of dual or multiple origins.¹⁵ It is this generation that most clearly articulates a pan-Caribbean perspective, as well as a sense of Canadianness.¹⁶

The New Zealand census contains a category for Pacific New Zealanders, and numerous strategies and policies exist across various sectors recognizing

Pacific identities. Among the more than 4.5 million people who live in New Zealand, nearly 300,000 are of Pacific descent.[17] The first Polynesians settled the islands now known as New Zealand "at least 1200 years ago."[18] Over time, an Indigenous culture evolved, and Māori are considered by others and understand themselves as distinct from other Polynesians and Pacific peoples. Most Pacific peoples migrated between the 1950s and 1980s, during New Zealand's labor shortages. The majority were Samoans who have a special status within New Zealand's immigration policies due to their former colonial dependency. Some moved from the Cook Islands, Tonga, and Niue, and, to a lesser extent, Fiji, Tokelau, and Tuvalu. There are also small communities originating from French Polynesia, Kiribati, Papua New Guinea, and the Solomon Islands.[19] Most Pacific New Zealanders live in Auckland, which is considered the "Polynesian capital of the world."[20] The diversity of Pacific New Zealand expressivities is evident in the city's annual Pasifika festival. Yet Pacific New Zealanders are still frequently perceived by others as Samoan and "brown"; and Polynesia is also often a synonym for the entire Pacific.[21] Today, most Pacific New Zealanders are born in New Zealand, and are frequently of mixed heritage.[22] Like Caribbean Canadians, this next generation increasingly identifies with a pan-Pacific standpoint, and has developed a distinct New Zealand–born identity.[23]

CELEBRITIZATIONS OF THE GOVERNORS-GENERAL AND MINORITY SUCCESSES

Fame can be "attributed" through publicity, "achieved" through open competition, or "ascribed" by birth.[24] Barack Obama's successful campaign for the US presidency earned him both attributed and achieved types of fame. But Britain's Queen Elizabeth II and her descendants probably best exemplify the type of ascribed recognition that attaches to aristocracy. The governors-general are therefore distinct from the monarch they represent, because their posts are nonhereditary and temporary, two defining features of the principles of "democracy" and "capitalism" through which celebritizations articulate.[25] On one hand, it is believed that everyone has the "potential" to succeed, regardless of social origin. On the other hand, success is also defined by the changes of the economic market, in which public figures are being "evaluated."[26] The positions of the governors-general are ambiguous, because they are neither chosen by the public nor contested in public. Although situated within the political sphere, they are not elected, as are the US president or the Canadian and New Zealand prime ministers. While the governors-general do not possess the kind of political influence that adheres to the executive functions of government, their "symbolic power" is important for those they (un)officially represent, because the selection for this office signifies a form of endorsement that can secure prestige and cultural continuity.[27]

Throughout the Commonwealth, each governor-general represents the British monarch, as well as the individual state and the respective nation. The office was formally established in Canada in 1867 and in New Zealand in 1840. Initially, governors-general were chosen by the sovereign, and drawn from the British military or nobility. Since the appointments of Vincent Massey in 1952 and Arthur Porritt in 1967, all governors-general have been and must be Canadian and New Zealand citizens, respectively. They now theoretically can come from all walks of life and various origins. Consequently, there have been more historic firsts in the selections of governors-general.[28] Since Georges Vanier's appointment in 1959, there has been a rotation between Anglophones and Francophones in Canada. In 1985, Paul Reeves became the first governor-general of New Zealand of Māori descent. In 1984, Jeanne Sauvé became the first woman in this position in Canada, and the first with a broadcasting background. In 1990, Catherine Tizard was the first woman governor-general for New Zealand. In 1999, Adrienne Clarkson was the first Asian Canadian appointed to the office, and the first to have come to Canada as a refugee. Between 2005 and 2010, Michaëlle Jean was the first governor-general of Canada of African-Haitian/Caribbean origin. Between 2006 and 2011, Anand Satyanand was the first governor-general of New Zealand of Indo-Fijian/Pacific descent. State formation in European settler societies such as Canada and New Zealand is a "vital prerequisite for nation creation."[29] To promote a national consciousness, "elites, therefore, seek to use the state to achieve a linkage between state formation and 'ethnic' components of nationhood."[30] Canada and New Zealand initially sought such unity through assimilation practices, but the integrative models of multiculturalism and biculturalism have become more effective in recent decades.

As governors-general, Jean and Satyanand occupied elite political positions, restricted to one individual at a certain time and place. Examining their diasporic identities, however, reveals that they are also members of minorities-within-minorities that do not tend to be associated with state power. Although her African-Caribbean heritage places Jean among the majority of Caribbean Canadians, as a Francophone she is a minority among Anglophones. While Haitians have not played an important role in the archipelagic identity formation of the Anglophone Caribbean, Haiti's historical significance lies in the abolition of slavery in the Caribbean and the Americas as a whole, and its landmark of becoming the world's "first black republic" in 1804.[31] In Satyanand's case, Indo-Fijians are a diasporic minority in Fiji, and Fijians are a minority among Pacific New Zealanders. Most Indo-Fijians trace their ancestry to Indian laborers indentured through the British colonial system.[32] When Fiji gained its independence in 1970, there was a tense balance between Indigenous Fijians and Indo-Fijians along with various ethnic minorities. Similar to Indo-Caribbean Canadians, who are generally subsumed under the South Asian or the African-Caribbean diasporas,[33] Indo-Fijian New Zealanders are situated between Asian and Pacific minorities in New Zealand.

In media reports, there were comments about how Jean's and Satyanand's appointments symbolized new pathways for their diasporic communities. On August 11, 2005, the black/Caribbean Canadian newspaper *Share* proclaimed that "history was made" when Jean became "the first Black to be elevated to the post," declaring that it "sends a clear message to the rest of the world that Canada is a diverse society." On October 8, 2005, the *Toronto Star* reported that Haitian Canadians felt "a deep sense of pride" because Jean's "appointment is a recognition of the achievements of Haitians and black people alike in Canada" and therefore "a symbol of possibilities and hope for our children." In a similar way, on October 9, 2006, the Indian Association of New Zealand was quoted in the *New Zealand Herald* to the effect that "it was time" Satyanand's "community was represented in Parliament." In its issue in March–April 2007, the Pacific/Māori New Zealand magazine *Spasifik* printed statements that Satyanand's "appointment symbolized the multicultural nature of contemporary New Zealand," and in its issue in July–August 2006, it reported that "this small group of around half a million [Indo-Fijian] people [worldwide] felt delight at the achievements of one of their sons." Jean's and Satyanand's success stories were clearly historically significant for their respective states, nations, and diasporas alike.

MULTICULTURALISM AND CARIBBEAN CANADIANS' TRANSNATIONAL OUTLOOK

The recognized Aboriginal peoples of the country now known as Canada are First Nations, Inuit, and Métis.[34] France asserted power in North America during the sixteenth century. Then, after the Seven Years' War and the signing of the Treaty of Paris in 1763, the British dominated the continent.[35] Throughout the eighteenth and the nineteenth centuries, the British settlers oppressed, deported, and/or killed many of the Indigenous populations and the French Acadians, and discouraged nonwhite/British migrants from entry through immigration legislation. Still, Canada's western expansion attracted migrants from diverse places. And with the help of the Underground Railroad, tens of thousands escaped US slavery by fleeing to Canada.[36] While the United States followed a republican path after its War of Independence, Canada became a dominion within the British Empire in 1867. After World War II, Canada loosened its colonial ties but remained a member of the Commonwealth, and retained the British monarch as head of state.[37] With the economic growth of the 1950s, Canada sought to fill its labor needs by accommodating non-Europeans or so called "visible minorities" in revised immigration policies.[38] Nonetheless, Caribbean immigrants experienced various forms of marginalization and racism,[39] despite their (post)colonial links with Canada. After its Quiet Revolution during the 1960s, Quebec obtained a special status within the Canadian Federation, and Francophones gained significant power alongside Anglophones.[40] Between the 1970s and 1980s, Canada officially adopted a multicultural discourse,[41] but its version of biculturalism continued to privilege the British and French diasporas.

Michaëlle Jean was born in Haiti and came to Canada as a refugee child with her family. In a speech she made at a diasporic art exhibition on September 21, 2009, she described herself as "a woman in whom many cultures and identities co-exist." She claimed the Aboriginal peoples of Haiti, enslaved Africans, and deported Acadians as her ancestors, and further stressed that although she had "put down [her] roots" in Quebec, "those roots reach right across Canada" now.[42] Jean thus demonstrated the complexities of her Caribbean Canadian identity, her positioning as a Québécoise within the Canadian context, and her responsibility as governor-general to represent the interests of all Canadians. Although Jean's allegiance to Canada was initially questioned in the national media, on August 6, 2005, the *Toronto Star* saw her appointment as "a tribute to multiculturalism," and between December 26, 2005, and January 2, 2006, *Maclean's* magazine believed her appointment called "for an end to ethnic and linguistic divisions." As part of fulfilling the usual duties of a governor-general, which aim to be inclusive, Jean attended several functions concerning First Nations and the African/Caribbean diasporas in Canada. Furthermore, her trips to Haiti, and the launch of the Michaëlle Jean Chair at the University of Alberta in 2009, were notable steps in bringing more attention to the Caribbean Canadian experience.

Although she was better-known in Quebec than in the rest of Canada, Jean already had a media profile prior to becoming governor-general, because she was a broadcaster, documentary filmmaker, and journalist. Jean entered Rideau Hall more than three years before Barack Obama took office in the White House, but during his presidential campaign, her popularity appeared to increase as well. While the media rarely acknowledged Jean as a Caribbean Canadian, and depicted her primarily as "black," on January 14, 2008, there was a major article in *Maclean's* that compared Jean with the influential African American television host and producer Oprah Winfrey. Jean's gender also attracted specific commentary. On October 10, 2005, the *Toronto Star* described her appointment as "an outstanding exception" that "masks Ottawa's woeful record on women," because "Canadian political parties continue to seek power men but poster women to lead them." Whereas women in positions of more active power are sometimes defeminized, Jean's image tended to be overfeminized. On October 31, 2005, *Maclean's* portrayed her as a "bombshell," exuding "Hollywood style glamour," and on January 8, 2009, the *Toronto Star* compared her hair to Michelle

Obama's. In repartee over her qualification for the post, on November 7, 2005, Jean herself was quoted in *Maclean's* saying that "she only got the job because she's 'hot.'" In these ways Jean's representational power was trivialized by concerns with style consumptions, and disassociated from concerns with racism or sexism. Comparing her role as governor-general to that of a politician, however, on January 14, 2008, Jean maintained in *Maclean's* that "there are things that I cannot change in this country," and "this position is exactly that. You stay outside politics. And you represent a moral authority." While her individual leadership style was described as an "unabashed appeal to emotion," it is a strategy that political figures increasingly use to connect with the public.[43] The way Jean was celebritized in the media thus demonstrated her affective and symbolic powers as governor-general of Canada. Moreover, it revealed the US influence on Canada in general, and the African American influence on Caribbean Canadians in particular.

BICULTURALISM AND PACIFIC NEW ZEALANDERS' REGIONAL GROUNDING

The ancestors of the Māori first populated the islands of New Zealand over one thousand years ago.[44] With the signing of the Treaty of Waitangi in 1840, Britain believed it had gained sovereignty in New Zealand, which increased conflicts between British settlers and Māori over land. In 1907, New Zealand became a dominion within the British Empire. After World War II, New Zealand started loosening its colonial ties, but, like Canada, it remained a member of the Commonwealth, and kept the British monarch as head of state. With the economic boom of the 1950s, New Zealand also sought to meet its labor shortages by relaxing immigration policies, particularly for citizens of Pacific Island nations in the neighborhood. Although there were significant numbers of non-British/European migrants, New Zealand maintained "a vestige of the 'White New Zealand Policy'" until the 1980s,[45] and Pacific New Zealanders experienced various forms of discrimination.[46] A Māori protest movement during the 1970s and 1980s led to the renaissance of Māori language and culture, which brought Māori special rights as Indigenous peoples vis-à-vis Pākehā (who are descendants of British settlers in New Zealand), and the Waitangi Tribunal was set up to settle grievances.[47] While New Zealand has become more culturally diverse, government has officially promoted a bicultural discourse since the 1980s.[48] Unlike Canada's strategy, New Zealand's bicultural policy focuses on the British diaspora and the Māori.

Anand Satyanand was born and raised in New Zealand of Indo-Fijian origin. During Birte Blascheck's interview with him in June 2008 at Government House, Satyanand described his ethnicity as "positive additions" to the role of the governor-general, but insisted that his "Pacificness is a secondary thing."

His comments revealed a ranking of his "twice diasporized" identity, with his Indian/Asian heritage coming first, and his Fijian/Pacific origin second. His view of himself as a "brown" person connected these multiple identities. Like Michaëlle Jean, Satyanand represented Queen Elizabeth II as head of state, and had a responsibility "to the whole of New Zealand," and "to be inclusive of everyone." Since he is neither Pākehā nor Māori, Satyanand's personal identity did not reflect New Zealand's biculturalism, but his role as governor-general made him accountable to it, because he attended numerous functions concerning both communities. In terms of New Zealand's multiculturalism, Satyanand said that he had found "evidence in the press" that his appointment was "seen as a really good thing," because it "speaks well of the country." Nonetheless, a controversy arose in October 2010, when a TVNZ broadcaster remarked that Satyanand did not "look" or "sound" like a New Zealander.[49] As governor-general, Satyanand officiated numerous ceremonies addressing all New Zealanders, but he also went to events that particularly concerned the Indian and Pacific communities. While he was mindful of his triangulated Asianness, Pacificness, and New Zealandness in many of his speeches, he maintained that he also greeted audiences in the Pacific languages of "the realm of New Zealand of which the [governor-general] has jurisdiction." Like Jean in Canada, Satyanand drew attention to New Zealand's cultural diversity.

Although he was a lawyer, judge, and ombudsman, Satyanand did not have much of a media profile prior to becoming governor-general. His swearing-in ceremony received hardly any media coverage in New Zealand, and there was less focus on his public personality than on Jean's in Canada. In the interview with Blascheck, Satyanand explained that the governor-general "does a range of set things," such as "constitutional," "legal," "ceremonial," and "community things." Therefore he believed that the media presented him "in an orthodox fashion," which is in "association with all of these events," and "separate from the individual personality" of the governor-general. Yet on April 4, 2006, when the *New Zealand Herald* announced that "'Satch'... wins top job," that might have been a sign of celebritization despite there being a prevailing sense of egalitarianism in New Zealand. Similar to the way that Jean's specific origins were elided in the media, Satyanand was rarely identified as Indo-Fijian in news coverage, and he was regularly assumed to be Asian. The media did not explicitly describe him as a brown/Pacific New Zealander, even though he was profiled in an exhibition on Pacific peoples in New Zealand in the national museum Te Papa. Reflecting on how his position was different from that of a politician, Satyanand pointed out in the interview that he was "not part of the domestic controversies or the political events of the day." Whereas "politicians are there to develop the policies of the day and to implement them," he said he made people "aware of the things the government is doing," and checked that "what they have passed is in accordance with the law." This again was "removed from whether I personally think the legislation is a good idea or not." As governor-general, Satyanand was "not trying to be popular," because in his role he was neither "seeking affirmation or peoples' votes," nor seeking out "celebrity." Compared to Jean in Canada, there were no US, Australian, or Asian/Pacific Australian influences on Satyanand's portrayals in the media, and the attention he received was more focused on his duties as a representative of the New Zealand state than on him personally.

THE NEXT GENERATION'S AMBIVALENT RELATIONS TO "SMALL ISLAND" AND STATE REPRESENTATIONS

Between April and December 2008, Birte Blascheck conducted twelve focus group interviews with seventeen Caribbean Canadians in Toronto and Montreal and with twenty Pacific New Zealanders in Auckland and Wellington, examining their perceptions of diasporic achievements.[50] In the media, the individual success stories of both governors-general were portrayed as new pathways for Caribbean Canadians and Pacific New Zealanders. Moreover, Michaëlle Jean made youth an explicit focus during her term in office, and Anand Satyanand stated in Blascheck's interview that he was "there to affirm what people are doing," to help youth develop their "potential."[51] As representatives of the next generation, however, focus group participants were less "inspired" by narratives of celebritized success than might have been expected. Like the governors-general themselves, they acknowledged that families and friends played a larger role in influencing and supporting them than public personalities. Nevertheless, they sympathized with the governors-general's stories of "struggle"[52] in "small island" communities, and some could see parallels between Jean's and Satyanand's parents and their own (grand)parents. While interviewees appeared ambivalent in their "evaluations"[53] of the governors-general, they carefully assessed Jean's and Satyanand's diasporic identities, their (inter)national settings, and their influence within the political sphere.

About half of the young Caribbean Canadians interviewed recognized Jean in a photograph, but most did not know her name. Although participants were generally well aware of the cultural diversity of their diaspora, they did not comment on Jean's Francophone identity. They rather saw her Haitian minority position as part of the "black" majority among Caribbean Canadians. Recalling Haiti's historical significance, one interviewee asserted, "Haiti is the first island to have gained independence in the Caribbean, and they have suffered a lot of hardship since." Considering negative images of Caribbean peoples in Canada, a mixed group of participants stated that "Haitians were seen as gang members," and another group maintained in solidarity that "we're not just shooting people." Interestingly, a group of Haitian Canadians was "not more passionate" about Jean than about Anglophone Caribbean Canadian celebrities. A participant of Indo-Trinidadian heritage was not happy that Caribbean peoples tend to be represented by "blacks." But a participant of Cuban origin figured, "I cannot get mad, because there aren't many [Hispanophone Caribbean Canadians]." A few participants seemed to have mixed feelings about how Jean figured as an instrument of Canadian state policy: one group wondered whether Jean was purposefully selected as "a person of color," to make a statement that Canada was "not racist," and suggested that Jean was "a puppet." While there had already been a Chinese Canadian governor-general, they cynically surmised that "next there will be an Indian, everyone gets a turn." More optimistically, another group emphasized that "Canada is multicultural," and therefore Jean's appointment "shows diversity." Hence participants considered Jean's influence in terms of the heterogeneous complexities of the Caribbean diaspora and of Canada's multicultural policy.

Caribbean Canadian interviewees recalled only a few Caribbean Canadian public personalities, but talked about several African American figures in the United States. One group stressed that Jean was "the first," and that they "have to give her respect for that," but they were "not too surprised, because today we can see Barack Obama [in the daily news about his presidential campaign at the time]." In much the same way as the media, interviewees seemed to see Jean as more credible because of Obama, even though he had made a later arrival on the celebritized public personality scene. While someone remembered that Jean had been "on the front of Caribbean newspapers," and two groups compared her with Oprah Winfrey as *Maclean's* had, one group felt that Jean's public profile was "not to the same extent as Michelle Obama, but she's our little version." Again, although Obama was not even in power yet, the next generation perceived his wife (as potential First Lady of the United States) as more influential than Jean. Reflecting on Jean's success story, however, most participants thought that it was "an excellent accomplishment" for a "woman," for a "black" person, and for someone from the "Caribbean," especially from "Haiti," to have been appointed as governor-general. One participant reiterated that it "is a great position, a person of authority." There was a commonly held belief that "usually they say that black people are only good in sports," and a few participants admitted that they were "more interested in sports or music," and wondered whether politics were "more important to our parents' generation." Yet several interviewees expressed curiosity about Jean's political power. Aware of official constraints, one group reflected that Jean "has the potential to be influential," but wondered, "If she rocks the boat, can she really speak out?" One interviewee was waiting to see whether Jean was "going to make us proud or look bad," while another believed that Jean embodied "a sense of pride" because she offered a positive representation of Caribbean Canadians. So research participants felt ambivalent about the ways they saw themselves represented through the state.

The majority of the young Pacific New Zealanders interviewed did not recognize Satyanand when shown his photograph, but during the discussions some recalled that they had heard of him or seen him at a community function, although very few remembered his name. While most participants initially perceived Satyanand as Indian, they eventually acknowledged his connection to Fiji over the course of the interview. A Niuean New Zealander sympathized with Satyanand's minority-within-a-minority status by saying that his "being Indian Fijian" is inspiring, because "there aren't many," just like Niueans. A participant of Indo-Fijian descent stated that Satyanand's appointment was "really important to me," because "for Indians we aren't Indian enough, and Pacific people think we're not Pacific enough." Two Pacific New Zealanders who also had Māori heritage, however, were not so convinced about Satyanand: one expressed "mixed feelings" about him "in that position," because "there could have been a Māori";[54] and another one thought that Satyanand was "not obvious . . . just based on his looks," but recalled that he had heard about him on TVNZ's *Tagata Pasifika* weekly program, which covers Pacific news. He stressed that "you don't necessarily gain respect, because of your role," and asked, "What has he done or contributed to the collective nature [of the Pacific community]?" Hence participants were assessing Satyanand's relevance to them in terms of the heterogeneity of the Pacific diaspora and New Zealand's bicultural policy.

In their discussions of various Pacific New Zealand public personalities, interviewees did not emphasize Satyanand's "historic first" symbolism, in the way that Caribbean Canadians had with Jean; nor did they link him with Obama, whose Hawaiian birthplace connects him to the Pacific. But similar to the Caribbean "small island" perspective, one group whose participants also mentioned their mixed Asian and European heritages argued that "knowing that he's not European . . . is really inspiring." One participant felt that it was important that Satyanand was governor-general: "It's awesome, a huge accomplishment, a high role." Another one emphasized that "sports and entertainment get more attention," and that "intellectual and academic PIs don't receive as much limelight."[55] Others were proud of Satyanand because he "might have an impact on politics" or "must be a big influence nationally and internationally." Someone noted that he "is sensitive to Pacific countries. In all his speeches he greets and acknowledges everyone." So despite not being recognized immediately as a Pacific New Zealander, Satyanand's approach to community representations was appreciated by some members of the next generation. A few interviewees, however, could not relate to him because, they said, "we're more into show business," and others commented, "we can relate more to younger people." One was explicitly skeptical "of the western government" because "they give them suits and they go all strange." Thus research participants demonstrated ambivalence toward state politics because they were concerned about the actual and symbolic representations of their diasporic matters and the interests of their generation.

CONCLUSION

While Barack Obama's success story is being mediated through the lenses of US celebrity culture, Michaëlle Jean's and Anand Satyanand's achievements deserve nuanced considerations on their own merits. As governors-general, their appointments showcased Canada's and New Zealand's bicultural and multicultural state policies of integration. Whereas the national media depicted Jean primarily as "black" and Satyanand primarily as "Asian," their viceregal tenures also signaled new pathways and positive recognitions for Caribbean Canadian and Pacific New Zealand diasporas. Although there are numerically more Caribbean Canadians than Pacific New Zealanders, proportionally the latter are in a relatively stronger position vis-à-vis their national population. While regional categories are useful in dealing with archipelagic complexities, Caribbean identities are not as recognized in Canada as Pacific identities are in New Zealand.

The young Caribbean Canadians and Pacific New Zealanders interviewed in this study were aware of their communities' heterogeneity, conscious of their geocultural circumstances, and critical about politics. As this essay has shown, the next generation's perceptions of Jean and Satyanand were filtered through social imaginations of "small island" connections that predate commercialized processes of celebritization. These were therefore not views of belittlement and isolation but relational approaches to minority and majority interdependencies. In this way, Jean's and Satyanand's individual success stories were not merely consumed by "affected" audiences, but also "evaluated"[56] by focus group participants in the ways they saw themselves "symbolically"[57] represented by these two public personalities. As an African-Caribbean Canadian, Jean mirrored the "twice diasporized" identities of most Caribbean Canadians, despite her Francophone minority position. As an Indo-Pacific New Zealander, Satyanand reflected the diasporic but not the "indigenous"[58] affiliations felt among most Pacific New Zealanders. While young Caribbean Canadian interviewees appeared to be more US-Americanized and influenced by African American links, Pacific New Zealand participants were more attuned to their distinct New Zealand context. Both diasporic groups of the next generation, however, seemed to find their archipelagic identifications empowering (inter)nationally.

As the current secretary-general of the Francophonie and the current chair of the Commonwealth Foundation, respectively, Jean and Satyanand remain influential in Francophone and British Anglophone worlds. Caribbean and Pacific pan-connections continue to be important within and outside these two archipelagoes. Canada and New Zealand, moving away from their colonial pasts, have repositioned themselves more assertively within the Americas and the Asia-Pacific. Although US celebrity culture is spreading globally and being imitated locally, the fact that family, friends, and community are still important for young Caribbean Canadians and Pacific New Zealanders, and are not replaced through celebritized role models, suggests that the work of archipelagic American studies is also being done outside of the academy.

NOTES

1. Edward W. Said, *Orientalism: Western Conceptions of the Orient* (London: Penguin, 2003); E. Kamau Brathwaite, *Contradictory Omens: Cultural Diversity and Integration in the Caribbean* (Mona, Jamaica: Savacou, 1974); and Epeli Hau'ofa, "Our Sea of Islands," in *A New Oceania: Rediscovering Our Sea of Islands,* ed. Eric Waddell, Vijay Naidu, and Epeli Hau'ofa (Suva, Fiji: University of the South Pacific, 1993), 2–16; on Canadian-US relations, see Patrick Lennox, *At Home and Abroad: The Canada-US Relationship and Canada's Place in the World* (Vancouver: University of British Columbia Press, 2010); on New Zealand–Australian relations, see Philippa Mein Smith, Peter Hempenstall, and Shaun Goldfinch, *Remaking the Tasman World* (Christchurch, NZ: Canterbury University Press, 2009).

2. Roberts argues that archipelagic diasporas "forge interlinkings of the planet's disparate cultural regions," in which the archipelago provides a geographically "formal" connection and the diaspora provides a connection through "cultural geography"; Brian Russell Roberts, "Archipelagic Diaspora, Geographical Form, and Hurston's *Their Eyes Were Watching God,*" *American Literature* 85, no. 1 (2013): 144. Although continental heritage might predate the archipelagic identities of some Caribbean Canadians and Pacific New Zealanders, in the context of this study, we view the archipelago as the source of origin for the diaspora in different nations.

3. Brian Russell Roberts and Michelle Stephens, "Archipelagic American Studies and the Caribbean," *Journal of Transnational American Studies* 5, no. 1 (2013): 5 and 14.

4. Esther Figueroa, Gerard A. Finin, Scott Kroeker, Katerina M. Teaiwa, and Terence Wesley-Smith, "Islands of Globalization: Pacific and Caribbean Perspectives," *Social and Economic Studies* 56, nos. 1–2 (2007): 32–40.

5. Rex Nettleford, "Ideology, Identity, Culture," in *General History of the Caribbean: The Caribbean in the Twentieth Century,* vol. 5, ed. Bridget Brereton (Paris, FR: UNESCO, 2004), 537–58; and Ron Crocombe, *The South Pacific* (Suva, Fiji: University of the South Pacific Press, 2008).

6. Teresia Teaiwa and Sean Mallon, "Ambivalent Kinships? Pacific Peoples in New Zealand," in *New Zealand Identities: Departures and Destinations,* ed. James H. Liu, Tim McCreanor, Tracey McIntosh, and Teresia Teaiwa (Wellington, NZ: Victoria University of Wellington Press, 2005), 207–8.

7. Graeme Robertson, "Island Studies Resources," in *A World of Islands: An Island Studies Reader,* ed. Godfrey Baldacchino (Charlottetown: University of Prince Edward Island Press, 2007), 539–78.

8. Stuart Hall, "Cultural Identity and Diaspora," in *Theorizing Diaspora: A Reader,* ed. Jana Evans Braziel and Anita Mannur (Oxford, UK: Blackwell, 2003), 233–46; Teresia Teaiwa, "Native Thoughts: A Pacific Studies Take on Cultural Studies and Diaspora," in *Indigenous Diasporas and Dislocations,* ed. Graham Harvey and Charles D. Thompson, Jr. (Burlington, VT: Ashgate, 2005), 15–35.

9. Stuart Hall, "Negotiating Caribbean Identities," *New Left Review* 209, no. 1 (1995): 5.

10. Statistics Canada, www.statcan.gc.ca, accessed October 4, 2016.

11. Guyana is not an island, but Guyanese have a strong presence among Caribbean Canadians.

12. Alissa Trotz, "Rethinking Caribbean Transnational Connections: Conceptual Itineraries," *Global Networks* 6, no. 1 (2006): 41–59.

13. Michel Plourde, Hélène Duval, and Pierre Georgeault, eds., *Le français au Québec: 400 ans d'histoire et de vie* (Quebec: Fides, 2003), 343–77.

14. Camille Hernandez-Ramdwar, "From TT to T.O.: Second-Generation Identities in the Caribbean Diaspora" (PhD diss., Toronto: University of Toronto, 2006), 236; Rinaldo Walcott, "Caribbean Pop Culture in Canada; Or, the Impossibility of Belonging to the Nation," *Small Axe* 9 (2001): 128.

15. Alan B. Simmons and Dwaine E. Plaza, "The Caribbean Community in Canada: Transnational Connections and Transformations," in *Transnational Identities and Practices in Canada,* ed. Lloyd Wong and Vic Satzewitch (Vancouver, BC: UBC Press, 2006), 142–44.

16. Walcott, "Caribbean Pop Culture," 125.

17. As New Zealand's Indigenous peoples, Māori are listed in a separate category, but in other places, such as Australia or the United States, they would also be considered "Pacific Islanders." Pacific New Zealanders whose ancestors have not been Indigenous to the Pacific, however, tend to fall into other categories, such as the Asian or European diasporas; New Zealand Statistics, www.stats.govt.nz, accessed October 4, 2016.

18. Cluny Macpherson, "Pacific Diaspora," in *Encyclopaedia of the Pacific,* ed. Brij V. Lal (Honolulu: University of Hawai'i Press, 2000), 114.

19. Teaiwa and Mallon, "Ambivalent Kinships," 208.

20. Steven R. Fischer, *A History of the Pacific Islands* (New York: Palgrave, 2002), 263.

21. Melani Anae, "From Kava to Coffee: The 'Browning' of Auckland," in *Almighty Auckland,* ed. Ian Carter, David Craig, and Steve Matthewman (Palmerston North, NZ: Dunmore Press, 2004), 89–110; a "Nesian" identity among younger Pacific New Zealanders also includes Melanesian and Micronesian as well as Māori identifications; Belinda Borell, "Living in the City Ain't So Bad: Cultural Identity for Young Maori in South Auckland," in Liu et al., *New Zealand Identities,* 202–3.

22. Ministry for Pacific Peoples, www.mpia.govt.nz/pacific-people-in-nz, accessed October 4, 2016.

23. Peggy Fairbairn-Dunlop and Gabrielle Makisi, eds., *Making Our Place: Growing Up PI in New Zealand* (Palmerston North, NZ: Dunmore Press, 2003).

24. Chris Rojek, *Celebrity* (London: Reaktion, 2001), 17–20.

25. David Marshall, *Celebrity and Power: Fame in Contemporary Culture* (Minneapolis: University of Minnesota Press, 1997), 4.

26. Marshall, *Celebrity and Power*, 246; Francesco Alberoni, "The Powerless 'Elite': Theory and Sociological Research on the Phenomenon of the Stars," in *The Celebrity Culture Reader*, ed. David Marshall (New York: Routledge, 2006), 115.

27. On occasion, however, the governors-general can make use of their discretionary powers.

28. Stuart Hall, "The Spectacle of the 'Other,'" in *Representation: Cultural Representations and Signifying Practices*, ed. Stuart Hall (London: Sage, 1997), 259; The Governor-General of Canada, www.gg.ca, accessed October 4, 2016; The Governor-General of New Zealand, https://gg.govt.nz, accessed October 4, 2016.

29. David Pearson, *The Politics of Ethnicity in Settler Societies: States of Unease* (Basingstoke, UK: Palgrave, 2001), 10.

30. Pearson, *Politics of Ethnicity*, 10.

31. Jana Evans Braziel, *Diaspora: An Introduction* (Malden, MA: Blackwell, 2008), 20.

32. On Indo-Fijian history, see Brij V. Lal, ed., *Bittersweet: The Indo-Fijian Experience* (Canberra, AU: Pandanus, 2004).

33. Dwaine E. Plaza, "The Construction of a Segmented Hybrid Identity among One and a Half and Second Generation Indo- and African-Caribbean Canadians," *Identity: An International Journal of Theory and Research* 6, no. 3 (2006): 207–30.

34. On Indigenous history in Canada, see Augie Fleras and Roger Maaka, *The Politics of Indigeneity: Challenging the State in Canada and Aotearoa* (Dunedin, NZ: University of Otago Press, 2005).

35. John A. Dickinson, "L'anglicisation," in Plourde, Duval, and Georgeault, *Le français au Québec*, 80.

36. For the history of the Underground Railroad, see David W. Blight, ed., *Passages to Freedom: The Underground Railroad in History and Memory* (Washington, DC: Smithsonian, 2006).

37. As a member of the Francophonie, Canada also holds close ties with France.

38. There are ambiguous power structures behind ideas of "visibility." In other places, such as South Africa, peoples of European heritage would be considered as "visible minorities." Moreover, the "nonvisible" masses in consumer societies might view celebrities as "visible" elites.

39. Simmons and Plaza, "Caribbean Community in Canada," 139–40.

40. Plourde, Duval, and Georgeault, *Le français au Québec*, 239–329.

41. On multiculturalism in Canada, see Augie Fleras, *The Politics of Multiculturalism: Multicultural Governance in Comparative Perspective* (New York: Palgrave Macmillan, 2009).

42. Michaëlle Jean, "Opening of the DiasporArt Exhibit," September 21, 2009, http://www.gg.ca/document.aspx?id=13252.

43. Sean Redmond, "Avatar Obama in the Age of Liquid Celebrity," *Celebrity Studies* 1, no. 1 (2010): 81–95.

44. On Indigenous history in New Zealand, see Fleras and Maaka, *Politics of Indigeneity*.

45. Arvind Zodgekar, "The Changing Face of New Zealand's Population and National Identity," in Liu et al., *New Zealand Identities*, 141.

46. Teaiwa and Mallon, "Ambivalent Kinships," 211.

47. Evan Poata-Smith, "The Treaty of Waitangi Settlement Process and the Changing Contours of Māori Identity," in *The Waitangi Tribunal,* ed. Janine Hayward and Nicola R. Wheen (Wellington, NZ: Bridget Williams, 2004), 168–83.

48. On biculturalism in New Zealand, see Augie Fleras and Paul Spoonley, *Recalling Aotearoa* (Auckland, NZ: Oxford University Press, 1999).

49. "Paul Henry Suspended," *Stuff,* accessed October 4, 2016, http://www.stuff.co.nz/entertainment/tv-radio/4197611/Paul-Henry-suspended.

50. The interviews were conducted on the condition that the interviewees' names remain confidential. Participants were of various island origins and frequently of mixed descent. Most were studying, some were working, and a few were unemployed.

51. Marshall, *Celebrity and Power,* 246.

52. Yiorgos Anagnostou, "Model Americans, Quintessential Greeks: Ethnic Success and Assimilation in Diaspora," *Diaspora* 12, no. 3 (2003): 288.

53. Alberoni, "Powerless 'Elite,'" 115.

54. Former governor-general Paul Reeves was Māori, but he seemed to be perceived more as a Pākehā. Jerry Mateparae, who succeeded Anand Satyanand, is also Māori.

55. New Zealanders, derogatorily, used to call peoples from Pacific islands other than New Zealand "Pacific Islanders." Pacific peoples have now in turn reappropriated the term "PI" as an expression of pride; Fairbairn-Dunlop and Makisi, *Making Our Place,* 9–18.

56. Marshall, *Celebrity and Power,* 203–41; Alberoni, "Powerless 'Elite,'" 115.

57. Hall, "Spectacle of the 'Other,'" 259.

58. Teaiwa, "Native Thoughts," 15–35.

18 | **LIVING THE WEST INDIAN DREAM**

ARCHIPELAGIC COSMOPOLITANISM AND TRIANGULATED ECONOMIES OF DESIRE IN JAMAICAN POPULAR CULTURE

Ifeoma Kiddoe Nwankwo

> We are not just nations. We are also neighbors.
>
> PRESIDENT BARACK OBAMA,
> University of the West Indies,
> Jamaica, April 9, 2015

THE HISTORY OF US-CARIBBEAN RELATIONS is a history of asymmetry, especially in terms of geography and power.[1] Natural forces produced the geographical differences, and, in conjunction with human mappings of these geographical differences, Atlantic slavery and empire created the economic disparities, establishing a hierarchical paradigm for the flow of money, goods, and people. Fundamental to this model is the idea that the archipelago is secondary to the continental nation—that, for the United States, relative geographical size indexes a divine affirmation of a relative right to dominion in and over all other arenas.[2] The notion that the geographically inferior islands constitute a blank slate upon which the United States can write whatever it wishes has long underpinned US policy in the region.[3]

Given this fact, it would be easy to sum up the US-Caribbean relationship with a blanket statement that the continental nation has been asserting and extrapolating from its purported geographical superiority by dominating the island nations, and leave it at that. That would, however, be reductive. The relationship between the United States and the Anglophone Caribbean, for instance, is also shaped by both the archipelago's and the continental nation's relationship with another island nation—England. As Carole Boyce Davies and Monica Jardine point out, the very development of Caribbean nations as such took place between the Scylla of a "retreating" British imperialism and the Charybdis of the United States' "rising regional imperialism."[4] Drawing on the words of Claudia Jones, Boyce Davies and Jardine note that there was a "family arrangement between U.S. imperialism and British imperialism whereby the U.S. as the first-born son would take over a substantial part of the family business (imperialism), while still allowing the father to manage others." As Jones put it, "the outward political responsibility (and cover) remains British, but . . . the United States controls the economic basis."[5]

Engagements between the United States and the Anglophone Caribbean are always undergirded, in significant part, by this triangulation. In US discourse, the Caribbean islands are places where the United States can carry on the "family business." Exoticization is a key aspect of that "family business," along with economic and political intervention. In British West Indian discourse, lively, loud, laughing, colorful US culture often appears as a desirable alternative to staid, laugh-like-a-lady English culture.

Triangulation has featured prominently in scholarship on the Caribbean for decades but primarily through discussions of the triangle created by the Atlantic slave trade—Africa, Europe, and the Americas. This triangle is continent-centered. An archipelagic approach to triangulation better explains representational engagements between the Anglophone Caribbean and the United States in the postcolonial era.[6] Thinking with the archipelago in our understanding of the relationships between and among the United States, the Anglophone Caribbean, and Britain facilitates greater attentivness to the perspectives coming from the Caribbean. It also, relatedly, unlocks the critical possibilities inherent in viewing all three as parts of and participants in an archipelago in which two are geographical island groups and one is a geographically continental nation composed of multiple metaphorical islands (including regional and racial ones).

Archipelagic thinking helps illuminate relational dynamics that might be missed with hierarchy-focused center-periphery analytical frameworks. It reveals approaches to representation and to identity conceptualization that are not concerned with talking back to, resisting, or revising "colonizing grammars of empire," as Elaine Stratford has termed empire's discursive technologies.[7] The Caribbean is not only an object of the gaze. It is also a gazer, as Krista Thompson also points out in *An Eye for the Tropics*.[8] Furthermore, it is not just an exoticized, consumed, represented, and constructed object. It is also an exoticizer, consumer, representer, and constructor of its Others. Those Others include the United States. The Caribbean can and does define, drive, and demand particularly configured conceptualizations and contours of interactions between itself and US-America, as well as between itself and England. Yes, the Caribbean has been the object of English and US colonialism and neocolonialism, but that fact cannot and should not hinder recognition of the ways Caribbean people are creating and circulating approaches to identity and relation that are not about resisting, mimicking, or revising English or US models.

PARADISE NEXT DOOR: THE UNITED STATES' COLONIAL INHERITANCE

Neoliberal economic policy, the predominant force in determining the course of US-Caribbean relations from the latter half of the twentieth century forward, has reinforced and drawn on the idea of the archipelago as a blank slate waiting to be written upon.[9] From the 1960s on, "differences" among the newly independent British Caribbean nations, England, and the United States over agricultural and trade policy have complicated the region's economic progress.[10] As a result, since the 1980s in particular, the Caribbean has turned to tourism as its key "export," to echo the curious terminology from a World Bank report on the region.[11] A consequence of the emphasis on this "export" has been an intensified reification of the (formerly) British Caribbean in US popular discourse as "paradise next door."[12]

Discourse on and about this neighboring idyll and, more specifically, on and about tourism to the region, is at once an extension and a revision of the mother island's relationship with the United States and Caribbean. The insistence on conceptualizing the islands as blank slates that can be made into ahistorical idylls recalls the logic of colonialism and, more specifically, its reliance on erasure. In that sense, the notion of the archipelago as the United States' "paradise next door" and its history as one of England's primary colonial outposts are linked. Colonialism relies on the idea that the colonized others are less than the colonizer and, further, that they should be thankful for the fact that the colonizer has decided to bestow his benevolence upon them. Tourism based on the "paradise next door" and "export" concepts encourages the othering of Caribbean people and the perception of them as needing and benefiting from tourists' generosity. Importantly, this tourism also fundamentally and inherently owes its very existence to a differentiation between self (tourist) and other (exotic so-called native) and, by extension, to a perceived distinction between the familiar and the unfamiliar (and therefore exotic). Stopping at that realization, however, does not leave room for noticing, let alone analyzing, perspectives from the archipelago. It does not leave room for calling attention to the role the archipelago has played in the constitution of either its continental sibling or its island parent. The archipelago, though, through its presence, its people, and its popular culture, demands this room. It deserves this room.

Thinking about the desire for the exotic in ways that go beyond centering hierarchy is an arena in which island-originated models are especially helpful. The concept and critique of Orientalism, for example, while important and historically necessary, carries within it a foregrounding of the "West's" perceptions of and perspectives on the "East." Missing is a vocabulary that facilitates the foregrounding of the "East's" view of the "West," a foregrounding that may begin with a framing that does not assume the West as the holder or center of the compass. For the Anglophone Caribbean, the vocabulary and models for thinking about relation between *this* place and *that* place arise out of a history of "migration in fact" and "migration by metaphor" (to use Edward Kamau Brathwaite's brilliant terminology) in which conceptualizing oneself as always already international is a fundamental and necessary element of life and identity.[13] This place and that place are both always already part of everyone's universe. Everyone is always already a citizen of the world, including especially of the Atlantic and global archipelagoes, in addition to being a citizen of his/her island nation.

The impact of this worldview on the modern-day circulation of desire between the Caribbean and the United States is particularly evident in appearances of the Anglophone Caribbean in US-American television, film, and advertising, and, reciprocally, appearances of the United States in Jamaican television, film, and advertising. To illustrate this point by way of specific examples, the remainder of this essay centers on popular media (music, television, and advertising) produced between 1990 and 2008, an era that saw a remarkable uptick in representations of the Anglophone Caribbean in US popular media. The moment was particularly unprecedented in terms of representations created by and featuring US African Americans. This was the era that saw the creation, to give a few of the many of possible examples, of *How Stella Got Her Groove Back* (1998) and the African American tourism boom it inspired; of Miss Cleo the "Jamaican" psychic that TV viewers could "call for you free readin'" (1997–2003); of the *Caribbean Rhythms* show on BET hosted by the often bikini-clad and always last-name-less "Rachel"; of Steven Seagal's movie *Marked for Death* (1990), featuring demonic Jamaican drug posse members; of *Cool Runnings* (1993), the John Candy- and Doug E. Doug–led movie based on the true story of the Jamaican bobsled team; of the Caribbean immigrant-focused "Hey Mon" skits on the Wayans family–driven sketch comedy show *In Living Color* (1990–1994); and of the initiation of long-running Parrot Bay and Malibu rum ads that used images of the Caribbean and partying as their primary selling point.

This was an era in which the US economy became increasingly focused on the other Americas (the North American Free Trade Agreement's passing is but one manifestation), and it was a moment that saw the popularity of black British musicians such as Soul II Soul, Mark Morrison, and Monie Love take off. This was the era in which, as Sean Goudie reminds us, Bill Clinton publicly described the United States as "a Caribbean nation."[14] The period is also bookended by president George H. W. Bush's hosting of Jamaican prime minister Michael Manley's first official visit to Washington in May 1990 and his granddaughter

Jenna Bush's official visit to Jamaica "on a fact-finding mission exploring issues concerning Jamaican children" in 2007.[15]

Economies of desire for the exotic undergird representational relations between the archipelago and the continental United States, and unfinished business with the "mother island" has a profound and continuing impact on those engagements. Probing them therefore challenges "the colonial myth that islands are peripheral to the march of world history"—and, more specifically, to the march of the continental behemoth that is the United States—and provides a way to think *with* rather than just about islands.[16] The United States' representational engagements with the Caribbean actually illuminate the continental nation's vulnerabilities, including particularly intranational fissures and postcolonial anxieties, buried in the discourses of the divinely, terrestrially united nation. This is the nation that because of its continental geography and economic power is conventionally understood as the more modern, more cosmopolitan, more *everything good* opposite of the presumably backward, insular, less-everything-modern islands. In quotidian US parlance in the late twentieth and early twenty-first centuries, "the islands" and "the Caribbean" are synecdochic, representing the "take it easy" life and the "no problem, mon" attitude presumed to be central to island weltanschauung.[17] At the same time, Caribbean representational engagements with the United States lay bare distinctive models for understanding why and how cosmopolitanism can be understood as fundamental to archipelagic identity and, further, why and how it might be useful for Americanists to envision US-Caribbean relations using an archipelagic model in which the United States is part of an archipelago and constitutes a "world of islands."[18] As Brian Russell Roberts and Michelle Stephens put it, "Landmasses traditionally conceived of as continents may be reframed as islands that are constituent parts, rather than continental administrators, of the global meta-archipelago."[19]

In her meditation on tourism in the Caribbean, Jamaica Kincaid opines, "Every native everywhere lives a life of overwhelming and crushing banality and boredom and desperation and depression, and every deed, good and bad, is an attempt to forget this. Every native would like to find a way out, every native would like a rest, every native would like a tour."[20] In Kincaid's model, in which the notion of nativeness refers not to Indigenous roots but to social construction, everyone is a native of somewhere. Only financial limitations prevent all natives from becoming tourists. In an analogous vein, US-born Marxist political theorist Fredric Jameson notes "the Utopian vocation"—Jameson could have just as easily made this observation about the Utopian vacation—"can be identified . . . by the persistent and obsessive [search for] a single-shot solution to all our ills. And this must be a solution so obvious and self-explanatory that every reasonable person will grasp it."²¹ Dreaming, whether of "find[ing] a way out . . . a rest [and a] tour" or of finding a "single-shot solution to all our ills," seems fundamental to human existence.

Both Kincaid and Jameson index a deep-seated desire for alternatives and escapes, for a more satisfying existence—a structure of desire that is fundamental to the inequalities and ideologies of a West born out of capitalism's intertwined relation to transatlantic slavery. Jameson explicitly states, "Utopias seem to be by-products of Western modernity."²² Kincaid repeatedly points to the air of superiority and willful obliviousness she identifies as endemic among the swarms of white tourists to the (formerly) British Caribbean as constituting a colonial palimpsest, as evidence of structures of relation erected during the era of chattel slavery. The escapist desire both writers spotlight has been a key factor shaping interactions between the peoples of the United States and the Caribbean. Financial concerns, on the part of states as well as of individuals, have operated alongside this entrenched need for exotic, alternative routes, resulting in economies of desire that manifest themselves in the ubiquity of the United States and the Caribbean in each others' popular discourses. These representations function as mirrors, albeit at times holographic ones, enabling people in each site to refine, validate, and occasionally critique their collective self-concepts and national imaginaries. The Caribbean is part of the (US) American Dream. The United States is part of the West Indian Dream.

THE EXOTIC UNITED STATES: PERSPECTIVES FROM "THE ISLANDS"

The very different yet linked relationships among the Caribbean island nations, the mother island, and the United States became particularly clear in the year 2002. That year saw the televising in Jamaica of the visit of Queen Elizabeth II to the island as part of her Golden Jubilee celebration. The Jamaican television coverage included extended live video of uniformed Jamaican schoolchildren cheering the queen as she moved through the capital city's streets in her motorcade and as she exited the motorcade for her visit to the island nation's Parliament. It also included live coverage of the official ceremonial welcome extended to the queen, the official head of the Jamaican state, by the Jamaican Parliament, and of her unsurprisingly paternalistic speech to Parliament. British Caribbean people were (and still are in some cases) taught to revere Mother England, who encourages us to bring out and show off our "proper" behavior—and who is definitely not seen as at the cutting edge of global youth culture.²³

But the United States is *el ultimo*, the essence of what's cool now. For Caribbean people, the United States—particularly the vision of it as the "happening place," regardless of whether one is trying to improve her economic situation or her coolness quotient—occupies a significant place in the mind and in daily life.[24] Debates about the impact of the US cultural presence on Caribbean youth are particularly intense, including the research-based conclusions of Fitzroy A. Baptiste that "whether intended deliberately or not, U.S. cable TV is waging U.S. cultural imperialism on the mind of Caribbean peoples."[25] The year of the queen's Golden Jubilee also saw the release of a song that Lady Saw (the Jamaican "queen of dancehall" music) recorded with US popular music group No Doubt (titled "Underneath It All"; released on No Doubt's album *Rock Steady*), as well as a few of the many Lady Saw solo songs that feature US-American vernaculars, accents, and references.[26] Popular culture is certainly a key arena in which the intertwined US and Caribbean economies of desire for the exotic show themselves.

There is absolutely no doubt about the ubiquity of US television in the West Indies. There is also no doubt that Caribbean people are making decisions about whether and how to incorporate aspects of US culture into their own—decisions based on particular notions of the value added by these foreign cultural elements. The United States is no less exotic to the Caribbean-based Caribbean person than the Caribbean is to the US-American. Certainly, historical and contemporary power disparities between the two have had a profound impact on their peoples' relative ability to widely disseminate and normalize their image of the other. This does not mean, however, that the exoticization goes one way or that the exoticized are simply passive objects. To succeed in thinking with and from the island rather than just about it, we have to consider the figurative ways in which the West Indian Dream—Caribbean desires for the United States—can be in fact very substantive.

Class and gender dimensions of the valuing of being overseas surface particularly clearly in the television work of a founding parent of contemporary Jamaican popular culture. Oliver Samuels (b. 1948) has for decades been one of the major figures on the Jamaican performance scene. He has been praised as "probably Jamaica's most beloved comedic figure, in large part because he represents that part of ourselves that we most like to mock and celebrate."[27] His wildly successful sitcom, *Oliver at Large*, further elevated his standing among Jamaicans and brought his talents to a wider audience than ever before.[28] One series of the sitcom's episodes represents the value among working-class Jamaicans of knowing about, traveling "very regular" to, and having items from or related to the "fareign" (or at least being successful at making a pretense of it). The main character, Olivius Adams (played by Samuels), goes to the airport to depart for his trip to the United States. The humor inheres in the gap between his knowledge and the actual mechanics of travel. When he first attempts to report for a flight, he does not even know that he needs a visa (and therefore does not have one). Nevertheless, he pretends to have the knowledge needed to help a fellow traveler who is not as knowledgeable as he is about traveling to 'Merica. Once his lie is discovered, she ends up mocking him for his lack of knowledge.

On his second attempt, we see that he now has a visa, along with all the other accoutrements he believes are needed for a visit to the United States, including "aise muffins" (earmuffs) and a scarf. He still does not know nearly enough, though, from the perspective of his fellow Jamaicans. He attempts to take a large box as a carry-on, and he fails to understand why they cannot just "strap it pon top of de plane," as one would on a country bus. In addition, he is terrified of the metal detector and initially refuses to go through it alone, screaming like a banshee when it beeps as he passes through. In order to be funny as presented, the episode clearly presumes an audience that is itself familiar with the information that Olivius lacks—they do, in fact, "travel regular, very regular," and would most certainly not find themselves in Olivius's neophyte position. Familiarity with traveling, then, becomes the glue that bonds the Jamaican audience members to each other. The value of the United States for Jamaicans is presented as epistemological and social, with the representation of travel to the States not about consuming (the country) or about having the freedom to consume (common in US-American popular discourses), but rather about being able to display a knowledge of the ins and outs of travel in particular, and about a cosmopolitan sophistication more generally. Travel to the United States is so basic to Jamaican life that anyone not knowing how it is done prompts laughter. The United States is at once exotic and familiar. It is at once a valuable foreign trinket that we want to show off that we own, epistemologically, and an object that is so familiar to us that we can laugh at others to whom it is not familiar. It is at once foreign enough that we can seek and get "respec'" for knowing about it and familiar enough that we can see knowing it as basic knowledge that every Jamaican should have, unless s/he wants to be laughed at. The United States is part of our archipelagic identity. It is part of our archipelago.

The *Oliver at Large* scenario therefore simultaneously mocks those who do not know and who do not "travel regular, very regular," magnifying the class commentary that underpins the episode. The situation is only funny because Olivius is lower class, as signaled at the very beginning by the camera shots of his home, by the fact that he must take a taxi to the airport rather than relying on his own car or on a friend with a car, and by the contrast between his language and that of the airline staff. The episode reveals, comments on, and rejects the idea that cosmopolitanism belongs only to, or should belong only to, formally educated, monied people. Through its representation of Olivius's lack of knowledge as humorous, the episode posits what might be termed a Jamaican Dream—a country full of Jamaican cosmopolites and devoid of people like Olivius Adams, who can only pretend to be in the know. Everyone knows. As if to emphasize the ubiquity of Jamaicans' international engagement and awareness, the person he is visiting in New York is a Jamaican woman. It is telling that Samuels's character Olivius is the only person in the whole airport and on the whole plane who is not familiar with the how-tos of air travel to the United States. By the end of the episode, though, the Jamaican Dream has been achieved and the now travel-savvy Olivius has settled into his journey to "Bronx, 'Merica."

This representation of working-class Jamaicans traveling also, however, highlights an ongoing anxiety about the damage to true "roots" Jamaicanness that could be caused by too much openness to interactions with the United States. Recall Baptiste's contention that, "whether intended deliberately or not, U.S. cable TV is waging U.S. cultural imperialism on the mind of Caribbean peoples."[29] Because of the "culture of migration" that is now part of the basic "cultural orientation" of people in the region, particularly in the mid- to late twentieth century, there has been the question of what all this movement means about the definition of Jamaicanness (as well as for other national identities). Neither Olivius nor those who work at the airport nor those who travel with him are portrayed as being in any way torn between being US-American and being Jamaican. The object of their national or linguistic allegiance is not in question. In addition, they are united in their valuing of travel and knowledge of how to travel to the United States, even though the disparities in their access to that knowledge are clear.

The most palpable tension in the episode occurs between Jamaicans of different classes—more specifically, between their different visions of propriety.[30] Jamaican media icon Fae Ellington plays the airline check-in agent, speaking in a fashion conventionally marked as indicative of an individual who is middle or upper class—someone who has been educated to speak the Queen's English, with all the flourishes, pronunciations, and inflections that mark the educated bourgeoisie. The contrast between Ellington's speech and Olivius's deep patois is heightened by her condescending tone when she is explaining to him why he cannot carry his cardboard box onto the plane. Throughout much of the episode, markers of Olivius's lower-class status are interwoven with indices of his ignorance about travel to the United States. The oversized boxes that he wishes to take with him set him off from the other passengers, an otherness only made more pronounced when he does not understand why they cannot be strapped onto the top of the plane. In his relationship to the bourgeois culture of manners, Olivius differs from the flight attendant on the plane (he calls her "waitress") and other characters marked by their language or comportment as being a class step above.

A working-class yet travel-savvy model is also presented, though, and illustrates the extent to which, despite profound class tensions, the Jamaican Dream argued for in the episode is not about having or not having money: it is about travel sophistication. Olivius's counterpart on the plane, Brenda, is a clearly working-class woman who has, in fact, traveled regular, very regular. After initial strife between them, due largely to Brenda's unwillingness to move out of Olivius's assigned seat and his concomitant insult-laden tirade (much could be said here in terms of the aforementioned disparate relationship with bourgeois culture's notion of propriety), they become bosom buddies. Significantly, the magnet that brings them together is real, home-cooked, quintessentially Jamaican food. She brings hers out, and Olivius salivates, but she refuses to share it with him. He then "cuts his eye" at her by bringing out his food, and she salivates. Their gastronomic Jamaicanness brings them together, striking a balance between roots and routes—between the desires to travel regular, very regular, to the United States and to stay steadfast in their true Jamaicanness at the same time.

The *Oliver at Large* episode's presentation of Brenda, a working-class woman, as the one who has the most knowledge about traveling regular, very regular, reveals a recurrent marking of cosmopolitanism as a female domain in West Indian literature, music, and popular performance culture. It is a gendered dimension that is also indexed in Lady Saw's collaboration with No Doubt and her uses of US African American ways of speaking and singing as one of her artistic registers. The world (of linguistic and artistic styles) is hers, and in drawing on it she posits an argument about how and why the international is valuable and how it should be connected and marked as intersecting with the local.[31] The United States is at once the foreign and the familiar. It is at once an exotic accoutrement and a key element of the local. We see further evidence of this in Lady Saw's song "Superstar," which includes the lines "Pimp Daddy, and mi a di Pimp Mummy," "'riches' gyal pon the block who run di Sout," "I got all the connections, to the biggest names in the nation," "Mi related to great Cecil Charlton," and "Mi have more money dan Paris Hilton." (Importantly the song also references the third point on the Anglophone Atlantic triangle to which I am calling attention in this essay: "mi new ride wey mi ship from Englan.'"[32]) Travel belongs to Lady Saw and Brenda: it is they, and their working-class women peers, who enable productive engagement between Jamaican people and the world beyond the island and ensure that that engagement does not lead to detachment from the local, the particular.

The Jamaica Tourist Board's website during the era under study here sought to reflect international intersections with the local, but had to work around the images of the region that permeate the discourses that educate potential tourists.

The website walks a fine line between catering to potential tourists and evincing national pride—in other words, it does not completely erase the cultural agency and dignity of the "natives." The tourism board even tempts nudists, saying, "If tan lines are a pet peeve or nudity a fetish, Jamaica is the place to bare it all with more nude beaches than any other Caribbean island. Our au-naturel beaches range from sedate and relaxing to wild and crazy, so pick a sandy patch that's right for you ... the perfect all-body tan waits for you on this tropic isle."[33] The language mirrors the ads in US tourist brochures and websites, invoking the hedonistic, healing, ready-to-be-consumed Caribbean. In describing and defining the tourist's experience in Jamaica in the way it does, the website plays into the white tourist–black native presumption indexed and criticized by Kincaid, among others.

While ensuring that those who desire the Caribbean see exactly what they want on the website, though, the tourism board has also attempted to provide a fuller picture of the nation and its people than US-based websites do. In particular, the site has aimed to foreground the complexity and diversity of the island by highlighting its different regions and through its "Meet the People" program. By highlighting the US-American artists scheduled to perform in Jamaica, the tourism board markets the country as a living intellectual and cultural museum and an active entertainment venue, not just a series of beaches, bodies, and bacchanalian celebrations. The site has even featured an "Island Trivia" question—Marcus Garvey has sometimes featured prominently. The point is that the perceived possibilities for the international projection of national identity are determined by the overwhelming power of not just US representations of the region but also of the nation's cash—more specifically, the funds brought by the tourists who desire the Caribbean as constructed by US popular discourse.

So although there is room for texts produced for Caribbean national and regional audiences to examine the dynamic relationship between national identity and "ovah sea," and even to incorporate the valuing of the foreign into definitions of national identity, the economic frameworks set in motion by Columbus's arrival in the Americas still raise the question of whether and how it will ever be possible to change the persistent images of the Caribbean in US popular discourse, particularly if those images are replicated, albeit with a difference and under financial duress, by Caribbean governments themselves. It is this representational bind that makes the issues discussed here not simply US-Caribbean but global. Desire flows throughout the American archipelago and in the "global meta-archipelago" in multiple directions.[34] The (US) American Dream and the West Indian Dream reinforce one another, and even trade on one another, continually rehearsing dynamics set in motion under English imperialism. At the same time, as evident in the preceding discussion of *Oliver at Large*, West Indian people have developed and are developing approaches to seeing and representing the United States as at once both foreign and familiar that are not so much, or even at all, about those dynamics as they are about naturalizing and showcasing a cosmopolitan awareness that is "broader than Broadway" (to use reggae and dancehall artist Barrington Levy's phrasing).

RETHINKING THE UNITED STATES' EXOTIC CARIBBEAN

The meaning of US-American national identity is as porous (all the while working to appear impermeable) as that of other nations in the Americas.[35] In general, as Julia Kristeva suggests in *Strangers to Ourselves*, the Other is a space for working through the self.[36] The historical relationships between the United States and other nations in the region—via the slave trade and Manifest Destiny and its offspring—have made this process even more complicated. Whether the image perpetuated is of bodies, beaches, and bacchanal, or of pitiful children who must be taken care of and protected from themselves and their own communities, or of laboring hands and bodies at US textile factories on the island, the fundamental hierarchy remains. Thinking archipelagically, we have to recognize that the reflexive US-Caribbean representations constitute a search on the parts of all parties for ways to order, make sense of, and make selves and nations out of the histories that continue to bind the national subjectivities to each other. It is not just that Jamaica is periphery to the US metropole: the Anglophone Caribbean and the US dream of each other, and Mother England is always already present in the shadows as a contrast to both US and Anglophone Caribbean visions of the ideal self and life.

A range of US businesses have sought to harness the Caribbean's symbolic value by attaching distinctively Caribbean words to products and services, regardless of whether they have any actual connection to the region. Their ads portray the Caribbean as ground zero in the "take it easy" life universe. This notion of the Caribbean as the ultimate antithesis of "taking life seriously" seems to be everywhere, from restaurant menus to clothing brands. The Seattle-based leisurewear label Tommy Bahama describes itself as a "purveyor of island lifestyles"; website visitors can join the label's online Paradise Nation community, the motto of which is "Relax." At Max and Erma's, an Ohio-based casual restaurant chain, flavor is added to a simple plate of grilled chicken breast with pineapples just by naming it "Caribbean Chicken" and anchoring the dish description with the phrase "like a little tropical vacation." Max and Erma's framing of this entrée exemplifies the simultaneous fungibility and fixity of "Caribbean" as a notion in the United States. Uses of the Caribbean are often bound up with two related, quintessentially US beliefs—that consumption is the answer to everything (and, therefore, the key to happiness) and that anything can be sold so long as it has consumer demand. If one can find the means, anything one wants—or at least a pared-down version of it—can be bought. If one cannot afford a real island getaway at this moment, at least one can have this Caribbean Chicken approximating a rather vague sense of what an island getaway should feel like. One can undertake what might productively be called virtual tourism, or synecdochic tourism.

In late twentieth- and early twenty-first century US popular discourse, the image of "the islands" as a site of endless partying and eternal joy, the materialization of the dream of having a rest, taking a tour, or finding something that will help you forget all ills, even if only temporarily, predominates.[37] This vision is reinforced by, among other media representations, a plethora of commercials. In one ad for Parrot Bay Rum in 2005, for example, the humor of the ad inheres in the ridiculous possibility that British Caribbean people would actually be concerned about serious issues affecting their daily lives. One version of the ad begins with semiserious discussion between two poor Caribbean men about the worth of a donkey. The conversation is interrupted by the arrival from the sky of a brightly colored party bus along with dozens of dancing Caribbean men and women partying as if there's no tomorrow. A white male tourist emerges from the bus, saying, "Now *this* is real island life," making the point that a conversation about one's basic means of transportation and livelihood is not the "real island life."[38]

A slightly more recent Parrot Bay Rum spot (from 2006) reiterates the association of the Caribbean with hedonism and with the "take it easy" lifestyle but also, curiously, detaches that from the Caribbean. By removing markers of Caribbean particularity and replacing them with synecdoches indexing "the islands," the ad's creators empty the Caribbean of its specificity and position it, instead, as a generic symbol. The commercial features a partying master of ceremonies, not unlike the happy, shouting master of pep familiar to visitors at the Caribbean's all-inclusive resorts. Of course, he is wearing the brightly colored shirt that tourists who never leave the safety of their resorts might be led to believe is the native garb of Caribbean people. Played by an individual whose horrific accent absolutely undercuts his pretension to Caribbeanness, the character's affect is somewhere between Al Jolson and a bad Harry "Day-O" Belafonte impression. The slightly but not quite brown, not quite green, not quite yellow, not quite right complexion of his skin and his clownish eyebrows make determining whether he is a brown man in islandface or a white man in brownface a special challenge. The point is made: bright colors plus semitropical accented pep master plus dancing equals freedom from one's cares. Parrot Bay Rum can get you there, regardless of how close to or far away you are (or he is) from the Caribbean Sea or Caribbeanness. The message is, buy this thing and get the "little tropical vacation," whether actual or metaphorical, you so desire.

The portrayal of the Caribbean in an ad for Malibu Rum (from 2006) is perhaps, however, the most revelatory—and insidious. It underscores the extent to which the persistence of the desire to represent the Caribbean in US popular discourse is bound up with US-American nationalist discourse. The ad begins with a Caribbean voice narrating, "Malibu asks, what if we Caribbeans took life as seriously as the rest of the world?" The Caribbean villagers discover cellular phones, albeit ancient and oversized ones. They begin to boast to each other about the features of personal phones—one man, for example, brags that his phone has an address book, and the camera cuts to the miniature lined notebook attached to his phone. Another man has a phone strapped to his head with what looks to be a shoelace. Another is proud of the fact that his phone has three hours of battery life, as the camera pans to the wires that connect his phone to an old dirty car battery. Yet another rides a donkey in circles while on his phone. The one woman, wearing a head-tie with a front knot, asks the person calling her to call her back because she is "busy." The spot ends with the whole village screaming in horror as one of the men stands in the sea with one of these antiquated phones saying, "Can you hear me now?" echoing the catch phrase of contemporaneous Verizon Wireless advertisements.[39]

The implication of the Malibu spot is that Caribbean people are the antithesis of today's globalized modernity—they are technologically retrograde, have no awareness of how far behind they are, and live in a bubble (or perhaps a crab barrel) in which they know about and compare themselves only to each other.[40] By simultaneously recalling the ongoing academic and popular conversations about the impact of cell phone usage on driving, the ad indexes the presumably huge intellectual, economic, cultural, and technological gulf between the United States and the Caribbean as imagined by a liquor company. The purported humor of the woman's statement that she is busy works because she is the opposite of busy as it is defined in the modern Western world, a world of which these people are represented as being at the periphery. In contrast, "busy" to Caribbean people apparently means just sitting in a shack on the beach.

The Caribbean characters—caricatures—in the Malibu ad are presented not just as being on the margins of the modern world or as unbelievably late to grasp the value of becoming modern: they seem fundamentally incapable of catching up because they lack the cultural and intellectual capital necessary to become truly modern. They are capable only of mimicking the real moderns by repeating their words ("I'll put you on hold," "My phone has a three hours' battery time," "Can you hear me now?"). This backward, bacchanaling Caribbean functions as a countermodel to the United States' notion of itself as the ultimate modern nation. At the same time, it creates a space for the surfacing of doubt about the ultimate worth of that pursuit and position. Recall that the Parrot

Bay campaign's catchphrase is "What if we took life as seriously as you do?" and that the Malibu ad's is a version thereof. A side effect of the ad, one likely not anticipated by the producers of this "iconic brand," is that this representation of the Caribbean allows US-Americans to ask whether there is such a thing as "too modern," and to consider—if only for six nights and seven days, and if only for the half of that period that they have their wits about them—whether the endless pursuit of the (US) American Dream is really the best possible way to live their lives. The portrayal of the Caribbean as at once an antithesis of and antidote to modernity also speaks to the urges toward both self-control and hedonism inherent in twentieth-century US-Americans—their nation is at once Puritan and prurient.[41] So, while the aforementioned portrayals of the Caribbean illustrate ethnocentric US-American notions of the Caribbean and its people, they also implicitly reveal fissures in US national ideology.

Figurations of the Caribbean such as those delineated earlier in this chapter pretend as if slavery never happened in the Caribbean.[42] At the end of the Malibu Rum spot, the commercial's catchphrase is repeated, with a slight twist: "If we Caribbeans took life as seriously as the rest of the world, we would not have invented Malibu." The absolute negation, erasure, and overwriting of the painful history of rum production in the Caribbean here reflects just the sort of conceptual contortions necessary for the production of contemporary images of the Caribbean in US popular discourse. According to the ad, these people are what would typically be characterized as lazy and shiftless based on Western work paradigms. The region has been productive only when its people have reveled in this antibusyness version of busyness. It is as if none of the horrible practices that have historically been concomitant with sugar and rum production in the region were continuing now, and certainly none during the production of that bottle of Malibu Rum that the ad encourages its target audience to buy: "Malibu coconut rum has its beginnings on the beautiful Caribbean island of Barbados.... The distillery overlooks the beach and white sands of Black Rock. The setting is wonderfully tropical and as easy going as Malibu rum itself.... Malibu adds the unique and subtle taste of the true Caribbean to your drink." Evacuating the history of conquest, slavery, and colonialism, and its contemporary offspring, in turn enables the envisioning of the Caribbean as "as easygoing as Malibu rum itself." In these portrayals, the Caribbean is a site of play, never of work.[43]

On the contrary, the generic representations of the region as a "take it easy" kind of place are narratives of the specific sorts of freedom the region has to offer to the US-American visitor. As with Max and Erma's "Caribbean Chicken" entrée, often the freedom promised is a classically US-American freedom—the freedom to consume. The (US) American Dream grants the freedom to consume Caribbean flora, fauna, and people, laying bare the bond between US-American tourism discourse and Manifest Destiny ideology; we even read that "Jamaica's fabulous Dunn's River Falls in Ocho Rios, its Blue Mountains National Park and the [eighteenth-century] plantation houses of Montego Bay offer a view that fulfills a Caribbean fantasy."[44] The chronologically unspecific location of the "Caribbean fantasy" illustrates how easy it is to slip between slavery-era and contemporary US ideas of the archipelago, linking colonialism and tourism.[45]

The center-periphery paradigm, while useful for pointing out the historical palimpsests at work here, including underlying links between US and English tropicalizations of the region (to mirror Frances Aparicio's and Krista Thompson's uses of the term),[46] is absolutely inadequate for explaining all of the motivating factors behind and implications of the coexisting US-American fantasy and of the Jamaican use of it to package the island for consumption. Center-periphery also does not provide a way to account for the Jamaican Dream of epistemologically possessing the United States or for the degree to which that dream rests on an idea of US-America as both foreign and familiar—as both an exotic other and as an already known quantity. Cosmopolitanism and triangulation, in contrast—as concepts that emphasize nonhierarchical relationality—are more useful. Françoise Lionnet's argument for a creole form of cosmopolitanism helps to illuminate why, in particular, such an idea is valuable for revealing dimensions and drivers of relationality that may be missed otherwise. She criticizes scholars who she sees as "wedded to a view of cosmopolitan universalism that excludes the possibility of its actual transformation . . . in the contact zones of the region and their creolized life worlds. These worlds, shaped by movement along intersecting axes that connected historical nodes of economic activity on land and at sea, remain a crucial part of contemporary geopolitics."[47] She points to an archipelago as consisting of "an ethnically diverse mix of creolized multilingual populations whose concrete experiences of 'actually existing cosmopolitanisms' . . . can serve to modify the parameters by which scholars construct the idea of the cosmopolitan."[48]

In a similar vein, I am arguing that "migration in fact" and "migration by metaphor" (Brathwaite's terms)—"concrete experiences of 'actually existing cosmopolitanisms'"—long fundamental to Caribbean life, along with transatlantic triangulation, have ensured that cosmopolitanism is regularly embedded in Anglophone Caribbean literature, cultural products, and worldviews, including those discussed in this essay.[49] The West Indian Dream of experiencing and taking epistemological possession of / knowing the world, along with the desire to publicly showcase that familiarity with the world, including the at once exotic and familiar United States, recurs as a key element of Caribbean individuals' approaches to conceptualizing, engaging, and visualizing themselves as imbricated in the world. It is an archipelagic cosmopolitanism that is continuously being defined, redefined, considered, or enacted. It is an archipelagic cosmopolitanism that is always there and always already rooted in Relation.

Archipelagic American studies offers a new avenue for documenting, contextualizing, and interpreting Relation through cosmopolitanism and triangulation at the same time. It facilitates recognition of the fact that people are conceptualizing and actuating Relation in ways that go beyond center-periphery, beyond resisting, mimicking, or revising, and into claiming citizenship within, among, and across lands, seas, and sensibilities.

NOTES

Epigraph: "President Barack Obama Town Hall at UWI, Jamaica—April 9, 2015," https://www.youtube.com/watch?v=K6wWyHikpBg

1. Anthony Maingot and Wilfredo Lozano, *The United States and the Caribbean: Challenges of an Asymmetrical Relationship* (Boulder, CO: Westview, 1994).

2. The works of Louis Pérez, Gwendolyn Midlo Hall, and Harvey Neptune stand out in their explication of the methodologies, manifestations, and mechanics of the impact in Cuba, Haiti, and Trinidad, respectively. Manifest Destiny and the Monroe Doctrine are visions linked by their positing of the Caribbean and Latin America as the United States' backyard, as an area over which the United States has dominion. These visions were not foreign policy statements but rather "a set of discourses through which US Americans formulated national identity as well as foreign policy," discourses that were reflective of and reflected in a wider cultural imagination; Gretchen Murphy, *Hemispheric Imaginings: The Monroe Doctrine and Narratives of US Empire* (Durham, NC: Duke University Press, 2005), 13, 17.

3. See, for example, Elaine Savory, "Utopia, Dystopia, and Caribbean Heterotopia: Writing/Reading the Small Island," *New Literatures Review* 47–48 (2011): 36.

4. Carole Boyce Davies and Monica Jardine, "Imperial Geographies and Caribbean Nationalism: At the Border between 'A Dying Colonialism' and US Hegemony," *New Centennial Review* 3, no. 3 (2003): 152.

5. Davies and Jardine, "Imperial Geographies," 161.

6. Anglophone Africa, of course, has also been a key player in this family relationship. The configuration of its role has changed over the centuries, though. It does not play as significant of a direct role in the relationship in the time period that is the primary focus of this essay—the late twentieth century.

7. Elaine Stratford, "The Idea of the Archipelago: Contemplating Island Relations," *Island Studies Journal* 8, no. 1 (2013): 4.

8. Krista Thompson, *An Eye for the Tropics: Tourism, Photography, and Framing the Caribbean Picturesque* (Durham, NC: Duke University Press, 2007).

9. As explicated in great, and horrifying, detail by a former Jamaican prime minister, the late Michael Manley (and unwittingly by an International Monetary Fund executive), in Stephanie Black's film *Life and Debt* (2002), the machinations of the IMF (and its partners the World Bank, the Inter-American Development Bank, and others), the US government, and US corporations locked Caribbean nations in an

economic bind (perhaps more appropriately called an economic bondage) from which they have yet to extricate themselves.

10. Clive Y. Thomas provides an in-depth analysis of how specific economic mechanisms set in motion by conquest and slavery laid the foundation for the economic situation of the twentieth century. See *The Poor and the Powerless: Economic Policy and Change in the Caribbean* (New York: Latin American Bureau, 1988). Also see Eric Williams, *Capitalism and Slavery* (1944; repr., New York: Russell and Russell, 1961).

11. World Bank, "OECS: Towards a New Growth Agenda," accessed October 11, 2016, http://go.worldbank.org/VROOGU0TT0. Although the IMF and World Bank contradict each other on whether the preferential trade pact the United States has made with the Caribbean has helped the Caribbean move closer to the agencies' goals for the region, their unanimity on recommendations for the Caribbean—liberalize trade policy, and make the local labor force more attractive, mobile, and available to internal and external business—is striking; World Bank, "A Time to Choose: Caribbean Development in the 21st Century," accessed May 19, 2006, http://go.worldbank.org/Q6CLMHE8G1; Office of US Trade Representative, *Sixth Report to Congress on the Operation of the Caribbean Basin Economic Recovery Act*, accessed May 19, 2006, http://ustr.gov/Trade_Development/Preference_Programs/CBI/Section_Index.html.

12. Paget, "Coco Reef Resort Bermuda: 'Paradise Next Door,'" accessed May 20, 2006. http://www.tripadvisor.com/ShowUserReviews-g147259-d148955-r4600798-Coco_Reef_Resort_Bermuda-Paget_Bermuda.html. That is not to say that tourism in the Caribbean began in the 1980s. Frank Fonda Taylor's *To Hell with Paradise: A History of the Jamaican Tourist Industry* (Pittsburgh: University of Pittsburgh Press, 1993) illustrates through the example of Jamaica the extent to which it was concomitant with the rise of US imperialism in the region in the mid- to late nineteenth century.

13. Edward Kamau Brathwaite, *Roots* (Ann Arbor: University of Michigan Press, 1993), 8.

14. Sean X. Goudie, *Creole America: The West Indies and the Formation of Literature and Culture in the New Republic* (Philadelphia: University of Pennsylvania Press, 2006), 1.

15. See George H. W. Bush, "Remarks following Discussions with Prime Minister Michael Manley of Jamaica," American Presidency Project, May 3, 1990, http://www.presidency.ucsb.edu/ws/?pid=18446; and Davia Morrison Panos, "Jenna Bush Bowls for Children on Visit to Jamaica," *Jamaica Observer*, May 22, 2007, http://www.jamaicaobserver.com/news/123317_Jenna-Bush-bowls-for-children-on-visit-to-Jamaica.

16. Elizabeth DeLoughrey, "Introduction: Of Oceans and Islands," special issue, *New Literature Review* 47–48 (2011): 2; the notion of thinking with and through islands and archipelagoes has been discussed by Elaine Stratford et al., "Envisioning the Archipelago," *Island Studies Journal* 6, no. 2 (2011): 113–30; John R. Gillis, *Islands of the Mind: How the Human Imagination Created the Atlantic World* (New York: Palgrave Macmillan, 2004); and Jonathan Pugh, "Island Movements: Thinking with the Archipelago," *Island Studies Journal* 8, no. 1 (2013): 9–24.

17. This is especially the case when the islands being discussed are not seen as politically threatening (Cuba) or as barbaric and lawless (Haiti).

18. Godfrey Baldacchino, ed., *A World of Islands: An Island Studies Reader* (Charlottetown, Canada: Institute of Island Studies, University of Prince Edward Island, 2007).

19. Brian Russell Roberts and Michelle Stephens, "Archipelagic American Studies and the Caribbean," *Journal of Transnational American Studies* 5, no. 1 (2013): 13.

20. Jamaica Kincaid, *A Small Place* (New York: Farrar, Straus, and Giroux, 1988), 18–19.

21. Fredric Jameson, *Archaeologies of the Future: The Desire Called Utopia and Other Science Fictions* (London: Verso, 2005), 11.

22. Jameson, *Archaeologies*, 11.

23. Compare this, for example, to President Obama's trip to Jamaica in April 2015, and most specifically to his town hall visit with Jamaican college students at the University of the West Indies. Obama demonstrated his coolness by beginning the town hall engagement speaking Jamaican patois, and, even group community-indexing Jamaican patois: "Greetings, massive. . . . Waah gwan?" (Greetings, family / my folks. . . . What's goin' on / What's happenin'?). Interestingly enough, Obama goes on to think with the island, verbally constructing an archipelagic link between Jamaica and his Hawaiian home: "It is great to be in beautiful Jamaica, not only because [I have to be here on official business] but because I just like the vibe here. I was born on an island and it was warm so I feel right at home [here]"; "President Barack Obama Town Hall at UWI, Jamaica—April 9, 2015," https://www.youtube.com/watch?v=K6wWyHikpBg.

24. Sociologists have done extensive work on how viewing US television programs affects Caribbean youth's attitudes, behaviors, and sense of national identity. Particularly insightful are the studies outlined in Ewart Skinner, "Empirical Research on Mass Communication and Cultural Domination in the Caribbean," in *Culture and Mass Communication in the Caribbean: Domination, Dialogue, Dispersion*, ed. Humphrey A. Regis (Gainesville: University Press of Florida, 2001), 37–62.

25. Fitzroy A. Baptiste, "United States–Caribbean Relations from World War II to the Present: The Social Nexus," in *U.S.-Caribbean Relations: Their Impact on Peoples and Culture*, ed. Ransford W. Palmer (Westport, CT: Praeger, 1998), 36.

26. Lady Saw also traveled and performed with No Doubt on the album tour. Video of their Worcester, Massachusetts, performance of "Underneath It All" on October 20, 2002, is posted on YouTube, https://www.youtube.com/watch?v=kLlK1TaUE84; these songs include the single "Tightness Supply," "I've Got Your Man" (released on the 2004 album *Strip Tease*), and "Darnest Things" (released on the 1998 album *Raw: The Best of Lady Saw*; the full first line is "Men say the darnest things"). The latter song title bears a remarkable resemblance to the title of the Bill Cosby comedy series *Kids Say the Darndest Things* (1995). Lady Saw is only one example. Others include Barrington Levy with "Here I Come (Broader than Broadway)," and Yellow Man with "Blueberry Hill."

27. Tanya Batson Savage, "Another Riotous Ride with Oliver," *Jamaica Gleaner* August 29, 2003, C3.

28. Tapes of the show are still treated like gold, especially among Jamaicans in diaspora. The year 2003 saw the production of a stage version of the program; "Oliver Gets Large Abroad," *Jamaica Gleaner*, July 18, 2003, C3.

29. Baptiste, "United States–Caribbean Relations," 36.

30. The reality is that "class and race still operate as functional mechanisms of minority rule–majority subordination in a society that has become a sort of modified plantation economy"; Gordon K. Lewis, "The Contemporary Caribbean," in *Caribbean Contours*, ed. Sidney W. Mintz and Sally Price (Baltimore: Johns Hopkins University Press, 1985), 238.

31. As I have argued elsewhere, this indexing of a cosmopolitanism on the part of working-class West Indian women goes all the way back to the first West Indian slave autobiography—that of Mary Prince (published in 1831), and includes the articulations of the speakers in several Louise Bennett poems; Ifeoma Kiddoe Nwankwo, *Black Cosmopolitanism* (Philadelphia: University of Pennsylvania Press, 2005); Ifeoma Kiddoe Nwankwo, "Rooted Routes and Routed Roots: Jamaican Patois Poet Louise Bennett and the Cosmopolitan Ideal," Modern Language Association Convention 2003, New York; and Ifeoma Kiddoe Nwankwo, "Cosmopolitan Consciousness" (PhD diss., Duke University 1999).

32. Lady Saw, "Superstar (Buckle up Riddim)," Dem Yute Deh, 2006.

33. Jamaica Tourist Board website, accessed August 25, 2006, http://www.visitjamaica.com/vacation_themes/beaches/au_naturel_beaches.aspx.

34. Roberts and Stephens, "Archipelagic American Studies and the Caribbean," 13.

35. Shalini Puri has a wonderful analysis of this phenomenon in the creation and articulation of Caribbean national identities, particularly with regard to the treatment of East Indian and other non-African populations; Shalini Puri, *The Caribbean Postcolonial: Social Equality, Post-Nationalism, and Cultural Hybridity* (New York: Palgrave Macmillan, 2004).

36. Julia Kristeva, *Strangers to Ourselves* (London: Harvester Wheatsheaf, 1991), 1.

37. This contrasts with images of the region in the work of British historians well into the twentieth century, who write the history as if blacks played no role in the development of the nations' economics, cultures, or histories. The racist paternalism evident in their writings differs from the exoticizing ethnocentrism evident in US popular texts, perhaps because of the differing goals of the US and British governments in the region. A comparison of US historians' writings with those of British historians may reveal that the issue is one of discipline or genre rather than the sort of imperialism being enacted. See Eric Williams, *British Historians and the West Indies* (London: Andre Deutsch, 1966).

38. It seems that these ads were specifically crafted to pique the interests of US consumers in new flavors launched in the country between 2004 and 2006.

39. "Malibu Mobile Phone Ad," YouTube video, last modified February 13, 2007, http://www.youtube.com/watch?v=UxfoAL-h4zI.

40. As a number of Bajan taxi driver Trevor Mapp's statements about himself exemplify, the reality is, of course, quite different: "I'm an island man, educated here. I can read and write, I have e-mail. I've traveled—I've been to Canada, to the States, and I've just come back from Japan. I get to see other cultures too. You learn a lot more from traveling than you do from listening to tourists talk about it . . . it ain't the same until you've seen it for yourself," and "A lot of visitors can't believe our history is 350 years old. They can't believe that this island once produced more riches than all of the North

American colonies.... I think a lot of people, when they hear about our heritage, change their opinion of Barbados. They realize that we're not just down here like a bunch of monkeys in grass skirts, but we're actually an industrialized and developing nation trying to come around and make honest livings. I really like the role of educating tourists about my island"; George Gmelch, *Behind the Smile: The Working Lives of Caribbean Tourism* (Bloomington: Indiana University Press, 2003), 59.

41. Peter Stearns makes a similar point, calling attention to the "tensions between a new insistence on self-restraint ... and a new delight in personal gratification" that arose at the turn of the century and that "we live still with"; Peter N. Stearns, *Battleground of Desire: The Struggle for Self-Control in Modern America* (New York: New York University Press, 1999), x.

42. Elaine Savory describes such approaches to the islands as reflecting an "impulse to suppress or repackage inconvenient truths in order to make [the island] into an idyll"; Savory, "Utopia, Dystopia, and Caribbean Heterotopia," 41.

43. Thanks to Gary Ashwill for bringing to my attention the recurrence of this opposition in these representations.

44. American Automobile Association, "Caribbean Vacation," accessed August 24, 2006, http://ww1.aaa.com/AAA_Travel/Vacations/caribbean_vacation.htm.

45. The particular impact of this historical connection becomes even clearer when we contrast the images of the Caribbean to that of India. Both are forms of fantasies, but profoundly different ones. See Bill Mullen, *Afro-Orientalism* (Minneapolis: University of Minnesota Press, 2004); and Balkrishna Govind Gokhale, *India in the American Mind* (Bombay, India: Popular Prakashan, 1989).

46. Thompson, *Eye for the Tropics*, 5; and Frances Aparicio and Susana Chávez-Silverman, eds., *Tropicalizations: Transcultural Representations of Latinidad* (Hanover, NH: Dartmouth College Press, 1997).

47. Françoise Lionnet, "Cosmopolitan or Creole Lives? Globalized Oceans and Insular Identities," *Profession* (2011): 24.

48. Lionnet, "Cosmopolitan or Creole Lives?," 38.

49. Like Françoise Lionnet's creole cosmopolitanism, it is a cosmopolitanism that does not preclude nationalism. In fact, as we saw with Oliver Samuels's decision to have the characters Olivius and Brenda bond over Jamaican food even while on the way to the exotic-familiar place of which they dream, nation remains of paramount importance/significance, even when cultural producers are articulating, or evincing an investment in, a sense of connection to the world beyond the shores.

19 OFFSHORE IDENTITIES

RUPTURES IN THE 300-SECOND AVERAGE HANDLING TIME

Allan Punzalan Isaac

Society for the Filipino is a small rowboat: the *barangay*. Geography for the Filipino is a small locality: the *barrio*. . . . Enterprise for the Filipino is a small stall: the *sari-sari*. Industry and production for the Filipino are the small immediate searchings of each day: *isang kahig, isang tuka* [one chicken scratch, one peck]. And commerce for the Filipino is the smallest degree of retail: the *tingi* [piecemeal].

NICK JOAQUIN, *Culture and History*

Some people still look onto overseas work as a solution to their financial woes and complained about the lack of lucrative employment opportunities within the country. Whilst, just under their noses is an industry hungry for their talent and willing to propel them out of poverty without the hassle of leaving the Philippines. The fact is the middle class is alive, and they are working in the Philippines as BPO [business processing organization] professionals. So if you work in the industry even as the new guy, be grateful as you are part of this emerging middle class and don't have to go through any long-distance thing with the people you love.

PIO GRANADA, "BPOs: The Rise of the New Middle Class," *After Call*

ON THE COVER OF THE ISSUE of *After Call* magazine from midsummer 2012, a beautiful mestiza model, well coiffed, water-beaded, and bejeweled, emerges from the water Venus-like without the clamshell (figure 19.1). The model is identifiably a call center agent on vacation with her headset decidedly disconnected. Playing on the idea of an offshore agent, she is indeed offshore, a sexualized feminine ideal outdoors in all her sartorial and sexual excess. *After Call* is a magazine created by a Filipino national lobby organization, the Business Processing Association of the Philippines (BPAP), for call center agents. The magazine is found in Starbucks or any other twenty-four-hour eatery in small glittering caffeinated and nicotined enclaves of clubs, bars, and restaurants that have sprouted all over

Figure 19.1. Front cover of *After Call* 5, no. 2 (Midsummer 2012).

the central business districts of Manila and Cebu to accommodate the call center industry and its nocturnal denizens. Across the Philippine archipelago, intimacy with strangers half a world away is performed by the voices of 400,000 call center agents in five-minute spurts, ten to twelve times per hour for seven hours, repeated an average of seventy to eighty times by each agent every night through dawn. By contrast, the particular summer issue above offers a visual rather than auditory rendering of the offshore call center agent in her postwork fantasy. The model agent's headset is unplugged, sensually draped over her palm, and in its place are oversized and overwrought gold rope earrings. Fittingly, her daytime bathing suit seems to verge on eveningwear with its cutout sides and fringes, wet from the warm waters of a beach resort. By proxy, this moment is her (and the agent reader's) midsummer's release, as the caption headline reads: it is her/the reader's "time to disconnect and relax."

Writing about another archipelago ten thousand miles away, Antonio Benítez-Rojo suggests that the Caribbean is a "meta-archipelago . . . and as a meta-archipelago it has the virtue of having neither a boundary nor a center. Thus the Caribbean flows outward past the limits of its own sea with a vengeance."[1] How might the Philippines embody what Benítez-Rojo refers to as a meta-archipelago? In what ways does the Philippines flow "outward past the limits of its own sea" in the contemporary moment? How might call centers then be a mode for understanding the capitalist regime that exploits the porousness of this meta-archipelago for its own means?

I argue that these precarities and disjunctures of time, like the precarities and disjunctures of the postcolonial archipelagic space, reveal the contested but textured outlines of this insular inhabitant—the offshore worker-subject. Ruled and measured as she is by several temporal and spatial attachments, the offshore agent as a liminal figure simulates being in synch as a sonic presence with corporate global time at night while living bodily in Philippine national time. Benedict Anderson in his classic work *Imagined Communities* has described the national imaginary as occupying, following Benjamin, "homogenous empty time" in which anonymous inhabitants march along the ever-present calendrical time of the nation-state.[2] As Anderson has suggested, nationalism is but one cultural-ideological construction of belonging and collectivity borne out of the shift in the modern era to print capitalism. I have argued elsewhere that "at issue in narrating the postcolonial nation is the accommodation not only of the plurality of spaces within 'homogenous empty time,' but also the tensile plurality of temporalities vying for hegemony in the island space and imagination."[3] This simultaneity of times, in this case bridged by twenty-first-century technology, is nonidentical with either national or global time. From this precarious time and space, the offshore identity emerges from the circuitry bridging global and national capital spaces and histories.

"I UNDERSTAND WHERE YOU'RE COMING FROM": MAKING OFFSHORE EMPATHS

It is 9 AM and "Carla" just arrived home from her shift a few hours ago. She is already quite busy with her children and new grandchild. Like the cover model, Carla usually works at night, from 8 PM to 5 in the morning. Luckily, today is her day off so she can spend time with me for the interview while catching up with the children and the day's household chores. Unlike the cover model, Carla is forty years old and lives in the nongated part of inner-city Manila, in a small, modest house and lot that has seen better days. The wooden house that once stood at the site was a typical old-style Filipino urban home elevated from the street, but it burned down a few years ago, and the lot suffered more damage with the recent hurricanes. With two years of college under her belt, Carla began working at a major call center company four years ago—two years servicing a US phone company, and the last year and half with a US cable company. The North American–based call center company will soon be entering into a contract with yet another major US phone company. The other phone company giant has chosen to consolidate its call center operations to the Philippines' second major city, Cebu. When I asked for an interview with Carla, her repeated request was to conduct the interview in Tagalog or Tag-lish (a vernacular mix of Tagalog and English) because, she said, she was so tired of speaking English that "dinudugo na ang ilong ko" (my nose is bleeding), a colloquial Tagalog phrase humorously used when a person is averse to being forced to speak English at length.[4] English, once the colonial language, was work, after all.

At the end of 2011, call center agents numbered 400,000 in the Philippines, up 20 percent from 2010, outpacing India in growth and number for voice operations.[5] Indian-owned companies such as Aegis have moved operations into the Philippine archipelago. In fact, in a rhetorical move whereby the Orient orientalizes other parts of the Orient, the chief executive of Mumbai-based Aegis has described the Philippines as "a unique combination of Eastern, attentive hospitality and attitude of *care and compassion* mixed with what I call Americanization."[6] The Philippines is number one in voice operations, and is valued for an English speaking population that imbibes American culture thanks to over one hundred years of colonial and neocolonial relationship with the United States. Call center agents make up 400,000 of the 630,000 business processing organization (BPO) employees, which in turn creates 3.2 million ancillary jobs that have generated a revenue of eleven billion dollars in 2011.[7] This revenue begins to rival the twenty billion dollars brought in by 10 percent of the population, the nine million Filipinos who work overseas and send remittances. The Business Processing Association of the Philippines (BPAP), in cooperation with investors and the Philippine government, has been pushing for the industry to employ one million Filipinos in BPOs by 2016 to generate twenty-five billion dollars in revenue, outpacing the remittance revenue.[8] They call on young people to enter the "industry hungry for their talent and willing to propel them out of poverty without the hassle of leaving the Philippines."[9]

Carla saw the advertisement for call center work "by accident," she said, when interviewing for another job in the southern part of Manila. Carla's sighting of the job notice was in fact not accidental but evidence of the ubiquity and aggressive placement of industry ads. The job calls are apparent in lower-middle- to middle-class malls, schools and colleges, local airports, and even in some upscale neighborhoods, locations where a population with some college education might congregate to shop, eat, study, or travel. These placements filter potential workers. Furthermore, the English-language skills exam during the interview also serves as a behavioral test to determine if the worker has the confidence and assertiveness presumed to be similar to those of the US callers the industry serves. In the job interview process with the call center company, Carla reports that "they are looking to see how you carry yourself and if you have a strong personality because *kausap mo Americano* [you will be speaking with Americans]. The motto of [the company] is 'Outthinking, Outdoing.'"[10] Before being hired she had already been prescreened and cast to deal with what was expected of American callers not simply for linguistic ability but also for behavioral competencies.

Like other call center agents I interviewed, Carla related how these affective ties across oceans are produced through improvisational scripting and management training. For example, Carla reports that the phone company with whom the call center contracted paid her well because the account required not only technical knowledge but also a "strong personality." According to Carla, a strong personality means that the agent is "dominant" and "aggressive": "[Callers might] curse you, but they train you *papano ikaw mag-dominate sa call* [how to dominate the call]."[11] Thus, it is not so much the so-called natural warmth of Filipinos that makes for successful call centers but the filtering, casting, and training process that has created an English-speaking pool of lower-middle- to middle-class workers. What the industry affords these potential workers who already wield the education and perhaps occupy precarious middle-class status is fiscal power that may be beyond reach without proper family and social connections. With a minimum two to four years of college, the agent can make approximately 23,000 Philippine pesos ($500) per month, a considerable amount for a college-educated Filipino without job experience. After social security and health care deductions, Carla is usually left with 11,000 to 15,000 pesos per month, a decent, though not extravagant, wage in Manila.

For consumers in the United States, the offshore agent is a disembodied empathetic voice for a US firm. Agents are taught to "personalize" the problem and perform emotional labor to practice empathy. The agent further creates an empathetic bond with reassuring stock phrases to calm customers—"I understand your frustration"; "We'll help you out"; or "I understand where you're coming from"—very much part of the US-American English idiom to facilitate this emotional connection. As an empath, the agent is to mute both her difference and her distance—which might mean the same thing from the US caller's point of view—and addresses irate caller's needs with culturally appropriate responses. Given her affective production and orientation toward US shores, the offshore subject then refers to serviceable voices just beyond the continental United States. Her offshoreness names the labor of creating a feeling of proximity and propinquity to the US continent, rather than Philippine archipelago. While this labor is peripheral to the manufacture of the material product, capital needs her offshore labor as the voice of humanity to smooth any bumps along the very strictly measured just-in-time delivery between capital production and consumption. Thus the seamlessness between land and sea that the offshore agent endeavors to produce in this "offshoreness" also performs her erasure from the center of capital.

300 SECONDS: ARCHIPELAGIC INTIMACIES

The sunrise industry of call centers in the Philippines produces these affective relationships with US consumers every 300 seconds, the average handling time, or AHT, of calls. In 300 seconds the third-world agent must identify the problem, pinpoint the caller's personality, strategize a rhetorical resolution, implement a logistical solution, and sustain the brand loyalty of the first-world, often US-American, consumer. Through the flows of technological circuitry, these connections follow an archipelagic logic, as Brian Russell Roberts and Michelle Stephens have argued in the Caribbean context, "a logic within which intermittent locales assume spatial forms."[12] These intermittent units of conversation are the affective bridges between the Philippines and the continental United States that make possible the flow of capital. Those 300 seconds are vital paracapitalist productions so that the global production-consumption cycle might be kept in motion. These intermittent relations are *vital* given their critical place in capitalist production, but *vital* also insofar as these corporate intimacies underscore how outsourced voices of the global South serve as the only human touch to the lightning speed of capital consumption of goods, technology, and services. The archipelagic logic of the call center industry makes and takes time, so to speak, for repeated and repetitive intimate negotiations over consumer relations across time zones and transnational locales.

These 300-second telematic bridges give a twenty-first-century spin to what Philippine writer, historian, and public intellectual Nick Joaquin has provocatively suggested in his oft-quoted but controversial 1966 essay "Heritage of Smallness." There he bemoans how Philippine culture seems to have given up on monumental national aspirations, suffering from the tendency to think in small terms, from micropackaging (*tingi*) of toothpaste and shampoo (despite being a survival mechanism for the poor) to envisioning our world in terms of the self-enclosed boat (*barangay*) as a social unit (despite the 21,500-mile coastline). He laments how creative energies exert "so much effort by so many for so little."[13] To Joaquin, the preponderance of small things everywhere keeps Filipinos insular, in the provincial sense, tantamount to the Philippines remaining a small place and a small nation. With such endeavors, the dream that the 7,100 islands of the Philippine archipelago could ever achieve greatness is cast further and further adrift from its shores. At issue, perhaps, is how national and global capital imagine differently the place of these liminal shores that Filipino workers navigate.

Outsourced voices provide small human moments in people's homes and handsets to make the quotidian possible for the first world. Beginning in the late twentieth century, the same economic and social conditions that have forced the mass dispersal of Filipino labor have been channeling educated middle-class workers into this domestic industry, generating controlled and commoditized

300-second off-shore relationships between Philippine agents and US consumers. Unlike their family and friends before them, who have had to migrate to find work across the planet—on cruise ships, on merchant vessels, in homes as domestics and caregivers—from Europe and the Middle East to East Asia and North America, these communications workers could stay home to work at night. However, *like* their migrating counterparts, they work in another time zone with another culture. Lobbyists offer the call center industry as the solution to Philippine economic woes and to the mass outmigration of educated working populations away from their families. Organizations such as BPAP offer the nationalist argument that these communication jobs keep citizens at home on Philippine shores where they belong while still servicing the global economy: "Just under their noses is an industry hungry for their talent and willing to propel them out of poverty without the hassle of leaving the Philippines," argues an article in *After Call*.[14] This emergence of a temporal rather than spatial migration of workers to serve the first world provides a different spin on dispersal and the hybridity of postcolonial states such as the Philippines.

In this manner the archipelagic logic of the offshore subject's living and working conditions refers not only to a disjuncture of space but also to a disjuncture of time. The offshore worker-subject is a hybrid subject emerging from the demands of national and global capital competing for her time. In her work on Indian call centers, Raka Shome reconceptualizes cultural hybridity without the spatial parameters of migration or diaspora having to refer to a "home" location.[15] In the night shift, Shome argues, "the present itself is multiply extended across geographies, nations, spaces through telematic communication, and it is this collision of times stretched over multiple geographies and spatial relations in one moment that creates the diasporic tension and articulates the subject as hybrid."[16] This immaterial industry produces and manages workers working on corporate time while living in nationalist time. The lived "con-fusion" and layering of temporal belonging in the call center industry creates subjects tethered to the global arena as the voice of goods and services ranging from cable and phone companies to travel agencies and banks for US-American consumers. Simultaneously, they are equally bound to nation by the Philippine economy as a highly sought-after citizen not only as a worker but also as an avid consumer. National and corporate global modes of temporality intersect and rift across geographic and geocultural spaces to vie for the way workers live and imagine their everyday lives.

While international call center companies mold, train, and measure the performance of offshore agents to refine their empathetic skills and responses to corporate clients, the national industry aggressively advertises to educated (often young) people not by calling for "caring" people to work but by projecting an image of the industry as a lifestyle choice. In its representation of the call center agent, the industry focuses on the other half of the potential worker's waking hours to produce a pleasure-seeking national(ist) consumer. While "offshore" for the global North describes labor "elsewhere" (somewhere off *its* coast), officially, "the Philippines claim that the waters in between and around the islands, and extending outward to a parametric boundary line, are their national waters."[17] As an archipelagic state, the Philippines is often claimed to be an island-studded sea rather than a group of islands with necessary appurtenances of adjacent waters.[18] This perspective shift reclaims the real and metaphorical space of the offshore not as liminal but as national territory ready to be settled by a new breed of Filipino cosmopolites.

"YOU NEED TO DISCONNECT": MAKING OFFSHORE BODIES

> The clock is indeed ticking, and you haven't hit the beach all summer long....
> You're on the edge, nearly burned out. Caffeine has lost its jolt, you become numb to nicotine, and every workday your nerves feel they are about to give way to a breakdown—you need to disconnect.
>
> PIO GRANADA, "Last Minute Summer: Four Fantastic Quick Weekend Getaways," *After Call*

Rather than inhabiting the global North's liminal "elsewhere," the BPO industry has created an imaginative space for this new inhabitant of the night who answers the call to remain in and remain true to the Philippines. Inside the midsummer 2012 issue of *After Call* magazine, the cover model's pleasure is elaborated with a photo spread of swimwear and the season's top beach getaways in the Philippines: "Here are four quick junkets. They're only about two hours away from Manila either by land, sea or air. That's faster than braving the weekend traffic to the usual quick weekend getaway. These four escape routes will get you out of Manila faster than your longest call. So bring out the weekend warrior and book the trip."[19]

Once disconnected, the national industry reorients the offshore subject bodily to the coastal shores of the archipelago as a domestic tourist. The BPAP representation of the offshore agent reterritorializes her as a national subject, a hedonistic one who looks to her own shores for her pleasure. Corporate nationalism offers a visual solution to what N. V. M. Gonzalez and Oscar Campomanes have signaled as a thematic conundrum in Filipino American and diasporic expressions around multiple dislocations: "To negotiate and map their 'communities' in the space of conflicting demands between 'a national longing for form' and a radically (anti)national predicament of formless dispersals."[20] The magazine presents an "alter-native" class geography and identity that offers a "way out" of social and economic stasis without leaving the Philippines' shores. The corporate visualization of the offshore inhabitant signals the multiple textures of the archipelagic space and typologies of belonging as informed not only by the island but also in conjunction with imagining shore, offshore, currents, histories, and class fantasies. The offshore identity here indexes the cosmopolitan aspirations of a class of people who have income and social mobility.

After Call's tagline descriptor is "The *Look* and *Feel* of the Outsourcing Industry" (emphases mine). The magazine envisages the offshore agent in her national and bodily form. The articles and advertisements inside are not about her work-life disembodiment or disaffection but about her *look* and *feel*, her beauty and pleasure, her visual and haptic life—senses that corporate metrics have no use for during the night. The magazine imagines the agents *after* the headphones come off—during their days and times off. *After* the call is where and when her modeling of her national citizenship happens. *After* the call, she is supposed to be able to reintegrate her body, her senses, her needs, and her social citizenship as a middle-class consumer of leisure. Once again an embodied subject, she surfaces on the national stage as a glamorous consumer—the flip side to the 300-second sonic theater of self-abnegation she performs continually throughout the night. Her recreational time is about the recreation of national geographies and cosmopolitan identities.

The magazine's producer, BPAP, calls on young people to "Work Abroad, Live Here" as a solution to stem the tide of outmigration (figure 19.2).[21] Addressing both nationalist desires and capitalist demands by creating jobs domestically, "Work Abroad, Live Here" articulates a spatial compromise to promise a redemptive status for those who work at night away from families. The corporate compromise offers not an alternative sociality but a consumer lifestyle to define the terms of their national belonging. While the slogan introduces the antonymic relationship between "abroad" and "here," it elides the rupture between work and family life that the time shift has introduced for many young people by figuring the terms as a false binary *such as* "here" and "abroad." In this industry of young flexible (and caffeinated) labor, the spatial border does not move through their bodies, as in formal colonialism, nor do bodies move through borders to become ethnic bodies, as in labor migration. Skipping the inconveniences of airports, visas, and immigration reviews, one can indeed be in two places at once: enjoy the glamour of working "abroad" while living "here."

The offshore agent, as an emergent national *and* transnational subject, is the product of a union between call center companies producing denizens of corporate time at night and national industry lobbyists producing consumer citizens during the day. She embodies the contradiction of the postcolonial body inhabiting a global telematic circuitry. Constructed as a nationalist by not migrating out of the physical confines of nation, her assimilation to a foreign culture

Figure 19.2. Cover photo of Information Technology-Business Processing Organization, *Facebook*, April 15, 2016, https://www.facebook.com/WorkAbroadLiveHere.

is temporary and simply a function of work, unlike the *balikbayan* (Filipino returnee), or overseas worker, who has had to live a different and often subordinated life as a migrant. For the nonmigrant cosmopolitan worker, her confidence, language, and communication skills are honed as tools to provide her mobility into other social spaces she might not otherwise have access to, such as beach resorts and other fantasies of Philippine consumerism. The diurnal denizen is depicted as a potential tourist of her own country. Offshore but at home, she can skirt around issues of racialization and national subordination faced by overseas or migrating counterparts, but her perceived social mobility within the nation potentially troubles notions of national order in terms of sexuality, gender, and class.

Outside the temperature-controlled and fluorescent-lit cubicle workplace and *after* the calls, the reconstruction not only of national but also class and sexual identities takes place. Right beside the model on the *After Call* cover is a headline for another feature article announcing a socioeconomic formation due to call centers: "BPOs: The New Middle Class." The space-saving editing of the headline makes the industry indistinct from the employees working in it, representing the model as the industry rather than the corporate forces driving it. The article optimistically and encouragingly reports, "In a nutshell, what the report says is that the BPO industries is one of the main pillars of the Philippines GDP growth, and this is for the expansion of the country's middle class over the past decade. A strong middle class is what the country needs to grow more and display stellar economic performance. The BPO industry is supplying exactly this, but what does it take to be in the middle class?"[22] The short piece goes on to cite national criteria from the National Statistical Coordination Board for the trappings of middle-class status in the Philippines, including an "annual income ranging between PhP 251,283 ($6,282) to PhP 2,045,280 ($51,132), live in a domicile made of strong materials, [and have] a refrigerator, and a radio."[23]

Radios notwithstanding, BPO workers, from call center agents to managers, could earn anywhere from three hundred to two thousand dollars per month, quite within the enormously wide range provided by the article. An anxiety to prove through statistical numbers that the reader belongs to this socioeconomic class permeates the article as well as the advertisements for affordable condos and vacations filling the pages of the magazine. Being part of the industry in the expansion of the middle class, the writer asserts, is to be a main pillar in Philippine national growth and development.

This anxiety was apparent among a group of call center agents and managers I interviewed in Cebu one very early morning over "dinner" after their shifts. Occupying various posts as agents, team leaders, and managers, the agents were only too aware of the way others perceive their membership in respectable middle-classness.

> A: But it was my choice—it was my decision. . . . It's been always normal [for] Filipinos that they would look down on call centers although they know that it's a high-paying job. . . . They would say, "Why only a call center—why did you not choose your own profession?" But if you come to think of it: yes, you are a manager in a bank, but your pay! Mine is 40 or 50 percent higher than yours. But I'm a manager here, too. So that's the big difference.

While the BPO worker has fiscal power with the same managerial title, as a call center agent she has no social capital. A lower-paid bank manager, however, is perceived to have chosen a respectable career track because finance and business administration are recognized "fields" that one can major in. According to the interviewees, others Filipinos feel that being a call center agent is a temporary job that the worker secures before a "real" or more permanent "career" in the Philippines or abroad. When asked why they stay in such stressful jobs based on continual time metrics and competition with each other, the agents expressed some ambivalence about staying on as well-paid but not well-respected urban professionals.

Aside from the pay differential, the temporal shift has constructed a difference around morality and cultural belonging. Working at night as "vampires" or "daywalkers," away from their families and friends (*barkada*), unlike "normal" people, negatively affects others' moral perception of the call center agents. When someone in the group interview would use terms such as "normal" and "vampire" to describe daytime and nighttime BPO workers, respectively, the rest would smile, chuckle, or simply nod in agreement at the colorful description. They seemed to understand that some may see them as youths living a culture of permissiveness with much disposable income and carousing into the night and early morning hours. Others, they report, see them as tolerating or partaking in nonmarital and nonheterosexual sex, accompanied by excessive smoking and drinking. In the media, call center agents continue to be characterized as promiscuous and even a main source of the spread of disease.

> B: I think they think you keep drugs because you have a lot of money.
> A: (mumbling) . . . Or that you have AIDS.

In 2010, a nonscientific news report made a splash in the local news about the rise in absolute numbers of HIV cases and STDs. The rise in *absolute* numbers meant a dramatic rise in infection *rates*, which became the focus of the reports and was then tenuously linked to call center agents and their presumed promiscuity as nighttime workers like prostitutes. When asked about this perception, one of my informants responded, "[They think] we don't get to follow the old Filipino way because we're talking with Americans."[24] The informant adds another layer to the perception of permissive or tolerant youth culture at night. These young people, some would claim, inhabit a foreign space and time zone. As they work in the very visible gleam of call center areas of the city, this visual separation exacerbates the anxieties around the nocturnal character of the offshore lifestyle.

Decidedly not a migrant or an overseas worker, not a native islander, a peasant, or a domestic here or abroad, the offshore subject is cosmopolitan barely leaving the shores of the Philippines, part of the consuming middle class that can buy leisure time like the elite, *balikbayans* and foreign tourists. With this consuming power, she is able to cleanse herself of her class origins or perhaps regain her once tenuous hold on middle-class respectability. Consumer citizenship is thus represented even by the industry as her claim to nationalism and national belonging. Yet, these reparative modes of bodily representation of the call center agent as a youthful, rich, pleasure seeker also produce social and cultural anxieties around the new identity. By paying such high wages in a nontraditional occupation, the industry has shifted the imagination and production of fiscal power, loosening it from the domain of land-owning families and of the colonial bureaucracy controlled by professional credentialing in elite universities. Call center firms and companies provide much of the training—not universities, whether elite or not. Part of the cultural anxiety then lies in fiscal power not acquired through the traditional channels established by a colonial history of higher education or an elite family network. As explained by the group of agents I spoke with,

A: I think they would say that it is easy to be recruited into a call center but it's actually not.
B: [They] think it makes you dumber because of the repetitiveness.
C: You don't need a bachelor's degree to get into the call center.
A: Only two years is needed.

Informants point to the perceived ease and lack of professional credentials (a bachelor's degree) required for positions in the industry. Their chosen jobs or careers do not follow the (neo)colonial routes to middle-class respectability as would being a doctor, lawyer, engineer, teacher, or nurse, particularly because institutional credentialing or imprimaturs have seemingly been bypassed. While commanding the attributes of the privileged with fraught "global" or "lightly accented" English, some college education, and much purchasing power, these offshore workers do not necessarily have the family or elite educational institutional network of other middle classes. Indeed, American studies scholar Jan Padios's excellent work on call centers has pointed out how the call center stigma devalues the very attributes of education, wealth, and body grooming that the elite have relied on as traditional status markers.[25] Their cosmopolitanism simulates and values "the promise of the foreign," to use Vicente Rafael's term, without having to leave the country.[26] However, these digital denizens are not legible as returnees (*balikbayan*) from overseas who have accumulated some wealth, a now common phenomenon dating from the 1970s. Hence, these cyberpark citizens who come from such dangerous proximity as "offshore" seem to threaten a social class order with promiscuity of a different sort: class promiscuity.[27]

HERITAGE OF SMALL PLACES: "ALTER-NATIVE" CLASS GEOGRAPHIES

Every native would like to find a way out, every native would like a rest, every native would like a tour. But some natives—most natives in the world—cannot go anywhere. They are too poor. They are too poor to go anywhere. They are too poor to escape the reality of their lives; and they are too poor to live properly in the place where they live, which is the very place you, the tourist, want to go—so when the native sees you, the tourists, they envy you, they envy your ability to leave your own banality and boredom.

JAMAICA KINCAID, *A Small Place*

The *After Call* article proclaims that young people "don't have to do the long distance thing with the people you love" to support themselves and their loved ones.[28] Through temporal migration into "IT parks" and "tech centers," the industry offers offshore agents some of the economic means by which to "live properly in the place where they live," transformed in the magazine pages into "the very place you, the tourist, want to go." Commanding wages $250 to $300 a month higher than her Indian counterpart, higher than some junior managers in Philippine banks, and higher than the minimum wage of five dollars a day, the call center agent can afford some pleasures of domestic tourism. Corporate expansion into and reterritorialization of the offshore space gives glamorous form to Campomanes and Gonzalez's "national longing," as well as a cosmopolitan magnitude to Joaquin's smallness of island space—at least for the industry's purposes.

Here lies a twist in Kincaid's observation around native animus against the (Western) tourist in the context of the reterritorialized offshore agent. While the call center industry offers a way for families to stay together in the same country, inhabitants of the offshore do not necessarily share the same circadian and quotidian rhythms as other citizens to make traditional family life a reality. Temporal migration has caused a cultural shift. Even when disconnected from the global circuitry, their disconnection extends to their own families. They no longer participate in reunions and other life-occasion markers. Like Carla and the group of agents I interviewed, shared waking hours are decidedly not spent in sand and surf but in playing catch-up with duties to children and other family members. Their families adjust to the agents' frequent absences and accommodate their sleeping and eating cycles, including creating special sleeping quarters in darkened, air-conditioned, and noise-free parts of the house. Though physically present, agents are often secreted and asleep during family activities that their income has made possible. Because of economic demands, these young workers violate this central duty of communality and sense of belonging, making the dislocation offshore more of an exile from the "everyday."

Thus, we may understand the 300-second average handling time that marks the intermittent relationships between the Philippines and the United States throughout the night as sedimented with colonial histories and fraught with cultural anxieties and transgressions as it remaps once again the geographies of national belonging. The offshore subject's temporal migration into the global simultaneity of times during the night shift produces otherness to nation not by leaving political borders; rather, the dislocation disrupts accepted social order in diurnal absence from family life and errant class mobility without traditional migratory movement for others in the traditional middle classes. In capital fantasy and in local practice of survival, the national ruptures in the offshore agent's nightly and repetitive "economic" performance, to echo Campomanes and Gonzalez once again, are elaborations of compressed narratives around the offshore subject and most markedly the anxieties that ebb and flow across the telematic circuitry. Read through Jamaica Kincaid's emotionally riven and "economic" work on Antigua as a "small place," Joaquin's "heritage of smallness" then reveals a complex of anxieties about legibility and belonging. In the sedimented and painful, but disavowed, colonial history of the Philippines, inhabitants continually appear and disappear in the violence of master visions and narratives. The offshore subject's *partial* relocation reveals yet another texture and another outline of the Philippine meta-archipelago and its "'dispersed nationality' and the experience of multiple dislocations."[29] As colonial and capital frames shift the contours of national belonging, the Filipino has always been there, to be sure, but she emerges intermittently more visible *and audible* in different forms—sometimes glamorous, sometimes unrecognizable—in her multiple connections and dislocations in and around the insular space: native, nationalist, citizen, expat, tourist, *balikbayan*, overseas worker, and offshore inhabitant.

NOTES

Epigraphs: Nick Joaquin, *Culture and History* (Manila: Anvil Publishing, 2004), 351; Pio Granada, "BPOs: The Rise of the New Middle Class," *After Call* 5.2 (Midsummer 2012), 10; Pio Granada, "Last Minute Summer: Four Fantastic Quick Weekend Getaways," *After Call* 5.2 (Midsummer 2012), 16.

1. Antonio Benítez-Rojo, *The Repeating Island: The Caribbean and the Postmodern Perspective,* 2nd ed., trans. James Maraniss (Durham, NC: Duke University Press, 1996), 4.

2. Benedict Anderson, *Imagined Communities: Reflections on the Origin and Spread of Nationalism* (London: Verso, 1983), 24.

3. Allan Punzalan Isaac, *American Tropics: Articulating Filipino America* (Minneapolis: University of Minnesota Press, 2006), 14.

4. "Carla" (call center agent) in discussion with the author, June 2012.

5. Vikas Bajaj, "A New Capital of Call Centers," *New York Times*, November 25, 2011, Business section.

6. Bajaj, "New Capital."

7. Business Processing Association of the Philippines representative in discussion with the author, July 2012.

8. Business Processing Association of the Philippines representative in discussion with the author, July 2012.

9. Pio Granada, "BPOs: The Rise of the New Middle Class," *After Call* 5, no. 2 (Midsummer 2012): 10.

10. "Carla" (call center agent) in discussion with the author, June 2012.

11. "Carla" (call center agent) in discussion with the author, June 2012.

12. Brian Russell Roberts and Michelle Stephens, "Archipelagic American Studies and the Caribbean," *Journal of Transnational American Studies* 5, no. 1 (2013): 14.

13. Nick Joaquin, *Culture and History* (Manila: Anvil Publishing, 2004), 351.

14. Granada, "BPOS," 10.

15. Raka Shome, "Thinking Through the Diaspora: Call Centers, India, and a New Politics of Hybridity," *International Journal of Cultural Studies* 9, no. 1 (2006): 105–24.

16. Shome, "Thinking Through the Diaspora," 114.

17. Muhammad Munavvar, *Ocean States: Archipelagic Regimes in the Law of the Sea* (Dordrecht, Netherlands: Martinus Nijhoff Publishers, 1995), 62.

18. Munavvar, *Ocean States*, 64. Munavvar also explains, "Topographically, the Philippines is broken up by the sea, which gives it one of the largest coastlands of any nation in the world. Its coastline of 34,600 km (21,500 statute miles) is highly irregular and fringed with numerous coral reefs, gulfs, and lagoons"; Munavvar, *Ocean States*, 21.

19. Pio Granada, "Last-Minute Summer," 16.

20. N. V. M. Gonzalez and Oscar V. Campomanes, "Filipino American Literature," in *An Interethnic Companion to Asian American Literature*, ed. King-Kok Cheung (Cambridge: Cambridge University Press, 1997), 100–101.

21. Information Technology-Business Processing Organization, "Work Abroad. Live Here," *Facebook,* April 15, 2016, https://www.facebook.com/WorkAbroadLiveHere.

22. Granada, "BPOS," 11.

23. Granada, "BPOS," 11.

24. Group of call center agents (Cebu) in discussion with the author, July 2012.

25. Jan Maghinay Padios, "Listening between the Lines: Culture, Difference, and Immaterial Labor in the Philippine Call Center Industry" (PhD diss., New York University, 2012). See also "Queer Confessions: Transgression, Affect, and National Crisis in the Philippines' Call Center Industry," *Center for Art + Thought,* January 2013. http://centerforartandthought.org/work/item/queer-confessions-transgression-affect-and-national-crisis-philippines%E2%80%99-call-center-industry; for excellent studies on sexuality and Philippine call centers, see Emmanuel David, "Transgender Workers and Queer Value at Global Call Centers in the Philippines," *Gender and Society* 29, no. 2 (2015): 169–94; Emmanuel David, "The Sexual Fields of Empire," *Radical History Review* 123 (2015): 115–43; and Emmanuel David, "Outsourced Heroes: Queering the Labor Brokerage State," *GLQ* 22, no. 3 (2016): 381–408.

26. Vicente L. Rafael, *The Promise of the Foreign: Nationalism and the Technics of Translation in the Spanish Philippines* (Durham, NC: Duke University Press, 2005).

27. Call center enclaves are often given technological-sounding names such as IT Park in Cebu, or Eastwood City Cyberpark in eastern Metro Manila.

28. Granada, "BPOS," 10. The epigraph for this section is taken from Jamaica Kincaid, *A Small Place* (New York: Farrar, Straus, and Giroux, 1988), 18–19. Because Kincaid is not referring to "native" in an Indigenous sense, the term "native" remains uncapitalized throughout this essay.

29. Gonzalez and Campomanes, "Filipino American Literature," 102.

AFTERWORD | **THE ARCHIPELAGIC ACCRETION**

Paul Giles

THE ARCHIPELAGIC IMPACT, as presented in this engaging collection of essays, depends upon an intersection of two complementary but in some ways antithetical vectors. One such vector, as Brian Russell Roberts and Michelle Ann Stephens suggest in their introduction, involves "metageographical remappings," the conceptual rearrangement of planetary space according to alternative geographies. The other, though, involves what they call, citing George B. Handley, a "phenomenological encounter with natural forms," a sense of the archipelagic environment as inherently different from more abstract continental designs. As J. Michael Dash indicates in his contribution here, this kind of "conflict between two antagonistic ideas," between "placeless thought or conceptual transparency," on the one hand, and "thought as matter in all its material specificity," on the other, was also fundamental to the work of Édouard Glissant, whose writings have probably helped shape the "archipelagic turn" more than anyone else's. The inherently paradoxical dimensions of Glissant's oeuvre, its capacity to move at the same time in two contrary directions, is replicated in the self-dissolving tendencies of an archipelagic imaginary that both evokes and revokes geographical premises simultaneously.

It is the second of these vectors, the material specificity of the archipelago, that has been evident most recently in the aspects of archipelagic thought that have circulated in the US academy. We witness this kind of oppositional stance in the section titled "Archipelagic Thought" in the *Las Américas Quarterly* issue of *American Quarterly* in September 2014, one predicated upon the idea of locality as resistance, of ethno-racialized subjects resisting the terms of official US subjecthood.[1] Appearing in the American Studies Association's house journal, the cluster of essays under the heading "Archipelagic Thought" used Caribbean nations as its starting point, putting Puerto Rico, Cuba, and Haiti into conversation with each other.[2] This book of essays collected by Roberts and Stephens engages in some ways with a similar kind of premise, but it also expands its geographical frame to encompass Hawai'i (Brandy Nālani McDougall), Guam (Craig Santos Perez), and the Philippines (Joseph Keith, Allan Punzalan Isaac), as well as connections between Maori peoples and the American Pacific Northwest (Hsinya Huang). The Caribbean also features prominently in the agenda of *Archipelagic American Studies*, as we see here in the contributions of Yolanda Martínez-San Miguel, Ramón E. Soto-Crespo, and Cherene Sherrard-Johnson. Nicole Waligora-Davis similarly comments on how US military presence in the Caribbean during the twentieth century was both romanticized and glossed over in popular music and film, while Matthew Pratt Guterl analyzes how the screen persona of Josephine Baker came to embody the spirit of "islands" more generally. Birte Blascheck and Teresia Teaiwa also note the efficacy of archipelagic American studies "outside of the academy" in relation to "'small island' communities," and a dominant paradigm informing many of these essays is of the United States as an imperial force. John Carlos Rowe's contribution, for instance, links Craig Santos Perez's poetry to the "anticolonial intentions" of James Joyce, in the way that the "Chamorro teacher, scholar, poet, and activist" sought creatively to refunction the metaphor of the "voyage" that "has for so long been invoked by poets to align their work with the boldness and daring of the imperial conqueror." Underlying these approaches is an implicitly utopian impulse given expression most famously in Epeli Hau'ofa's essay "Our Sea of Islands," a frequent critical touchstone here, as well as in Albert Wendt's projections of the Pacific, as expressed in his lyrical prose piece "Towards a New Oceania" (1976) and other works.[3] Such utopianism of "island form" was framed specifically as a counterpart to "postcolonial geopoetics" by University of Cyprus scholar Antonis Balasopoulos, who hails the island's theoretical emergence from a "reified entity" through "the call, from off the shore, of an islandness to come."[4] Along similar lines, Brandy Nālani McDougall's contribution here on Hawai'i follows Elaine Stratford's notion that "thinking with the archipelago" allows for "multiple emancipatory narratives that enunciate exceptions to colonizing grammars of empire that rendered islands remote, isolated and backward," and one obvious benefit of this essay collection is to give voice to supposedly "remote" communities marginalized by conventional continental cartographies.

Representation is, however, a slippery phenomenon. When, for example, Walt Whitman in "Salut au Monde" (1856) hails "All you on the numberless islands of the archipelagoes of the sea!," it is not clear that this sweeping poetic rhetoric can be incorporated unproblematically, or without the risk of some reductive element, into a unilinear narrative of imperial appropriation.[5] John Ashbery again uses the image of "archipelagoes" in an idiosyncratically elusive and self-conscious manner in his long poem "Self-Portrait in a Convex Mirror" (1975):

> Whispers of the word that can't be understood
> But can be felt, a chill, a blight
> Moving outward along the capes and peninsulas
> Of your nervures and so to the archipelagoes
> And to the bathed, aired secrecy of the open sea.[6]

For Ashbery, this figure of the archipelago involves a retreat from the normative conditions of "mapped space," although, by a typical Ashbery mise en abyme, the "archipelagoes" then become in themselves another form of mapped space, not so much an alternative to closure as its textual, metaphorical corollary. This exemplifies what Roberts and Stephens call the "metageographical" aspects of their collection, its inquiry into ways in which the spatial dimensions of this term can provide theoretical groundings that differ from more established conceptions such as the hemispheric, transnational, or indeed postcolonial. As Lanny Thompson suggests here, the archipelagic method reworks an area studies model by moving away from the idea of a "spatially bounded unit," and, rather than the "double consciousness" characteristic of "border epistemology," it typically emphasizes instead flows that are "multiple and relational."

Such an approach involves, of course, the refurbishment for our contemporary world of various comparative methods that can be seen as relatively traditional in their provenance. Susan Gillman helpfully points out here how Benedict Anderson's work on comparative nationalisms was shaped in part by his early "training in Southeast Asia and his focus on Rizal's Philippines," something that leads him "to characterize the Philippines of the 1890s as the 'westernmost part of Latin America.'" To recognize Anderson in this way as "an unrecognized theorist of archipelagoes" is to accord him honorary status as a godfather of archipelagic studies (where the archipelagic topography of Southeast Asia, seen in Anderson's scholarly focus on Indonesia and the Philippines, becomes an activating terraqueous space), and in this light it becomes easier to track the intellectual genealogy of this theoretical impulse.[7] Rather than a hemispheric trajectory driven by the interests of Latin Americanists or a transnational model impelled by the juxtaposition of discrete "contact zones," in Mary Louise Pratt's famous phrase, what we find in the archipelagic turn is a relative obliteration of geographical distance and a problematization of conventional binary oppositions between center and margin, near and far.[8] Hau'ofa's ancestral insistence on viewing the world not as "islands in a far sea" but rather "a sea of islands" serves systematically to traduce the concept of spatial distance while privileging instead an idea of immersion. As Hau'ofa says, the Western academy, and indeed Western society in general, has tended to "belittle" the notion of Oceania, to regard it as "deficient in resources," as inherently marginal to the civilized world's wider concerns.[9] However, in a twenty-first-century environment that lays more stress on geocentric resistance to imposed political designs, the archipelagic turn signals the intellectual revenge of the planet upon the bounded nation, the putative overwhelming of continental space by an all-encompassing sea.

In his work *In Oceania*, the Australian-born anthropologist Nicholas Thomas took issue specifically with Edward Said's notion of orientalist subjugation, arguing that such a received version of colonization was "not helpful for the Pacific," since this oceanic space is predicated upon shifting boundaries of identity and a ubiquity of "exchange practices" rather than on any kind of centralized or panoptical authority.[10] Despite its perspicacity, Thomas's analysis runs the risk of both Pacific exceptionalism and archipelagic pastoralism, as though these constellations of islands were somehow immune from global sources of Western power. By contrast, one of the positive aspects of Ifeoma Kiddoe Nwankwo's fine contribution to this volume is to posit an intersection between archipelagic and transnational designs, thereby indicating the complex triangulation processes that have linked the Caribbean historically with the United Kingdom as well as the United States, and so suggesting "how it might be useful for Americanists to envision US-Caribbean relations using an archipelagic model in which the United States is part of an archipelago." Such forms of reciprocity seem endemic to the archipelagic enterprise, and, even as Roberts and Stephens in their introduction point toward transnationalism's "tendency to paper over difference" and its preference for "tracing cultural continuums across national borders," it might be most useful to consider ways in which the archipelagic works to reframe the transnational within a planetary context. While a critical "anxiety of influence" typically seeks to create discursive space for the promotion of some new critical method, in fact this valuable archipelagic constellation is, appropriately enough, constructed in a more organic way around spatial and temporal accretion rather than theoretical parricide.[11] Transnationalism has always been committed to elucidating points of friction as well as congruence, but the particular contribution of this archipelagic method involves incorporating such local crossovers into a global framework shaped by the ecological demands of an ocean-based planet. Stratford points out here how only five states are formally categorized as "archipelagic" under the legal terms of the United Nations Convention, but in terms of the metaphorical implications of this idea, the archipelagic has come to assume a much wider and more amorphous resonance.

One of the more striking and surprising aspects of this collection, though, is the way it suggests how the development of archipelagic consciousness was also tied to cultural and technological changes that had nothing to do with the phenomenology of the sea. Etsuko Taketani's excellent contribution links the emergence of an "archipelagic black global imaginary" to the identification of "air-age globalism" in the wake of innovative cartography that adopted an aerial perspective, something that came to public attention particularly during World War II. The aerial cartographers of this era thought that the flat Mercator maps tended to overemphasize spatial differences between continents and thus to lull their insular populations into a false sense of security. These new aerial maps showed how shorter distances could be navigated across the poles, making Washington, DC, considerably closer to Berlin than it was to Buenos Aires, a cartographic reordering that made the East Coast of the United States seem more vulnerable to transatlantic attack than the old atlases might have suggested. Taketani aptly notes here how Paul Gilroy's *The Black Atlantic* (1993) is implicitly "theorized within and against Mercator's Eurocentric codification of the modern world," since Gilroy "fixes on the image of the sailing ship, evocative of the Middle Passage of the slave trade," as an emblem of the Atlantic Ocean, and his book actually says little about ways in which land and sea have recently been brought into a more adjacent proximity through aeronautical and other technologies. In this sense, what Roberts has elsewhere called the motifs of "planetary connectivity" and "planetary relationality" can be traced back specifically to the projections in the mid-twentieth century of a modernist outlook in which, as Taketani suggests, the reconfiguration of terrestrial space from aerial perspectives provoked a different kind of global understanding.[12] James Joyce deploys archipelagic imagery in *Finnegans Wake* (1939)—"Procreated on the ultimate ysland of Yreland in the encyclical yrish archipelago"—and this speaks not only to his emphasis in this all-encompassing book on an ontological fluidity centered around "the regeneration of all man by affusion of water," but also to the author's imaginative vision of the planet as systematically interlinked through an interpenetration of universal currents.[13]

Alice Te Punga Somerville's essay in this volume alludes to Elizabeth McMahon's important article "Archipelagic Space and the Uncertain Future of National Literatures," in which McMahon points to the significant "coincidence of John Donne's pronouncement that 'no man is an island' in 1623 being the same year the British claimed their first island colony in the Caribbean."[14] McMahon also makes reference in the same essay to Gillian Beer's scholarship on how Donne's phrase became "well known and used," indeed a kind of "cliché," around the time of World War II.[15] The structural double bind here involves a recognition of the inherently isolated condition of the island only in simultaneously acknowledging the dissolution of that insular space, a *fort/da* process that brings to mind Frederick Jackson Turner's invocation of the US-American frontier in a celebrated lecture of 1893 at precisely the time when the West was changing and the frontier itself was officially being closed.[16] Beer points out how the origins of the word "island" itself involved two elements: "'Isle' in its earliest forms derived from a word for water and meant 'watery' or 'watered.' In Old

English 'land' was added to it to make a compound: 'is-land': water-surrounded land." This makes the word "island" itself "a kind of pun," as Beer suggests, and it implies by extension how the island, like the frontier, is by definition a chimerical or antithetical conception, something that can be defined only by what it is not. As Beer explains, Donne's words "No man is an island" effectively "take their charge from their quality of paradox. They presuppose that the individual *is* ordinarily understood to be like an island."[17] Concomitantly, part of the burden of a modernism inflected by the specter of global conflict was to convey—in novels such as Hemingway's *For Whom the Bell Tolls* (1940), which drew specifically on Donne's famous phrase for its title—how the world was in fact now inherently interconnected in all kinds of previously unforeseen ways.[18] Beer herself also links this reconfiguration of space to aeronautical technology, citing how Gertrude Stein's book *Picasso* (1938) "comments on the formal reordering of the earth when seen from the aeroplane—a reordering which does away with centrality and very largely with borders."[19]

If it was the modernist period that recalibrated terrestrial space, the postmodern era has developed this archipelagic perspective by taking the theme of air travel one stage further. Balasopoulos has observed how what he calls the "postmodern reinvention of the island imaginary" was shaped by the "tremendously influential iconicity of the photographs of the earth generated by the Apollo missions of 1968 and 1972," photographs that produced "a pictorial language of the global that highlighted the ocean-dominated, islanded status of the planet earth, surrounded by the silent, hostile blackness of outer space."[20] Many of the contributors to this collection follow the pioneering work of Elizabeth M. DeLoughrey in drawing upon Barbadian poet Edward Brathwaite's theory of "tidalectics" to disavow the binary opposition of land and water and to emphasize instead, in DeLoughrey's words, a "cyclical" rather than "synthesizing" model, one reflecting the "continual movement and rhythm of the ocean."[21] But it is important also to recognize how this broader reconfiguration of island space, and in particular the projection of continental space as archipelagic, is molded in part by more abstract technologies of transport and communication, from space travel to the Internet. Allan Punzalan Isaac's concluding essay in this volume speaks appositely to this conundrum, describing how call centers in the Philippines, and the flow of capital associated with them, produce a different kind of spatial logic among these "cyberpark citizens," who live in a state of relative dislocation from their proximate environment while simultaneously being connected to distant others across oceanic space. In this light, Isaac's description of the "archipelagic logic of the call center industry" testifies to ways in which an archipelagic design has morphed from Hau'ofa's tribute to the phenomenology of the sea into a condition driven by virtual artifice of various kinds.

As Stratford observes in the "Theories and Methods" section, then, part of the theoretical thrust behind this volume involves considering what it might "mean to decenter US continentalism and imagine the United States' complex spatiality in archipelagic terms." Such a move "to unsettle overpowering discourses of continentalism" necessarily involves a contrarian aspect, and within such a countersuggestible framework it might be seen as apt that a cumbersome word with an antithetical prefix, "decontinentalizing," is built into the rubric of this book through Roberts and Stephens' introduction. There has of course been distinguished work before on this archipelagic conundrum, but it has always tended, as in the historical writings of J. G. A. Pocock, to bear an inherently revisionist or adversarial slant. Pocock's work positions itself self-consciously outside national formations, using the trope of oceanic conjunction to dislodge insular assumptions of US-American exceptionalism, Anglocentrism, and "the Eurocratic mind" alike. In Pocock's words,

> "Britain," or "the Atlantic archipelago," situated as "it" is, should be capable of existing in more than one history and recognizing the claims and contests arising between them. . . . We do not understand the American Revolution until we understand that American history is not its only outcome; Caribbean . . . histories claim a parity of esteem, derived from the sheer facts of their existence and their complicated continuity, and they still figure in a British history conceived as a history of empire in more than one sense of the term.[22]

As Pocock himself recognized, it is no coincidence that he was born and initially trained in New Zealand before moving later in his career to the United States. Drawing on this antipodean background, he describes his 2005 book *The Discovery of Islands* as "formed partly in an archipelago of the Southern Ocean" and as presenting "the islands including Britain as another archipelago . . . not the promontory of a continent."[23] Extrapolating from a specific geographic location, in other words, Pocock's archipelagic perspective is reorganized conceptually into a more abstract theoretical method of writing cultural history.

In his own book *Archipelagic English*, however, John Kerrigan quotes Pocock acknowledging ruefully how his innovatory formulation of "the Atlantic archipelago" had generally "failed to catch on."[24] It may perhaps be that the inherently oppositional nature of this term lends it an institutional outsideness, a perpetual spiral whereby any given object is analyzed from an always already alien position. Though such outsideness might not be methodologically inevitable, it is important from a practical perspective to acknowledge how continents enclose not only landmasses but also a hefty weight of vested interests, academic as well as bureaucratic, that have long been concerned to shore up the political as well as epistemological boundaries of nation and continent. Kerrigan himself, in another gesture of structural belatedness, argues that seventeenth-century English literature is "amenable to archipelagic re-reading" in the light of the use of "the three kingdoms" as "the standard seventeenth-century formula for England/Wales, Scotland, and Ireland." Curiously enough, though, he does not choose to extend this logic of "archipelagic Englishness" across the Atlantic, arguing that "the literature of America did not, despite such luminaries as Edward Taylor and Jonathan Edwards, have anything like the mass and quality of the British-Irish archipelago, until well after 1707."[25] One of the consequences of archipelagic logic is precisely the kind of disorienting mise en abyme illuminated by Ashbery's "Self-Portrait in a Convex Mirror," in which one concentric circle blurs disarmingly into the next, but Kerrigan's work might be said to represent an example of this archipelagic critical impulse circumscribed firmly by more traditional national designs.

However this conception is framed or geographically bounded, the archipelagic tends to involve an excess of significations, a disruption of stable entities, the overwhelming of static land masses by multidirectional flows of oceanic space. If postcolonialism focused on power structures, and transnationalism on power exchanges of one kind or another, then the archipelagic imaginary might be said to involve a more fluid system, one that disrupts solid foundations and reinscribes them as ontologically evanescent. The archipelagic's belated quality speaks intellectually to its capacity to turn the subject inside out, to redescribe islands as empires and vice versa. The American continent, like every other continent, contains its own insular quality, but, as the essays in this collection abundantly show, an archipelagic logic has the capacity to enable an imaginative inversion of the domestic premises that have traditionally underpinned the field of American studies.

NOTES

1. See section 5, "Archipelagic Thought," in *American Quarterly* 66, no. 3 (September 2014): 801–73. This includes essays by Arnaldo Manuel Cruz-Malavé, José Quiroga, Régine Michelle Jean-Charles, and Alexandra T. Vazquez.

2. Macarena Gómez-Barris and Licia Fiol-Matta, "Introduction: *Las Américas Quarterly*," *American Quarterly* 66, no. 3 (September 2014): 501.

3. Epeli Hau'ofa, "Our Sea of Islands," in *A New Oceania: Rediscovering Our Sea of Islands*, ed. Eric Waddell, Vijay Naidu, and Epeli Hau'ofa (Suva, Fiji: University of the South Pacific, 1993), 2–16; Albert Wendt, "Towards a New Oceania" (1976), in *Readings in Pacific Literature*, ed. Paul Sharrad (Woolongong, Australia: New Literatures Research Centre, University of Woolongong, 1993), 9–15.

4. Antonis Balasopoulos, "Nesologies: Island Form and Postcolonial Geopoetics," *Postcolonial Studies* 11, no. 1 (2008): 23.

5. Walt Whitman, "Salut au Monde," in *Leaves of Grass*, ed. Sculley Bradley and Harold W. Blodgett (New York: Norton, 1973), 147.

6. John Ashbery, "Self-Portrait in a Convex Mirror," in *Self-Portrait in a Convex Mirror: Poems by John Ashbery* (1975; repr., Manchester, UK: Carcanet New Press, 1977), 75.

7. See, for example, Benedict Anderson, *The Spectre of Comparisons: Nationalism, Southeast Asia, and the World* (London: Verso, 1998).

8. Mary Louise Pratt, *Imperial Eyes: Travel Writing and Transculturation* (New York: Routledge, 1992), 4.

9. Hau'ofa, "Our Sea of Islands," 7, 16, 11.

10. Nicholas Thomas, *In Oceania: Visions, Artifacts, Histories* (Durham, NC: Duke University Press, 1997), 17, 188.

11. Harold Bloom, *The Anxiety of Influence: A Theory of Poetry* (New York: Oxford University Press, 1973). Bloom's theory of "misprision" (19), applied primarily in this analysis to Romantic poetry, has taken on a wider resonance within the world of critical theory.

12. Brian Russell Roberts, "Archipelagic Diaspora, Geographical Form, and Hurston's *Their Eyes Were Watching God*," *American Literature* 85, no. 1 (March 2013): 125, 132.

13. James Joyce, *Finnegans Wake* (London: Faber, 1939), 605, 606.

14. Elizabeth McMahon, "Archipelagic Space and the Uncertain Future of National Literatures," *Journal of the Association for the Study of Australian Literature* 13, no. 2 (2013), n.p.

15. Gillian Beer, "The Making of a Cliché: 'No Man Is an Island,'" *European Journal of English Studies* 1, no. 1 (1997): 37, 39–40.

16. Frederick Jackson Turner, "The Significance of the Frontier in American History" (1893), in *The Turner Thesis: Concerning the Role of the Frontier in American History*, ed. George Rogers Taylor, rev. ed. (Lexington, MA: D. C. Heath, 1956), 1–18.

17. Gillian Beer, "The Island and the Aeroplane: The Case of Virginia Woolf" (1990), in *Virginia Woolf: The Common Ground* (Edinburgh: Edinburgh University Press, 1996), 156–57.

18. Ernest Hemingway, *For Whom the Bell Tolls* (New York: Scribner's, 1940). Hemingway's novel, published during World War II, is set during the Spanish Civil War of 1936 to 1939.

19. Beer, "Island and Aeroplane," 150.

20. Balsopoulos, "Nesologies," 18.

21. Elizabeth M. DeLoughrey, *Routes and Roots: Navigating Caribbean and Pacific Island Literatures* (Honolulu: University of Hawai'i Press, 2007), 2.

22. J. G. A. Pocock, "The New British History in Atlantic Perspective: An Antipodean Commentary," *American Historical Review* 104, no. 2 (April 1999): 493, 492, 498.

23. J. G. A. Pocock, *The Discovery of Islands: Essays in British History* (Cambridge: Cambridge University Press, 2005), 23.

24. John Kerrigan, *Archipelagic English: Literature, History, and Politics, 1603–1707* (Oxford: Oxford University Press, 2008), 83.

25. Kerrigan, *Archipelagic English*, 12, 57.

SELECTED BIBLIOGRAPHY

Alaimo, Stacy. "States of Suspension: Trans-corporeality at Sea." *Interdisciplinary Studies in Literature and Environment* 19, no. 3 (2012): 476–93.

Alcoff, Linda Martín. "Mignolo's Epistemology of Coloniality." CR: *The New Centennial Review* 7, no. 3 (2007): 79–101.

Allen, Chadwick. *Blood Narrative: Indigenous Identity in American Indian and Maori Literary and Activist Texts.* Durham, NC: Duke University Press, 2002.

———. *Trans-Indigenous: Methodologies for Global Native Literary Studies.* Minneapolis: University of Minnesota Press, 2012.

Allewaert, Monique. *Ariel's Ecology: Plantations, Personhood, and Colonialism in the American Tropics.* Minneapolis: University of Minnesota Press, 2013.

Amar, Paul. *The Security Archipelago: Human-Security States, Sexuality Politics, and the End of Neoliberalism.* Durham, NC: Duke University Press, 2013.

Anae, Melani. "From Kava to Coffee: The 'Browning' of Auckland." In *Almighty Auckland,* edited by Ian Carter, David Craig, and Steve Matthewman, 89–110. Palmerston North, NZ: Dunmore Press, 2004.

Anagnostou, Yiorgos. "Model Americans, Quintessential Greeks: Ethnic Success and Assimilation in Diaspora." *Diaspora* 12, no. 3 (2003): 279–327.

Anderson, Ben, Matthew Kearnes, Colin McFarlane, and Dan Swanton. "On Assemblages and Geography." *Dialogues in Human Geography* 2, no. 2 (2012): 171–89.

Anderson, Benedict. *Imagined Communities: Reflections on the Origins and Spread of Nationalism.* London: Verso, 1983.

———. *The Spectre of Comparisons: Nationalism, Southeast Asia, and the World.* London: Verso, 1998.

Andrew, Dale. "Archipelagos and the Law of the Sea: Island Straits States or Island-Studded Sea Space?" *Marine Policy* 2, no. 1 (1978): 46–64.

Andrews, H. Gordon. "'White Trash' in the Antilles." In *Negro: An Anthology,* edited by Nancy Cunard, 303–7. 1934. Reprint, London: Bloomsbury Academic, 1996.

Appadurai, Arjun. *Modernity at Large: Cultural Dimensions of Globalization.* Minneapolis: University of Minnesota Press, 1996.

Appiah, Kwame Anthony. *Cosmopolitanism: Ethics in a World of Strangers.* New York: W. W. Norton, 2007.

Appleby, Joyce. *Shores of Knowledge: New World Discoveries and the Scientific Imagination*. New York: Norton, 2014.
"Archipelago." *Oxford English Dictionary*. 2nd ed. Oxford: Clarendon Press, 1989.
Arias, Santa. "Rethinking Space: An Outsider's View of the Spatial Turn." *GeoJournal* 75, no. 1 (2010): 29–41.
Axford, Barrie. *Theories of Globalization*. Cambridge: Polity Press, 2013.
Balasopoulos, Antonis. "Nesologies: Island Form and Postcolonial Geopoetics." *Postcolonial Studies* 11, no. 1 (2008): 9–26.
Baldacchino, Godfrey. "Islands, Island Studies, Island Studies Journal." *Island Studies Journal* 1, no. 1 (2006): 3–18.
———. "Studying Islands: On Whose Terms? Some Epistemological and Methodological Challenges to the Pursuit of Island Studies." *Island Studies Journal* 3, no. 1 (2008): 37–56.
———, ed. *A World of Islands: An Island Studies Reader*. Charlottetown, Canada: Institute of Island Studies, University of Prince Edward Island, 2007.
Baldacchino, Godfrey, and David Milne, eds. *The Case for Non-Sovereignty: Lessons from Sub-National Island Jurisdictions*. New York: Routledge, 2008.
Baldoz, Rick, and César Ayala. "The Bordering of America: Colonialism and Citizenship in the Philippines and Puerto Rico." *Centro Journal* 25, no. 1 (2013): 76–105.
Baptiste, Fitzroy A. "United States–Caribbean Relations from World War II to the Present: The Social Nexus." In *U.S.-Caribbean Relations: Their Impact on Peoples and Culture*, edited by Ransford W. Palmer, 7–52. Westport, CT: Praeger, 1998.
Batongbacal, Jay L., ed. *Archipelagic Studies: Charting New Waters*. Diliman, Quezon City, Philippines: UP Systemwide Network on Archipelagic and Ocean Studies in cooperation with the UP Center for Integrative and Development Studies, 1998.
———. "Defining Archipelagic Studies." In Batongbacal, *Archipelagic Studies*, 183–94.
Beer, Gillian. "The Island and the Aeroplane: The Case of Virginia Woolf" (1990). In *Virginia Woolf: The Common Ground, Essays by Gillian Beer*. 149–78. Edinburgh: Edinburgh University Press, 1996.
———. "The Making of a Cliché: 'No Man Is an Island.'" *European Journal of English Studies* 1, no. 1 (1997): 33–47.
Belnap, Jeffrey, and Raúl Fernández, eds. *José Martí's "Our America": From National to Hemispheric Cultural Studies*. Durham, NC: Duke University Press, 1998.
Benítez-Rojo, Antonio. *La isla que se repite: El Caribe y la perspectiva posmoderna*. Hanover, NH: Ediciones del Norte, 1989.
———. *The Repeating Island: The Caribbean and the Postmodern Perspective*. 2nd ed. Trans. James E. Maraniss. Durham, NC: Duke University Press, 1996.
Bevacqua, Michael Lujan. "Ghosts, Chamorros and Non-Voting Delegates: Guam! Where the Production of America's Sovereignty Begins." PhD diss., University of California, San Diego, 2010.
———. "My Island Is One Big American Footnote." In *The Space Between: Negotiating Culture, Place, and Identity in the Pacific*, edited by Marata Tamaira, 120–22. Honolulu, HI: Center for Pacific Islands Studies, Occasional Paper 44, 2009.

Blanco, John D. *Frontier Constitutions: Christianity and Colonial Empire in the Nineteenth-Century Philippines*. Berkeley: University of California Press, 2009.

Blank, Paul W. "The Pacific: A Mediterranean in the Making?" *Geographical Review* 89, no. 2 (1999): 265–77.

Blum, Hester. "Introduction: Oceanic Studies." *Atlantic Studies* 10, no. 2 (2013): 151–55.

———. "The Prospect of Oceanic Studies." *PMLA* 125, no. 3 (2010): 670–77.

Bonilla, Yarimar. *Non-Sovereign Futures: French Caribbean Politics in the Wake of Disenchantment*. Chicago: University of Chicago Press, 2015.

Borell, Belinda. "Living in the City Ain't So Bad: Cultural Identity for Young Maori in South Auckland." In *New Zealand Identities: Departures and Destinations*, edited by James H. Liu, Tim McCreanor, Tracey McIntosh, and Teresia Teaiwa, 191–206. Wellington, NZ: Victoria University of Wellington Press, 2005.

Bosch, Juan. *De Cristóbal Colón a Fidel Castro: El Caribe frontera imperial*. Santo Domingo, Dominican Republic: Editora Alfa y Omega, 1981.

Boyce Davies, Carole, and Monica Jardine. "Imperial Geographies and Caribbean Nationalism: At the Border between 'A Dying Colonialism' and U.S. Hegemony." *New Centennial Review* 3, no. 3 (2003): 151–74.

Brathwaite, Edward Kamau. *Contradictory Omens: Cultural Diversity and Integration in the Caribbean*. Mona, Jamaica: Savacou, 1974.

Brickhouse, Anna. *The Unsettlement of America: Translation, Interpretation, and the Story of Don Luis Velasco, 1560–1945*. New York: Oxford University Press, 2014.

Britton, Celia M. *Édouard Glissant and Postcolonial Theory: Strategies of Language and Resistance*. Charlottesville: University of Virginia Press, 1999.

Buhle, Paul. *C. L. R. James: The Artist as Revolutionary*. London: Verso, 1988.

Bulosan, Carlos. *America Is in the Heart*. 1946. Reprint, Seattle: University of Washington Press, 1976.

———. *On Becoming Filipino: Selected Writings of Carlos Bulosan*. Edited by E. San Juan Jr. Philadelphia: Temple University Press, 1995.

Burnett, Christina Duffy, and Burke Marshall. "Between the Foreign and the Domestic: The Doctrine of Territorial Incorporation, Invented and Reinvented." In Duffy and Marshall, *Foreign in a Domestic Sense*, 1–36.

———, eds. *Foreign in a Domestic Sense: Puerto Rico, American Expansion, and the Constitution*. Durham, NC: Duke University Press, 2001.

Butcher, John C. "Becoming an Archipelagic State: The Juanda Declaration of 1957 and the 'Struggle' to Gain International Recognition of the Archipelagic Principle," 28–48. In *Indonesia beyond the Water's Edge: Managing an Archipelagic State*. Singapore: Institute of Southeast Asian Studies, 2009.

Byrd, Jodi. *The Transit of Empire: Indigenous Critiques of Colonialism*. Minneapolis: University of Minnesota Press, 2011.

Camacho, Keith L. "After 9/11: Militarized Borders and Social Movements in the Mariana Islands." *American Quarterly* 64, no. 4 (2012): 685–713.

———. *Cultures of Commemoration: The Politics of War, Memory, and History in the Mariana Islands*. Honolulu: University of Hawai'i Press, 2011.

Carrera, Magali. *Traveling from New Spain to Mexico: Mapping Practices of Nineteenth-Century Mexico*. Durham, NC: Duke University Press, 2011.

Carroll, Jeffrey, Brandy Nālani McDougall, and Georganne Nordstrom, eds. *Huihui: Navigating Art and Literature in the Pacific.* Honolulu: University of Hawai'i Press, 2014.

Carter, Paul. "Dark with Excess of Bright: Mapping the Coastlines of Knowledge." In *Mappings*, edited by Denis Cosgrove, 125–47. London: Reaktion Books, 1999.

Césaire, Aimé. *A Tempest.* Translated by Richard Miller. New York: TCG Translations, 2002.

Chang, David A. *The World and All the Things upon It: Native Hawaiian Geographies of Exploration.* Minneapolis: University of Minnesota Press, 2016.

Clifford, James. *Routes: Travel and Translation in the Late Twentieth Century.* Cambridge, MA: Harvard University Press, 1997.

Cohen, Margaret. "Literary Studies on the Terraqueous Globe." *PMLA* 125, no. 3 (2010): 657–62.

Colón, Jesús. *A Puerto Rican in New York and Other Sketches.* New York: Arno Press, 1975.

Constantakopoulou, Christy. *The Dance of the Islands: Insularity, Networks, the Athenian Empire, and the Aegean World.* New York: Oxford University Press, 2007.

Coquia, Jorge R. "Development of the Archipelagic Doctrine as a Recognized Principle of International Law." *Philippine Law Journal* 58, no. 2 (1983): 13–41.

Corbett, Debra G., Christine Lefevre, and Douglas Siegel-Causey. "The Western Aleutians: Cultural Isolation and Environmental Change." *Human Ecology* 25, no. 3 (September 1997): 459–79.

Cribb, Robert, and Michele Ford. "Indonesia as an Archipelago: Managing Islands, Managing the Seas." In *Indonesia beyond the Water's Edge: Managing an Archipelagic State,* 1–27. Singapore: Institute of Southeast Asian Studies, 2009.

Crocombe, Ron. *The South Pacific.* Suva, Fiji: University of the South Pacific Press, 2008.

Cruz-Malavé, Arnaldo Manuel. "'Under the Skirt of Liberty': Giannina Braschi Rewrites Empire." *American Quarterly* 66, no. 3 (2014): 801–18.

Curry, David Park. *Childe Hassam: An Island Garden Revisited.* New York: W. W. Norton and Company, 1990.

Curtin, Philip D. *The Rise and Fall of the Plantation Complex: Essays in Atlantic History.* Cambridge: Cambridge University Press, 1990.

D'Arcy, Paul. *The People of the Sea: Environment, Identity, and History in Oceania.* Honolulu: University of Hawai'i Press, 2006.

Dash, J. Michael. "Remembering Édouard Glissant." *Callaloo* 34, no. 3 (2011): 671–75.

Dautel, Susan. "Transoceanic Trash: International and United States Strategies for the Great Pacific Garbage Patch." *Golden Gate University Environmental Law Journal* 3, no. 1 (2009): 181–208.

Davidson, Emily F. "Among Spectators and Agents of History: Navigating through the Memory Sites of the Panama Canal." *Global South* 6, no. 2 (2013): 130–53.

Davis, Gregson. *Aimé Césaire.* Cambridge: Cambridge University Press, 1997.

Davis, Jeffrey Sasha. "Representing Place: 'Deserted Isles' and the Reproduction of Bikini Atoll." *Annals of the Association of American Geographers* 95, no. 3 (2005): 607–25.

de Waal Malefijt, Annemarie. *The Javanese of Suriname: Segment of a Plural Society.* Assen, Netherlands: Van Gorcum, 1963.

Deleuze, Gilles. *Desert Islands and Other Texts, 1953–1974.* Los Angeles: Semiotext(e) Foreign Agents Series, 2004.

DeLoughrey, Elizabeth. "Heavy Waters: Waste and Atlantic Modernity." PMLA 125, no. 3 (2010): 703–12.

———. "Introduction: Of Oceans and Islands." *New Literatures Review* 47–48 (2011): 1–15.

———. "Island Writing, Creole Cultures." In *The Cambridge History of Postcolonial Literature,* edited by Ato Quayson, 802–32. Cambridge: Cambridge University Press, 2014.

———. "'The litany of islands, The rosary of archipelagoes': Caribbean and Pacific Archipelagraphy." ARIEL: *A Review of International English Literature* 32, no. 1 (2001): 21–51

———. *Routes and Roots: Navigating Caribbean and Pacific Island Literatures.* Honolulu: University of Hawai'i Press, 2007.

Dening, Greg. *Beach Crossings: Voyaging across Times, Cultures, and Self.* Philadelphia: University of Pennsylvania Press, 2004.

Diaz, Vicente M. *Repositioning the Missionary: Rewriting the Histories of Colonialism, Native Catholicism, and Indigineity in Guam.* Honolulu: University of Hawai'i Press, 2010.

———. "Voyaging for Anti-Colonial Recovery: Austronesian Seafaring, Archipelagic Rethinking, and the Re-mapping of Indigeneity." *Pacific Asia Inquiry* 2, no. 1 (2011): 21–32.

Diaz, Vicente, and J. Kēhaulani Kauanui. "Native Pacific Cultural Studies on the Edge." *Contemporary Pacific* 13, no. 2 (2001): 315–42.

Duany, Jorge. *The Puerto Rican Nation on the Move: Identities on the Island and in the United States.* Chapel Hill: University of North Carolina Press, 2002.

Dunn, Richard S. *Sugar and Slaves: The Rise of the Planter Class in the English West Indies, 1624–1713.* London: Jonathan Cape, 1972.

Edmond, Rod, and Vanessa Smith, eds. *Islands in History and Representation.* London: Routledge, 2003.

Elden, Stuart. "How Should We Do the History of Territory?" *Territory, Politics, Governance* 1, no. 1 (2013): 5–20.

———. "Missing the Point: Globalization, Deterritorialization and the Space of the World." *Transactions of the Institute of British Geographers* n.s., 30, no. 1 (2005): 8–19.

Fairbairn-Dunlop, Peggy, and Gabrielle Makisi, eds. *Making Our Place: Growing Up PI in New Zealand.* Palmerston North, NZ: Dunmore Press, 2003.

Feinberg, Richard, et al. "'Drawing the Coral Heads': Mental Mapping and Its Physical Representation in a Polynesian Community." *Cartographic Journal* 40, no. 3 (2003): 243–53.

Figueroa, Esther, Gerard A. Finin, Scott Kroeker, Katerina M. Teaiwa, and Terence Wesley-Smith. "Islands of Globalization: Pacific and Caribbean Perspectives." *Social and Economic Studies* 56, nos. 1–2 (2007): 32–40.

Fischer, Steven Roger. *A History of the Pacific Islands.* Houndmills, UK: Palgrave, 2002.

———. *Islands: From Atlantis to Zanzibar.* London: Reaktion Books, 2012.

Fishkin, Shelley Fisher. "Crossroads of Cultures: The Transnational Turn in American Studies—Presidential Address to the American Studies Association, November 12, 2004." *American Quarterly* 57, no. 1 (2005): 17–57.

Fleras, Augie, and Paul Spoonley. *Recalling Aotearoa.* Auckland, NZ: Oxford University Press, 1999.

Fluck, Winfried. "A New Beginning? Transnationalisms." *New Literary History* 42, no. 3 (2011): 365–84.

Fonkoua, Romuald. *Aimé Césaire.* Paris: Perrin, 2010.

Gaynor, Jennifer L. "Maritime Ideologies and Ethnic Anomalies: Sea Space and the Structure of Subalternity in the Southeast Asian Littoral." In *Seascapes: Maritime Histories, Littoral Cultures, and Transoceanic Exchanges,* edited by Jerry H. Bentley, Renated Bridenthal, and Kären Wigen, 53–68. Honolulu: University of Hawai'i Press, 2007.

Giles, Paul. "Antipodean American Literature: Franklin, Twain, and the Sphere of Subalternity." *American Literary History* 20, nos. 1–2 (2008): 22–50.

Gillis, John R. "Islands in the Making of an Atlantic Oceania, 1500–1800." In *Seascapes: Maritime Histories, Littoral Cultures, and Transoceanic Exchanges,* edited by Jerry H. Bentley, Renated Bridenthal, and Kären Wigen, 21–37. Honolulu: University of Hawai'i Press, 2007.

———. *Islands of the Mind: How the Human Imagination Created the Atlantic World.* New York: Palgrave Macmillan, 2004.

———. "Island Sojourns." *Geographical Review* 97, no. 2 (2007): 274–87.

———. "Not Continents in Miniature: Islands as Ecotones." *Island Studies Journal* 9, no. 1 (2014): 155–66.

Gillman, Susan. "Oceans of Longue Durées." *PMLA* 127, no. 2 (2012): 328–34.

Gilroy, Paul. *The Black Atlantic: Modernity and Double Consciousness.* Cambridge, MA: Harvard University Press, 1993.

Glissant, Édouard. *La cohée du Lamentin.* Paris: Gallimard, 2005.

———. *Le discours antillais.* Paris: Gallimard, 1997.

———. *L'intention poétique.* Paris: Gallimard, 1997.

———. *Monsieur Toussaint.* Translated by J. Michael Dash and Édouard Glissant. Boulder, CO: Lynne Rienner, 2005.

———. *Philosophie de la Relation.* Paris: Gallimard, 2009.

———. *Poetics of Relation.* Translated by Betsy Wing. Ann Arbor: University of Michigan Press, 1997.

———. *Soleil de la conscience.* Paris: Seuil, 1956.

———. *Traité du Tout-monde.* Paris: Gallimard, 1997.

———. *Tratado de todo-mundo.* Translated by María Teresa Gallego Urrútia. Barcelona: El Cobre Ediciones, 2006.

———. *Une nouvelle région du monde.* Paris: Gallimard, 2006.

———. "The Unforeseeable Diversity of the Word." In *Beyond Dichotomies: Histories, Identities, Cultures, and the Challenge of Globalization,* edited by Elisabeth Mudimbe-Boyi, 287–98. Albany: State University of New York Press, 2002.

Glover, Kaiama L. *Haiti Unbound: A Spiralist Challenge to the Postcolonial Canon.* Liverpool, UK: Liverpool University Press, 2010.
Gómez-Barris, Macarena, and Licia Fiol-Matta. "Introduction: *Las Américas Quarterly.*" *American Quarterly* 66, no. 3 (2014): 493–504.
Gonzalez, N. V. M., and Oscar V. Campomanes. "Filipino American Literature." In *An Interethnic Companion to Asian American Literature,* ed. King-Kok Cheung (Cambridge: Cambridge University Press, 1997): 62–124.
González-Vélez, Mirerza. "Mapping Points of Origin in the Transnational Caribbean: The Foundational Narrative of the Puerto Rican Pioneer Family in the Virgin Islands." *Revista Umbral* 8 (2014): 46–63.
Goudie, Sean X. "'Our Nation Is a Caribbean Nation: The West Indies and Early U.S. America." In *Creole America: The West Indies and the Formation of Literature and Culture in the New Republic.* Philadelphia: University of Pennsylvania Press, 2006.
Gruesz, Kirstin Silva. *Ambassadors of Culture: The Transamerican Origins of Latino Writing.* Chapel Hill: University of North Carolina Press, 2002.
Guilbault, Jocelyne. *Governing Sound: The Cultural Politics of Trinidad's Carnival Musics.* Chicago: University of Chicago Press, 2007.
Guterl, Matthew Pratt. *American Mediterranean: Southern Slaveholders in the Age of Emancipation.* Cambridge, MA: Harvard University Press, 2008.
Hagimoto, Koichi. *Between Empires: Martí, Rizal, and the Intercolonial Alliance.* New York: Palgrave, 2013.
Hall, Robert B. *Area Studies: With Special Reference to Their Implications for Research in the Social Sciences.* New York: Social Science Research Council, 1949.
Hall, Stuart. "Negotiating Caribbean Identities." *New Left Review* 209 (1995): 3–14.
Hammond, Joyce D. "Hawaiian Flag Quilts: Multivalent Symbols of a Hawaiian Quilt Tradition." *Hawaiian Journal of History* 27 (1993): 1–26.
Hanai, Colleen. "Hae Hawaii." *Hawaiʻi Historical Review* (October 1963): 93–103.
Hantel, Max. "Rhizomes and the Space of Translation: On Édouard Glissant's Spiral Retelling." *Small Axe* 17, no. 3 42 (2013): 100–112.
Harris, Peter. "Decolonising the Special Relationship: Diego Garcia, the Chagossians, and Anglo-American Relations." *Review of International Studies* 39, no. 3 (2013): 707–27.
Harris, Susan K. *God's Arbiters: Americans and the Philippines, 1898–1902.* New York: Oxford University Press, 2011.
Hauʻofa, Epeli. "The Ocean in Us." *The Contemporary Pacific* 10, no. 2 (1998): 391–410.
———. "Our Sea of Islands." In *A New Oceania: Rediscovering Our Sea of Islands,* edited by Eric Waddell, Vijay Naidu, and Epeli Hauʻofa, 2–16. Suva, Fiji: University of the South Pacific/Beake House, 1993.
———. *We Are the Ocean: Selected Works.* Honolulu: University of Hawaiʻi Press, 2008.
Hay, Peter. "A Phenomenology of Islands." *Island Studies Journal* 1, no. 1 (2006): 19–42.
Hayward, Philip. "Aquapelagos and Aquapelagic Assemblages." *Shima: International Journal of Research into Island Cultures* 6, no. 1 (2012): 1–11.

Headley, Clevis. "Glissant's Existential Ontology of Difference." CLR *James Journal* 18, no. 1 (2012): 59–101.

Hezel, Francis X. "From Conversion to Conquest: The Early Spanish Mission in the Marianas." *Journal of Pacific History* 17, no. 3 (1982): 115–37.

Hiepko, Andrea Schwieger. "Creolization as a Poetics of Culture: Édouard Glissant's 'Archipelic' Thinking." In *A Pepper-Pot of Cultures: Aspects of Creolization in the Caribbean*, edited by Gordon Collier and Ulrich Fleischmann, 237–59. New York: Editions Rodopi, 2003.

Holt, John Dominis. *On Being Hawaiian.* 1964. Reprint, Honolulu, HI: Ku Pa'a, 1995.

Hoskins, Janet, and Viet Thanh Nguyen. *Transpacific Studies: Framing an Emerging Field.* Honolulu: University of Hawai'i Press, 2014.

Hsu, Hsuan L. "Guåhan (Guam), Literary Emergence, and the American Pacific in *Homebase* and *from unincorporated territory*." *American Literary History* 24, no. 2 (2012): 281–307.

Huang, Hsinya. "Toward Trans-Pacific Ecopoetics: Three Indigenous Texts." *Comparative Literature Studies* 50, no. 1 (2013): 120–47.

Hulme, Peter. "Writing on the Land: Cuba's Literary Geography." *Transactions of the Institute of British Geographers* 37, no. 3 (2012): 346–58.

Iannini, Chris. *Fatal Revolutions: Natural History, West Indian Slavery, and the Routes of American Literature.* Chapel Hill: University of North Carolina Press, 2012.

Irving, Washington. *History of the Life and Voyages of Christopher Columbus.* Vols. 1–2. Philadelphia, PA: Lea & Blanchard, 1841.

Irwin, Bernice Pi'ilani. *I Knew Queen Lili'uokalani.* 1960. Reprint, Honolulu, HI: Native Books, 2000.

Isaac, Allan Punzalan. *American Tropics: Articulating Filipino America.* Minneapolis: University of Minnesota Press, 2006.

James, C. L. R. *At the Rendezvous of Victory: Selected Writings.* London: Allison and Busby, 1984.

———. *The Black Jacobins: Toussaint L'Ouverture and the San Domingo Revolution.* 2nd ed., rev. New York: Vintage/Random House, 1963.

———. *The Future in the Present: Selected Writings.* London: Allison and Busby, 1977.

———. *Mariners, Renegades, and Castaways: The Story of Herman Melville and the World We Live In.* Hanover, NH: University Press of New England, 2001.

———. *Modern Politics.* Detroit, MI: Bewick/Ed, 1973.

Jetnil-Kijiner, Kathy. "United Nations Climate Summit Opening Ceremony—A Poem to My Daughter," *Iep Jeltok: A Basket of Poetry and Writing from Kathy Jetnil-Kijiner.* Accessed Oct. 16, 2016. https://jkijiner.wordpress.com/2014/09/24/united-nations-climate-summit-opening-ceremony-my-poem-to-my-daughter/.

Johnson, Chalmers. *The Sorrows of Empire: Militarism, Secrecy, and the End of the Republic.* New York: Henry Holt, 2004.

Kaplan, Amy. "'Left Alone with America': The Absence of Empire in the Study of American Culture." In *Cultures of United States Imperialism,* edited by Amy Kaplan and Donald E. Pease, 3–21. Durham, NC: Duke University Press, 1993.

———. "Violent Belongings and the Question of Empire Today." *American Quarterly* 56, no. 1 (2004): 7–18.

———. "Where Is Guantánamo?" *American Quarterly* 57, no. 3 (2005): 831–58.

Kauanui, J. Kēhaulani. *Hawaiian Blood: Colonialism and the Politics of Sovereignty and Indigenity.* Durham, NC: Duke University Press, 2008.

Keown, Michelle. *Pacific Islands Writing: The Postcolonial Literatures of Aotearoa / New Zealand and Oceania.* New York: Oxford University Press, 2007.

———. *Postcolonial Pacific Writing: Representations of the Body.* New York: Routledge, 2005.

Kerrigan, John. *Archipelagic English: Literature, History, and Politics, 1603–1707.* Oxford: Oxford University Press, 2008.

Kincaid, Jamaica. "On Seeing England for the First Time." *Transition* 51 (1991): 32–40.

———. *A Small Place.* New York: Farrar, Straus, and Giroux, 1988.

Kirk, Gwen, and Lisa Natividad. "Fortress Guam: Resistance to U.S. Military Mega-Buildup." *Asia-Pacific Journal.* May 10, 2010. Accessed August 15, 2010. http://japanfocus.org/-Gwyn-Kirk/3356.

Knight, Franklin W. *The Caribbean: The Genesis of a Fragmented Nationalism.* 2nd ed. New York: Oxford University Press, 1990.

Kuptana, Rosemarie. "The Inuit Sea." *Nilliajut: Inuit Perspectives on Security, Patriotism and Sovereignty* (Ottowa: Inuit Tapiriit Kanatami, 2013): 10–12.

Kurochkin, Oleg. *The Annexation of Micronesia: US Colonialism in the Twentieth Century.* Moscow: Novosti, 1986.

Kuwada, Bryan Kamaoli. "E Mau nō Kou Welo ʻana: The Appropriation of the Hawaiian Flag." *ʻŌiwi: A Native Hawaiian Journal* 4 (2009): 22–30.

Lai, Paul. "Discontiguous States of America: The Paradox of Unincorporation in Craig Santos Perez's Poetics of Chamorro Guam." *Journal of Transnational American Studies* 3, no. 2 (2011): 1–28.

Lal, Brij V., ed. *Bittersweet: The Indo-Fijian Experience.* Canberra, AU: Pandanus Books, 2004.

Lamming, George. *The Pleasures of Exile.* 1960. Reprint, New York: Alison and Busby, 1984.

Lee, Maurice S. "Deserted Islands and Overwhelmed Readers." *American Literary History* 26, no. 2 (2014): 207–33.

Leibowitz, Arnold H. *Defining Status: A Comprehensive Analysis of United States Territorial Relations.* Netherlands: Martinus Nijhoff, 1989.

Lennox, Patrick. *At Home and Abroad: The Canada-US Relationship and Canada's Place in the World.* Vancouver: University of British Columbia Press, 2010.

Lewis, Martin W. "Dividing the Ocean Sea." *Geographical Review* 89, no. 2 (1999): 188–214.

Lewis, Martin W., and Kären E. Wigen. *The Myth of Continents: A Critique of Metageography.* Berkeley: University of California Press, 1997.

Lionnet, Françoise. "Continents and Archipelagoes: From *E Pluribus Unum* to Creolized Solidarities." PMLA 123, no. 5 (2008): 1503–15.

———. "Cosmopolitan or Creole Lives? Globalized Oceans and Insular Identities." *Profession* (2011): 23–43.

Llenín-Figueroa, Carmen Beatriz. "Imagined Islands: A Caribbean Tidalectics." PhD diss., Duke University, 2012.

Lyons, Paul, and Ty P. Kāwika Tengan. "Introduction: Pacific Currents." *American Quarterly* 67, no. 3 (2015): 545–73.
Macpherson, Cluny. "Pacific Diaspora." In *Encyclopaedia of the Pacific*, edited by Brij V. Lal, 106–8. Honolulu: University of Hawai'i Press, 2000.
Magallona, Merlin M. "Reflections on Strategic Research: Towards an Archipelagic Studies and Ocean Policy Program." In Batongbacal, *Archipelagic Studies*, 7–10.
Maldonado-Torres, Nelson. "Thinking through the Decolonial Turn: Post-Continental Interventions in Theory, Philosophy, and Critique—An Introduction." *Transmodernity: Journal of Peripheral Cultural Production of the Luso-Hispanic World* 1, no. 2 (2011): 1–15.
Malkin, Irad. *A Small Greek World: Networks in the Ancient Mediterranean*. New York: Oxford University Press, 2011.
Mandelbrot, Benoit. *The Fractal Geometry of Nature*. New York: Freeman, 1983.
———. *Fractals: Form, Chance, and Dimension*. San Francisco: Freeman, 1977.
———. "How Long Is the Coast of Britain? Statistical Self-Similarity and Fractional Dimension." *Science*, n.s. 156, no. 3775 (1967): 636–38.
Martínez San Miguel, Yolanda. *Coloniality of Diasporas: Rethinking Intra-Colonial Migrations in a Pan-Caribbean Context*. New York: Palgrave Macmillan, 2014.
Matsuda, Matt K. *Pacific Worlds: A History of Seas, Peoples, and Cultures*. New York: Cambridge University Press, 2012.
McCall, Grant. "Nissology: A Proposal for Consideration." *Journal of the Pacific Society* 17, no. 2–3 (1994): 1–14.
McCall, Grant, and John Connell, eds. *A World Perspective on Pacific Islander Migration: Australia, New Zealand, and the USA*. Sydney: University of New South Wales, 1993.
McKeown, Adam. *Chinese Migration Networks and Cultural Change: Peru, Chicago, Hawaii*. Chicago: University of Chicago Press, 2001.
McMahon, Elizabeth. "Archipelagic Space and the Uncertain Future of National Literatures." *Journal of the Association for the Study of Australian Literature* 13, no. 2 (2013), http://www.nla.gov.au/openpublish/index.php/jasal/article/viewArticle/3154.
Mein Smith, Philippa, Peter Hempenstall, and Shaun Goldfinch. *Remaking the Tasman World*. Christchurch, NZ: Canterbury University Press, 2009.
Metzger, Sean, Francisco-J. Hernández Adrián, and Michaeline Crichlow. "Introduction: Islands, Images, Imaginaries." *Third Text* 28, nos. 4–5 (2014): 333–43.
Mignolo, Walter. *Local Histories / Global Designs: Coloniality, Subaltern Knowledges, and Border Thinking*. Princeton, NJ: Princeton University Press, 2000.
Millett, Nathaniel. "Borderlands in the Atlantic World." *Atlantic Studies* 10, no. 2 (2013): 268–95.
Mohammed, Patricia. "Mapping the West Indies." In *Imaging the Caribbean: Culture and Visual Translation*, 52–90. Oxford: Macmillan, 2009.
Moretti, Franco. *Distant Reading*. London: Verso, 2013.
Morillo-Alicea, Javier. "Uncharted Landscapes of 'Latin America': The Philippines in the Spanish Imperial Archipelago." In *Interpreting Spanish Colonialism: Empires, Nations, and Legends*, edited by Christopher Schmidt-Nowara and John Nieto-Phillips, 25–53. Albuquerque: University of New Mexico Press, 2005.

Munavvar, Muhammad. *Ocean States: Archipelagic Regimes in the Law of the Sea.* Dordrecht, Netherlands: Martinus Nijhoff Publishers, 1995.

Murphy, Gretchen. *Hemispheric Imaginings: The Monroe Doctrine and Narratives of U.S. Empire.* Durham, NC: Duke University Press, 2005.

Neptune, Harvey. *Caliban and the Yankees: Trinidad and the United States Occupation.* Chapel Hill: University of North Carolina Press, 2007.

———. "Manly Rivalries and Mopsies Gender, Nationality, and Sexuality in United States-Occupied Trinidad." *Radical History Review* 87 (2003): 78–95.

Niedenthal, Jack. *For the Good of Mankind: A History of the People of Bikini and Their Islands.* Majuro, Marshall Islands: Bravo Publishers, 2001.

Noudelmann, Francois. "Entretien avec Édouard Glissant: La relation, imprédictible et sans morale." *Rue Descartes* 37 (2002): 76–95.

Novak, Maximillian E. "Robinson Crusoe and Economic Utopia." *Kenyon Review* 25, no. 3 (1963): 474–90.

Oldenziel, Ruth. "Islands: The United States as a Networked Empire." In *Entangled Geographies: Empire and Technologies in the Global Cold War,* edited by Gabrielle Hecht, 13–41. Cambridge, MA: MIT Press, 2011.

Osorio, Jonathan Kay Kamakawiwoʻole. *Dismembering Lāhui: A History of the Hawaiian Nation to 1887.* Honolulu: University of Hawaiʻi Press, 2002.

Pease, Donald. "C. L. R. James, *Moby Dick,* and the Emergence of Transnational American Studies." *Arizona Quarterly* 56, no. 3 (2000): 93–123.

———. "Re-thinking 'American Studies after US Exceptionalism.'" *American Literary History* 21, no. 1 (2009): 19–27.

Peattie, Mark R. *Nanʻyō: The Rise and Fall of the Japanese in Micronesia, 1885–1945.* Honolulu: University of Hawaiʻi Press, 1988.

Pedreira, Antonio. *Insularismo.* Río Piedras, Puerto Rico: Editorial Edil, 1992.

Perez, Craig Santos. "Blue-Washing the Colonization and Militarization of Our Ocean." *Hawaiian Independent.* July 26, 2014. http://hawaiiindependent.net/story/blue-washing-the-colonization-and-militarization-of-our-ocean.

———. *from unincorporated territory [guma'].* Richmond, CA: Omnidawn Publishing, 2014.

———. *from unincoporated territory [hacha].* San Diego, CA: Tinfish Press, 2008.

———. *from unincorporated territory [saina].* Richmond, CA: Omnidawn Publishing, 2010.

———. "The Page Transformed: A Conversation with Craig Santos Perez." *Lantern Review* (2010). Accessed Oct. 15, 2016. http://www.lanternreview.com/blog/2010/03/12/the-page-transformed-a-conversation-with-craig-santos-perez/.

———. "The Poetics of Mapping Diaspora: Navigating Culture and Being from Part 1" (2011). Accessed Oct. 15, 2016. http://www.doveglion.com/2011/04/craig-santos-perez-the-poetics-of-mapping-diaspora-navigating-culture-and-being-from-part-1/.

———. "Surviving Our Fallen: Chamorros, Militarism, Religiosity, and 9/11." Published 2011. Accessed Oct. 15, 2016. https://craigsantosperez.wordpress.com/2011/09/11/surviving-our-fallen-chamorros-militarism-religiosity-and-911-part-1/

———. "Transterritorial Currents and the Imperial Terripelago." *American Quarterly* 67, no. 3 (September 2015): 619–24.

Perloff, Marjorie. "Removing the Eggshells: Rereading Wittgenstein on a Desert Island." *Genre* 33 (2000): 269–77.
Pinet, Simone. *Archipelagoes: Insular Fictions from Chivalric Romance to the Novel.* Minneapolis: University of Minnesota Press, 2011.
Pocock, J. G. A. "British History: A Plea for a New Subject." *Journal of Modern History* 47, no. 4 (1975): 601–21.
———. *The Discovery of Islands: Essays in British History.* Cambridge: Cambridge University Press, 2005.
———. "The New British History in Atlantic Perspective: An Antipodean Commentary." *American Historical Review* 104, no. 2 (1999): 490–500.
Prentice, Chris. "'A Knife through Time': Robert Sullivan's *Star Waka* and the Politics and Poetics of Cultural Difference." *ARIEL* 37, no. 2–3 (2006): 111–35.
Pugh, Jonathan. "Island Movements: Thinking with the Archipelago." *Island Studies Journal* 8, no. 1 (2013): 9–24.
Puri, Shalini. *The Caribbean Postcolonial: Social Equality, Post-Nationalism, and Cultural Hybridity.* New York: Palgrave Macmillan, 2004.
Quiroga, José. "The Cuban Exile Wars: 1976–1981." *American Quarterly* 66, no. 3 (2014): 819–33.
Rafael, Vicente. *The Promise of the Foreign: Nationalism and the Technics of Translation in the Spanish Philippines.* Durham, NC: Duke University Press, 2005.
Raustiala, Kal. *Does the Constitution Follow the Flag? The Evolution of Territoriality in American Law.* New York: Oxford University Press, 2009.
Reckin, Anna. "Tidalectic Lectures: Kamau Brathwaite's Prose/Poetry as Sound-Space." *Anthurium: A Caribbean Studies Journal* 1, no. 1 (2003): article 5.
Rediker, Marcus. "The Red Atlantic; or, 'A Terrible Blast Swept over the Heaving Sea.'" In *Sea Changes: Historicizing the Ocean,* edited by Bernhard Klein and Gesa Mackenthun, 111–30. New York: Routledge, 2004.
Renda, Mary A. *Taking Haiti: Military Occupation and the Culture of U.S. Imperialism, 1915–1940.* Chapel Hill: University of North Carolina Press, 2001.
Retamar, Roberto Fernández. "Caliban: Notes toward a Discussion of Culture in Our America." In *Caliban and Other Essays,* translated by Edward Baker, 3–45. Minneapolis: University of Minnesota Press, 1989.
Roberts, Brian Russell. "Abolitionist Archipelago: Pre- and Post-emancipation Islands of Slavery and Emancipation." *Atlantic Studies* 8, no. 2 (2011): 233–52.
———. "Archipelagic American Literary History and the Philippines." *American Literary History* 27, no. 1 (2015): 128–40.
———. "Archipelagic Diaspora, Geographical Form, and Hurston's *Their Eyes Were Watching God.*" *American Literature* 85, no. 1 (2013): 121–49.
———. "(Ex)Isles in the Harlem Renaissance: The Insular and Archipelagic Topographies of Wallace Thurman's *The Blacker the Berry.*" *Arizona Quarterly* 67, no. 3 (2011): 91–118.
Roberts, Brian Russell, and Michelle Stephens. "Archipelagic American Studies and the Caribbean." *Journal of Transnational American Studies* 5, no. 1 (2013): 1–20.
Roberts, W. Adolphe. *The Caribbean: Our Sea of Destiny.* Indianapolis: Bobbs-Merrill, 1940.

———. *These Many Years: An Autobiography,* edited with introduction by Peter Hulme. Kingston, Jamaica: University of West Indies Press and National Library of Jamaica, 2015.
Robertson, Graeme. "Island Studies Resources." In Baldacchino, *A World of Islands,* 539–78.
Rodriguez, Dylan. *Suspended Apocalypse: White Supremacy, Genocide, and the Filipino Condition.* Minneapolis: University of Minnesota Press, 2009.
Rogers, Robert F. *Destiny's Landfall: A History of Guam.* Honolulu: University of Hawai'i Press, 1995.
Rohlehr, Gordon. *Calypso and Society in Pre-Independence Trinidad.* Port of Spain, Trinidad: Gordon Rohlehr, 1990.
Rowe, John Carlos. "Transpacific Studies and the Cultures of U.S. Imperialism." In *Transpacific Studies,* edited by Janet Hoskins and Viet Nguyen, 134–50. Honolulu: University of Hawai'i Press, 2014.
Rowe, John Carlos, et al. Introduction to *Post-Nationalist American Studies,* edited by John Carlos Rowe, 1–21. Berkeley: University of California Press, 2000.
Saldívar, José David. *Trans-Americanity: Subaltern Modernities, Global Coloniality, and the Cultures of Greater Mexico.* Durham, NC: Duke University Press, 2011.
Sandiford, Keith. *Theorizing a Colonial Caribbean Atlantic Imaginary: Sugar and Obeah.* New York: Routledge, 2011.
San Juan, Epifanio. *The Philippine Temptation: Dialectics of Philippines-U.S. Literary Relations.* Philadelphia: Temple University Press, 1996.
Savory, Elaine. "Utopia, Dystopia, and Caribbean Heterotopia: Writing/Reading the Small Island." *New Literature Review* 47–48 (2011): 35–56.
Schmitt, Robert C. "Holidays in Hawai'i." *Hawaiian Journal of History* 29 (1995): 141–46.
Schulten, Susan. "Richard Edes Harrison and the Challenge to American Cartography." *Imago Mundi* 50 (1998): 174–88.
Schwarz, Bill. "Breaking Bread with History: C. L. R. James and *The Black Jacobins:* Stuart Hall Interviewed by Bill Schwarz." *History Workshop Journal* 46 (1998): 17–31.
Schwyzer, Philip. Introduction to *Archipelagic Identities: Literature and Identity in the Atlantic Archipelago, 1550–1800,* edited by Philip Schwyzer and Simon Mealor, 1–7. Hampshire, UK: Ashgate, 2004.
Shell, Marc. *Islandology: Geography, Rhetoric, Politics.* Stanford, CA: Stanford University Press, 2014.
Sherrod, Robert. *On to Westward: War in the Central Pacific.* New York: Duell, Sloan and Pearce, 1945.
Siler, Julia Flynn. *Lost Kingdom: Hawaii's Last Queen, the Sugar Kings, and America's First Imperial Adventure.* New York: Atlantic Monthly Press, 2012.
Silva, Noenoe. *Aloha Betrayed: Native Hawaiian Resistance to American Colonialism.* Durham, NC: Duke University Press, 2004.
Simmons, Alan B., and Dwaine E. Plaza. "The Caribbean Community in Canada: Transnational Connections and Transformations." In *Transnational Identities and Practices in Canada,* edited by Lloyd Wong and Vic Satzewitch, 130–49. Vancouver: UBC Press, 2006.

Skaggs, Jimmy M. *The Great Guano Rush: Entrepreneurs and American Overseas Expansion.* New York: St. Martin's, 1994.
Smith, John. *Generall Historie of Virginia, New-England, and the Summer Isles.* London: Blackmore, 1632.
Soekarno. "Lahirnja Pantjasila" (*The Birth of Pantjasila*): *An Outline of the Five Principles of the Indonesian State.* [Jakarta]: Ministry of Information, Republic of Indonesia, 1952.
Song, Yann-Huei, and N. Elias Blood-Patterson. "Likelihood of U.S. Becoming a Party to the Law of the Sea Convention during the 112th Congress." *Journal of Maritime Law and Commerce* 43, no. 4 (2012): 447–66.
Soto-Crespo, Ramón. *Mainland Passages: The Cultural Anomaly of Puerto Rico.* Minneapolis: University of Minnesota Press, 2009.
Starosielski, Nicole. "Critical Nodes, Cultural Networks: Re-mapping Guam's Cable Infrastructure." *Amerasia Journal* 37, no. 3 (2011): 18–27.
Steinberg, Philip E. "Lines of Division, Lines of Connection: Stewardship in the World Ocean." *Geographical Review* 89, no. 2 (1999): 254–64.
———. "Of Other Seas: Metaphors and Materialities in Maritime Regions." *Atlantic Studies* 10, no. 2 (2013): 156–69.
———. *The Social Construction of the Ocean.* Cambridge: Cambridge University Press, 2001.
Steinberg, Philip E., Elizabeth Nyman, and Mauro J. Caraccioli. "Atlas Swam: Freedom, Capital, and Floating Sovereignties in the Seasteading Vision." *Antipode* 44, no. 4 (2012): 1532–50.
Stephens, Michelle. "Federated Ocean States: Archipelagic Visions of the Third World at Mid-Century." In *Beyond Windrush: Rethinking Postwar Anglophone Caribbean Literature,* edited by J. Dillon Brown and Leah Rosenberg, 222–37. Jackson: University of Mississippi Press, 2015.
———. "What Is an Island? Caribbean Studies and the Contemporary Visual Artist." *Small Axe* 17, no. 2 41 (2013): 8–26.
Stevens-Arroyo, Anthony. "The Inter-Atlantic Paradigm: The Failure of Spanish Medieval Colonization of the Canary and Caribbean Islands." *Comparative Studies in Society and History* 35, no. 3 (1993): 515–43.
Stratford, Elaine. "Flows and Boundaries: Small Island Discourses and Challenges of Sustainability, Community and Local Environments." *Local Environment* 8, no. 5 (2003): 495–99.
———. "The Idea of Archipelago: Contemplating Island Relations." *Island Studies Journal* 8, no. 1 (2013): 3–8.
Stratford, Elaine, Godfrey Baldacchino, Elizabeth McMahon, Carol Farbotko, and Andrew Harwood. "Envisioning the Archipelago." *Island Studies Journal* 6, no. 2 (2011): 113–30.
Taketani, Etsuko. *The Black Pacific Narrative: Geographic Imaginings of Race and Empire between the World Wars.* Hanover, NH: Dartmouth College Press, 2014.
Taylor, Frank Fonda. *To Hell with Paradise: A History of the Jamaican Tourist Industry.* Pittsburgh, PA: University of Pittsburgh Press, 1993.

Teaiwa, Teresia. "bikinis and other s/pacific n/oceans." *Contemporary Pacific* 6, no. 1 (1994): 87–109.

———. "Native Thoughts: A Pacific Studies Take on Cultural Studies and Diaspora." In *Indigenous Diasporas and Dislocations,* edited by Graham Harvey and Charles D. Thompson Jr., 15–35. Burlington: Ashgate, 2005.

Teaiwa, Teresia, and Sean Mallon. "Ambivalent Kinships? Pacific Peoples in New Zealand." In *New Zealand Identities: Departures and Destinations,* edited by James H. Liu, Tim McCreanor, Tracey McIntosh, and Teresia Teaiwa, 207–29. Wellington, NZ: Victoria University of Wellington Press, 2005.

Te Punga Somerville, Alice. "Our Sea of Anthologies: Collection, Display, and the Deep Blue Sea." In *Cultural Crossings: Negotiating Identities in Francophone and Anglophone Pacific Literature /A la croisée des cultures: De la négociation des identités dans les litteratures francophones et anglophones du Pacifique,* edited by Raylene Ramsay, 217–34. Brussels, Belgium: Peter Lang, 2010.

Thomas, Nicholas. *In Oceania: Visions, Artifacts, Histories.* Durham, NC: Duke University Press, 1997.

Thompson, Lanny. *Imperial Archipelago: Representation and Rule in the Insular Territories under U.S. Dominion after 1898.* Honolulu: University of Hawai'i Press, 2010.

———. *Nuestra Isla y su gente: La construcción del otro puertorriqueño en "Our Islands and Their People."* Río Piedras, PR: Centro de Investigaciones Sociales, 2007. http://edicionesdigitales.info/biblioteca/lanny.pdf.

Trask, Haunani-Kay. *From a Native Daughter: Colonialism and Sovereignty in Hawai'i.* 1993. Reprint, Honolulu: University of Hawai'i Press, 1999.

Trask, Haunani-Kay, and Mililani Trask. "Speeches for the Centennial of the Overthrow, 'Iolani Palace 1993." In Carroll, McDougall, and Nordstrom, *Huihui,* 99–114.

Trotz, Alissa. "Rethinking Caribbean Transnational Connections: Conceptual Itineraries." *Global Networks* 6, no. 1 (2006): 41–59.

Tuason, Julie A. "The Ideology of Empire in *National Geographic Magazine*'s Coverage of the Philippines, 1898–1908." *Geographical Review* 89, no. 1 (1999): 34–53.

Vannini, Phillip, et al. "Reterritorializing Canada: Arctic Ice's Liquid Modernity and the Imagining of a Canadian Archipelago." *Island Studies Journal* 4, no. 2 (2009): 121–38.

Vazquez, Alexandra T. "Learning to Live in Miami." *American Quarterly* 66, no. 3 (2014): 853–73.

Veracini, Lorenzo. *Settler Colonialism: A Theoretical Overview.* Houndmills, UK: Palgrave Macmillan, 2010.

Vine, David. *Island of Shame: The Secret History of the U.S. Military Base on Diego Garcia.* Princeton, NJ: Princeton University Press, 2009.

Walcott, Derek. "Isla Incognita." In *Caribbean Literature and the Environment: Between Nature and Culture,* edited by Elizabeth M. DeLoughrey, Renée K. Gosson, and George B. Handley, 51–57. Charlottesville: University of Virginia Press, 2005.

———. "The Sea Is History." In *Selected Poems.* New York: Farrar, Straus, Giroux, 2007.

Walcott, Rinaldo. "Caribbean Pop Culture in Canada; Or, the Impossibility of Belonging to the Nation." *Small Axe* 5, no. 1 (2001): 123–39.

Warrior, Robert Allen. "A Room of One's Own at the ASA: An Indigenous Provocation." *American Quarterly* 55, no. 4 (2003): 681–87.

Weaver, Jace. *The Red Atlantic: American Indigenes and the Making of the Modern World, 1000–1927.* Chapel Hill: University of North Carolina Press, 2014.

Weigert, Hans W. "Strategic Bases and Collective Security." *Foreign Affairs,* 25, no. 2 (1947): 250–62.

Wendt, Albert. "Towards a New Oceania." *Mana* 1, no. 1 (1976): 49–60.

Wharton, Glenn. *The Painted King: Art, Activism, and Authenticity in Hawaiʻi.* Honolulu: University of Hawaiʻi Press, 2012.

Whitman, Walt. "Passage to India" (1871). In *Leaves of Grass and Other Writings,* edited by Michael Moon, 345–53. New York: W. W. Norton and Co., 2002.

Williams, Eric. *British Historians and the West Indies.* London: Andre Deutsch, 1966.

———. "Impact of the International Crisis upon the Negro in the Caribbean." *Journal of Negro Education* 10, no. 3 (July 1941): 536–44.

Wilson, Rob. *Reimagining the American Pacific: From "South Pacific" to Bamboo Ridge and Beyond.* Durham, NC: Duke University Press, 2000.

Wineera, Vernice. "This Island." In *Into the Luminous Tide,* 4. Provo, UT: Brigham Young University, 2009.

Wolfe, Patrick. *Settler Colonialism and the Transformation of Anthropology: The Politics and Poetics of an Ethnographic Event.* London: Cassell, 1999.

———. "The Settler Complex: An Introduction." *American Indian Culture and Research Journal* 37, no. 2 (2013): 1–22.

Wynter, Sylvia, and Katherine McKittrick. "Unparalleled Catastrophe for Our Species? Or, to Give Humanness a Different Future: Conversations." In *Sylvia Wynter: On Being Human as Praxis,* edited by Katherine McKittrick, 9–89. Durham, NC: Duke University Press, 2015.

Yu, Henry. "Los Angeles and American Studies in a Pacific World of Migration." *American Quarterly* 56 no. 3 (2004): 531–43.

CONTRIBUTORS

BIRTE BLASCHECK is an independent scholar who holds a PhD from Victoria University of Wellington, New Zealand. Her contribution to this volume stems from interdisciplinary research on diaspora and popular celebrity culture, in which she examined the various meanings of Caribbean Canadian and Pacific New Zealand public personalities in arts, sports, and politics for the next generation.

J. MICHAEL DASH is Professor of French at New York University and has worked extensively on Haitian and French Caribbean writers, especially Édouard Glissant, whose works *The Ripening* (1985); *Caribbean Discourse* (1989); and *Monsieur Toussaint* (2005) he has translated into English. His publications include *Literature and Ideology in Haiti* (1981); *Haiti and the United States* (1988); *Édouard Glissant* (1995); and *The Other America: Caribbean Literature in a New World Context* (1998). His most recent books are *Libète: A Haiti Anthology* (1999), with Charles Arthur, and *Culture and Customs of Haiti* (2001).

PAUL GILES is Challis Professor of English at the University of Sydney, Australia. Among his books are *Antipodean America: Australasia and the Constitution of U.S. Literature* (2014), *The Global Remapping of American Literature* (2011); *Transnationalism in Practice: Essays on American Studies, Literature, and Religion* (2010); *Atlantic Republic: The American Tradition in English Literature* (2006); *Virtual Americas: Transnational Fictions and the Transatlantic Imaginary* (2002); *Transatlantic Insurrections: British Culture and the Formation of American Literature, 1730–1860* (2001); *American Catholic Arts and Fictions: Culture, Ideology, Aesthetics* (1992); and *Hart Crane: The Contexts of* The Bridge (1986).

SUSAN GILLMAN teaches nineteenth-century US literature and world literature and cultural studies at the University of California, Santa Cruz. She has worked collaboratively on several essay collections, most recently (with coeditor Russ

Castronovo) *States of Emergency: The Object of American Studies* (2009). Her current book-in-progress, *Our Mediterranean: American Adaptations, 1820–1975*, is a project on adaptation and translation, linguistic and cultural, in the Americas context.

MATTHEW PRATT GUTERL is Professor of Africana Studies and American Studies at Brown University. He is the author, most recently, of *Seeing Race in Modern America* (2013) and *Josephine Baker and the Rainbow Tribe* (2014), and, with Caroline Field Levander, *Hotel Life* (2015).

HSINYA HUANG is Provost for Faculty Enhancement and Academic Affairs and Professor of American and Comparative Literature, National Sun Yat-sen University, Taiwan. She is author or editor of several works, including *(De)Colonizing the Body: Disease, Empire, and (Alter)Native Medicine in Contemporary Native American Women's Writings* (2004); *Huikan beimei yuanzhumin wenxue: Duoyuan wenhua de shengsi* (*Native North American Literatures: Reflections on Multiculturalism*) (2009); *Aspects of Transnational and Indigenous Cultures* (2014); and *Ocean and Ecology in the Trans-Pacific Context* (2016). She serves on the National Council of the American Studies Association, on the advisory boards of *Journal of Transnational American Studies* and Routledge series on Transnational Indigenous Perspectives, and on the editorial board of *Transmotion*.

ALLAN PUNZALAN ISAAC is Associate Professor of American Studies and English and Chair of American Studies at Rutgers University-New Brunswick. He is the author of *American Tropics: Articulating Filipino America* (2006), which received the Association for Asian American Studies Cultural Studies Book Award. He has taught at LaSalle University in Manila as a Fulbright Senior Scholar.

JOSEPH KEITH is Associate Professor of English at Binghamton University, SUNY, where he specializes in twentieth-century literatures of the United States, comparative race and ethnic studies, and Marxist and postcolonial theory. He is the author of *Unbecoming Americans: Writing Race and Nation from the Shadows of Citizenship, 1945–1960* (2013). His work has appeared in such journals as *Interventions*, *The Black Scholar*, and *Postmodern Culture,* as well as in *The Cambridge Companion to Asian American Literature*. He is completing a book project titled *America's Archipelago: Islands and the Anomalous Geography of Empire.*

YOLANDA MARTÍNEZ-SAN MIGUEL is Professor in the Department of Latino and Caribbean Studies and the Program in Comparative Literature at Rutgers University–New Brunswick. She is the author of *Saberes americanos: Subalternidad y epistemología en los escritos de Sor Juana* (1999); *Caribe Two Ways: Cultura de la migración en el Caribe insular hispánico* (2003); *From Lack to Excess: "Minor"*

Readings of Colonial Latin American Literature (2008); and *Coloniality of Diasporas: Rethinking Intra-Colonial Migrations in a Pan-Caribbean Context* (2014). She is coeditor of the Critical Caribbean Studies book series at Rutgers University Press.

BRANDY NĀLANI MCDOUGALL is from Kula, Maui, and is of Kanaka 'Ōiwi, Chinese, and Scottish descent. She is author of *The Salt-Wind, Ka Makani Pa'akai* (2008) and coeditor of *Huihui: Navigating Art and Literature in the Pacific* (2014), an anthology on Pacific aesthetics and rhetorics. Her monograph *Finding Meaning: Kaona in Contemporary Hawaiian Literature* was published by the University of Arizona Press in 2016. Specializing in Indigenous studies, she is Associate Professor in the American Studies Department at the University of Hawai'i at Mānoa.

IFEOMA KIDDOE NWANKWO is Associate Provost for Strategic Initiatives and Partnerships; Chancellor's Higher Education Fellow; and Associate Professor of English at Vanderbilt University. Her work centers on intercultural and intergenerational relations, particularly as they surface in the literary texts, oral narratives, and popular music of Afro-descendants in the United States, the Caribbean, and Latin America. Her publications include *Black Cosmopolitanism* (2005; 2014); *"Globally Engaged" Scholarship, Pedagogy, and Creative Practice* (2016; coedited with Jan Cohen and Jeff Hou); "Bilingualism, Blackness, and Belonging" (2015); "Race and Representation in the Digital Humanities" (2014); *Rhythms of the Afro-Atlantic World* (2010; coedited with Mamadou Diouf); and *African Routes, Caribbean Roots, Latino Lives* (2009). She is founding director of the Voices from Our America and Wisdom of the Elders public scholarship projects.

CRAIG SANTOS PEREZ is a native Chamorro from the Pacific Island of Guam. He earned a PhD in ethnic studies from the University of California, Berkeley, and is currently Associate Professor in the English Department at the University of Hawai'i, Mānoa. He is the author of three collections of poetry, most recently, *from unincorporated territory [guma']* (2014), which received the American Book Award.

BRIAN RUSSELL ROBERTS is Associate Professor of English and Coordinator of the American Studies Program at Brigham Young University. He has published on archipelagic topics and regions in *American Literature, Atlantic Studies, American Literary History*, PMLA, and elsewhere. He is on the editorial board of Rowman and Littlefield's Rethinking the Island series. His books include *Artistic Ambassadors: Literary and International Representation of the New Negro Era* (2013) and, with Keith Foulcher, *Indonesian Notebook: A Sourcebook on Richard Wright and the Bandung Conference* (2016). He received *African American Review*'s 2009 Darwin T. Turner Award and was a 2015 Fulbright Senior Scholar in Indonesia.

JOHN CARLOS ROWE is USC Associates Professor of the Humanities, and Professor of English, American Studies and Ethnicity, and Comparative Literature at the University of Southern California. He is the author of nine books, more than 150 essays and reviews, and editor or coeditor of ten books, including *Literary Culture and U.S. Imperialism: From the Revolution to World War II* (2000); *A Concise Companion to American Studies* (2010); *Afterlives of Modernism* (2011); and *The Cultural Politics of the New American Studies* (2012). He is now completing *The Ends of Transnationalism and U.S. Cultural Imperialism*.

CHERENE SHERRARD-JOHNSON is Sally Mead Hands-Bascom Professor of English at the University of Wisconsin–Madison, where she teaches African American literature, visual culture, and feminist theory. She is the author of *Portraits of the New Negro Woman: Visual and Literary Culture in the Harlem Renaissance* (2007) and *Dorothy West's Paradise: A Biography of Class and Color* (2012). She is the editor of an annotated edition of Jessie Redmon Fauset's *Comedy: American Style* (2011) and *A Companion to the Harlem Renaissance* (2015).

RAMÓN E. SOTO-CRESPO is Associate Professor of English at the University of Illinois at Urbana-Champaign. He is the author of *Mainland Passage: The Cultural Anomaly of Puerto Rico* (2009). His essay in *Archipelagic American Studies* is part of a book-length manuscript, "Hemispheric Trash: Despised Forms in the Cultural History of the Americas."

MICHELLE ANN STEPHENS is Chair of the Department of English and Professor of Latino and Caribbean Studies at Rutgers University, New Brunswick, where she teaches courses on American, Caribbean, and black diaspora literature and culture. She is the author of *Black Empire: The Masculine Global Imaginary of Caribbean Intellectuals in the United States, 1914 to 1962* (2005) and *Skin Acts: Race, Psychoanalysis and The Black Male Performer* (2014). She is also co-editor with Tatiana Flores of *Relational Undercurrents: Contemporary Art of the Caribbean Archipelago* (2017). She sits on the editorial boards of Rowman and Littlefield's Rethinking the Island book series and Rutgers University Press's Critical Caribbean Studies book series and writes regularly on Caribbean art, the intersections of race and psychoanalysis, and the emerging field of archipelagic American studies.

ELAINE STRATFORD is Professor and Director of the Peter Underwood Centre for Educational Attainment at the University of Tasmania, a center of excellence for improving educational outcomes in Tasmania and raising young people's aspirations for tertiary education throughout their lives. Her research seeks to identify the conditions in which people flourish in place, in their movements, in daily life, and over the course of life—not least in island places. Elaine is also editor in chief of *Geographical Research* and lead editor of Rowman and Littlefield International's Rethinking the Island series.

ETSUKO TAKETANI is Professor of American Literature at the University of Tsukuba (Japan). She is the author of *U.S. Women Writers and the Discourses of Colonialism, 1825–1861* (2003) and *The Black Pacific Narrative: Geographic Imaginings of Race and Empire between the World Wars* (2014).

ALICE TE PUNGA SOMERVILLE (Te Ati Awa, Taranaki) writes and teaches at the intersections of Indigenous, Pacific, literary, and cultural studies. Her first book was *Once Were Pacific: Māori Connections to Oceania* (2012), and she is working on two book projects, "Indigenous-Indigenous Encounters" and "Ghost Writers: The Maori Books You've Never Read." With Daniel Justice and Noelani Arista she recently convened a major transnational project "Indigenous conversations about biography" and co-edited a special issue of *Biography* (39.3 Summer 2016) on the topic. She has taught English at Victoria University of Wellington (New Zealand) and University of Hawai'i-Mānoa (United States) and Indigenous studies at Macquarie University (Australia). She also writes the occasional poem.

TERESIA TEAIWA teaches at Victoria University of Wellington (New Zealand). Her research interests span from militarism and gender in the Pacific to contemporary culture and politics, and pedagogy. Over a twenty-year career she has produced several influential articles and essays in the field of Pacific studies. She is currently working on her first monograph, a history of Fiji women soldiers. In 2014 she received an Ako Aotearoa Tertiary Teaching Excellence Award, and in 2015 was one of two recipients of the inaugural Pacific Peoples Award for contributions to education in New Zealand.

LANNY THOMPSON is Professor in the Department of Sociology and Anthropology, University of Puerto Rico, Río Piedras. He is the author of *Imperial Archipelago* (2010); *Nuestra isla y su gente* (2007); and the prize-winning article "Imperial Republic" (2002). His current projects include historical research on the configurations of governmentality and the systems of education in the United States' overseas colonies.

NICOLE A. WALIGORA-DAVIS is Associate Professor of English at Rice University specializing in late nineteenth- and twentieth-century African American and American literary and cultural criticism, legal studies, critical race theory, and visual culture. She is the author of *Sanctuary: African Americans and Empire* (2011). She is associate editor of the award-winning *Remembering Jim Crow*

(2001), and her essays have appeared in numerous publications, including *The Cambridge History of African American Literature*, *The Cambridge Companion to American Literature after 1945*, *Centennial Review*, *African American Review*, *Modern Fiction Studies*, and the *Mississippi Quarterly*.

INDEX

Abercrombie, Neil, 274
"Ac-Cent-Tchu-Ate the Positive" (Andrews Sisters), 191
accretion, 42–43, 427–35
Acoma, 366
Act of Havana, 194
Affair in Trinidad, An (Sherman), 197, *197*
African Americans, 37, 113–29, 232–56, 341–46, 349, 380
After Call (magazine), 411, *412*, 417–19, 423–25
Agrihan, 103
Aguijan, 103
Aguinaldo, Emilio, 82
Aguon, Julian, 112n81
AHT (average handling time), 416–18, 424
Aimé Césaire (Gregson), 369n19
Air and Missile Defense Task Force, 106
Akaka Bill, 274
Alaimo, Stacy, 328
Alamagan, 103
Ala Press, 223
Alaska, 79, 81
Aleutian Islands, 5, 79
Alexie, Sherman, 332
Allen, Chadwick, 288, 291
Allewaert, Monique, 255n13
alter-Native models. *See* Indigenous peoples
America (United States of). *See* US-America

America, A Prophecy (Blake), 77, 87
America Is in the Heart (Bulosan), 38, 174–89
"The American Imperial Disease" (Lukas), 196
American Progress (Gast), 76
American Quarterly, 3, 53n137, 101–2, 427
American Sāmoa, 3, 32, 81, 101–2, 105, 214–15, 285, 329, 376
American Studies: archipelagic thinking and, 9–11, 35–43, 85–87, 334–35, 353; continental thinking and, 9–19, 42–43; methodologies of, 37, 57–73, 78, 97–98, 133–48, 177, 235, 433–35; postexceptionalist, 2–3, 11–13; scale questions and, 25–26; transnationalism and, 9–10, 36, 43n4, 430. *See also* archipelagic thinking; ASA (American Studies Association)
America's Town Meeting of the Air, 115, 126
"America the Beautiful" (song), 325–26, 337n26
Amsterdam, Morey, 192, 199
Amyot Crime, The (Nicole), 314
Amyot's Cay (Nicole), 314
Anatahan, 103
Andersen, Hans Christian, 246
Anderson, Benedict, 83, 145–47, 307, 311, 342, 413, 429
Andrews, H. Gordon, 304
Andrews, Maxine, 202

Andrews Sisters, 39, 191–207
Anglo-American Caribbean Commission, 193
Annexation Treaty (Hawai'i), 260
Anson, George, 222–23
anticolonialism, 39, 106–8, 133–37, 141–44, 157, 165–69, 199–203, 217–30, 273–75
anti-explorer methodology, 20–29
antifoundationalism, 40–41, 307, 310–11, 313–17. *See also* archipelagic thinking; mobility; navigation practices
Antigua, 156, 193, 237
Antilles, the, 4, 6–7, 35, 80, 134–35, 159–60, 192–93, 356–58, 363–64, 375. *See also specific islands and states*
Anzaldúa, Gloria, 9, 224
Aotearoa, 32, 35, 40, 102, 281, 288, 291, 297, 330, 333. *See also* New Zealand
Aparicio, Frances, 405
Appadurai, Arjun, 59
Archipelagic English (Kerrigan), 433
"Archipelagic Space and the Uncertain Future of National Literatures" (McMahon), 431
Archipelagic Studies (collection), 16
archipelagic thinking: American Studies and, 2–3, 35–43, 433; assemblages and, 11, 29–37, 74–88, 228, 283, 304, 324, 341; auto-archipelagos and, 37, 98, 103; colonialism and, 38, 155–69, 241–47, 341–55; comparative methods and, 37–38, 133–48; continentalism and, 9–19, 38, 74–78, 390, 394–95; cosmopolitanism and, 42, 177, 184–85, 282, 342–46, 350–51; definitions of, 6–8, 62, 71n22, 103–4, 135, 177, 215–16, 260–61, 318n6, 322–23, 428–29; diasporas and, 213–15, 235, 329–34, 373–86, 386n2; epistemologies of, 19–29, 85, 194–95, 405–6; Indigenous peoples and, 15–16, 33–34, 39–41, 156, 281–83, 286–97; maps of, 272; meta-archipelago and, 21, 31, 61, 108, 240–47, 412–13, 425; moving islands and, 100–103, 283–86, 292–93; navigation and, 33, 175–76, 178–80, 183–85, 223, 281–83, 329–30,

430; racial regimes and, 115–30, 216–17, 249–50, 302–17, 338n36; relationality and, 12, 14, 17–35, 37–38, 40, 57–58, 61–69, 101, 136–37, 165–69, 184–85, 236–47, 250–54, 259–60, 272–75, 281–86, 322–25, 329–30, 358–65, 392–95; rhetoric and, 259–75; scholarship and, 35–43, 66–69; spatiality and, 1, 4, 29–35, 37, 46n30, 62–70, 427, 429; temporality and, 1, 4, 69–70, 352; topology and, 14–15; trash and, 303–17, 320–35; US-American narratives and, 1–2, 4–5, 82–84, 87–88, 90n29, 97–110, 174–89, 235, 259–60, 268–72, 334–35, 434. *See also* borders; boundedness; colonialism; continental thinking; islands; navigation practices; Relation, the
"archipelago principle," 15, 148
archipelagraph, 80
archipe-logics, 62–70
Arctic Archipelago, 5, 84
area studies, 58–59
Armitage, David, 321
Armstrong, Louis, 199
Arrow Books, 306
Artero, Antonio, 123
ASA (American Studies Association), 3, 101–2, 427
Ashberry, John, 428–29, 434
(APEC) Asia-Pacific Economic Cooperation, 221
assemblages, 11, 29–35, 37, 74, 77–88, 228, 283, 304, 324, 341
Associated Negro Press, 125, 307
Asuncion, 103
Atlantic economy, 60, 65, 113–15, 253, 305–17, 325–26, 351, 391
Australia, 32, 62, 331, 338n39
Austronesian Taiwan, 281–82, 293–97, 299n14
auto-archipelagos, 37, 98, 103
Azores, 34, 155, 187

Bachelard, Gaston, 356
Bahamas, 35, 82, 84, 193

Bajo Nuevo Bank, 83
Baker, Josephine, 41, 341–55, 428
Baker Island, 81
Balaspoulos, Antonis, 428, 432
Balaz, Joseph P., 13–14
Baldacchino, Godfrey, 60
Bali Hai Series-II (Buehler), *33*, 34–35
Baptiste, Fitzroy A., 396, 398
Baron, Paul, 199
Barreiro, José, 336n8
Bates, Katherine Lee, 325–26
Batongbacal, Jay, 16, 62
"The Battle of the Summer Islands" (Waller), 236
Bautista, Lola Quan, 337n34
Beam, Dorri, 256n39
Beard, J. R., 139
Beer, Gillian, 431–32
Belasco, Lionel, 191, 199
Benítez-Rojo, Antonio, 15, 21, 31, 60–61, 80, 189, 216–17, 241, 256n28, 282, 354n6, 412
Benjamin, Walter, 283, 413
Bennett, Jesi Lujan, 112n81
Bennett, Louise, 409n31
Bermuda, 193, 198, 236–39, 241
Bevacqua, Michael Lujan, 99–100, 102–3, 226
Bhabha, Homi, 224, 353n1
Biak, 115
biculturalism, 380–82, 385
Bikini Atoll. *See* Pikini Atoll
bildungsromans, 176–89
Black, Stephanie, 406n9
Black Atlantic, The (Gilroy), 351, 431
"The Black Beach" (Glissant), 358
blackbirding, 330
black countermoderns, 349–50, 352
Black Current, 293–97
Black Jacobins, The (James), 133–34, 138, 140, 142
Black Midas (Carew), 313
Black Napoleon, The (Waxman), 139–40
Black Skin, White Masks (Fanon), 369n18
Blake, William, 77, 87

Blascheck, Birte, 42, 373–89, 428
Block, Herbert, 127–28
Blood Amyot (Nicole), 314
Blood-Patterson, Elias, 84
blood quantum, 215, 236
Blum, Hester, 10, 85, 237, 324
Boke of Idrography (Rotz), 21
Bolívar, Simón, 147
Book of the Dead, The (Rukeyser), 220
borders: borderlands scholarship and, 9–10; as confining, 30, 40–41, 57–62, 69, 97, 137, 143, 175, 194–95, 232–35, 322–27, 335, 359, 363, 375, 428; mobile nature of, 80–82, 329, 429; permeability of, 401–6; US-American law and, 102; water-based, 7–9, 14, 35, 241, 272–75
Borja-Kicho'cho', Kisha, 107–8
Bosch, Juan, 156
boundedness, 30, 40–41, 57–62, 69, 97, 137, 143, 175, 194–95, 232–35, 322–27, 335, 359, 363, 375, 428
Bourdieu, Pierre, 318n7
BPAP (Business Processing Association of the Philippines), 411, 414, 417, 419
Brathwaite, Edward Kamau, 97–98, 235, 283, 393, 405–6, 432
Braudel, Fernand, 12
Brave Marti Gras (Roberts), 134, 141
Bridge, The (Crane), 228
"The Bridge Stories" (Yanique), 165–69
Bringhurst, Robert, 287–88
Britain, 23–24; as archipelago, 433–34; coastline of, 21–23; colonial holdings of, 1, 5, 9, 63, 118–20, 308–17; Commonwealth of, 373–74, 380–82, 385–86; slavery and, 308–9; US-American Caribbean management and, 193–95; War of 1812 and, 76–77
British Columbia, 87
"British History" (Pocock), 16
Brown, John, 233, 248
Brown, Marie Alohalani, 277n25
Brown, William Wells, 246
Buehler, Fidalis, *33*, 34–35
Bulosan, Carlos, 38–39, 174–89

INDEX | 461

Bush, George H. W., 393
Bush, Jenna, 394
Byas, Vincent, 195
Byrd, Jodi, 229n3

Cahir d'un retour au pays natal (Césaire), 362–63
call centers, 42, 411–26, 432
Calvo, Oscar Lujan, 122
calypso, 191–207
Camacho, Keith, 226
Campomanes, Oscar, 418, 424–25
Canada, 5, 14, 35, 40, 42, 62, 87, 331, 373–86
Canary Islands, 155–56, 164–65
canoes, 40, 222–24, 227–28, 236, 250, 284–89
Cape Cod, 234
Cape Hatteras, 235
capitalism, 216, 395, 424–25. *See also* colonialism; neoliberalism; slavery
Carby, Hazel, 244
Carew, Jan, 304, 313
Carey, Henry, 90n29
Caribbean, the: African Americans and, 200–203, 380; British colonialism in, 1, 373–74; center-metropole dynamic and, 341–55; continental thinking and, 9, 38; desire for US-America and, 395–401; maps of, *136, 144, 159*; Mediterraneanization of, 134–48; as node in transcontinental flows, 5, 155–69, 282, 374–76; slavery and, 5, 60, 63–65, 78, 113–14, 235–38, 248, 256n41, 304–17, 390–95, 401–6, 431; spatiality in, 356–58, 360–65; tourism and, 18–19, 24–235, 392–95, 399–406; US-American imperialism in, 1–2, 4, 10–11, 38–39, 80, 145–48, 165–69, 191–207, 349, 390–410; whiteness in, 302–18. *See also* colonialism; plantations; *specific places*
Caribbean, The (W.A. Roberts), 133–35, 138, 141–44
Caribbean Discourse (Glissant), 15, 365–66
Caribbean Philosophical Association, 68
Caribbean Rhythms, 393

Caroline Islands, 124
Cartagena, 162
Carter, Ashley, 304
Carter, Paul, 86
Casa de Contración, 160–61, 171n30
Cassini, Jacques Dominique, 17, *18*, 31
Castilian Spanish, 145–46
Castro, Fidel, 138
catachresis, 30–31
Catherwood, Hartwell, 258n77
Cato, Nancy, 304
celebrity, 42, 343, 346–58, 373–78, 380–85
center-periphery dynamics, 18, 42, 158, 162–63, 175, 341–55, 405–6
Césaire, Aimé, 41–42, 356, 360–65, 367–68, 369n18
Chagos Archipelago, 34, 83
Chamorro populations, 49n67, 97–108, 112n81, 122–23, 217–31, 330
"Chamorros, Ghosts, Non-Voting Delegates" (Bevacqua), 100
Chamorro-Spanish Wars, 222
Champlain, Samuel, 164, 172n42
Chang, David, 51n90, 262, 311–12
Channel Islands, 87
chaos-monde, 21, 63–66, 72n33
Chicago Defender, 121–24, 194
Children of Kaywana (Mittelholzer), 303, 313
China, 5, 79, 127
China Sea, 5, 84
Christophe (Césaire), 361
chronotopes, 113–14, 282
circum-Atlantic movements, 303–17
citizenship (US-American), 81, 99, 104–5, 165, 175–80, 185–87, 254, 331–34, 421–22
Clarke, Jacob, 302
Clarkson, Adrienne, 377
class, 42, 302–18, 409n31, 411–26
Clement, Michael, 112n81
Clifford, James, 284
Clotel (Brown), 246
coastlines, 19–29, 62, 82, 85–87, 234, 362–63
Cohen, Margaret, 77

Coker, Elizabeth Boatwright, 304
Cold War, 1, 58–59, 79, 115, 126–27, 187, 197
Cole, Nat King, 199
Coleman, Lonnie, 304
Coleman, Ornette, 208n38
colonialism: Age of Discovery and, 7–8, 60–61; anticolonialism and, 39, 106–8, 133–37, 157, 165–69, 199–203, 236–39, 273–75; capitalism and, 411–26; center-periphery discourses and, 18, 42, 60–61, 155–69, 175, 341–55, 373–86, 405–6; coastlines and, 19–29; competing Empires and, 2–3, 9, 67–68, 390–91; continental domains and, 1–11, 38–39; desert island trope and, 18–19, 24–25, 38–39, 77, 174–89, 247–54, 283; diasporic experiences and, 15, 373–86, 418–23; embodiments of, 348; epistemology of, 11, 51n90, 60–61, 63–66, 342–46, 352–53, 405–6; Guam and, 98–110; language and, 137, 139–43, 145–48, 214; maps and, 21, 113–14, 157–63, 169, 171n23, 197–98; naming practices and, 31, 101; nationalism and, 341–42; neocolonialism and, 145–48; performativity and, 41–42; postcolonial conditions and, 214–16, 283, 309–17, 360–65, 382–85, 412–24; race and, 60, 177, 179–83, 185–87, 198–203, 214–16, 240–47, 250–54, 303–17, 324–25, 342–46, 360–65, 375, 391; settler, 49n67, 85, 89n17, 90n28, 102–3, 214, 247–50, 333, 377–80; sexual politics and, 200–203, 208n47; slavery and, 5, 63–65, 78, 113–14, 235–38, 248, 256n41, 312, 390–95, 401–6, 431; sovereignty and, 214–15; Spanish, 5, 155–69; spatiality of, 67–68; temporality of, 67–68, 70, 297, 341–42, 349–50, 416–18; tourism and, 18–19, 24–235, 238–39, 392–95, 399–406; US-American laws and, 2, 4, 174–90, 259–60
Colored American Magazine, 233, 239
Columbus, Christopher, 172n40
Comacho, Keith L., 102
Community Writers Collective, 223

comparative methods, 37–40, 133–48. *See also* American Studies; archipelagic thinking
Congo, the, 367
Conrad, Earl, 307
Consejo de Indias, 160–61
Constantakopoulou, Christy, 16
Constitution (US-American), 104
contact zones, 235, 282, 429
Contending Forces (Hopkins), 232–36, 240–47, 245, 249, 253
continental thinking: American Studies and, 11–19; archipelagic thinking and, 9–19, 35–43, 194–95, 390, 394–95; boundedness and, 30, 40–41, 57–62, 69, 97, 137, 143, 175, 194–95, 232–35, 322–27, 335, 359, 363, 375, 428; coastlines and, 19–29, 85–87; continents as islands and, 12; definitions of, 6–7; foundationalism and, 40–41, 59, 155, 303–17; islands and, 232–33, 250–54, 392–95, 401–6; mainland ideology and, 13–14, 178–83; Manifest Destiny and, 1–4, 11, 37, 78, 82, 194, 401, 404–5, 406n2, 431–32; nationalism and, 6–7, 193–96; representations of, 32; trash and, 320–35; US-American expansion and, 1, 11, 74–75, 80–81, 87–88, 104–5, 181, 206n11, 259–75, 325–27, 336n21, 431–32. *See also* borders; maps; nationalism; settler colonialism
Cook Islands, 4, 285, 376
Cool Runnings (film), 393
Cooper, James Fenimore, 258n79
copyright infringement, 191, 199–205, 209n52
Coquia, Jorges R., 92n55
Coronelli, Vincenzo, 158, 171n25
cosmopolitanism, 42, 177, 184–85, 282, 342–46, 350–51, 390–410, 409n31
counterautobiography, 184–85
Crane, Hart, 228
Creole Dusk (Roberts), 134
creolization, 65–66, 72n41, 233–34, 242–47, 256n48, 315, 342, 349, 356, 405, 410n49. *See also* race

Crichlow, Michaeline, 24
"Crossroads of Cultures" (Fishkin), 102
Cuba, 4, 10, 35, 38, 80, 82–83, 101, 133–44, 157, 161–63, 427
Cultures of United States Imperialism (Pease and Kaplan), 80
cummings, e. e., 218

Dames, Vivian, 112n81
Darwin, Charles, 5
Dash, J. Michael, 41, 356–70, 427
David, George, 289
David, Joe, 285, 289
Davies, Carole Boyce, 390
Davies, Mike, 39
Davis, Gregson, 361, 369n19
Davis, Mike, 54n144
Davis, Thadious, 247, 255n14
Dean, Tim, 317
de Balbuena, Bernardo, 162
decapitalized whiteness, 40, 301–17
decolonization, 157, 165–69, 216, 222–23, 225, 307–8, 335, 373–74. *See also* anticolonialism; colonialism
Decolonization (journal), 49n67
decolonization efforts, 106–8
decontinentalization, 11–19, 77
Defoe, Daniel, 39, 77, 89n17, 128, 174–77, 183, 186, 248
de Lacroix, Pamphile, 140
de Las Casas, Bartolomé, 163–64
Deleuze, Gilles, 63, 72n30, 77, 216, 283
de Lisser, Herbert, 304, 312
Dell (publisher), 306
DeLoughrey, Elizabeth, 17, 37, 62, 80, 97, 105, 175, 223, 236–37, 250, 260, 345–46, 363, 432
Dening, Greg, 20
Denning, Michael, 9
Derrida, Jacques, 221, 230n26, 341–42
desire, 42, 390–410, 424–25
Desmond, Jane C., 101
Dessalines, Jean-Jacques, 233, 368
Destiny's Landfall, 97
Día del Galeón Festival, 5, 6

Diamond Rock, 358
diasporas: archipelagic, 235, 374, 386n2; center-periphery dynamics and, 18, 228; colonial subjects and, 15, 137–39, 373–86, 418–23; internal, 213–15, 329–34, 374–76; intracolonial, 67–68, 79; jetsam and, 328–29; twice-diasporized dynamic and, 374, 381
Diaz, Vicente, 67, 100–101, 223, 226, 283–84, 292–93
Diego Garcia, 83
Dimock, Wai Chee, 12, 254n3
"Discontiguous States of America" (Lai), 105
Discovery of Islands, The (Pocock), 433
distant reading, 28–36, 52n117, 305
Distant Reading (Moretti), 29, 52n117, 305
"Dividing the Ocean Sea" (Lewis), 6–7
Does the Constitution Follow the Flag? (Raustiala), 104
domestic diasporas, 213–14
Dominguez, Virginia R., 101
Dominica, 167–68, 364
Dominican Republic, 4
Donne, John, 282–83, 326, 431–32
"Don't Fence Me In" (Andrews Sisters), 191
double consciousness, 68, 429
Drake, James D., 206n11
Drexler, Michael, 233
Drinnon, Richard, 1–2
Dubai, 331
Du Bois, W. E. B., 10
Duchamp, Marcel, 228
Dutch East Indies, 8
Dymaxion map, 31, 32, 33

echo-monde, 360
ecology, 26, 39, 108, 234–37, 282, 286–97, 320–35. *See also* archipelagic thinking; nonhuman, the
economies of desire, 42, 390–410, 424–25
Edwards, Jonathan, 434
EEZ (exclusive economic zone), 9, 62, 84, 105–6

El filibusterismo (Rizal), 146
Eliot, T. S., 218, 226
Elizabeth II, 376, 381, 396
Ellington, Fae, 398
Ellis, Julie, 304
Ellison, Ralph, 352
Emancipation Act (Britain), 309
empathy, 413–15
epistemology. *See* archipelagic thinking; colonialism; continental thinking; maps; Relation, the; spatiality; temporality
Equiano, Olaudah, 254
erasure, 203–5, 221, 273, 400, 409n37
errancy, 28, 65–66, 360
etak, 100–101, 293
Et leschiens se taisient (Davis), 369n19
exoticization, 391–95, 401–6
Eye for the Tropics, An (Thompson), 391
Eyes of the Sky (Rapongan), 281, 293–97

Fanon, Frantz, 369n18
Farallon Islands, 87, 103
Faulkner, William, 303, 306
Fawcett Crest, 306
"53" (Sullivan), 292
Fiji, 15, 32, 84, 285, 329, 331, 333, 376, 384
films, 321–55
Finnegans Wake (Joyce), 218, 431
First Nations, 40, 285–89, 378
Fischer, Steven Roger, 283
Fishkin, Shelley Fisher, 9, 102
Fitzgerald, Ella, 199
flags, 260–61, 266–67. *See also* Hae Hawai'i
Flores, Alfred, 112n81
Flores, Evelyn, 112n81
flota system, 5, 6, 38, 161–62, 220
flotsam, 328–30
flying fish, 293–97, 300n56
Fonds-Massacre, 367
Fonkoua, Romuald, 361
Fornander, Abraham, 262
For Whom the Bell Tolls (Hemingway), 432
Fractal 3 (Stephens), 26, 28

fractal geometry, 21–25, 28–29
Fractal Geometry of Nature (Mandelbrot), 23, 25
Fractals (Mandelbrot), 21–23
France: colonial holdings of, 9, 35, 63, 133–34, 138–39, 142, 157, 349–50; diasporic subjects and, 342–51; language of, 139–43; Louisiana Purchase and, 1, 11, 74; postcolonial relationality and, 364–65; Revolution of, 133–34, 138, 140. *See also* Haiti; Martinique
Franco, Francisco, 134
Frank, Gunder, 162
Freedom, 198–99
Frisbie, Florence "Johnny," 26, 30
From a Native Daughter (Trask), 273
"*from* Organic Acts" (Perez), 220
from unincorporated territory [guma'] (Perez), 217–18, 225, 227
from unincorporated territory [hacha] (Perez), 217, 222
from unincorporated territory [saina] (Perez), 217–19, 222, 224–25, 227
frontier ideology, 187–90, 431
FSM (Federated States of Micronesia). *See* Micronesia
Fuchs, Barbara, 162
Fukushima nuclear plant, 324
Fuller, Richard Buckminster, 31–33

Gabrys, Jennifer, 324
Galeón de Manila, 5, 6, 161
Gandhi, Mohandas K., 119
garden figure (of continents), 12
Garvey, Marcus, 350, 400
Gast, John, 76
gender, 42, 240–47, 252–53, 379, 396, 409n31
genealogies, 260–67, 291, 294–95
General History of Trade, A (Defoe), 89n17
General History of Virginia, New England, and the Summer Isles, The (Smith), 5
Geneva Convention, 124–25
geography. *See* spatiality
geography of reason, 68–70, 71n22

Germany, 63, 103
Gibson, Walter Murray, 264
Gilchrist, Rupert, 304
Giles, Paul, 39–40, 42–43, 235, 427–35
Giles, Raymond, 304
Gillis, John R., 46n30, 84, 334–35
Gillman, Susan, 37–38, 133–51, 342–43, 346, 429
Gilroy, Paul, 113–15, 349, 351–53, 431
Glissant, Édouard, 15, 20–29, 41, 63–69, 135–36, 236, 249, 283–86, 356–60, 364–68, 427. *See also* Relation, the; specific works
globalization, 69–70, 169, 385–86, 430–31
global studies, 59
Goetzfridt, Nicholas, 112n81
Gonzalez, N. V. M., 418, 424–25
Good Neighbor Policy, 194, 349
Gould, Thomas, 265
Graham, Alice Walworth, 304
Graham, Fred, 288–89
Granada, Pio, 411
Grand Isle, 87, 249–50
Grant, Rupert Westmore, 191. *See also* Invader, Lord
Graphs, Maps, Trees (Moretti), 305
Grau, Shirley Ann, 304
Great Salt Lake, 14
Grimshaw, Anna, 139
Grotius, Hugo, 77
Growth of the Modern West Indies, The (Lewis), 310
Guadeloupe, 375
Guam (Guåhan), 3, 35, 37, 81–82, 97–115, 121–23, 128, 217–31, 229n15, 326–29, 428
Guanahani, 5
Guano Islands Act, 4, 81
Guantánamo Bay, 54n144, 83
Guattari, Félix, 216
Guguan, 103
Guiana, 4, 193–94, 375
Gulliver (bomber), 117, *118*, 118–19
Guterl, Matthew Pratt, 41, 341–55, 428
gyres, 320–21

Hachey, Thomas, 119
Hae Hawaiʻi, 262–63, 266–67, 269
Haida Gwaii, 35, 281, 286–89, 297
Haiti, 4, 83, 133–34, 138–42, 233, 318n3, 349–50, 367–68, 378–79, 382, 427
Halifax (Viscount), 118
Hall, Gwendolyn Midlo, 406n2
Hall, Lisa Kahaleole, 102
Hall, Robert, 58
Hall, Stuart, 375
hallucinations, 9–10
Handley, George B., 10–11, 427
Hanlon, David, 226
Hantel, Max, 358, 364–65, 368
Harding, Sandra, 68
Harley, Brian, 86, 157–58
Harootunian, Harry, 136–37
Harris, Susan K., 214
Harrison, Richard Edes, 113, *114*, 114–15
Hartman, Saidiya, 244
Hassam, Childe, 74, *75*, 87–88
Hauʻofa, Epeli, 15, 29, 31, 62–63, 227, 281–82, 284, 297, 329, 337n22, 428–29, 432
Hawaiʻi, 4–10, 32, 40, 79–81, 99–107, 115, 155, 215, 226, 259–75, 322, 326, 428
Hay, Peter, 20
Headley, Clevis, 72n30
Hearne, John, 304
"Heavy Waters" (DeLoughrey), 105
Heckert, Eleanor, 304
Heidegger, Martin, 230n26
Henrikson, Alan K., 113
"Heritage of Smallness" (Joaquin), 416
Hernández Adrián, Francisco-J., 24
Herring, Terrel Scott, 25
heuristics, 31, 37, 57–73, 78, 177, 235
Hiawatha (Longfellow), 249–50
Hilton Head Island, 87
Hiroshima, 120, 127
Hispaniola, 82, 162
History of Mary Prince, a West Indian Slave, The (Prince), 238–39
Holt, John Dominis, 322
Honduras, 4
Hopa, Ngapare, 334

Hopkins, Pauline, 39, 232–58
Horner, Lance, 304
Hoskins, Janet, 177
Howland Island, 81
"How Long Is the Coast of Britain" (Mandelbrot), 21–23
How Stella Got Her Groove Back (film), 393
Hsu, Hsuan L., 121
Huang, Hsinya, 40, 281–301, 428
Hughes, Langston, 352
Hunt, Gregory, 270
Hurd, Charles, 126
Hurston, Zora Neale, 235, 252–53
hybridity, 214, 224, 234
hyperobjects, 51n103

Imagined Communities (Anderson), 342, 413
immigration, 175–77, 180–83, 186–90, 336n20, 373–86, 419–23
imperial archipelagoes, 4, 76
imperialism. *See* colonialism
India, 118–20, 127, 410n45
Indigenous peoples: anticolonialism and, 39–40, 90n28, 106–8, 233, 235–36, 268–75; archipelagic thinking and, 41, 156; blood quantum and, 215, 236; Caliban figure and, 360–65, 367–68; capitalization decisions and, 49; cartographic practices of, 33, 34, 53n134, 86–87, 100–101, 290–95; definitions of, 215; diasporas of, 327–35, 338n39, 374–76, 423–25; Guam and, 98–110; Hawai'i and, 259–75; Manifest Destiny and, 1–4, 11, 37, 77–78, 82, 194, 401, 404–5, 406n2, 431–32; racialization of, 216–17, 249–50, 338n36; relations among, 283–89; spatiality and, 15–16, 281–84, 293–97, 322–23; US-American policies toward, 249–50, 258n79, 259–75, 278n51; World War II and, 120–21. *See also* archipelagic thinking; colonialism; navigation practices; *specific peoples*
Indonesia, 7–9, 14–15, 84, 429

Ingold, Tim, 86
In Living Color, 393
In Oceana (Thomas), 430
inspiration, 382–85
Insular Cases, 2, 43n8, 92n56, 104–5, 179, 181
Insularismo (Pedreira), 156, 170n11
insularity: critical, 17–19; definitions of, 12–13
International Journal of Okinawan Studies, 17
In the Break (Moten), 244
intimacy, 416–18
Inuit, 5, 378
Invader, Lord, 191, 199–201, 205
invisibility (of the Pacific), 320–35
Isaac, Allan Punzalan, 42, 411–26, 428, 432
"Isla Incognita" (Walcott), 20
island hopping, 114–15, 119–26
islands: boundedness of, 30, 40–41, 57–62, 69, 97, 137, 143, 175, 194–95, 232–35, 322–27, 335, 359, 363, 375, 428; coastlines and, 19–29; desert island trope, 18–19, 38–39, 52n123, 77, 174–89, 232, 247–54, 283, 346, 375, 428, 431–32; as fantasy elements, 18–19, 29–35, 52n123, 60, 100, 177, 181–83, 191–209, 232, 236, 250–51, 342–46, 391–95, 401–6; as infinite, 23–26, 33–34; insular imaginary and, 11, 177, 183–85, 249, 284, 335, 359, 365–68, 432; loneliness and, 342–46; as methodological heuristic, 37; moving, 100–103, 283–86, 292–93; navigation practices and, 33, 79, 236–39; near-shore, 85–87; as openings, 15, 39, 41, 141, 234–36, 240–47, 359, 363, 368; performativity and, 40–41; repeating, 26–35, 60–61, 69–70, 216–17, 256n28, 343; temporality and, 233, 282; topology of, 232; tourism and, 18–19, 24–235, 392–95, 399–406; US-America as mythological, 12. *See also* archipelagic thinking; *specific places*
island studies, 16–17, 60–61, 69–70, 155
Island Studies Journal, 17, 60

Islas de los Ladrones, 103
Isle of Palms, 87
Isle Royale, 87
Isthmus Canal Commission, 92n56
isthmuses, 79–80, 134, 143, 359

Jackson, Helen Hunt, 147–48
Jamaica, 42, 82, 133–34, 138–44, 163–64, 193, 239, 308, 375, 390–410
Jamaica Progressive League, 138
James, C. L. R., 15, 38, 133–34, 137–44, 187
Jameson, Fredric, 184–85, 311, 317, 395
Jane Eyre (Brontë), 308
Japan, 79, 99, 106–8, 120, 122, 124–25, 132n51
"Japan from Alaska" (Harrison), *114*
"Japan from the Solomons" (Harrison), *114*
Jardine, Monica, 390
Jarvis Island, 81
Java, 5, 7, 30
Jean, Michaëlle, 373–74, 376–79, 381–83, 385
Jefferson, Thomas, 1
Jetnil-Kijiner, Kathy, 34–35
jetsam, 328–30
Jim Crow laws, 115–21, 124–26, 208n47
Joaquin, Nick, 411, 416, 425
Johnson, Chalmers, 219
Johnston Island, 81, 115
Jones, Claudia, 390–91
Joyce, James, 218, 428, 431
Juan Fernandez Islands, 89n17

Ka'ano'i, Patrick, 263
Ka Hae Hawaii, 266
Kaleikuahulu, 262
Kalukaua, 265
Kamehameha: I, 260–67, 269; III, 266; IV, 264
"Ka Moolelo Hawaii Kahiko" (Poepoe), 260
Ka Mooolelo Hawai'i, 262
Ka Na'i Aupuni, 260
Kansas-Nebraska Act, 248

Ka Nupepa Kuokoa, 266, *267*
Kaplan, Amy, 39, 54n144, 80, 101–2, 189
Katherine E. Nash Gallery, 33
Kauanui, J. Kēhaulani, 67, 278n51, 283
Kau Inoa, 274
Kaywana Blood (Mittelholzer), 302
Keith, Joseph, 38–39, 174–90, 428
Keli'imaika'i, 264
Kenna, Pardaic, 54n144
Kerrigan, John, 433–34
Khan, Mohamed, 198–200
Khan v. Feist, 199, 201
Kincaid, Jamaica, 156, 394–95, 423–25, 426n28
King, Martin Luther, Jr., 196
Kingman Reef, 81
kinship relations, 33, 184, 214, 228, 235–36, 250, 258n76, 288, 375
Kipling, Rudyard, 127
Kiribati, 34, 285, 330, 376
Kirk, Gwen, 226
Kissinger, Henry, 321
Knight, Alisha, 248
Korean War, 79
Kristeva, Julia, 401
Kukutai, Tahu, 338n38
Kuper, Kenneth Gofigan, 112n81
Kuwada, Bryan Kamaoli, 268
Kwajalein, 115

labor movements, 185–87
Lacan, Jacques, 24
Lady Saw, 396, 399, 408n26
Lai, Paul, 105
Lake Texcoco, 6, 14
Lambert, David, 308
Lamming, George, 31, 369n18
language, 137, 139–43, 145–48, 214, 217–18, 225–26, 260–61, 293–97, 411–26, 428
"L'année passé" (Belasco), 191
Las Américas Quarterly, 3, 46n36, 427
La siréne des tropiques (film), 342–46, 348–50
Latte Stone Park, 129
leapfrogging, 114–15

Le Dictionnaire Phraésologique Royal, 160
Le Grand Dictionaire Historique (Moreri), 160
Leo Feist Incorporated, 199, 201–5
Leon-Guerrero, Victoria, 226
Levine, Jesse, 17
Levy, Barrington, 401
Lewis, Edmonia, 251
Lewis, Gordon K., 310, 409n30
Lewis, Martin W., 6–7, 227
Leyte, 115
Liberation Day, 107, 219–20, 226
Life, 200
Life and Debt (Black), 406n9
Linebaugh, Peter, 255n21
Lionnet, Françoise, 15, 50n78, 405, 410n49
Lipman, Jana K., 102
literary canons, 302–17
Little Mermaid (Andersen), 246
Llenín-Figueroa, Beatriz, 50n89
Lloyd, David, 17
Lloyd, Stephen, 142
Lochard, Metz, 194
loneliness, 342–46, 350
Longfellow, Henry Wadsworth, 250, 258n79
Look at the World (Harrison), *114*
"Los Angeles and American Studies in a Pacific World of Migration" (Yu), 102
Louisiana Purchase, 1, 11, 74, 81–82, 193
L'Ouverture, Toussaint, 138–39, 233, 349
Lukas, J. A., 196
Lumumba, Patrice, 367
Lunalilo, William Charles, 264
Luta, 223
Luzon, 115

MacArthur, Douglas, 120
Macéo, Antonio, 142
Maclean's, 379–80, 383
Magellan, Ferdinand, 98, 103, 220
Mahan, Alfred, 62
mainland discourses, 13–14, 179–83, 270, 272–75
"Da Mainland to Me" (Balaz), 13–14

Malibu Rum, 402–3
Malkin, Irad, 16
Mallarmé, Stéphane, 357
Malo, David, 262
Manawa (exhibit), 284, 288
Man Called White, A (White), 120–21
Mandelbrot, Benoit, 20–25, *25*, 28–30, 33
Mandingo (book), 307
Manhattan Island, 5, 87, 283
Manifest Destiny, 1–4, 11, 37, 78, 82, 194, 401, 404–5, 406n2, 431–32
Manley, Michael, 406n9
Manley, Norman, 138
Mannoni, Octave, 369n18
Maori populations, 223, 281–92, 294, 332–34, 338n38, 376, 380–82, 387n17, 428
Mapp, Trevor, 409n40
maps: aerial, 37, 113–19, 126–29, 430–31; archipelagos and, 2, 5, 37, 427; decontinentalization efforts and, 17, *18–19*; epistemologies of, 57–58, 157–63, 169, 171n23; Indigenous practices and, 33, *34*, 53n134, 86–87, 100–101, 282, 284; Mercator maps and, 37, 113–14, 129, 431. *See also* colonialism; spatiality; *specific places*
"Maps, Knowledge, and Power" (Harley), 158
Marco Island, 87
Mare Liberum (principle), 77
Marianas Trench Marine National Monument, 271
Marked for Death (film), 393
Marsh, Kate, 80–81
Marshall Islands, 3–4, 33, 53n134, 83–84, 105, 107–8, 124, 128, 215, 285
Martha's Vineyard, 87, 234
Martí, José, 14, 35, 38, 133–37, 142, 145–48, 205
Martínez, Enmanuel, 166
Martínez-San Miguel, Yolanda, 38, 155–73, 428
Martinique, 157, 358, 364–68, 375
Marx, Karl, 89n17, 140–41
Marx, Leo, 54n140

masks, 361–62
Massachusetts, 234
Massey, Vincent, 377
materiality: assemblages and, 11, 29–37, 74–88, 228, 283, 304, 324, 341; call center bodies and, 418–23; formality and, 10–11; the nonhuman and, 242–46, 286–97; of the ocean, 10, 85; of symbols, 260–61, 264, 266–67; of thought, 356–57, 427
Matinicus, 87
Maug, 103
Mauritius, 15, 239
Max and Erma's, 401, 404
Maxwell, William, 72n45
McCall, Grant, 18
McDaniel, Antoinette Charfauros, 112n81
McDougall, Brandy Nālani, 40, 259–78, 428
McKinley, William, 79
McMahon, Elizabeth, 326, 431
McNeill, George, 304
Mediterraneanizing, 38, 134–35, 141
Meinig, Donald, 74–75, 79, 82, 90n29
Melanesia, 7, 330, 337n34
Mémoires pour servir à l'Historie de la révolution de Saint-Domingue (de Lacroix), 140
Mercator maps, 37, 113–14, 129, 431
méstissage, 65–66, 72n41
meta-archipelago, 7–8, 21, 31, 61, 108, 240, 412–13, 425
metamorphosis, 63, 263, 288–89, 305
metaphors (geographical), 7–8, 57–61, 77, 158, 165–69, 320–35, 391, 393
Métis, 378
Metzger, Sean, 24
Mexico, 5–6, 38, 98–99, 157–63
Michener, James A., 52n123
Micronesia, 1, 3–4, 7–8, 32, 105, 124, 223, 321
Midsummer Night's Dream (Shakespeare), 348
Midway Atoll, 81
Mignolo, Walter, 68, 222, 224

"Militarization and Resistance from Guåhan" (Na'puti and Bevacqua), 102–3
"Militarized Borders and Social Movements in the Mariana Islands" (Camacho), 102
Mingus, Charles, 208n38
minority successes, 42, 343, 346–58, 373–85
"Miss Calypso," 198
Missouri Compromise, 248
Mittelholzer, Edgar, 302–4, 307–8, 311–14, 316
mobility: of borders, 80–82, 329, 429; citizenship and, 331–34; class membership and, 390–410, 409n31; insular imaginary and, 33, 40, 46n30, 100–101, 178–80, 183–85, 222–24, 290–93, 329–30; by metaphor, 393, 405–6; racial politics and, 113–32. *See also* center-periphery dynamics; colonialism; cosmopolitanism; kinship relations
Moby Dick (Melville), 187
Modern Epic (Moretti), 316
modernization, 349, 352–53
Mohammed, Patricia, 158
Mokumanamana, 271
Moll, Herman, 159–60
Monnig, Laurel A., 112n81
Monroe Doctrine, 76, 194, 196, 406n2
Monsieur Toussaint (Glissant), 356, 360–61, 365–68
Moore, Charles, 323, 327–28
Moreri, Louis, 160
Moretti, Franco, 28–29, 40–41, 54n140, 178, 305–6, 316
Mormons, 330, 333
Morris, Paula, 334
Morrison, Toni, 254
Morton, Timothy, 51n103
Moten, Fred, 200, 208n38, 244
moving islands, 100–103
"Moving Islands of Sovereignty" (Diaz), 284, 293
mulatto figure. *See* creolization; race
multiculturalism, 378–80, 385

Munavvar, Muhammad, 426n18
"My Island Is One Big American Footnote" (Bevacqua), 99
myth-and-symbol school, 36, 54n140
Myth of Continents, The (Lewis and Wigen), 6, 227

NAACP (National Association for the Advancement of Colored People), 114–15, 125
NAFTA (North American Free Trade Act), 221
Nagasaki, 120, 127
Naholowaʻa, Leiana, 112n81
Naʻi Aupuni, 274
naming practices, 31, 101
Nantucket, 87, 234
Naone, Kahu Lyons, 275
Napoleon Bonaparte, 90n35
Naʻputi, Tiara R., 102–3, 112n81
Narrative of a Voyage to the West Indies and Mexico in the Years 1599–1602 (Champlain), 164
National Gallery of Art, 74
National Geographic, 325
nationalism: antifoundationalism and, 40–41, 307, 310–11; corporate, 418–25; diasporas within, 213–15, 329–34, 374–76; immigration discourses and, 42; mainland formulations and, 13–14; postcolonial movements and, 138, 145–48, 360–68; postnational space and, 188–90; race and, 215, 236, 249–50; rhetoric and, 260–75; sovereignty concerns and, 35, 40, 57–58, 81, 84, 104–5, 194–96, 269, 294; state formation and, 376–78; temporality and, 341–42, 353n1. *See also* anticolonialism; boundedness; citizenship (US-American); continental thinking; Cuba; Philippines
Native Americans, 78, 87, 219, 226, 249–50, 258n79
Native Hawaiian Government Reorganization Act, 273–74
Natividad, Lisa, 112n81, 226

NATS (Naval Air Transportation Service), 120–21
Navassa, 83
navigation practices, 33, 40, 46n30, 100–101, 183–85, 222–24, 290–93
negritude, 350, 362
Nehru, Jawaharlal, 119, 127
neoliberalism, 392, 407n11, 411–26
Neptune, Harvey, 406n2
Netherlands, 5, 8–9, 63, 375
New Guinea, 7, 32, 84, 115, 376
Newlands Resolution, 260
New Literatures Review, 17
New Mexico Territory, 8
New Oceania, A (collection), 15
New Region of the World, A (Glissant), 358
New Spain. *See* Mexico
New York Herald Tribune, 127
New York Inquirer, 203
New York Post, 120–21
New York Times, 123
New Zealand, 32, 35, 40, 42, 292, 330–31, 333, 338n39, 373–86
New Zealand Herald, 378, 381
Nguyen, Viet Thanh, 177
NH&OPI (Native Hawaiian and other Pacific Islanders), 328–29, 331–32
Nicole, Christopher, 304, 313–17
Nihoa, 271
nissology, 18–29
Niue, 376, 384
"No Deal" (Won Pat-Borja), 106–7
No Doubt, 396, 399, 408n26
Noguchi, Yone, 183–84
nomadology, 216. *See also* Deleuze, Gilles; mobility
nonhuman, the, 232, 240–44, 246, 286–97
Northern Mariana Islands, 3, 81, 102, 105, 108, 124, 223, 322
Northwest Ordinance, 104
Noudelmann, François, 360
Nous étions assis sur le rivage du monde (Pliya), 356, 364
Nova Scotia, 87
"No Walk in the Park" (Flores), 102–3

nuclear testing, 83–84, 107, 127–28, 215
"Nuestra América" (Martí), 14, 147–48, 205
Nunan, Seamus, 201
Nuñez de Balboa, Vasco, 325
Nwankwo, Ifeoma Kiddoe, 42, 390–410, 430

Oak Island, 87
Obama, Barack, 5, 47n49, 84, 271, 373, 376, 379, 383–85, 408n23
Obama, Michelle, 383
objects, 10, 40, 66, 198–203, 213, 236–46, 281–83, 328, 396. *See also* colonialism; Indigenous peoples; materiality; nonhuman, the; trash
O'Callahan, Evelyn, 312
oceans. *See* archipelagic thinking; Blum, Hester; borders; coastlines; continental thinking; materiality; navigation practices
Office of Insular Affairs, 3–4
offshoring, 411–24
Of One Blood (Hopkins), 256n44
Ojibwa, 87
Oklahoma Territory, 8
Oliver at Large, 396–401
Olson, Charles, 218, 227
Omiya Jima. *See* Guam (Guåhan)
One World (Willkie), 117
"One World, One War" (Harrison), 113
Onstott, Kyle, 304
opacity, 66, 356
Organic Acts, 99, 165, 219–20, 260
Orientalism, 392, 430
Ortiz, Fernando, 148
Osorio, Jonathan, 264
"Our Sea of Islands" (Hau'ofa), 15, 284, 428
outsourcing, 411–26

Pacific, the: Atlantic comparisons and, 283–86; black Pacific trope and, 115; colonial views of, 177; garbage patch in, 41, 320–35; Indigenous conceptions of, 15–16, 213–29, 374–76; migrations in, 281–301; nuclear testing in, 83–84, 107–8, 126–29, 215, 321; scholarship on, 36–37; US-American imperialism in, 1–4, 10–11, 98–110, 174–90, 268–72. *See also* colonialism; Guam (Guåhan); Hawai'i; New Zealand; Philippines; Spain
Pacific Currents, 3
Pacific Remote Islands National Monument, 271
Padios, Jan, 423
Padrón, Ricardo, 158
Pagan, 103
Pågat, 106
Paine, Thomas, 12
Pakui, 262
Palau, 3–4, 105
Palmyra Atoll, 4, 81
Panama Canal, 79, 81, 165, 195, 197–98, 208n41
Pan American World Airways, 126
Papahānaumokuākea National Monument, 271
Papua, 7, 32, 84, 376
parallax zones, 39–40, 235
Paris Treaty, 82, 220, 378
Parrot Bay Rum, 402–4
"Passage to India" (Whitman), 228
Pavletich, JoAnn, 258n77
Pease, Donald, 2, 80, 187
Pedreira, Antonio S., 156, 170n11
Peleliu, 115
Perez, Craig Santos, 37, 39, 97–112, 213–29, 428
Perez, Helen, 222
Pérez, Louis, 406n2
Perez, Michael, 112n81
performativity, 40–41, 60, 281–301
Perloff, Marjorie, 249, 257n73
Perthes, Justus, *311*
Petrie, George, 85
Philippines, 4–15, 35–42, 79–84, 98–101, 136–37, 145–48, 155–65, 175–89, 214–31, 411–26, 428
Philosophy of Relation (Glissant), 359

Picasso (Stein), 432
"Pikes Peak" (Bates), 325–26
Pikini Atoll, 6, 83, 128, 215
Pinet, Simone, 19–20, 24
"Pious Sites" (Diaz), 101
plantations, 4–5, 60–61, 63–64, 255n13, 303–4, 306–9, 313–17, 318n3
Pleasures of Exile (Lamming), 369n18
Pliya, José, 41–42, 356, 364
Pocock, J. G. A., 16, 433
Poepoe, Joseph, 260, 276n8
Poetic Intention, The (Reverdy), 357
poetics, 165–69, 295–96, 359–60
Poetics of Relation (Glissant), 15, 25, 29, 63, 72n33, 358–59
Polynesians, 31, 285–86, 291–97, 330, 332–34, 376
Pomare, Maui, 333
Pongso no Tau, 35, 281, 293–97, 300n46
pookof, 101
Poppies, Isles of Shoals (Hassam), 74, 75, 87–88
Porritt, Arthur, 377
Portugal, 63
postexceptionalist American studies, 2, 12–13
Pound, Ezra, 218, 310
Pratt, Mary Louise, 235, 429
Prentice, Chris, 291
primitivism, 342, 345, 350, 394–95, 402–3
Prince, Mary, 238–39, 409n31
Prince, Nancy, 254
Provisional Government of Hawai'i, 268
Psychologie de la colonisation (Mannoni), 369n18
Puerto Rico, 2–3, 43n8, 68–69, 81–82, 101–7, 156–57, 162–64, 168, 179, 326, 427
Pugh, Jonathan, 17, 63, 157, 263, 323
Pukapuka, 4, 26

Quayle, Ada, 304
Quebec, 379
Quiet Revolution, 379
Quintilian, 30

race: blood quantum and, 215, 236; celebrity and, 42, 343, 346–58, 373–78, 380–85; class and, 302–18, 390–410; colonialism and, 60, 177, 179–83, 198–203, 208n47, 240–47, 250–54, 324–25, 360–65, 375; creolization and, 65–66, 233–34, 240–47, 256n48, 315, 342; decapitalized whiteness and, 40, 301–17; Indigenous peoples and, 216–17, 249–50, 338n36; nationalism and, 249–50; sexual politics and, 200–203, 208n47, 244, 251–52, 307, 312, 314–15, 342–46; slavery and, 5, 63–65, 78, 113–14, 235–38, 248, 256n41, 312, 390–95, 401–6, 431; spatial politics of, 37, 40, 430–31; state formation and, 376–78; tourism and, 18–19, 24–235, 392–95, 399–406. *See also* African Americans; colonialism; Indigenous peoples; slavery; US-America
Radway, Janice, 10, 54n139, 101
Rafael, Vicente, 145–46, 423
Ramona (Jackson), 147–48
Rapongan, Syaman, 40, 281, 293–97
Raustiala, Kal, 104
Reading, Nigel, 285
Real, the, 24, 37
Rediker, Marcus, 77–78, 255n21
Reframing Islandness (special issue), 17
Reid, Bill, 40, 281, 297
Relation, the, 21, 24–25, 63–64, 66, 69–70, 136, 283–86, 356
Re-Occupation Day, 107, 219–20, 226
"Re-Occupation Day (aka 'Liberation Day')" (Borja-Kicho'cho'), 107
Repeating Island, The (Benítez-Rojo), 216, 354n6
repeating islands (figure), 26–27, 29–35, 60–61, 69–70, 216–17, 256n28, 343
Republic of Hawai'i, 268
resistance. *See* anticolonialism
"Resituating American Studies in a Critical Internationalism" (Desmond and Dominguez), 101
Rethinking the Island (series), 17
Return to Guam (US Navy), 122

INDEX | 473

Reverdy, Pierre, 357
rhetoric, 40, 259–78
rhizomatics, 216, 364
Rhys, Jean, 304, 307–9
Riggio, Christine, 23
A Rising Wind (White), 114–19
Rizal, José, 35, 38, 133–34, 137, 145–48, 429
RMI (Republic of the Marshall Islands). *See* Marshall Islands
Roanoke Island, 5
Roberts, Brian Russell, 1–54, 97, 125, 181, 194–95, 206n11, 235, 253, 270, 328, 353, 386n2, 394, 416, 427–30, 433
Roberts, W. Adolphe, 38, 133–48
Robeson, Paul, 198–99
Robinson Crusoe (Defoe), 39, 77, 89n17, 128, 174–77, 181, 185–86, 189, 248
Robinson Crusoe, USN (Tweed), 122
Rock Steady (No Doubt), 396
"A Room of One's Own" (Warrior), 101
Roosevelt, Eleanor, 117–18
Roosevelt, Franklin D., 1, 117, 192–93, 349
Roosevelt, Theodore, 76, 143
Roosevelt Corollary, 194
ROP (Republic of Palau). *See* Palau
Rose Atoll Marine National Monument, 271
Rosenberg, Emily, 75
Rota, 103
Rotz, Jean, 21
Routes and Roots (DeLoughrey), 97, 216
Rowe, John Carlos, 39, 213–31, 428
Royal Street (Roberts), 134, 141
Rukeyser, Muriel, 220, 227
"Rum and Coca-Cola" (Andrews Sisters), 39, 191–207
Rusert, Brit, 258n76

Said, Edward, 175, 430
Saint Lucia, 193, 359, 364
Saipan, 103, 115, 124, 132n51, 330
Saison (Césaire), 361
Sakmans, 222–24, 227
Saldívar, José David, 4–5, 162, 167
"Salut au Monde" (Whitman), 428

Samuels, Oliver, 396
San Juan, E., Jr., 179
Santos, Jonathan Pangelinan, 220–21
Santos-Bamba, Sharlene, 112n81
Sargasso Sea, 40, 307–11, *310–11*, 314, 317
Sargassum, 309
Sarigan, 103
Sartre, Jean Paul, 364
Satyanand, Anand, 373–74, 376–78, 380–81, 384–85
Sauvé, Jeanne, 377
Savory, Elaine, 410n42
scale, 23–25, 33–34, 59, 64, 78, 331–34, 416–18, 423–25. *See also* archipelagic thinking; center-periphery dynamics; colonialism; maps
Schwyzer, Philip, 16
Scott, David, 141, 149n14
sea, the. *See* archipelagic thinking; Atlantic economy; coastlines; continental thinking; islands; materiality; navigation practices
Seacole, Mary, 254
"The Sea is History" (Walcott), 15
seashells, 26, 28, 243
Sea Venture, 237, 251, 255n21
Second Gulf War, 221
Sein und Zeit (Heidegger), 230n26
"Self-Portrait in a Convex Mirror" (Ashberry), 428–29, 434
Selkirk, Alexander, 89n17
Serranilla Bank, 83
settler colonialism, 42, 343, 346–58, 373–78, 380–85. *See also* colonialism
Seven Years' War, 378
Seward, William Henry, 165
sexuality, 200–203, 208n47, 244, 251–53, 307, 312, 314–15, 342–46
Shakespeare, William, 348, 361
Share, 378
Shell, Marc, 20, 24, 46n30
Sherman, Vincent, 196
Sherrard-Johnson, Cherene, 39–40, 232–58, 428
Sherrod, Robert, 122, 124–25

Shetland Islands, 187
Shima, 17
Sholokhov, Mikhail, 183–84
Shome, Raka, 417
Signet (publisher), 306
Sikau, Manny, 223
Silva, Noenoe, 337n27
The Single Star (Roberts), 134, 138, 142
Skinner, Ewart, 408n24
slavery, 5, 63–65, 78, 113–14, 235–38, 248, 256n41, 312, 390–91, 395, 401–6, 431. See also Atlantic economy; colonialism; plantations
Small Axe, 319n29
Small Place, A (Kincaid), 156
Smith, Henry Nash, 54n140
Smith, John, 5
social sciences, 57–58, 60–61, 64, 133–48
Solomon Islands, 333, 376
Somers, George, 237
Sommer, Doris, 40–41, 307, 311, 316–17
Song, Yann-Huei, 84
Soto-Crespo, Ramón E., 40–41, 302–19, 428
South China Sea. *See* China Sea
Southerly, 17
South Pacific (Rodgers and Hammerstein), 29, 33–34, 52n123
sovereignty, 35, 40, 57–58, 79–84, 104–8, 155, 194–96, 214–15, 266–69, 273–75, 294
Sovereignty Restoration Day, 266
Soviet Asia Mission (Wallace), 117
Soviet Union, 126–27
Spain: anticolonial movements and, 141–44; Civil War in, 134; colonial administration systems of, 5, 38, 63, 79, 98–99, 134–37, 145–48, 155–69, 220, 325. See also Caribbean, the; Guam (Guåhan); Philippines
Spanish-American War, 2, 79, 82, 98–99, 103–5, 220, 326
Spasifik, 378
spatiality: aerial mapping and, 37, 113–19, 126–29, 430–31; geographical metaphors and, 57–69; Indigenous conceptions of, 15–16, 281–83, 293–97, 322–23; island space and, 82–84, 233, 240–47, 427; mobility and, 178–80; navigation practices and, 33, 40, 46n30, 100–101, 183–85, 222–24, 290–93; ocean expanses and, 84–85; racial politics and, 113–29; relationality and, 29–35; the Relation and, 41; representations of, 17, 21, 31–33, 37, 46n30, 113–15, 157–63, 169, 342–46, 429; social mobility and, 175–76; technology and, 37–40, 432; temporality and, 12, 67–68, 70, 345–50; thinking and, 356–57; topography/topology distinction and, 11–12. *See also* archipelagic thinking; continental thinking; maps
Spectre of Comparisons, The (Anderson), 145–47
spill, 330
Spillers, Hortense, 199
Spirit of Haida Gwaii, The (Reid), 281, 286–89
Star Waka (Sullivan), 281, 290–94
statues, 264, 265, 266, 269
Stearns, Peter, 410n41
Stein, Gertrude, 432
Steinberg, Philip, 85, 89n13, 324
Stephens, Michelle Ann, 1–54, 60–62, 97, 181, 194–95, 206n11, 270, 328, 353, 394, 416, 427–30, 433
Stephens, Sandra, 26, 27–28
Steward, Julian, 58
stick charts, 33, 34, 53n134
Strachey, William, 232, 237
Strangers to Ourselves (Kristeva), 401
"Strategies of Erasure" (Hall), 102
Stratford, Elaine, 37, 74–94, 157, 272, 391, 428, 430, 433
substantial presence, 331–34
Successors of the Unknown (Kane), 27
Sugarloaf Key, 87
Sullavan, Jeri, 203, 297
Sullivan, Robert, 40, 281, 290–93
Summer Isles, 5, 236–37
Sun of Consciousness (Glissant), 358
"Superstar" (Lady Saw), 399

Surinam, 4–5
"Surviving Our Fallen" (Santos), 221
Swan Islands, 4
System of Geography, A (Moll), 159

Taft, Howard, 92n56
Tagalog (language), 137, 145–46, 414
Tagata Pasifika, 384
Tahiti, 283
Taiwan, 35, 40, 281, 283, 285, 300n46
Taketani, Etsuko, 37, 113–32, 430–31
Talbot, Paul, 306–7
Taylor, Edward, 434
Teaiwa, Teresia, 42, 373–89, 428
tectonic plates, 6–7
Tempest, A (Césaire), 356, 360–65, 367
Tempest, The (Shakespeare), 236–37, 361, 364
temporality: archipelagic thinking and, 12, 70, 345–46, 349–50; capitalism and, 416–18; Enlightenment versions of, 67–68; imperial time and, 341–42, 349–50, 352; island time and, 233, 254n3, 282; national time and, 341–42, 352
Tenochtitlan, 6, 14
Te Punga, Hamuera, 333
Te Punga Somerville, Alice, 36, 41, 320–35, 431
Te Rangihiroa, 333
territory. *See* continental thinking; settler colonialism; US-America
Thaxter, Levi and Celia, 74
Their Eyes Were Watching God (Hurston), 252–53
"Theories and Methods" (Stratford), 433
Theresa—A Haytien Tale, 233
thinking-with, 10, 19–35, 50n81, 52n118, 66–69, 272, 324, 396, 407n16, 428, 472
Third Text, 17
Thomas, Clive Y., 407n10
Thomas, Nicholas, 430
Thomas, Richard, 266
Thompson, Krista, 391, 405
Thompson, Lanny, 4, 37, 57–73, 156, 429
Through Other Continents (Dimock), 12

Ticknor, Como, 148
tidalectics, 62, 97–98, 247–48, 283
Time magazine, 119
Times Literary Supplement, 321
Tinian, 103, 115
Tizard, Catherine, 377
Tokelau, 376
Tommy Bahama, 401
Tonga, 329, 333, 376
topography (definitions of), 11–12, 39, 187
topology (definitions of), 11–12
Toronto Star, 378–80
totalité-monde, 65, 72n33
tourism, 18–19, 24–235, 238–39, 392–95, 399–406
tout-monde, 356
"Towards a New Oceana" (Wendt), 428
Trachtenberg, Alan, 54n140
tragedy, 365–68
Traité du Tout Monde (Glissant), 136
translation, 147–48, 149n14
transnational turn, 9, 235, 430
Trans-Pacific Partnership, 108, 221, 272
transpacific studies, 174–90, 213–29
Transpacific Studies (Nguyen), 177
trash: Pacific garbage patch and, 41; people as, 40, 302–19, 324–25
trash fiction, 303–17
Trask, Haunani-Kay, 259–60, 273, 329
Treatise of the Tout-Monde (Glissant), 356–57, 359
Treaty of Waitangi, 380
Tresillian, Richard, 304
triangulation, 39–40, 100–101, 390–410
Trinidad and Tobago, 34, 156, 191–207, 375
Trinidad News Tips, 208n47
Truman, Harry S., 1, 120
Trust Territory of the Pacific Islands, 4, 8, 103
Turks and Caicos, 238–39
Turnabout Map of the Americas, 19
Turner, Frederick Jackson, 337n28, 431
Turtle Island, 5
Tuvalu, 376

476 | INDEX

Tweed, George Ray, 121–24
12 Million Black Voices (Wright), 125
Tydings-McDuffie Act, 179

UN (United Nations), 4, 8, 103, 124–25
UNCLOS (Law of the Sea), 15, 62, 84, 86, 92n57, 105–6
Under Three Flags (Anderson), 147
unincorporated organized territories, 81, 104–5, 165, 179, 215, 219. *See also* colonialism; US-America; *specific places*
University of Hawai'i at Mānoa, 3, 102, 217, 221
Untalan, Faye, 112n81
US-America: American Dream and, 396–404; archipelagic thinking and, 1–5, 8, 35–43, 62–63, 74–78, 82–84, 87–88, 90n29, 92n56, 101–6, 115–30, 175–76, 185–87, 235, 268–72, 326–27, 334–35, 433–34; borderwaters and, 7–9, 14, 187–90; citizenship and, 81, 99, 104–5, 165, 177–80, 185–87, 214–15, 254, 331–34, 421–22; continental thinking and, 1–11, 13–14, 74–78, 83, 87–88, 178–83, 193–96, 270, 320–35, 336n21, 431–32; exceptionalism of, 2–3, 11–12, 178, 180, 282; immigration discourses and, 175–77, 180–83, 186–90, 336n20; laws of, 2, 4, 15, 57–58, 81, 102–6, 115–19, 191, 199, 205n4, 219, 274–75; military of, 79, 81, 99, 105–8, 114–32, 191–209, 214–15, 219–29, 243; neocolonialism and, 145–48, 165–69, 174–90, 192–207, 214–31, 237–39, 268–72, 390–410; as object of desire and, 395–401; racial politics and, 36, 39, 78, 113–29, 141, 185–87, 208n47, 235–36, 248–50, 325–26, 328–34; slavery and, 5, 63–65, 78, 113–14, 235–38, 248, 256n41, 312, 390–95, 401–6, 431; terminological preferability of, 35–36, 46n36, 88n44. *See also* American Studies; Atlantic economy; citizenship (US-American); colonialism; continental thinking; World War II; *specific places*
US Virgin Islands, 3, 81, 105, 157, 165

Variety Magazine, 203
Vazquez, Alexandra T., 44n11, 434n1
Venezuela, 162
Venuti, Lawrence, 147–48
Veracini, Lorenzo, 214
Veracruz, 162
Victory Calypsoes 1943 Souvenir Collection, 192
Vieques, 107
Viernes, James, 112n81
Vietnam War, 226
"Violent Belongings and the Question of Empire Today" (Kaplan), 101–2
Vizenor, Gerald, 288
Voyage of the Beagle, The (Darwin), 5
"Voyages" (Crane), 228

Wake Island, 81
Walcott, Derek, 15, 20, 237
Waligora-Davis, Nicole, 39, 191–209, 428
Wallace, Henry A., 117
Waller, Edward, 236
War of 1812, 76–77
"The War Reparations Saga" (Leon-Guerrero), 226
Warrior, Robert, 101
Washington Post, 127–28
Waste Land, The (Eliot), 226
Waxman, Percy, 139
We Are the Ocean (Hau'ofa), 227
Weaver, Jace, 283
Weigert, Hans, 196
Wendt, Albert, 31–32, 335, 336n10, 428
West Indian Federation, 167
Whakamutunga (Graham), 288
Whale Rider, The (film), 292
Wharton, Glenn, 264
"What's in a Name?" (Radway), 10, 47n42, 101
Whidbey Island, 87
whipping posts, 236, 239, 245–46
White, Walter, 113–29
White Islander, The (Catherwood), 258n77
white trash, 302–18

INDEX | 477

"'White Trash' in the Antilles" (Andrews), 304
White Witch of Rose Hall, The (de Lisser), 312
Whitman, Walt, 183, 228, 428
Wide Sargasso Sea (Rhys), 307–9
Wigen, Kären E., 6–7, 227
Williams, Eric, 191, 205
Willkie, Wendell L., 117, *118*, 118–19
Wilson, Ivy, 254n5
Wineera, Vernice, 334–35
Winfrey, Oprah, 379, 383
Wini, H. M., 266
Winona (Hopkins), 232–36, 241, 247–54, 258n77
Wolfe, Patrick, 214
Women Writing the West Indies (O'Callahan), 312
Wong, Sau-ling Cynthia, 178
Won Pat-Borja, Melvin, 106–8
Woodward, Clark Howell, 193–94
World Bank, 392, 406n9, 407n11
World War II, 4, 8, 37, 99, 113–32, 132n51, 191–92, 215, 220, 431
Wray, Matt, 318n3
Wright, Richard, 125, 183, 307, 352
Wyatt, Gary, 285
Wynter, Sylvia, 15

Yanique, Tiphanie, 157, 165–69
"Yankee Dollar" (Invader), 201–2
Yu, Henry, 102

Zouzou (film), 346–51

www.ingramcontent.com/pod-product-compliance
Lightning Source LLC
Chambersburg PA
CBHW061340300426
44116CB00011B/1929